# Interior Construction & Detailing

## Disclaimer

This book is intended to be used by knowledgeable professionals as a general reference source and as a guide for developing their own details within the context of their specific designs. Where appropriate, the reader should seek additional professional advice or consult original sources for more detailed information.

The information presented in this book has been compiled from many sources including industry standards, building codes, manufacturer's literature, and technical reference works, as well as the author's own experience. Every effort has been made to present reasonably accurate information; however, it is difficult to ensure that all the information given is entirely accurate and the possibility of error cannot be entirely eliminated. The publisher and the author do not warrant the techniques and methods presented in this book. This book and the materials contained herein have not been examined for safety engineering, consumer or workplace safety, or similar or dissimilar laws or regulations. The author and publisher assume no liability or responsibility for any injury and/or damage to persons or property that is incurred as a consequence, directly or indirectly, of the use and application of any of the contents of this book.

## Trademark List

| | |
|---|---|
| CinemaScope® | Twentieth Century Fox Film Corporation |
| Green Seal® | Green Seal |
| LEED® | U.S. Green Building Council |
| Lexan® | General Electric Company |
| MasterFormat™ | Construction Specification Institute, Inc. and Construction Specifications Canada |
| Monel® | Inco Alloys International, Inc. |
| Permalam® | American Laminators Association |
| PowerPoint® | Microsoft Corporation |
| Romex® | GK Technologies, Incorporated |
| Teflon® | E.I. DuPont De Numours and Company |

# Interior Construction & Detailing for Designers and Architects

Fourth Edition

**David Kent Ballast, AIA**

Professional Publications, Inc. • Belmont, CA

## How to Locate Errata and Other Updates for This Book

At Professional Publications, we do our best to bring you error-free books. But when errors do occur, we want to make sure that you know about them so they cause as little confusion as possible.

A current list of known errata and other updates for this book is available on the PPI website at **www.ppi2pass.com/errata**. We update the errata page as often as necessary, so check in regularly. You will also find instructions for submitting suspected errata. We are grateful to every reader who takes the time to help us improve the quality of our books by pointing out an error.

**INTERIOR CONSTRUCTION & DETAILING FOR DESIGNERS AND ARCHITECTS**
**Fourth Edition**

Current printing of this edition: 1

**Printing History**

| edition number | printing number | update |
|---|---|---|
| 2 | 3 | Minor corrections. |
| 3 | 1 | CSI MasterFormat™ numbers updated. |
| 4 | 1 | New edition. Code updates. |



Printed in the United States of America

PPI
1250 Fifth Avenue, Belmont, CA 94002
(650) 593-9119
www.ppi2pass.com

ISBN-13: 978-1-59126-105-6
ISBN-10: 1-59126-105-8

Library of Congress Control Number: 2007924253

# TABLE OF CONTENTS

# LIST OF FIGURES

# LIST OF TABLES

# PREFACE AND ACKNOWLEDGMENTS

Since the first edition of *Interior Construction and Detailing* was published, many changes in the construction industry have affected interior designers. Most notably, the International Building Code (IBC) was first published in 2000 and is being adopted by most jurisdictions in the United States. The Americans with Disabilities Act (ADA) continues to evolve, and a new version of the *ADA Accessibility Guidelines* (ADAAG) was published in 2004 by the U.S. Access Board. Although at the time of this writing the Department of Justice had not yet formally adopted the new guidelines, it is only a matter of time before the new ADAAG will be in use.

Change is also occurring as clients and designers alike become more interested in environmentally responsible design. Many clients, including governmental agencies, are requiring that their architects and interior designers conform to the requirements of the Leadership in Energy and Environmental Design (LEED®) Green Building Rating System. Trade associations and standards-writing organizations are revising their standards. And, as always, new materials continue to come on the market.

To respond to these changes, I expanded the second edition of this book to include more information on the 2000 IBC, a new chapter on structural coordination and the required updates to industry standards, and some information on environmental issues. In the third edition, I updated code information to conform to the 2003 edition of the IBC, and added the changed requirements of the 2004 edition of ADAAG. I also updated the Construction Specification Institute's 2004 revision to its MasterFormat™ system and added new material to various chapters.

In this fourth edition, I have updated the code information to conform to the 2006 IBC as well as to various industry standards that have changed. I have completely revised the chapter on audiovisual systems because technology in this area continues to evolve rapidly. Finally, I have added a chapter on sustainable design, as this is now a vitally important area of knowledge that must be applied to design, interior construction, and specifying.

I thank the many people who helped me with the development and publication of this book. Credit goes to Michele Guest, Registered Interior Designer, and

Hubert I. McDaniel, ASID, IBD, IDEC, for their reviews of the initial proposal and early chapters. Thanks also goes to Robert D. Troy, architect and Registered Interior Designer, for his thorough technical review of the first edition and his many helpful suggestions that have made the material clearer, and to Holly Williams Leppo, RA/CID for her technical review of the updated material, codes, and standards in the fourth edition.

The great people at PPI did a great job, as always, of getting everything on paper and between the covers in the right way. For this fourth edition, I would like to thank Sarah Hubbard, director of new product development; Scott Marley, editor; Jenny Lindeburg, copy editor and proofreader; Amy Schwertman, typesetter and cover designer; and Tom Bergstrom, illustrator.

The Construction Specifications Institute (CSI) and Construction Specifications Canada (CSC) also graciously allowed me to use both the MasterFormat™ system, for numbering many of the sections, and the MasterFormat™ index.

Economic conditions continue on a roller coaster ride, resulting in employment fluctuations that interior design and architectural professionals are used to. Success goes to those with the most knowledge and the flexibility to do a variety of tasks in the office. I hope this book provides you with the knowledge to work smarter and better and to improve the service the interior design profession gives to the public.

David Kent Ballast, AIA, CSI, NCARB certified, NCIDQ certified

# INTRODUCTION

Good interior construction design and detailing requires a broad range of knowledge about materials, finishes, construction assemblies, mechanical and electrical systems, building codes, and planning standards. *Interior Construction and Detailing* is a comprehensive reference text on such topics for interior designers and architects involved in commercial and residential construction.

Interior architecture is a specialty in itself; however, until now no book has covered the broad spectrum of knowledge required for competent interior design and detailing. Many books on interior design lack data about construction, mechanical and electrical systems, code requirements, and other subjects that were once thought to be the exclusive province of the architect. Architectural books stop short of covering all of the specialty materials and methods necessary for sophisticated interior detailing. This book brings together information from the two fields.

The merger of what has typically been thought of as strictly architectural or interior design knowledge reflects the changes now taking place in the professional design fields. Three of the most prominent changes are given here.

First, the required knowledge base of interior designers is continually expanding. This is reflected in the increasingly complex work interior designers are undertaking, the knowledge needed to take the National Council for Interior Design Qualification (NCIDQ) examination, the rigorous standards set by the Foundation for Interior Design Education Research (FIDER) for accreditation of interior design schools, and expanding title and practice legislation for interior designers across the United States and Canada.

Second, many architectural and interior design firms are merging as a result of economic conditions along with the need to practice more efficiently and to offer a broad range of services. Whatever the reasons, architects and interior designers need to better understand each other's specialized knowledge so that they can work together.

Finally, more architectural firms are limiting themselves to interior design work as a way to either survive difficult economic times or increase business and profits. Architects, previously untrained in the specialized area of interior design, need additional information to practice competently.

Even though fields that have historically been thought of as separate (i.e., interior design and architecture) are merging, regulatory constraints have been slow to keep up. Most building departments still require the stamp of a licensed architect for many types of interior construction work described in this book. The inclusion of a specific type of work in this book does not mean that the work is the province of the interior designer or that a licensed architect is not required to assist with design and drawing preparation. However, the interior designer should know what is required both when working with an architect and for accurate preliminary design purposes, so that the design project gets started in the right direction.

The subject matter in this book is generally organized in the same way interiors are constructed. The early chapters describe construction components that give form to all interior spaces in all types of interior construction. These include the elements of partitions, ceilings, doors, hardware, glazing, and woodwork. Chapters in the middle of the book cover finish materials applied to the structure of the building. Finally, supplemental topics such as acoustics, security systems, mechanical and electrical coordination, barrier-free design, building codes, and sustainable design are discussed.

Throughout the book, more detailed, supplemental information is given in separate sidebars. This allows the main text to be read without interruption by reference information, which not all readers want to review on the first reading.

Although the scope of the book includes much more than just product and construction information, six-digit MasterFormat numbers have been included in headings when appropriate. These are the standard numbers developed by the Construction Specifications Institute, Inc. (CSI) as part of their MasterFormat system, which is a system of numbers and titles for organizing construction information. A separate MasterFormat index is included at the back of the book.

Because the United States has been slow to convert to the metric system, the measurements in this book are based on the customary U.S. (or English) units of measure. The corresponding metric, or SI (Système International d'Unités), units are included in parentheses immediately after the customary U.S. units to accommodate readers who are already using this system and to familiarize others with it. In addition, because the Department of Commerce requires all federal designs for renovation and new construction to be done only in metric units, many designers and architects are required to use the SI system.

In the text, the SI values are followed by the units, such as mm for millimeters or kg for kilograms. However, to avoid clutter, only the numerical values are given for SI dimensions on the illustrations (in parentheses immediately after the English units); units such as millimeters are not included. Following standard conventions, all distance measurements in the illustrations are in millimeters, unless specifically indicated as meters. For example, a dimension on a drawing may be shown as 4½" (114), which means that it is 4½ in in customary U.S. units and 114 mm in SI units. A distance of 30' (9.1 m) means that the distance in customary U.S. units is 30 ft and the distance in SI units is 9.1 m.

This book uses different abbreviations for pounds of force and pounds of mass in customary U.S. units. The abbreviation used for pounds of force (pounds-force) is lbf, and the abbreviation used for pounds of mass (pounds-mass) is lbm.

# 1

# PARTITIONS

Partitions define space, support doors and interior glazing, interface with ceilings, anchor woodwork, contain electrical and plumbing systems, and provide the base for a majority of decorative finishes. The commonly used partition types include gypsum wallboard, lath and plaster, masonry, and glass block.

## GYPSUM WALLBOARD PARTITIONS [092116]

Gypsum wallboard is the most common and most versatile of all partition types. It consists of a gypsum core sandwiched between heavy paper or other materials. Wallboard is factory-formed into standard-size sheets ready for dry application to a variety of framing methods. Because of its many advantages, wallboard is the most common material used for constructing partitions and ceilings in both residential and commercial construction. New products include wallboard manufactured with gypsum and fiber from recycled newspaper.

Gypsum wallboard is used on studs for partitions, over furring to cover other rough walls or columns, and on structural or suspended framing for ceilings. In some situations it can be directly applied to concrete block and other substrates with mastic.

However, the use of mastic requires the application surface to be smooth, flat, and free of oil, grease, paint, and other foreign substances that would prevent secure bonding. Concrete walls must be free of ridges, fins, depressions, and high spots. Masonry walls must be smooth and free of mortar protrusions. Generally, it is best to avoid mastic application of wallboard to surfaces other than another layer of wallboard.

### Wallboard components

Although the term "gypsum wallboard" (or "gyp board" for short) is often used to describe a construction component, such as "a gyp board ceiling," the component is actually an assembly of several individual pieces. A typical gypsum wallboard system consists of framing to which the gypsum wallboard is attached. The corners and exposed edges of the frame are covered with trim, and then the joints are finished with reinforcing tape and joint compound. This results in a smooth surface that is ready for final finishing with paint, wall covering, or some other decorative finish.

## Gypsum wallboard

Gypsum wallboard is manufactured in panels 4 ft and 4½ ft (1200 mm and 1372 mm) wide and 8, 10, 12, and 14 ft long (2400, 3000, 3600, and 4200 mm). Special 1 in (25 mm) thick core board used for shaft enclosures is manufactured in 2 ft widths. The length depends on the requirements of the job, but contractors generally use the longest practical length to minimize the number of joints.

Standard gypsum wallboard is available in thicknesses of ¼, ⅜, ½, and ⅝ in (6.4, 9.5, 12.7, and 15.9 mm). A relatively new product that is ¾ in (19 mm) thick is also available, which carries a 2-hour fire rating. This allows a 2-hour-rated partition to be constructed with a single layer without resorting to a standard two-ply application.

The thickness used depends on the particular application, frame spacing, and building code requirements. For most commercial and high-quality residential work, ⅝ in (16 mm) thick wallboard is used. A thickness of ½ in (12.7 mm) is commonly used in residential projects and for some commercial applications, such as furred walls. Table 1.1 gives general guidelines for determining wallboard thickness based on frame spacing.

Other applications require different wallboard thicknesses. For example, a ⅜ in (9.5 mm) thickness is used in some double-layer applications or when wallboard is applied over other finished walls in remodeling work. A thickness of ¼ in (6.4 mm) is used for forming curved surfaces and for providing new finishes over old wall and ceiling surfaces. Double-layer applications are used when additional fire resistance is required or for extra acoustical benefits.

Gypsum wallboard is available in a variety of types and edge treatments. The most common wallboard has tapered edges on the face side along the long dimension of the panel and square edges at the ends. The tapered edges allow for application of reinforcing tape and joint compound without causing bulges at the joints. Square-edge panels are used where appearance is not a factor, for base layers of two-layer applications, and for veneer plaster work.

In addition to the standard paper-faced gypsum wallboard, several other types are available. The types commonly used for interior construction are discussed.

### Fire-rated gypsum wallboard

Fire-rated gypsum wallboard, commonly designated as Type X, must be used where

**Table 1.1** Wallboard thickness based on frame spacing

| application | frame spacing (in (mm)) | |
|---|---|---|
| | 16[1] (406) | 24[1] (610) |
| partitions | ½[2] (12.7) | ⅝ (15.9) |
| ceilings | ½[2] (12.7) | ⅝ (15.9) |
| furring | ½ (12.7) | ½ (12.7) |
| mastic applied | ⅜[3] (9.5) | ⅜[3] (9.5) |

[1] On center.
[2] Required fire rating may dictate the use of ⅝ in (15.9 mm) Type X wallboard in some cases.
[3] No frame.

fire-rated partitions or coverings are required. It has a specially formulated core containing mineral additives that improve the wallboard's fire resistance.

### Water-resistant wallboard

Water-resistant wallboard is used as a backing for adhesive-applied ceramic tile and similar finishes in moist areas, such as showers or where the wallboard may be exposed to moisture during construction. However, for heavy-duty commercial showers and applications that are continuously wet, it is better to use ceramic tile on a Portland cement plaster setting bed or a glass mesh mortar unit as described in Ch. 10. Today, for most residential and commercial construction, other types of cementitious panel products are used in place of gypsum wallboard in showers. Water-resistant wallboard is also available as a fire-rated product.

### Abuse-resistant wallboard

*Abuse resistance* is the ability of a material or assembly to resist three basic types of damage: surface scratching or indentation, penetration into the stud cavity, and security breaches through the entire partition. Specialty wallboard products are available that can minimize damage from surface abuse and penetration into the stud cavity. For more information on security partitions, refer to Ch. 14.

Materials that resist surface damage are commonly used in hotel lobbies, restaurant dining rooms, waiting rooms, classrooms, and similar areas. Materials that resist penetration into the stud cavity are commonly used in hospital corridors, gymnasiums, and locker rooms, around loading docks, and in similar high-abuse areas.

Gypsum wallboard manufacturers produce various types of abuse-resistant materials by mixing paper fibers or other additives into the core, by using abrasion-resistant face papers and heavy back liners, by applying thin sheets of fiberglass or Lexan® to the backs of panels, by requiring the application of a coat of veneer plaster, or by some combination of all these methods. The required level of protection must be determined before selecting one of the many products available. In some cases only a modest degree of scratch and abrasion resistance is required, while other situations require a very high level of penetration resistance.

For example, if impact and penetration resistance are required, one manufacturer offers products that will resist from 60 ft-lbf (single layer of ⅝ in Type X wallboard) to over 2100 ft-lbf (⅝ in proprietary product with a 0.080 in backing layer of Lexan).

### Foil-backed wallboard

Foil-backed wallboard provides a vapor barrier to prevent the transmission of water vapor into exterior wall and ceiling spaces. It is installed with the foil-backed side facing the framing members. It is not commonly used for interior construction, but may be required when remodeling exterior walls or ceilings.

### Pre-finished gypsum wallboard

Pre-finished gypsum wallboard is available with various types of vinyl wallcovering already applied. However, instead of being installed like regular wallboard, it is used with demountable partition systems. It slips into bottom and top runners, and various types of concealed clips connect the edges to each other. Once installed, a thin vertical joint exists where one panel is butted up against the next. For very large projects, the wallboard can be manufactured with a custom wall covering of the type, pattern, and color specified by the designer.

## Framing

Gypsum wallboard framing for vertical construction, such as walls or furring, can be either wood or metal. (For ceiling framing, see Ch 2.) Wood is used in residential construction and occasionally in smaller

## Detailing curved partitions with gypsum wallboard

Gypsum wallboard partitions may be constructed with single curved surfaces by bending thin wallboard and attaching it to closely spaced studs. The amount of curvature (minimum radius) depends on wallboard thickness and whether the wallboard is applied dry or wet. When applied dry, the wallboard is usually installed horizontally and is gently bent while being attached to the studs. When applied wet, the wallboard face is moistened and then attached to studs. After drying, the panels regain their original hardness. Generally, ¼ in (6.4 mm) or ⅜ in (9.5 mm) panels are used in multiple layers. Table 1.2 gives the minimum radii possible when using wallboard for curved surfaces, both wet and dry. These dimensions are approximate. Exact numbers may vary depending on individual manufacturer's recommendations.

**Table 1.2** Minimum bending radii for standard gypsum wallboard

| application | minimum radius | | |
|---|---|---|---|
| | panel thickness, (in (mm)) | long dimension perpendicular to framing (ft (mm)) | long dimension parallel to framing (ft (mm)) |
| dry bending | ¼ (6.4) | 5 (1500) | 15 (4600) |
| | ⅜ (9.5) | 7.5 (2290) | 25 (7600) |
| | ½ (12.7) | 20 (6100) | — |
| | ½ [2¼ in layers] | 5 (3050) | — |
| wet bending [(1)] | ¼ (6.4) | 2 (600) | — |
| | ⅜ (9.5) | 3 (900) | — |
| | ½ (12.7) | 4 (1200) | — |
| | ½ [2¼ in layers] | 2 (600) | — |

[(1)] Dimensions are for gypsum wallboard applied to a 4 in (100 mm) partition.

Source: United States Gypsum Company.

Some manufacturers produce flexible ¼ in (6.4 mm) panels that are specially formulated for bending. These products can be used with a dry or wet application to achieve radii significantly less than those achieved with standard wallboard. Table 1.3 shows the ranges possible with these products.

## Detailing curved partitions with gypsum wallboard (cont.)

**Table 1.3** Minimum bending radii for flexible gypsum wallboard

| application | | lengthwise bend radii (in (mm)) | lengthwise max. stud spacing (in (mm)) | widthwise bend radii (in (mm)) | widthwise max. stud spacing (in (mm)) |
|---|---|---|---|---|---|
| dry | inside bend | 32–46 (823–1168) | 9 (225) | 20–34 (508–864) | 9 (225) |
| | outside bend | 32–34 (813–864) | 9 (225) | 11–18 (279–457) | 6–8 (152–203) |
| wet | inside bend | 20–34 (508–864) | 9 (225) | 10–12 (254–305) | 6 (152) |
| | outside bend | 14, 15 (356–381) | 6 (152) | 7, 8 (178–203) | 5, 6 (127–152) |

Note: Verify exact bending limitations with manufacturer.

Source: Manufacturers' literature.

## Composition of Type X gypsum wallboard

In general, gypsum wallboard is an excellent fire barrier because of its basic composition, hydrous calcium sulfate. Gypsum is about 50% water by volume, and when subjected to heat the water of crystallization is turned into steam. Because this process takes time and requires a great deal of heat, the gypsum remains incombustible and insulates the nonexposed side against heat transfer. However, because the gypsum shrinks as the crystallized water is driven off during a fire, pure gypsum board develops cracks and allows fire and heat to pass through. Type X gypsum board is manufactured with vermiculite, glass fiber, and other additives that offset shrinkage and increase durability.

commercial projects. Metal studs are commonly used in commercial construction because they are noncombustible, lightweight, and easy to work with. Metal framing may be used in residential construction; however, residential contractors prefer wood stud walls because they can double as loadbearing walls.

### Wood framing

Wood framing for gypsum wallboard partitions consists of 2 × 4 wood studs (actual size 1½ in by 3½ in [38.1 mm by 88.9 mm]) spaced 16 in (406 mm) or 24 in (610 mm) on center, although 16-in spacing is more common, especially for residential construction. These spacings are used because they are even subdivisions of the 4 ft width and 8, 10, and 12 ft lengths of gypsum wallboard. For ceilings, the wallboard is generally attached directly to wood joists or ceiling rafters, which are also spaced 16 in on center.

### Metal framing

Metal framing is light-gage, galvanized steel formed in a variety of sizes and shapes. Although metal stud partitions are usually nonloadbearing they can be loadbearing if heavy gage, structural steel studs are used. Loadbearing walls require calculations and sizing by a structural engineer, but the gypsum wallboard is applied directly to the studs as with any other partition.

Metal studs are available in several gages (thicknesses). The most common thicknesses are 25 gage (0.0175 in or 0.455 mm), 22 gage (0.0270 in or 0.69 mm), and 20 gage (0.0329 in or 0.836 mm). The 25-gage thickness is used most often for studs and other metal framing. Heavier gages are used for very tall partitions, when the partitions must support unusual loads, and for framing door openings. For loadbearing partitions, exterior walls, and other heavy loading conditions, 12-, 14-, 16-, or 18-gage structural steel studs can be used.

Metal studs are manufactured in a C shape with small flanges, as shown in Fig. 1.1. Openings are prepunched along the length to allow for the passage of electrical conduit and other wiring. Metal studs are available in depths of 1⅝, 2½, 3⅝, 4, and 6 in (41.3, 63.5, 92.1, 101.6, and 152.4 mm). These depths are the sizes labeled on construction drawings. The exact width of a stud is not critical and varies slightly depending on the manufacturer. It is usually about 1¼ in (32 mm).

Metal studs are placed vertically and, like wood studs, are spaced either 16 in or 24 in (406 mm or 610 mm) on center. However, 24 in spacing is commonly used for most nonloadbearing commercial construction because it is more economical and minimizes construction time. Metal studs must be framed into runners both at the floor and ceiling, as shown in Fig. 1.1(a). The runners are C-shaped metal fabrications, without flanges or prepunched holes, and are the same width as the studs. The runners are attached to the floor and upper support first

**Figure 1.1**
Metal stud wall framing

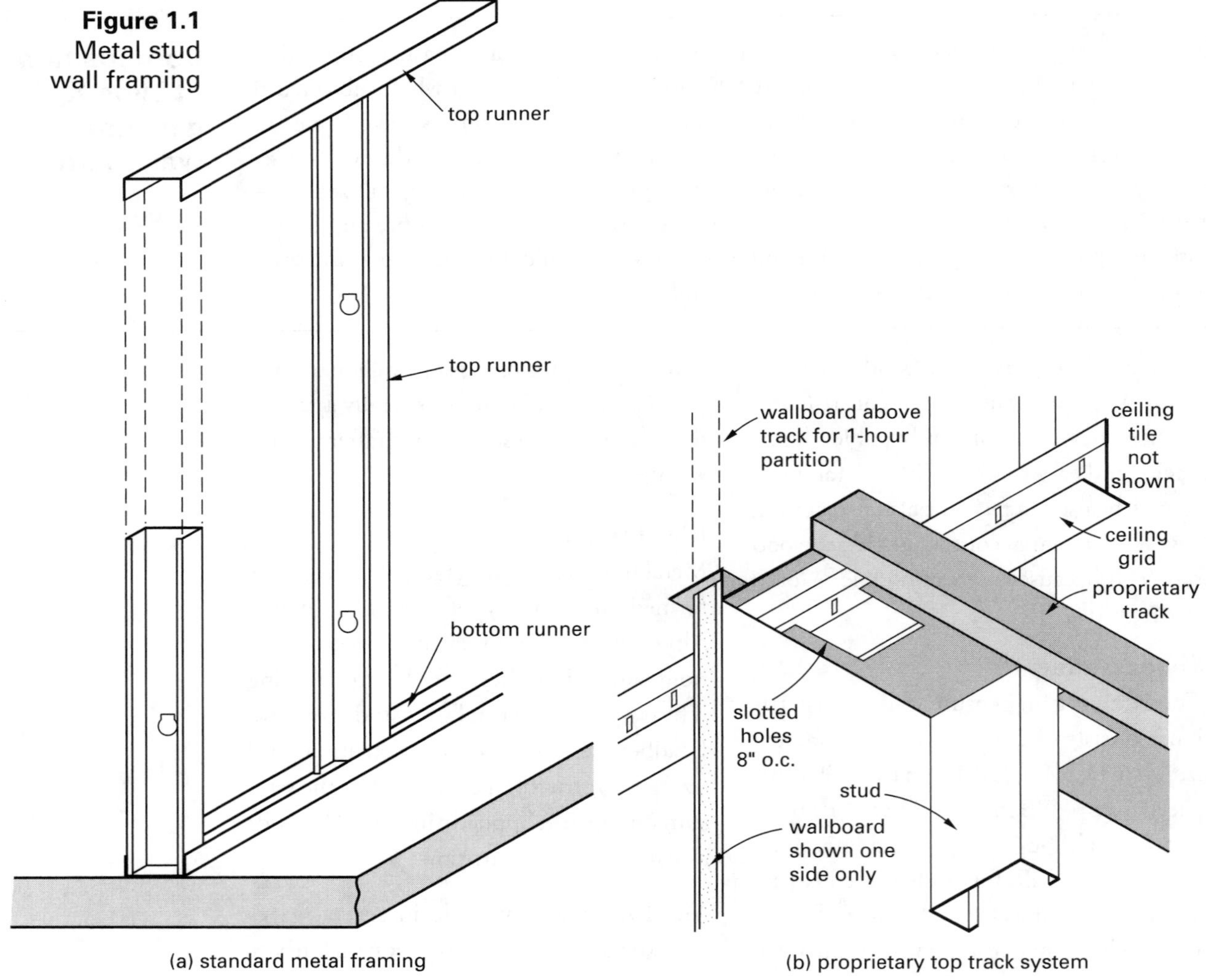


(a) standard metal framing

(b) proprietary top track system

and then the studs are slipped into the runners and attached with self-tapping screws or a crimping device. Other stud shapes are also available for special uses, such as stairway shaft framing.

The depth of a steel stud is generally determined by the height of the partition. The most common metal stud size (depth) used in commercial construction is 2½ in (63.5 mm), although 3⅝ in (92.1 mm) studs are also frequently used. A 2½ in stud is generally adequate for normal ceiling heights (8 ft to 10 ft) and also allows clearance for electrical boxes, wiring, and small plumbing pipes. Table 1.4 gives an abbreviated listing of maximum partition heights based on stud depth. Although one stud size may be sufficient for structural purposes, larger sizes may be required to accommodate plumbing pipes and recessed items, such as medicine cabinets or pocket doors.

## Special framing

Specially shaped metal studs are used for specialized partitions. For example, various configurations of proprietary studs are used for shaft wall liners in fire stairs, elevators,

**Table 1.4 Maximum partition heights based on stud depth[1]**

| stud depth (in (mm)) | structural criteria[2] | | | |
|---|---|---|---|---|
| | *L*/120[3] height (ft-in (mm))[5] | | *L*/240[4] height (ft-in (mm))[5] | |
| | 25-gage studs | 20-gage studs | 25-gage studs | 20-gage studs |
| 1⅝ (41.3) | **8 ft 9 in**[6] **(2670)** | 11 ft 2 in (3400) | 7 ft 11 in (2410) | 8 ft 11 in (2720) |
| 2½ (63.5) | **11 ft 3 in (3430)** | 15 ft 1 in (4600) | 10 ft 7 in (3230) | 11 ft 9 in (3580) |
| 3⅝ (92.1) | **13 ft 6 in (4110)** | 19 ft 1 in (5820) | 13 ft 5 in (4090) | 15 ft 2 in (4620) |
| 4 (101.6) | **14 ft 3 in (4340)** | 20 ft 11 in (6380) | 14 ft 2 in (4320) | 16 ft 7 in (5050) |
| 6 (152.4) | **15 ft 0 in (4570)** | 27 ft 5 in (8360) | 15 ft 0 in (4570) | 21 ft 9 in (6630) |

(1) The heights in this table are based on various industry sources and represent conservative values. The exact limiting height varies depending on manufacturers' values and which dated version of ASTM C754 may be required by the local building code. Some manufacturers' values also vary depending on whether one or two layers of gypsum wallboard are being used and whether stud spacing is 16 in or 24 in on center.
(2) The values in this table assume a 5 psf (240 Pa) load, stud spacing of 24 in on center, and a single layer of gypsum wallboard on each side of the partition. A 5 psf loading is typically the minimum required by most codes.
(3) *L*/120 refers to the maximum allowable deflection based on the length, *L*, of the stud. Partition heights are the heights from the bottom runner to the top runner, not the finished ceiling height. *L*/120 is the maximum deflection limit allowed by most building codes. Some manufacturers recommend a maximum of *L*/240.
(4) *L*/240 is the *recommended* maximum deflection for partitions with brittle finishes, such as veneer plaster. Some manufacturers also recommend this value for all partitions. For partitions with brittle finishes, some manufacturers recommend a maximum deflection value of *L*/360. The *L*/240 deflection is also the maximum deflection *mandated* by the 1997 UBC for partitions with brittle finishes.
(5) Heights in mm are rounded to the nearest 10 mm from the ft-in values.
(6) Figures shown in **bold type** are the most common.

and dumbwaiters. See Fig. 1.2(a). These allow the wallboard to be applied from one side only and provide a 2-hour-rated separation, as required by building codes. H-shaped studs are used for area separation walls to provide a firebreak between adjacent apartments or condominiums, or anywhere such a partition is required. They can be used with other metal stud construction or with wood frame construction, as shown in Fig. 1.2(b).

Other types of special framing include proprietary top track used for slip joints, top track used to frame partitions to existing ceiling grids, and flexible runners used for framing curved partitions. As discussed in a later section of this chapter, slip joints are required where a fire-rated partition abuts a structural floor above to allow for deflection of the floor above without placing stress on the partition and cracking the wallboard. Figure 1.9(a) shows one way of doing this with standard components, but other systems are available. Figure 1.9(b) illustrates one type of top track that allows a section of gypsum wallboard to be fastened to the proprietary track and to slip past the main portion of the partition while maintaining the fire rating and accommodating a fluted metal deck. This manufacturer's system is available in a variety of configurations for both 1-hour and 2-hour-rated partitions.

Another manufacturer makes long-leg top tracks with slotted holes for slip joints. The slotted holes allow the wallboard to be attached to the studs while enabling the top track to deflect without putting stress on the partition.

In order to simplify the task of attaching studs to an existing ceiling grid, one manufacturer makes a punched top track with holes for studs spaced 8 in (203 mm) on center. This track provides a snap-lock attachment of studs without the need for screws and gives the wallboard a finished edge by using a lip that extends over its top edge. See Fig. 1.1(b). The top track is first attached to the ceiling grid. Then the studs are snapped into place. Finally, the wallboard is attached and finished. If constructed according to the manufacturer's instructions, one variation of this partition system with the studs extending to the structure above has a 1-hour rating. This is the only partition system in which the ceiling grid penetrates the wall that carries a 1-hour rating.

For curved partitions, one manufacturer makes an adjustable track with hinged sections that can be curved to fit nearly any radius. Once formed, the track sections are

**Figure 1.2** Special wallboard studs

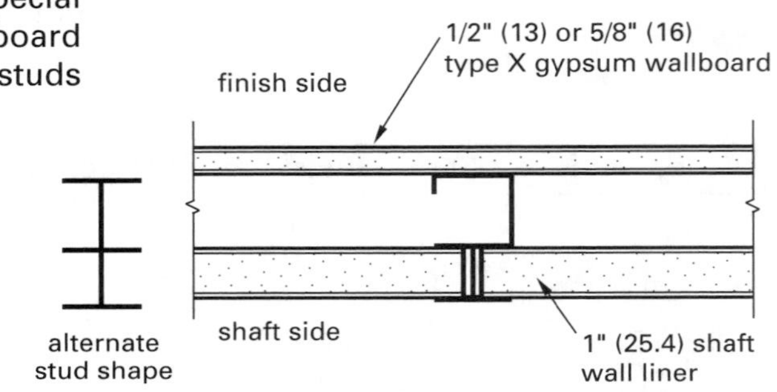


(a) proprietary stud for shaft liners

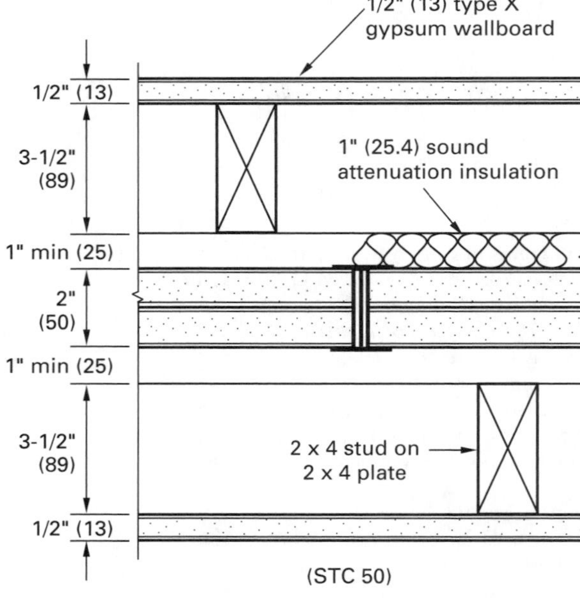


(b) H stud for area separation partitions

fixed in position by placing screws through the legs of the track and into a continuous metal band. The track is then fixed to the floor and ceiling to receive studs.

Although many of these specialty products cost more than the basic wallboard components, they can cut costs in some situations by reducing the amount of labor required to build some types of partitions.

## Wood and metal furring

Furring consists of smaller framing members, either wood or metal, that only provide a base for attachment of gypsum wallboard to one side of some other construction, which is not appropriate for direct attachment of the wallboard. First, the furring is attached to the substrate behind it, such as a concrete or masonry wall, and then the wallboard is screwed to the furring. The furring can also be free-standing when the application is to use wallboard to cover up some other construction. For example, a finished, square column can be built around a rough, unfinished, structural concrete column.

There are several types of furring, as shown in Fig. 1.3. When wood furring is used, it measures a minimum of 1 × 2 (actual size ¾ in by 1½ in [19.1 mm by 38.1 mm]) if it is directly attached to another solid wall, such as concrete block. If the furring is applied perpendicular to the other studs, or if a greater depth is required, a 2 × 2 (51 ×51) piece must be used.

There are three common types of metal furring. The most common is the metal furring channel, sometimes called a hat channel because of its cross-sectional shape. See Figure 1.3(b). The channel is attached to other construction, such as a concrete block wall or ceiling framing, providing a surface to which the gypsum wallboard can be screw-attached. Furring channels are usually spaced 16 in or 24 in (406 mm or 610 mm) on center. Resilient channels are similar to hat channels but are manufactured with legs of unequal length so that only one edge touches the framing. See Fig. 1.3(c). This avoids a rigid connection between the gypsum wallboard and the stud wall or ceiling structure and reduces sound transmission through the wall or ceiling. To accommodate electrical conduit, switch boxes, and insulation, Z-furring channels provide more depth than standard metal furring channels. See Fig. 1.3(d).

**Figure 1.3**
Common types of furring

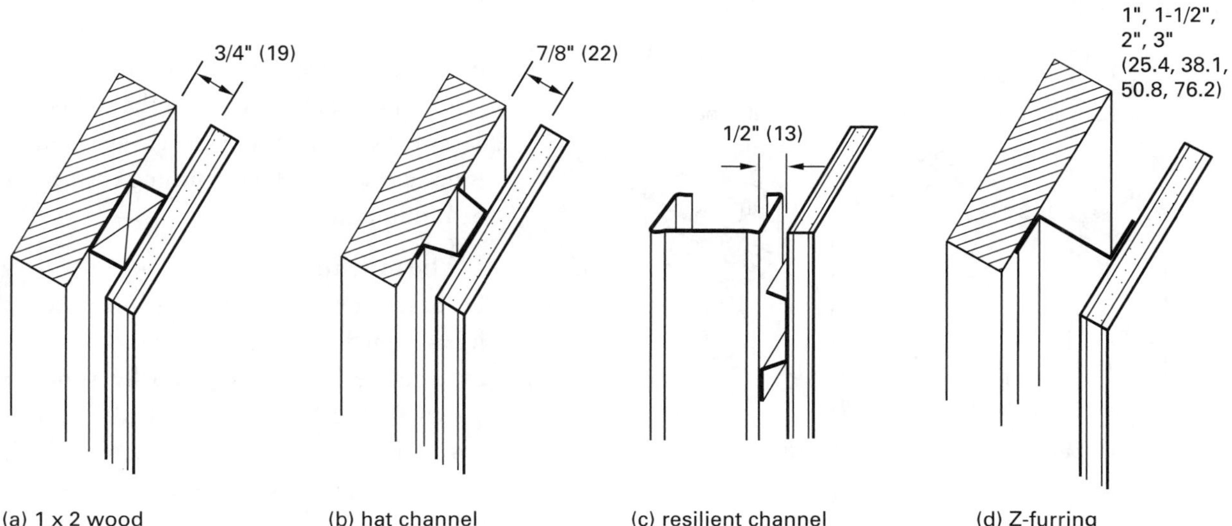

## Standard trim [092116]

Because the edges of gypsum wallboard are ragged when cut, they must either be concealed or finished with prefabricated trim. The most common trim is made from galvanized steel in a few common configurations. Other types of proprietary trim are available in aluminum in a variety of shapes to accommodate many detailing conditions. Vinyl trim is also made to finish off common edge conditions. There are six common trim shapes used for gypsum wallboard.

**Figure 1.4** Standard wallboard trim types

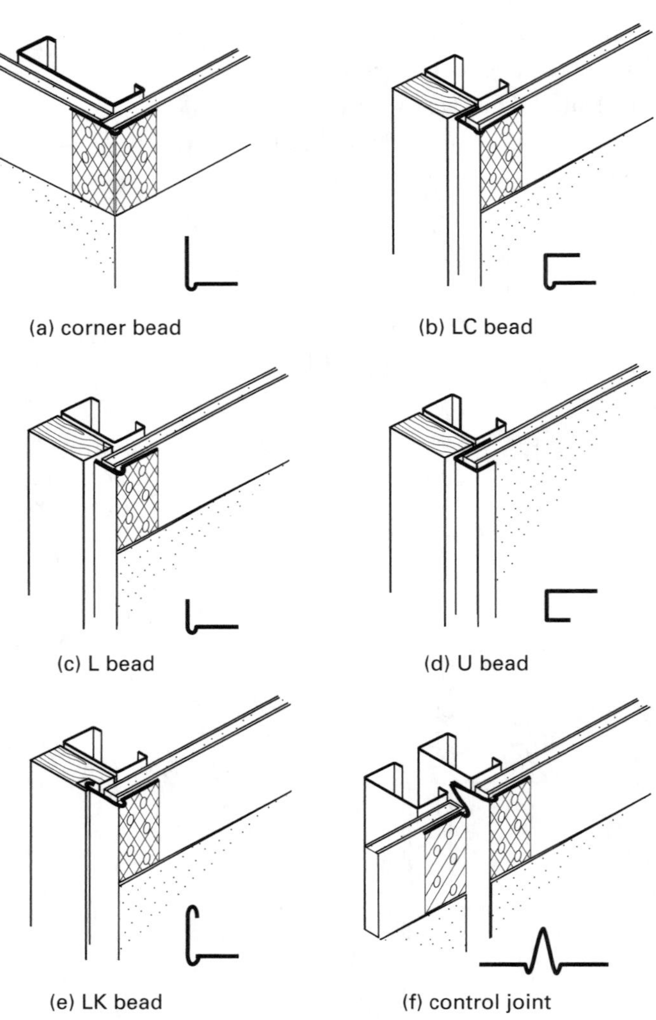

(a) corner bead (b) LC bead (c) L bead (d) U bead (e) LK bead (f) control joint

### Corner bead trim

Corner bead trim is L-shaped with legs of equal length, about 1 in (25.4 mm) long. See Fig. 1.4(a). It is used at all exposed exterior corners. Once applied, the metal is covered with joint compound and then sanded smooth, ready for painting or other finishing.

### LC bead trim

LC bead trim is used where the edge of the gypsum wallboard is exposed. See Fig. 1.4(b). This trim requires finishing with joint compound; however, once finished, it gives a neat, clean edge that does not look like a metal edge. Because of its U shape, LC bead trim must be installed before the wallboard is installed, or at the same time. LC bead is its generic name, and contractors sometimes call it U-bead or J-bead. Also, manufacturers have different numerical designations for it.

### L bead trim

L bead trim is similar to LC bead but does not have the back flange; therefore, it can be installed after the wallboard. See Fig. 1.4(c). This is an advantage when remodeling and when trim is used to make final dimensional fits next to millwork, door frames, and other construction. Like LC bead, L bead must be finished with joint compound.

### U bead trim

Like LC trim, U bead trim fits over the edge of the wallboard; however, it does not require finishing. See Fig. 1.4(d). As a result, the metal is visible on the wallboard surface. This trim is used where appearance is not critical or where finishing costs must be minimized.

### LK bead trim

LK bead trim is similar to LC trim; however, it has a small V edge that must be fitted into a slot in the construction (usually wood) to which the wallboard is attached. See Fig. 1.4(e). Because of this installation method, LK bead trim is adjustable and can be used for wallboard measuring ⅜, ½, or ⅝ in (9.5, 12.7, or 15.9 mm), or in situations where the wood trim is not exactly plumb. This trim must also be finished with joint compound.

### Control joints

A control joint is used when movement in large expanses of gypsum wallboard is expected. See Fig. 1.4(f). Generally, this is not a problem with interior construction for two reasons. First, there is very little expansion and contraction caused by temperature variations; second, most wallboard surface areas are limited by the size of rooms and spaces. Occasionally, on surfaces such as ceilings in very long corridors, in large rooms, or where there is a building expansion joint, wallboard expansion joints are required. They are generally used at distances not to exceed 50 ft (15 m) when an unbroken surface exceeds that dimension, or when movement is expected.

## Proprietary gypsum wallboard trim

For situations where the standard wallboard trim will not work, there are various types of proprietary trim available from several manufacturers. Proprietary trim is usually made from extruded aluminum and allows detailing of reveals, rounded edges, and other configurations that would otherwise not be feasible. Fig. 1.5 gives four examples of proprietary wallboard trim.

## Reinforcing tape, joint compound, and finishing

After gypsum wallboard is nailed or screwed to the framing, the holes and joints must be covered. For joints, joint compound is placed along the crack, and either paper or fiberglass reinforcing tape is embedded in the compound and troweled smooth. After the compound has dried, another layer of compound is applied, troweled smooth and feathered farther out onto the wallboard, allowed to dry, then sanded. This process is repeated. At this point, when the joint compound blends smoothly with the wallboard, the surface is ready for finishing. A similar three-coat process is used to cover nail or screw holes, except that no tape is used.

Once the wallboard is installed and readied for finishing, it can be primed and painted for a smooth finish. Textured coating, which is applied before painting, provides an alternative to a smooth finish and is often preferred by contractors because it hides minor

**Figure 1.5** Proprietary wallboard trim

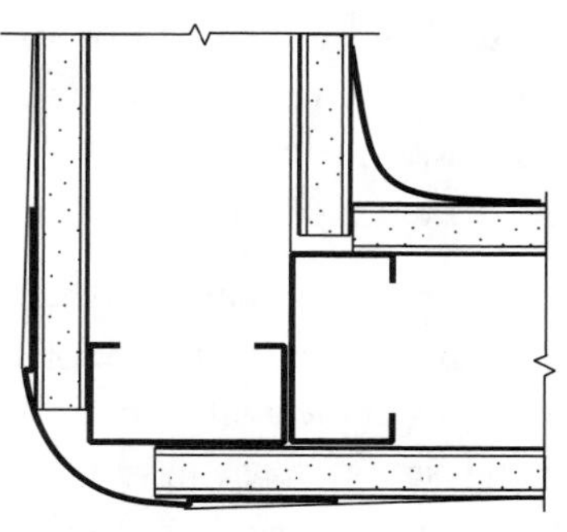

(a) outside and inside radius forms

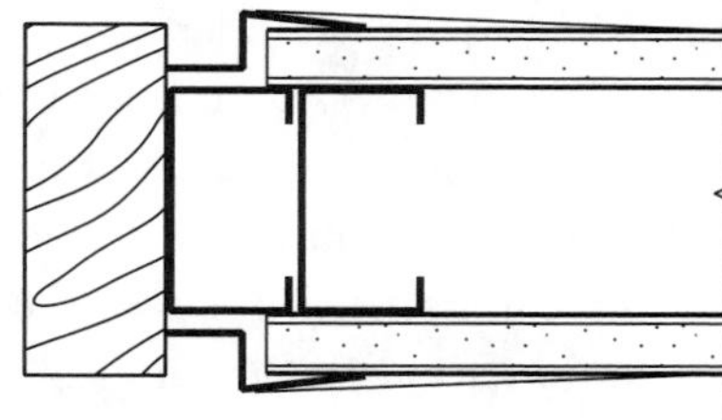

(b) reveal at door or opening trim

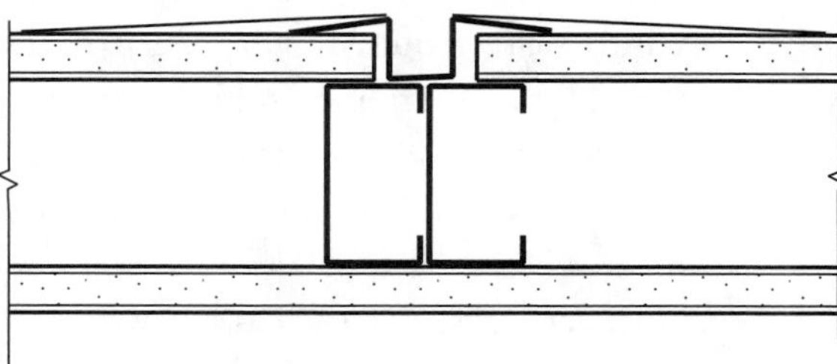

(c) reveal in field of partition

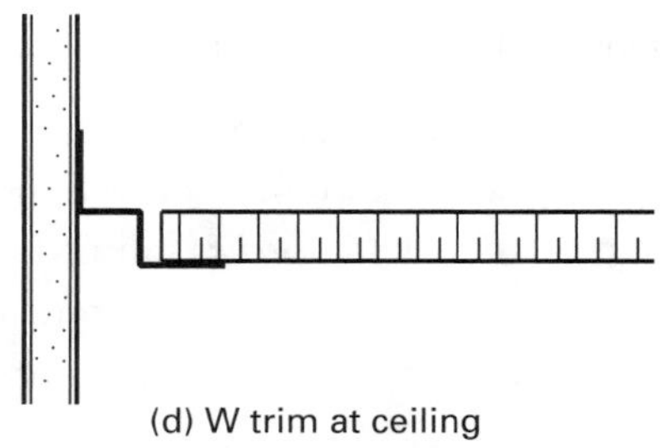

(d) W trim at ceiling

surface imperfections. A variety of treatments is available, from a fine, sandy finish to a heavy, coarsely textured finish. One of the most common is the "orange peel" texture.

## Fire and sound ratings

Two of the most important qualities of gypsum wallboard partitions are fire resistance and sound rating. Gypsum wallboard is a good material for both because gypsum is inherently fire resistant, as described previously, and is very dense, making it a good barrier for sound transmission. Because there are dozens of ways a partition can be built, knowing what type of fire resistance (if any) and acoustic qualities are needed helps determine the exact partition construction.

Partition fire ratings are specified as 1-hour, 2-hour, 3-hour, and 4-hour. A 1-hour partition, for example, will theoretically prevent fire and smoke from passing through the partition for a period of at least one hour. The ratings are established by an independent testing laboratory. A partition is built and subjected to a standard test fire, and the results are measured. In addition to partitions, gypsum wallboard can also be used to protect columns, beams, and other building components. Refer to Ch. 19 for more information on fire ratings.

For interior construction 1-hour-rated partitions, and occasionally 2-hour-rated partitions, are required. 1-hour partitions are used for separating corridors from lease space, separating houses from their attached garages, and separating one type of occupancy from another. 2-hour partitions are used to enclose vertical shafts, such as stairways and elevators. Some architectural applications, such as some types of occupancy separations, require 3-hour or 4-hour protection.

Partitions are also given sound ratings based on laboratory testing. These ratings usually appear along with the fire ratings in various reference tables and publications. In most cases, the rating is the STC number, or sound transmission class. This is an average rating of the resistance to transmission over a wide range of frequencies. The higher the number, the better the partition is in reducing sound transmission. Some approximate STC ratings are given in Table 1.6. Refer to Ch. 11 for more information on acoustics.

## Typical partition construction

Figures 1.6–1.8 show three of the most common types of gypsum wallboard partitions. One is the standard wood frame partition used in residential construction. The other two are metal frame partitions commonly used in commercial construction.

Figure 1.6 illustrates a residential wood frame partition. These partitions are constructed with 2 × 4 studs 16 in (406 mm) on center, covered with one layer of gypsum wallboard on each side. Because of the way the board is installed, there is usually about a ¼ in to ½ in (6 mm to 12 mm) gap at the floor, which is concealed by the base.

Figure 1.7 shows a typical nonrated partition used in commercial construction to economically divide spaces when fire separation, sound control, and security are not critical considerations. The partition is built from the floor to the underside of the suspended ceiling, with the plenum space above the ceiling left open.

This standard partition is constructed by attaching the bottom runner to the floor with power-actuated fasteners (or other means) and attaching a corresponding top runner to the ceiling grid with screws or rivets (or other types of fasteners). The studs are slipped between the runners and attached to them with self-tapping metal screws. Application of the gypsum wallboard and finish base completes the construction.

In most cases, ⅝ in (15.9 mm) wallboard is used because of the typical 24 in (610 mm) spacing of studs, but ½ in (12.7 mm)

## Standard types of gypsum wallboard finish

The following levels of wallboard finish have been standardized in the gypsum wallboard industry and are described in *Recommended Levels of Gypsum Board Finish*, published by the Gypsum Association. The levels provide a way to specify the exact requirement for any project. This is important because factors such as lighting conditions and paint type can affect the appearance of the surface if it is not finished properly. For example, strong sidelighting from a window perpendicular to a partition can accentuate minor flaws and dents in the wallboard.

**Level 0:** Requires no taping, finishing, or accessories.

**Level 1:** Joints and interior angles have tape embedded in joint compound with the surface free of excess joint compound. This level is used for plenums above ceilings and other areas not normally open to view.

**Level 2:** All joints and interior angles have tape embedded in joint compound and one separate coat of compound applied over all joints, angles, fastener heads, and accessories. This level is used where water-resistant backing board is used as a substrate for tile and in other areas where appearance is not critical.

**Level 3:** Similar to Level 2, except that two coats of joint compound are used and the surface is free of tool marks and ridges. This level is used where the surface will receive heavy- or medium-textured finishes or where heavy-grade wall coverings are to be applied.

**Level 4:** Similar to Level 3, except that three coats of joint compound are used. This level is used where light textures or wall coverings will be applied or where economy is of concern. Gloss, semigloss, and enamel paints are not recommended over this level of finish.

**Level 5:** Similar to Level 4 except that a thin skim coat of joint compound is applied over the entire surface. This level is used where gloss, semigloss, enamel, or nontextured flat paints are specified or where severe lighting conditions exist.

## Building code requirements for gypsum wallboard

The International Building Code (IBC) and other model codes specify the exact requirements for the application of both single-ply and two-ply gypsum wallboard, including framing member spacing, wallboard thickness, types and spacing of fasteners, and joint treatment. Some of these are specified in Tables 720.1(2) and 720.1(3) of the International Building Code (and similar tables in other model codes). Detailed construction requirements can also be found in such publications as the Underwriters Laboratories' *Building Material Directory,* the Gypsum Association's *Fire Resistance Design Manual,* and manufacturers' product literature, as well as other reference books.

In addition, the IBC requires water-resistant gypsum board to be used as a base for tile and wall panels, tub and shower enclosures, and water closet compartment walls. However, water-resistant gypsum wallboard cannot be used over vapor barriers, in areas of high humidity (such as saunas, steam rooms, or gang showers), or on ceilings.

wallboard may be applied to studs spaced 16 in (406 mm) on center. Wallboard ½ in (12.7 mm) thick is sometimes applied to metal studs 24 in (610 mm) on center to reduce costs.

Steel studs that measure 2½ in (63.5 mm) are generally used for usual ceiling heights of 8 ft to 9 ft (2438 mm to 2743 mm), but 3⅝ in (92.1 mm) studs can be used when additional cavity depth is needed for pipes or recessed items. The exposed edge of the wallboard near the ceiling should be finished with some type of trim.

Although wallboard may be applied with the length parallel to the studs (vertically) or with the length perpendicular to the studs (horizontally), most contractors prefer to apply it horizontally. For partitions, if the ceiling height is 8 ft 1 in (2464 mm) or less, it is best to apply wallboard horizontally in the longest lengths practicable for the following reasons.

- It results in fewer joints, which means faster and less-costly finishing.
- It places the horizontal joint at a convenient height for finishing.
- It ties more studs together, making the installation stronger.
- It puts the strongest dimension of the wallboard across the studs.

**Figure 1.6** Standard wood frame partition

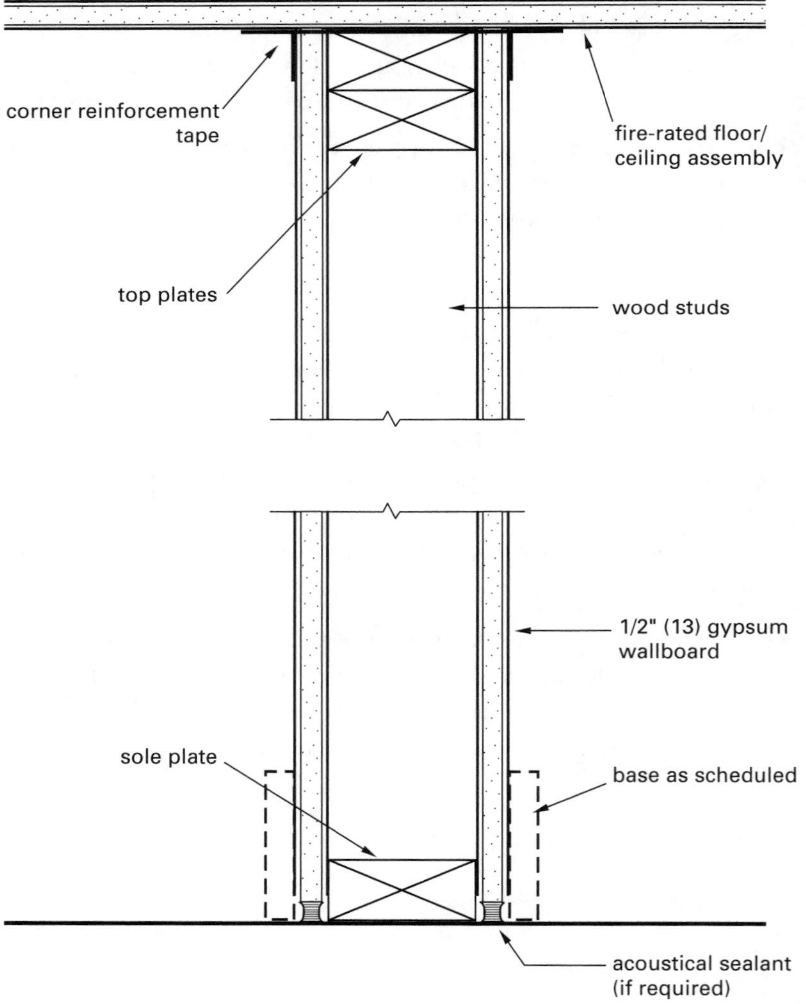

If ceiling heights are 9 ft, two horizontal rows of 54 in wide wallboard may be used.

Figure 1.8 shows a 1-hour fire-rated partition used in commercial construction. This partition type is commonly used to separate an exit corridor from adjacent spaces and when the building code requires a 1-hour separation. It is also used when acoustical control, but not a fire separation, is needed between two spaces. If the partition is used for sound control, acoustical insulation should be detailed within the stud space as well. Refer to the next section on special partition construction for examples of acoustical partitions. There are other construction assemblies that provide 2-hour, 3-hour, and 4-hour ratings; however, these are seldom encountered in most interior construction. One exception is 2-hour-rated partitions that are required around vertical enclosures, such as stairways.

Although there are many variations of 1-hour-rated partitions, all these partitions must be built with Type X gypsum wallboard and must extend to the structure above. All joints, edges, and penetrations must be sealed. If ducts pass through the

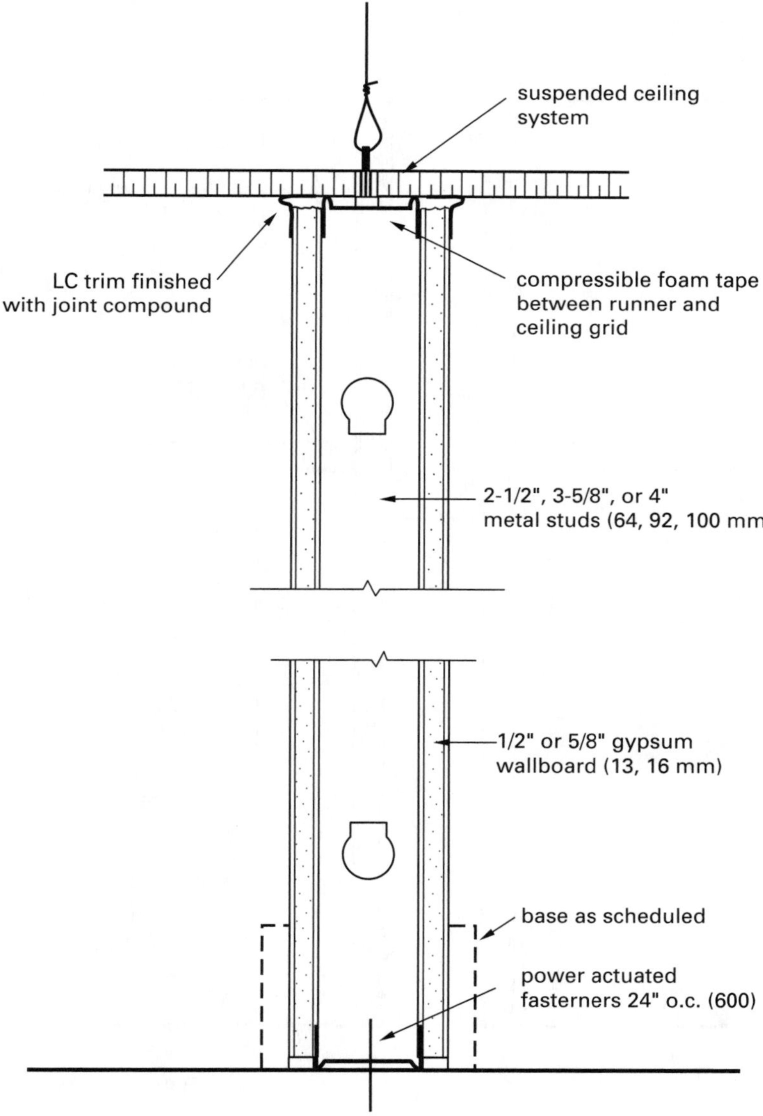


**Figure 1.7** Standard floor-to-ceiling steel stud partition

wall, they must have a fire damper at the wall line. Electrical boxes may be placed in the wall but are limited to one box on one side of the wall in each space between studs.

This kind of partition should be provided with a slip joint at the structural floor or roof, as shown in Fig. 1.9(a) or 1.9(b). The space between the structural slab and the top of the gypsum board must be sealed with fire-rated caulking compound. In addition, if the top of the partition abuts a fluted metal deck, the voids must be sealed with appropriate fire-rated material.

Two other common partition details include 2-hour-rated partitions and chase walls. Figure 1.12 illustrates a typical 2-hour-rated partition developed by using a double layer of Type X wallboard on each side of metal studs. It is also possible to use proprietary ¾ in (19.1 mm) thick wallboard in a single layer.

**Figure 1.8**
One-hour-rated slab-to-slab partition

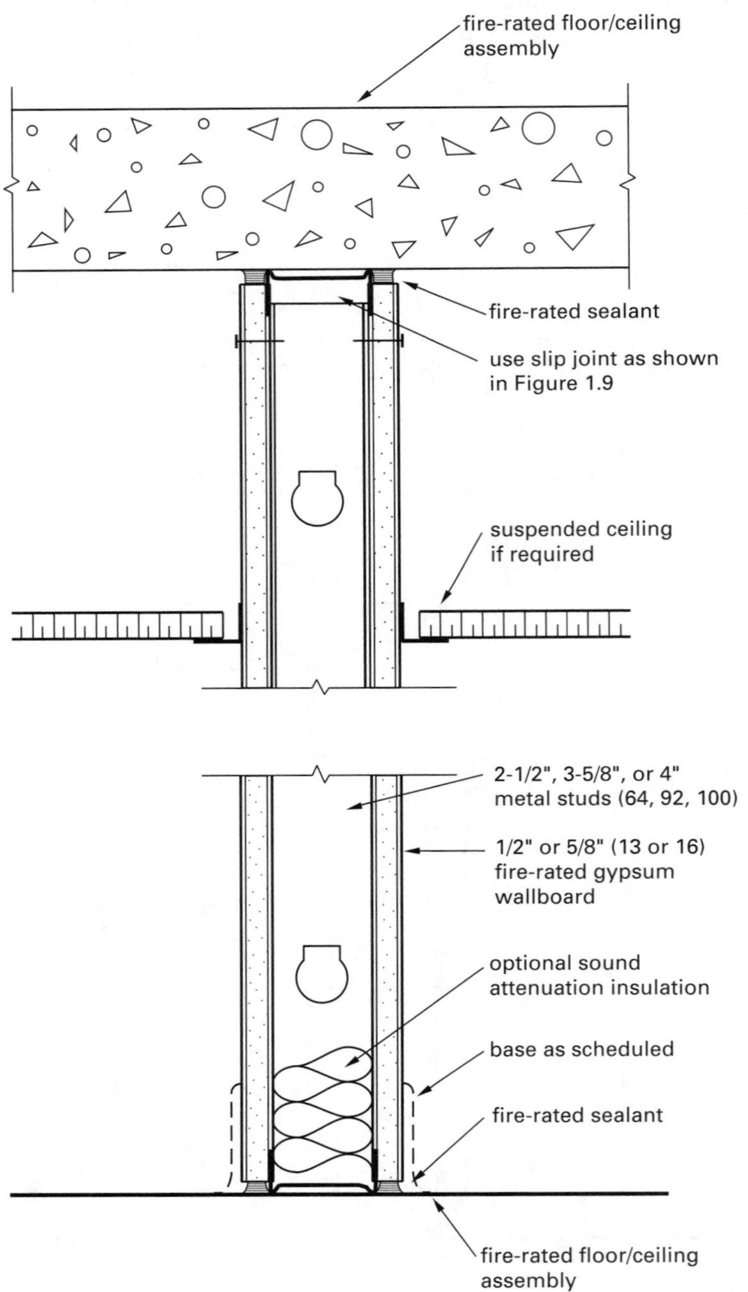

## Partition cracking in high-rise buildings

All buildings move to some extent, thus causing cracking of materials that are rigidly attached to the structure. This problem is especially prevalent in high-rise buildings where structural movement, movement caused by floor deflection, and expansion and contraction are more pronounced than in residential and smaller commercial buildings.

Most wallboard cracking in high-rise buildings is caused by partitions that are rigidly attached to walls, columns, beams, or floor slabs without provisions for such movement. When a floor slab deflects it can put enough pressure on a slab-height partition to cause it to crack. This can be avoided by detailing a slip joint as shown in Fig. 1.9(a). This joint seals the partition to the slab while allowing some movement. Also refer to Fig. 1.9(b).

In addition, when high-rise buildings sway under wind load, they move from side to side. Figure 1.10 shows another type of joint that can be used between the edge of a partition and an exterior window mullion. Figure 1.11 shows a perimeter relief joint where a partition abuts a column or structural wall.

**Figure 1.9**
Slip joints under structural floor

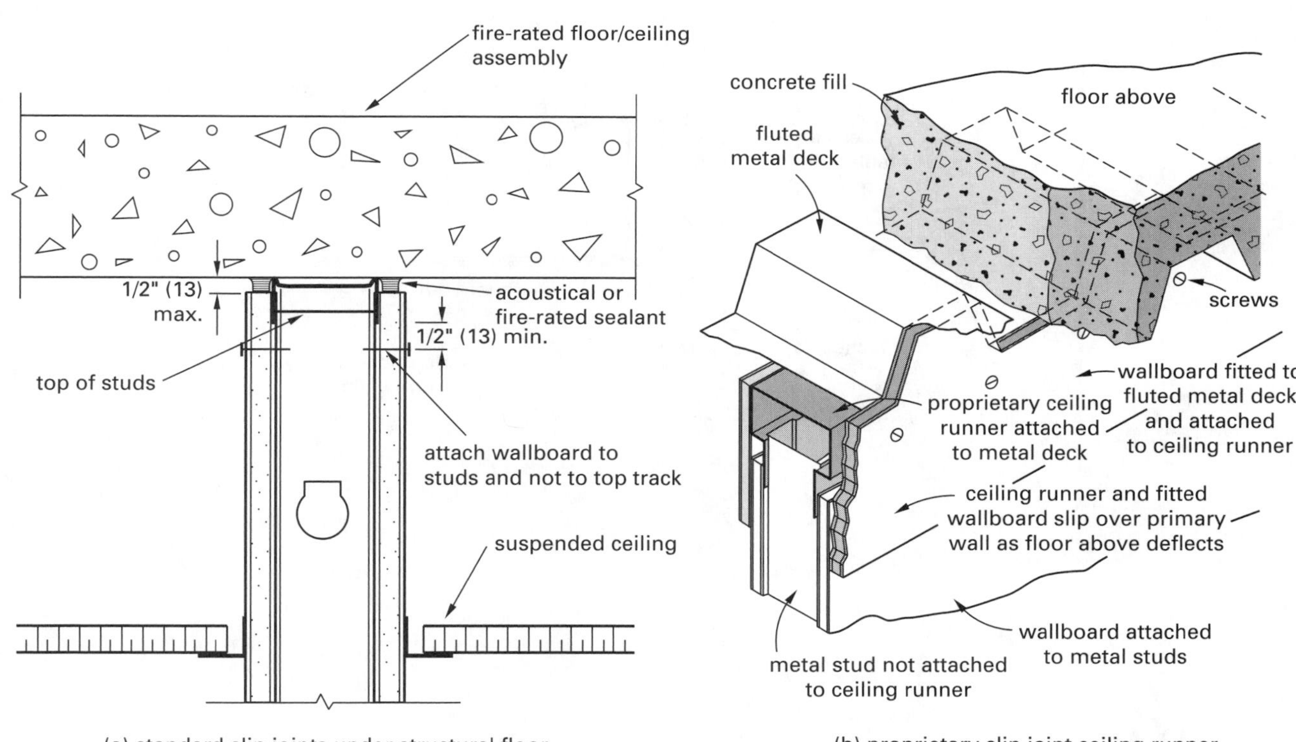

**Partition cracking in high-rise buildings (cont.)**

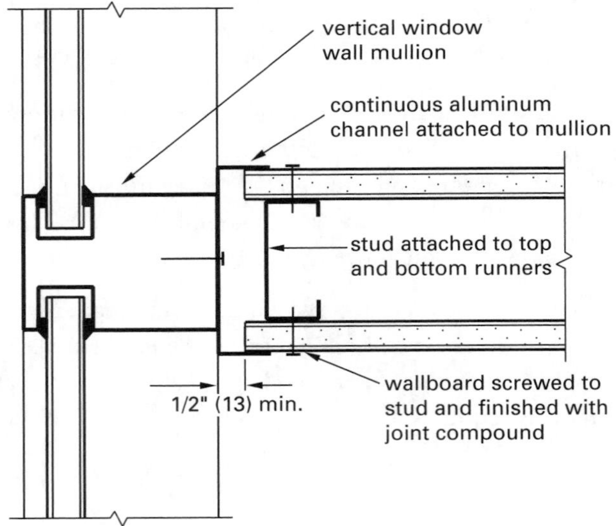


**Figure 1.10**
Relief joint at mullion

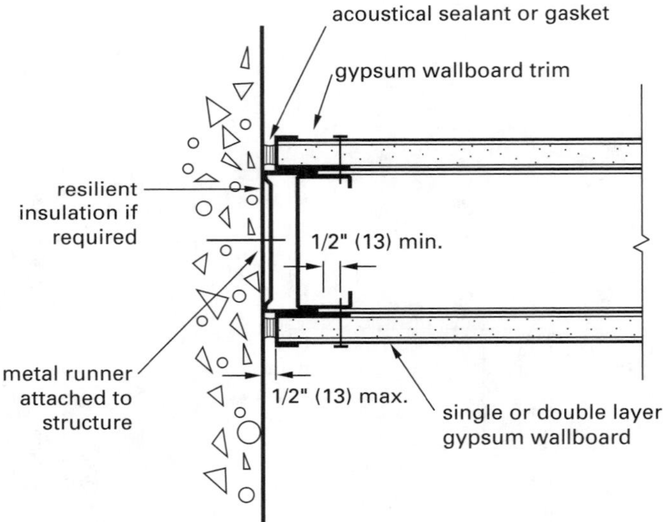


**Figure 1.11**
Relief joint at structural wall or column

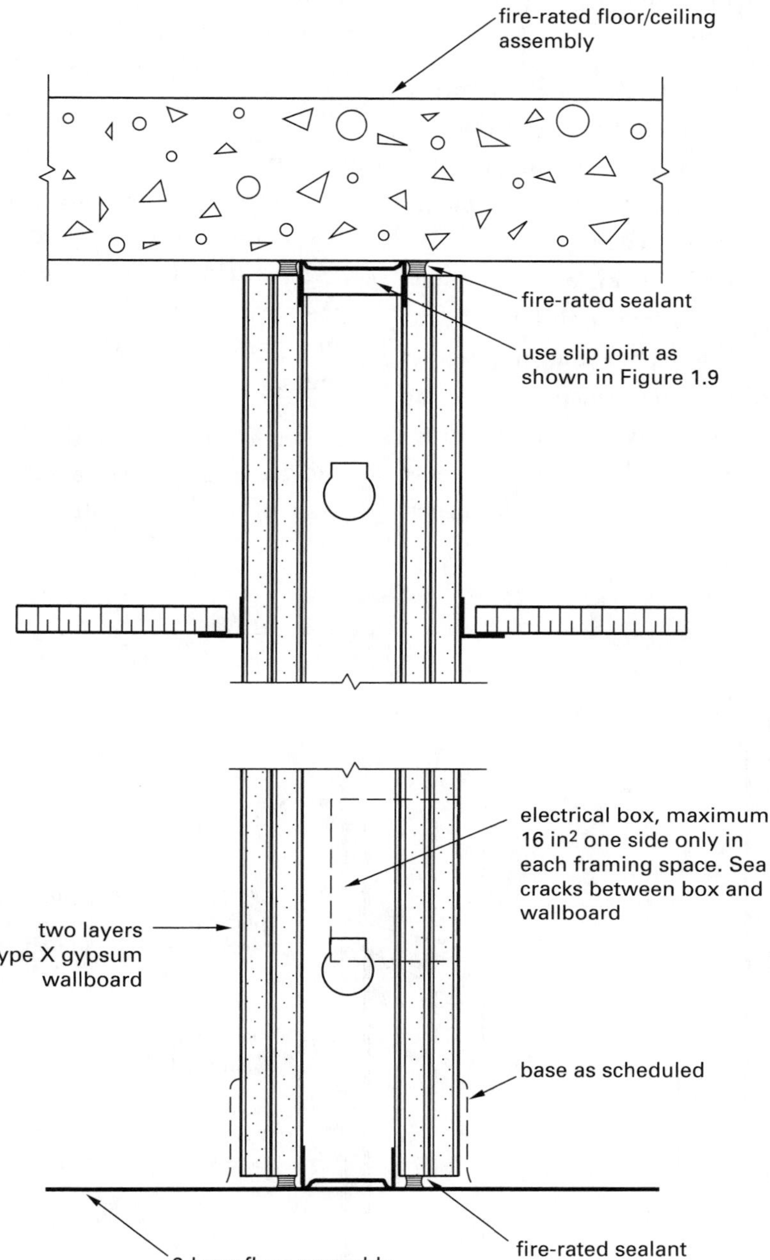


**Figure 1.12**
Two-hour-rated partition

Figure 1.13 shows a chase wall, which is a double row of studs braced together and spaced far enough apart to accommodate plumbing pipes. Chase walls can also be used to recess large elements, such as bookcases and cabinets. If sound control is required, extra layers of wallboard are applied or resilient furring channels are used.

For soffits above cabinets, lockers, and similar items, gypsum wallboard can be framed down from the ceiling, as shown in Fig. 1.14. In residential construction, 2 × 2s or 2 × 4s are used instead of the metal framing shown in the commercial detail of Fig. 1.14.

## Special partition construction

Detailing often requires special partition construction for acoustical separation, shaft linings around stairways and dumbwaiters in high-rise buildings, and column enclosures to maintain the required fire ratings for structural elements.

There are many acoustical partition designs available; the right choice depends on the degree of sound reduction desired. Some of the more common ways of detailing partitions are illustrated in Figs. 1.15–1.20. For partitions with a single row of studs, additional sound attenuation for standard partitions is achieved by adding more layers of wallboard, by using resilient channels, by using batt insulation within the stud cavity, or with some combination of all these methods. High-attenuation partitions, such as those shown in Figs. 1.17 and 1.18, usually require a double row of studs to physically separate one side of the partition from the other.

In all types of acoustic partitions, simply detailing the partition is not enough. Special attention must also be placed on observing the construction to verify compliance with the drawings, sealing all penetrations, and using the appropriate types of doors and frames.

Although 2-hour-rated shaft lining partitions are usually part of the architectural design of a building, interior construction

**Figure 1.13**
Chase wall

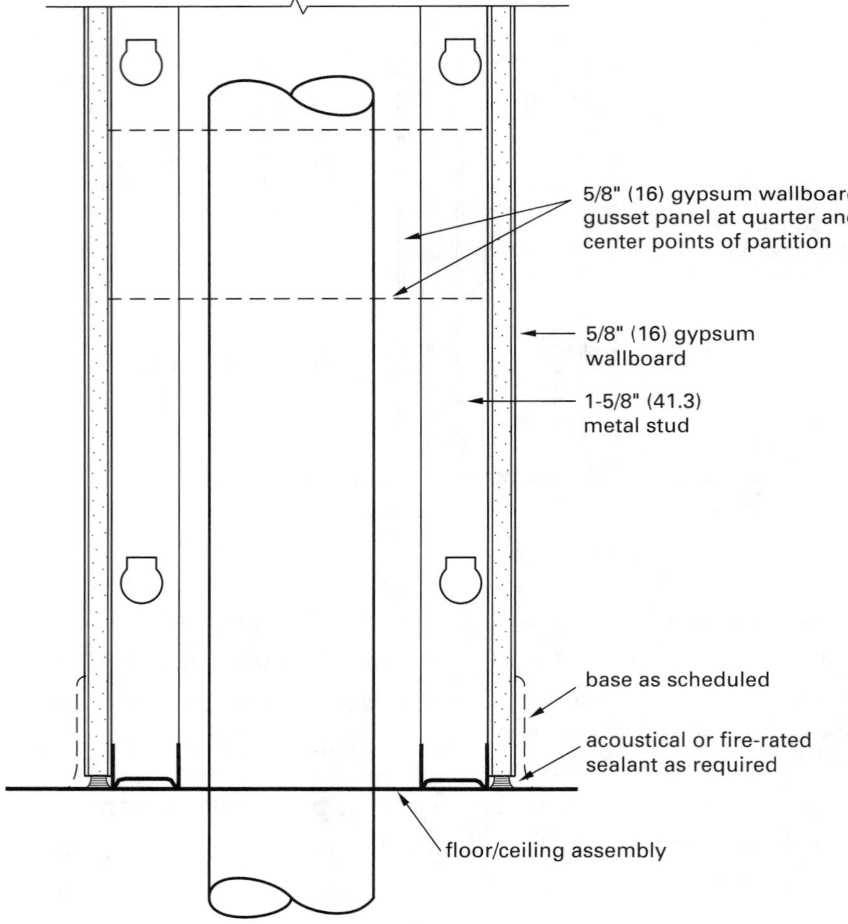

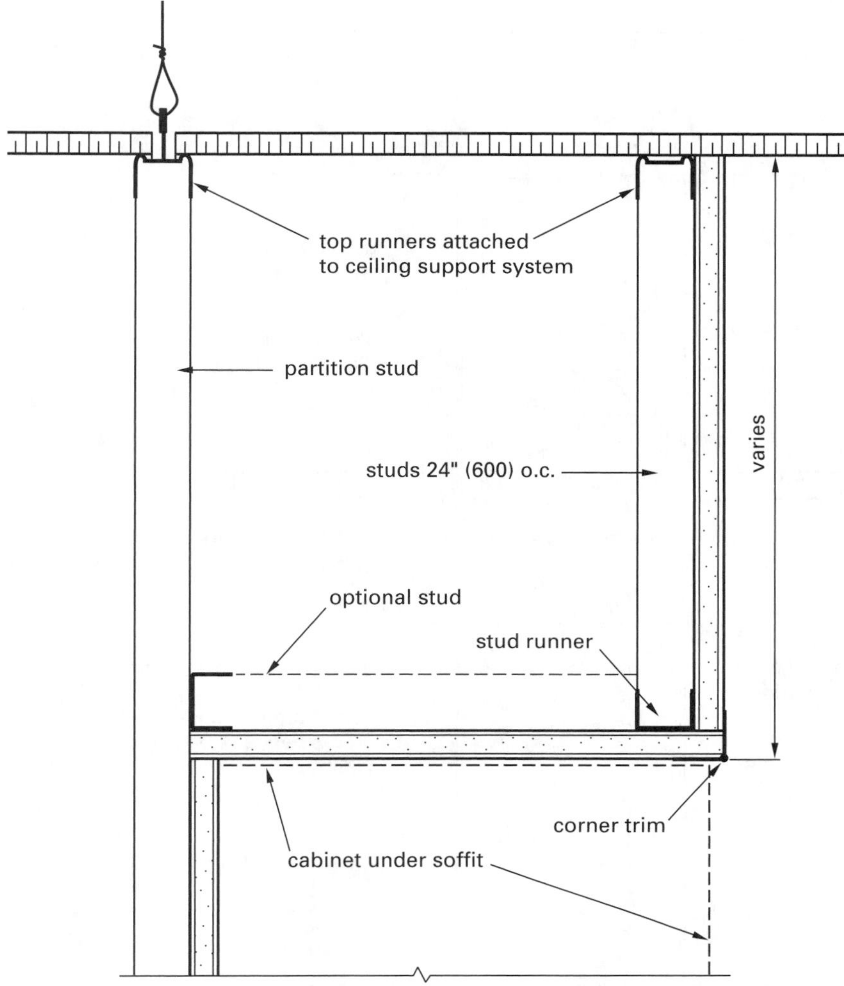


**Figure 1.14**
Soffit detail

sometimes requires an enclosed stairway. This usually occurs when a new stairway is constructed in a high-rise building for a multifloor tenant. Two-hour-rated shafts are also required for vertical transportation systems, such as dumbwaiters. It is useful to know the size requirements for detailing such an opening so that plenty of space can be provided early in the design phase. One method of detailing a partition around a stairway that bypasses an intermediate floor is shown in Fig. 1.19. The exact configuration may vary depending on the structural system used.

Fire protection of structural elements is another condition that is usually part of the architectural design of a building. However, new construction is often required during remodeling when old column covers are stripped away. Figure 1.20 shows one method of enclosing a steel column that otherwise had not been protected with spray-on fireproofing. Refer to Ch. 19 for more information on how to determine hourly rating requirements for structural elements.

There are many varieties of gypsum wallboard partitions, but the partitions discussed in this section are the most common for the majority of interior construction. The final decision usually accounts for cost, fire-rating requirements, acoustical separation needs, and ease of construction.

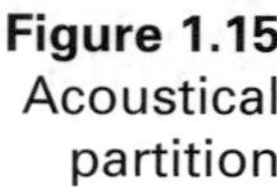

**Figure 1.15**
Acoustical partition

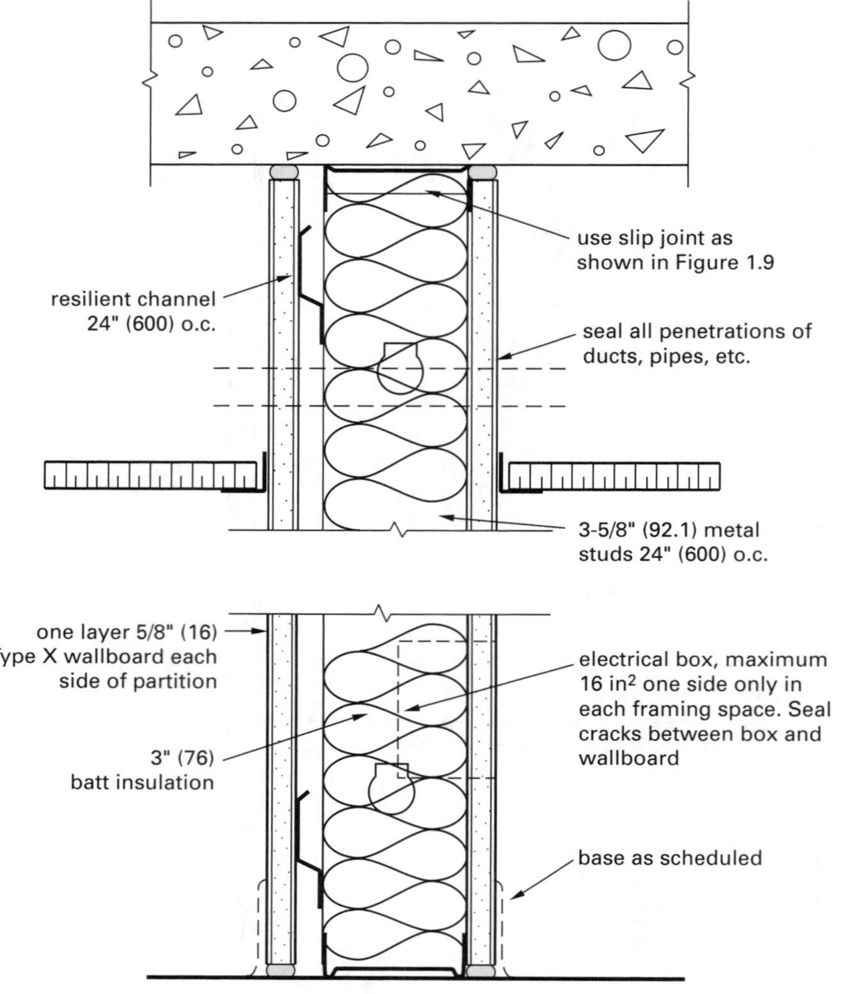


STC: 54
1-hour rated

**Figure 1.16**
Acoustical partition at suspended wallboard ceiling

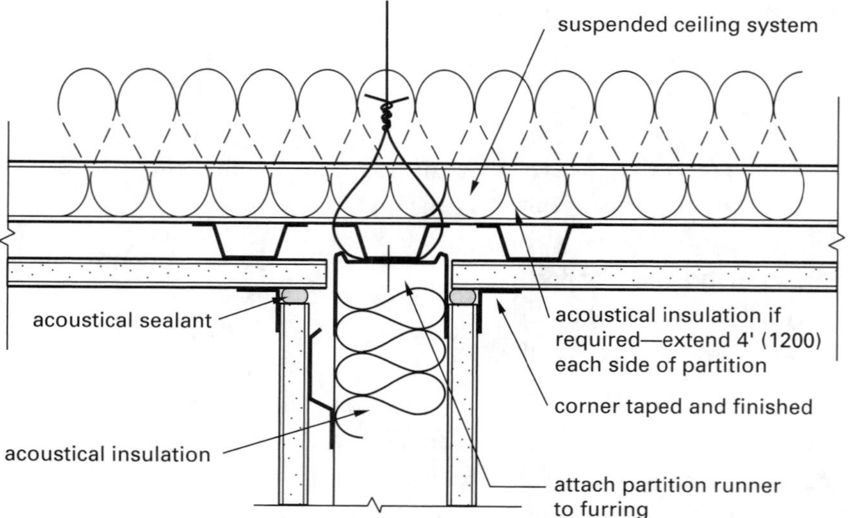

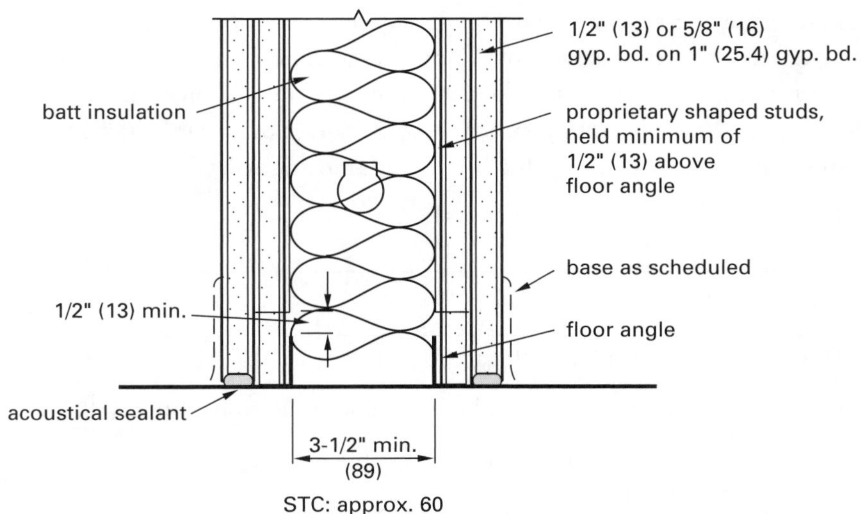


**Figure 1.17** High-attenuation partition

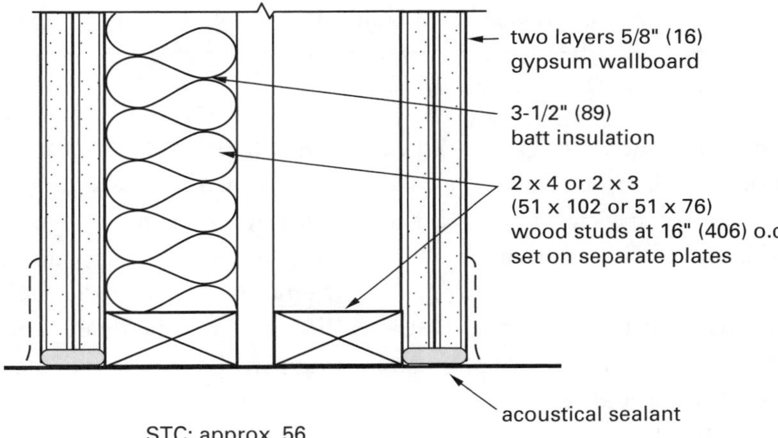


**Figure 1.18** Wood-framed high-attenuation partition

The partitions discussed in this section are sketched in Table 1.6 along with a description of their construction, their fire ratings, and their acoustical STC ratings. Some additional partitions that are variations of the ones discussed are also included.

## Coordination with other construction components

Developing partition details requires coordination with other construction elements and conditions. Some of the things to consider in addition to fire and sound ratings include the following: vertical deflection of floor structures, horizontal movement, support for heavy loads, total partition depth, and partition anchors.

### Vertical deflection

In many cases, it is simply a matter of nailing, screwing, or using power-actuated fasteners to rigidly attach the bottom and top runners of a partition to the floor and ceiling. In other cases, movement of the structure must be provided for, as discussed in the previous section.

### Horizontal movement

In tall buildings, wind loading on the exterior wall or windows causes a slight horizontal

## STC ratings and what they mean

The sound transmission class (STC) of a construction assembly is a quick way to evaluate the relative effectiveness of the assembly in reducing sound transmission. It uses a single number to represent the average sound loss. For more information on acoustics, refer to Ch. 11. Table 1.5 gives some STC ratings and a subjective description of their effect on speech. Higher ratings may be required to reduce the sound transmission of music, machinery, and other types of noise.

**Table 1.5**
STC ratings and what they mean

| STC | subjective effect |
|---|---|
| 25 | Normal speech can be clearly heard through the barrier. |
| 30 | Loud speech can be heard and understood fairly well. |
| 35 | Loud speech is not intelligible but can be heard. |
| 42–45 | Loud speech can only be heard faintly. Normal speech cannot be heard. |
| 46–50 | Loud speech is not audible. Loud sounds other than speech can only be heard faintly, if at all. |

movement. If a partition is rigidly attached to a window mullion or flexible wall, the gypsum wallboard may crack. This was also discussed in the previous section.

### Support for hanging heavy loads

Standard gypsum wallboard partitions constructed with metal studs will only support moderate loads. Although there are various types of screws and bolts that can be used to hang pictures and lightweight shelving, blocking must be shown on the drawings when heavy loads are involved. This blocking is either ¾ in (19 mm) plywood or solid wood and is placed within the wall cavity, set between the studs and attached to them. The wood blocking provides a solid substrate into which screws can be driven to support cabinets, paneling, and other wall-hung items.

### Partition depth

If plumbing pipes, recessed equipment, or other large items must be built into the walls, a stud size must be specified that accommodates the largest item. For very deep built-in items, a chase wall must be detailed, as shown in Fig. 1.13.

### Partition anchoring

In commercial construction, partitions are often only built to the underside of the suspended acoustical ceiling. The top runner is fastened to the ceiling grid, and this is all that holds the upper portion of the partition in place. When heavy doors or cabinets are placed on the wall, it is often necessary to provide additional braces extending from above the ceiling to the structural floor above. These braces are called *kickers* and are usually metal studs that can be screwed to the top partition runner through the ceiling.

### Environmental considerations

Because gypsum wallboard is produced in such large quantities (over 36 billion square feet [3.36 billion m$^2$] in 2005), its manufacture, use, and disposal have an effect on the environment. Since the 1950s, gypsum wallboard manufacturers have been using recycled paper to manufacture the surfaces of wallboard. In addition, some manufacturers are using recycled newspaper mixed with gypsum as the core material to yield a product that is more rigid than standard

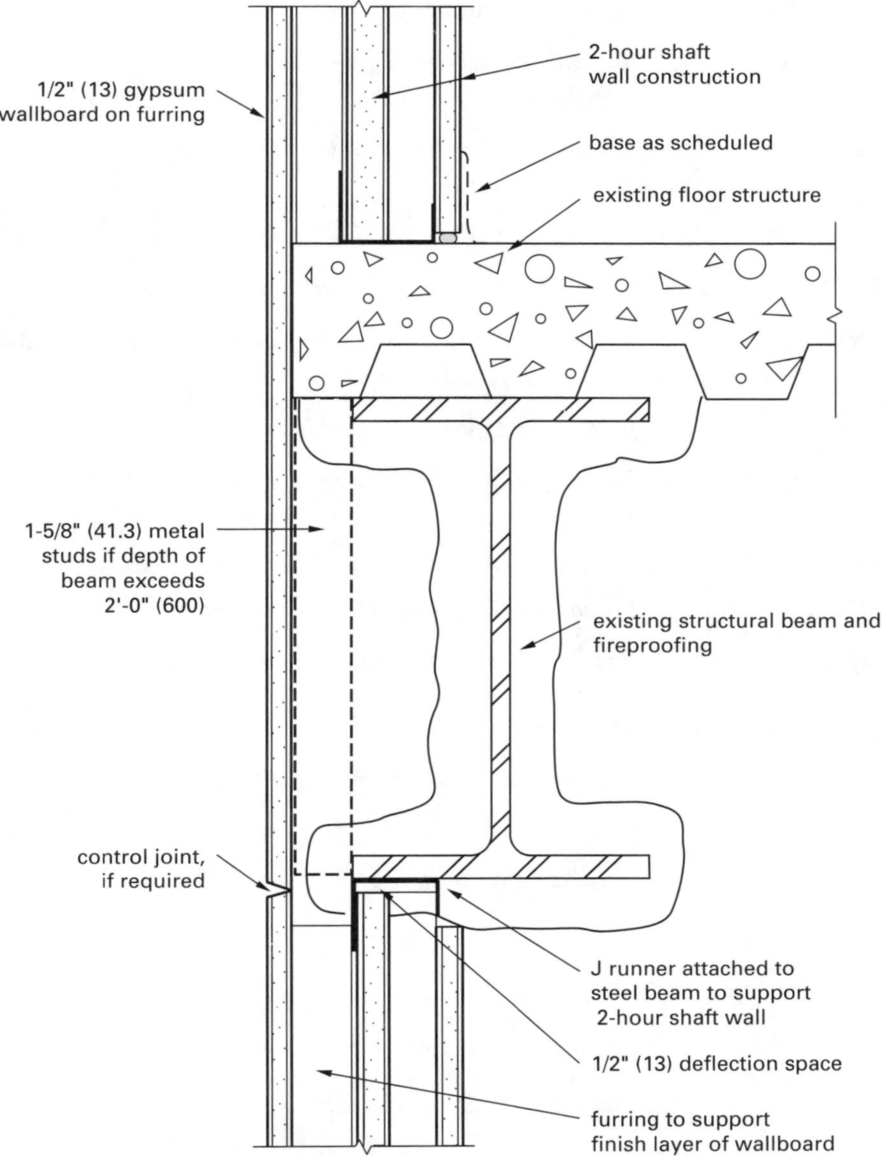


**Figure 1.19**
Two-hour-rated partition at stair opening

wallboard yet still maintains all the other advantages of the product. In addition, about 7% of the industry's total use of natural gypsum is synthetic gypsum. Synthetic gypsum is chemically identical to natural, mined gypsum, but is a byproduct of various manufacturing, industrial, or chemical processes. The main source of synthetic gypsum in North America is flue gas desulfurization. This is the process whereby power generating plants (and similar plants) remove polluting gases from their stacks to reduce emission of harmful materials into the atmosphere. Using this by-product allows the efficient use of refuse material that would otherwise have to be discarded.

The larger environmental concern involves the disposal of used gypsum wallboard, which cannot be reused for its original purpose when it is ripped out of an old building or a renovation project. There are some gypsum wallboard plants around the country that are recycling old drywall. The only condition is that the wallboard must be free of screws, nails, asbestos, and lead paint. Currently,

## Applicable standards for gypsum wallboard partitions

American Society for Testing and Materials (ASTM):

| | |
|---|---|
| ASTM A653 | *Specification for Sheet Steel, Zinc-Coated (Galvanized) or Zinc-Iron Alloy-coated by the Hot-Dip Process* |
| ASTM C475 | *Specification for Joint Compound and Joint Tape for Finishing Gypsum Board* |
| ASTM C514 | *Specification for Nails for the Application of Gypsum Wallboard* |
| ASTM C645 | *Specification for Nonstructural Steel Framing Members* |
| ASTM C754 | *Specification for Installation of Steel Framing Members to Receive Screw-Attached Gypsum Panel Products* |
| ASTM C840 | *Specification for Application and Finishing of Gypsum Board* |
| ASTM C1002 | *Specification for Steel Self-Piercing Tapping Screws for the Application of Gypsum Panel Products or Metal Plaster Bases to Wood Studs or Steel Studs* |
| ASTM C1178 | *Specification for Glass Mat Water-Resistant Gypsum Backing Panel* |
| ASTM C1278 | *Specification for Fiber Reinforced Gypsum Panel* |
| ASTM C1396 | *Standard Specification for Gypsum Board* |

Gypsum Association (GA):

| | |
|---|---|
| GA-214 | *Recommended Levels of Gypsum Board Finish* |
| GA-216 | *Application and Finishing of Gypsum Board* |
| GA-600 | *Fire Resistance Design Manual* |

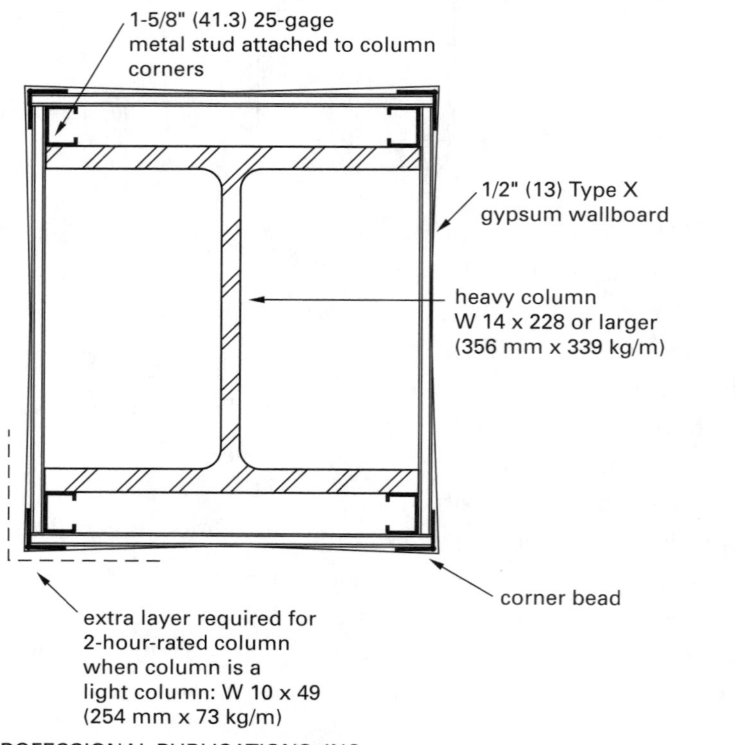


**Figure 1.20** Two-hour-rated column cover

**Table 1.6**
Common partition types

| partition | description | fire rating | STC | figure reference |
|---|---|---|---|---|
| 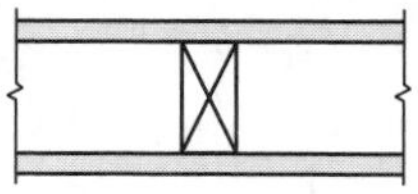 | ½ in (12.7 mm) wallboard each side 2 × 4 (51 × 102) wood studs 16 in (406 mm) on center. One-hour rating with ⅝ in (15.9 mm) Type X wallboard. | 3/4 hr | +30 | 1.6 |
| 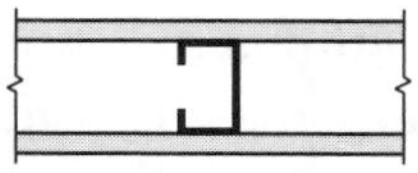 | ⅝ in (16 mm) wallboard each side 2½ in (64 mm) metal studs 24 in (610 mm) on center to underside of suspended ceiling. | None | ±40 | 1.7 |
|  | ⅝ in (16 mm) Type X wallboard each side 2½ in (64 mm) metal studs 24 in (610 mm) on center built to underside of slab above with 1½ in (38 mm) sound attenuation insulation. | 1 hr | ±47 | 1.8 |
| 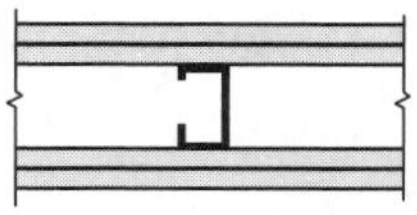 | Two layers ⅝ in (16 mm) Type X wallboard each side 2½ in (64 mm) metal studs 24 in (610 mm) on center built to underside of slab above. Adding 2 in (51 mm) sound attenuation insulation blanket raises STC to about 56. | 2 hr | ±48 | 1.12 |
| 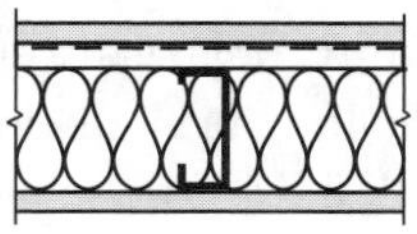 | ⅝ in (16 mm) Type X wallboard each side 3⅝ in (92 mm) metal studs 24 in (610 mm) on center. Wallboard one side mounted on resilient channels 24 in (610 mm) o.c. with 3 in (76 mm) sound attenuation insulation in stud cavity. | 1 hr | ±54 | 1.15 |
| 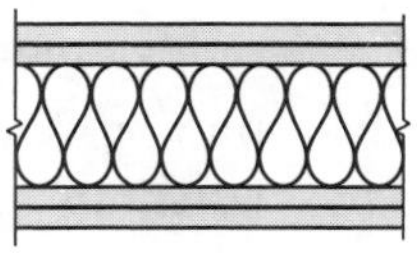 | ½ in (13 mm) wallboard on 1 in (25.4 mm) wallboard liner panels on proprietary studs. Liner panels spaced 3½ in (89 mm) apart with cavity filled with 3 in (76 mm) sound attenuation insulation. Bead of acoustical sealant on vertical center line between panel edges. | 3 hr | ±60 | 1.17 |
| 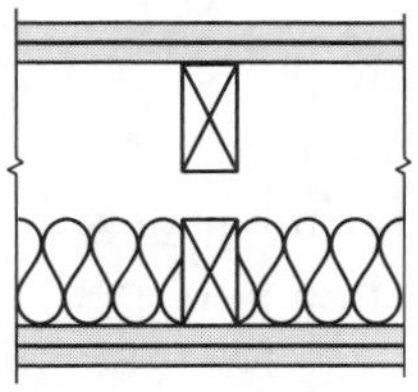 | Two layers ⅝ in (16 mm) Type X wallboard on 2 × 4 studs 16 in (406 mm) o.c. on separate plates. 3½ in (89 mm) sound attenuation insulation in cavity. | 2 hr | ±56 | 1.18 |
| 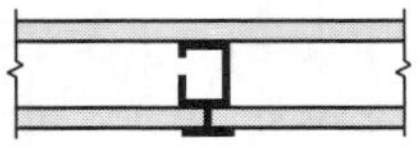 | ⅝ in (16 mm) Type X wallboard on proprietary studs 24 in (610 mm) o.c. with 1 in (25.4 mm) wallboard panel on shaft side. | 1 hr | ±35 | 1.2(a) |
| 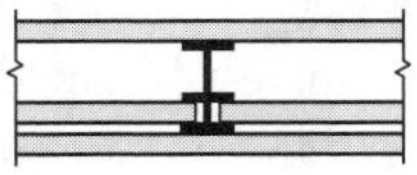 | ⅝ in (16 mm) Type X wallboard each side proprietary studs 24 in (610 mm) o.c. with 1 in (25.4 mm) wallboard liner panel set between studs. | 2 hr | ±41 | 1.19 |
| 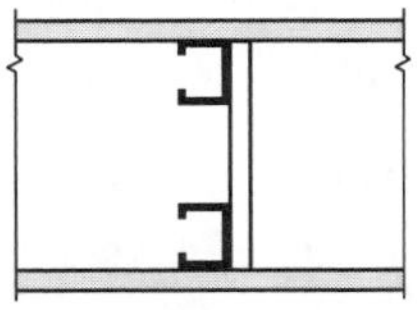 | ⅝ in (16 mm) Type X wallboard each side 1⅝ in (41.3 mm) studs 24 in (610 mm) o.c. with ⅝ in (16 mm) wallboard gusset panel attached at quarter points and center point. Adding 3½ in (89 mm) sound attenuation insulation raises STC to about 52. | 1 hr | N/A | 1.13 |
| 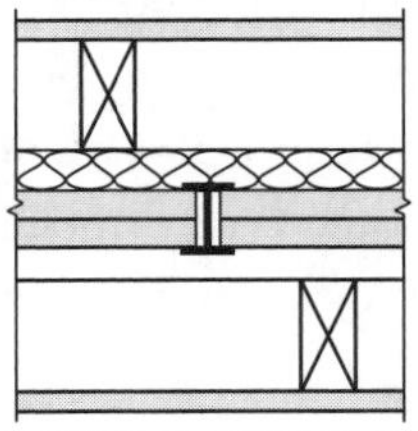 | ½ in (13 mm) wallboard on 2 × 4 studs 16 in (406 mm) o.c. with two layers 1 in (25.4 mm) wallboard set between H-studs 24 in (610 mm) o.c. 1 in (25.4 mm) sound attenuation insulation on one side of double 1 in panels. | 2 hr | ±50 | 1.2(b) |

Source: United States Gypsum Company.

the cost of collecting and transporting the old wallboard is a disincentive for recycling.

Old wallboard can also be pulverized into pieces equal to or smaller than ½ in and worked into the ground as a soil additive. Farmers in California and parts of Colorado use recycled gypsum as a soil conditioner for grapes, peas, and peanuts. It is also possible to work the gypsum directly into the soil around a job site as long as the land has adequate drainage and aeration and local and state regulations allow it.

## LATH AND PLASTER PARTITIONS [092113]

Gypsum wallboard has supplanted plaster as the typical partition material because it costs less, is easier and faster to apply, and is readily available, and because many workers know how to install it. However, plaster has many advantages that gypsum wallboard cannot duplicate: it can be applied to form single or double curves, it can be molded into ornate decorative pieces for either new or remodeling work, and it can be finished with a wide variety of textures. Functionally, it is very abrasion resistant, and it is water resistant if portland cement is used.

### Plaster partition components

Plaster is a cementitious material that is applied to a surface in a plastic state and subsequently sets, or hardens, to a rigid state. The most common plasters used today for interior finishing are some combination of a cementitious binder, either gypsum or portland cement, with lime, water, and aggregates of sand, vermiculite, or perlite.

The two cementitious binders used represent the two broad categories of plasters: gypsum and portland cement. Gypsum plaster is used for most interior applications. Portland cement plaster is used in interiors where wetting, steam, or severe dampness is expected. When portland cement plaster is used on the exterior of a building it is often called stucco.

#### Plaster

There are various formulations of plastering material to suit different conditions and to enhance the material's strength, abrasion resistance, and water resistance. Most partitions can be constructed with gypsum plaster troweled to a smooth finish. When water resistance is required, portland cement plaster over metal lath is used because moisture can cause gypsum plaster to deteriorate. When extreme abrasion resistance is needed, Keene's cement is used. This is a mixture of pure, completely dehydrated gypsum and lime putty.

For added texture, strength, sound reduction, and workability, various gradations of sand are added to the mixture. Aggregates of pumice, perlite, or vermiculite can also help reduce shrinkage, extend finish coverage, lower cost, and increase plasticity. Unique decorative effects can be achieved by adding unusual materials, such as straw or wax. Pigments can be added to the plaster mix to create integral color.

Special effects available with plaster include scagliola, sgraffito, marezzo, and fresco. Scagliola is plaster applied and painted to give the appearance of marble. Sgraffito is a plastering process that uses two or more layers of different-colored plasters. While the plasters are still soft, part of the top layer is scratched off to expose the layer or layers below. Marezzo is another type of imitation material formed with colored Keene's cement and precast on a glass or marble bed. Fresco is the painting of freshly spread plaster before it sets.

The two basic types of plaster construction are standard lath and plaster and veneer plaster over gypsum board lath. The standard lath and plaster construction method is the traditional type, where several coats of plaster are applied over some type of open lath that is attached to studs or some other type of framing. It is even possible to form solid plaster partitions two or more inches thick; however, this technique is seldom used today. The veneer plaster method substitutes a special type of gypsum wallboard for the open lath. The wallboard is applied to wood or metal studs, and a very thin coat of plaster from 1/16 in to 1/8 in (1.6 mm to 3 mm) thick is applied over the wallboard to form a uniform, homogenous surface.

Portland cement plaster can also be applied directly to concrete or masonry surfaces, but this is not a common use for interior applications. It is generally preferable to attach furring strips over the wall and apply a veneer plaster system onto the furring.

### Metal lath [092236]

Expanded metal lath is used in standard lath-and-plaster construction. There are various types, but the three most common for interior use are shown in Fig. 1.21. Diamond mesh lath as shown in Fig. 1.21(a) is used over studs or other framing by attaching it with wire ties. This type of lath can be shaped into single curves or shaped and molded into complex, double curves. It is also available in a self-furring type for use in column fireproofing and replastering old surfaces.

Flat rib metal lath, shown in Fig. 1.21(b), is more rigid than diamond mesh lath and is used for flat ceilings and in other applications where extra rigidity is needed. Rib metal lath, shown in Fig. 1.21(c), is available with either 3/8 in (10 mm) or 3/4 in (19 mm) ribs spaced about 4 in (100 mm) apart. This is used for studless, solid partitions or where rigidity is needed over widely spaced framing.

### Gypsum lath [092236]

Gypsum lath is used for veneer plaster installations. This is similar to gypsum wallboard, with the exception that the paper surface is specially formulated to provide a good plaster bond. The paper face is usually light blue and is sometimes referred to as "blueboard." Fire-rated gypsum lath must be used for rated partitions.

### Trim

For both types of plaster construction various trim types are used for outside corners, in framed openings, and where the plaster abuts another material. These trim pieces are very similar to those used for gypsum wallboard construction.

## Typical plaster construction

In the standard lath and plaster construction method, plaster is applied in three coats over wire lath. See Fig. 1.22. The first coat is called the *scratch coat* and is about 1/2 in (12 mm) thick. Before it sets, the scratch coat is roughened with deep ridges to provide a good base for mechanical bonding of the next coat. The second coat, or *brown coat,* is

**Figure 1.21**
Expanded metal lath

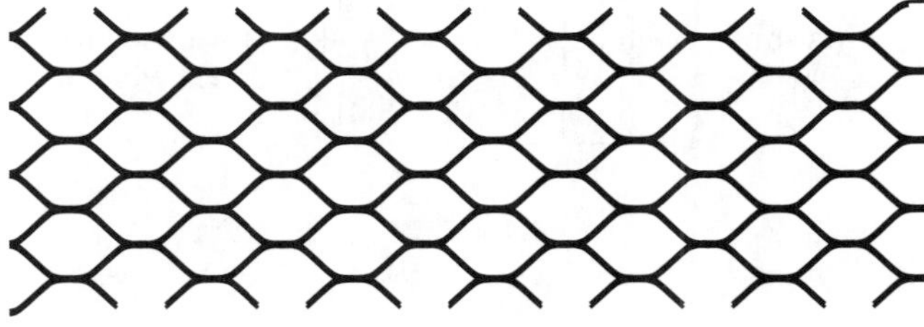

(a) diamond mesh lath

(b) flat rib metal lath

(c) rib metal lath

**Building code provisions for plaster construction**

Building codes specify the requirements for plaster mixes for various applications, frame spacing, the types and application of gypsum and metal lath, and the exact method of applying the lath and plaster. Refer to the appropriate model code for specific requirements.

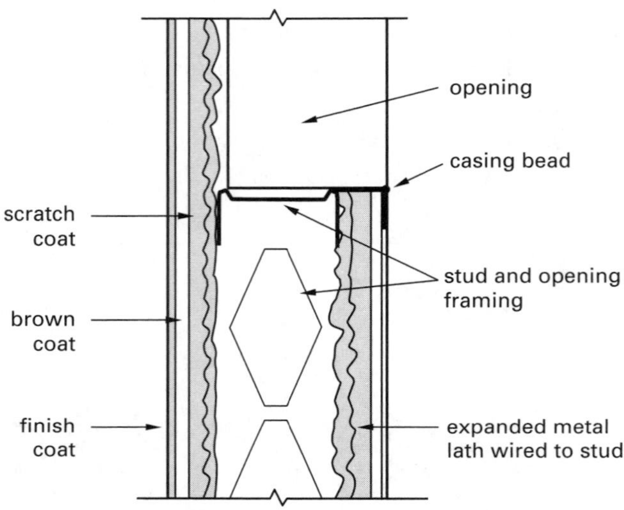


**Figure 1.22** Traditional three-coat plaster partition

about ¼ in (6 mm) thick and is used to bring the surface to a true level and near its final position. The *finish coat* of about ⅛ in (3 mm) provides the final smoothing and surface texture. Sometimes only two coats are used, primarily in preparation for applying ceramic tile.

Veneer plaster has many of the advantages of three-coat plaster, but only one of its disadvantages. It provides a very hard, durable surface that can be treated with a variety of textures and finishes and is faster and less expensive to construct. In addition, there is not as much moisture involved during interior construction. The only disadvantage is that gypsum lath is not appropriate as a base in wet areas such as showers and around tubs. Cement backing boards are used in residential construction or in other moderately wet construction areas. Standard lath and plaster systems are used for extremely wet, commercial applications. A typical veneer plaster partition is shown in Fig. 1.23. The veneer may be applied in one or two coats.

Variations of the typical partition shown in Fig. 1.23 include using two layers of fire-rated gypsum lath to achieve a 2-hour rating, adding batt insulation to improve the sound attenuation properties of the partition, and using resilient channels to further improve sound attenuation.

Stud spacing depends primarily on the type and weight of the lath and the weight of any surfacing material, such as ceramic tile. Metal studs measuring 2½ in (63.5 mm) should be spaced 16 in (406 mm) on center. See Table 1.7 for recommended stud spacing.

## Glass-reinforced gypsum [092713]

The term *glass-reinforced gypsum* (GRG) refers to a broad class of products manufactured from high-strength, high-density gypsum reinforced with continuous filament glass fibers or chopped glass fibers. It is also known as *fiberglass-reinforced gypsum* (FRG) and *glass-fiber-reinforced gypsum* (GFRG).

GRG products are used for decorative elements, such as column covers, arches, coffered ceilings, ornate moldings, light troughs, and trim. They are premanufactured products made by pouring GRG into molds. After setting, the products are shipped to the job site for installation and final finishing. They can be finished with any kind of material that can be put on plaster or gypsum wallboard. An unlimited variety of shapes can be manufactured that would otherwise be too expensive or impossible to achieve with site-fabricated lath and plaster.

**Table 1.7** Maximum spacing of studs for plaster partitions

| lath type | wood studs (in (mm)) | metal studs (in (mm)) |
|---|---|---|
| diamond mesh, 2.5 psy[1] | 16 (406) | 12 (305) |
| diamond mesh, 3.4 psy [1] | 16 (406) | 16 (406) |
| flat rib lath, 2.75 psy [1] | 16 (406) | 16 (406) |
| flat rib lath, 3.4 psy [1] | 19 (483) | 19 (483) |
| ⅜ in rib lath, 3.4 psy [1] | 24 (610) | 24 (610) |
| ⅜ in gypsum lath | 16 (406) | 16 (406) |
| ½ in gypsum lath, 1-coat system | 16 (406) | 16[3] (406) |
| ½ in gypsum lath, 2-coat system | 16/24[2] (406/610) | 16/24[3] (406/610) |
| ⅝ in gypsum lath, 1-coat system | 16/24[2] (406/610) | 16/24[3] (406/610) |
| ⅝ in gypsum lath, 2-coat system | 24[2] (610) | 24[3] (610) |

(1) psy = weight of lath in pounds per square yard. Verify with specific manufacturer's recommendations.
(2) Spacing of 24 in may require special joint treatment. Follow manufacturer's recommendations.
(3) Assemblies using metal studs and gypsum base require paper joint tape and setting-type joint compound.

Source: United States Gypsum Company.

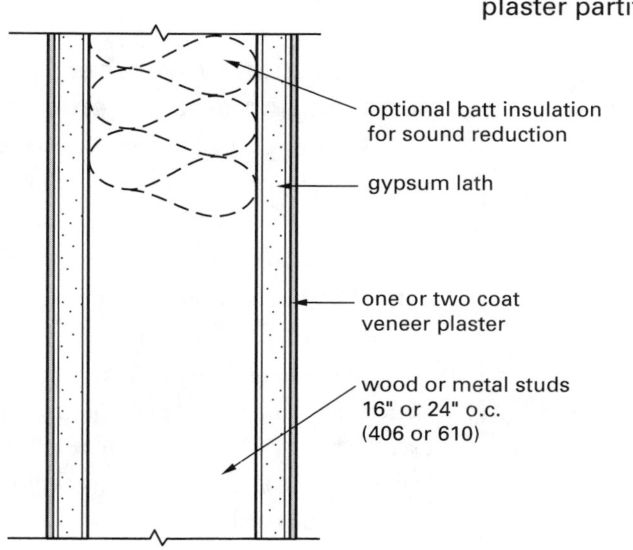


**Figure 1.23** Veneer plaster partition

## Design tips

Here are some design tips for glass-reinforced gypsum that will save time and reduce costs.

- Design GRG components so that only one side is exposed. Because of the way GRG is molded, the back side is rough and shows the reinforcing and stiffing ribs.
- Minimize the number and detail of components on a job. The more unique the molds that have to be made, the higher the cost will be.

**Security partitions**

For durable, thin, smooth-finish partitions in jails, vaults, and other security areas, it is possible to construct a solid plaster partition that resists breakthrough and ballistic attack. A special, heavy-gage, perforated steel sheet is used in the center of the partition, and high-strength plaster is applied to the steel sheet. A finish coat of 3000 psi or 20,684 kPa (psi-pounds per square inch; kPa-kilopascals) compressive strength plaster is then applied over the solid base coat. Although not appropriate in every instance, this type of partition is thin (from 3½ in to 4½ in (89 mm to 115 mm), lightweight, and easy to maintain and repair.

- GRG shapes should only be used as decorative covers—not for bearing loads.
- Detail corners so that components can be removed easily from the molds. This means providing curves or draft angles and avoiding 90° angles or details that make it impossible to remove a casting from a mold.
- GRG components are attached to framing with screws, adhesive, or hanging. Follow the manufacturer's recommendation for specific details.
- Openings for mechanical and electrical penetrations can be made in the field.
- Transitions from curved GRG shapes to flat gypsum wallboard should be made so that the GRG curved component extends about 2 in (50 mm) into the flat wallboard. This allows the joint to be floated together easily.
- Joint alignment tolerances should not exceed ⅛ in (3 mm), and joint width should not exceed ⅜ in (10 mm).

### Coordination with other construction components

- Mounting strips or wood cleats for attachment of medium to heavy cabinets and other loads should be bolted to metal studs.
- Steel door frames used with plaster partitions should be at least 16-gage steel.
- Control joints or relief joints should be placed where a plaster partition abuts a structural element, where a partition run exceeds 30 ft (9.1 m), and where a building expansion or control joint occurs. Full-height doors can be used as control joints.
- Metal studs for partitions faced with ceramic tile should be a minimum of 20-gage, 3⅝ in (92.1 mm) deep, spaced 16 in (406 mm) on center.
- The total thickness of the scratch and mortar coating as the base for ceramic tile should not exceed 1 in (25.4 mm).

## MASONRY PARTITIONS

Masonry is a term that includes brick, concrete block, glass block, structural clay tile, terra cotta, and gypsum block. Masonry is usually part of the architectural design of a building. However, there are times when interior construction requires a masonry, nonloadbearing partition for special purposes or to match existing construction. Most often, masonry partitions are concrete block or glass block.

### Concrete block [042200]

Concrete block is manufactured with cement, water, and various types of aggregate, including gravel, expanded shale or slate, expanded slag or pumice, or limestone cinders. It is hollow and its size is based on a nominal 4 in (100 mm) module that includes an allowance for ⅜ in mortar joints. One of the most common sizes is an 8 × 8 × 16 unit (203 × 203 × 406), which is actually 7⅝ in (193.7 mm) wide, 7⅝ in high, and 15⅝ in (396.9 mm) long. Common nominal thicknesses are 4, 6, 8, and 12 in (102, 152, 203, and 305 mm). Various sizes and shapes are manufactured for particular uses.

Concrete block is laid up in a staggered bond with horizontal joint reinforcement placed every 16 in (406 mm) on center vertically. As the partition is being laid, door and glass frames are set in place and anchored with special masonry anchors laid in the joints.

### Structural clay tile [042123]

For interior partitions, glazed structural clay tile is typically used where a hard, durable, nonstaining, easily cleaned partition is required, such as in hospitals, institutions, and food processing plants. Glazed tile is available in 8 × 16 and 6 × 12 sizes (203 × 406 and 152 × 305), in thicknesses of 2, 6, and 9 in (51, 152, and 225 mm). It is available in several preformed trim shapes, such as bull-nose, wall and end caps, curved inside corners, and curved outside corners. It is also available in a variety of colors and finishes. Specified in the correct thickness for the height, glazed structural clay tile provides a finished partition in one construction operation.

### Coordination with other construction components

- The loadbearing capacity of existing floors for new masonry must be verified by a structural engineer.
- In existing construction, new steel reinforcing may need to be anchored to existing floors and walls to tie new masonry walls to the existing building. This must be designed by a structural engineer.
- Electrical and plumbing requirements may increase the difficulty and cost of using masonry for interior partitions.

## Applicable standards for plaster partitions

American Society for Testing and Materials (ASTM):

| | |
|---|---|
| ASTM C28 | *Specification for Gypsum Plasters* |
| ASTM C35 | *Specification for Inorganic Aggregates for Use in Gypsum Plaster* |
| ASTM C59 | *Specification for Gypsum Casting Plaster and Gypsum Molding Plaster* |
| ASTM C61 | *Specification for Gypsum Keene's Cement* |
| ASTM C150 | *Specification for Portland Cement* |
| ASTM C206 | *Specification for Finishing Hydrated Lime* |
| ASTM C207 | *Specification for Hydrated Lime for Masonry Purposes* |
| ASTM C587 | *Specification for Gypsum Veneer Plaster* |
| ASTM C631 | *Specification for Bonding Compounds for Interior Gypsum Plastering* |
| ASTM C841 | *Specification for the Installation of Interior Lathing and Furring* |
| ASTM C842 | *Specification for the Application of Interior Gypsum Plaster* |
| ASTM C843 | *Specification for the Application of Gypsum Veneer Plaster* |
| ASTM C844 | *Specification for the Application of Gypsum Base to Receive Gypsum Veneer Plaster* |
| ASTM C847 | *Specification for Metal Lath* |
| ASTM C897 | *Specification for Aggregate for Job-Mixed Portland Cement-Based Plasters* |

• Increased sound attenuation properties can be achieved by filling the hollow cells of concrete block with sand or grout.

• Rough wood framing is required in a masonry opening to provide a solid base for wood doors and frames.

• Whenever possible, the heights and widths of openings in masonry should be based on the nominal module of the masonry, usually 4 in (102 mm), so that excessive cutting of masonry is not required.

## GLASS BLOCK PARTITIONS [042300]

Glass block is manufactured either as a hollow or solid unit with a clear, textured, or patterned face. It is a popular choice for interior use when a combination of light transmission, privacy, and security is required. Solid block can also be used for flooring if the flooring is supported correctly.

Generally, glass block does not provide rated fire resistance; however, some assemblies are now available that qualify as 30-minute and 45-minute opening protectives in 1-hour-rated walls. Underwriters Laboratories has given some manufacturer's blocks 60-minute or 90-minute ratings in openings up to 100 ft$^2$ (9.29 m$^2$) if no dimension is greater than 10 ft (3050 mm). Exact requirements vary, and some controversy exists concerning fire-rated glass block used for interior walls and openings; therefore, check with local codes.

### Glass block components

Glass block is manufactured in a nominal thickness of 4 in (102 mm) and in face sizes of 6 × 6, 8 × 8, 12 × 12, and 4 × 8 (152 × 152, 203 × 203, 305 × 305, and 102 × 203). The two standard thicknesses are 3⅛ in and 3⅞ in (79.4 mm and 98.4 mm). The thinner block is commonly used for interior partitions. Other sizes are available from manufacturers outside the U.S. Glass block is available in clear, textured, or patterned

**Building code requirements for glass block**

Building codes limit the maximum size and maximum unsupported length of unsupported glass block panels. These requirements are summarized in Table 1.8. When panels larger than these sizes are required, stiffeners similar to those shown in Figs. 1.25 or 1.26 must be provided. The International Building Code also requires that at least a 3 in (76 mm) thick block be used, that reinforcement be of minimum size W1.7 wire, and that mortar joints be from ¼ in to ⅜ in (6 mm to 10 mm) thick. The IBC requires a glass block partition to have expansion joints along the top and sides at all structural supports and to provide at least ⅜ in (10 mm) displacement.

**Table 1.8** Maximum glass block panel sizes for interior partitions based on building code limitations

| | interior walls | | |
|---|---|---|---|
| International Building Code | area (ft$^2$ (m$^2$)) | height (ft (mm)) | width (ft (mm)) |
| standard unit panel[(1)] | 250 (23.2) | 20 (6096) | 25 (7620) |
| thin unit panel[(2)] | 150 (13.9) | – | – |
| solid unit panel[(1)] | 100 (9.3) | 20 (6096) | 25 (7620) |

[(1)] Standard units have a minimum thickness of 3⅞ in (98 mm), while solid units have a minimum thickness of 3 in (76 mm).
[(2)] Thin walls are blocks 3⅛ in (79 mm) thick.

faces, and special blocks made by most manufacturers can be used to form 90° angles and end caps.

## Standard glass block assemblies

Glass block walls are laid in stack bond (with joints aligned rather than staggered) with mortar and horizontal and vertical reinforcement in the joints. Because of the glass expansion coefficient and the possibility of floor structure deflection and other building movement, it is good practice to provide expansion strips at the tops and sides of glass block partitions. Figure 1.24 shows typical detailing for the sill and head of an interior glass block wall, and Fig. 1.25 shows jamb and vertical joint details. A steel stiffener similar to the section shown in Fig. 1.25 is required when a block partition exceeds the maximum sizes allowed by the building code. An alternate type of stiffener is illustrated in Fig. 1.26.

Because glass block cannot be loadbearing, standard unit individual interior panels are limited by code to 250 ft$^2$. Thin unit panels are limited to 150 ft$^2$. Each panel must be supported both horizontally and vertically by a suitable structure and by expansion joints provided at the structural support points.

## Custom glass block assemblies

If the appearance of a frame overlapping the block is objectionable, the block can be set flush with the steel frame if special detailing is used. This is done by both horizontal and vertical reinforcement using panel anchors that are rigidly attached to the bottom and top framing members. See Fig. 1.27. This detailing also eliminates the need for intermediate vertical stiffeners, if allowed by the local building code

## Curved glass block partitions

The minimum radius of a partition is determined by the block thickness. Assuming that a wedge-shaped head joint measures

**Figure 1.24**
Glass block partition at sill and head

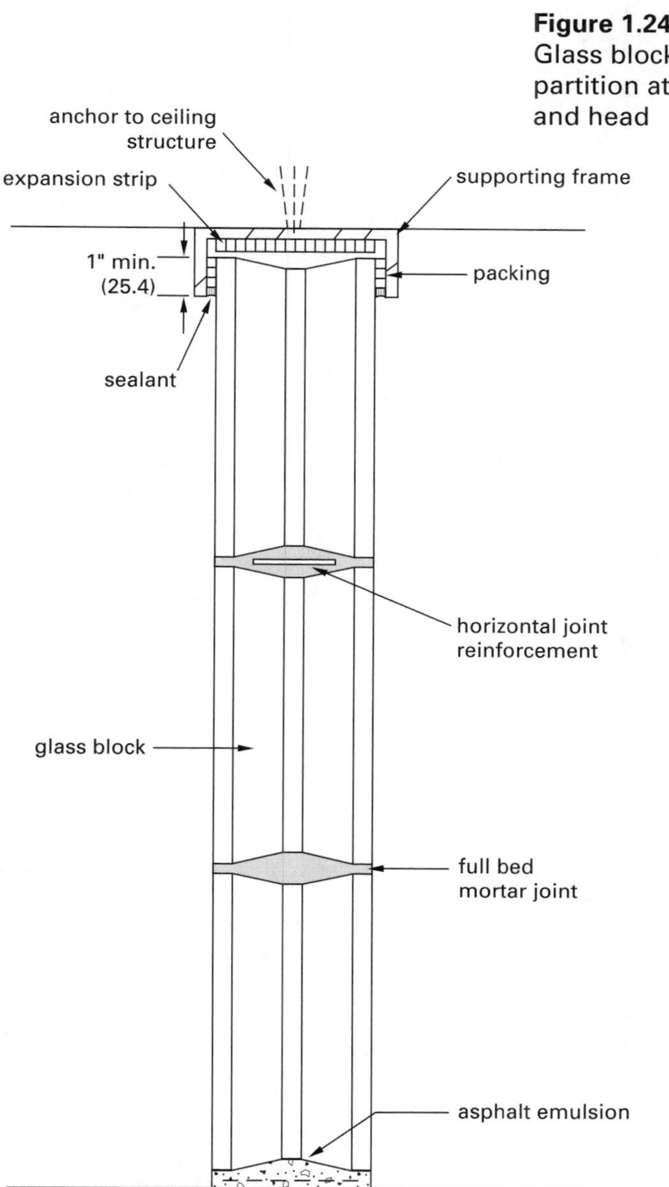


⅛ in (3 mm) on the inside and ⅝ in (16 mm) on the outside, the minimum radii for curved partitions are shown in Table 1.9.

## Coordination with other construction components

- The width and height of the opening should be an even multiple of the size of the glass block used.
- The deflection of the floors, beams, or other structural members supporting the glass block must not exceed L/600. Verification by a structural engineer is necessary.

**Table 1.9**
Minimum radii for curved glass block partitions

| block size (in (mm)) | minimum radius inside (in (mm)) |
|---|---|
| 4 (100) | 32 (813) |
| 6 (150) | 48½ (1232) |
| 8 (200) | 65 (1650) |
| 12 (300) | 98½ (2500) |

• Intermediate vertical stiffeners, as shown in Fig. 1.25 or 1.26, are required at every change of direction in a multicurved wall and at every location where a curve joins a straight section.

**Figure 1.25**
Glass block partition at jamb and vertical joint

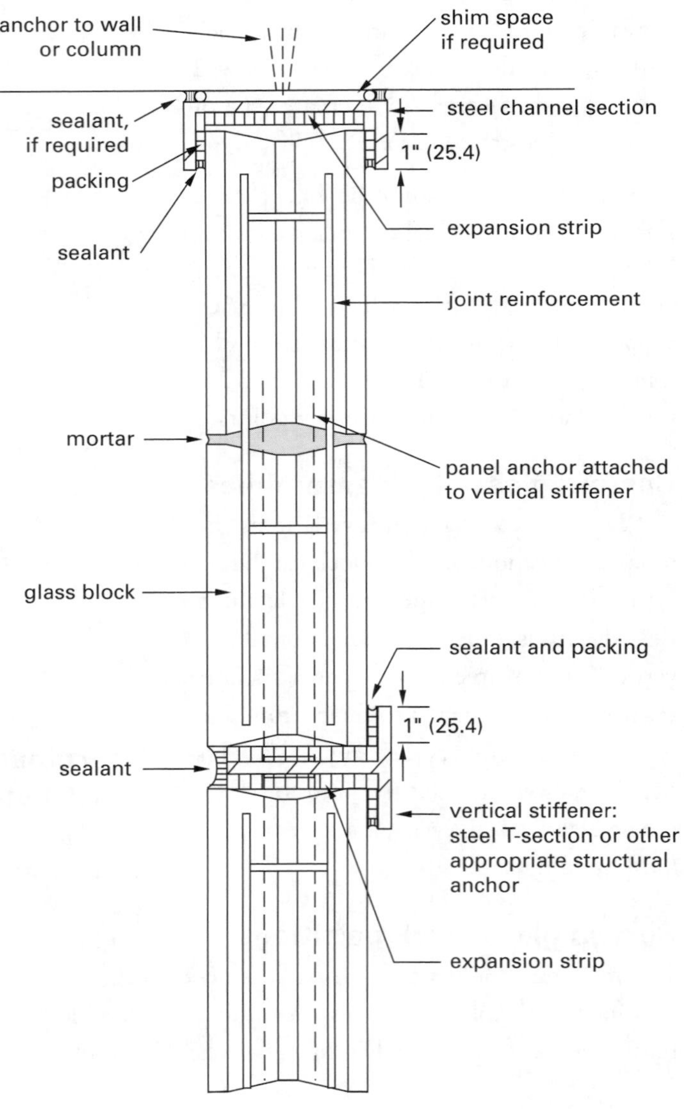

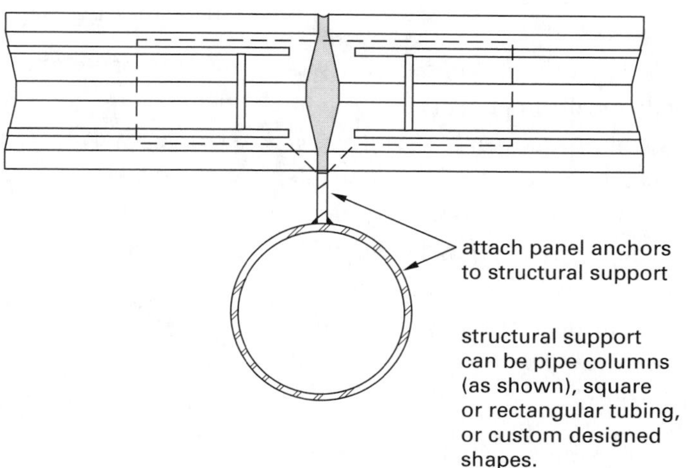


**Figure 1.26** Intermediate stiffener behind glass block partition

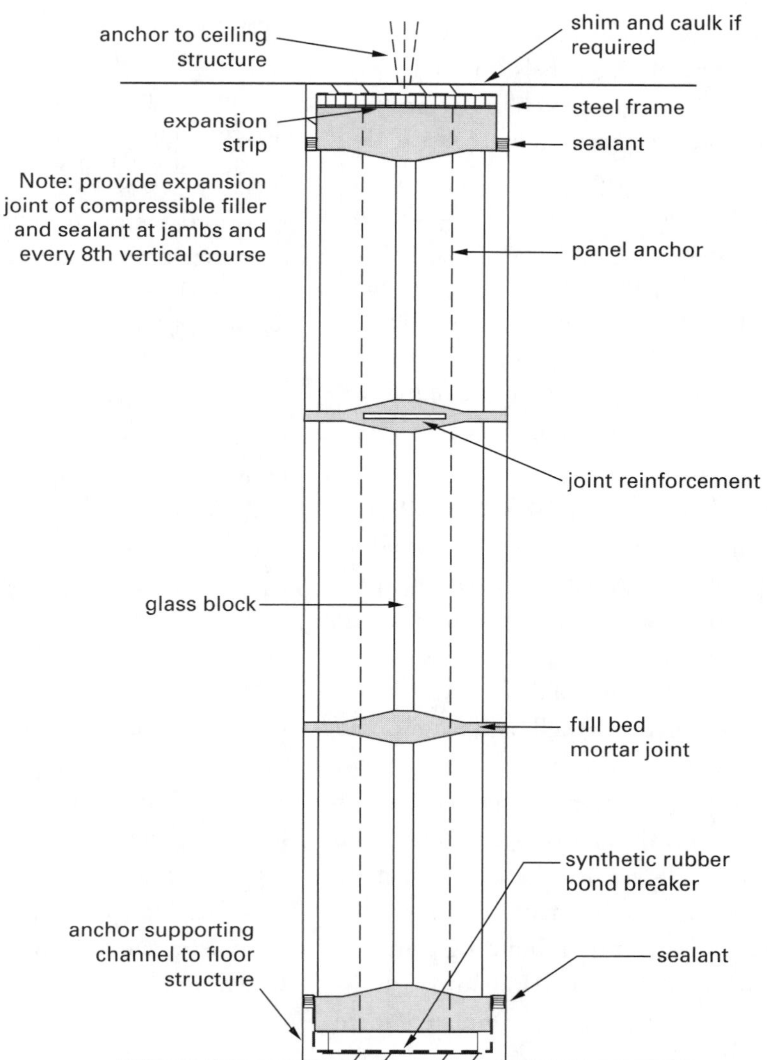


**Figure 1.27** Alternate glass block partition detail

# DEMOUNTABLE PARTITIONS [102219]

## Demountable partition components

Demountable partitions consist of a system of individual components that can be quickly assembled, disassembled, and reused with near-total salvageability. Demountable partitions differ from operable partitions, as described in Ch. 3, in that demountable partitions are intended to remain in place as standard partitions, while operable partitions act as special doors to open and close space frequently.

Demountable partitions allow space to be reconfigured quickly and easily as needs change. Because the components are prefinished and designed as a system, they can be rearranged and combined with new components, such as doors and glazing panels, without messy demolition and damage to adjacent construction. They can also make initial construction faster because flooring, ceilings, lighting, and mechanical work can be completed first, and the partitions can be installed later. Although demountable partitions have higher initial costs than standard partition construction, where space plans are changed frequently, life-cycle costs are lower because of the savings in material and labor costs.

## Typical partition construction

The configuration and design of individual components varies with each manufacturer but generally consist of four components: floor runners, ceiling runners, stud sections with clips to hold the panels, and prefinished gypsum wallboard panels. The panels are typically covered with vinyl wallcovering in a range of standard colors and patterns, although custom finishes are possible on large jobs. Panels are usually 24 in or 30 in (610 mm or 762 mm) wide to work with common building planning modules of 4 ft or 5 ft (1220 mm or 1524 mm). When a partition is completed, there are small vertical joints between the panels, and the top track is visible as it overlaps the panels at the ceiling. A manufacturer's standard base trim snaps on at the floor line.

In addition to the basic components, all manufacturer's systems have door frames, glazing, bank rails, openings, and similar common components. Some manufacturers also provide for hanging shelves and furniture components in slots between the panels.

The bottom track can rest directly on the structural floor or finished floor like a standard gypsum wallboard floor runner. As shown in Fig. 1.28, tracks are also available with spikes extending below the runner, allowing the runner to be placed directly over carpeting without crushing it. When the partition is moved, the previous partition's location is less noticeable. The top track is attached directly to the suspended ceiling system, as with standard construction, except that the flange of the track overlaps the panel and is visible in the final installation.

Partition systems can be either progressive or nonprogressive. In a progressive system the first panel must be placed before the second panel, which must be placed before the third panel, and so on. When the partition is taken down, the reverse order must be followed. In a nonprogressive system the panels are independent and can be removed or replaced individually. Although progressive systems have a lower initial cost than nonprogressive panels, they are much less flexible.

## Coordination with other construction components

Demountable partition systems are only cost-effective if they are coordinated with other building components and systems, including lighting, HVAC (heating, ventilating, and air conditioning), window mullions, and a suspended ceiling system. Space plans should be laid out on the building grid, which should also coincide with the ceiling grid. In this way, the relocation of lights,

HVAC diffusers and grilles, and sprinkler heads is minimized when partitions change. Slotted suspended ceiling grids should be used, which allow the top track to be screwed into the grid without damaging its appearance when the track is moved.

**Figure 1.28** Demountable partition

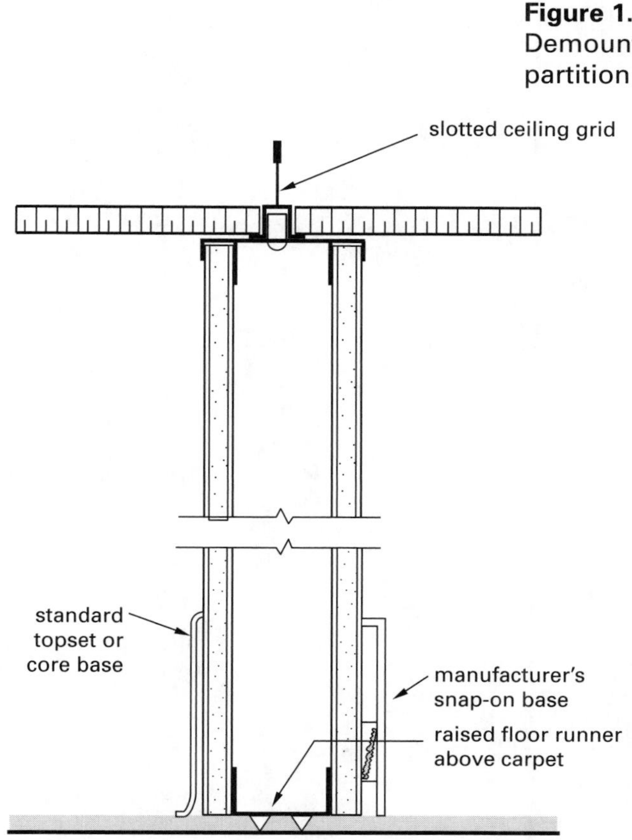

# 2

# CEILINGS

In addition to providing the finish surface for a space, ceilings form part of a system that accommodates lighting, partition attachments, supply- and return air grilles and diffusers, speakers, and other construction components. Because ceilings are dominant design features and have many functional requirements, their detailing is critical.

Ceilings can be classified into three groups based on how they are attached to the structure. They can be suspended from the structure, they can be attached directly to the structure, or the structure and the finish ceiling can be the same component. Figure 2.1 illustrates this ceiling classification system and the variations possible within each group. The most common construction method for residential ceilings is gypsum wallboard placed directly on the floor joists or ceiling joists with mechanical attachment using screws or nails. In most commercial construction, the ceiling is a wire-suspended system supporting a finished surface of acoustical tile, gypsum wallboard, or other decorative material. This provides a flat ceiling surface for partition attachment, lights, and acoustical treatment and allows the space above the ceiling, called the *plenum*, to be used for mechanical systems, wiring, and other services.

## SUSPENDED ACOUSTICAL CEILINGS [095100]

Suspended acoustical ceilings are the most common type for commercial construction. They consist of thin panels of wood fiber, mineral fiber, or glass fiber set in a support grid of metal framing that is suspended by wires from the structure. The tiles are perforated or fissured in various ways to absorb sound. Although acoustical ceilings absorb sound, they do not prevent sound transmission to any appreciable extent. The advantages of suspended acoustical ceilings include low cost, fast installation, sound control, flexibility, adaptability to lighting and mechanical services, and easy accessibility to the plenum.

### Acoustical ceiling components

Acoustical ceiling tiles and the metal grids that support them are available in a variety of sizes and configurations. The most common type is the lay-in system in which panels are simply laid on top of an exposed T-shaped grid system. See Fig. 2.2(a). A variation of this is the tegular system, which uses panels with rabbeted edges, as shown in Fig. 2.2(b).

Systems are also available in which the grid is completely concealed. Concealed systems

**Figure 2.1**
Ceiling classification

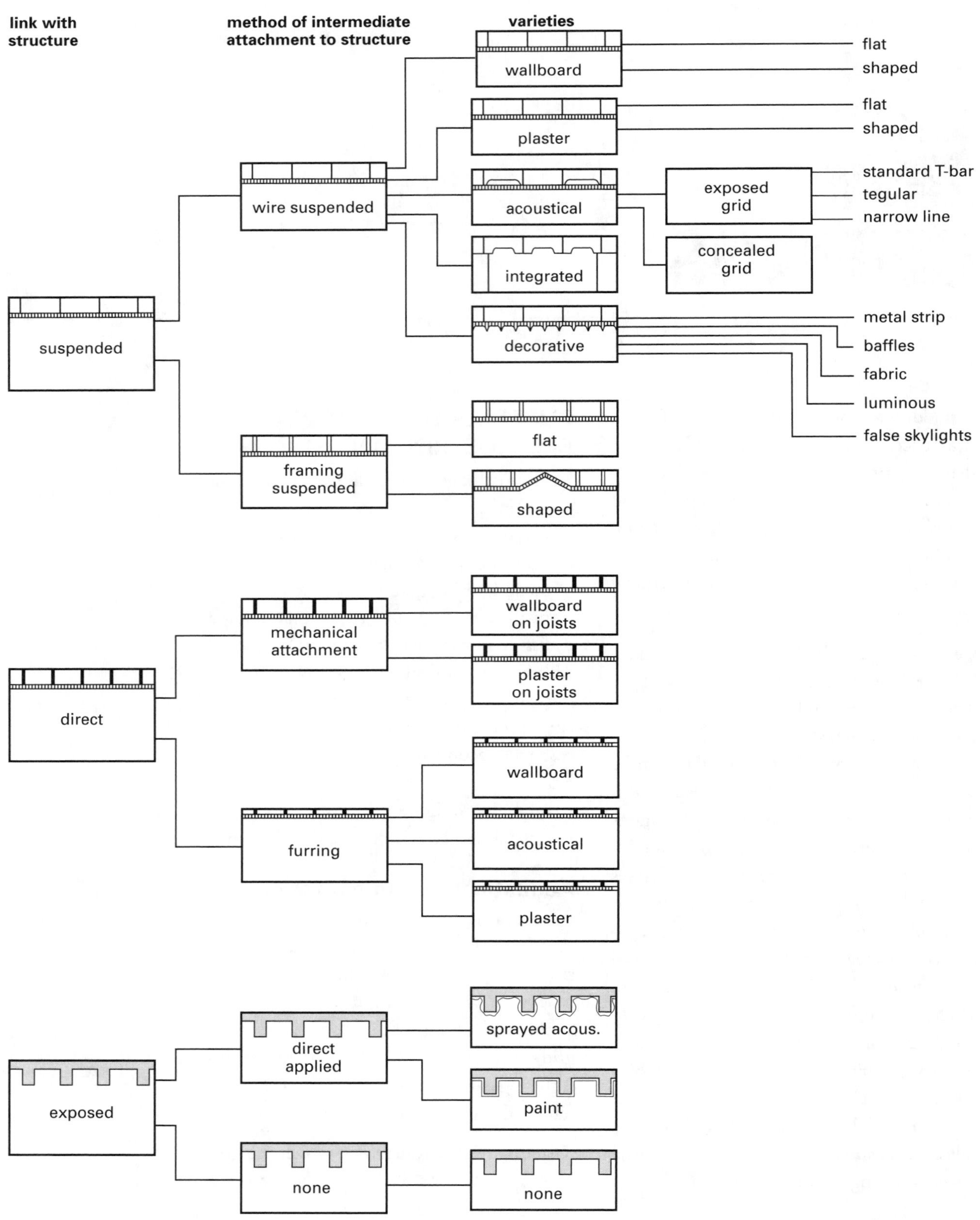

typically use 1 × 1 (300 × 300) tiles with either square or beveled edges. Beveled-edged tiles are better than square-edged tiles because the slight bevel helps prevent edge chipping and conceals minor misalignments between tiles. See Fig. 2.2(c). Whichever system is used, the tile at the perimeter walls is supported by a ceiling angle. This angle is also used to support light fixtures mounted next to the wall.

Manufacturers offer many types of grid shapes and sizes. Some of these are shown in Fig. 2.3. Refer to manufacturer's catalogs for current information on the availability of acoustical tiles and support systems.

The most common tile and grid sizes for lay-in acoustical ceiling systems are 24 × 24 (600 × 600) and 24 × 48 (600 × 1200).

A 20 × 60 (500 × 1500) size is also available for use in buildings with a 5 ft working module so that three panels fit within one 60 in (1500 mm) grid. This allows office partitions to be laid out on the 5 ft module lines without interfering with HVAC (heating, ventilating, and air conditioning) registers and special 20 × 48 (508 × 1219) light fixtures located in the center of a module. The system is most often employed when demountable partitions are used. Partitions can be moved easily without disturbing most of the lighting and HVAC system. See Fig. 2.4.

Other types of suspended systems that provide acoustical properties are also available. These include metal strip ceilings, wood grids, and fabric-covered acoustical batts. All serve the same purpose: they provide a finished ceiling to absorb rather than reflect sound (like a gypsum wallboard ceiling does) to reduce noise levels within a space while providing easy plenum access.

## Standard ceiling assemblies

Suspended acoustical ceilings are installed by attaching hanger wires to the structural floor or roof and using these wires to support lengths of the grid system spaced 4 ft (1200 mm) on center. Cross tees are then snapped into prepunched holes in the main runners every two feet. If the grid size is 24 × 24 (610 × 610), additional cross tees are placed in the center of the 24 × 48 (610 × 1219) grid. A ceiling angle is placed around the perimeter of the room and around columns and other obstructions. See Fig. 2.5. The tiles are placed within the grid and odd-sized tiles are cut to fit nonstandard

**Figure 2.2** Standard acoustical ceiling systems



(a) standard T-bar

(b) tegular tile

(c) concealed grid

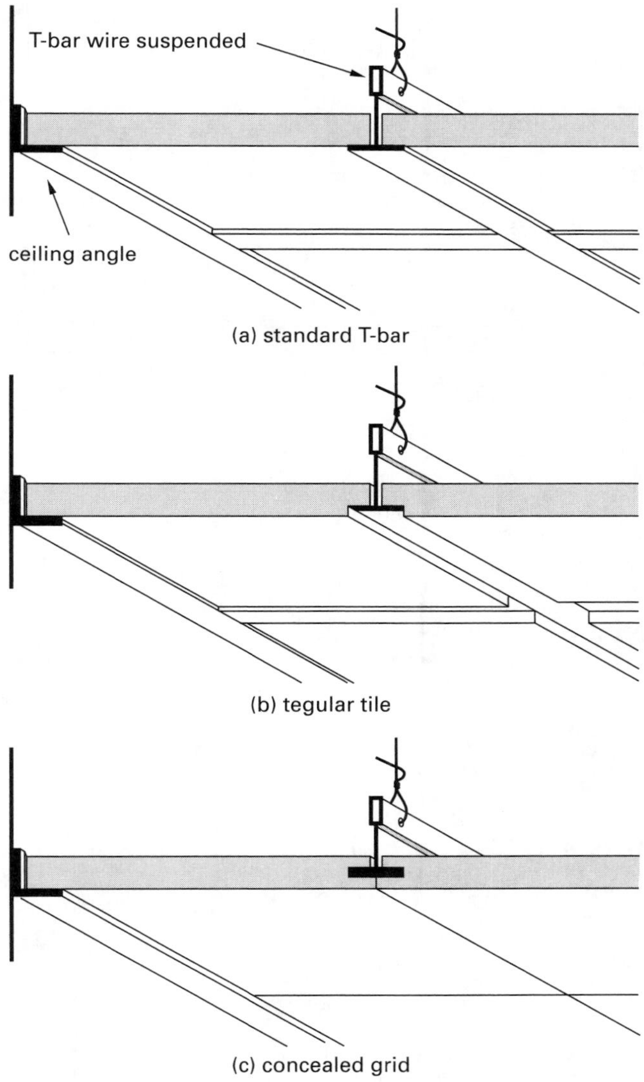

openings. Tiles are easily cut to accommodate holes for lights, sprinklers, and other penetrations. Retention clips can be installed above the ceiling to prevent people from pushing the tiles out of the grid or for fire-rated ceiling assemblies when retention is required.

Concealed spline ceilings use a similar suspension system, with the exception that special cross members are required. These cross members fit within slots that have been cut into the edges of the tiles. Various systems are used to install the last pieces of tile and close up the ceiling. In addition, special components are required that allow tiles to be removed so that workers can gain access to the space above. Although the exact details vary with each manufacturer, there are two types: downward accessible and upward accessible.

**Figure 2.3** Ceiling grid types

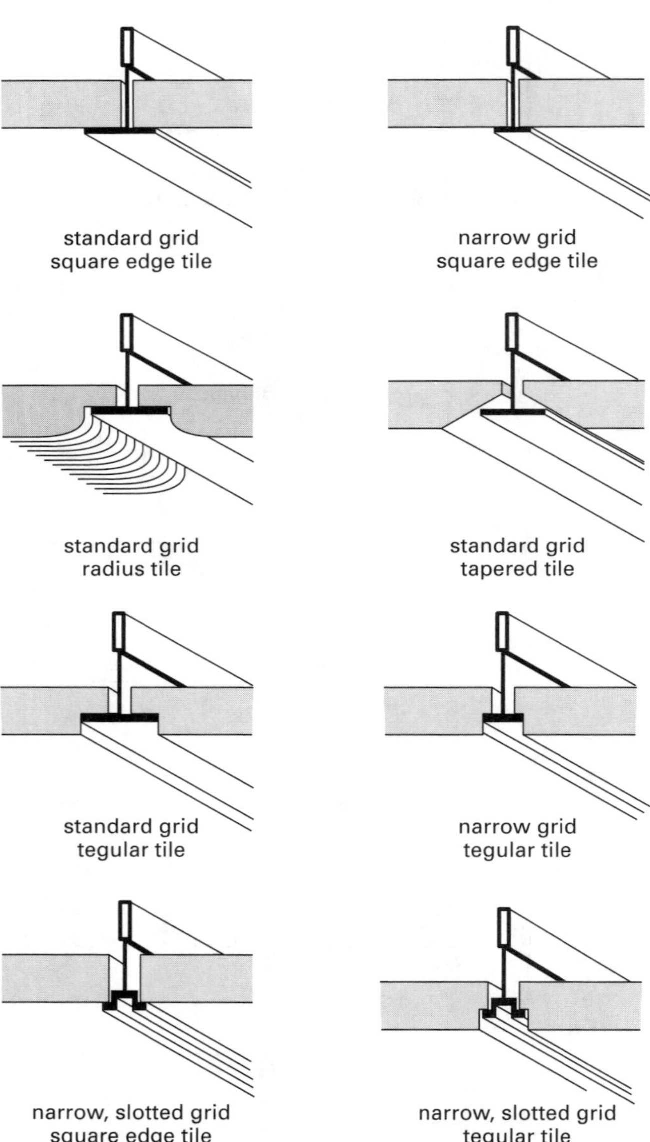


In the downward accessible system, an access clip mounted to the framing or a special tool is required to pull a unit of two tiles loose by pivoting them from one end. After the unit is removed, the adjacent tiles can be removed if necessary. In an upward accessible system, a unit of two tiles is pushed up from a pivot point at one end and removed. Additional tiles can then be removed by slipping out intermediate splines.

In either system, the percentage of the total ceiling area that is accessible can be specified based on the amount of access required. For example, if a 25% accessible ceiling is specified, then one-fourth of the tiles should consist of units of two tiles that can be easily removed. Upward accessible ceilings are preferable to downward accessible ceilings because the tool used to pull down the tiles usually causes the tile edges to chip. After a time the ceiling becomes unsightly. In an upward accessible system, the tiles rest in place on concealed Z-clips, and all that is required to remove them is a push up. In order to identify which tiles are accessible, some manufacturers place a small pin in the corner of the removable tile.

Suspended ceilings are installed level to a tolerance of ⅛ in in 12 ft (3 mm in 3660 mm). Because ceilings are almost always more level than floors, critical dimensions are often measured from the ceiling down. In addition to flat ceilings, suspended acoustical systems can accommodate vertical rises and sloped sections with standard suspension system components.

In commercial construction, the space above a suspended ceiling is frequently used as a return air plenum. Return air grilles are set

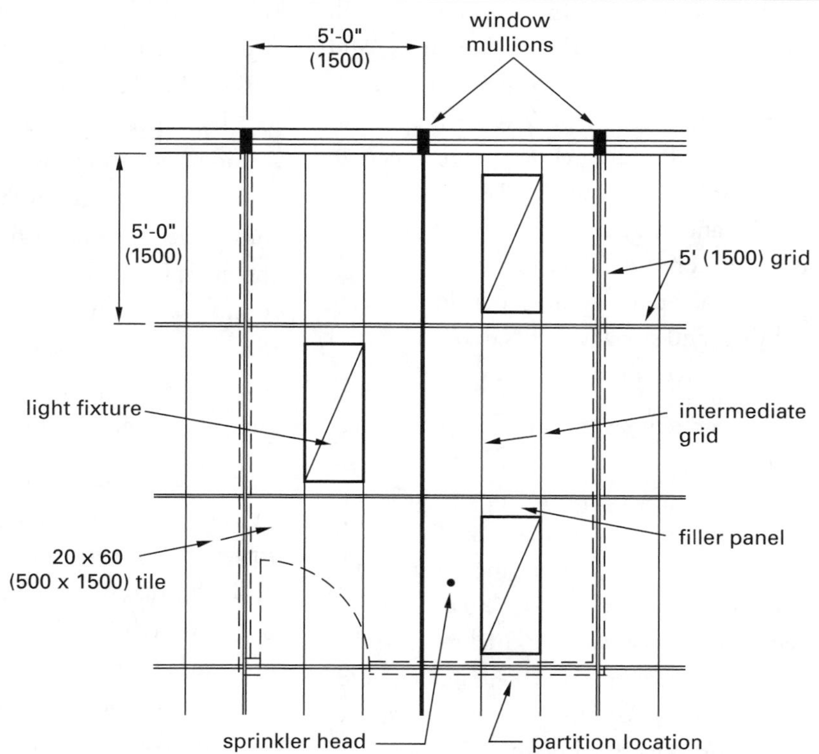


**Figure 2.4**
20 × 60 ceiling grid for modular layout

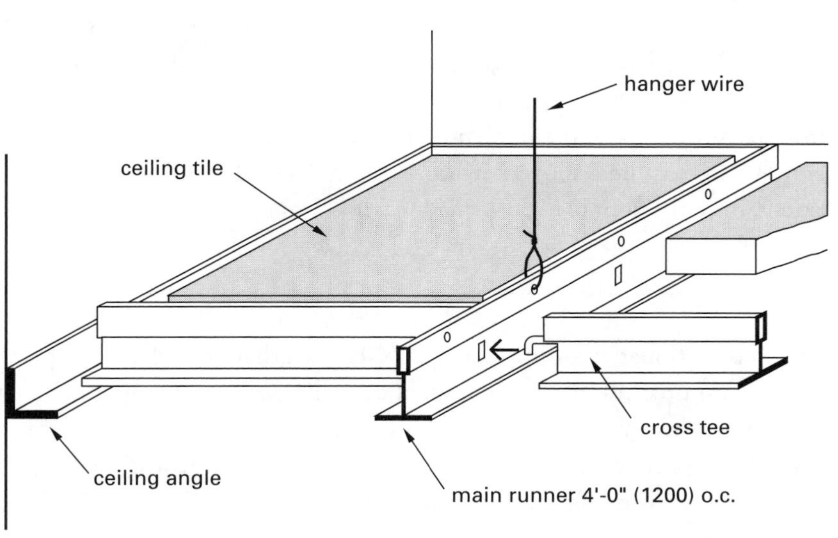


**Figure 2.5**
Lay-in suspended acoustical ceiling

## Maintaining the flush appearance of concealed spline ceilings

Although adjacent tiles of concealed spline ceilings are installed nearly flush, tolerances between tiles can be critical if artificial or natural light grazes across the ceiling. Variations between tiles of as little as 0.005 in (0.127 mm) can cause objectionable shadows that emphasize any joint unevenness. Ambient lighting or rooms with a lot of reflected light are preferable. If grazing light is going to be present, cardboard splines can be installed in all joints of a concealed spline ceiling. Although it adds to the initial cost and makes removal more difficult, the splines force the tiles into closer alignment. Bevel-edged tiles can also be used to conceal misalignment.

in the grid, and return air passes through the grilles, through the ceiling space, and back to a central return air duct or shaft that connects to the HVAC system. If this is the case, building codes require that no combustible material be placed above the ceiling and that all plastic wiring be run in metal conduit. Some codes allow wiring used for telephone, computer, low-voltage lighting, and signal systems to be exposed if it is approved plenum-rated wiring.

Suspended ceilings may be rated or nonrated. If they are fire rated, it means that they are part of a complete floor/ceiling or roof/ceiling assembly that is rated. Ceiling systems in themselves cannot prevent the spread of fire from one floor to the next. Rated acoustical ceiling systems consist of rated mineral tiles and rated grid systems, which include hold-down clips to keep the panels in place and expansion slots to allow the grid to expand when subjected to heat.

### Special ceiling assemblies

Because acoustical ceilings cannot stop sound from passing through them, plenum sound barriers are required above partitions that extend from the floor to the underside of the suspended ceiling when acoustical privacy is needed. There are several ways to achieve this without breaking the ceiling grid. The easiest and least expensive way is to lay fire-rated sound attenuation insulation on top of the ceiling tile for a distance of about 4 ft (1200 mm) on either side of the partition line, as shown in Fig. 2.6. While this provides some sound control, noise can still pass through the ceiling of one space into the plenum, through the plenum over the insulation, and into the adjacent room.

If the ceiling grid cannot be broken, a better solution is to suspend a partition from the structural floor above down to the top of the ceiling grid and apply one layer of gypsum wallboard to it. The crack between the bottom runner and the top of the ceiling tile is filled with sound-attenuation insulation. Alternately, sheet lead can be suspended from the structural floor above down to the ceiling. Both of these methods are awkward to build and add to the cost of the ceiling; however, they offer better sound attenuation than insulation laid on ceiling tile. Refer to Ch. 11 for more information on acoustical design and details of plenum barriers.

## Building code requirements for suspended acoustical ceilings

The International Building Code (IBC) and other model codes specify the finish and construction requirements for suspended ceilings. As with any finish material, ceiling tile must meet the particular flame-spread limitations for the occupancy group and space in the building where the ceiling is being used. Nearly all acoustical ceiling tiles have a Class A rating; therefore, this usually is not a problem.

The IBC requires that acoustical ceiling systems be designed, fabricated, and installed in accordance with generally accepted engineering practice and according to the manufacturer's recommendations. Specifically, it requires that suspended acoustical ceiling systems be installed in accordance with the provisions of ASTM C635 and ASTM C636. Further, systems that are part of a fire-resistance-rated construction must be installed in the same manner used in the assembly tested and must conform to the applicable provisions of the fire-resistance-rated construction chapter (Ch. 7) of the IBC.

Seismic restraint may also be required, as discussed in the next section.

In some areas of the United States, special seismic restraint detailing is required for suspended ceilings. Because seismic restraint requirements are evolving, check with the local building code and building official to determine current rules.

Under the 2006 International Building Code, each structure is assigned to a seismic design category based on its occupancy category and the severity of the design earthquake ground motion at the site. The occupancy category is used to determine structural requirements based on occupancy. There are four occupancy categories, based on how important the site is to post-earthquake recovery and how essential it is. Hospitals and fire stations, for example, rank highly on this scale and are assigned an occupancy category of IV, while minor storage facilities have an occupancy category of I. There are six seismic design categories labeled A through F, with A being the least restrictive and F the most restrictive. Seismic design categories D, E, and F have the most stringent requirements for earthquake design, including ceiling detailing.

Although the IBC now publishes very detailed maps that engineers use to design buildings and that determine many aspects of interior design construction, in general, the most severe locations in the United States are what were formerly known as earthquake zones 3 and 4. These are roughly indicated in the map shown in Fig. 2.7, which was used by the 1997 UBC.

Designers working on projects in or near these areas should verify the exact seismic design category classification of the building they are working on and should then obtain specific design requirements for ceilings and other interior components from the local authority having jurisdiction. If necessary, the services of a qualified structural engineer or other design professional should be consulted.

Depending on the seismic design category, certain interior components must be designed according to requirements given in

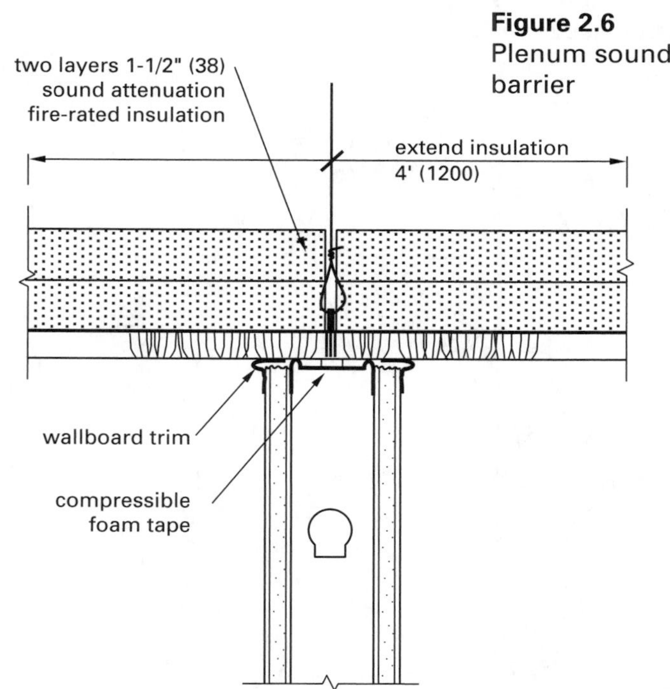


**Figure 2.6**
Plenum sound barrier

the IBC. These components include nonstructural walls and partitions, ceilings, cabinets, access floors, sprinkler pipes, and bookcases, among others. In seismic design category C, suspended ceilings must be designed in accordance with CISCA 0–2, *Recommendations for Direct-Hung Acoustical Tile and Lay-in Panel Ceilings, Seismic Zones 0–2*, published by the Ceilings and Interior Systems Construction Association. Suspended ceilings in seismic design categories D, E, and F must be designed in accordance with CISCA 3–4, *Guidelines for Seismic Restraint Direct-Hung Suspended Ceiling Assemblies, Seismic Zones 3 & 4*. The zones referred to in these publications relate to the zones on the map shown in Fig. 2.7. The IBC is stricter than the UBC and adds some requirements to those found in CISCA 3–4.

The detailed provisions of seismic design of architectural components can be found in ASCE-7, *Minimum Design Loads for Buildings and Other Structures*, published by the American Society of Civil Engineers.

For zones 0 and 1, CISCA recommends that individual light fixtures or other types of equipment that weigh 56 lbm (25.4 kg) or

**Figure 2.7**
Earthquake zones

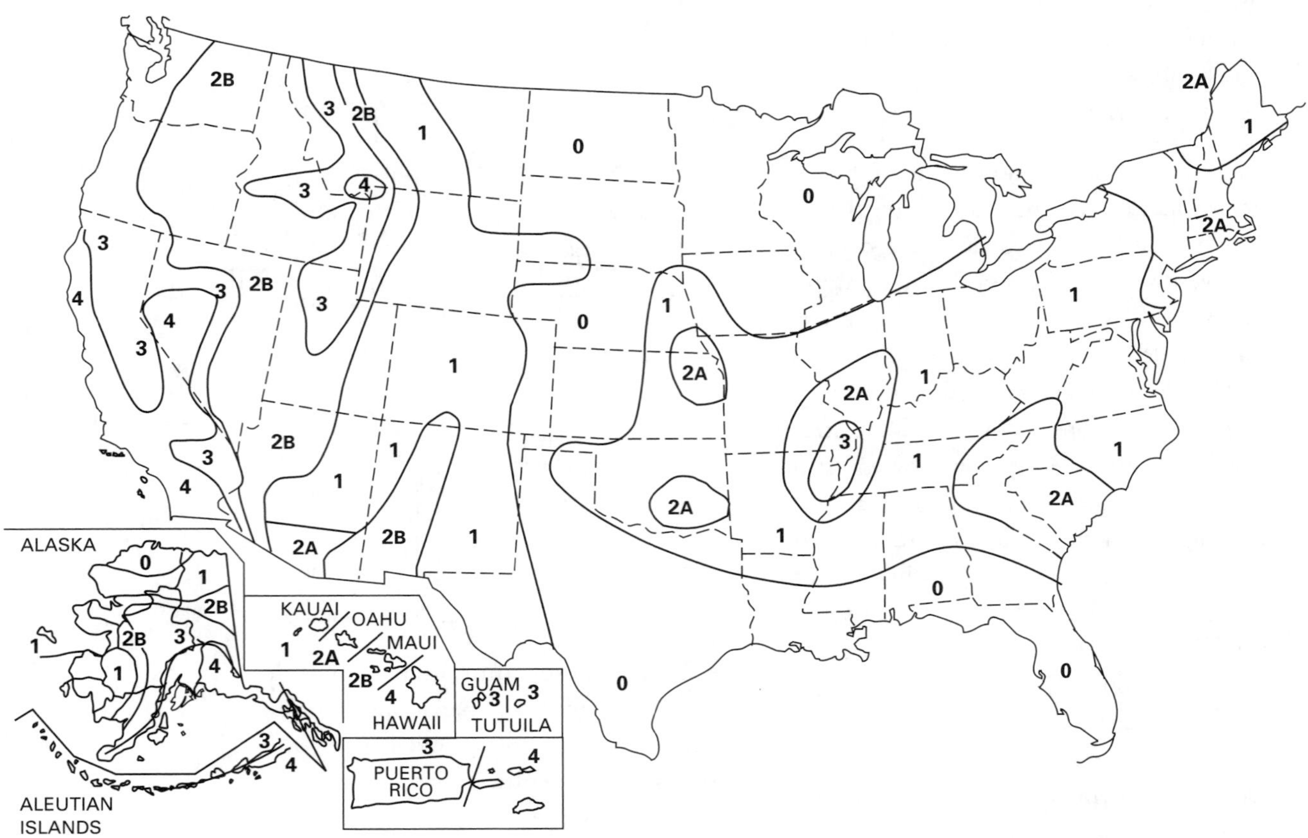




less and that are typically supported by the ceiling grid have two no. 12 gage wire hangers attached at opposite corners. Although these wires must be slack, they would prevent the fixture from falling if the ceiling grid deformed or broke. Fixtures heavier than 56 lbm should be supported independently of the structure. Additionally, CISCA recommends that the intersection of the main runner and cross runners have an average ultimate test strength of 60 lbm (27.2 kg) or more in both tension and compression.

For buildings in zone 2, CISCA recommends the same specifications as for zones 0 and 1 along with four others, summarized here; however, exact requirements must be verified with the local building code.

- The actual average weight of the ceiling system, including lights and air terminals, should be 2.5 lbm/ft$^2$ (12.2 kg/m$^2$) or less. All other items should be supported independently.

- The ceiling system should not be used to provide lateral support for partitions. Instead, the partitions should be braced with detailing similar to that shown in Fig. 2.8 so that the ceiling membrane can move laterally.

- Ceiling angles should provide at least a ⅞ in (22 mm) ledge, and there must be at least a ⅜ in (10 mm) clearance from the edge of the tile to the edge of the wall. This is shown in Fig. 2.9.

- The perimeter main runners and cross runners must be prevented from spreading without relying on permanent attachment to the ceiling angle.

The requirements for buildings in zones 3 and 4 are much stricter and require more elaborate detailing. The suspension system must be a heavy-duty type and must have lateral force bracing 12 ft (3600 mm) on center in both directions, with the first point within 6 ft (1800 mm) from each wall. As illustrated in Fig. 2.10, these points of lateral bracing must provide support in all four directions and must have rigid struts connected to the structure above to prevent uplift as well as to support gravity loads. Additional wire supports are also required for all runners at the perimeter of the room within 8 in (200 mm) of the wall. Clearances from the end of the runners to the partition must be ½ in (13 mm) instead of ⅜ in (9.5 mm). The IBC now requires a minimum clearance of ¾ in (19 mm) in zones 3 and 4 and a minimum 2 in (50 mm) wide ceiling angle. Complete detailing recommendations can be found in the *Guidelines for Seismic Restraint Direct Hung Suspended Ceiling Assemblies, Seismic Zones 3 & 4,* published by CISCA.

**Figure 2.8**
Partition bracing for zones 3 and 4

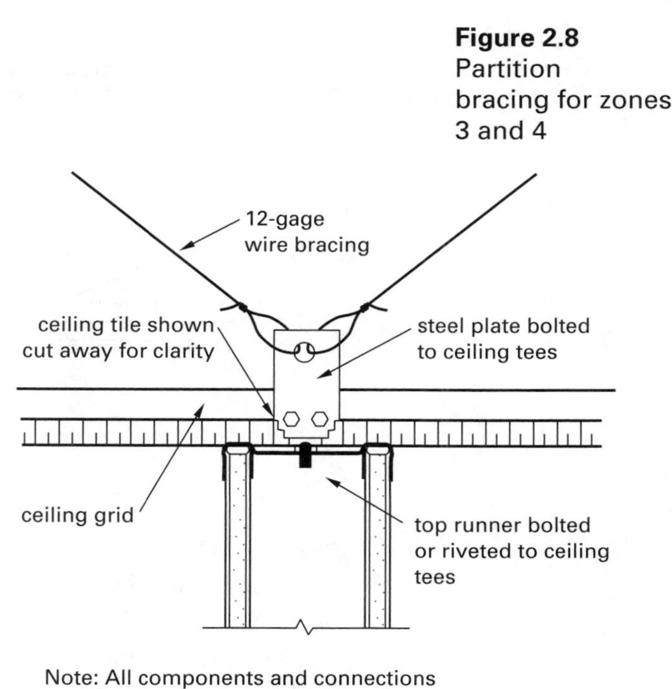


**Figure 2.9**
Detail of runners at perimeter partition

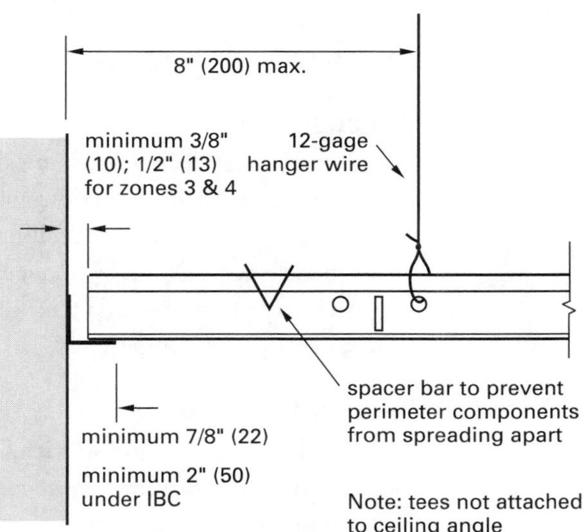


## Coordination

Because ceilings serve so many purposes in modern construction in addition to acoustical control, there are many elements that must be coordinated with the selection and detailing of ceiling systems. These elements can include recessed lights, duct work, sprinkler piping, fire alarm speakers, smoke detectors, drapery pockets, and other recessed items.

### Surface-mounted items

All the mechanical, electrical, and architectural items that must be mounted on the ceiling should be considered. They must be located consistent with the design plan, while satisfying the limitations of function and code requirements. These items may include lighting fixtures, HVAC air grilles and registers, speakers, smoke detectors, sprinkler heads, fire alarms, and signs.

**Figure 2.10**
Ceiling grid bracing

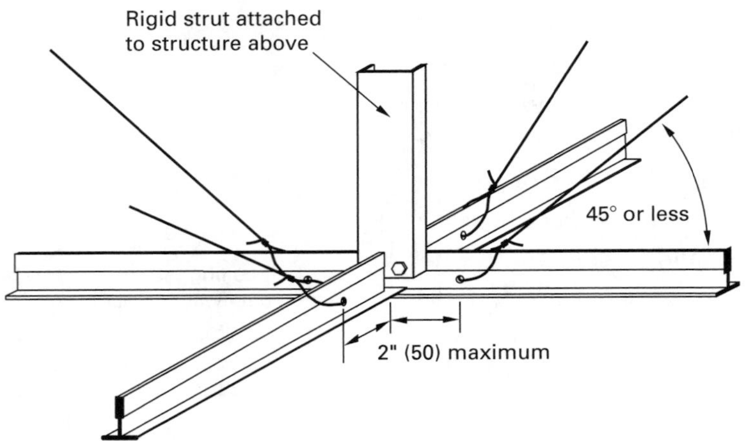


### Recessed lights

The space above suspended ceilings is packed with ducts, conduit, and piping. It must be verified that there is sufficient clearance for recessed lights, coffers, and other specified design features.

### Plenum space

If the plenum is being used for return air as part of the mechanical system, only non-combustible materials can be used in the plenum space. For example, the use of wood blocking, even if it is fire-retardant treated, is generally not permitted. Wiring must be in conduit or be the approved plenum-rated type. Exact requirement must be verified with the local building code.

### Access

If there is a great deal of mechanical equipment, valves, electrical junction boxes, and other items requiring access, a ceiling system must be selected that is easy to open up and return into place without damage or soiling the visible system components.

### Remodeling work

In remodeling work, painting existing acoustical tiles is sometimes seen as an economical way to refinish ceilings. However, painting may destroy the acoustical value of the tiles. Instead, replacing or cleaning the tiles should be considered.

### Heavy loads

When partitions extend only to the suspended ceiling, additional bracing may be required for heavy loads suspended on the partition, such as bookcases. Additional bracing will prevent wall shake from heavy doors being closed and can be used for earthquake bracing in zones 3 and 4. Bracing may consist of diagonal studs screwed through the ceiling into the top runner of the partition and secured to the structural floor above.

### Demountable partitions

If a demountable partition system is used, a ceiling suspension system with a continuous slotted grid or other provisions for attachment should be selected. Doing so will prevent marring of the grid when the top runner of the partition is removed and reinstalled.

### Drapery pockets

It must be verified that there is enough clearance to recess drapery track or horizontal blinds if required by the design.

## GYPSUM WALLBOARD CEILINGS [092116]

### Gypsum wallboard ceiling components

Gypsum wallboard for ceilings is either ½ in (13 mm) or ⅝ in (16 mm) thick depending on the frame spacing. Wallboard

½ in thick is generally used for framing 16 in on center (406 mm); wallboard ⅝ in thick is used for framing 24 in (600 mm) on center. As with partitions, contractors prefer to use the longest lengths practicable to minimize the number of joints.

When wallboard is attached directly to structural framing, such as joists, the only other components to the assembly are fasteners, tape, and joint compound. Screws are almost always used for both ceiling and partition construction because they are faster and easier to install and do not pull out of the framing.

When wallboard is suspended, a framing grid of 1½ in (38 mm) steel channels and furring channels is suspended from the structure above like an acoustical ceiling. These components are discussed in the next section.

### Standard ceiling assemblies

Gypsum wallboard ceilings are either directly attached to structural framing or suspended like an acoustical ceiling. For residential construction, wallboard is screwed directly to the ceiling joists. Wiring and heating ducts are concealed between the joists. If a small additional space below the joists is required, furring is used. Larger spaces for ducts or dropped soffits are made by boxing in with wood framing and applying the wallboard over it.

Because commercial construction typically requires clear space above the ceiling for piping, electrical conduit, HVAC duct work, and sprinkler pipes, gypsum wallboard ceilings are applied to a suspended grid of framing members. Fig. 2.11 shows the typical construction. Steel channels measuring 1½ in (38 mm) are located 4 ft (1200 mm) on center and are suspended from the structural floor or roof above with wires spaced 4 ft on center. Metal furring channels (hat channels) are attached to the main runners either 16 in or 24 in on center, with the wallboard screwed to them. For most commercial construction 24 in (600 mm) spacing is used with ⅝ in (16 mm) wallboard.

Although gypsum wallboard ceilings in commercial construction provide a smooth, uninterrupted finished ceiling, they lack the easy accessibility of suspended acoustical ceilings. Because of this, where access to valves, junction boxes, fire dampers, or other equipment or services is required, access panels must be installed in the ceiling. These are prefabricated steel units with a hinged

**Applicable standards for suspended acoustical ceiling systems**

**American Society for Testing and Materials (ASTM):**

| | |
|---|---|
| ASTM C423 | *Test Methods for Sound Absorption and Sound Absorption Coefficients by the Reverberation Room Method* |
| ASTM C635 | *Standard Specification for the Manufacture, Performance, and Testing of Metal Suspension Systems for Acoustical Tile and Lay-in Panel Systems* |
| ASTM C636 | *Standard Practice for Installation of Metal Ceiling Suspension Systems for Acoustical Tile and Lay-in Panels* |
| ASTM E580 | *Standard Practice for Application of Ceiling Suspension Systems for Acoustical Tile and Lay-in Panels in Areas Requiring Moderate Seismic Restraint* |
| ASTM E1264 | *Standard Classification for Acoustical Ceiling Products* |

**Ceilings & Interior Systems Construction Association (CISCA):**

*Recommendations for Direct-hung Acoustical Tile and Lay-in Panel Ceilings, Seismic Zones 0–2*

*Guidelines for Seismic Restraint for Direct-hung Suspended Ceiling Assemblies, Seismic Zones 3 & 4*

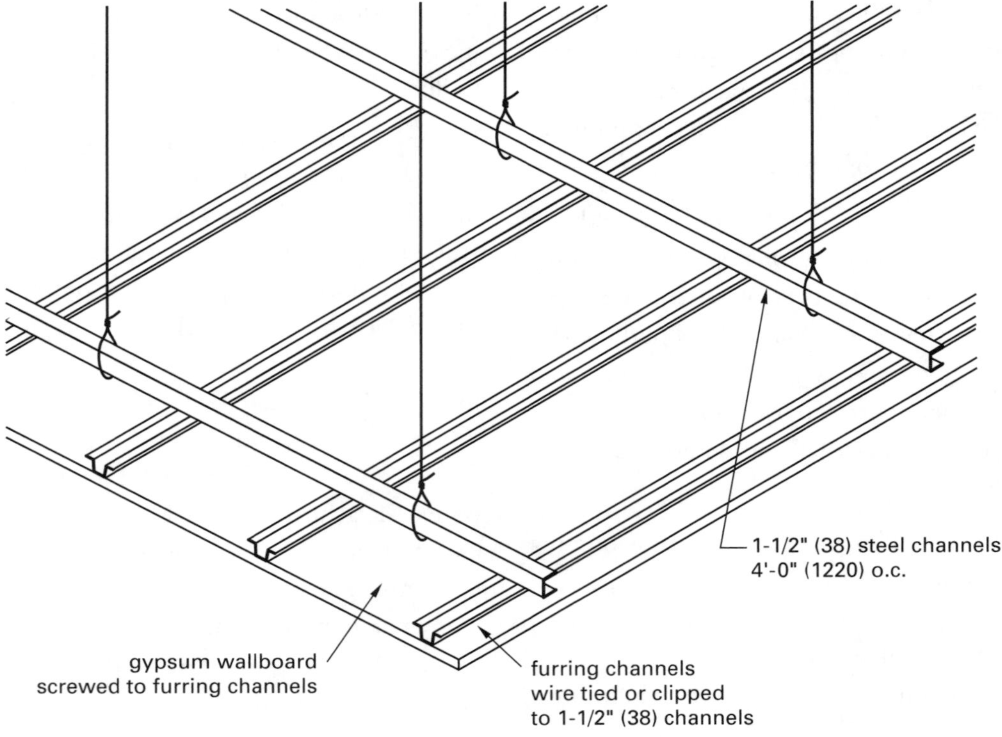


**Figure 2.11** Suspended gypsum wallboard ceiling

door that allow the wallboard to be framed into them. They are available in several standard sizes, but a 24 in (600 mm) square door is usually sufficient. Unfortunately, if the design intent is to build a smooth ceiling, access panels interrupt the appearance and become unsightly after they are used a few times. Cracks develop in the joint compound around the frame, and the finish becomes soiled. If possible, wallboard ceilings should be limited to areas not requiring access panels, or the mechanical and electrical engineers should be requested to locate new equipment away from intended wallboard ceilings.

## Custom ceiling assemblies

In addition to a flat ceiling, gypsum wallboard can be formed into nearly any configuration. Stepped, sloped, coffered, vaulted, and arched ceilings are all possible using various combinations of suspended framing and studs to form the basic shape. For curved shapes, the minimum radii for forming curved partitions given in Tables 1.2 and 1.3 are applicable.

When acoustical control is required in residential construction, resilient channels are attached to the joists, and sound attenuation insulation is placed between the joists. One typical assembly is shown in Fig. 2.12.

## Coordination

- Fire-rated floor/ceiling assemblies require the use of Type X gypsum wallboard.
- Light troffers, air terminals, and other heavy equipment should be supported separately.
- In commercial construction, the locations of valves, junction boxes, and other mechanical and electrical equipment should be coordinated to eliminate or minimize the need for access panels.
- For sloped, vaulted, or arched ceilings, it must be verified that there is no interference from duct work, piping, or other obstructions.

**Building code requirements for gypsum wallboard ceilings**

As with acoustical ceilings, model codes require that the entire suspension system be noncombustible. The codes also specify the minimum size of hanger wires based on the type of installation and the area of ceiling that is supported.

All gypsum wallboard ceilings are required to be installed in conformance with GA 216, *Applications and Finishing of Gypsum Board*, as well as ASTM C840, ASTM C754, and ASTM C1007.

For ceilings that are part of a rated floor/ceiling assembly, certain construction details must be followed as they relate to the penetration of horizontal ceiling membranes. For example, if a supply air diffuser penetrated a ceiling, the diffuser would have to have a ceiling radiation damper. Also, access doors must be fire rated and match the rating of the floor/ceiling assembly. However, in most commercial construction, the fire rating of the floor/ceiling assembly is provided by the structural floor and is not dependent on the suspended ceiling, so no special detailing needs to be provided. If modifications are being made to existing construction, the interior designer should verify with the building architect or the local building official whether or not the ceiling is part of a rated assembly, so the designer can make the correct decisions about ceiling penetrations and other ceiling detailing.

Seismic restraint may also be required.

## PLASTER CEILINGS [092113]

### Plaster ceiling components

Lath and plaster ceilings are constructed similarly to lath and plaster partitions. Like their partition counterparts, lath and plaster ceilings cost more than gypsum wallboard ceilings and are more difficult to construct. However, they can easily be curved in two directions to form complex shapes. Full, three-coat portland-cement plaster ceilings are used most often when ceramic tile must be applied in a continuously wet environment, such as a public shower or a steam room. They are also used in remodeling work when ornate or complex moldings and decorative castings are required.

### Standard ceiling assemblies

A typical commercial plaster ceiling assembly is shown in Fig. 2.13. A framework is suspended from the structure like a gypsum wallboard ceiling. However, instead of using wallboard, expanded metal lath is wired to the framework and the plaster is applied, usually in a three-coat application process. In a traditional plaster ceiling for residential construction, metal lath is attached to the ceiling joists and a two- or three-coat plaster application process is used. Refer to Ch. 1 for information on standard plaster construction.

When curved shapes are required, the suspended framing is shaped into the approximate configuration of the ceiling, and wire lath is bent to conform to the final profile. The application of the plaster completes the final shape. Large templates are sometimes used to ensure the entire length of a curved shape has a consistent profile. Like plaster partitions, a ceiling can be finished in a variety of textures.

As with partitions, veneer plaster construction can also be used. Gypsum lath is screwed to the framing, and a thin veneer coat of plaster approximately ⅛ in (3 mm) thick is applied.

### Custom ceiling assemblies

For decorative work, complex moldings are formed by cutting a piece of sheet metal or wood to conform to the desired profile. A large amount of plaster is applied in place, and the metal template is run along the

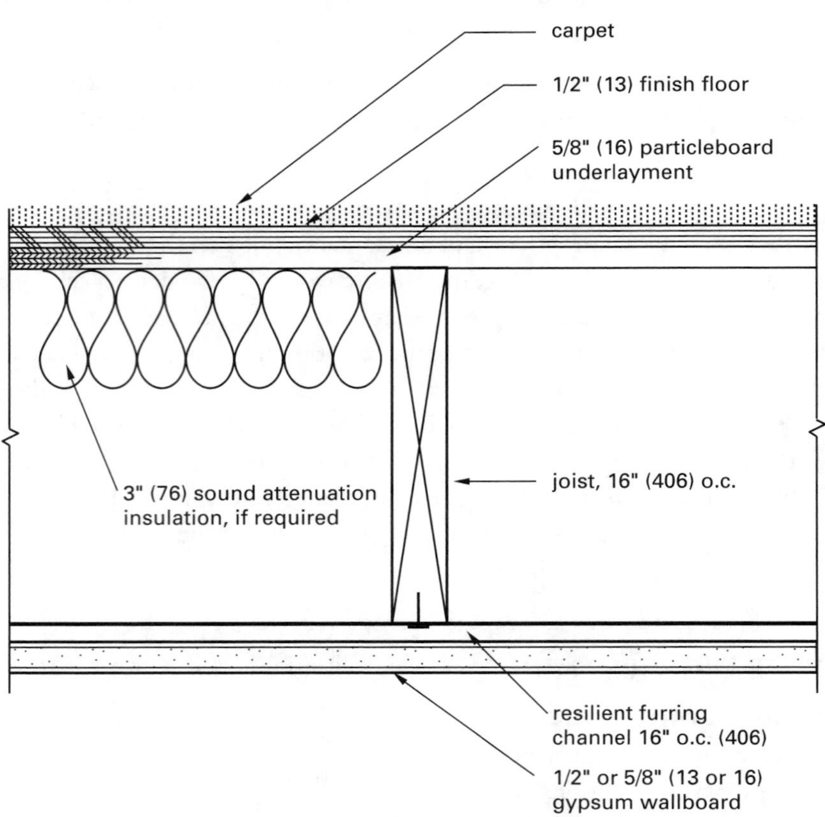


**Figure 2.12** Gypsum wallboard ceiling on wood framing

length of the molding to shape it. When moldings cannot be formed in place, they can be cast in molds and attached to the walls and ceilings.

## Coordination

• In commercial construction, heavy loads, such as large light fixtures and mechanical equipment, should be suspended independently from the structure above.

• Perimeter isolation joints, as shown in Fig. 2.13, should be used where the ceiling is adjacent to a structural element or dissimilar partition, where other vertical penetrations occur, and where building movement can be expected.

• Control joints should be detailed when a ceiling dimension exceeds 50 ft (15 m) in either direction when perimeter relief joints are used, or when a ceiling dimension exceeds 30 ft (9 m) when perimeter relief joints are not used.

## LINEAR METAL CEILINGS [095423]

Linear metal ceilings are suspended systems that use lengths of prefinished aluminum sections. These sections are clipped to carrier sections that are suspended with wires attached to the structure above. The exact configuration of linear metal ceilings varies with each manufacturer, but a typical section is shown in Fig. 2.14. The visible pieces are available in a variety of sizes and shapes and in painted and anodized finishes. There is usually a gap between each piece to provide for both some sound absorption and return air movement. If additional acoustical control

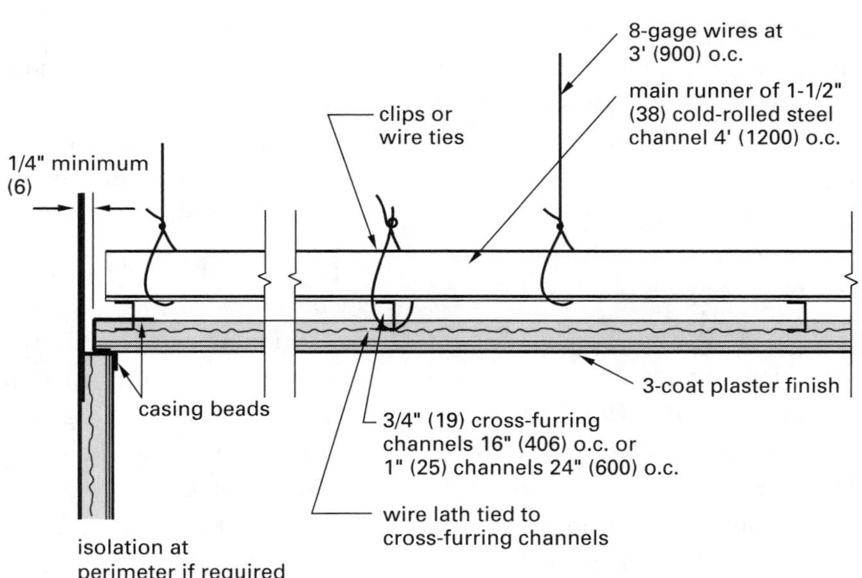


**Figure 2.13**
Typical plaster ceiling construction

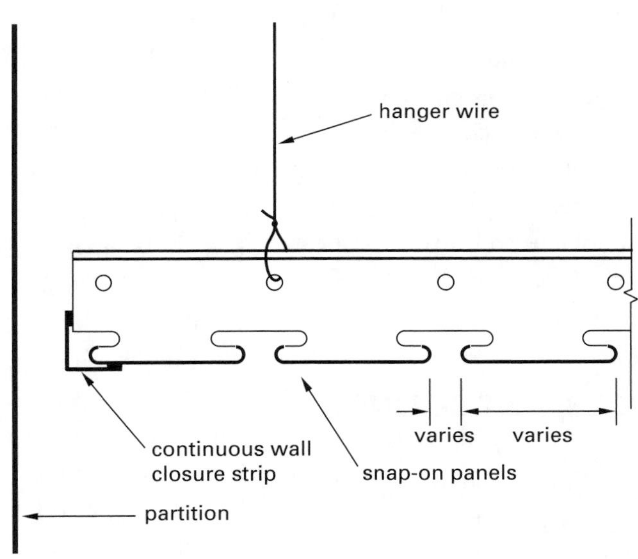


**Figure 2.14**
Linear metal ceiling

is needed, acoustical batts can be laid on top of the ceiling. Each manufacturer provides accessories for trimming around walls, light fixtures, and other openings.

## DECORATIVE SUSPENDED CEILINGS [095433]

Many other types of decorative suspended ceilings are available. They are all suspended with either wires or threaded rods anchored to the structure above. The visible, finished portion of the ceiling can be vertical metal baffles, wood strips, mirrored panels, open grids of aluminum or wood, or other proprietary systems. Refer to manufacturer's catalogs for availability and exact installation details.

## INTEGRATED CEILINGS [095800]

Integrated ceilings are suspended ceiling systems specifically designed to accommodate acoustical ceiling tile, light fixtures, supply and return air grilles, fire sprinklers, and partition attachment in a consistent, unified way. There are many proprietary systems, each with its own characteristics; however, all are intended to be used in commercial applications where the partitions, lights, and other elements connected with the ceiling change frequently. Most of the systems are designed to work with standard building planning grids of 4 ft (1200 mm) or 5 ft (1500 mm).

All of the components are designed for maximum reusability and flexibility. Light fixtures usually have plug-in connectors, and HVAC system air terminals are connected with flexible ducts so all services can be relocated easily. The top track of a demountable partition screws or clips onto a specially designed grid. Refer to manufacturer's catalogs for availability and exact installation details.

Integrated ceilings are more expensive than standard acoustical ceilings but can be economical when frequent changes to space plans are made. However, before deciding on an integrated ceiling system, a life-cycle cost analysis should be made to determine if the cost savings of frequent changes offsets the higher initial cost.

## ABUSE-RESISTANT CEILINGS [095700]

Abuse-resistant ceilings include a range of products that are designed to resist one or more of the following kinds of abuse.

- environmental damage such as humidity, atmospheric corrosion, and surface moisture
- contact from objects striking the ceiling such as balls, mop handles, and other thrown objects
- frequent access to the plenum
- deliberate abuse such as vandalism
- deliberate attempts to gain unauthorized access to the ceiling space

Abuse-resistant ceilings are commonly detailed and specified for areas in schools, hospitals, industrial plants, and security or detention facilities. They include various types of acoustical suspended-ceiling systems as well as plaster and built-up gypsum wallboard systems.

Suspended acoustical abuse-resistant ceiling systems use several types of tiles depending on the severity and type of abuse expected. For light abuse such as in commercial kitchens, the tiles are mineral-based or glass-fiber-based construction with plastic, fiberglass, fabric, aluminum, or other metal-membrane-faced overlays. For heavier use there are snap-in metal panels with perforated steel, stainless steel, or aluminum facings backed with acoustic material. For maximum security and durability, metal plank systems can be used. These consist of linear pans of heavy-gage steel securely attached to wall-mounted angles with tamper-resistant fasteners.

As with standard suspended-ceiling systems the grid is supported with wires, but where penetration to the plenum space must be restricted, compression members are typically installed at 48 in (1220 mm) on center to resist uplift of the grid. To resist incidental uplift, the panels are attached to the grid with clips. For more-secure installations, special metal panels can be used that snap under a bulb tee of the grid, locking the tile in place and making removal impossible except with obvious damage.

Plaster systems use a hard finish coat over plaster base coats that are spread on heavy, expanded metal lath. Gypsum wallboard systems use multiple layers of wallboard separated by heavy-gage expanded metal lath. A veneer coat of dense plaster is applied to the exposed surface to increase surface durability. Although both plaster and wallboard systems provide the necessary degree of abuse resistance, they result in poor acoustical performance.

# 3

# DOORS

Doors are available in a variety of materials and use a range of operating methods to meet many functional and aesthetic needs. There are dozens of standard designs for interior use. Doors and frames can also be custom detailed to meet particular project requirements. This chapter discusses how to select and detail the best door assembly for any situation and then reviews the various types of doors available for interior use.

## SELECTION AND DETAILING PROCEDURES

### Door classifications

A door can be classified by the function it serves, its operation, and the material from which it is made. Each classification is helpful in its own way in the selection of the best door type for a particular situation. Doors for interior use can serve one or more of the following functions.

- control passage
- provide visual privacy
- provide sound privacy
- provide security
- provide fire and smoke resistance
- provide light control
- provide radiation shielding
- serve a decorative function

Door operation refers to the way a door opens and closes. The common operation types and variations are shown in Fig. 3.1. Each operating method has its own advantages and disadvantages, as summarized in Table 3.1.

### Swinging doors

Swinging doors provide easy and convenient operation, are simple to install, can be fire rated, and can accommodate many people. The three common variations of swinging doors are classified by suspension method. These include the typical hinged door; pivoted doors, either center-hung or offset; and balanced doors, which reduce the force required to open the door. Balanced doors are typically used as entrance doors where wind or air pressure makes it difficult to open the door.

The double-acting door is another type of swinging door. It uses special hinges or center-hung pivots that allow it to operate in either direction. Double-acting doors are good for situations requiring quick passage without the use of an opening device, such as a commercial kitchen. Because of the nature of their operation they cannot be used as exit doors and cannot be sealed against sound or light.

## Sliding doors

Sliding doors are appropriate when space is tight. They have many disadvantages. They are not good for frequent use, are awkward to open and close, and are difficult to seal against sound and light. In addition, they are not acceptable for exit doors.

## Folding doors

Folding doors are also good where space is limited. However, like sliding doors, they have disadvantages. They are not good for normal passage and are best used for closets and other minor spaces. Accordion folding doors can be used as space dividers but are limited in maximum size to about 20 ft (6 m) high by 40 ft (12 m) wide.

## Special doors

Movable walls can be classified as special doors. They are used to divide very large spaces. They are composed of individual solid sections of material that fit tightly together when closed. When open, the sections come apart and slide into a storage area. Movable walls are suspended from ceiling tracks and usually include provisions for sealing against sound transmission.

Other types of special doors can be used for interior construction, but they are not commonly used. Overhead coiling doors, for example, are sometimes used for securing large openings during off-hours. They can also act as automatic-closing fire doors for large openings.

**Figure 3.1** Door classification by operation

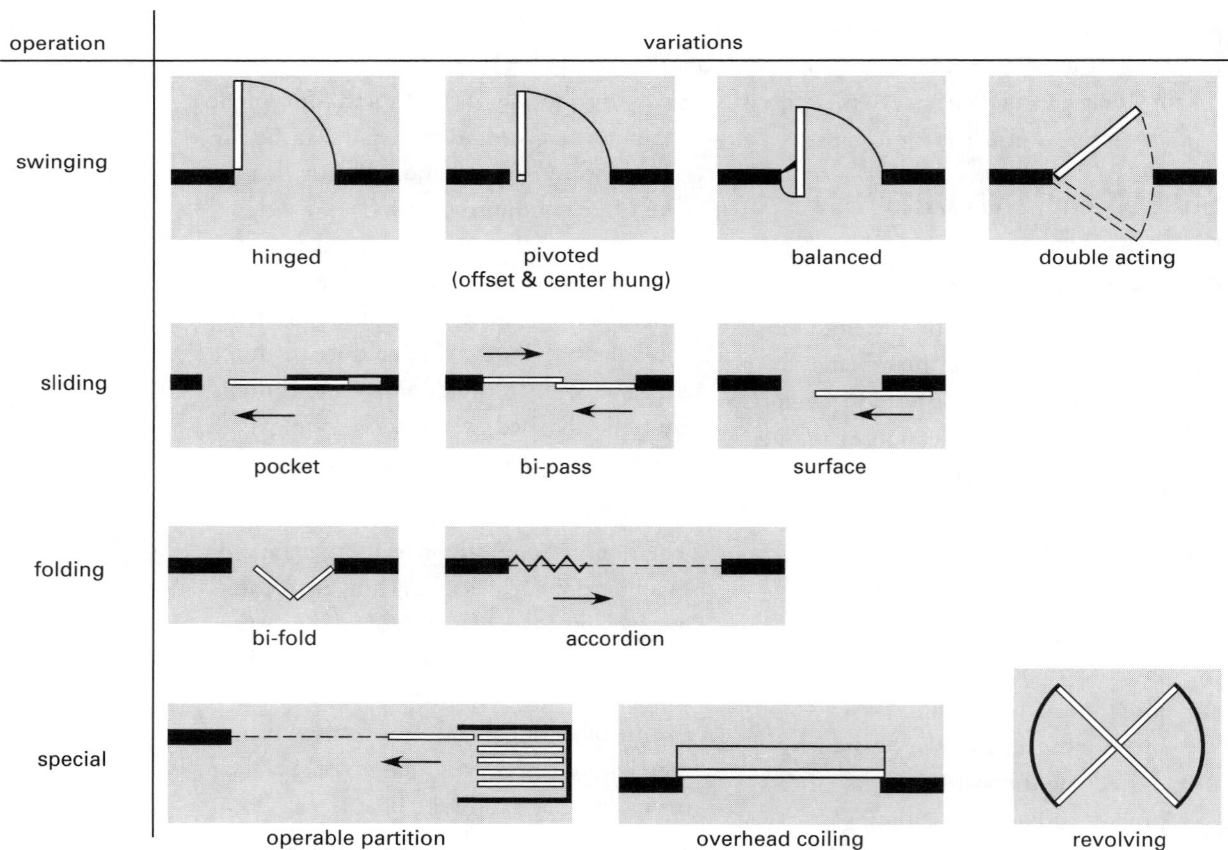

**Table 3.1**
Door types—advantages and disadvantages

| door operation type | advantages | disadvantages |
|---|---|---|
| **swinging** | | |
| hinged | Ease of use and installation<br>Inexpensive<br>Can be fire rated<br>Wide variety of hinge styles | Appearance of hinges sometimes undesirable |
| offset pivoted | Ease of use<br>Closer can be part of pivot<br>Can be fire rated<br>Can accommodate very heavy doors<br>Minimal hardware appearance | More expensive than hinges<br>Floor closers require solid flooring and adequate thickness to accommodate closer |
| center-hung pivoted | Ease of use<br>Closer can be part of pivot<br>Allows door to swing both ways<br>Support hardware is fully concealed<br>Can be fire rated<br>Can accommodate very heavy doors | More expensive than hinges<br>Floor closers require solid flooring and adequate thickness to accommodate closer<br>Height limitations required to avoid bowing |
| balanced | Little effort required to operate | Expensive<br>Clear width reduced when open |
| double acting | Easy operation both ways | Cannot be used as exit door<br>Dangerous unless glass light provided |
| **sliding** | | |
| pocket | No operating space required | Awkward for frequent use<br>Difficult to seal against light or sound<br>Cannot be used as exit door |
| bi-pass | No operating space required | Awkward for frequent use<br>Difficult to seal<br>Cannot be used as exit door |
| surface | No operating space required | Appearance of hardware<br>Cannot be used as exit door |
| **folding** | | |
| bi-fold | Minimum operating space | Awkward to use<br>Cannot be used as exit door |
| accordion | Useful for subdividing space<br>Inexpensive | Poor as a sound barrier<br>Cannot be used as exit door<br>Limited finishes and colors available |
| **special** | | |
| operable partition | Good for very large openings<br>Good sound barrier<br>Wide choice of finishes | Expensive<br>Cannot be used as exit door |
| overhead coiling | Automatic closing of large openings for security or fire separation | Appearance when closed<br>Requires large space for housing<br>Cannot be used as exit door |
| revolving | Accommodates large numbers<br>Prevents air infiltration<br>Types available for darkrooms | Only appropriate for entrance doors<br>Requires large space<br>Expensive<br>Cannot be used as exit door |

## Door handing

The standard method of referring to the way a door swings is called the *door hand* or the *handing* of the door. Handing is used by designers, specifiers, and hardware suppliers to communicate how a door swings and what kind of hardware must be supplied for a specific opening. Some hardware will only work on a door that swings a particular way because of the way the strike side of the door is beveled. Hardware that can work on any hand of door is called *reversible*, or *nonhanded*.

The door hand is determined by standing on the outside of the door, as shown in Fig. 3.2. The exterior of a building is considered the outside, as is the hallway side of a room door, the lobby side of a door opening into a room, or the room side of a closet door. In situations where the distinction is not clear, such as between two offices, the outside is considered the side of the door where the hinge is **not** visible.

**Figure 3.2**
Door handing

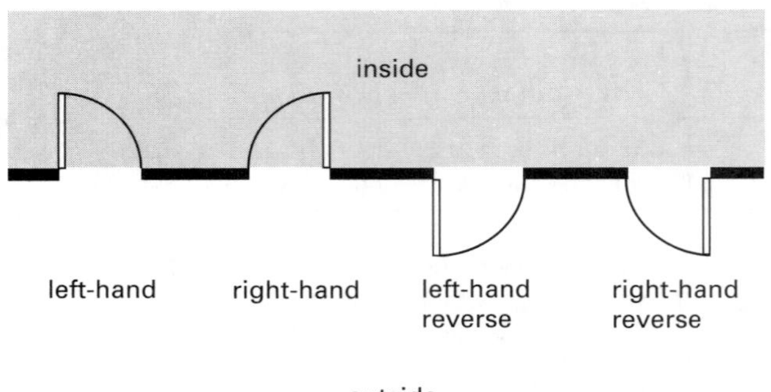


When standing on the outside looking at the door, if the door hinges on the left and swings away, it is a *left-hand door*. If it hinges on the right and swings away, it is a *right-hand door*. If the door swings toward you, it is considered a *left-hand reverse* or a *right-hand reverse*, depending on the hinge location. Sometimes a left-hand reverse door may be referred to as a right-hand door and a right-hand reverse door as a left-hand door, but it is better to use the correct terminology.

Revolving doors are commonly used for building entrances to prevent air infiltration and to accommodate many people. However, they are not acceptable as exit doors or accessible doors. Smaller revolving doors are available that provide seals against light for darkrooms.

### Door types and materials

Doors are also classified by their type and the material from which they are made. Common door types include flush, panel, louvered, sash, glass, and Dutch. Common materials for doors include wood (and wood with plastic laminate facing), steel (also called *hollow metal*), aluminum, glass, and other metals, such as brass, bronze, and stainless steel. Combinations are also possible, such as ornamental sheet metal laminated to wood or steel doors. Not all door types are available or possible in all materials. The common type and material combinations are shown in Fig. 3.3. Many variations are possible within most of the type/material combinations.

### Components of opening assemblies

There are four major components of a door system: the door itself, the frame, the hardware, and the partition in which the frame and opening are placed. Each must be coordinated with the others and must be appropriate for the function of the door as well as the design intent. This concept is especially important when detailing and specifying fire-rated opening assemblies. As with door types and materials, there are many possible combinations and variations of these four components, but some are never used. For example, a steel door is never placed in a wood frame, but wood doors are commonly set in steel or aluminum frames.

The most common types of partitions for interior construction include gypsum wallboard on either wood or metal studs, plaster on either wood or metal studs, and masonry, either exposed or covered with gypsum wallboard or plaster. Specific detailing conditions for these partition types are shown in the following sections.

## Design and detailing

Selecting, designing, and detailing a door assembly follows a logical sequence of steps. The order of decision may vary slightly from one project to the next, but all of the steps must be considered.

1. Determine the primary function or functions of the door and the method of operation. The spaces or rooms on either side of the door and specific programmatic requirements determine what function the door will serve. Operating types are determined by considering the following.

- code requirements
- frequency of use
- opening size
- ease of operation
- security
- sound privacy
- light control
- cost
- availability

Table 3.2 shows the commonly used types and materials for the required functions and can be used as a guide in making preliminary selections.

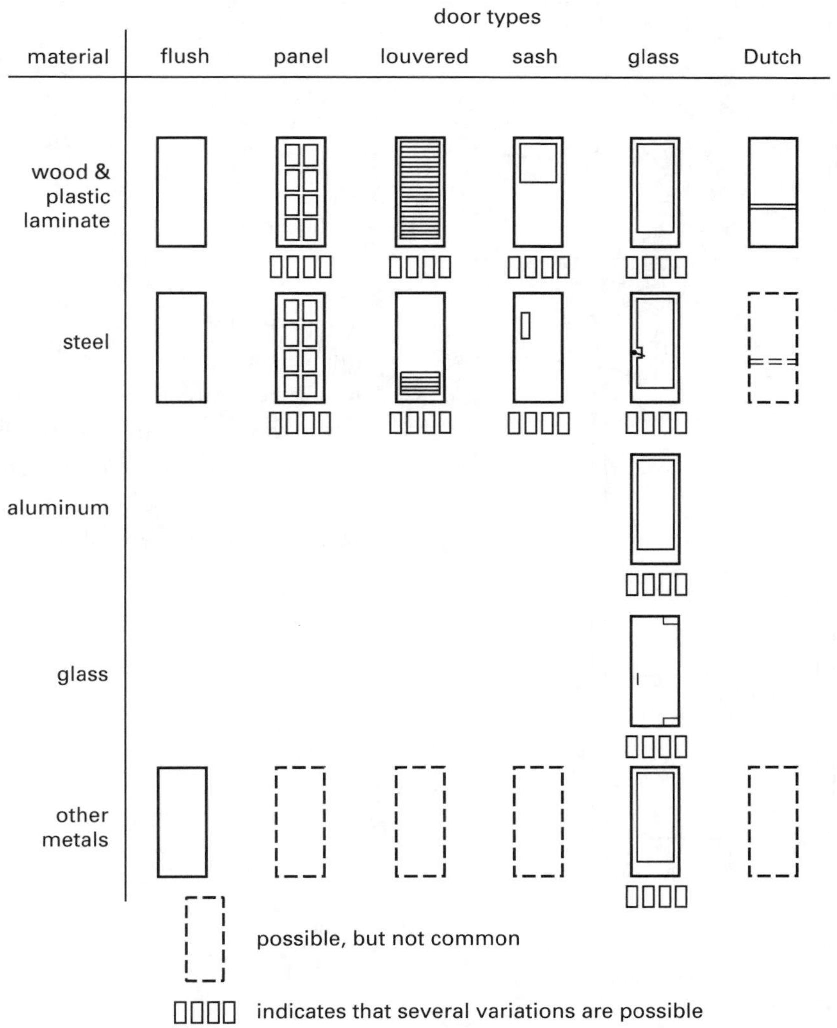

**Figure 3.3**
Door classification by types and materials

**Table 3.2** Door classifications by function, operation, and material

| | operation | control passage | visual privacy | audio privacy | security | control fire/smoke | control light | control radiation |
|---|---|---|---|---|---|---|---|---|
| swinging | hinged | W, S, A, B, T | W, S, A, B, T | W, S, B, T | W, S, B, T | W, S, B, T | W, S, B, T[1] | S[2] |
| swinging | pivoted | W, S, A, G, B, T | W, S, A, B, T | W, S, B, T | W, S, B, T | W, S, B, T[1] | | |
| sliding | pocket | W | W | | | | W | |
| sliding | bi-pass | W | W | | | | | |
| folding | bi-fold | W | W | | | | | |
| folding | accordion | W, V | W, V | | | | | |
| special | movable wall | W, S, A | W, S, A | W, S | W, S | | W, S | |
| special | overhead coiling | S | S | | S | S[3] | | |
| special | revolving | S, A, G, B | | | S, A, G, B | | | |

W = Wood
S = Steel
A = Aluminum
G = Glass

B = Bronze, brass, etc.
T = Stainless steel
V = Vinyl

[1] Limited fire ratings with wood.
[2] Special shielding required.
[3] Not for exiting.

## Door terms

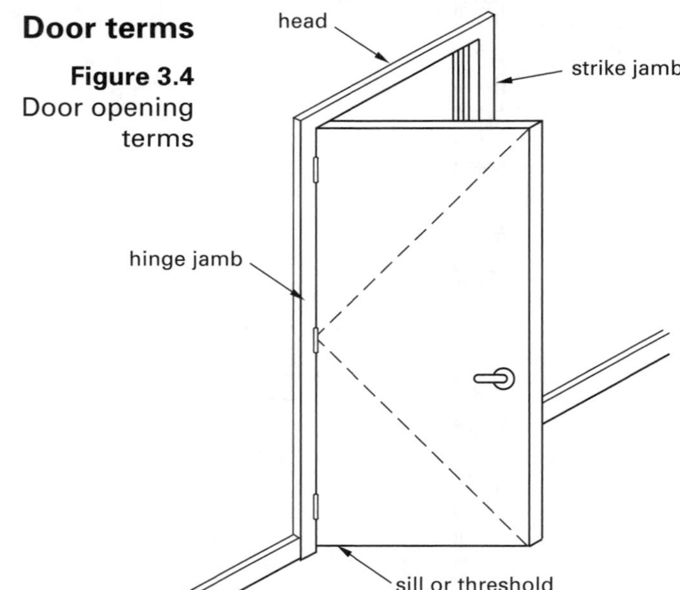


**Figure 3.4** Door opening terms

Note: dashed lines used on construction drawings to indicate how door swings when drawn on a two-dimensional elevation.

The terms used to describe parts of a door opening are illustrated in Fig. 3.4. To differentiate between the two jambs, the side where the hinge or pivot is installed is called the *hinge jamb,* or *hinge side,* and the jamb where the door closes is called the *strike jamb, strike side,* or *latch side* of the door.

Often, the specific functional requirements determine what door and frame material to use when several types are possible. For example, a low level of security can be accomplished with a solid core wood door, while greater security requirements may require a heavy-gage steel door.

2. Determine the desired appearance of the door and the opening. This is a design decision based on the program and the design concept of the entire project. Some questions to ask include: Should the opening be emphasized, standard, or concealed? Should the door finish match or contrast with the partition? Should the frame be emphasized or minimized? Should the hardware be emphasized, standard, or concealed? What finish should the hardware have? Does it meet accessibility requirements?

3. Determine the type and material of the door. This depends on both the functional requirements and the aesthetic goals of the project. For example, if a wood door is used, a paneled door may be more appropriate than a flush door for a traditional design.

4. Decide on the door size. Door width is primarily determined by functional requirements; door height is generally determined by cost and aesthetic considerations. A 36 in (914 mm) door provides the minimum 32 in (813 mm) clear opening required for an exit door. A 36 in door also provides a 32 in (813 mm) clear opening that is required for accessibility. Wider doors may be needed where large objects will be moved through; narrower doors may be acceptable for infrequently used doors, such as closets and residential bathrooms.

While 80 in (2032 mm) and 84 in (2134 mm) high doors are standard sizes, taller doors may be desirable. For instance, many designers prefer full-height doors, which are as high as the ceiling.

5. Decide on the frame type. Considerations for this decision include the desired appearance, fire-rating requirements, security needs, partition type, and anchorage for closers. In some cases, frames are not even required. Blind doors, for example, can be mounted on pivots, finished the same way as the partition, and set in openings without any trim, thereby minimizing their presence.

6. Determine hardware types for the desired appearance and functional requirements. How a door is hung and operated affects both its appearance and how the construction is detailed. In some cases, such as with fire-rated door assemblies, only certain types of hardware can be used; in other cases, there is a wide variety to choose from. Refer to Ch. 4 for more information on hardware.

7. Determine frame substrate conditions. All frames must be attached to the partition framing. The conditions on all four edges of a door opening can affect how the frame is detailed. For example, heavy doors or doors that receive rough use may require extra studs or other bracing to prevent wall shake or cracked finishes.

Some of the more important detailing considerations for a door opening are summarized in Fig. 3.5. Additional questions to consider when planning and detailing doors include the following.

- For doors in corners, is the hinge jamb far enough away from the wall and perpendicular to the door to allow the door to open at least a full 90°, with space for the door handle, door stop, and other hardware?
- For doors serving many people, do the doors open at least 110°?
- Are vision panels included in double-acting doors?
- Is protection required on the door in the way of armor plates, kick plates, edge guards, and similar hardware?
- Will the door swing clear of carpeting, uneven floors, and other obstructions?

- If used, can gaskets and sound seals be readjusted after a period of use?

- If the frame and door are wood, is the wood species compatible with surrounding wood trim and other millwork and furniture on the job?

- Will concealed doors operate freely after the application of finish material?

- Does the door operate within the maximum force requirements for accessibility?

- Is there sufficient space on either side of the door to meet accessibility requirements?

- Do door tolerances need to be specified differently from industry standards?

- Are doors recessed so that they do not interfere with traffic on the opening side?

## Fire-rated doors

When a building code requires that a partition be fire rated, then all openings, such as doors, glazing, ducts, and louvers, in that partition must also be fire rated. A protected opening is considered an *opening assembly*, but in the case of doors it is usually referred to as simply a fire-rated door.

### Fire door classifications and ratings

A *fire-door assembly* is defined as a door assembly that has been tested by an independent laboratory to determine that it is

**Figure 3.5**
Door detailing considerations

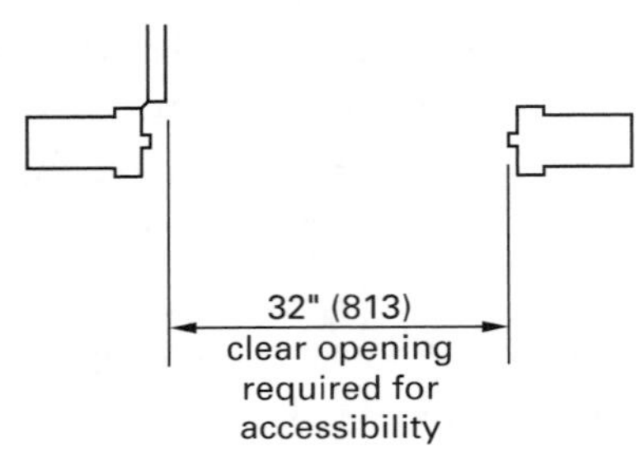


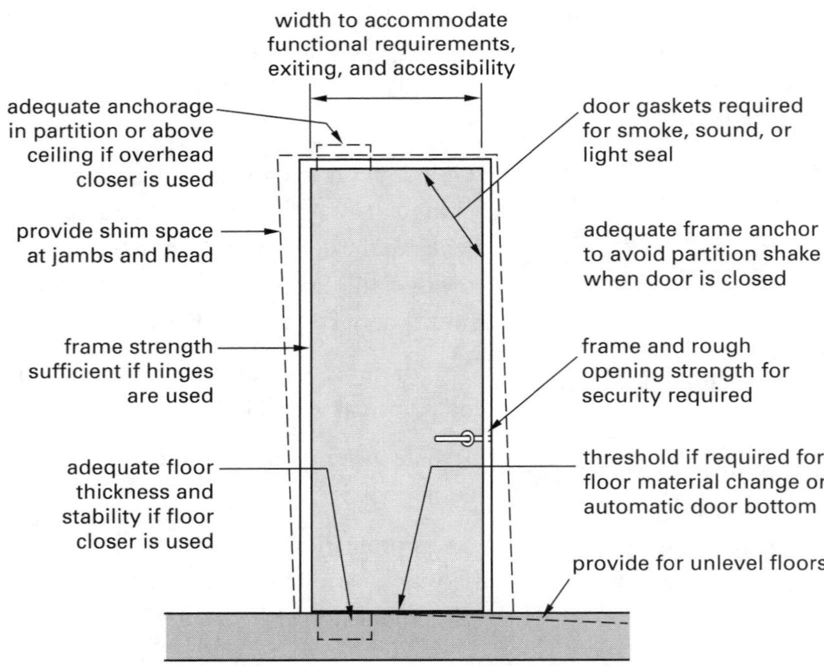

capable of withstanding a measured temperature without failure for a specific length of time. The assembly consists of the door itself, the frame, and the hardware used on the door and frame. The classification is stated in hours or minutes, and some doors are also given a corresponding letter designation. The required rating for a door depends on the rating of the wall or partition in which it is placed and the use of the wall or partition. Table 3.3 lists fire-door classifications and highlights the three types most commonly used in interior design work.

Most commercial interior design only requires the use of a 20-minute-rated door in a 1-hour-rated corridor or where a smoke and draft assembly is required; or a ¾-hour-rated door in a 1-hour exit passageway or in a 1-hour fire-resistive partition. For multifloor projects, a 1½-hour-rated door must be used in a 2-hour-rated exit enclosure (stairway).

In recent years, codes have been modified to include a requirement for positive-pressure fire testing. This testing simulates actual fire conditions where there is positive pressure on the fire side of the door above a certain point on the door (called the neutral pressure level) and negative pressure below this point. Under such conditions, there is a greater tendency for smoke and gases to be forced through the crack between the door and frame. There are two standards that provide for this type of testing: UL 10C and NFPA 252. The IBC references UL 10C and NFPA 252 (with the neutral pressure level set at 40 in (1016 mm) above the floor).

When a door must meet the requirements of positive-pressure fire testing, it must have

**Table 3.3**
Fire-door classifications

| fire-door rating (hr) | use of wall | rating of wall (hr) |
|---|---|---|
| 1½ to 3 | fire walls<br>fire-barrier wall | 1½ to 4 |
| 1½ | exit stairs<br>occupancy separations | 2 |
| 1 | exit passageways<br>exit stairs | 1 |
| ¾ | fire-resistive partitions<br>occupancy separations<br>hazardous areas | 1 |
| ½ | limited application | 1 or less |
| ⅓ | corridors<br>smoke barriers | 1 or less |
| 1½ | severe exterior exposure | 2 or more |
| ¾ | exterior exposure | 1 or less |

Note: Classifications in the shaded areas are those most commonly used for interior design. Because exact provisions vary among building codes, the requirements must be verified with the code having jurisdiction.
See Table 20.6 for glazing restrictions in fire doors.

approved gasketing or intumescent material along its edge or frame. An *intumescent material* is one that swells and chars to form a smoke and fire barrier when exposed to heat.

Doors in corridors and smoke barriers must meet the requirements for a smoke-and-draft-control door assembly tested in accordance with UL 1784, *Standard for Safety for Air Leakage Tests for Door Assemblies.* Local jurisdiction may require that they carry an S label.

For fire-door assemblies, either wood or hollow metal doors may be used. Wood doors are available with fire ratings up to 1½ hours (with mineral cores) from some manufacturers, while hollow metal doors are required for ratings higher than 1½ hours. More commonly, wood doors are used for 20-minute, 30-minute, and 45-minute-rated doors, while hollow metal doors are used for ratings above 45 minutes.

Fire-door assemblies must be installed in accordance with NFPA 80 and must carry a label of a recognized testing laboratory. Installation of smoke doors must be in accordance with NFPA 105. Light-gage steel frames may be used for ratings up to 1½ hours. 18-gage or heavier steel frames are required for ratings up to 3 hours. Aluminum frames may be used for up to a 45-minute rated assembly. Wood frames may be used if they meet the testing standards used by the code in force. Some manufacturers supply wood frames that have fire ratings of 20, 45, 60, and 90 minutes. More commonly, wood frames are used on 20-minute doors, and metal frames are used on doors with ratings higher than 20 minutes. Verify the availability of ratings with individual manufacturers.

Because exact provisions vary among local building codes, the exact requirements must be verified with the code having jurisdiction. Refer to Ch. 19 for more information on code requirements for opening assemblies.

## Additional considerations for detailing fire-rated doors

- Nearly all requirements for fire-rated doors apply to other than one- and two-family dwellings. Most codes require the use of a solid core door to separate a house from an attached garage.

- Combustible floor coverings cannot extend through the door opening unless the flooring has, at minimum, a Class II rating.

- The type and amount of glass used in fire-rated doors is limited. Refer to Ch. 20 and Table 20.6 for exact requirements.

- Generally, modifications to a fire-rated door cannot be made on the job site. All cutting, fitting, and hardware preparation must be done in the factory.

- There is a maximum allowable dimension of ⅜ in (9.5 mm) from the bottom of a single door to the top of the floor and a maximum of ¼ in (6.4 mm) for pairs of doors.

- The maximum size of a single-leaf, fire-rated door is 48 in (1219 mm) wide and 96 in (2438 mm) high for doors with panic hardware. The maximum height is increased to 10 ft (3048 mm) when other types of hardware are used. Pairs of doors can be up to 8 ft wide.

- A minimum of 6 in (152 mm) must be maintained between the edge of a door and any cutouts for glazing and louvers.

- If assemblies must conform to NFPA 252 or UL 10C for positive pressure, fire-rated intumescent material may need to be mortised into door edges or frames.

## Labels and listing for fire ratings

When a door opening assembly is used, the door, frame, and closer are required to be labeled, and the other hardware must be labeled or listed. A *label* is a permanent identifying mark attached to the door or frame by a testing organization that indicates the component is in compliance with

## Core types for wood doors

There are four basic types of cores for flush wood doors: hollow core, particleboard core, staved core, and mineral core. Figure 3.6 illustrates these types and some of their variations as classified by the Architectural Woodwork Institute (AWI).

A standard hollow core door has either one or three plies of veneer on either side of a ladder, mesh, or cellular core. The door is framed with a 2¼ in (57 mm) thick rail on the top and bottom and 1 in (25 mm) thick stiles. A solid lock-block is provided on each side for application of hardware. Institutional hollow core doors are also available that have wider stiles and rails and an intermediate crossrail.

Particleboard core doors use mat-formed particleboard with a density of 28 lbm/ft$^3$ to 32 lbm/ft$^3$ (448 kg/m$^3$ to 513 kg/m$^3$). These doors are faced with two or three plies of wood veneer, plastic laminate, or hardboard that is suitable for painting.

Staved core doors use solid blocks of wood with the end joints staggered in adjacent rows. Like particleboard core doors, the facing can be multiple plies of wood veneer, plastic laminate, or hardboard. Both particleboard core and staved core doors can be used where a 20-minute or ½-hour fire-rated door is required.

Mineral core doors are used when fire ratings of ¾, 1, and 1½ hours are required. The core is a mineral composition within a frame of treated, solid wood stiles and rails (see the section on panel doors) faced with wood veneer or plastic laminate constructed according to NFPA 80 and designed to meet the test requirements of UL 10B and NFPA 252.

**Figure 3.6**
Wood door core types

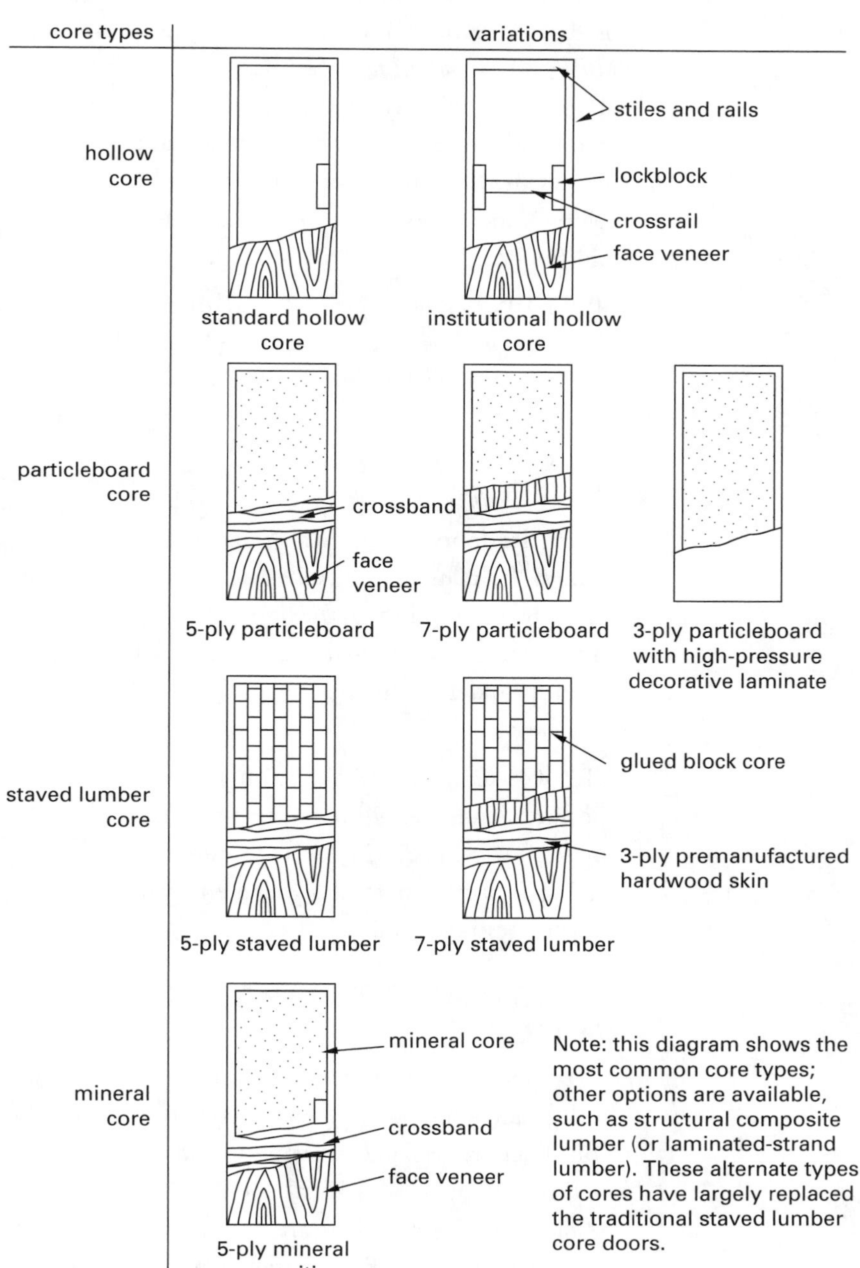

the standard tests for fire doors and with the National Fire Protection Association's Standard NFPA 80, which governs the installation of fire doors. A *listed* device is a product that has been shown to meet applicable standards for use in fire-rated assemblies (including NFPA 80) or that has been tested and found suitable for use in a specific application.

### Tests for fire-rated doors

There are three primary industry standards used in connection with fire-door assemblies. NFPA 80, *Standard for Fire Doors and Fire Windows*, establishes minimum criteria for installing and maintaining assemblies and devices used to protect openings in walls, ceilings, and floors from the spread of fire and smoke.

NFPA 105, *Standard for the Installation of Smoke Door Assemblies and Other Opening Protectives*, covers the requirements for doors that will limit smoke spread.

NFPA 252, *Standard Methods for Fire Tests of Door Assemblies*, is the standard method for testing fire doors and assigning them hourly ratings. It includes the hose stream test, which tests the ability of the door assembly to withstand the thermal shock produced when sprinklers or fire hoses rapidly cool a door heated by a fire.

UL 10C is similar to NFPA 252 but includes specific requirements for positive-pressure fire testing. NFPA 252 allows the authority having jurisdiction to designate positive-pressure testing conditions.

## WOOD DOORS AND FRAMES [081400]

Wood doors are the most common type for both residential and commercial construction. They are available in a variety of styles, methods of operation, sizes, and finishes. As shown in Fig. 3.3, there are six common types of wood doors: flush, panel, louvered, sash, glass, and Dutch.

## Types of wood doors

### Flush wood doors

Flush wood doors are made of thin, flat veneers laminated to various types of cores. They are either hollow core or solid core. Hollow core doors are made of one or three plies of veneer on each side of a cellular interior. The frame is made of solid wood, with larger blocks of solid wood where the latching hardware is located. Hollow core doors are used where only light use is expected and cost is a consideration. They cannot be fire rated.

Solid core doors are made with a variety of core types depending on the functional requirements of the door. Cores may be particleboard, staved lumber (solid blocks of wood), or mineral core for fire-rated doors. Solid core doors are used for their fire-resistive properties, as acoustical barriers, for security, and for their superior durability. They are available with fire ratings of 20, 30, 45, 60, and 90 minutes.

Solid core doors can either be bonded or nonbonded. With a *bonded core*, the stiles and rails are glued to the core material and the whole assembly is sanded as a unit before the faces are applied. This reduces the likelihood of telegraphing of the core. With a *nonbonded core*, the elements can vary slightly in thickness and can telegraph through the faces noticeably. Five-ply doors are typically made with a bonded core, while seven-ply doors are made with a nonbonded core.

The face veneers of wood doors are made from any available hardwood species using rotary-cut, plain-sliced, quarter-sliced, or rift-cut methods, just as with wood paneling discussed in Ch. 6. Veneers of hardboard suitable for painting and plastic laminate are also available.

### Special function wood flush doors

A sound-retardant door is often thicker than 1¾ in (44 mm) and has a core with a special damping compound. Sound-retardant doors are usually furnished with special gasketing and automatic door bottoms to complete the installation. They are specified by including the required sound transmission class coefficient (see Ch. 11).

Lead-lined doors are manufactured with a continuous lead sheet in the center of the door or between the crossbanding and the core. The thickness of the lead may be specified to meet the functional requirements of the project.

Electrostatic shield doors are manufactured with wire mesh in the center or between the crossbanding and the core. The mesh is grounded with electrical leads through the hinges to the frame.

## Standards for flush wood door

Two organizations develop the most commonly used standards for flush wood doors. One is the Window and Door Manufacturers Association (WDMA), and the other is the Architectural Woodwork Institute (AWI). The WDMA publishes I.S. 1-A, *Architectural Wood Flush Doors* and I.S. 1-R, *Residential Wood Flush Doors.* I.S. 1-A is similar to AWI standards and includes three grades of doors: Premium, Custom, and Economy. The WDMA standards are considered the minimum requirements for construction and can be used by themselves to specify wood doors for many interior applications. The AWI standards are classified into the same three groups, but they generally exceed the WDMA standards and have a different method of specifying doors. For most commercial interior design work it is best to use the AWI standards or WDMA I.S. 1-A for specifying wood doors.

Premium grade should be specified when the highest level of materials, workmanship, and installation is required. Custom grade is suitable for most installations and is intended for high-quality work. Economy is the lowest grade and is intended for work where price is a primary factor.

## Panel doors

Panel doors are constructed of solid pieces of wood that frame various types of panels. Because the vertical wood frame pieces are called *stiles* and the horizontal framing members are called *rails,* paneled doors are also called stile and rail doors. Any number of panels can be constructed, and the door is described by the number of panels it has. For example, a door with six panels is called a six-panel door. The WDMA has also developed standard number designations for doors with typical panel configurations.

The panels can be framed into the stiles and rails in a number of ways. Figures 3.7(a) and 3.7(b) show two typical panel door constructions. A wide variety of panel doors is available. These doors, including doors with glass panels, can be purchased as catalog items from many manufacturers. Panel doors can also be custom designed and detailed.

## Louvered doors

A louvered door has a solid wood stile and rail frame with wood slats set at an angle to allow airflow through the door. The slats can be set to prevent all vision or to allow some vision. They can also be adjustable. They are commonly used for closet doors and other areas where ventilation is required.

## Sash doors

Sash doors are flush- or panel-type doors having one or more pieces of glass. Standard sash doors are available from a variety of manufacturers, and custom sash sizes and configurations can be designed. The glass lights are framed into the stiles and rails in much the same way as they are for panel doors, but with the addition of removable stops that allow the glass to be installed and replaced. When most of the door consists of multiple sash lights it is called a French door.

## Glass doors

Glass doors differ from sash doors in that most of the door is one piece of glass set in a

**Figure 3.7** Panel door construction

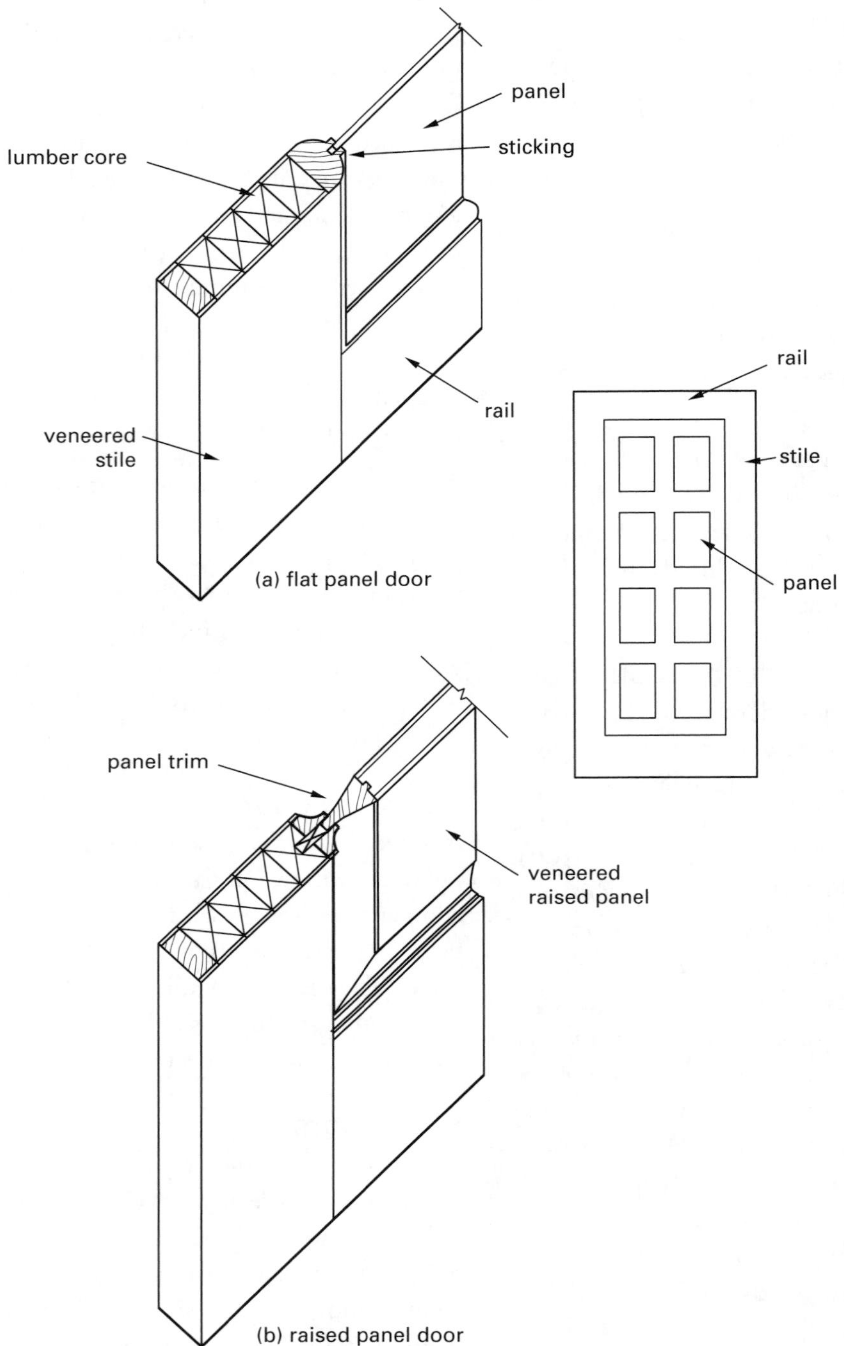


solid wood frame. Sash doors and glass doors allow vision and light to pass through, while controlling passage.

## Dutch doors

Dutch doors are two-piece doors that allow the top half to be opened while the bottom half remains latched. The two halves can be latched so that the entire door operates as a standard door. The halves can be flush, paneled, or sash type. Dutch doors prevent, or at least discourage, passage when the lower half is latched, provide an unobstructed view, and allow objects to be passed through the opening.

## Wood door specifications

Wood doors can be custom made to any size. However, standard widths are 1 ft 6 in, 2 ft, 2 ft 4 in, 2 ft 6 in, 2 ft 8 in, and

3 ft (457, 610, 711, 762, 813, 914 mm). Standard heights are 6 ft 8 in (2032 mm) and 7 ft (2133 mm). Higher doors, often used in commercial construction, are available. Hollow core doors are commonly 1⅜ in (35 mm) thick and solid core doors 1¾ in (44 mm) thick.

Frames for wood doors can be wood, steel (hollow metal, discussed in the next section), or aluminum. In custom details, wood doors can also be set on pivots in an opening without a frame as described later in this chapter.

The following are standard clearances between a wood door and its frame. Clearance dimensions are subject to a tolerance of ± 1/32 in (0.8 mm); however, no plus tolerance is allowed for fire doors.

at hinge jamb: ⅛ in (3 mm)
at lock jamb: ⅛ in (3 mm)
at head: minimum ⅛ in (3 mm)
at meeting edges of door pairs: ⅛ in (3 mm)

Undercut dimensions can be labeled on the drawings, but for fire doors there is a maximum of ⅜ in (9.5 mm) from the bottom of the door to the floor for single doors and a maximum of ¼ in (6.4 mm) clearance for double doors.

## Standard assemblies

In addition to the door and the partition, standard wood door assemblies consist of three major parts: the head/jamb frame itself, casing trim to cover the space between the frame and the partition, and the stop. In addition, all wood frames require a shim space so that the frame can be set plumb and level within the rough opening of the partition. Wood doors are beveled at 3° or ⅛ in in 2 in (3.2 mm in 50.8 mm) on the strike side to prevent the edge of the door from scraping the jamb as the door opens. A common wood frame jamb is illustrated in Figs. 3.8(a) and 3.8(b). Although the stop and casing trim are shown as simple shapes, any molding profile can be used. Pre-hung doors are available that include the door, frame, and hinges in one package.

The decision concerning the type of frame to use for a wood door depends on the appearance desired, the type of partition the opening is being installed in, fire rating requirements, the security needed, and the durability desired. For example, wood frames are generally only available for use in 20-minute fire door assemblies. Doors that require higher ratings must be set in steel frames. When appearance is important, labeled steel frames are available that are covered with a thin lamination of real wood veneer.

Figures 3.9(a)–3.9(f) illustrate several possible combinations of wood frame profiles set in various types of partitions.

## Custom assemblies

By definition, custom wood door frame assemblies include a limitless variety of configurations. Some or all three of the major component parts of a standard assembly may be omitted, but certain functional requirements must be met. First, there must be some way to hang the door, either with hinges, pivots, or an overhead track. Some type of jamb frame is required if hinges are used. For frameless openings, the door must be supported with a pivot or track. Second, there must be some way to stop the door. If a standard continuous trim stop is not used, a metal angle or block must be provided either in the head section or the strike jamb. In some cases, stopping action can be provided by a door closer. Third, there must be some way to operate the door with a handle, knob, pull, or other hardware, as discussed in Ch. 4.

Optional components of a custom opening detail include a method to lock the door and a method to seal the openings between the door and frame. However, for many interior door assemblies these options are not required.

Figs. 3.11–3.13 illustrate some commonly used custom door opening details. The

**Figure 3.8**
Standard wood door frame

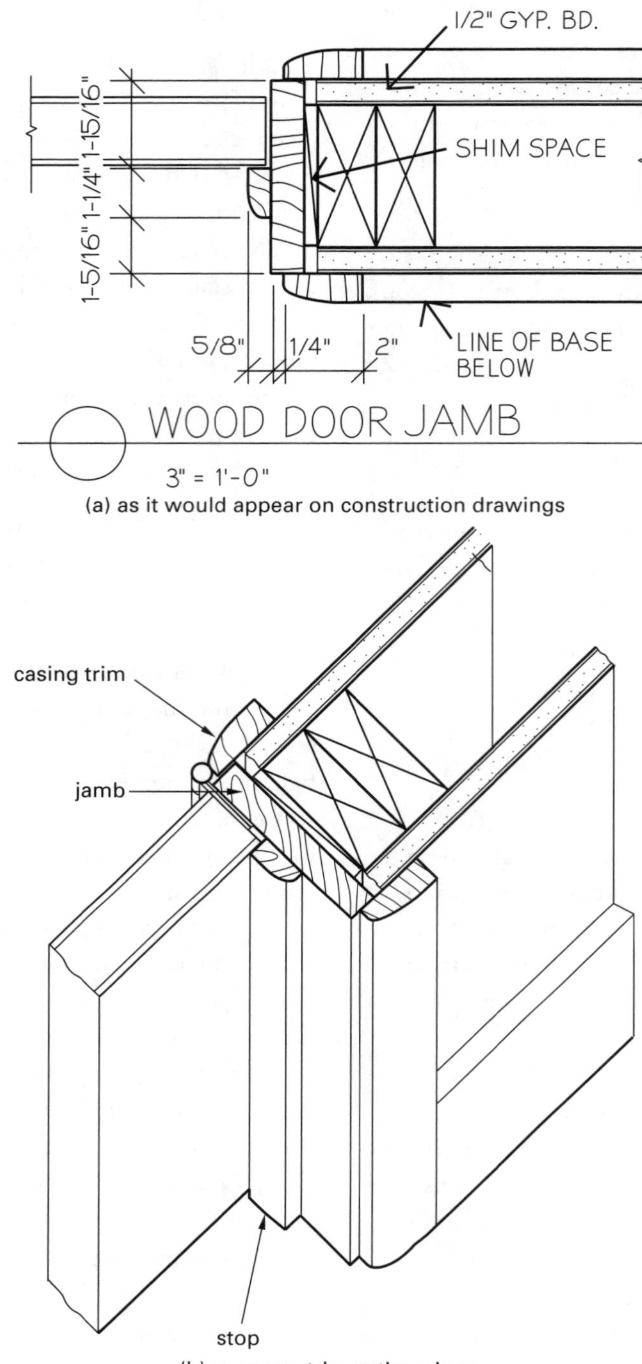


(a) as it would appear on construction drawings

(b) axonometric section view

drawings show jamb details, but the head details are similar. If a threshold is required it can be set flush with adjacent flooring materials or raised slightly above the finish floor. Thresholds of wood, stone, and metal are commonly used. Standard aluminum thresholds can also be used where cost is a consideration or where a special sound, weather, or light seal is required.

## Coordination

Designing and detailing custom door assemblies, and even some standard door assemblies, requires coordination between

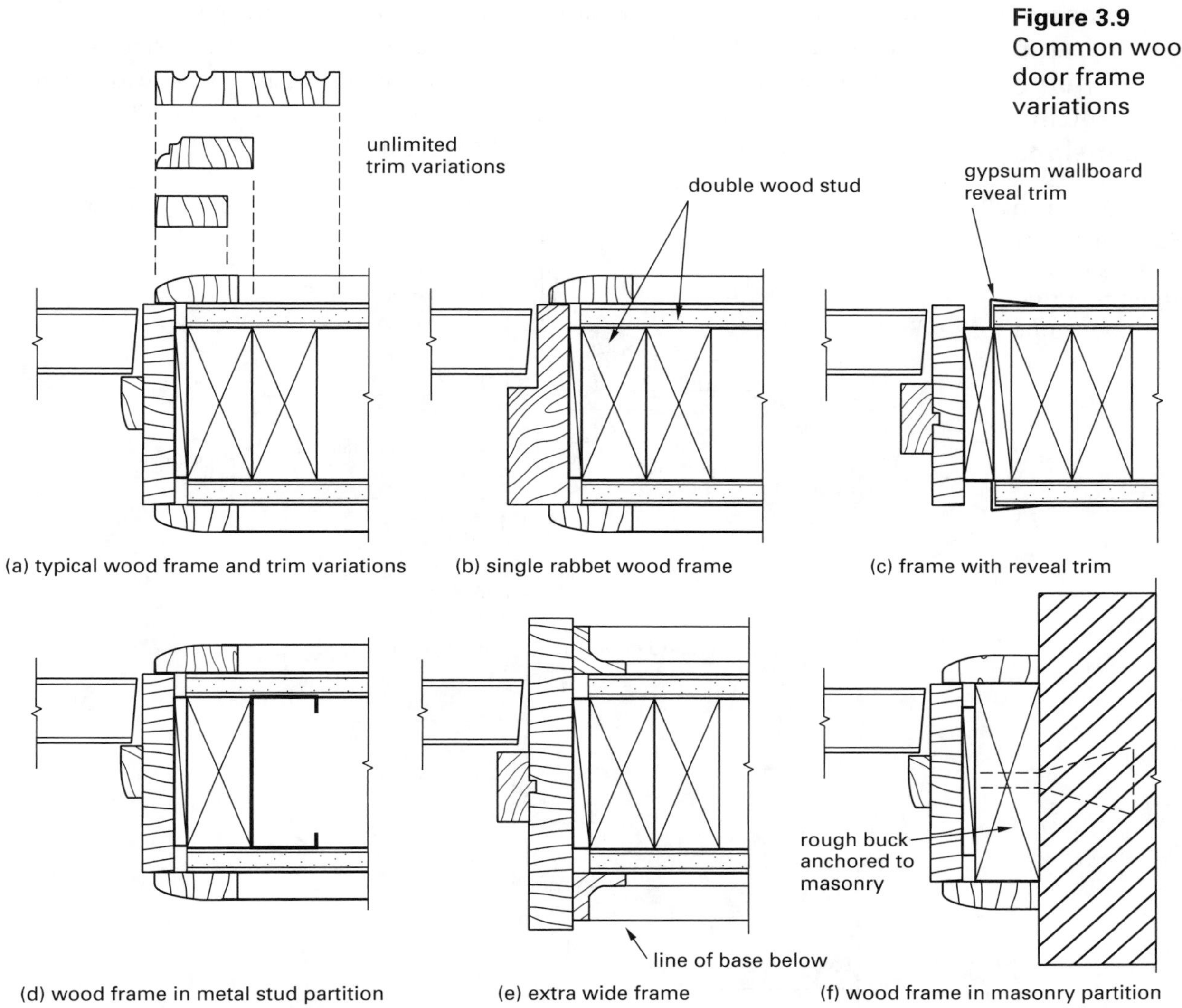


**Figure 3.9** Common wood door frame variations

the door components and other construction elements. The following list summarizes some of the considerations.

- Wood blocking at jambs is generally required for wood jambs set in metal stud partitions.
- Casing trim should be thick enough to provide a stopping point for the wall base.
- Hardware, louvers, and glass lights must be listed or labeled to be used in a labeled door.
- Smoke gaskets may be required for some fire-rated doors.
- A steel or aluminum frame may be required for some fire-rated doors.
- Floors must be of adequate thickness and stability to support floor closers.
- Partitions or ceilings must be of adequate stability to support overhead closers.
- Hard-surfaced thresholds should be used when automatic door bottoms are installed.

## Standard door frame and hinge setting dimensions

Figures 3.10(a) and 3.10(b) show the industry-standard dimensions for wood door frames, along with ways in which hinges are applied to doors and frames. These dimensions are useful when standard hinges and doors are used, but they may be modified when detailing a door within a custom frame assembly. Maintaining standard dimensions simplifies detailing and minimizes the cost and difficulty of building the detail.

**Figure 3.10**
Standard door frame details and hinge fitting dimensions

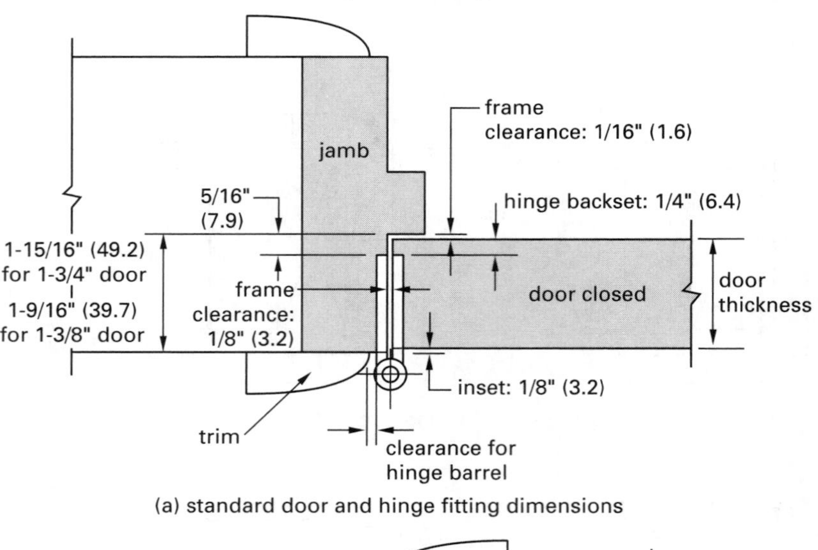


(a) standard door and hinge fitting dimensions

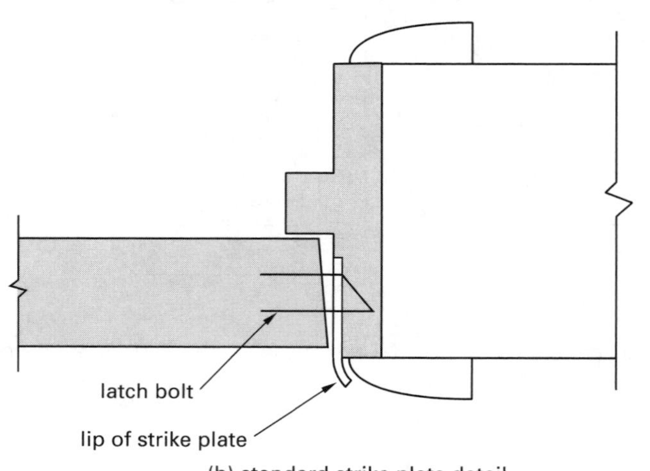


(b) standard strike plate detail

**Figure 3.11**
Wood frame without casing trim

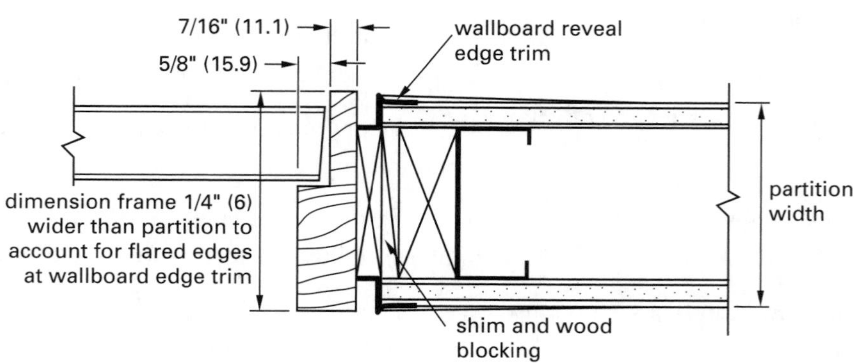

**Applicable standards for wood doors and frames**

**American National Standards Institute (ANSI):**

ANSI A117.1 — *Specifications for Making Buildings and Facilities Accessible to and Usable by Physically Handicapped People*

**Architectural Woodwork Institute (AWI):**

*Architectural Woodwork Quality Standards*, Section 900, Frames and Jambs; Section 1300, Architectural Flush Doors; Section 1400, Stile and Rail Doors; Section 1500, Factory Finishing

**American Society for Testing and Materials (ASTM):**

ASTM E119 — *Fire Tests of Building Construction and Materials*

**Door and Hardware Institute (DHI):**

DHI-WDHS-3 — *Recommended Hardware Locations for Wood Flush Doors*

**National Fire Protection Association (NFPA):**

NFPA 80 — *Standard for Fire Doors and Windows*
NFPA 105 — *Standard for the Installation of Smoke Door Assemblies and Other Opening Protectives*
NFPA 252 — *Standard Methods for Fire Tests of Door Assemblies* (same as UL 10B)

**Window and Door Manufacturers Association (WDMA):**

I.S. 1-A — *Industry Standard for Architectural Wood Flush Doors*
I.S. 6 — *Industry Standard for Wood Stile and Rail Doors*
I.S. 6-A — *Industry Standard for Architectural Stile and Rail Doors*

**Underwriters Laboratories (UL):**

UL 10B — *Standard for Safety for Fire Tests of Door Assemblies* (same as NFPA 252)
UL 10C — *Standard for Safety for Positive-Pressure Fire Tests of Door Assemblies*
UL 1784 — *Standard for Safety for Air Leakage Tests for Door Assemblies*

**Figure 3.12**
Wood frame with center-hung door

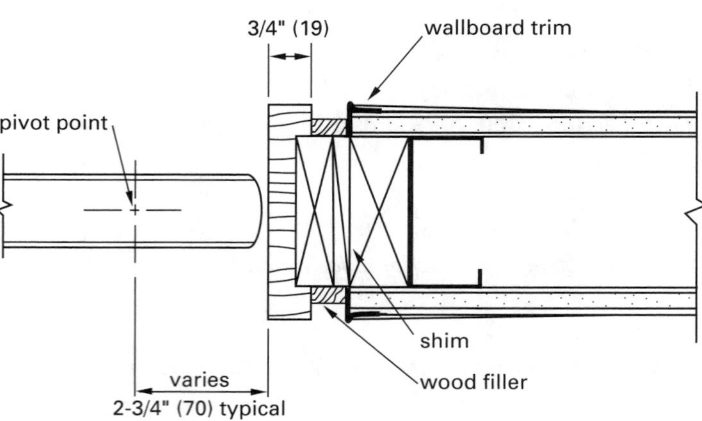


**Figure 3.13**
Blind door detail

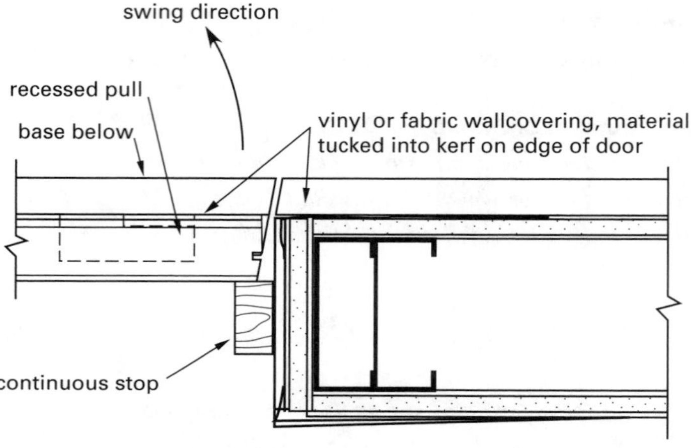


Strike side shown. Door can be hung with center hung pivots or offset pivots depending on direction of swing.

## STEEL DOORS AND FRAMES [081113]

Steel doors and frames, often referred to as *hollow metal*, are the most common type of metal door assemblies. Aluminum, stainless steel, and bronze (discussed in later sections), are also used. Steel doors are seldom used for residential construction but are frequently used in commercial construction because of their durability, security, and fire-resistive qualities. However, steel doors manufactured to resemble paneled doors and filled with polyurethane or polystyrene insulation are being used more often for residential entrance doors because of their added durability and insulative qualities.

### Steel door construction

Steel doors are constructed with faces of cold-rolled sheet steel. The steel face is attached to cores of honeycomb kraft paper, steel ribs, mineral fiberboard, polyurethane, polystyrene, or other materials. The edges are made of steel channels, with hardware locations reinforced by heavy gage steel.

Mineral wool or other materials are used to provide sound-deadening qualities, if required.

## Steel door grades and models

Steel doors are classified into four levels based on the thickness of their face sheets and their durability, which is based on a standardized test. The four levels are Level I, standard duty; Level II, heavy duty; Level III, extra heavy duty; and Level IV, maximum duty. Level I doors are only available in 1⅜ in (35 mm) thickness, while the other levels are only available in 1¾ in (44 mm) thickness. Steel doors are further classified into models, which refer to their construction method. Model 1 is full flush, which means that there is a visible seam on the edge of the door where the face sheets meet. Model 2 is called seamless. There is no visible seam on the edge of the door. Model 3 is a stile and rail door. These levels and models, along with their corresponding face sheet thicknesses, are summarized in Table 3.4.

The durability of a steel door is based on tests conducted in accordance with ANSI A250.4, *Test Procedure and Acceptance Criteria for Physical Endurance for Steel Doors and Hardware Reinforcings.* This test includes swing testing and twist testing of a representative specimen of production doors and frames. It establishes three performance levels: A, B, and C. A Level A door is subjected to 1,000,000 cycles; a Level B door is subjected to 500,000 cycles; and a Level C door is subjected to 250,000 cycles of the test. Performance-level C doors are used in Level I, standard duty doors. Level B doors are used in Level II, heavy-duty doors, and Level A doors are used in both Level III and Level IV doors.

The choice of which level of door to use in a particular circumstance is left to the designer's judgment. However, recommendations

**Table 3.4**
Standard steel door grades and models

| | level | model | construction | full flush or seamless | | |
|---|---|---|---|---|---|---|
| | | | | MSG no. | IP (in) | SI (mm) |
| I | standard duty | 1 | full flush | 20 | 0.032 | 0.8 |
| | | 2 | seamless | | | |
| II | heavy duty | 1 | full flush | 18 | 0.042 | 1 |
| | | 2 | seamless | | | |
| III | extra heavy duty | 1 | full flush | 16 | 0.053 | 1.3 |
| | | 2 | seamless | | | |
| | | 3 | stile and rail[(1)] | | | |
| IV | maximum duty | 1 | full flush | 14 | 0.067 | 1.6 |
| | | 2 | seamless | | | |

[(1)] Stiles and rails are 16 gage; flush panels, when specified, are 18 gage.
For complete standard steel door construction specifications and available sizes, refer to *Steel Door Institute Technical Data Series*, ANSI A250.8-03 (SDI-100), and *Test Procedure and Acceptance Criteria for Physical Endurance for Steel Door and Hardware Reinforcements*, ANSI A250.4-01.

Reprinted with permission from SDI 108-1998, copyright © 1999 by the Steel Door Institute.

for some building uses are given in Table 3.5. The level of door and frame thickness that is finally selected depends on the width of the opening, the expected frequency of use, the security needs, and the severity of service, along with availability and cost.

## Steel door and frame thicknesses

Traditionally, steel thickness has been referred to with the term "gage" (or gauge). Unfortunately, several different gage-sizing systems have developed throughout the history of the metals industry, so the same gage number may refer to a different thickness depending on which system is being used. Some of the different gage sizes are shown in Table 7.4. The MSG (manufacturers' standard gage) system previously used by the door industry is yet another system in addition to those shown in Table 7.4. The steel door industry, as well as other industries that use metal, have adopted the more accurate method of describing metal thickness with actual dimensions, either customary U.S. (English) units of decimals of an inch, or SI (metric) units of millimeters. Technically, the use of gage sizes is obsolete. However, because gages are still used by many in the industry, both actual thickness and gage numbers are used in this chapter.

### Steel door frames

Steel door frames are used for either steel doors or wood doors and are made from sheet steel bent into the shape required for installation of the door. Frames are constructed of 18-, 16-, 14-, or 12-gage steel depending on the grade level of the door and the specific application. Table 3.6 gives the recommended frame thickness based on the door grade level. Table 3.4 also gives the recommended frame gages for various applications. Different types of anchoring devices are used inside the frame to attach it to the partition. A floor anchor is also used at each jamb when the frame is installed before the partition.

Steel frames are manufactured as one-piece frames, welded frames, knock-down (KD) frames, where the two jamb sections and the head section are shipped to the job site as separate pieces, or drywall slip-on frames. One-piece frames must be set in place before the partition is constructed; knock-down and drywall slip-on frames can be set after gypsum wallboard partitions are built. Drywall slip-on frames are not available with welded corners and should be avoided if the appearance of a joint is objectionable.

### Specifications

Steel doors and frames are available in the full range of fire ratings, from 20-minute to 3-hour ratings. Steel frames are used almost exclusively for openings that must be rated over 20 minutes, although qualifying aluminum frames may be rated up to 45 minutes, and some wood frames are available with higher ratings.

Although metal doors can be custom made in almost any practical size, standard widths are from 2 ft (600 mm) to 4 ft (1200 mm) in multiples of 2 in (50 mm). Standard opening sizes are listed in Table 3.7.

The following are standard clearances between a door and its frame for steel doors. Clearance dimensions are subject to a tolerance of ±1/32 in (0.8 mm) for nonrated doors. No tolerance is allowed for fire doors.

- at hinge jambs: 1/8 in (3 mm), maximum
- at head: 1/8 in (3 mm), maximum
- at meeting edges of door pairs: not more than 1/4 in (6 mm) but 1/8 in (3 mm) for fire-rated door openings
- undercut dimension: 3/4 in (19 mm) for nonrated doors and 3/8 in (9.5 mm) for single fire doors.
- between door face and door stop: 1/16 in (1.6 mm)

**Table 3.5** Recommended gages for steel doors and frames

| building type | door levels recommended | frame gage[1] |
|---|---|---|
| **apartments** | | |
| main entrances | II, III | 16 or 14 |
| apartment entrances | II, III | 16 or 14 |
| bedrooms | I | 18 or 16 |
| bathrooms | I | 18 or 16 |
| stairwells | II, III | 16 or 14 |
| **schools** | | |
| entrances | III, IV | 16, 14, or 12 |
| classrooms | II | 16 |
| toilets | II, III | 16 or 14 |
| gymnasiums | III, IV | 16, 14, or 12 |
| cafeterias | II, III | 16 or 14 |
| stairwells | II, III | 16 or 14 |
| **hotels/motels** | | |
| main entrances | II, III | 16 or 14 |
| room entrances | I, II | 18 or 16 |
| bathrooms | I | 18 or 16 |
| closets | I | 18 or 16 |
| stairwells | II, III | 16 or 14 |
| storage and utility rooms | II, III | 16 or 14 |
| **hospitals** | | |
| main entrances | III | 16 or 14 |
| patient rooms | II | 16 |
| stairwells | II, III | 16 or 14 |
| operation and exam rooms | II, III | 16 or 14 |
| kitchens | II, III | 16 or 14 |
| **industrial** | | |
| entrances | III, IV | 16, 14, or 12 |
| offices | I, II | 18 or 16 |
| production | III | 16 or 14 |
| toilets | II, III | 16 or 14 |
| tool and trucking | III, IV | 16, 14, or 12 |
| **offices** | | |
| entrances | III | 16 or 14 |
| individual offices | I | 18 or 16 |
| closets | I | 18 or 16 |
| toilets | II, III | 16 or 14 |
| stairwells | II, III | 16 or 14 |
| mechanical rooms | II, III | 16 or 14 |

(1)These are manufacturer's standard gages. See Table 3.5.

Source: adapted from recommendations of the Steel Door Institute

**Table 3.6**
Steel thicknesses for frames

| level | MSG no. | thickness (in) |
|---|---|---|
| 1 | 18 or 16 | 0.042/0.053 |
| 2 | 16 | 0.053 |
| 3 | 16 or 14 | 0.053/0.067 |
| 4 | 14 or 12 | 0.067/0.093 |



**Table 3.7**
Standard opening sizes for steel doors

| 1¾ in (44 mm) doors (ft-in (mm)) | | 1⅜ in (35 mm) doors (ft-in (mm)) | |
|---|---|---|---|
| width | height | width | height |
| 2 ft (610) | 6 ft 8 in (2032) | 2 ft (610) | 6 ft 8 in (2032) |
| 2 ft 4 in (711) | 7 ft (2134) | 2 ft 4 in (711) | 7 ft (2134) |
| 2 ft 6 in (762) | 7 ft 2 in (2184) | 2 ft 6 in (762) | 7 ft 2 in (2184) |
| 2 ft 8 in (813) | 7 ft 10 in (2388) | 2 ft 8 in (813) | |
| 2 ft 10 in (864) | 8 ft (2438) | 2 ft 10 in (864) | |
| 3 ft (914) | 8 ft 10 in (2692) | 3 ft (914) | |
| 3 ft 4 in (1016) | 10 ft (3048) | | |
| 3 ft 6 in (1067) | | | |
| 3 ft 8 in (1118) | | | |
| 3 ft 10 in (1168) | | | |
| 4 ft (1219) | | | |

## Standard assemblies

The three most common types of metal doors are flush, sash, and louvered. Flush doors have a single, smooth surface on both sides; sash doors contain one or more glass lights; and louvered doors have an opening with metal slats to provide ventilation. Many standard configurations of sash and louvered doors are available, as well as doors with both louvers and glass.

Steel frames are generally made from one piece of sheet steel bent into the required profile. Figures 3.14(a) and 3.14(b) show one of the most common frame profiles, along with some standard dimensions and the terminology used to describe the parts. Frames can also be custom fabricated into a variety of sizes and shapes within the limits of the machinery used to form them. Figures 3.15(a)–3.15(e) illustrate several possible combinations of steel door frames set in various types of partitions.

Light-gage steel frames are also available. These consist of a single frame piece that slips over the partition. Separate casing trim pieces are then snapped onto the edges of the frames. These frames are available in 18-, 20-, and 22-gage thicknesses (which measure 0.042, 0.032, and 0.025 in (1.0, 0.8, and 0.4 mm), respectively).

## Custom assemblies

Most custom steel door assemblies are unique because of the size or shape of the frame. The frame profile shown in Fig. 3.14 is the most common. Other profiles are possible; however, the minimum face dimension is usually 1 in because of limitations on the brake presses used to form the frame. An unusual design must be verified with a hollow metal door manufacturer to be sure that its fabrication is possible. Figures 3.16(a) and 3.16(b) show some examples of custom frames.

**Figure 3.14**
Standard steel door frame

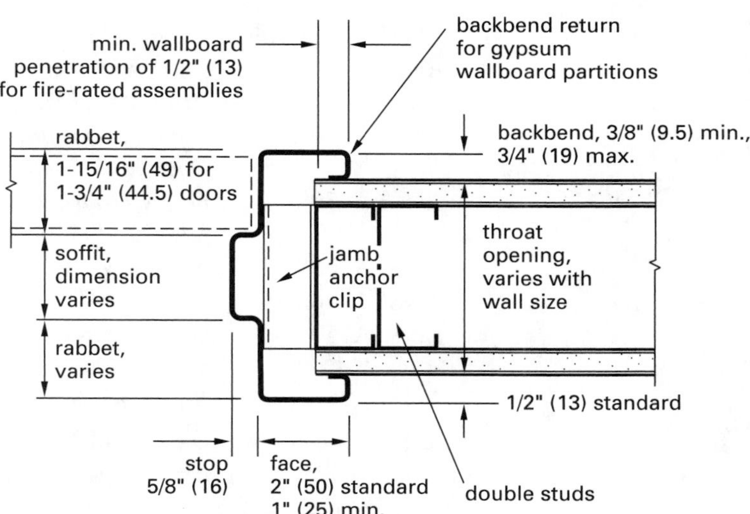


(a) orthographic view

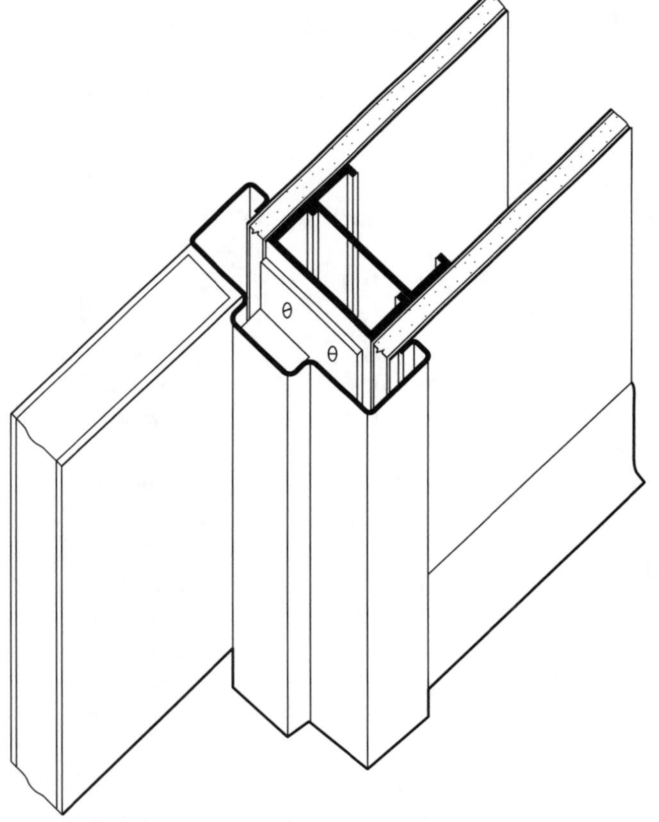

(b) axonometric view

## Applicable standards for steel doors and frames

**American National Standards Institute (ANSI):**

| | |
|---|---|
| ANSI/ISDSI 100 | *Door Size Dimensional Standard and Assembly Tolerance for Insulated Steel Door Systems* |
| ANSI/ISDSI 102 | *Installation Standard for Insulated Steel Door Systems* |
| ANSI/ISDSI 103 | *Acoustical Performance Standard for Insulated Steel Door Systems* |
| ANSI A250.3 | *Test Procedure and Acceptance Criteria for Factory-Applied Finish Painted Steel Surfaces for Steel Doors and Frames* |
| ANSI A250.4 | *Test Procedure and Acceptance Criteria for Physical Endurance for Steel Doors and Hardware Reinforcings* |
| ANSI A250.6 | *Recommended Practice for Hardware Reinforcing on Standard Steel Doors and Frames* |
| ANSI A250.7 | *Nomenclature for Steel Doors and Steel Door Frames* |
| ANSI A250.8 | *Recommended Specifications for Standard Steel Doors and Frames* |
| ANSI A250.10 | *Test Procedure and Acceptance Criteria for Prime Painted Steel Surfaces for Steel Doors and Frames* |
| ANSI A250.11 | *Recommended Erection Instructions for Steel Frames* |

**American Society for Testing and Materials (ASTM):**

| | |
|---|---|
| ASTM E119 | *Fire Tests of Building Construction and Materials* |

**Door and Hardware Institute (DHI):**

*Recommended Locations for Builders' Hardware for Custom Steel Doors and Frames*
*Recommended Locations for Architectural Hardware for Standard Steel Doors and Frames*

**National Fire Protection Association (NFPA):**

| | |
|---|---|
| NFPA 80 | *Standard for Fire Doors and Windows* |
| NFPA 105 | *Standard for the Installation of Smoke Door Assemblies and Other Opening Protectives* |
| NFPA 252 | *Standard Methods for Fire Tests of Door Assemblies* |

**Steel Door Institute (SDI):**

| | |
|---|---|
| SDI-106 | *Recommended Standard Door Type Nomenclature* |
| SDI-108 | *Recommended Selection and Usage Guide for Standard Steel Doors and Frames* |
| SDI-109 | *Hardware for Standard Steel Doors and Frames* |
| SDI-110 | *Standard Steel Doors and Frames for Modular Masonry Construction* |
| SDI-111 | *Recommended Selection and Usage Guide for Standard Steel Doors, Frames, and Accessories* |
| SDI-112 | *Zinc-Coated (Galvanized/Galvannealed) Standard Steel Doors and Frames* |
| SDI-117 | *Manufacturing Tolerances for Standard Steel Doors and Frames* |
| SDI-118 | *Basic Fire Door Requirements* |
| SDI-122 | *Installation and Troubleshooting Guide for Standard Steel Doors and Frames* |
| SDI-124 | *Maintenance of Standard Steel Doors and Frames* |
| SDI-128 | *Guidelines for Acoustical Performance of Standard Steel Doors and Frames* |
| SDI-129 | *Hinge and Strike Spacing* |

**Underwriters Laboratories (UL):**

| | |
|---|---|
| UL 63 | *Standard for Safety for Fire Doors and Frames* |
| UL 10B | *Standard for Safety for Fire Tests of Door Assemblies* |
| UL 10C | *Standard for Safety for Positive-Pressure Fire Tests of Door Assemblies* |

**Figure 3.15**
Common steel door frame variations

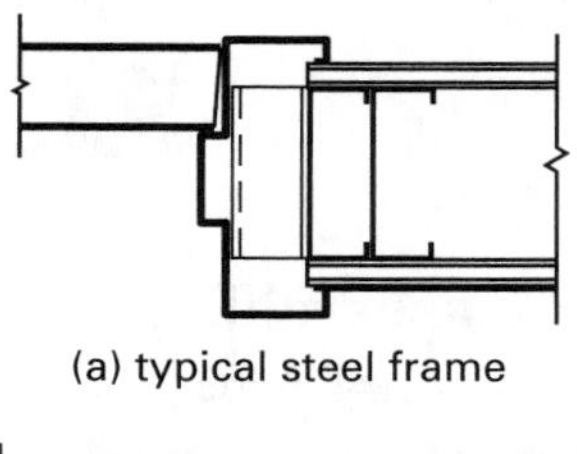
(a) typical steel frame

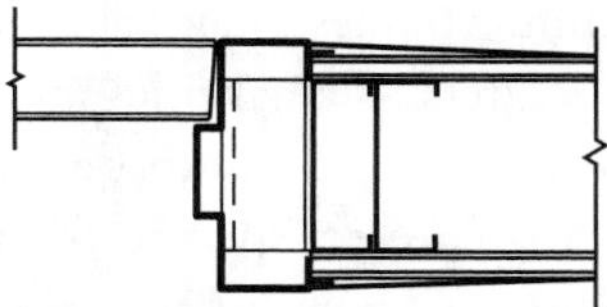
(b) flush frame application

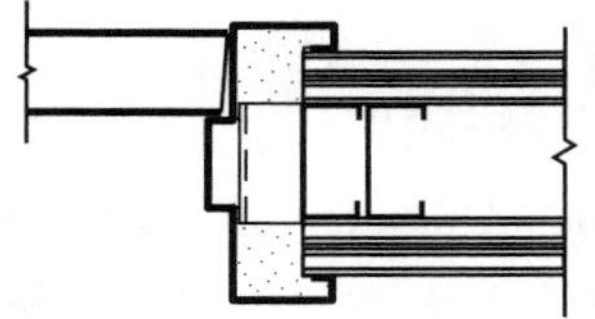
(c) frame in 2-hour-rated partition

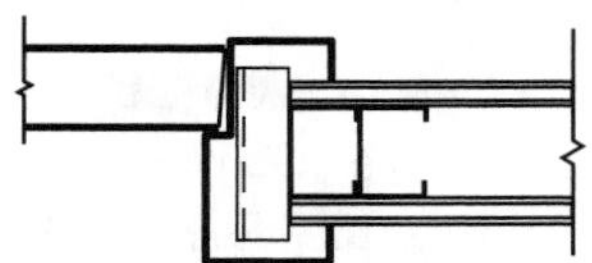
(d) single rabbeted frame in narrow partition

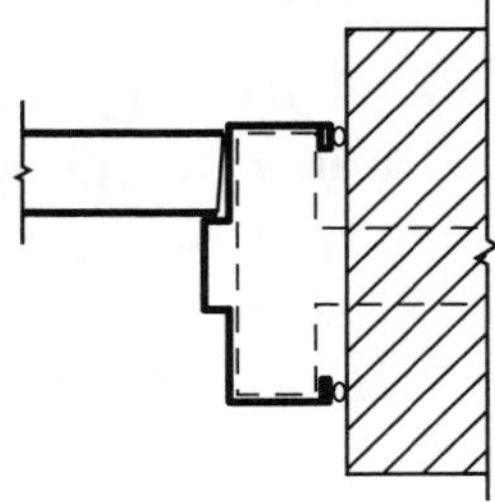
(e) frame in masonry wall

**Figure 3.16**
Custom steel frame applications

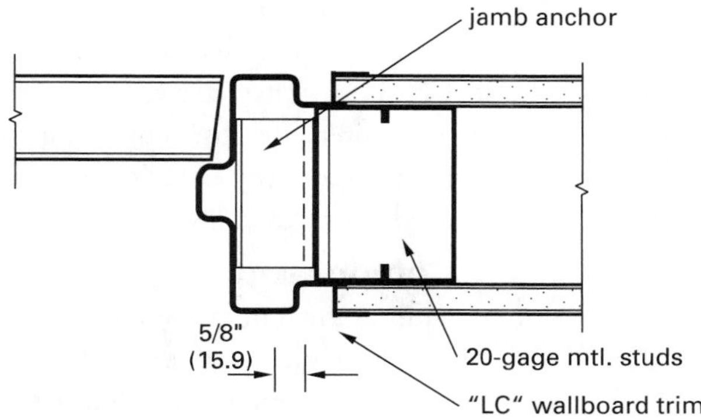

(a) frame shaped for flush application with reveal

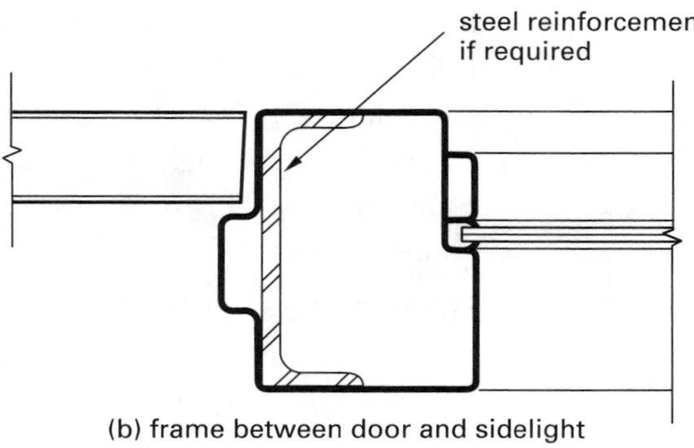

(b) frame between door and sidelight

## Coordination

Designing for hollow metalwork requires some of the same coordination as for wood doors and frames. In addition, consider the following items in detailing.

- Knock-down or drywall slip-on frames are easier to install than one-piece welded frames in gypsum wallboard partitions, but the joints are visible.
- Cutoff (or sanitary) stops that do not extend to the floor should be used where ease of cleaning around the frame is important.
- Mineral-core, flush wood doors may be used with steel frames for fire ratings up to 1½ hours.
- Rubber silencers must be provided in the strike sides of door frames.
- Full-height doors in partitions that extend only to a suspended ceiling may require extra bracing from the head frame to the structure above the ceiling.

## ALUMINUM DOORS AND FRAMES [081116]

Aluminum is commonly used as stile and rail material for glass doors and as door frame material for both aluminum glass doors and wood doors. A few manufacturers also offer flush, sash, and louvered doors faced with aluminum. Aluminum door frames are most commonly used in interior construction to frame wood doors when a lightweight, easily assembled frame is required. Aluminum frames are also used in many demountable partition systems (see Ch. 1) or when a complex frame profile is required. Because aluminum frames are manufactured by extrusion, intricate shapes can be formed easily.

### Components

Aluminum frames are constructed of one or more pieces of extruded aluminum. The exact configuration and size of a frame depends on the manufacturer's proprietary system, but most are a double-rabbeted shape with a continuous stop, similar to a steel door frame. One noticeable difference is that aluminum frames have sharp corners, as opposed to the slightly rounded corners of steel frames. This is because aluminum frames are extruded.

### Standard assemblies

Figure 3.17 shows a typical aluminum frame with a separate, continuous anchor member that is attached to the gypsum wallboard partition. The finished jamb and the door stop are attached to the anchoring subassembly to complete the installation. Other types of aluminum frames have separate jamb pieces and casing trim, similar to wood frames. The door stops may have individual silencers or a continuous wool pile sealer.

Aluminum frames are available for 20-minute fire-rated opening assemblies. Smoke gaskets are also available where they are required by code.

### Custom assemblies

Many proprietary shapes, sizes, and finishes of aluminum frames are available from several manufacturers. If quantities are sufficient, custom extrusion dies can be made to order so that project-specific frame profiles can be manufactured. Curves, angles, and ornate profiles are all possible with custom extrusions.

### Coordination

- Most manufacturers offer a complete system of extrusion sizes and shapes for door frames as well as glass sidelight framing, bank railing, and partition track.
- Other metals in contact with the frame should be stainless steel or zinc. Contact with other dissimilar metals should be prevented with bituminous paint or nonmetallic gaskets to prevent galvanic action.
- Aluminum framing used with demountable partition systems may be used with prefinished panels of gypsum wallboard in place of standard wallboard construction.

**Figure 3.17**
Typical aluminum frame

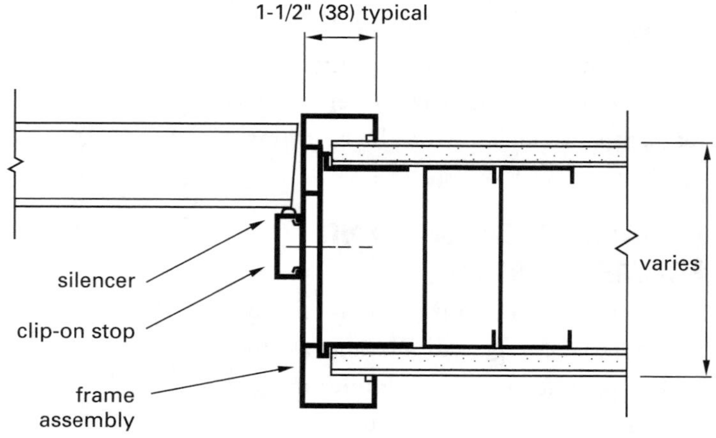


## GLASS DOORS [084226]

Glass doors refer to those constructed primarily of glass with fittings to hold the pivots and other hardware. Sometimes they are called *all-glass doors*. Their strength depends on the glass rather than the framing. Doors with large lights of glass framed with wood, steel, aluminum, or other metals are discussed in other sections.

### Components

Glass doors are generally constructed of ½ in (13 mm) or ¾ in (19 mm) tempered glass with fittings and operating hardware as required by the installation. Common door sizes are 36 in (914 mm) wide and 7 ft (2134 mm) high, although many designers prefer to specify glass doors at the same height as the ceiling.

Some typical glass door configurations are shown in Figs. 3.18(a)–3.18(d). The minimum configuration requires some type of door pull and a corner fitting at the top and bottom (sometimes called the *shoe*) to hold the pivots. In lieu of corner fittings, some manufacturers provide hinge fittings that clamp on the glass and support the door in much the same way as a standard hinged door. If a lock is required, the bottom fitting may be continuous across the door to allow for a dead bolt to be installed. Some designers prefer continuous fittings on both the top and bottom.

Because a full glass door is a potential hazard and extra strength is required, the glass must be tempered. Any holes, notches, or other modifications to the glass must be made before it is tempered. As a result, the design and detailing of glass doors must be finalized when the construction drawings are issued. Before glass doors are manufactured, the designer receives shop drawings to confirm that the manufacturer will make the door according to the original design intent.

The glass may be clear, tinted, or patterned, depending on the design requirements. Special designs, lettering, and logos can be etched into the glass as well, if deep etching is done before the glass is tempered.

**Figure 3.18** Standard glass door configurations

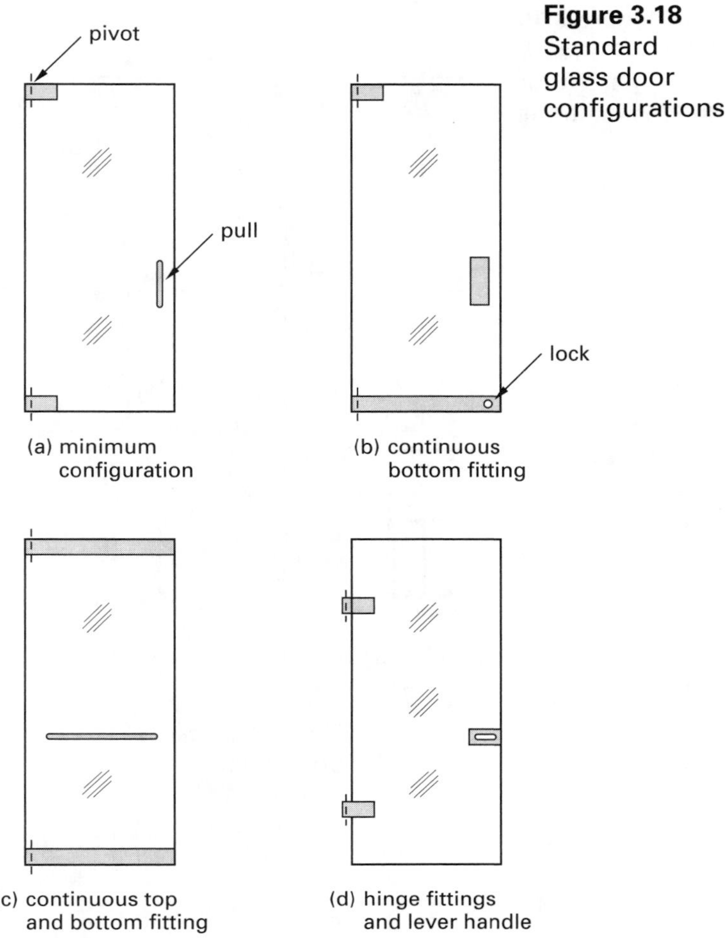


## Standard assemblies

Glass doors can be used alone and set within a wall opening with or without a frame, or they can be installed between glass sidelights. If glass sidelights are used, the same type of fitting used on the door is generally used to support the sidelights. Although jamb frames of aluminum, wood, or ornamental metal can be used, they are not necessary and the glass sidelights can be butted directly to the partition or held away a fraction of an inch. Figures 3.19(a)–3.19(c) shows some standard glass door jamb assemblies and associated jamb details. Figure 3.20 illustrates a typical vertical section through a full-height glass door.

## Custom assemblies

In a sense, all glass doors and their associated framing are custom designs because each installation is manufactured to meet the specific project requirements of size, metal finish, door pull type, and so forth. However, the most common assemblies described in the preceding section may be considered standard because they are used so often and present no significant manufacturing or installation challenges.

Custom assemblies generally involve installations with unusually large doors or sidelights, bent glass, custom-designed fittings,

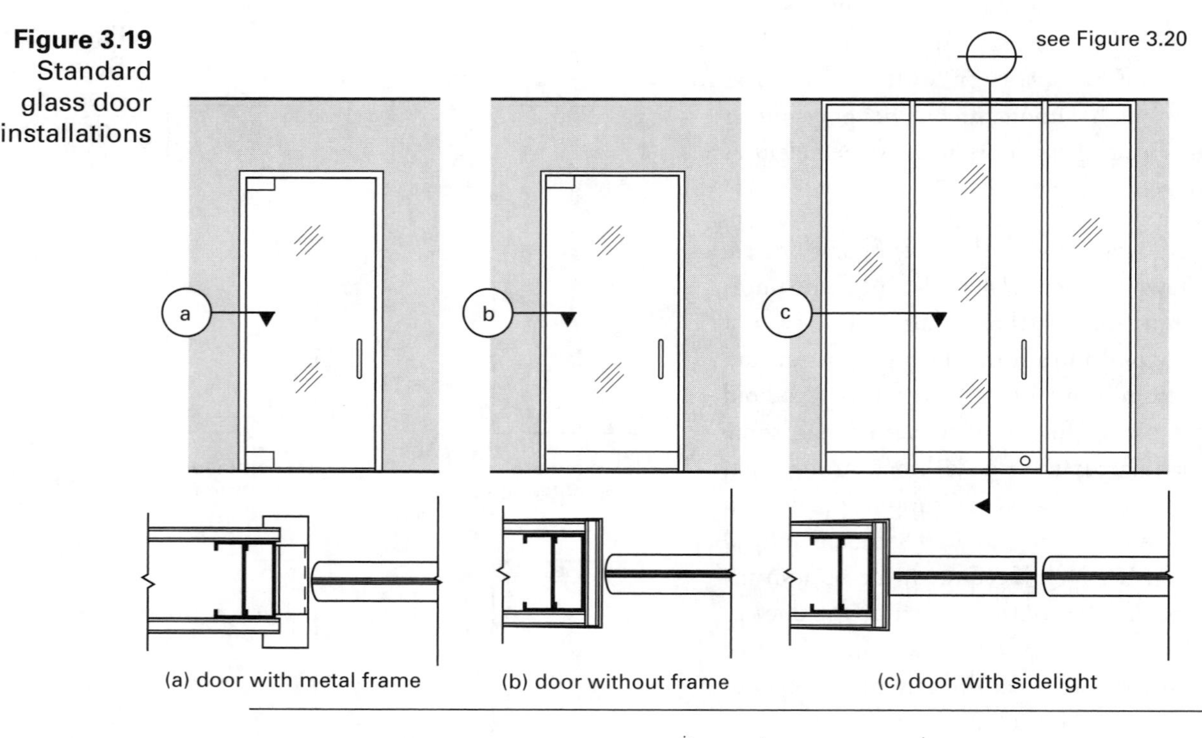

**Figure 3.19**
Standard glass door installations

see Figure 3.20
a
b
c
(a) door with metal frame
(b) door without frame
(c) door with sidelight

**Figure 3.20**
Full-height glass door head and sill

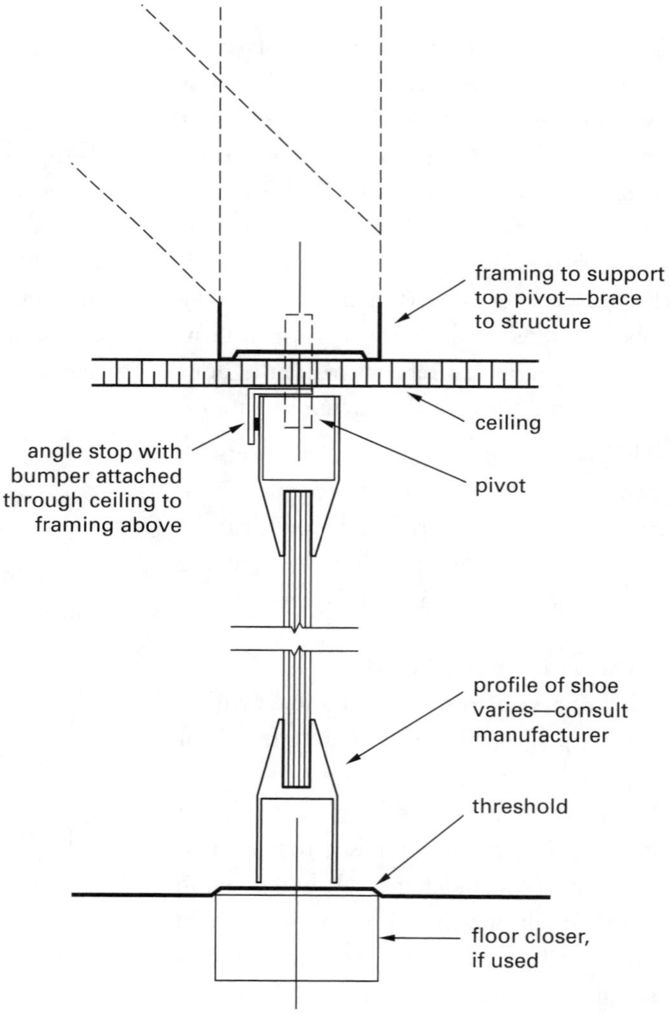

framing to support top pivot—brace to structure
ceiling
angle stop with bumper attached through ceiling to framing above
pivot
profile of shoe varies—consult manufacturer
threshold
floor closer, if used

## Building code requirements for all-glass doors

Because all-glass doors cannot be fire rated, they cannot be used where a protected opening is required in a fire-rated partition. When they are allowed and serve as exit doors, the type of hardware used must conform to the requirements of the building code in force. Some codes and local amendments are more restrictive than others and may prohibit the use of a simple dead bolt in the bottom rail fitting. Instead, special panic-type hardware is available for glass doors that allows the door to be locked from the outside (and operated with card keys or keypads, if necessary) but still allows the door to be unlatched and opened from the inside in a single operation without any special knowledge or effort, if handicapped accessability is not a consideration. See Fig. 3.21.

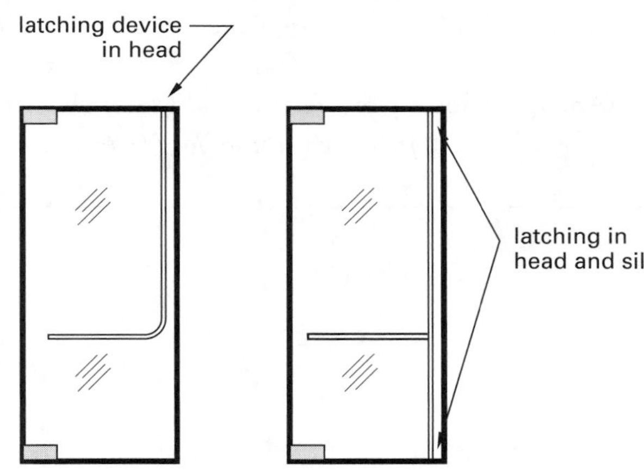


**Figure 3.21** Glass door panic hardware

unusual glass support or suspension systems, or special hardware. Some custom assemblies require the use of a specific manufacturer's proprietary system, while others can be built using standard component parts installed by a glazing contractor.

Glass doors may be part of an all-glass entrance system that does not use visible framing members. Instead, special fittings clamp onto the surrounding glass and contain the top pivot for the door and latching hardware. See Fig. 3.22. The glass panels surrounding the door are usually set in framing that is flush with the floor and ceiling so it is not visible. Refer to Ch. 5 for information on concealed glazing framing.

### Coordination

Glass doors, their hardware, and any glass sidelights are usually supplied by one manufacturer and installed by the glazing contractor as a complete package. Therefore, most of the required coordination of design elements is verified during bidding and production of shop drawings. However, there are several items that the designer should consider during design and construction document production.

- Verify if glass doors are allowed by the local building code and what type of hardware is required.

- If the door extends to the underside of a suspended ceiling, adequate bracing for the top pivot must be provided. If the space above the ceiling is a return air plenum, wood blocking is not allowed; all bracing must be noncombustible.

- If a floor closer is used, verify that the floor structure is thick enough and provides enough support for the depth of the closer housing.

- Thresholds are optional for glass doors; however, access to the cover plate over any floor closer mechanism must be maintained.

- Overhead closers may be located in the top rail fitting or in a transom bar if sufficient anchorage is provided. Verify availability with the manufacturer.

## METAL DOORS [081100]

Metal doors include those constructed primarily of some metal other than steel or aluminum. This includes bronze, brass, and stainless steel or doors clad with sheets of

**Applicable standards for glass doors**

**Consumer Product Safety Commission (CPSC):**
CPSC 16 CFR 1201 *Safety Standards for Architectural Glazing Materials*

**American National Standards Institute (ANSI):**
ANSI Z97.1 *Safety Glazing Material Used in Buildings, Safety Performance Specifications, and Methods of Test*

**American Society for Testing and Materials (ASTM):**
ASTM C1048 *Specification for Heat Treated Flat Glass*

**Figure 3.22** All-glass entrance system

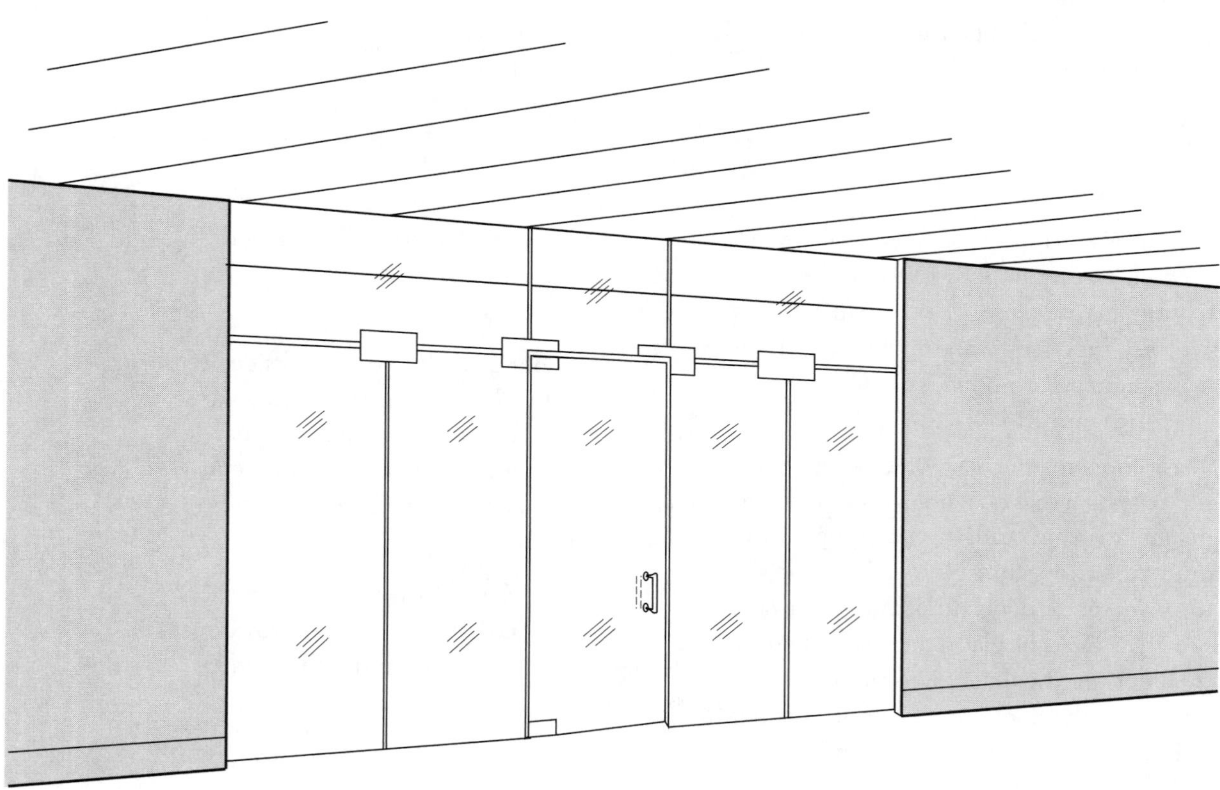

decorative metal. In some cases, wood, aluminum, or steel doors are used for structural support and are simply clad with thin sheets of the finish metal. If door framing is required, it is clad with the same material.

Metal doors may be custom fabricated to the designer's plans, or one of several manufacturer's proprietary decorative metal doors may be selected from a catalogue. If decorative metal is being added to a standard door, the hinges or pivots must be capable of supporting the extra weight, and the framing must allow for the increased thickness of the door. If hinges are used, wider hinges than normal may be required to accommodate the extra thickness.

## Stainless steel doors

Stainless steel doors are the third most common type of metal door, after hollow metal and aluminum. The advantages of stainless steel doors include corrosion resistance (to humidity, coastal salt spray, and industrial environments), low maintenance, durability, cleanability, and appearance. For interior applications, stainless steel doors are commonly specified for food preparation areas, clean rooms, industrial plants, swimming pools, and public areas where intentional or accidental damage is expected. For example, a stainless steel door with a swirl or distressed finish hides scratches and is easy to maintain.

Stainless steel doors are constructed similarly to hollow metal doors, with face sheets bonded to honeycomb or vertical stiffener cores. Polystyrene insulating cores can also be used. The most common steel alloy used is 304, but for more corrosion resistance, alloy 316 should be specified. Whatever type of alloy and construction is used, all components of the door and hardware should be of stainless steel to avoid galvanic corrosion.

While any standard stainless steel finish can be specified for doors, a no. 4 finish is quite common. This consists of fine parallel lines giving a dull finish that hides minor scratches. Refer to Table 7.3 for a listing of common stainless steel finishes. However, many other finishes are possible. These include swirl, distressed, and abrasive blast finishes as well as selective etching and embossing. Coloring is also possible, but it is easily scratched so it should be limited to the recessed portions of embossed finishes.

## SPECIAL DOORS

### Folding and accordion doors [083500]

Two types of special doors commonly used to close large openings or divide rooms are folding doors and accordion doors. When they are used as room dividers, they are called *folding* or *accordion partitions.*

Folding doors are made of multiple units of relatively narrow vertical slats hinged together so that the door can be folded against the jamb. They are made from a wood core and are covered with wood veneer, vinyl, or plastic laminate. Accordion doors have a folding steel framework and are covered with a continuous sheet of vinyl. See Figs. 3.23(a)–3.23(c).

Both folding and accordion doors are suspended from a track mounted on or concealed within the ceiling, as shown in Fig. 3.23(d). They can be used singly or in pairs for very large openings. The leading edge of the door has a continuous latching strip that mates with a closure strip mounted on the jamb. If the folding door is concealed within a pocket, it usually has a sliding jamb, as shown in Fig. 3.23(c), that pulls out flush with the finished wall when the door is completely closed.

Folding and accordion doors are relatively inexpensive and are a good choice for dividing small openings. However, their maximum size is limited to about 40 ft (12 m) wide and 20 ft (6 m) high. Some manufacturers make accordion partitions that can close off a 60 ft (18 m) wide opening. They can be used in straight runs or on a curved path. Electrically driven doors are available. The range of available colors and materials is also limited to what each manufacturer provides, unless the supplier offers custom color choices.

Although some types of these doors are manufactured to reduce sound transmission, their sound attenuation capabilities are limited to provide a sound transmission coefficient (STC) of about 40. Therefore, they should not be used where acoustical control is critical. (See Ch. 11 for a discussion of STC values.) In these situations operable partitions should be used instead.

Folding doors and accordion doors cannot be used as exit doors, and they are not typically fire rated as an opening assembly. One manufacturer, however, does make electrically driven, automatic-closing partitions that have been tested and approved for ⅓-, ¾-, 1-, and 1½-hour fire ratings. Most manufacturers do offer finishes with a Class I fire rating.

**Figure 3.23**
Folding doors

(a) V-type (commonly wood)

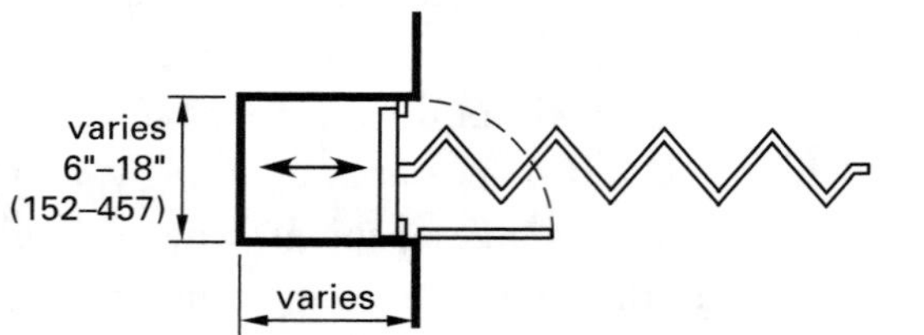


(b) folding door with sliding jamb

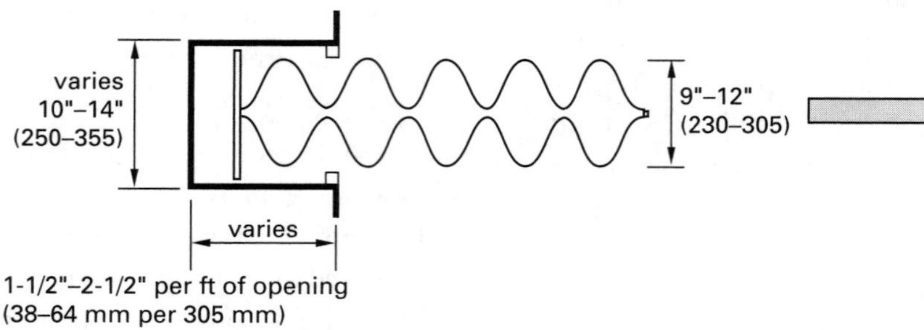


(c) accordion type (vinyl covered) with sliding jamb

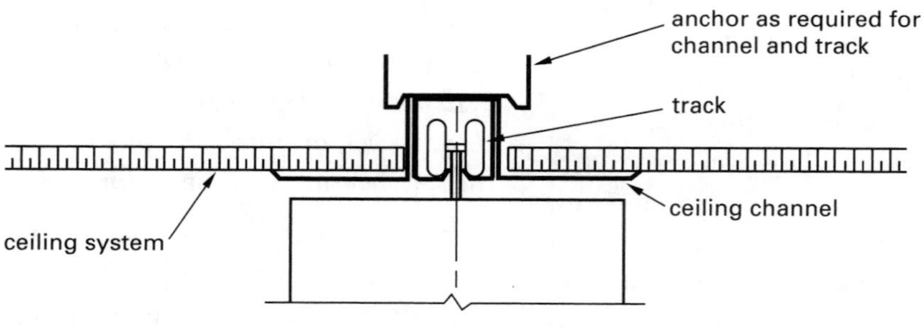


(d) typical ceiling detail

## Operable partitions [102226]

When very large rooms must be subdivided and sound control is critical, such as in meeting rooms or hotel ballrooms, an operable partition should be used. These are systems of individual panels suspended by a track in the ceiling, similar to folding doors. Unlike folding doors, however, operable partitions use fairly wide panels, typically from 3 ft to 5 ft (0.914 mm to 1.52 mm), that move independently (some systems use individual pairs of panels that are hinged). The panels can be manually operated or electrically driven. When fully closed, the edges of each panel are tightly sealed against the adjacent panels. Special sealing methods at the floor and top track provide a tight sound seal at these locations as well. Operable partitions can close off openings up to 48 ft (15 m) high with unlimited widths.

The panels are much thicker (typically from 3 in to 6 in [76 mm to 152 mm]) and heavier than folding doors, and with STC ratings up to 58, they provide a more massive barrier to

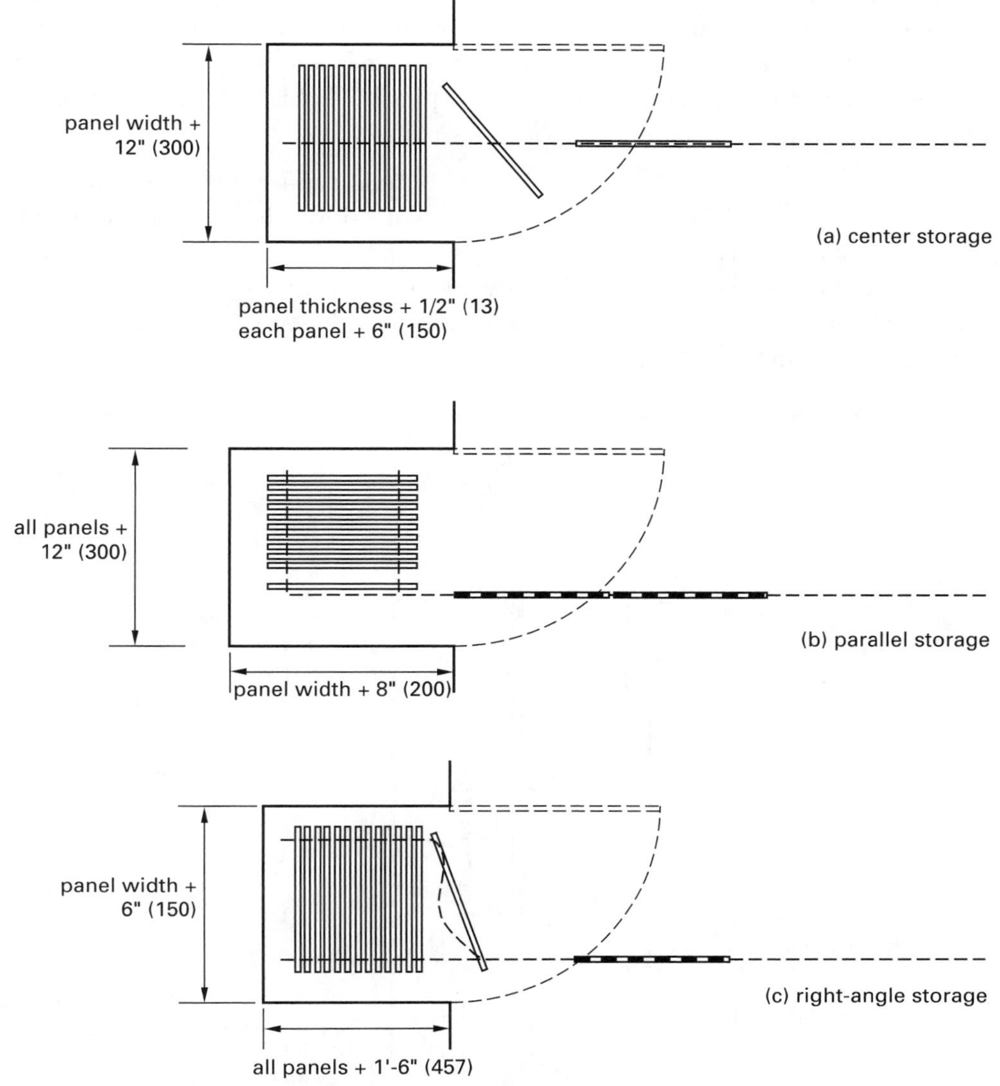


**Figure 3.24** Common operable partition stacking configurations

sound transmission. Generally, the panels can be finished to match the other walls in the room. When necessary, passage doors can be placed within one panel to allow access through the wall without opening the entire assembly.

Operable partitions are usually concealed within a separate pocket space. The exact method of stacking and track arrangement varies with each manufacturer and the requirements of the individual project. Figures 3.24(a)–3.24(c) show some common stacking configurations.

Because operable partitions are heavy, each manufacturer's track must be supported by structural steel above the ceiling. This must be designed by a structural engineer and coordinated with the partition manufacturer's track system. Figure 3.25 shows a "generic" detail of a suspension track. All details and dimensions must be verified for specific installations.

## Overhead coiling doors [083323]

When large openings need to be closed for fire separation or security reasons and appearance is not a consideration, overhead coiling doors can be used. They are not intended for frequent passage, but to close off an opening for an extended period of time or to automatically close off an opening during a fire. For example, a private stairway opening may require an automatically closing fire-rated door to isolate one floor from another. Because an overhead coiling door is not intended for passage, it cannot be used in an exit corridor unless an approved exit door is located adjacent to it.

Overhead coiling doors require a large space above the ceiling for the housing and motor, as well as steel tracks on each side of the opening. With careful detailing, however, only a narrow slot is required at the ceiling, and the jamb tracks can be recessed within the walls. Figures 3.26(a) and 3.26(b) show a typical head and jamb detail for an overhead coiling door.

Overhead doors can be manually operated or motor driven. For interior design applications a motor-driven door should be used with a fail-safe feature so it will close during a fire even if power is interrupted.

**Figure 3.25** Operable partition suspension track

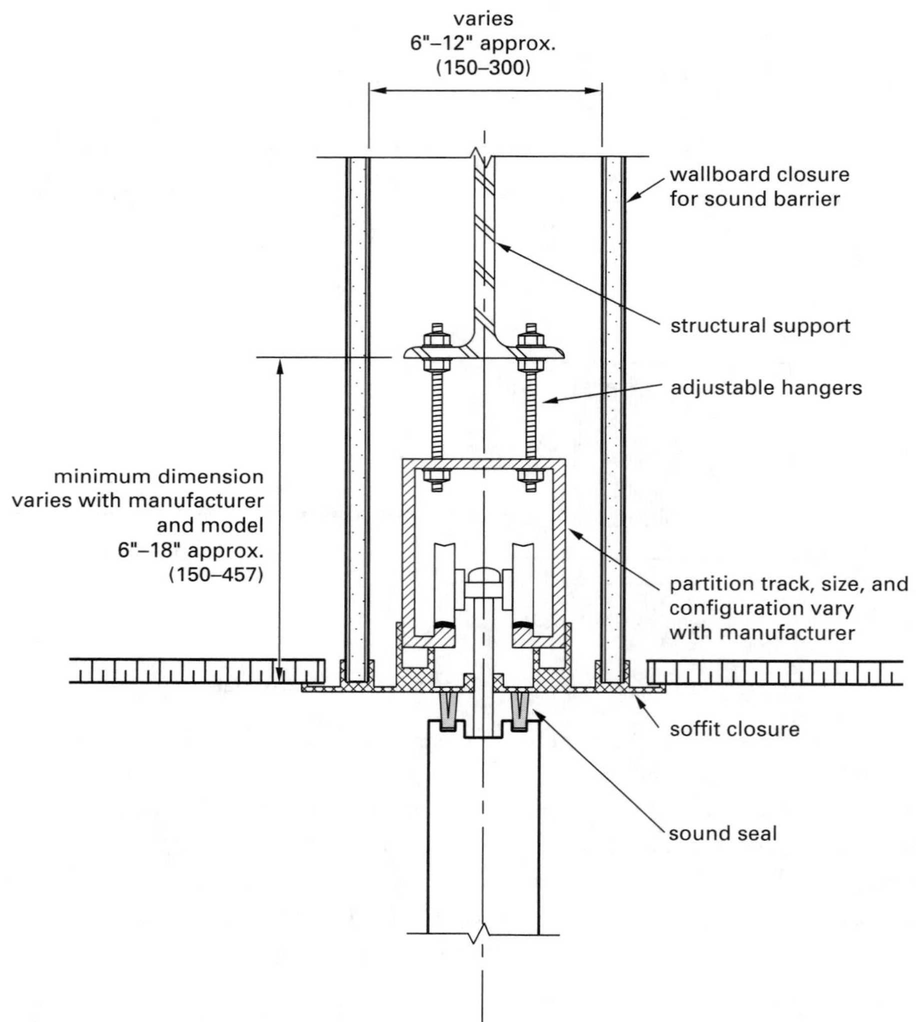

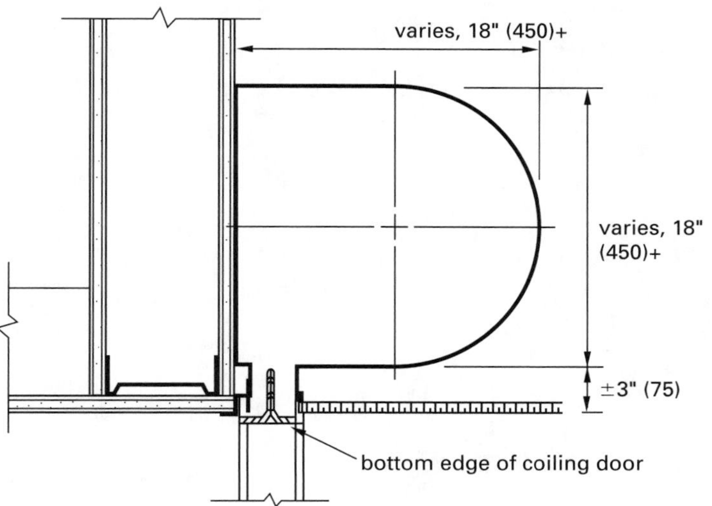

(a) detail at ceiling

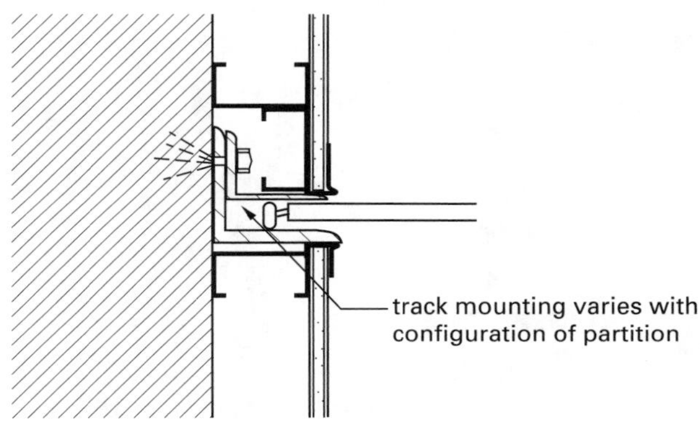


(b) detail of jamb

**Figure 3.26** Overhead coiling door details

# 4

# HARDWARE

There are two major categories of hardware: finish hardware and cabinet hardware. The former includes all hardware required to support and operate full-size doors, while the latter is used for smaller cabinet doors and other architectural woodwork. This chapter discusses finish hardware only.

Hardware is critical to door functioning, accessibility, and life-safety requirements, and is also a major design feature. Its style, detailing, and finish should complement other design features.

In most situations, the interior designer can be assisted with hardware selection and detailed specification writing by hardware suppliers or hardware consultants. However, every designer should know enough about hardware availability, function, and application to make intelligent preliminary decisions that are consistent with the functional and aesthetic needs of a project.

Selection of hardware involves the following criteria.

- *Opening constraints.* These include the door type, the frame type, the size of the opening, and the frequency of use.

- *Code requirements.* Hardware being used on a fire-rated door must be listed or certified for use on such doors.

- *Accessibility.* The hardware must be usable by the physically disabled, as prescribed by the local building code and the Americans with Disabilities Act. Refer to Ch. 18 for detailed information on accessibility requirements.

- *Security.* The degree of security required affects not only the type of lock used but also the method of hanging the door and installing other components.

- *Appearance.* The style and finish of hardware should be consistent with the design concept of the space in which the doors are used.

- *Special considerations.* Requirements such as light proofing, radiation protection, acoustic control, concealed door design, or other unusual design criteria dictate special hardware.

## DOOR MOUNTING

### Hinges [087100]

The typical way to mount a door is to use hinges. The most common type of hinge consists of two leaves with one or more knuckles on each leaf. The knuckles are attached with a pin that can be either removable (the standard) or nonremovable for security installations. The knuckles and pin form the barrel of the hinge, which is finished with a tip. Most hinges have three knuckles on one leaf and two on the other. There are four standard types of hinges: full-mortise, half-mortise, half-surface, and full-surface.

## Standard hinges

The full-mortise hinge is also called a butt hinge (or butt, for short). It is the most common type and is designed so that both leaves are fully mortised into the frame and the edge of the door. See Fig. 4.1(a). When the door is closed, only the barrel of the hinge is visible. Full-mortise hinges are used

**Figure 4.1** Common hinge types

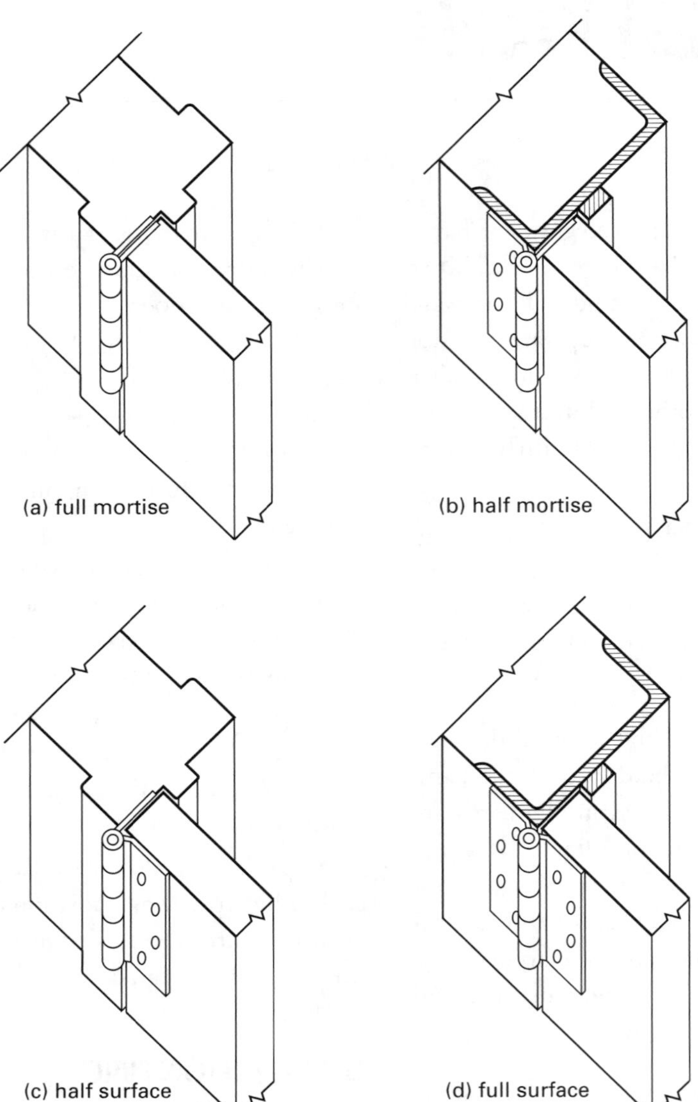

when both the door and the frame can be mortised.

Half-mortise hinges are designed so that one leaf is mortised into the edge of the door, while the other leaf is surface mounted to the frame. See Fig. 4.1(b). These are used when the frame cannot be cut away, such as in a steel channel frame.

In half-surface hinges, one leaf is mortised into the frame. The other is surface applied to the door face and secured with through bolts. See Fig. 4.1(c). These are used on extremely large doors and other types of composite doors that cannot be mortised.

Full-surface hinges are designed to be surface mounted to both the frame and the door when mortising is not possible, such as on a kalamein (metal-clad) door hung on a steel channel frame. See Fig. 4.1(d). Full-surface hinges are seldom used for interior applications.

## Special hinges

There are also special types of hinges. Raised barrel hinges are used when there is no room for the barrel to extend past the door trim. The barrel is offset from its normal position to allow one leaf to be mortised into the frame. This is shown in Fig. 4.2. Swing clear hinges have a special shape that allows the door to swing 90° or 95° so that the full opening of the doorway is available, as shown in Fig. 4.3. Without a swing clear hinge, standard butt hinges decrease the opening width by the thickness of the door when it is open 90°.

Other types of specialty hinges are also available, as illustrated in Figs. 4.4(a)–4.4(d). Electric hinges allow low-voltage power to be run from the frame into the door to control electric locks, hold-open devices, or security alarms. Invisible hinges are completely concealed within the edge of the door and frame and are only partially visible when the door is open. Wide throw hinges are used where the barrel of the hinge and the door in the open position must clear molding or other protrusions. Pivot-reinforced hinges have an integral plate on one of the leaves perpendicular to the leaf that is screwed into the top or bottom of the door. They are used to support doors subject to a high frequency of use and abuse, such as in schools, institutions, and public buildings. Continuous hinges are also available that support the door along its entire length, distributing the weight along a much larger area and eliminating localized stress.

**Figure 4.2**
Raised barrel hinge

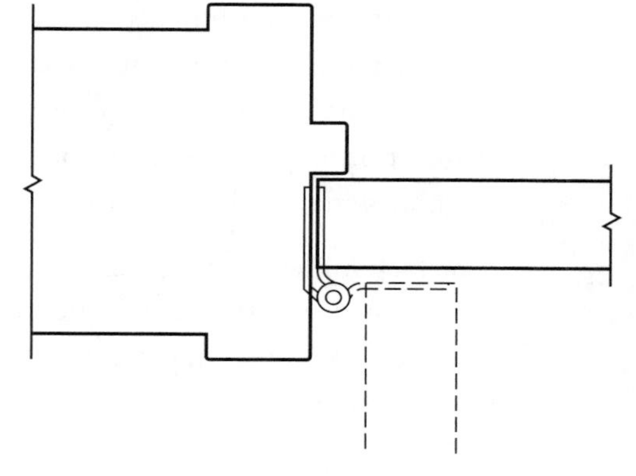

**Figure 4.3**
Swing clear hinge

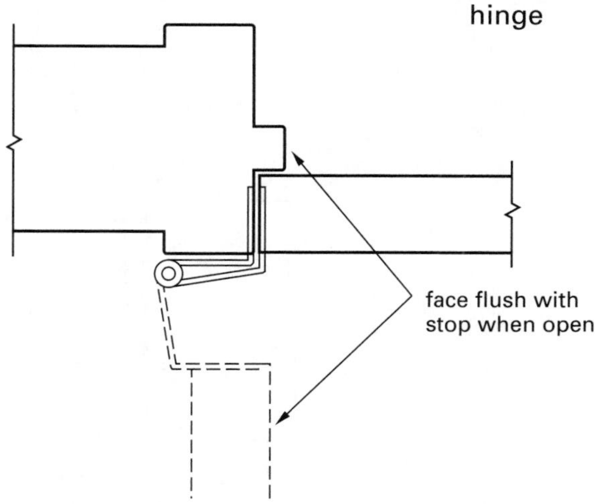

face flush with stop when open

## Selecting hinges

A standard procedure is used to determine the type, size, and number of hinges to be used on a door.

1. Determine the hinge type. This depends on the type of door and frame and includes the full-mortise, half-mortise, half-surface, full-surface, or other specialty hinges as required.

2. Determine the weight and bearing of the hinge. This depends on the door weight and frequency of use. Hinges are available with or without ball bearings in three types: standard weight, plain bearing; standard weight, ball bearing; and heavy weight, ball bearing. Table 4.1 gives some common applications and the recommended hinge type. Ball-bearing hinges are required for fire-rated assemblies and on all doors with closers.

3. Determine the hinge size. Hinge sizes are described by two numbers, such as 4¼ × 4½. The first number represents the height of the hinge in inches, not including tips. The second number represents the width of the hinge in inches when it is open. Standard widths include 3½, 4, and 4½ in (89, 102, and 114 mm). Standard heights include 3, 3½, 4, 4½, 5, 6, and 8 in (76, 89, 102, 114, 127, 152, and 203 mm).

The required width for full-mortise hinges is determined by the width of the door and the clearance required around the jamb trim. One rule of thumb is that the width of the hinge equals twice the door thickness, plus trim projection, minus ½ in (13 mm). If the fraction falls between standard sizes, use the next larger size.

The height of the hinge is determined by the door thickness and the door width, as indicated in Table 4.2.

4. Determine the number of hinges required. The number of hinges is determined by the height of the door. Numbers of hinges are commonly referred to by pairs; one pair meaning two hinges. Doors up to 60 in high (1500 mm) require two hinges (one pair), although some lightweight

**Figure 4.4**
Specialty hinges

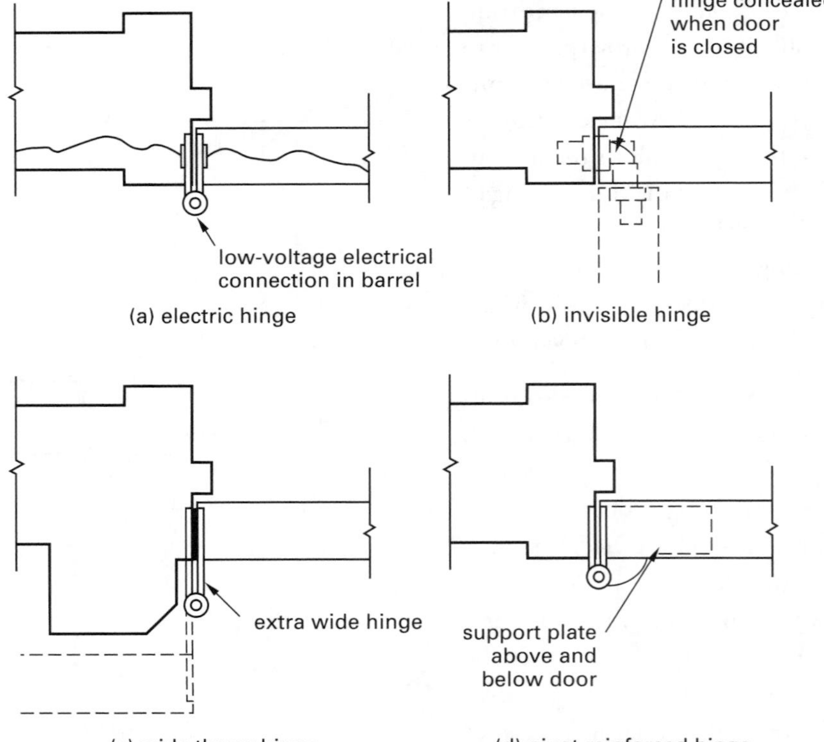

**Table 4.1**
Hinge weight selection

| application | estimated frequency (daily) | frequency classification | hinge type |
|---|---|---|---|
| large department store entrance | 5000 | high | heavy weight, ball bearing |
| large office building entrance | 4000 | | |
| school entrance | 1250 | | |
| school toilet door | 1250 | | |
| theater entrance | 1000 | | |
| store or bank entrance | 500 | | |
| office stairwell | 500 | | |
| office building door | 400 | | |
| school corridor door | 100 | medium | standard weight, ball bearing |
| office building corridor | 75 | | |
| store toilet door | 60 | | |
| residential entrance | 40 | | |
| residential door | 25 | low | standard weight, plain bearing |
| residential corridor door | 10 | | |
| residential closet door | 6 | | |

**Table 4.2**
Hinge sizing for height

| door thickness (in (mm)) | door width (in (mm)) | height of hinge (in (mm)) |
|---|---|---|
| ¾ to 1⅛ (19 to 29) | to 24 (610) | 2½ (64) |
| 1⅜ (35) | to 32 (813) | 3½ (89) |
| 1⅜ (35) | over 32 to 37 (over 813 to 940) | 4 (102) |
| 1¾ (44) | to 36 (to 914) | 4½ (114) |
| 1¾ (44) | over 36 to 48 (over 914 to 1219) | 5 (127) |
| 1¾ (44) | over 48 (over 1219) | 6 (152) |
| 2, 2¼, 2½ (51, 57, 64) | to 42 (to 1067) | 5 (heavy weight) (127) |
| 2, 2¼, 2½ (51, 57, 64) | over 42 (over 1067) | 6 (heavy weight) (152) |

residential doors over 60 in can be mounted with only two hinges. Doors from 60 in to 90 in (1500 mm to 2290 mm) require three hinges (1½ pair), and doors 90 in to 120 in (2290 mm to 3050 mm) require four hinges (two pair).

5. Determine the type of base metal. The base metal comprises the structural part of the hinge and is the metal to which the finish is applied. The type of base metal required is determined by atmospheric conditions, fire-rating requirements, and the final appearance desired. The available base metals include steel, brass, bronze, and stainless steel. For interior applications, any of these base metals may be used. However, fire-rated doors must have hinges with a base metal of steel or stainless steel. Not all finish coatings are available on every base metal. Refer to the section on materials and finishes near the end of this chapter for more information.

6. Determine the finish coating on the hinges. The available hardware finishes are listed at the end of this chapter.

7. Determine the tip design desired or required. Most manufacturers offer a variety of tip designs for the barrels of hinges. See Figs. 4.5(a)–4.5(f). Typical types are the flat button, hospital, and oval head. Flat button tips are the most common and are furnished if not specified otherwise. Flush tips are concealed within the knuckle. Hospital tips have a sloped end to make cleaning easy and to prevent attachment of ropes or cords in psychiatric wards and jails. Other tips available from some manufacturers include ball tips, steeple tips, and flush tips. Other decorator tips are available for some hinge varieties. Consult individual manufacturer's catalogs for availability.

**Figure 4.5**
Hinge tip designs

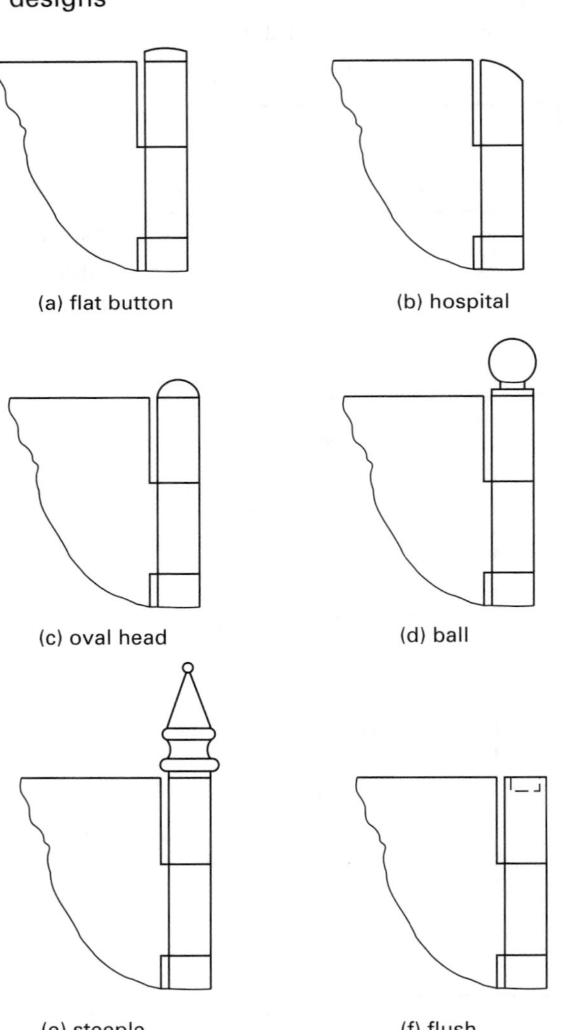


## Pivots

Pivots provide an alternative way to hang doors, where the appearance of hinges is objectionable or where a frameless door design may make it impossible to use hinges. Pivots are used in pairs with the bottom pivot mounted in or on the floor and a corresponding unit mounted in the head frame. They may be center hung or offset. Tall and heavy doors require offset pivots with one or more intermediate pivots. Tall doors require intermediate pivots to prevent warping, and heavy doors require them for additional support. Center-hung pivots allow the door to swing in either direction and are completely concealed. Offset pivots allow the door to swing 180°, if required. Pivots can be used alone, as shown in Figs. 4.6(a)–4.6(d), or they can be part of a closer assembly, as discussed in the section titled Closing Devices.

Because of the way they operate, center-hung pivots cannot be used with a door stop on the same side of the door on both jambs. This makes it difficult to seal the door against sound or light transmission on the hinge and strike sides, although a flexible strip of wool pile or synthetic stripping can be rabbeted into the edges of the door. The rotation point of a center-hung pivot is typically located 2¾ in (70 mm) from the edge of the frame, but it can be located anywhere along the door. For example, a series of doors with the pivot located in the center of the door width can be used to make a "louvered" opening between two rooms. See Fig. 4.7.

**Figure 4.6**
Door pivots

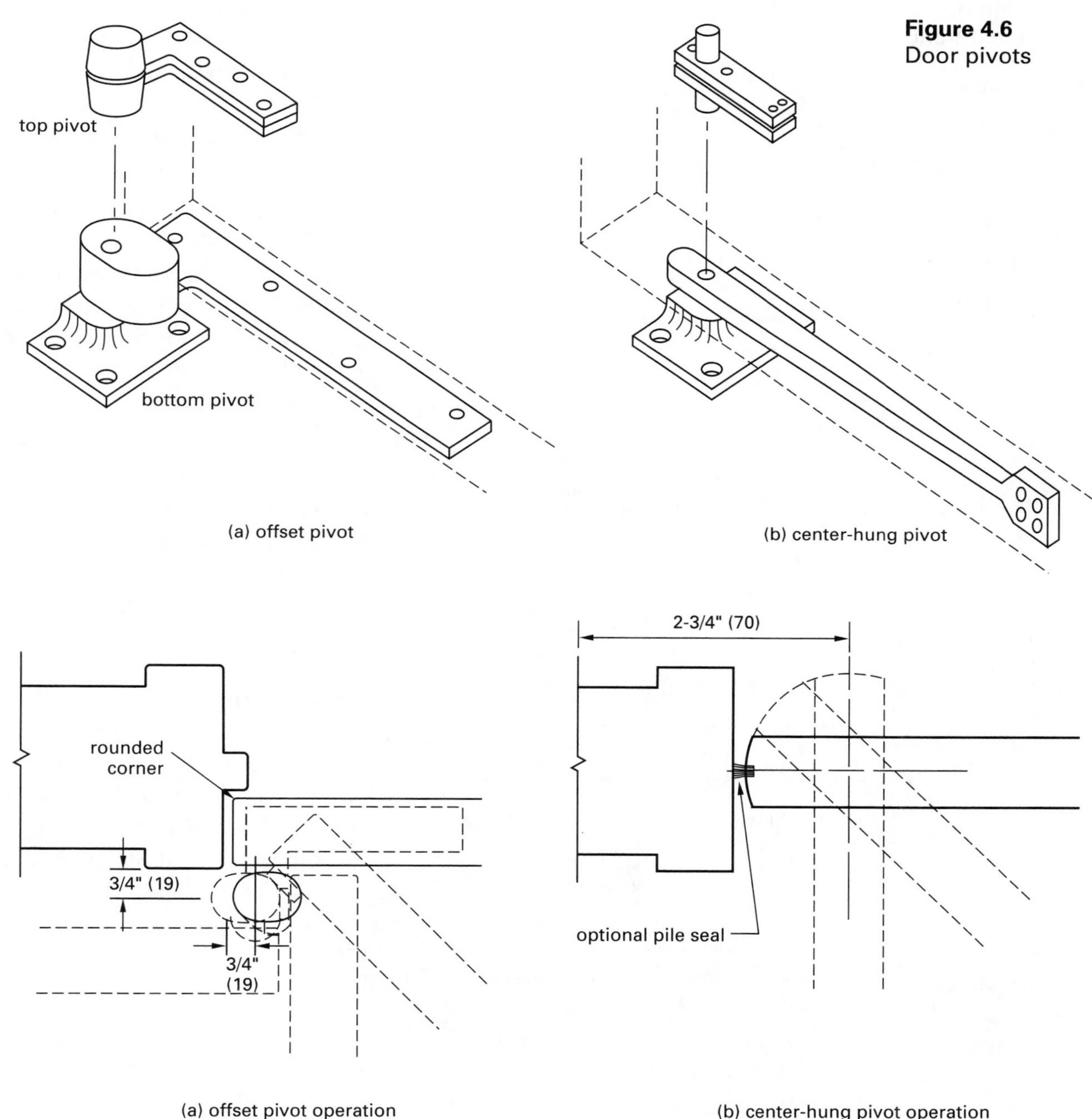

As shown in Fig. 4.6, offset pivots can be used in standard framed openings with door stops, but the corner of the door opposite the pivot must be slightly rounded so this corner does not scrape against the stop as the door opens.

## Concealed door detailing

Pivots are often used to detail concealed doors, those designed to appear to be part of the partition in which they are placed. Center-hung pivots, or closers, are especially useful because they are completely concealed by the top and bottom edges of the door and require no door frame. Figure 4.8 illustrates one method of detailing a door that is flush with the partition and that uses a minimum of visible hardware.

**Figure 4.7**
Center-hung pivots used in multiple door opening

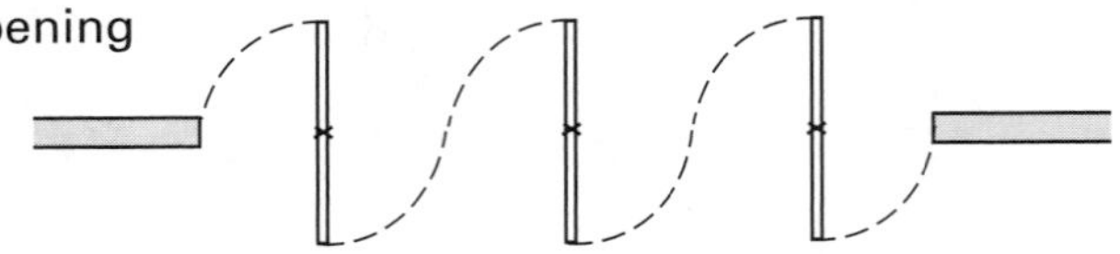

**Figure 4.8**
Concealed door details

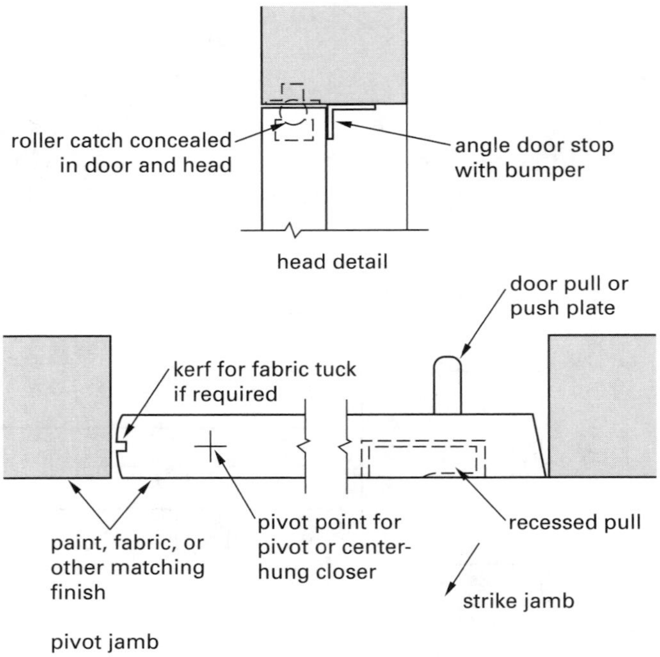

roller catch concealed in door and head

angle door stop with bumper

head detail

door pull or push plate

kerf for fabric tuck if required

paint, fabric, or other matching finish

pivot point for pivot or center-hung closer

recessed pull

strike jamb

pivot jamb

## Other mounting hardware

Pocket doors and sliding doors are suspended with rollers from tracks in the head frame. Hardware is also available to allow doors to be supported by rollers that run on floor tracks. These are used for very heavy doors or where movement of the bottom edge of the door must be restricted.

Special proprietary pocket pivot and continuous hinges are available that can be used on fire-rated doors while concealing much of the hardware. These are used where appearance is important but where building codes require labeled hardware.

# OPERATING DEVICES [087100]

Operating devices are used to open and close doors. These devices can range from simple push plates to power-assisted mechanisms. In some cases, such as with locksets, the method of securing the door is integrated with the method of operating the door.

## Latchsets and Locksets

A latchset is a device that operates a door and holds it in the closed position by means of a retractable latch. A doorknob or lever handle can be used both to provide a gripping surface and to operate the latching device. In most cases, a lever handle is needed to meet accessibility requirements. A lockset

**Applicable standards for hinges and pivots**

American National Standards Institute (ANSI):

| | |
|---|---|
| ANSI/BHMA A156.1 | *Butts and Hinges* |
| ANSI/BHMA A156.7 | *Hinge Templates* |
| ANSI/BHMA A156.17 | *Self Closing Hinges and Pivots* |
| ANSI/BHMA A156.20 | *Strap and Tee Hinges and Hasps* |
| ANSI/BHMA A156.26 | *Continuous Hinges* |

does the same job, but also has a method for locking the door.

There are four types of latches and locks: mortise, preassembled, bored, and interconnected. These are shown in Figs. 4.9(a)–4.9(d). Another type, the integral, is no longer produced in the United States but is still found in older buildings. Each of the four types is designated by a corresponding series number, as standardized by the American National Standards Institute (ANSI). Mortise locks are designated as Series 1000, preassembled locks as Series 2000, bored locks as Series 4000, and interconnected locks as Series 5000. Series 3000 was used for integral locks.

## Mortise locks

A mortise lock or latch is installed in a rectangular area cut out of the door. It is generally more secure than a bored lock and offers a much wider variety of locking options. Mortise locks allow the use of a deadbolt and a latchbolt, both of which can

**Figure 4.9**
Types of latches and locks

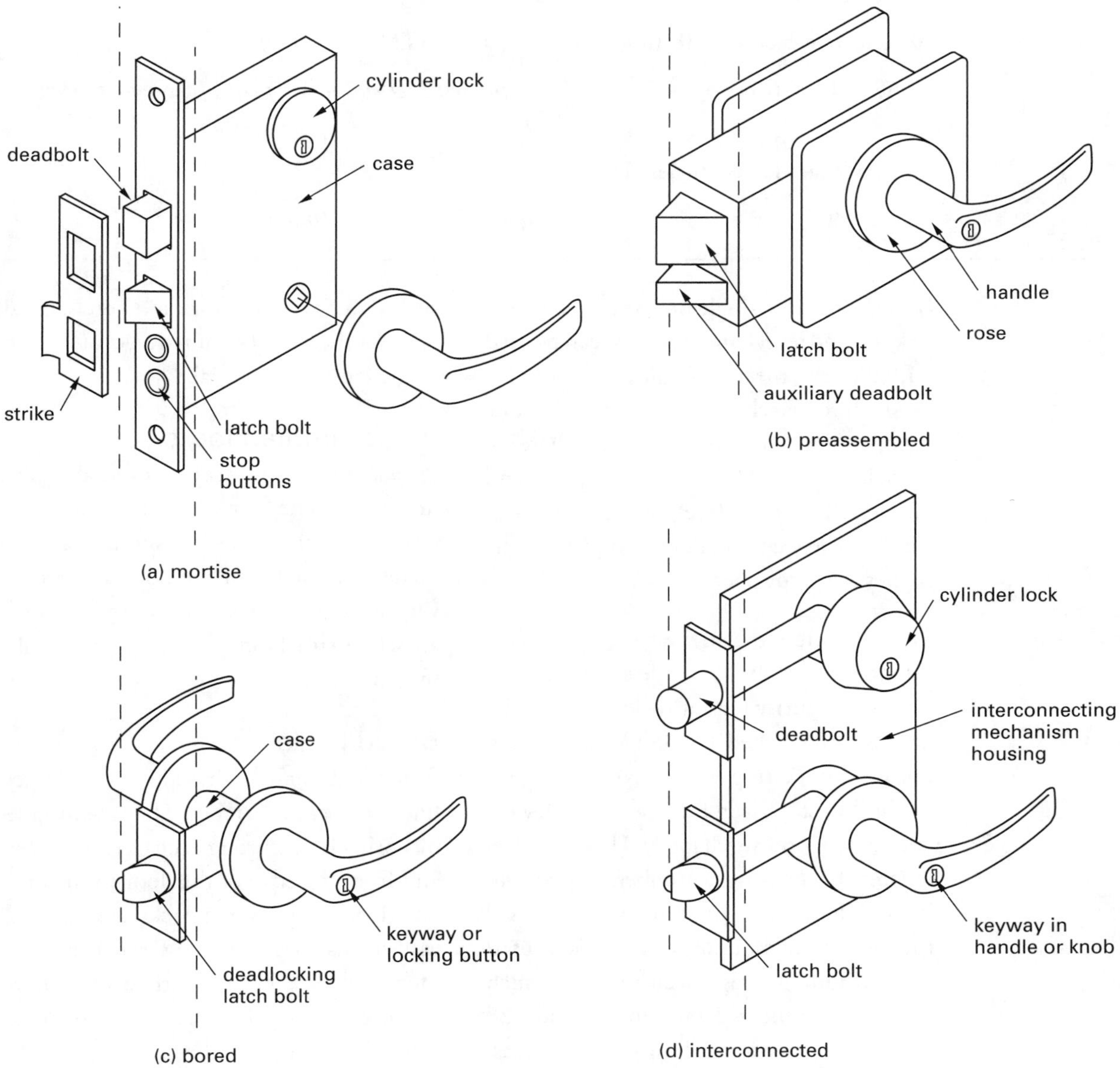

## Applicable standards for operating devices and locking

**American National Standards Institute (ANSI):**

| | |
|---|---|
| ANSI/BHMA A156.2 | *Bored and Preassembled Locks and Latches* |
| ANSI/BHMA A156.3 | *Exit Devices* |
| ANSI/BHMA A156.5 | *Auxiliary Locks and Associated Products* |
| ANSI/BHMA A156.10 | *Power Operated Pedestrian Doors* |
| ANSI/BHMA A156.12 | *Interconnected Locks and Latches* |
| ANSI/BHMA A156.13 | *Mortise Locks and Latches* |
| ANSI/BHMA A156.19 | *Power Assist and Low-Energy Power-Operated Doors* |
| ANSI/BHMA A156.23 | *Electromagnetic Locks* |
| ANSI/BHMA A156.24 | *Delayed Egress Locking Systems* |
| ANSI/BHMA A156.25 | *Electrified Locks* |

**American Society for Testing and Materials (ASTM):**

| | |
|---|---|
| ASTM F476 | *Standard Test Methods for Security of Swinging Door Assemblies* |

**Underwriters Laboratories (UL):**

| | |
|---|---|
| UL #305 | *Standard for Safety for Panic Hardware* |

be retracted in a single operation. A variety of knob and level handle designs can be used with the basic mechanism. Mortise locks are available in two classifications of grades, one for operation and one for security. There are three levels for each, Grade 1, Grade 2, and Grade 3. The grade level for each classification is expressed separately. Grade 1 is the highest level for operation.

Grade 1 offers the highest security, while Grade 3 offers the lowest level of security. Levels of security for entire door assemblies are also established by ASTM (American Society for Testing Materials) F-476. (See applicable standards for operating devices and locking in this chapter).These are designated by two-digit numbers. Grade 40 is the highest level of security and is used for commercial buildings. Grade 30 is used for medium- to high-security areas, such as small commercial buildings. Grade 20 is used for low- to medium-security areas, such as apartment houses and hotels. Grade 10 is for the lowest required level of security, single family residential.

### Preassembled locks

Preassembled locks and latches are also called unit locks. They arrive from the factory as a complete unit. They are slid into a notch made in the edge of the door and require very little adjustment. Preassembled locks are seldom used today and are only available in Grade 1.

### Bored locks

Bored locks and latches are also called cylindrical locks or latches. They are installed by boring holes through the face of the door and from the edge of the door to the other bored opening. Bored locks are relatively easy to install and are less expensive than mortise locks; however, they offer fewer operating functions than mortise locks. Bored locks are generally used in residential and small commercial projects. Like mortise locks, they are available in three grades.

### Interconnected locks

Interconnected locks have a cylindrical lock and deadbolt. The two locks are interconnected so that only a single action of turning a knob or lever on the inside releases both bolts.

With all types of latches and locks, either a doorknob or lever handle may be used to operate the latching device. In most cases, a lever handle must be used to meet accessibility requirements.

## Standard function designations

When used in the context of hardware, the word *function* refers to the mechanical operation of a lock or latch, the method of locking and unlocking, and the position, rigidity, and operability of the various parts of the hardware. Function designations have been standardized by the American National Standards Institute (ANSI) as sponsored by the Builders Hardware Manufacturers Association (BHMA). These function designations can be used to specify the desired operation without using specific proprietary manufacturer's names or numbers. However, many manufacturers make special latchsets and locksets that do not have corresponding ANSI function numbers.

Each function is specified with a number, a description of its common application, and a detailed explanation of the function. The detailed explanation describes three elements: (1) the operation of the lock or latch from either side of the door in the unlocked mode, (2) the method of locking from the outside and inside, and (3) the method by which unlocking is accomplished from the outside and inside. Although the description indicates the function's common usage, it does not restrict the function's use. For example, a store door lock can be used in applications other than retail stores. Overall, there are 54 different functions described by the ANSI standards.

Latchset and lockset functions are summarized in App. A-1. Full descriptions are given in App. A-2.

### Exit devices

Exit devices, commonly called *panic hardware*, are used where required by building code for safe egress by many people. Push bars extending across the width of the door on the push side operate side latches or vertical rods that disengage latches at the top and bottom. The vertical rods can be surface mounted or concealed in the door. Exit devices are intended to operate the door by pushing on a horizontal bar or push pad without any special knowledge or complex actions in the event of panic. Electrified panic hardware can be used where access from the outside is controlled with keypads or card readers, but where completely fail-safe, manually operated exiting is required from the inside.

### Pulls and push plates

Push plates and pull bars are used to operate doors that do not require automatic latching. Push plates and pull bars are available in a variety of designs and are commonly used on doors to toilet rooms and commercial kitchens. For doors that swing only in one direction, a combination push plate and pull bar can be used.

### Power-assisted openers

Power-assisted doors are activated by a push button, pressure pad on the floor, infrared beam, or other electronic means. They are most often used for interior construction where handicapped accessibility is required. Several types of openers are available, including those mounted at the head of the door and those concealed in the floor. The head-mounted door openers are usually surface-applied to the head of the door frame and operate the door with an arm assembly similar to a standard door closer. These are commonly used in retrofit applications where installation is fairly easy.

In-floor power-assisted openers are completely concealed but generally have to be installed at the same time the door and frame are installed. They are available in either center-hung or offset-hung styles and can operate doors mounted on pivots or butt hinges. These openers require a large pit in a concrete floor for mounting. Required pit depth ranges from about 6 in to 7 in (152 mm to 175 mm). For other types of floor construction or where the required depth is not available, the power mechanism can be mounted from the ceiling of the floor below with a drive shaft extending through the floor to the door.

## CLOSING DEVICES

Closers are devices that automatically return a door to its closed position after it is opened. They also control the distance a door can be opened, thereby protecting the door and the surrounding construction from damage.

Closers can be surface mounted on either side of the door or on the head frame. They also can be concealed in the frame or in the door. In addition, closers can be integrated with pivots mounted in the floor or ceiling.

### Surface-mounted closers [087100]

There are four basic types of surface-mounted door closers. They are categorized as to how they are mounted to the door and jamb and where the hardware is located, that is on the push or pull side of the door. Figure 4.10 illustrates regular arm, slide track, top jamb, and parallel arm door closers.

The regular arm application is used where a door swings into a room and the closer is mounted on the pull side of the door (the

**Figure 4.10** Surface-mounted door closers

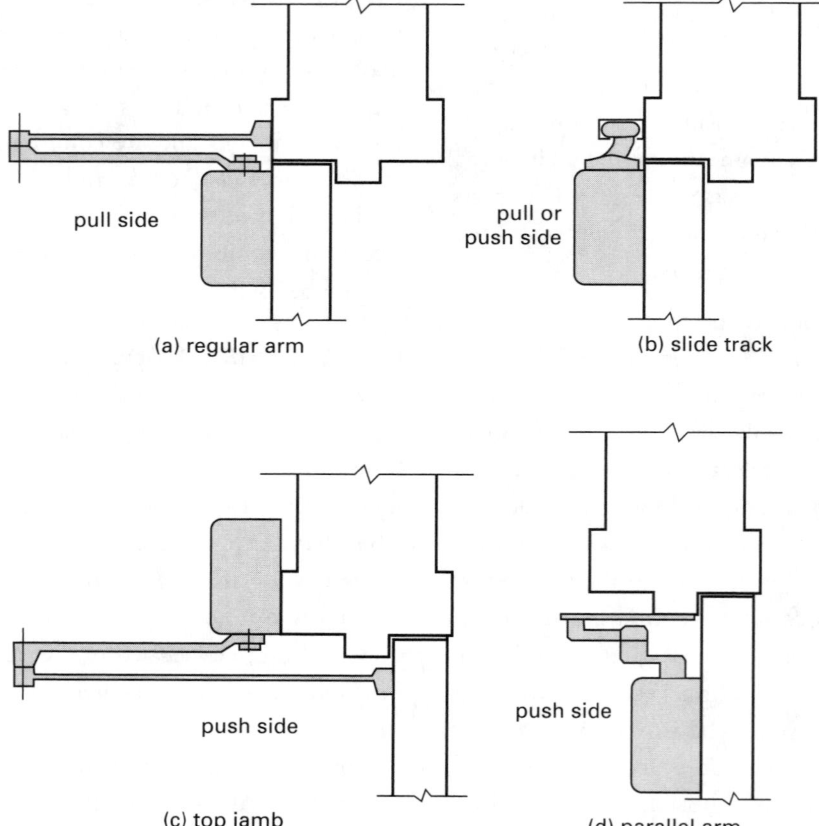

room side). When a door opens out and the closer should be mounted on the push side (inside the room), either a top jamb or parallel arm application can be used. A parallel arm application helps prevent vandalism because the arms are mostly concealed below the head frame. However, the power efficiency of the parallel arm application is less than that of the regular arm application.

Closers are available in three grades, Grades 1 to 3. Grade 1 is the most durable and is used for doors that have a high frequency of use and abuse. Closers are also rated by "size," which refers to the size of the internal spring mechanism that determines the closing force. Sizes range from 2 to 6; the higher the number, the greater the closing force. Closers with greater closing force are required for wide doors or heavy doors. Two types of adjustable closers are available, the 50% adjustable and the fully adjustable. 50% adjustable closers are furnished with springs between sizes 2 and 6, but the closing force can be increased 50% above the spring size. Fully adjustable closers are not sized but can be adjusted through the complete range of sizes. Adjustable closers are available for barrier-free applications so that the maximum opening resistance can be set to 5 lbf (2.2 N) for interior, non-fire-rated doors.

Closers are spray-painted in aluminum, bronze or tan colors. The Builders Hardware Manufacturers Association (BHMA) finish designations include 689, aluminum paint; 690, dark bronze paint; 691, light bronze paint; and 692, tan paint. They may also be specified as 600, prime paint.

## Concealed closers

As illustrated in Fig. 4.11, door closers can be concealed in the head frame or the door itself. However, it is generally best to avoid closers concealed in the door because anchoring is not as strong as it is in the head frame. Doors measuring 1¾ in (44 mm) must be used so that the entire mechanism can be concealed without the use of face plates. The head frame must be large enough to accommodate the closer selected.

A number of options are available for both surface-mounted and concealed closers. Hold-open closers have arms that can be set to hold the door in the open position until it is disengaged. However, these types cannot be used on fire-rated doors. Delayed-action closers momentarily hold the door open before starting the closing cycle, to make it easier for people to pass through the opening.

**Figure 4.11**
Concealed door closers

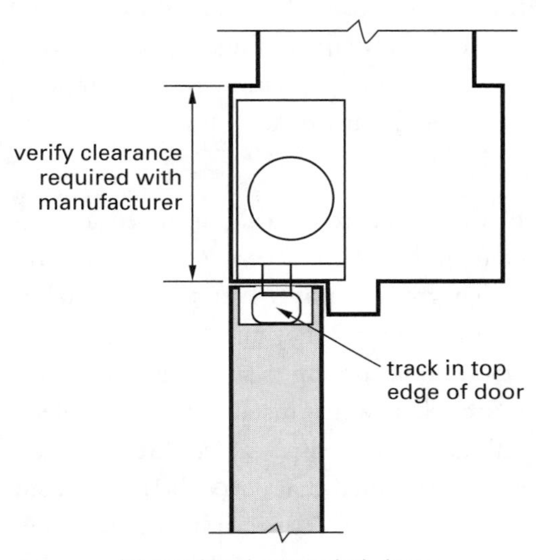


(a) overhead concealed closer

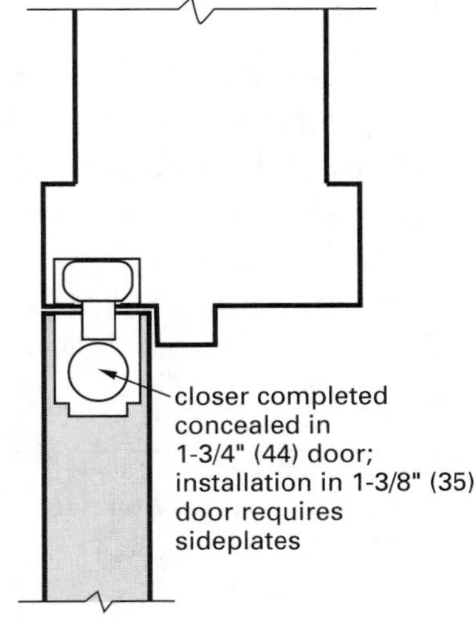


(b) closer concealed in door

### Pivot closers

Pivot closers incorporate both a pivot and a door closer in one mechanism. The door operation works in the same way described earlier in the section on pivots. Pivot closers are available for either center-hung or offset-hung doors. Pivot closers can be mounted either in the floor or above the door for center-hung doors, while floor closers can only be used for offset-hung doors. Because a closer is subjected to a great deal of torque during operation, overhead closers should only be used on lightweight doors up to about 200 lbm (91 kg). If a frameless door installation is used, the overhead closer must also be securely mounted in the door frame or above the ceiling. Floor mounting is the preferred installation method for pivot closers and must be used for heavy or very wide doors.

Floor closers are typically installed in concrete floors with a cement case, around which grout is poured to securely anchor the mechanism. They can be installed below wood floors as long as sufficient anchorage is provided. When installation is complete, only an access plate is visible. Thresholds can also be specified that cover the mechanism and extend across the width of the door. Low-profile closers are available for thin-slab concrete floors or for areas where clearance is limited.

Floor closers are available in different models to support weights of up to 1250 lbm (567 kg) for offset-hung doors and 1000 lbm (454 kg) for center-hung doors. Hold-open and nonhold-open floor closers are available, with openings limited to 85°, 90°, 95°, or 105°. For high traffic areas, heavy-duty models are available.

### Closers with integrated smoke detectors

Surface-mounted closers can be used to hold open a door under normal circumstances, but can also be used to automatically close a door when smoke is detected. These closers can be wired to sound an alarm upon activation and to close other doors without built-in smoke detectors. The limitations of use on these types of closers must be verified with local building and fire codes.

All types of closers must satisfy accessibility requirements. Closers must have their sweep periods adjusted so that, from an open position of 70°, the door will take at least 3 sec to move to a point 3 in (75 mm) from the latch, as measured to the leading edge of the door.

## DOOR SEALS [087100]

Door seals are used along the edges of doors to provide tight seals against smoke, light, and sound. Different types of neoprene, felt, metal, polyurethane, and vinyl are available in many configurations, three of which are shown in Figs. 4.12(a)–4.12(c). Refer to manufacturers' catalogs for specific sizes, materials, and available configurations.

### Smoke seals

Fire-rated seals are required on fire doors to prevent both smoke and drafts from passing through. They are similar to light and sound seals, but have been tested by an approved laboratory and certified for use on fire doors. They are used on the head and jamb sections.

### Light and sound seals

As with smoke seals, door seals for blocking the passage of light or sound are available in

**Applicable standards for closing devices**

**American National Standards Institute (ANSI):**

| | |
|---|---|
| ANSI/BHMA A156.4 | *Door Controls—Closers* |
| ANSI/BHMA A156.15 | *Closer Holder Release Devices* |

many configurations for jambs, head, and threshold. The compressible material used most often is neoprene. Double door seals can be used, when a high level of sound isolation is needed as illustrated in Fig. 4.13. This type of construction is usually limited to sound studios, stages, and other occupancies where sound isolation is critical.

## Intumescent seals

When doors must meet the requirements of positive-pressure fire testing, as discussed in Ch. 3, intumescent material must be used. Intumescent material expands upon exposure to heat and forms a tight, fire-resistant seal against the passage of smoke, gasses, and heat. There are two types used in the construction industry: hard puff and soft puff. Hard-puff intumescents begin to intumesce at approximately 500°F (260°C) and expand with an explosion-like force. These are used around penetrations of pipes and similar construction elements. Soft-puff intumescents are used for door openings and begin to expand at approximately 250°F to 300°F (121°C to 149°C). They expand very slowly, which prevents the door from being forced open.

Two types of soft-puff intumescent gasketing are currently used for door openings: expandable graphite in a polymeric binder, and sodium silicate. The expandable graphite type is produced in thin strips that fit within the allowable edge clearances around a door and are approximately 1/16 in (1.6 mm) thick and 1/2 in (12.7 mm) wide. It is available with a self-adhesive backing that allows for installation at various locations on the door. It can be painted to match the door frame. Sodium silicate requires some type of housing or carrier, which calls for special preparation of the door or frame. Sodium silicate has been known to degrade and fail over time.

If intumescent gasketing is required, it cannot be used alone. Some type of elastomeric gasketing must also be used for protection

**Figure 4.12** Smoke and sound seals

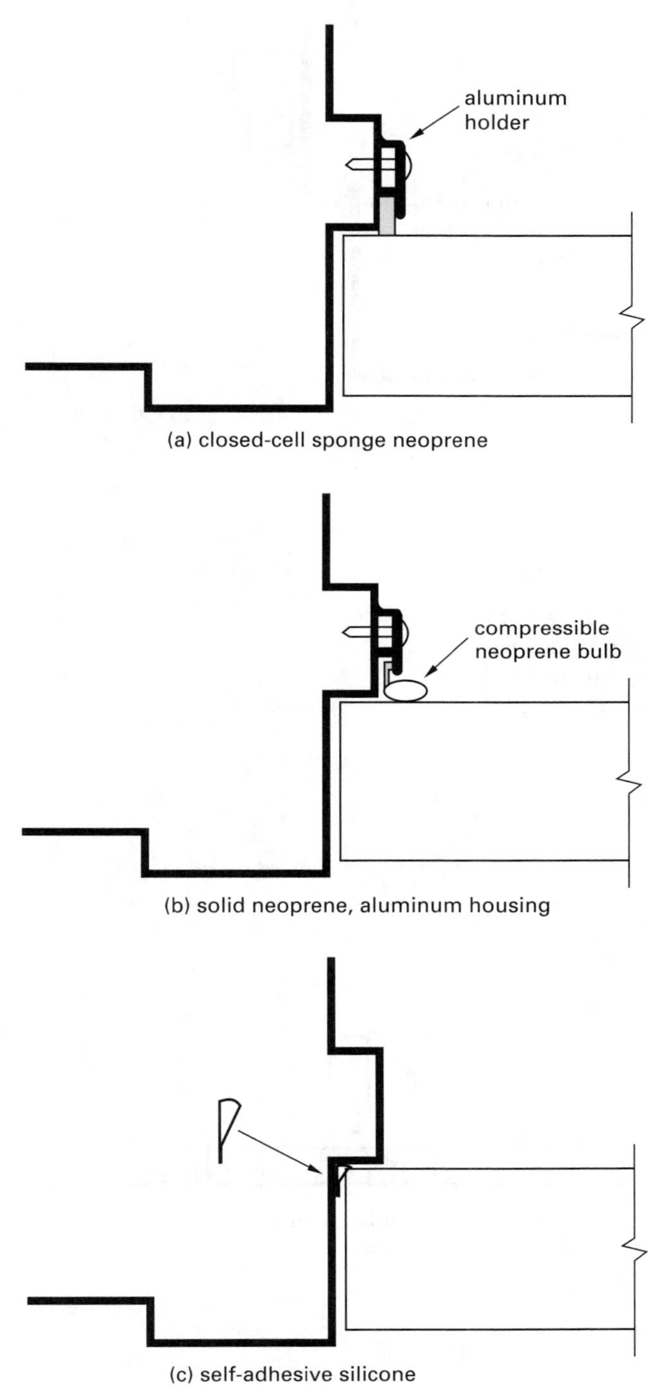

**Figure 4.13**
Double sound seal

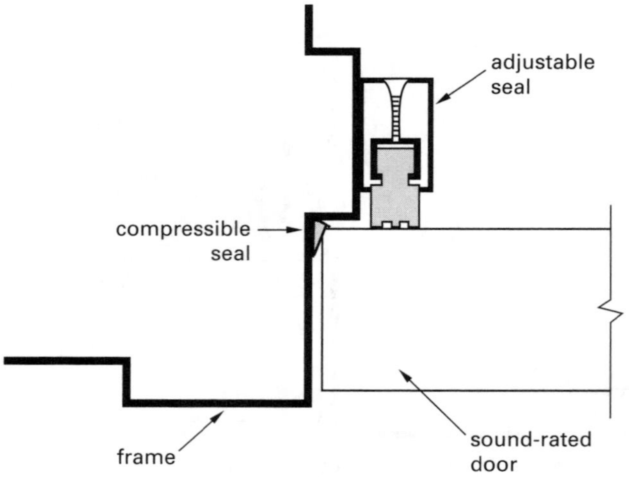

adjustable seal
compressible seal
frame
sound-rated door

**Figure 4.14**
Automatic door bottoms and threshold seal

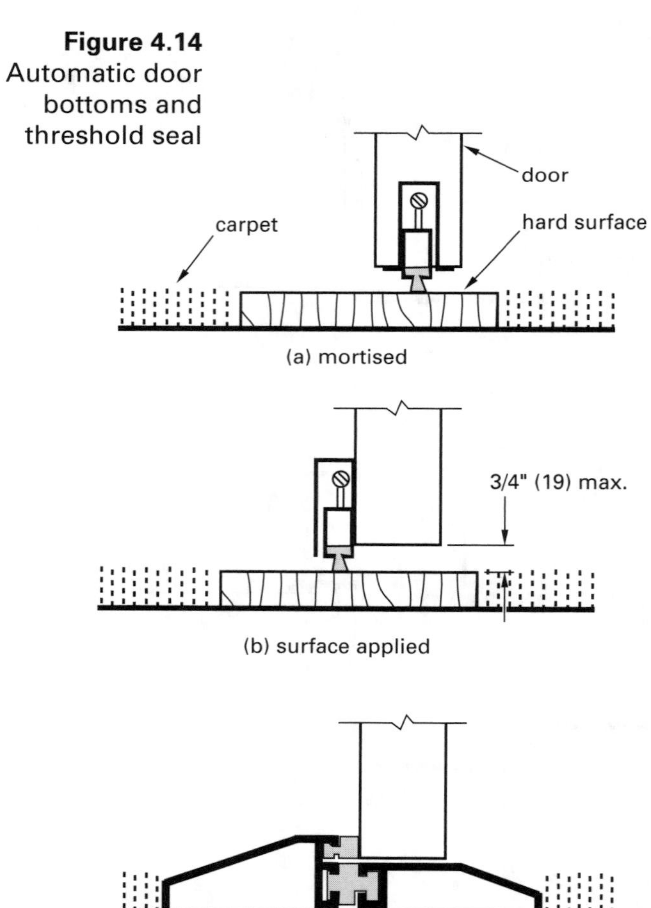


below 300°F (149°C), before the intumescent material activates.

### Automatic door bottoms

Figures 4.12 and 4.13 both show construction methods only at the jambs and head of a door. When the undercut between the bottom of a door and the floor or threshold needs to be sealed (as with all light and sound seals and some fire doors), an automatic door bottom must be used.

Automatic door bottoms are devices that are mortised or surface-applied to the bottom of the door to provide a seal against sound or light. When the door is open, the seal is up; as the door is closed, a plunger strikes the jamb and forces the seal down against the floor. See Figs. 4.14(a)–4.14(c). If carpeting is being used in two rooms separated by a sound door, the opening should be detailed so that there is a solid, smooth surface below the door bottom. This provides for a tight seal against the floor. Alternately, a threshold can be used to provide for a double seal as shown in Fig. 4.14(c); however, this is usually less desirable for most applications because it projects above the plane of the floor.

## DOOR SECURITY [087153]

Several types of manual and electrically operated locking hardware are available. This section discusses manual locks; electrically operated locks are discussed later in this chapter.

### Locksets

Locksets combine an operating device, either a knob or lever handle, with a mechanism for locking a door. The four major types of locksets are discussed in the section on operating devices. The most appropriate lockset type must be selected based on the degree of security required. Bored locksets are sufficient for residential and many types of commercial projects. Mortise locksets and interconnected locks provide greater security and a broader range of functions for many commercial applications.

## Deadbolts

A deadbolt is a lock component with an end that extends from the lock front by action of the lock mechanism. When the door is closed and locked, the bolt cannot be retracted with end pressure.

Deadbolts are used for added security, but their use is limited to single family residences and guest rooms of hotels and motels by most building codes. Even when their use is allowed, most codes require that deadbolts be operable from the inside without a key or tool, which means they must have a thumb turn on the inside. If the extra security of a deadbolt is required, a mortise lock with a deadbolt or an interconnected lock can be used. Both are constructed so that all the latches and bolts are retracted with a single operation of the knob or lever handle. Refer to Table 4.3 for a summary of the standard deadbolt functions.

## Flush bolts

Flush bolts are devices mortised into the edge of the door that allow a bolt to be extended into the head frame or the floor by manually flipping a lever. See Fig. 4.15. Flush bolts are used on pairs of doors so that the inactive leaf can be locked, thereby providing a fixed strike against which the active leaf can lock. Flush bolts require both an awkward manual operation to unlatch and the active leaf to be open before unlatching can occur. Because of these requirements, flush bolts are prohibited on exit doors and on many other doors by most building codes. Their use is generally limited to openings where an occasional wide opening is needed for access but where only the active leaf is used on a daily basis. Automatic flush bolts, however, may be used on exit doors.

## Keying

Keying refers to a system of matching keys to specific locks and door openings and determining which key will operate which lock. For example, everyone in an office must have his or her own key that operates both the occupant's personal office door and the front door. Furthermore, that key should not open other personal office doors or doors to rooms with restricted access. However, one person may need a key that can operate everyone's office door. In addition, building management must have a key that opens every door in the building.

Keying is based on different levels of access to locks as diagrammed in Fig. 4.16. At the lowest level is the change key, which operates an individual lock. Change keys may be keyed alike or keyed differently. If keyed alike, one key operates two or more locks. If keyed differently, each lock has a different key. A master key operates any number of locks with different change keys. A grand master key operates all locks operated by two or more master keys. A great grand master key operates all the locks operated by the various master keys and the grand master keys.

For very large buildings or multiple building complexes, it is also possible to have a great great grand master key. During construction there may be a construction key that temporarily operates all locks until the permanent keying system is established. This prevents construction workers and others

---

**Applicable standards for door locks**

American National Standards Institute (ANSI):

ANSI A156.2 *Bored and Preassembled Locks and Latches*
ANSI A156.3 *Exit Devices*
ANSI A156.12 *Interconnected Locks and Latches*
ANSI A156.13 *Mortise Locks and Latches*

---

**Table 4.3**
Selected hardware finishes

| BHMA no. | finish description | base material | BHMA category | nearest former US no. designation |
|---|---|---|---|---|
| 605 | bright brass, clear-coated | brass | A | US3 |
| 606 | satin brass, clear-coated | brass | A | US4 |
| 609 | satin brass, blackened, relieved, clear-coated | brass | C | US5 |
| 611 | bright bronze, clear-coated | bronze | A | US9 |
| 612 | satin bronze, clear-coated | bronze | A | US10 |
| 613 | satin bronze, dark-oxidized, oil-rubbed | bronze | B | US10B |
| 616 | satin bronze, blackened, relieved, clear-coated | bronze | C | US11 |
| 617 | bright bronze, dark-oxidized, relieved, clear-coated | bronze | C | US13 |
| 618 | bright nickel, clear-coated | brass, bronze | A | US14 |
| 619 | satin nickel-plated, clear-coated | brass, bronze | A | US15 |
| 620 | satin nickel, blackened, relieved, clear-coated | brass, bronze | C | US15A |
| 623 | light-oxidized, statuary bronze, clear-coated | bronze | C | US20 |
| 624 | dark statuary bronze, clear-coated | bronze | C | US20A |
| 625 | bright chromium-plated over nickel | brass, bronze | A | US26 |
| 626 | satin chromium-plated over nickel | brass, bronze | A | US26D |
| 627 | satin aluminum, clear-coated | aluminum | A | US27 |
| 628 | satin aluminum, clear-anodized | aluminum | A | US28 |
| 629 | bright stainless steel | stainless steel | A | US32 |
| 630 | satin stainless steel | stainless steel | A | US32D |
| 632 | bright brass-plated, clear-coated | steel | 605E | US3 |
| 633 | satin brass-plated, clear-coated | steel | 606E | US4 |
| 639 | satin bronze-plated, clear-coated | steel | 612E | US10 |
| 640 | oxidized satin bronze-plated over copper plate, oil rubbed | steel | 613E | US10B |
| 645 | bright nickel-plated, clear-coated | steel | 618E | US14 |
| 646 | satin nickel-plated, clear-coated | steel | 619E | US15 |
| 648 | nickel-plated, blackened, relieved, clear-coated | steel | 621E | US17A |
| 649 | light-oxidized bright bronze-plated, clear-coated | steel | 623E | US20 |
| 651 | bright chromium-plated over nickel | steel | 625E | US26 |
| 652 | satin chromium-plated over nickel | steel | 626E | US26D |
| 656 | light-oxidized satin bronze, bright relieved, clear-coated | steel | 655E | US13 |
| 666 | bright brass-plated, clear-coated | aluminum | 605E | US3 |

Compiled from ANSI/BHMA A156.18-2000, copyright 2000, by Builders Hardware Manufacturers Association.

**Figure 4.15**
Flush bolts

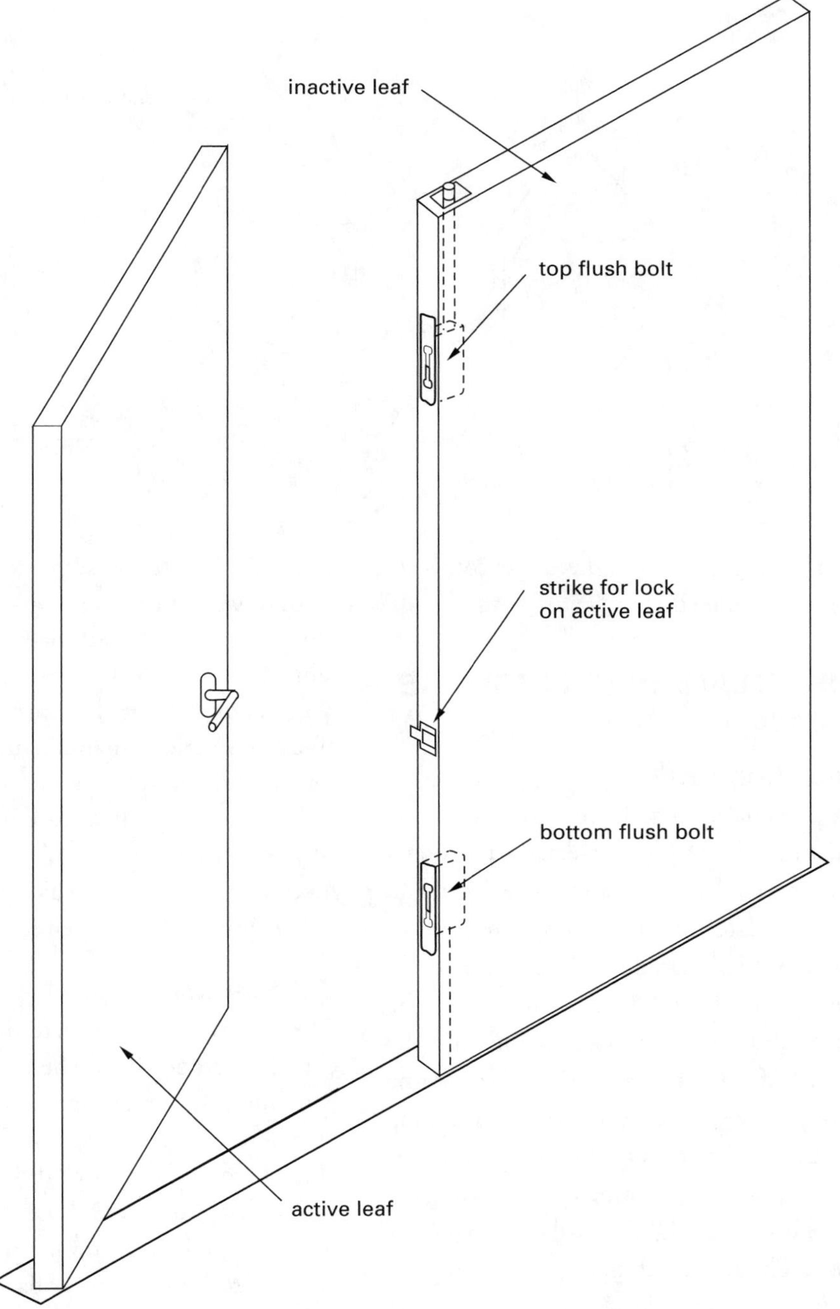

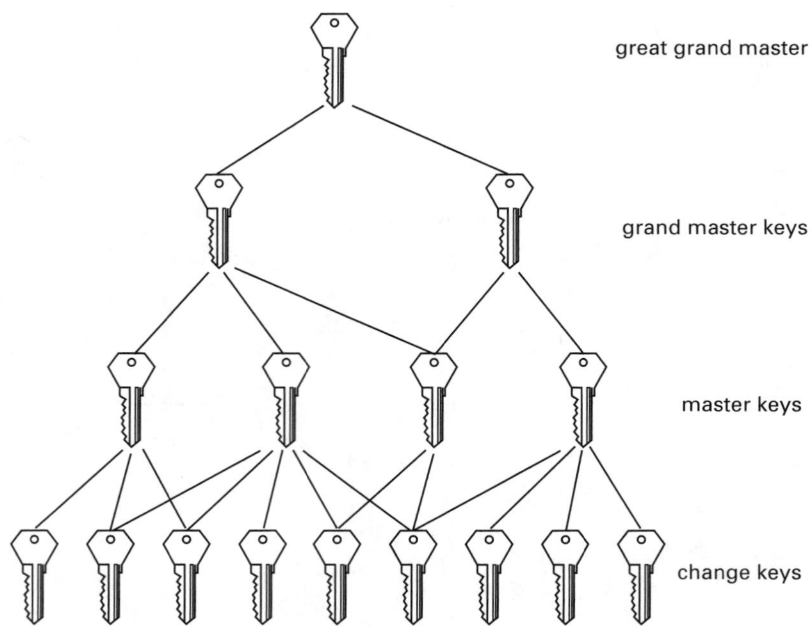


**Figure 4.16**
Keying

from having functioning keys after construction is completed.

## MISCELLANEOUS HARDWARE [087100]

### Coordinators

For pairs of doors to be fire rated, building codes require the gap between the two doors to be covered with an astragal. An astragal is a flat plate mounted along the edge of one door (designated as the active leaf) that overlaps the second door (designated as the inactive leaf) when the doors are closed. If the active leaf closes before the inactive leaf, the astragal prevents the inactive leaf from closing completely. A door coordinator prevents this from happening by momentarily holding the active leaf open slightly until the other door closes. The active leaf then closes, sealing the opening. Coordinators are mounted on the head frame and usually work in conjunction with automatic flush bolts, which latch the doors to the head frame and the floor.

### Door stops and bumpers

Some method of keeping doors from damaging adjacent construction is required. Closers will do this to some extent, but floor stops or wall bumpers provide more consistent protection. These devices are small metal fabrications with rubber bumpers attached. Several types of stops and bumpers are available from various manufacturers. Some of the more common ones are shown in Figs. 4.17(a)–4.17(c). Metal door frames also use silencers, which are small pads of rubber mounted into small holes along the door stop to cushion the door when it is closed.

### Thresholds

Thresholds are used where floor materials change at a door line, where a hard surface is required for an automatic door bottom, or where minor changes in floor level occur. There are dozens of different types of thresholds, but only those that conform to accessibility requirements should be used. Refer to Ch. 18 for barrier-free code requirements.

### Astragals

Astragals are vertical members used between double doors to seal the opening, act as a door stop, or provide extra security when the doors are closed. An astragal may be attached to one door leaf or may be a separate unit against which both doors close. If the pair of doors is fire rated and an overlapping astragal is used, the doors must be provided with a door coordinator, as described previously.

### Protective coverings

Metal plates can be attached to wood doors to protect the surface from damage. Mop plates extend the full width of the door, minus 1 in, and are about 6 in (150 mm) high. As the name implies, a mop plate protects the bottom of the door from damage during cleaning operations. Kick plates are similar but are placed slightly higher. Armor plates also extend the full width of the door, but are mounted higher to protect against damage caused by people pushing the door open with trays and other objects held at waist level.

### Door holders

Overhead holders are devices used to hold doors open until they are manually released. Usually they are straight bars or telescoping bars with a pivot that slides along a track that is recessed in the top edge of the door. Pushing the door slightly beyond its open position will disengage the hold-open device. Door holders cannot be used on fire-rated doors where codes require automatic-closing doors.

## ELECTRONIC HARDWARE [087400]

Electronic hardware includes devices that control or monitor door openings using electric or electromechanical means. Because electronic hardware and security systems can be complex, a qualified hardware or security consultant should be employed for

**Figure 4.17** Miscellaneous door hardware

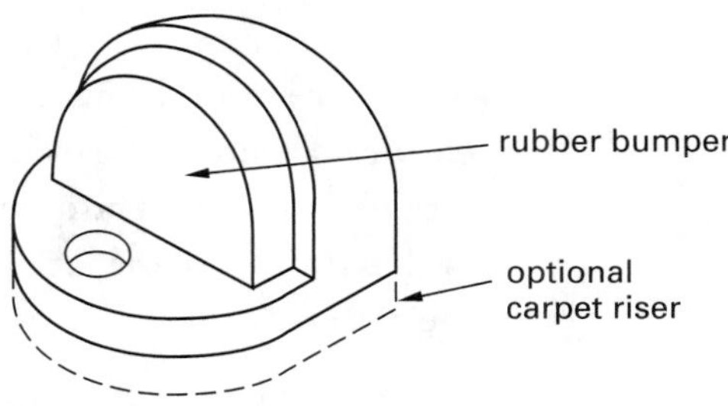


(a) dome floor stop

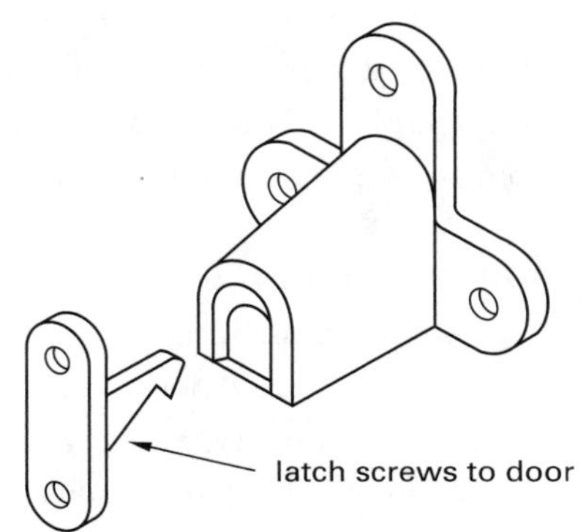


(b) combination stop and hold open

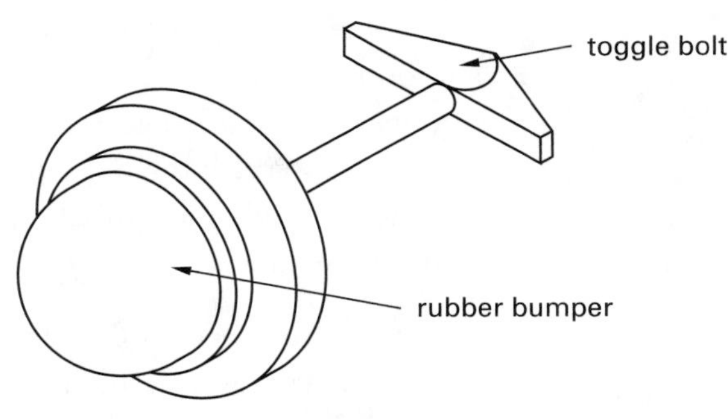


(c) wall bumper

**Applicable standards for miscellaneous hardware**

American National Standards Institute (ANSI):

| | |
|---|---|
| ANSI/BHMA A156.6 | *Architectural Door Trim* |
| ANSI/BHMA A156.8 | *Door Controls—Overhead Stops and Holders* |
| ANSI/BHMA A156.14 | *Sliding and Folding Door Hardware* |
| ANSI/BHMA A156.16 | *Auxiliary Hardware* |
| ANSI/BHMA A156.21 | *Thresholds* |
| ANSI/BHMA A156.22 | *Door Gasketing Systems* |

specialty installations. Local building codes must also be consulted because some electronic hardware devices do not qualify as allowable exit devices. If an exit door is electronically locked and controlled from the outside, most codes require that exiting be possible from the inside by a purely mechanical action of the locking device. This action must not depend on any power supply or deactivation of the lock on the inside by the person exiting.

There are hundreds of products available, ranging from simple intrusion detection devices to biometric readers than can unlock doors by identifying a person's retina, voice, or fingerprint. This section briefly describes some of the commonly used devices.

### Electric locks

An electric lock maintains a mortise or bored lockset in the locked position until a signal is activated by some type of regulating device. Regulating devices can include wall switches, push buttons, card readers, key switches, computerized controls, automatic timing devices, security consoles, and other sophisticated control devices. Electric locks can also be specified so that they automatically open if there is a power failure. In either case, the inside knob or handle mechanically unlatches the door for exiting at any time.

A variation of the electric lock is the electric latch. This device is typically in a position to hold the latchbolt of the lock so that the door cannot be opened. On activation, the electric latch pivots slightly, allowing the door to be opened. From the inside, the mechanical operation of the knob or handle retracts the latch, allowing exit regardless of the position of the electric latch. Electric latches have the advantage of not requiring any power to be run to the door; all wiring is done in the door jamb. Electric locks require the use of electric hinges or other power-transfer devices to make the low-voltage wiring connections from the door frame to the mechanism in the door.

### Electric bolts

Electric bolts are devices separate from the operating hardware of a door. They can be mounted in the strike jamb or head of a door. In the typical locked position, a bolt extends from the unit into a strike in the door. A push button, card reader, or other regulating device activates a solenoid, which retracts the bolt. Fail-safe units are available that open when there is a power failure. Electric bolts are generally not allowed on exit doors because there is no sure way to mechanically open the door if the bolt does not retract.

### Card readers

A card reader is one type of regulating device that reads a magnetic code on a small plastic card when the card is inserted into the reader. If the reader detects a valid code, the switch is activated and the door is unlocked. Card readers can also be used to send a signal to a central monitoring computer. The computer keeps track of whose card was used to open which door and when the entry was made. In addition, the computer can control the times of the day particular doors can be opened by particular cards. Card readers are usually mounted on the partition near the door they control. They also can be part of the lockset, such as the card readers typically used in hotels. Card readers can also be concealed behind the finish of the partition. To gain access the person must know where the card reader is concealed. The device is activated by pressing the card against the partition.

### Keypad devices

An alternative to the card reader is the keypad in which a coded number must be entered to gain access. The keypad device can be a separate unit mounted near the door or can be part of the door knob or lever. For additional security, keypads can be used with card readers.

## Magnetic hold-open devices

While exit doors must have closers, most codes allow them to be held in an open position if they can be closed automatically upon activation of a smoke detector or other approved fire signal. One method of doing this is to use a closer with an integrated smoke detector, as described previously. Another way is to use a magnetic hold-open device, which is an electromagnet mounted on a wall or the floor that makes contact with a metal plate attached to the door. Upon activation by a central alarm signal or a smoke detector, or upon a power failure, the electromagnet releases and the door closes.

## Delayed-exit devices

Delayed-exit devices resemble standard exit devices (panic hardware) but are designed to stay locked for a fixed time (usually 15 to 30 sec) after the bar is depressed. During that time an alarm sounds to allow response to an unauthorized door opening. Delayed-exit devices are used where both security and life safety are required. In an actual emergency, the delay is bypassed and the device unlocks upon activation from the building's fire alarm or other emergency system.

For more information on building security systems refer to Ch. 14.

# MATERIALS AND FINISHES

Hardware is available in a wide variety of finishes, the choice of which depends primarily on the desired appearance and the required durability. Standards for describing and comparing finishes are detailed in *Hardware—Materials and Finishes* (ANSI/BHMA A156.18), published by the American National Standards Institute (ANSI) and sponsored by the Builders Hardware Manufacturers Associations (BHMA). This standard provides a three-digit code to describe the finish and the base metal on which the finish is applied. These are summarized

### Comparing hardware finishes

Because various finishes can be applied to different base materials and some finishes are considered unstable, the ANSI/BHMA A156.18 standard establishes five categories of finishes, A, B, C, D, and E, and describes a method for comparing finishes on different hardware items. The Builders Hardware Manufacturers Association has match-plate samples available for purchase with samples of categories A, B, and C finishes.

When comparing category A finishes, such as chrome, brass, and stainless steel, with a match-plate sample, the two finishes are considered comparative if they appear the same when viewed 2 ft apart (600 mm) and 3 ft away (900 mm) under the same lighting conditions and on the same relative plane. The finishes in category A offer the highest potential for consistency in appearance on different hardware items throughout a project.

Category B finishes are considered unstable. One such finish is 613, oil-rubbed bronze. Finish inconsistencies can occur based on variations in alloys and base materials. Category B finishes are required to match only when compared to the same finish on the same alloy or base material.

Because category C finishes are hand applied, they are intended to be compatible with each other rather than to match exactly. Category D finishes are for protective applications only and are not considered for appearance. Category E finishes are intended to be matched with comparable finishes from categories A, B, and C. Many finishes applied to steel, aluminum, and plastic are category E finishes.

in Table 4.3, along with the older U.S. (United States) designations that are sometimes found in the literature.

There are 10 base material categories listed for hardware in ANSI/BHMA 156.18: (1) cast, forged, or extruded brass or bronze, (2) sheet, coil, or extruded brass or bronze, (3) cast, forged, or extruded aluminum, (4) sheet, coil, or strip aluminum, (5) stainless steel, (6) malleable iron, (7) cast iron, (8) steel, (9) zinc alloy, and (10) optional material, as determined by the manufacturer. The four base metals used for most finish hardware include steel, stainless steel, bronze, and brass. In many instances, the base metal can be important in specifying the hardware. For example, fire-rated doors must have hinges made from steel or stainless steel, even though any plated finish can be applied over the base metal. In other instances, plated finishes on pulls, levers, and other frequently used items can wear off with time; therefore, it is better to specify a finish with the same type of base metal even though the base metal may cost more. Some finishes, such an oil-rubbed bronze, wear and change color with time from the salt content in perspiration.

Some hardware finishes are more commonly used than others; therefore, manufacturers keep these items in stock. Other infrequently used finishes must be manufactured based on a specific order, and the lead time in getting hardware can be substantial.

## COORDINATION

### Mounting heights

Although hardware can be mounted anywhere on a door, there are standard heights for various hardware items. These are shown in Fig. 4.18. Unless otherwise noted on the drawings or specifications, door and hardware suppliers and contractors locate the hardware as shown in the illustration.

---

**Building code requirements for exit door hardware and accessibility**

All model codes refer to standards developed by the National Fire Protection Association, which include NFPA 80, *Standards for Fire Doors and Windows*, NFPA 252, *Fire Tests of Door Assemblies*, and NFPA 105, *Recommended Practice for the Installation of Smoke-Control Door Assemblies.*

The International Building Code requires exit doors to meet the following requirements. The other model codes have similar requirements.

- Exit doors must be operable from the inside without the use of a key or any special knowledge or effort.
- Panic hardware must be mounted at a height between 34 in and 48 in (864 mm and 1219 mm) above the floor. The unlatching force cannot exceed 15 lbf (67 N).
- Panic hardware is required for Group A occupancies or Group E occupancies with occupant loads greater than 50 and for any occupancy of Group H. (See Ch. 19 for information on occupancies and occupant loads.)
- Exit doors must have closers or other approved self-closing or automatic-closing devices. Any device that holds open a door must release upon activation of a smoke detector or power failure.
- Hinges must be steel or stainless steel and of the ball bearing type.
- Doors must be provided with an automatic latch that secures the door when it is closed.
- The floor level at a door cannot be less than ½ in (13 mm) below a threshold if the door is part of an accessible route.

Finally, hardware for doors must meet the requirements of the Americans with Disabilities Act and applicable provisions of ICC/ANSI A117.1, *Accessible and Usable Buildings and Facilities.*

---

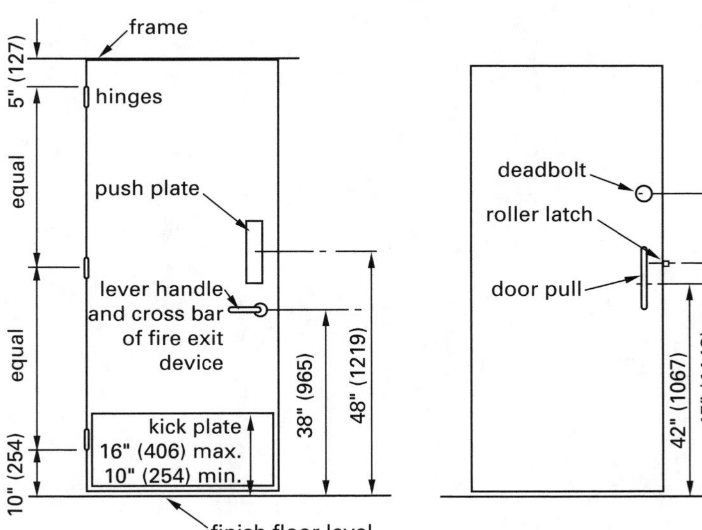


**Figure 4.18** Standard hardware mounting heights

Maximum mounting height for any accessible hardware is 48 in (1220 mm).

## Hardware schedules

Before a project can be bid on or a construction price can be negotiated, the interior designer must prepare a hardware specification list, which gives a general listing of the items necessary for the operation of doors and the level of quality desired for a particular project. Later, based on this specification, the hardware supplier compiles a thorough hardware schedule that contains all the details necessary to order from the factory.

On the hardware specification list, the various hardware items needed for each type of door on the job are grouped into hardware sets, and each set is given a sequential number. Each set includes a unique collection of hardware that may apply to one door or to several doors. The door schedule contains a separate column, which lists the hardware group that each door requires.

# 5

# GLAZING

## COMMON GLASS TYPES [088100]

In the building trades *glazing* is the installation of glass in framing. The word *glazing* also refers to glass used in the construction of a building. There are a number of common glass types available for interior use. Common glass types are described in this section. Special glazing will be discussed in the next section.

### Float glass

Float glass is the most common type of glass produced. It has replaced plate glass, which was in common use until the mid-1960s. Float glass is manufactured by flowing molten glass onto a bed of molten tin until the glass floats to a smooth surface. It is then slowly cooled, or *annealed*, and cut into the required lengths for further processing. Float glass is produced clear, but it can be tinted blue, bronze, gray, or green. For interior use, it is employed in small openings or where safety glazing is not required.

Float glass is available in thicknesses of 1/8, 3/16, 1/4, 3/8, 1/2, 5/8, and 3/4 in (3.0, 5.0, 6.0, 10.0, 12.0, 16.0, and 19.0 mm). Other thicknesses are available, but these are not frequently used for interior applications.

When higher strengths are required, heat-strengthened glass can be used. However, this type of float glass is generally used only for exterior windows and is about twice as strong as annealed glass.

### Tempered glass

Tempered glass is produced by subjecting float glass to a special heat treatment. The glass is heated to about 1200°F (650°C), after which both surfaces are cooled rapidly. This produces compressive forces on the surfaces and tensile forces in the core. Under uniform loading, tempered glass is about four times stronger in tensile bending strength than float glass of the same thickness. Therefore, it resists impact much better than float glass does. In addition to its extra strength for normal glazing, tempered glass is considered to be safety glass, so it can be used in hazardous locations (discussed later in this chapter). It breaks into very small, cubical pieces instead of into dangerous shards.

Tempered glass is available in thicknesses from 1/8 in (3.0 mm) to 7/8 in (22.0 mm). For interior use a 1/4 in (6.0 mm) thickness is common. The maximum dimensions for tempered glass vary depending on thickness, ranging from 42 × 84 for ⅛ in glass to 74 × 110 for ⅞ in glass (1067 × 2134 for 3.0 mm glass to 1880 × 2794 for 22.0 mm glass).

One of the disadvantages of tempered glass is that it must be ordered to the exact size required for the final installation because once it is tempered it cannot be cut, drilled, or deeply etched. In addition, tempering may produce slight distortions in the field of the glass as well as near the tong marks for vertically tempered glass.

Tempered glass also bows or warps slightly during the heat treatment. The distortion can take the form of a slight S shape or, more commonly, a long arch. When two or more large pieces of tempered glass are butt-joined without a frame, the bows should be oriented the same way so there is not a gap perpendicular to the plane of the glass at the midpoint.

### Bow tolerances for tempered glass

Glass can be tempered in a horizontal position or by suspending it vertically with tongs. If tongs are used, there will be marks near one edge of the glass that should be concealed with framing. For glass thicknesses up to ⅜ in (9.5 mm), the center line of the tong marks cannot be more than ½ in (12.7 mm) from the edge of the glass. For glass thicknesses over ⅜ in, the center line of the tong marks cannot be more than ¾ in (19 mm) from the edge of the glass. Regardless of which method is used, some distortions occur, the most noticeable of which is bowing. Bow tolerances depend on the glass thickness and the length of the longest edge. Table 5.1 shows some selected values for thicknesses and sizes normally used in interior design work.

## Laminated glass

Laminated glass consists of two or more layers of glass bonded together by an interlayer of polyvinyl butyral. The glass can be clear or tinted float glass, tempered glass, or heat-strengthened glass. When exceptional impact or ballistic resistance is required, heat-strengthened glass can enclose one or more layers of polycarbonate laminated with interlayers of polyvinyl butyral or polyurethane. Polycarbonates are thermoplastic resins that are dimensionally stable and have high impact strength.

Traditionally, laminated glass used for interior applications has been clear. However, recent developments have provided the interior designer with a wide range of decorative possibilities. These are discussed in the next section on special glazing.

When laminated glass is broken, the interlayer holds the pieces together even though the glass itself may be severely cracked. Laminated glass fabricated with tempered glass or polycarbonate is used where very strong glazing is required. Float glass or tempered glass can be used where acoustical control is needed. It can be bullet resistant and provides high security against breakage (intentional or accidental). Some combinations of glass and plastic thickness qualify as safety glazing and can be used in hazardous locations.

Laminated glass is available in thicknesses from 13/64 in to 3 in (5.2 mm to 76 mm). Most typically, thicknesses used for interior design projects range from 9/32 in to ¾ in (7.1 mm to 19.0 mm). These thicknesses consist of from two plies of ⅛ in (3.0 mm) glass to two plies of ⅜ in (10.0 mm) glass. Maximum sheet size is 84 × 160 (2134 × 4064). The polyvinyl butyral interlayer thickness can be specified from 0.015 in to 0.090 in (0.381 mm to 2.286 mm) or more.

Laminated glass is excellent where high strength or acoustical control is required. It qualifies as safety glazing and can be cut in the field. However, its impact resistance is low unless tempered or heat-strengthened glass is used. Refer to Ch. 11 for more information

**Table 5.1**
Selected bow tolerances for tempered glass[1]

| length of edge (in (mm)) | nominal glass thickness (in (mm)) | | | |
|---|---|---|---|---|
| | ⅛ in (3 mm) | ¼ in (6 mm) | ⅜ in (10 mm) | ½ in to ⅞ in (12 mm to 22 mm) |
| >20–35 (>500–900 ) | 0.16 (4.0) | 0.12 (3.0) | 0.08 (2.0) | 0.08 (2.0) |
| >35–47 (>900–1200) | 0.20 (5.0) | 0.16 (4.0) | 0.08 (2.0) | 0.08 (2.0) |
| >47–59 (>1200–1500) | 0.28 (7.0) | 0.20 (5.0) | 0.16 (4.0) | 0.08 (2.0) |
| >59–71 (>1500–1800) | 0.35 (9.0) | 0.28 (7.0) | 0.20 (5.0) | 0.16 (4.0) |
| >71–83 (>1800–2100) | 0.47 (12.0) | 0.35 (9.0) | 0.24 (6.0) | 0.20 (5.0) |
| >83–94 (>2100–2400) | 0.55 (14.0) | 0.47 (12.0) | 0.28 (7.0) | 0.20 (5.0) |
| >94–106 (>2400–2700) | 0.67 (17.0) | 0.55 (14.0) | 0.35 (9.0) | 0.28 (7.0) |
| >106–118 (>2700–3000) | 0.75 (19.0) | 0.67 (17.0) | 0.47 (12.0) | 0.39 (10.0) |
| >118–130 (>3000–3300) | – (–) | 0.75 (19.0) | 0.55 (14.0) | 0.47 (12.0) |

[1] Refer to ASTM C1048 for additional values for other thicknesses of glass and larger edge lengths.

Source: ASTM C1048, copyright ASTM. Reprinted with permission.

## Applicable standards for glazing

**American Society for Testing and Materials (ASTM):**

ASTM C1036 *Specification for Flat Glass*
ASTM C1048 *Specification for Heat-Treated Flat Glass*

**Consumer Product Safety Commission (CPSC):**

16 CFR 1201 *Safety Standard for Architectural Glazing Material*

**National Fire Protection Association (NFPA):**

NFPA 80 *Standard for Fire Doors and Windows*

on the use and detailing of laminated glass for acoustical control. Refer to Ch. 14 for more information on security glazing.

## Wired glass

Wired glass has a mesh of wire embedded in the middle of the sheet. The two wire patterns generally available are hexagonal and square shapes. The surface can be either smooth or patterned. Wired glass is used primarily in fire-rated opening assemblies, if it is not in a hazardous location. To be used as fire-protection-rated glazing, it must meet the requirements of the National Fire Protection Association's NFPA 80 or be classified by Underwriters Laboratories as a fire-protection-rated glazing. Wired glass cannot be tempered and, therefore, does not qualify as safety glazing for hazardous locations.

Fire-rated wire glass openings are limited to a maximum size of 1296 $in^2$ (0.836 $m^2$) and a maximum dimension between framing of 54 in (1372 mm).

## Figured/patterned glass

Figured or patterned glass is made by passing a sheet of molten glass through rollers on which the desired pattern is pressed, which may be on one or both sides. Vision through the panel is diffused but not totally obscured; the degree of diffusion depends on the type and depth of the pattern. The exact type of pattern and the available sizes depend on the individual manufacturer.

## Mirrored glass

Mirrored glass is produced by depositing a thin film of metal or metallic oxide on one surface of the glass. Because the reflective surface is fragile, a protective backing is applied. Mirrors can be made from standard float glass or from tempered glass, where safety glazing is required.

Mirrors should be installed using mechanical methods rather than simply applying the mirror to a backing with mastic. J-moldings, frames, or clips can be used. Mirrors can also be installed by drilling holes and using screws or special rosettes. A rubber sleeve should be placed around the fastener to prevent direct contact between the glass and fastener.

Transparent, or two-way, mirrors can be used to provide vision through the glass from one direction and a mirrored appearance from the other. These are used where undetected observation is required, such as in detention facilities, psychiatric centers, and gambling casinos. In order for transparent mirrors to work, the lighting level in the room to be observed must be at least five times greater (10 times is even more effective) than in the observation room. The mirror should be installed with the coated side to the observed (lighter) room.

## Decorative glass

Decorative glass differs from the glass types mentioned previously in that it is installed and, in most cases, manufactured by artists or craftspersons as a one-of-a-kind installation. The design possibilities of decorative glass are limitless and give the designer a large palette from which to work. There are dozens of different types of decorative glass. Some of the more common ones are described in this section.

### Beveled glass

Beveling produces a decorative edge to a sheet of glass. The most common treatment is a simple, sloped, polished surface. However, more elaborate carvings are possible, such as multifaceted bevels, bull-nose shapes, or more complex curved profiles. The beveled portion can be smooth or etched. The angle and length of the bevel can also be specified.

### Etched glass

Etched glass is created by using acid or sandblasting techniques to remove a portion of the glass surface. When the etching becomes very deep, it is often called carved glass. Glass can be etched uniformly (frosted) or in geometric patterns, with lettering or with elaborate designs, as the skill of the artist allows. When properly illuminated and positioned in front of the correct color and shade of background, carved glass has a dramatic, luminescent quality.

Etching can be done on several types of glass, depending on the depth of the etch and the thickness of the glass. Light etching, such as frosting, can be done on float glass, tempered glass, laminated glass, and insulated glass as thin as ⅛ in (3 mm). Slightly deeper etching must be done on glass at least ¼ in (6 mm) thick. Medium etching or carving requires at least ⅜ in (9 mm) glass, while some heavy carving may only be done on glass ½ in (12 mm) or thicker. If tempered glass is required for deep etching, the etching or carving must be done before the glass is tempered. Light etching may be done after tempering.

## Stained glass

As one of the most common forms of decorative glazing, stained glass can produce vivid, dynamic murals or area separation partitions. Used against an exterior window, stained glass can reveal a never-ending combination of colors and patterns. Although traditionally used in religious settings, stained glass has been applied to all types of residential and commercial design by artists working in a variety of areas.

Stained glass is produced by adding metal oxides to the glass during manufacturing. It is typically used in relatively small pieces to create a particular pattern or image. The individual glass pieces are set in H-shaped *cames* made from lead or zinc. The entire assembly is set in a heavier frame, which the interior designer needs to accommodate in the construction detailing. If stained glass is used in a ceiling or a location where it might be damaged, an additional piece of clear tempered or laminated glass or plastic (if allowed by the local building codes) should be placed over it for protection.

## Hand-blown glass

Hand-blown flat glass is made by blowing a large bubble or cylinder of glass with a traditional blow pipe and then cutting the cylinder and unrolling it flat. Because of the way they are made, hand-blown glass sheets are fairly small but have unique irregularities that make them desirable for decorative glass designs.

Hand-blown glass may be clear or colored, and there are several effects that can be created. Flashed glass uses a double layer, with one clear layer and a thin layer of colored glass. Crackle glass is made by dipping hot glass in water to produce a webbed pattern. Seedy glass is produced by blowing the glass before the silica and other material are completely refined. The effect is one of small particles on the glass that scatter light.

## Cathedral glass

Cathedral glass is machine formed by rolling molten glass across rollers that impress

---

### Lighting etched glass

Because of the reflective and transparent qualities of glass, special care needs to be taken when illuminating space or objects near glass. For most clear glass, light should be directed at objects and surfaces beyond the glass rather than at the glass itself. However, for etched glass, the frosted part of the glass needs to be illuminated for maximum effect.

There are two ways to do this. One way is to use directional lights from above on the etched side of the glass so that the light interacts with the rough surfaces, highlighting them and causing them to "glow." The other way is to use edge lighting with fluorescent lights. One or more edges of the glass are detailed in such a way that the light is centered on the thickness of the glass. Unfortunately, because the glass absorbs so much of the light coming from the edge, edge lighting is not effective past about 18 in (457 mm) from the light source.

---

patterns or textures on one side while the other side remains smooth. After cooling, the glass is textured and transparent.

### Opalescent glass

Opalescent glass is machine formed by mixing one or more colors with the glass. The final product is translucent and has a marbleized appearance.

### Painted glass

Painted glass is made by applying vitreous paints to clear glass and then firing the glass in a kiln until the applied material fuses to the glass. The same piece may be fired several times to create layers of color and texture. Because of the technique used, painted glass can have smaller and more intricate designs than stained glass.

### Dichroic Glass

Dichroic glass is manufactured by depositing a stack of very thin layers (3 to 5 millionths of an inch) of metal oxides on a sheet of glass using vacuum thin-film deposition. Although the stack of oxide films is clear, it acts as a filter to reflect one color of light and transmit other colors depending on the angle of view. The film acts a selective color mirror to reflect some light energy and transmit the rest. In the most commonly used single stack of film, the reflected colors are similar to a rainbow as the angle of view is varied. However, red and green are not present. To achieve these colors, a more complex, two-stack design is used to achieve all the colors of the rainbow. Custom glass can be manufactured to achieve a desired color.

### Cast glass

Cast glass pieces are produced by pouring molten glass into a mold that is made by pressing a positive model into specially prepared sand. The resulting piece is usually fairly thick and can be used for exterior as well as interior applications.

Cast glass can be made in a variety of colors, but in general the pieces must be fairly small. Although cast glass is usually done on a custom basis, some manufacturers mass-produce cast glass for wall and floor tiles.

### Kiln-formed glass

Kiln-formed glass is flat glass that is heated just enough to cause it to sag over a mold. The resulting piece has the sculptural relief and texture of the mold while the other side remains smooth. Typical thicknesses range from ¼ in to ½ in (6 mm to 12 mm). Pieces up to 4 ft (1200 mm) wide by 8 ft (2400 mm) long can be formed. Kiln-formed glass can be tempered, drilled, notched, and fitted into other building components, making it a functional as well as decorative construction element.

## SPECIAL GLAZING [088100]

Glazing technology is one of the fastest growing areas of building product innovation. There are dozens of products under development and on the market that provide a variety of functional and decorative possibilities. This section reviews special glazing that is useful for interior design applications.

### Fire-rated glazing

There are five types of glazing that can be used in fire-rated partitions: wired glass, clear ceramic, gel-filled glass, tempered glass, and some types of glass block. Glass block is discussed in Ch. 1.

Wired glass has traditionally been the only type of glazing permitted in fire-rated assemblies, such as partitions, doors, and windows. Wired glass is ¼ in (6 mm) thick and, when installed in a steel frame, carries a 45-minute fire rating in sizes up to 1296 in$^2$ or 9 ft$^2$ (0.84 m$^2$) with no dimension exceeding 54 in (1372 mm). Although its use is allowed by the 2006 IBC, wired glass must now meet the safety-glazing requirements of 16 CFR 1201 when used in hazardous locations. Previously, the codes allowed wired glass to meet the less stringent standards of the ANSI Z97.1 test standard when used in hazardous locations if the glass was required as a fire barrier.

## Building code requirements for fire-rated, glazed opening assemblies

Fire barriers, such as partitions, doors, and glazing, must meet three critical functional requirements: (1) they must restrict the passage of flame, (2) they must limit the spread of smoke, and (3) they must retard the transmission of heat. One of the reasons why it is difficult for glazing assemblies to have very high fire ratings in large sizes is that, while they can restrict the passage of flame and limit smoke spread (assuming the glazing stays intact), most products do not provide insulation against heat transmission. During a fire, if a combustible object is near one side of a piece of glazing, it is possible for the transmitted heat alone to ignite the object. It is not necessary for a flame to penetrate an opening.

Most codes require that 1-hour-rated corridor partitions have 45-minute-rated opening protection. This includes doors and glazing. Other types of 1-hour-rated partitions require 60-minute-rated opening protection. These partitions include occupancy separations and 1-hour-rated stairways. Refer to Ch. 19 for more information on code requirements.

Hazardous locations are discussed later in this chapter. Typically, wired glass can meet the 16 CFR 1201 requirements only if it is either laminated to tempered float glass or coated with a special surface-applied film. Because of changes in the IBC and the availability of newer glazing materials that are both fire rated and safety rated, wired glass is not being used as much as it once was.

The second type of glazing is not a glass at all but a clear ceramic that has a low expansion coefficient and a higher impact resistance than wired glass. The ceramic "glass" produced from one manufacturer carries a 1-hour fire rating in sizes up to 1296 $in^2$ (0.84 $m^2$) and a 3-hour rating in sizes up to 100 $in^2$ (0.0645 $m^2$). It is only 3/16 in (4.8 mm) thick and is available in sizes up to 48 in by 96 in (1200 mm by 2400 mm). It is available with polished or patterned surfaces. Although some forms of ceramic glass do not meet safety glazing requirements, there are laminated assemblies that are rated up to 2 hours and are impact safety-rated, meeting the requirements of both ANSI Z97.1 and 16 CFR 1201. For the exact thicknesses required, maximum sizes, and safety requirements for various fire ratings, manufacturers' catalogs should be consulted.

The third type of glazing is gel-filled glass, which uses two or three layers of tempered glass with a clear polymer gel between them. This type of glazing is also known as a transparent wall panel or technically as fire-resistance-rated glazing. When subjected to fire, the gel turns opaque and acts as an insulator against the passage of heat. This type of glazing is tested in accordance with ASTM E119 (see Ch. 19 for a description of this test) instead of the tests used for door glazing and fire-protection-rated glazing. It resists thermal shock from the hose stream part of the test, resists the transfer of heat, and passes the impact tests for safety glazing. Although it is expensive, this type of glazing is available in fire ratings up to 2 hours. It must be installed in strict accordance with the manufacturer's directions. A representative listing of maximum sizes available from one manufacturer for interior use is shown in Table 5.2.

The fourth type of fire-rated glazing is tempered fire-protective glass. It is rated at a maximum of 30 minutes because it cannot pass the hose stream test, but it does meet the impact safety standards of 16 CFR 1201. It is 1/4 in (6 mm) thick with maximum areas of 2905 $in^2$ (1.87 $m^2$) for use in doors and 4626 $in^2$ (2.98 $m^2$) for use in areas other than doors. The maximum dimension of any one length is 35.75 in (908 mm) for doors and 49.875 in (1267 mm) for other areas.

As of 2006, the IBC requires all fire-rated glazing to be labeled by the manufacturer according to a standard system. This label

**Table 5.2**
**Maximum sizes and thicknesses for fire-resistance-rated glazing**

| fire rating (minutes) | maximum area ($in^2$ ($m^2$)) | maximum size (in (mm)) | thickness (in (mm)) |
|---|---|---|---|
| 45 | 4500 (2.903) | 95 × 95 (2413 × 2413) | ¾ (19) |
| 60 | 5605 (3.616) | 95 × 95 (2413 × 2413) | 15/16 (23) |
| 90 | 3724 (2.403) | 90 × 90 (2286 × 2286) | 1 7/16 (37) |
| 120 | 3724 (2.403) | 111 × 111 (2819 × 2819) | 2⅛ (54) |

Note: These dimensions represent only one manufacturer and are for interior use for transparent wall units. Other sizes apply for use in doors or for exterior glazing. All uses require special framing as tested to achieve the fire ratings listed. Verify specific limitations and requirements prior to designing and specifying.

Source: Manufacturers' literature.

consists of a symbol W, OH, or D followed by the fire rating of the glazing in minutes. A W designation means the glazing is appropriate for use as a wall and has been tested in accordance with ASTM E119, including all the fire, hose stream, and temperature rise requirements. An OH designation means the glazing is appropriate for openings, including window, sidelite, and transom openings, and has been tested in accordance with NFPA 257 for fire and hose stream requirements. A D designation means the glazing is for use in doors and has been tested in accordance with NFPA 252. Refer to Chap. 19 for a description of these test procedures.

For doors, there are additional letters to indicate whether the glazing meets the hose stream test and temperature rise requirements. An H indicates the glazing meets the hose stream test and NH means it does not. A T indicates the glazing meets the temperature rise requirements and NT means it does not. For example, if glazing in a door were labeled D-H-NT-45, this would mean that the glazing is appropriate for use in a door, meets the hose stream requirements, does not meet the temperature rise requirements, and has been tested for a 45-minute rating.

## Bent glass

Bent glass is flat glass that has been shaped while hot into cylindrical or other curved surfaces. Bent glass can be plain annealed glass up to 1 in (25.4 mm) thick, or tempered, laminated, insulating, wire, or patterned glass. The maximum sizes available in different types depend on the capabilities of individual manufacturers, as do the minimum and maximum radii for bends. Maximum sizes are about 4 ft by 8 ft (1200 mm by 2400 mm). Generally, the minimum radius depends on the thickness. For ¼ in (6 mm) glass, the minimum radius for a 90° bend is about 8 in (200 mm); the maximum radius is about 60 in (1500 mm).

## Decorative laminated glass

Several manufacturers now offer laminated glass with an interlayer of opaque or translucent colored film, wire mesh, rice paper, fabric, and other materials. One product uses a film with a tiny dot pattern printed black on one side and colored on the other. The effect is that when viewed from one side the glass looks transparent (but slightly tinted), and when viewed from the other side the glass looks opaque. This offers visual privacy. In order for the effect to work, the opaque side (which can be printed with colors and patterns) must be at least 30% brighter than the transparent side.

## Electrochromic glazing

Electrochromic glazing is the general term for a type of glazing that changes when electric current is applied from either a dark tint or an opaque milky white to clear. When the current is on, the glass is transparent; when the current is turned off, the glass darkens or turns white (depending on its type). There are three distinct types of this glazing on the market as of this writing, only one of which is technically known as electrochromic glazing.

The other two types are suspended particle devices (SPD) and polymer-dispersed liquid crystal film. The distinction is important because each of the three types has slightly different characteristics, although all three depend on the application of a low electric current to keep them clear.

*Electrochromic glazing* uses an inorganic, ceramic thin-film coating on glass, and can be manufactured to range from transparent to heavily darkened (tinted). However, it is never opaque, so it cannot be used as privacy glass. It is intended for control of light, ultraviolet energy, and solar heat gain. The tinting is not just an on or off condition; the degree of it can be controlled with a simple rheostat switch.

*SPD glazing* uses a proprietary system in which light-absorbing microscopic particles are dispersed within a liquid suspension film, which is then sandwiched between two pieces of transparent conductive material. The appearance of the product can range from clear to partially darkened to totally opaque, so it can be used for privacy as well as for light control and energy conservation. It can also be variably controlled with a rheostat.

*Polymer-dispersed liquid crystal film glazing* is fabricated by placing a polymer film between two pieces of glass. The transparency can range from transparent to cloudy white. In its translucent state, this product offers total visual privacy but still allows a significant amount of light to pass through, so it cannot be used for exterior light control.

All types of electrochromic glazing are very expensive, but the first two types do offer the potential for significant energy savings, in the range of 20% to 30%.

### Other special glazing types

There are several other types of special glazing, but most of them are designed for exterior windows, to reduce solar heat gain and loss and otherwise modify the effects of climate on energy requirements. Photochromic glass, for example, changes its tint in response to changes in light level. Thermo-chromic glass changes in response to temperature changes.

Other glass products provide electromagnetic shielding to protect sensitive computer or communications equipment from interference from outside sources such as radar waves. Traditionally, glass with a wire mesh was used to prevent interference, but one manufacturer now has a clear glass product that provides the same shielding.

The type of glass used for exterior windows can have a significant effect on interior materials. Clear float glass allows ultraviolet light to enter. Fabrics and other finishes fade as a result, including many types of window coverings. If clear glass is present, fade-resistant window coverings should be specified and detailed in such a way as to protect interior furnishings and finishes. An alternative is that the furnishings and finishes themselves should be fade resistant. If the windows use tinted or reflective glass, or any glass that minimizes ultraviolet transmission, fading of interior materials is less of a problem.

## FRAMED GLAZING [088100]

The most common interior glazing installation consists of glass set in wood, steel, or aluminum frames. Because interior glass does not have to withstand wind loads or be weather sealed, the size of the framing members is not as critical as for windows, and it can be eliminated in some cases. This is frameless glazing and is discussed in the next section. If the glazed opening must be fire rated, most codes require that a steel frame be used and that fastening and other details meet particular criteria.

### Wood framing

Figures 5.1 and 5.2 illustrate jamb details for two common interior glass framing methods. Figure 5.3 shows the corresponding sill and head detail for the jamb shown in Fig. 5.2. As with wood doors (Ch. 3), the exact profile

**Figure 5.1**
Wood glazing jamb

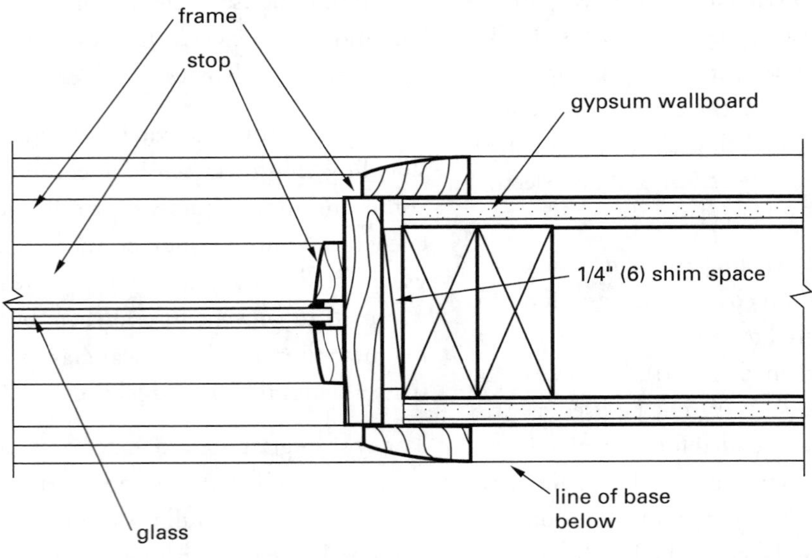


**Figure 5.2**
Wood glazing jamb with flush stop

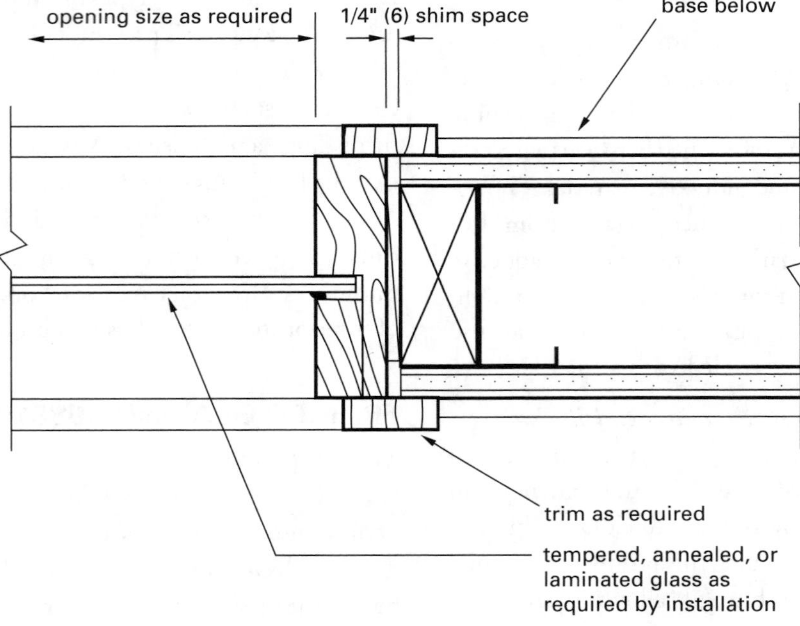


of the frame and trim can vary according to the functional and aesthetic needs of the installation.

Some detail requirements are common to all wood frames. Like door framing, a glass frame should have at least ¼ in (6 mm) of shim space on all sides of the rough opening to allow the frame to be leveled and plumbed. The glass frame should also allow some way to conceal the space between the frame and the partition. At least one of the stops holding the glass in place must be removable to allow for original installation and subsequent glass replacement. If the glazing is installed in a metal stud partition, most mill shops and carpenters prefer to have solid wood blocking into which they can attach the jamb frame.

In most cases, the glass should not come in contact with the frame. The glass should rest on setting blocks located at the quarter points of the sill (two setting blocks one-quarter of the way in from the edges of the glass). The space between the face of the glass and the

tempered, annealed, or laminated glass as required by installation

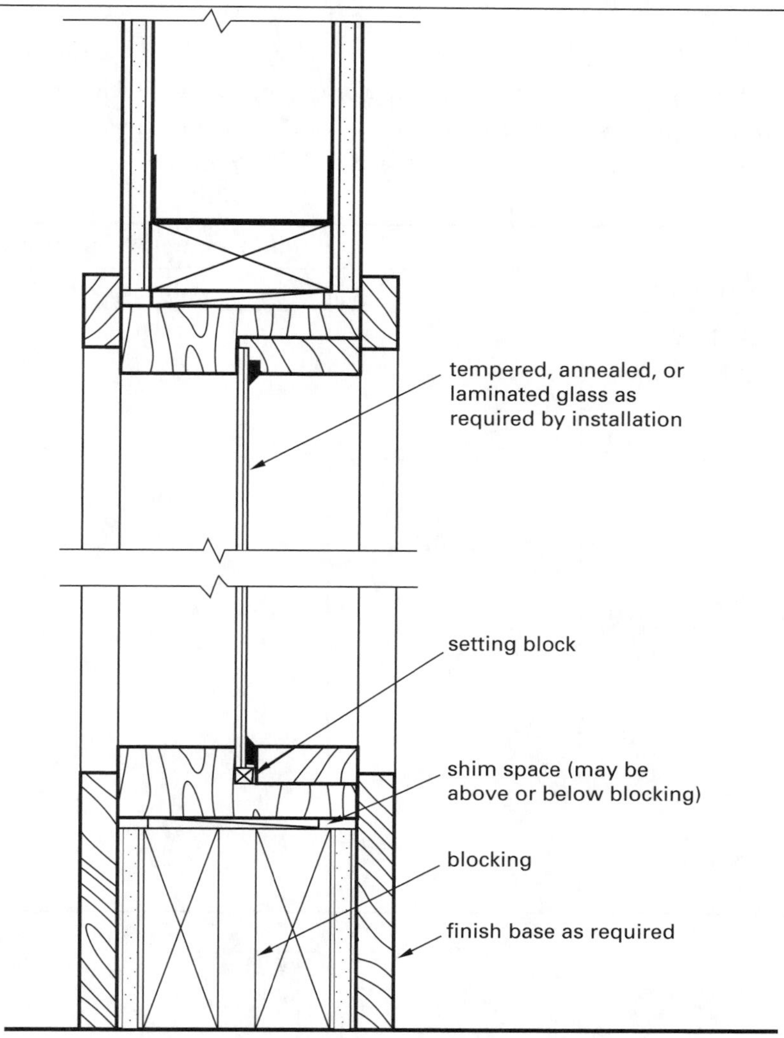

setting block

shim space (may be above or below blocking)

blocking

finish base as required

Note: If the sill is raised much above the height of the base, the space below the sill is framed as a partition instead of with blocking.

**Figure 5.3**
Head and sill of wood frame

stops should be filled with one of several appropriate glazing compounds. For interior glazing, this is usually silicone sealant or a preformed glazing tape of neoprene or another elastomeric material. In some instances, small pieces of glass can be held in place directly against wood stops. However, this is generally not recommended because uneven or point pressures can cause the glass to crack.

Generally, ¼ in thick (6 mm) glass should be used for most interior glazing. Small openings, such as pass-through windows and observation ports, can be glazed with double-strength ⅛ in (3 mm) or $\frac{3}{16}$ in (5 mm) glass. Thicker glass is used for very large openings or where the glass is adjacent to a glass door without a frame. Tempered or laminated glass must be used in hazardous locations. Refer to a later section of this chapter for detailed requirements for safety glazing.

## Steel framing

Interior steel glass framing (also called hollow-metal framing, like door framing) is typically required for fire-rated openings or where the designer wants to match nearby hollow-metal door framing. Frames are fabricated of 16- or 18-gage steel bent to standard or custom profiles. Because they are fabricated by bending, the corners have

## Framing clearances for interior glass

For standard glazing methods, framing clearances are the dimensions from the face and edges of the glass to the frame. For interior glazing, these dimensions are not as critical as for windows because there is no wind load or thermal movement. However, some recommended minimum dimensions are shown in Table 5.3.

**Table 5.3** Recommended face and edge clearances for interior glass

| thickness (in (mm)) | minimum clearance (in (mm)) | | |
|---|---|---|---|
| | face | edge | bite |
| 1/8 (3) | 1/8 (3.2) | 1/4 (6.4) | 3/8 (9.5) |
| 3/16 (5) | 1/8 (3.2) | 1/4 (6.4) | 3/8 (9.5) |
| 1/4 (6) | 1/8 (3.2) | 1/4 (6.4) | 3/8 (9.5) |
| 5/16 (8) | 3/16 (4.8) | 5/16 (7.9) | 7/16 (11.1) |
| 3/8 (10) | 3/16 (4.8) | 5/16 (7.9) | 7/16 (11.1) |
| 1/2 (12) | 1/4 (6.4) | 3/8 (9.5) | 7/16 (11.5) |
| 3/4 (19) | 1/4 (6.4) | 1/2 (12.7) | 5/8 (15.9) |

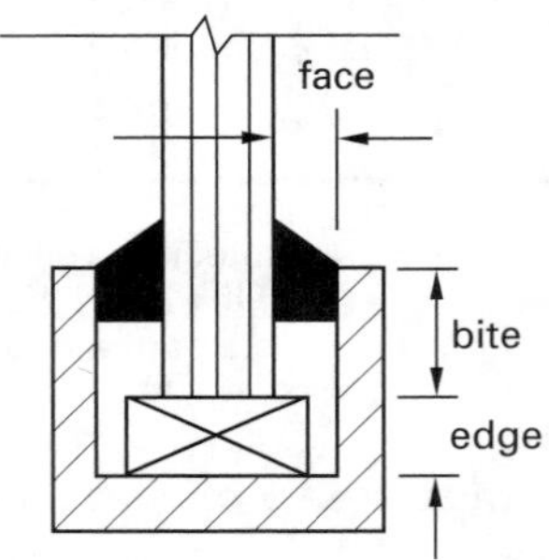


Note: Verify the dimensions with the manufacturer.

Reprinted with permission from the GANA *Glazing Manual,* copyright 1997, Glass Association of North America, 2945 SW Wanamaker Drive, Suite A, Topeka, KS 66614-5321, phone: (785) 271-0208, fax: (785) 271-0166, www.glasswebsite.com.

a slightly rounded profile. Figures 5.4 and 5.5 show two standard glass frame profiles similar to door frame profiles.

Like wood frames, there must be a removable stop to provide for glass installation and replacement. Most hollow-metal glass frames have visible screw heads where the stop is attached to the frame.

### Aluminum framing

Aluminum glass frames are used where a fire rating is not required, but where the other advantages of a metal frame are needed: durability, easy fabrication, and compatibility with aluminum door framing. Because they are extruded, aluminum frames have sharp corners, which some designers prefer over the rounded corners of steel frames. In

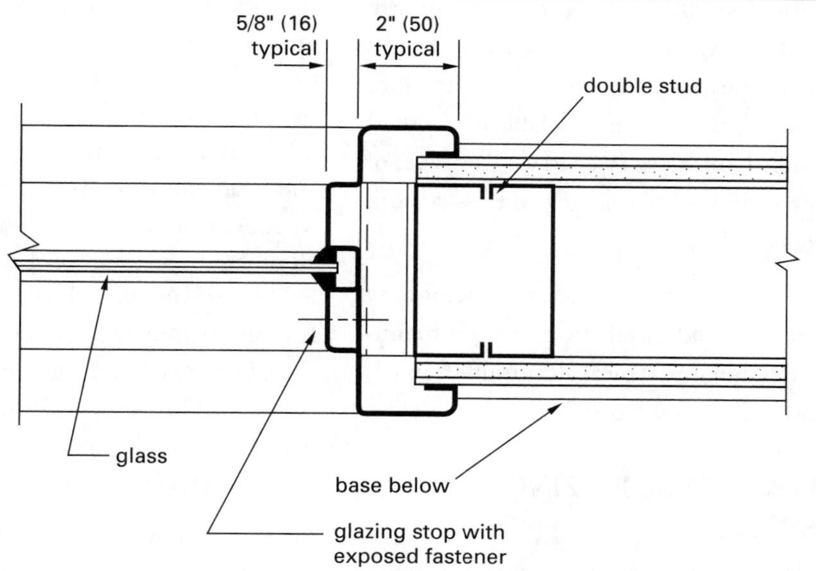


**Figure 5.4**
Double-rabbet steel frame

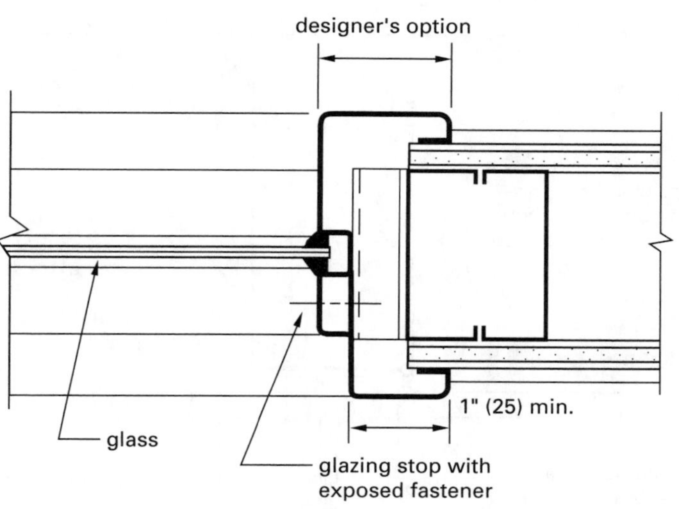


**Figure 5.5**
Single-rabbet steel frame

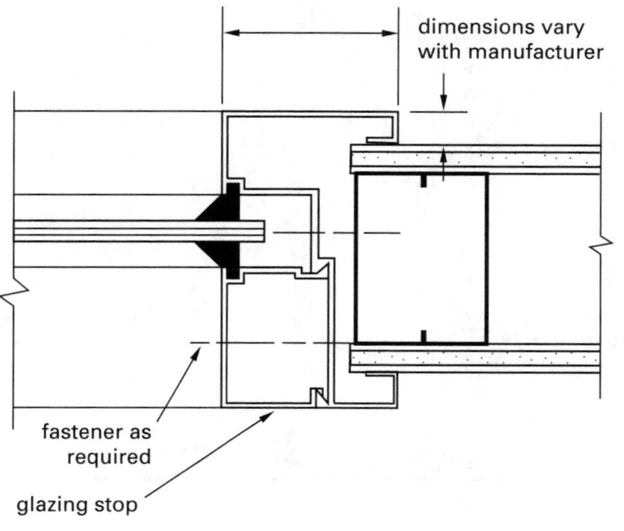


**Figure 5.6**
Typical aluminum frame

addition, glazing stops on most aluminum framing snap into place so there are no unsightly exposed fasteners. As with door frames, glass frames are available in standard anodized finishes, as well as various types of colored finishes. For large projects, custom colors can be specified.

Exact shapes, sizes, finishes, and methods of fabrication and installation vary by manufacturer, but one typical aluminum frame is illustrated in Fig. 5.6.

## FRAMELESS GLAZING [088100]

Frameless glazing minimizes the appearance of head, sill, and jamb framing for glass. Instead, the glass seems to float within an opening with the finish materials appearing to continue uninterrupted from one side of the glass to the other. In most situations, minimal framing is provided at the sill and head and is recessed into the structure to conceal it. Jamb framing is completely eliminated, and the edge of the glass is simply held away from the wall a fraction of an inch. If more than one panel of glass is required, the edges are butted together, and the joint is filled with silicone sealant. In some cases, where sound or draft control are not required, the joints are left open.

Figure 5.7 shows a common method of framing the sill and head of a single piece of glass that extends from the floor to a suspended

**Figure 5.7** Frameless glazing at head and sill

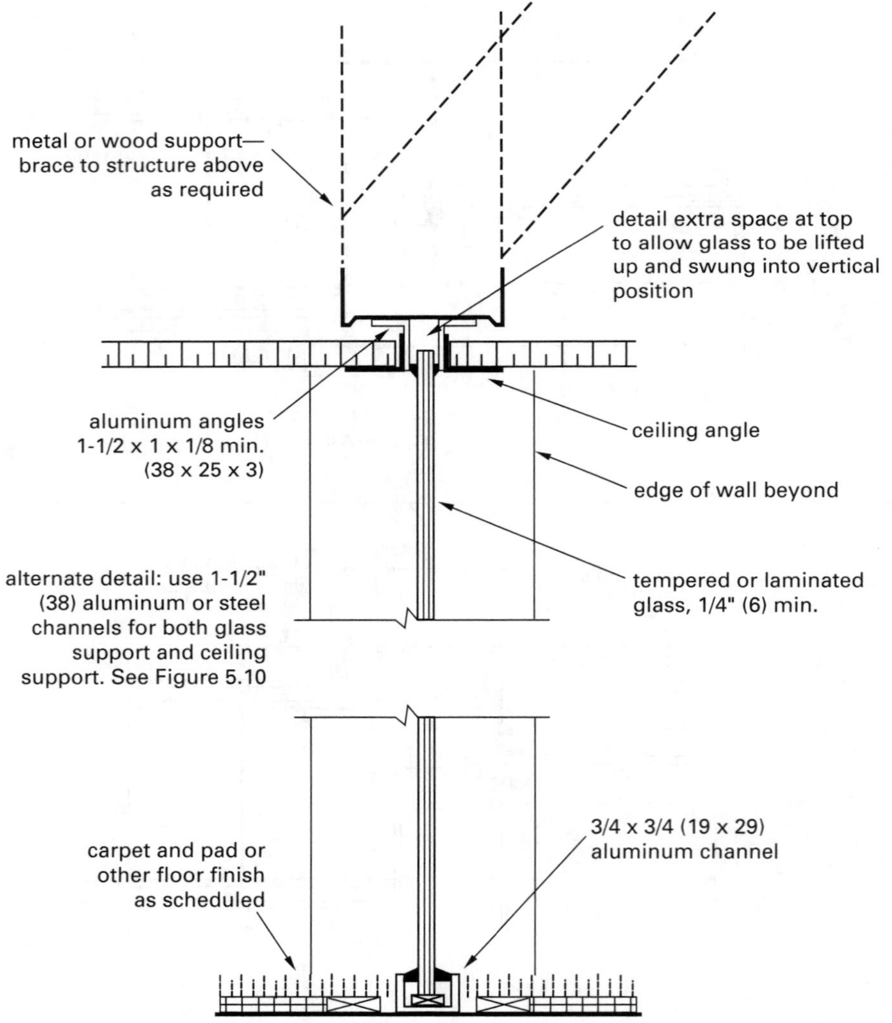

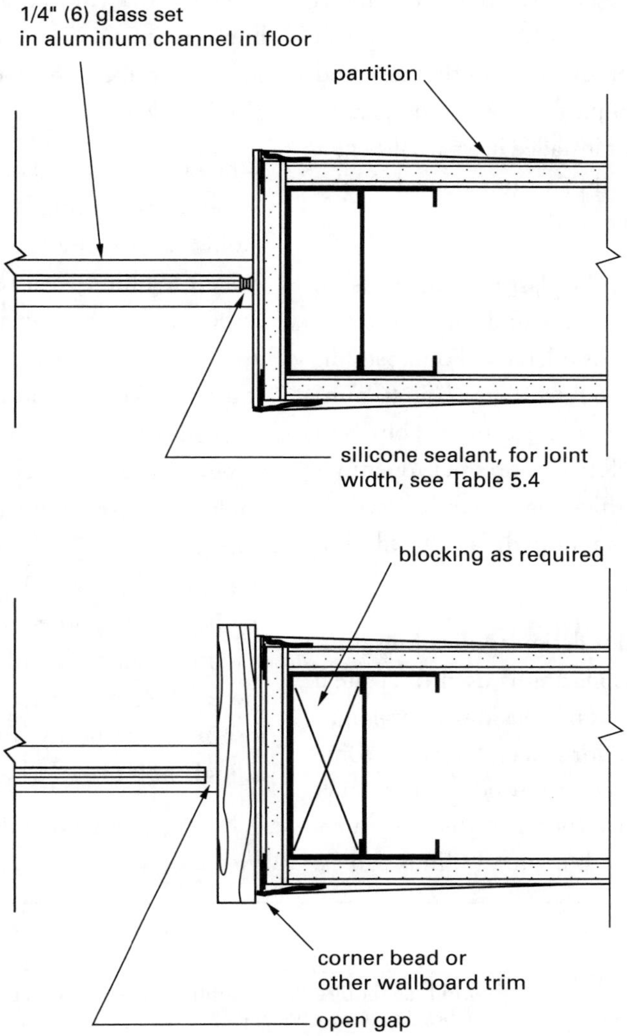

**Figure 5.8**
Frameless glazing at jamb

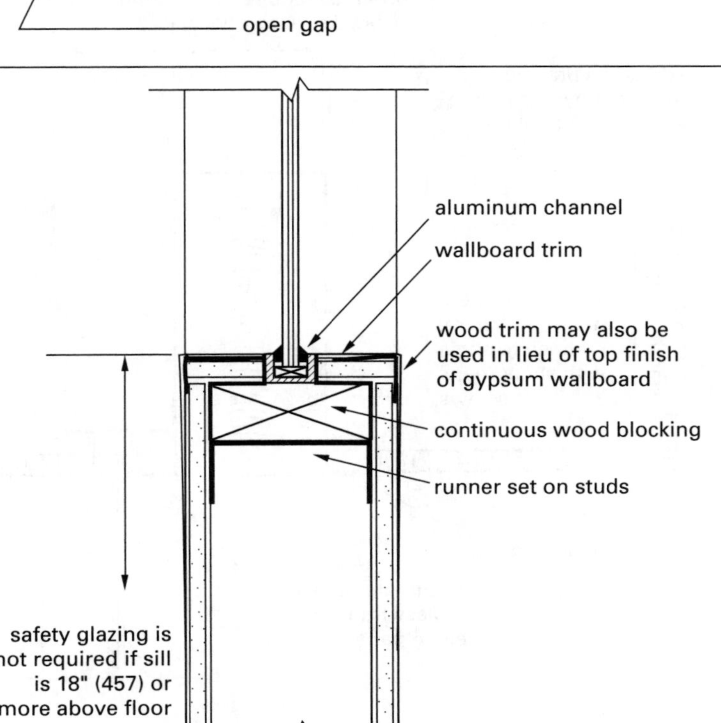


**Figure 5.9**
Glass in a partial-height partition

ceiling. Figure 5.8 shows two possible methods of treating the jamb: by letting the wall finish continue through the plane of the glass, and by installing a simple frame without a glazing stop. If the glass is installed in a partial-height gypsum wallboard partition, a detail similar to Fig. 5.9 can be used.

The thickness of the glass used depends on the size of the opening and the amount of glass "shake" that is tolerable. For most full-height glazing of 8 ft to 10 ft, a ¼ in (6 mm) thick tempered glass is acceptable, but ⅜ in (10 mm) is preferred. For small openings 3/16 in (5 mm) thick glass may be used. If sound control is required, laminated glass should be used.

For many interior design applications, full-height frameless glazing is used to create a sense of openness and to allow natural light to penetrate interior spaces. However, some provisions for privacy may be required, such as in a conference room. In this case, a recessed pocket for horizontal blinds can be installed adjacent to the glass to conceal the blinds when they are retracted. Figure 5.10 shows one method of detailing a recessed blind pocket.

When the edges of glass are butted together without any framing, minimum dimensions should be maintained to allow adequate space for filling with sealant, if it is used. Either clear or black silicone sealant can be used, but clear sealant often shows bubbles and can be visually more objectionable than black silicone. Figures 5.11(a)–5.11(d) show some common frameless joint configurations. Table 5.4 gives recommended joint widths for butt-joint glazing. The T-joint illustrated in Fig. 5.11(d) shows one piece of glass extending beyond the other two. This is generally a better way to handle three intersecting pieces of glass, because it is very difficult to install sealant neatly if three edges meet at a single point.

When very large openings must be glazed without frames, or when two or more pieces

**Figure 5.10**
Recessed blind pocket

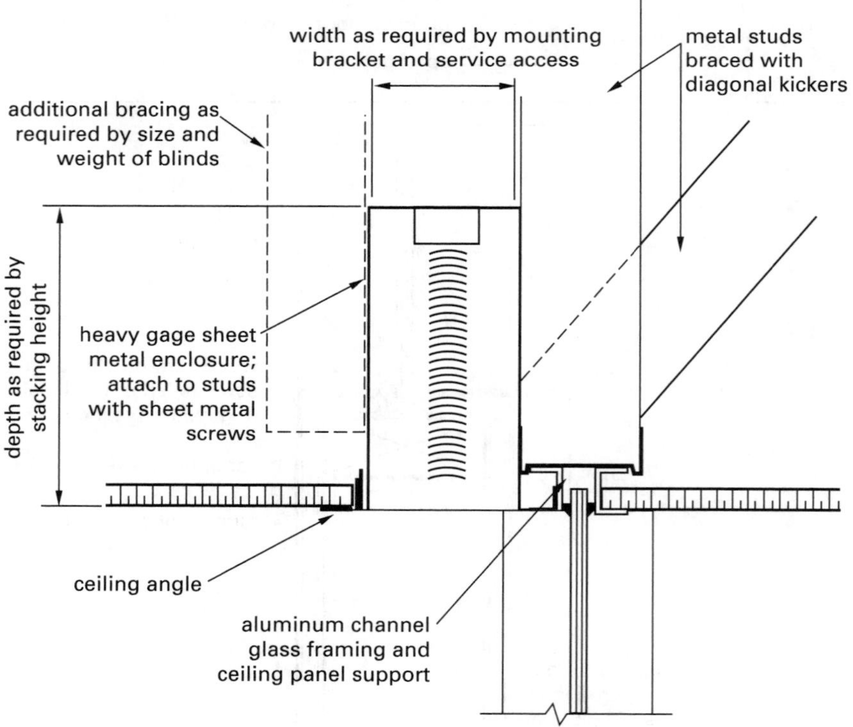

**Figure 5.11** Frameless glazing joints

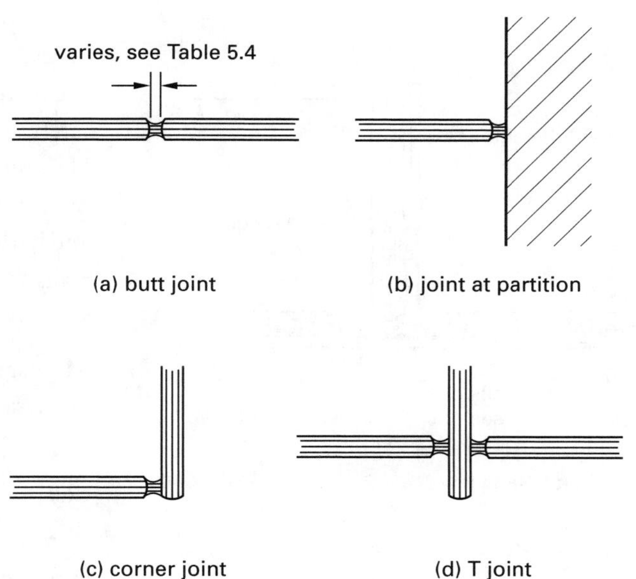


**Table 5.4** Recommended joint widths for butt-joint glazing

| glass thickness (in (mm)) | joint width, minimum (in (mm)) | joint width, maximum (in (mm)) |
|---|---|---|
| 3/8 (10) | 3/8 (10) | 7/16 (11) |
| 1/2 (12) | 3/8 (10) | 7/16 (11) |
| 5/8 (16) | 3/8 (10) | 1/2 (12) |
| 3/4 (19) | 1/2 (12) | 5/8 (15) |
| 7/8 (22) | 1/2 (12) | 5/8 (15) |

Reprinted with permission from the GANA *Glazing Manual,* copyright 1997, Glass Marketing Association of North America.

of glass must be stacked on top of one another without frames, an all-glass glazing system is used. This type of glazing system consists of glass walls supported only at the top and bottom by framing with lateral support provided by glass fins mounted perpendicular to the primary glass plane. Individual pieces of glass are connected with special patch fittings, and joints are sealed with silicone sealant. All-glass systems are capable of spanning vertically up to 30 ft (9 m) if the weight of the glass is carried by the base, and up to 75 ft (23 m) if the upper sections of glass are suspended from special clamps attached to an adequate structural support.

Because the vertical supports are glass and the top and bottom framing members can be recessed into the ceiling and floor, this system provides an almost completely

**Figure 5.12**
All-glass glazing system

glass mullion
structural support
line of finished wall
as required by wind loading
glass
silicone sealant
patch fitting

(a) plan view

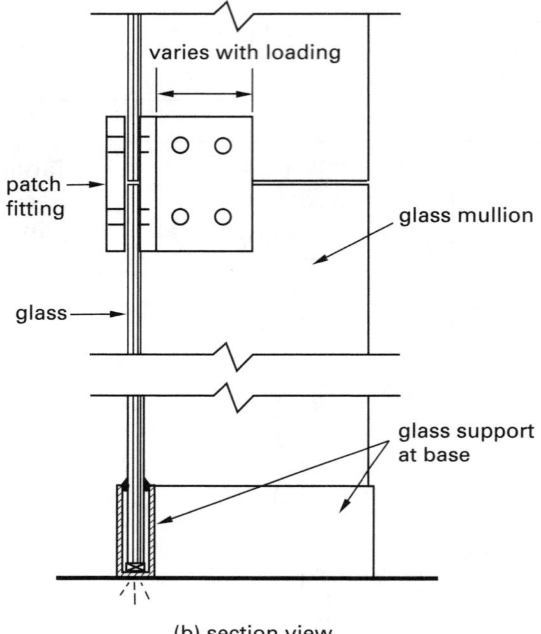


(b) section view

unobstructed view opening. Glass doors can be used with the system by using special patch fittings that are similar to those described in Ch. 3 and shown in Fig. 3.22.

Figures 5.12(a) and 5.12(b) show typical vertical and horizontal sections for an all-glass system. For many interior applications where the vertical span is not great, the glass can be supported by the floor framing and the patch fittings without using glass mullions.

## SAFETY GLAZING [088100]

In addition to regulating the type and amount of glass in fire-rated assemblies, building codes and federal regulations require that safety glazing be used in hazardous areas. Hazardous locations are those subject to human impact, such as glass in doors, shower and bath enclosures, and certain locations in walls. Tempered glass and laminated glass are considered safety glazings.

More specifically, hazardous locations that require safety glazing include the following.

- swinging doors (including storm doors), except jalousies
- fixed and sliding panels of sliding doors and panels in sliding and bi-fold closet doors
- unframed swinging doors
- doors and enclosures for hot tubs, whirlpools, saunas, steam rooms, bathtubs, and showers. This includes glass in any portion of a building wall enclosing these compartments where the bottom exposed edge of the glazing is less than 60 in (1524 mm) above a standing surface.
- guards and railings, including structural baluster panels and nonstructural in-fill panels, regardless of area or height above a walking surface
- panels within 36 in (914 mm) of a walking surface measured horizontally to the plane of the glazing. There are several conditions and exceptions to this requirement, shown graphically in Fig. 5.13.
- panels adjacent to a door where the nearest exposed edge of the glazing is within 24 in (610 mm) of the door. See Fig. 5.13.

To be considered safety glazing, glass must be tested in accordance with the requirement of 16 CFR 1201, *Safety Standard for Architectural Glazing Materials*. This standard establishes two categories of glazing: category I and category II. Category I material is tested using an impact load of 150 ft-lbf (203 N·m), and category II material

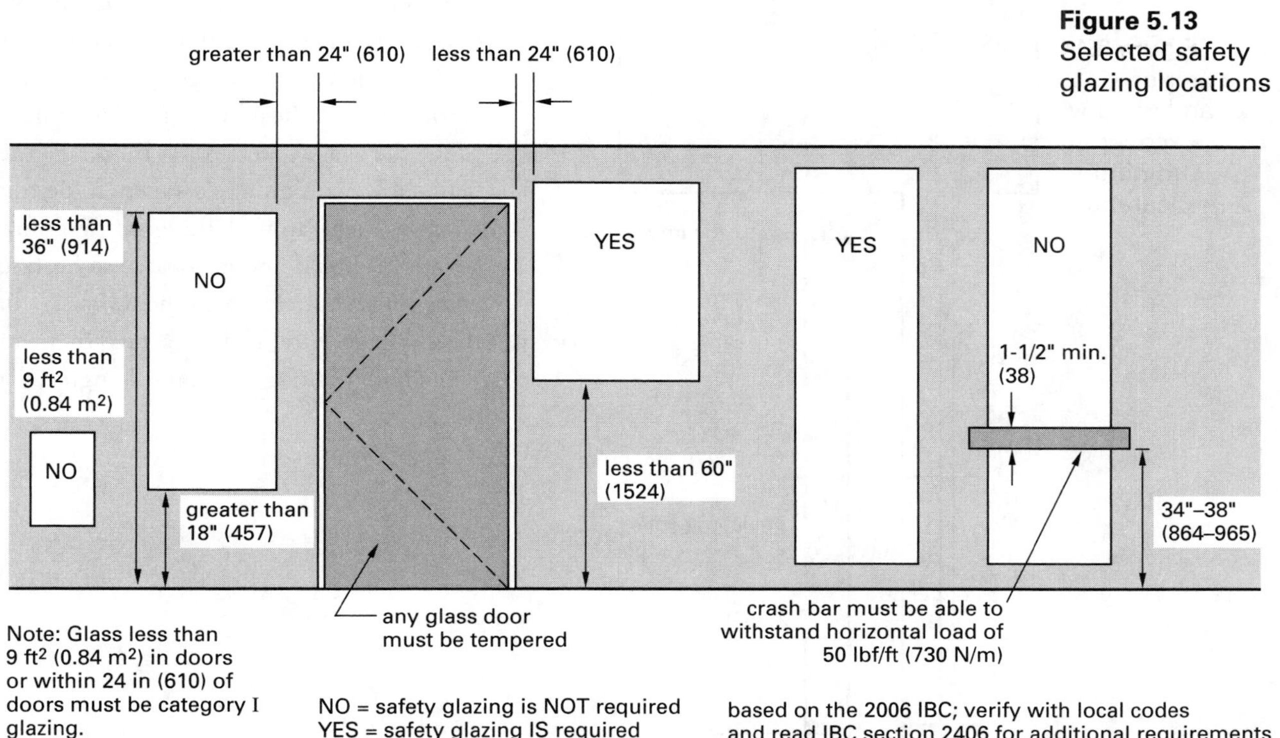


**Figure 5.13**
Selected safety glazing locations

is testing with an impact load of 400 ft-lbf (542 N·m). For hazardous locations greater than 9 ft² in area (0.836 m²), category II glass must be used. Category II glass must also be used in panels less than 9 ft² if they are in doors and enclosures around pool and sauna areas or if they are in sliding patio doors. Otherwise, panels less than 9 ft² in area are only required to have category I glass. There are no requirements for fixed panels less than 9 ft² adjacent to a walking surface.

Refer to Sec. 2406 of the IBC for complete requirements and exceptions.

The National Building Code of Canada is a little less prescriptive. It requires tempered or laminated glass in doors, shower enclosures, and glass sidelights greater than 500 mm (1 ft 7⅝ in) wide.

## COORDINATION

- For large sheets of glass, verify the maximum size that can be transported into the building through stairways or elevators.
- Specify horizontally tempered glass to avoid visible tong marks in frameless glazing.
- If patterned or etched glass is used, include in the details which way the patterned or etched side should face.
- If frameless glazing is used adjacent to a glass door, the thickness of the glass should match the thickness of the door, for the best appearance.
- Consider a design for markings on full-height glass to prevent people from running into large glazed areas. Even though the glass is tempered and strong enough to withstand impact, people are injured trying to walk through what looks like an opening. Alternately, furniture, plants, or other objects can be designed for placement in front of glazing.
- Detail glass stops for the side of the partition where appearance is least important, because fasteners, joints, and glazing tape or sealant on the stop side are usually not as neat as they are on the opposite side.

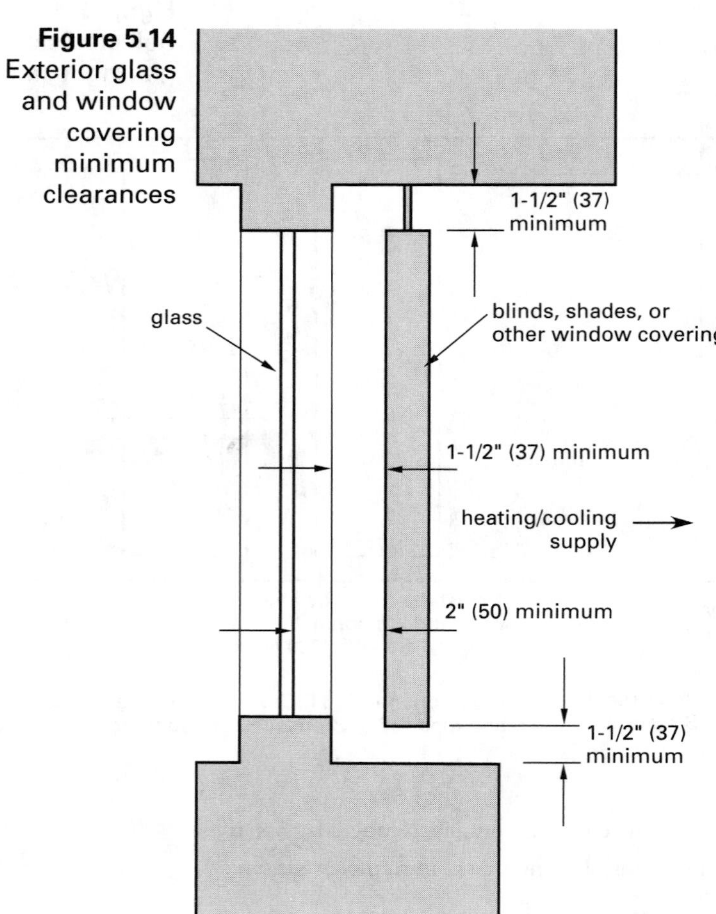


**Figure 5.14** Exterior glass and window covering minimum clearances

• When detailing and specifying window coverings, maintain sufficient clearances between the window covering and exterior glazing to avoid heat buildup, which might cause the glass to crack or break. Figure 5.14 shows minimum clearances to permit air movement around the glass. Window coverings should also be located so heating and cooling outlets are on the room side of the shading device. Verify exact requirement with the building's mechanical engineer if necessary.

# 6

# ARCHITECTURAL WOODWORK

Architectural woodwork is custom, shop-fabricated millwork built of lumber, finished wood, and other materials. It typically includes cabinetry, paneling, custom doors and frames, shelving, stair work and handrails, blinds and shutters, custom furniture, and special interior trim. Architectural woodwork makes it possible to produce superior wood items because most of the work is done under carefully controlled factory conditions with machinery and finishing techniques that cannot be duplicated on a job site.

Two related types of woodwork are finish carpentry and modular casework. However, architectural woodwork differs from these types in that it is custom designed and fabricated for a particular job and it is built in a factory.

Finish carpentry is woodwork assembled at the job site by finish carpenters. It includes such items as installation of doors and windows, door and window trim, standard wood base, site-built stairways, and handrails. Finish carpentry is commonly used in residential construction and commercial construction where there is a limited amount of woodwork or where cost is a consideration.

Modular casework is mass-produced cabinetry from a manufacturer's standard set of details adapted for a particular project. Although it is fabricated in a factory, there are a limited number of sizes and styles from which to select. Modular casework is typically used in institutional buildings, such as schools, hospitals, and laboratories, where economy, consistent appearance, and serviceability are important considerations. On a residential scale, prefabricated kitchen and bath cabinets are a type of modular casework.

Many aspects of architectural woodwork fabrication have been standardized by the Architectural Woodwork Institute (AWI), a nonprofit trade association representing its member architectural woodwork manufacturers of the United States and Canada and by the Woodwork Institute of California. They are described in great detail in the *Architectural Woodwork Quality Standards, Guide Specifications and Quality Certification Program. Quality Standards* provides information about standard construction techniques, describes standards and tests that can be used to ensure compliance, and provides a means of specifying by using the *Standards* as reference specifications. Although the AWI *Quality Standards* are voluntary, they are widely used in the commercial interior construction industry.

## FINISH CARPENTRY [062000]

Although finish carpentry cannot be installed with the same level of quality as factory-built architectural woodwork, it is adequate for a variety of interior finishes in residential and some commercial construction. However, the types of materials used and specification methods are different from those of architectural woodwork.

### Materials and grading

Lumber used for finish carpentry is a regional material, and the available species vary depending on location. Common species include Douglas fir, ponderosa pine, sugar pine, Idaho white pine, southern pine, western red cedar, poplar, oak, and redwood, among others. Local suppliers can provide information on available species and grades.

For interior construction, one of the most important aspects of specifying finish carpentry is the grade, which determines the type and number of allowable defects. Grading rules vary depending on the species and the trade organization responsible. Some of the more common grades for softwood shop lumber are summarized in Tables 6.1–6.3. For most species, B & Better is the highest

**Table 6.1**
Selected grades for appearance grades of western lumber

| grade category | grade | description |
|---|---|---|
| selects | B & Better | Highest quality of select grade lumber available with many pieces absolutely clear and free of defects. |
| | C Select | Appearance only slightly less than B & Better. Recommended for high-quality interior trim and cabinetwork with natural stain or enamel finishes. |
| | D Select | Allows more defects than C Select grade but is suitable where finish requirements are less exacting. |
| finish | Superior; Superior VG | Highest quality of Finish grade lumber available with many pieces absolutely clear. Used for high-quality trim and cabinetwork where natural, stain, or enamel finishes are used and the finest appearance is required. Can be specified as VG for vertical grain. |
| | Prime; Prime VG | Allows slightly more defects than Superior, but can be used where finishing requirements are less exacting. Can be specified as VG for vertical grain. |
| | E | Boards in this grade can be cut in such a way as to produce pieces of Prime or Superior grades. E-grade boards must contain two-thirds or more of such cuttings 2 in (50 mm) or wider and 16 in (406 mm) or longer. |
| paneling | any select or finish grade | C Select or any other grade can be used to produce paneling. |
| | Select 2 common for knotty paneling | Grade reserved for knotty paneling made from number 2 Common grade boards (not shown in this table). |

Note: Additional grades are available but they are commonly used for other architectural purposes.

available grade and is excellent for natural finishes or painted finishes. However, its supply is limited. C Select has only slightly more defects and is usually the best grade to specify for painting and some natural finishes. It is also possible with some species to specify either vertical or flat grain, which describes how the board is cut from the tree. Vertical grain wood is cut so that the annual growth rings are perpendicular, or almost perpendicular, to the face of the board. Vertical grain boards tend to warp less, are more abrasion resistant, and stain more uniformly than flat grain boards. The grades in the Finish category are similar to the Select grades and are usually used to grade Douglas fir and hem-fir, which is a combination of hemlock and fir.

## Plywood

Plywood is a panel product made from an odd number of layers of thin veneer glued together under heat and pressure. Each adjacent ply is laid in a direction perpendicular to the ply next to it. Plywood suitable for natural, stain, and painted finishes is commonly used in finish carpentry construction. Plywood is available in several thicknesses, including ¼, ⅜, ½, ⅝, and ¾ in (6, 10, 13, 16, and 19 mm). The standard sheet size is 4 ft by 8 ft (1219 mm by 2438 mm). Common finished surfaces are softwoods (such as fir), but surfaces of birch and oak veneer are also available where a smooth, finished surface suitable for painting or stain, respectively, is required. Medium density overlay (MDO) is also used where a smooth surface is needed for painting.

Plywood is graded based on the quality of the face veneer. The grades suitable for interior construction include N, A, and B. N grade is the highest quality and is intended for natural finishes. It is cut from 100% heartwood and is free from knots and splits, with only minor defects permitted. The veneer is well matched

**Table 6.2** Finish lumber grades for southern pine

| grade | description |
|---|---|
| B & Better | Highest quality available. Generally clear of defects, although a limited number of pin knots are permitted. Used for finest quality for natural or stain finish. |
| C | Almost clear but permits limited number of small tight knots and surface checks. Excellent grade for painted or natural finish where requirements are less exacting. |
| C & Better | Combination of B & Better and C grades. |
| D | More defects allowed, but usable for painted finishes where appearance is not critical. |

**Table 6.3** Redwood lumber grades for interior use

| grade | description |
|---|---|
| Clear, all heart | Highest quality of redwood available. Free of defects on one face although the reverse face may have slight imperfections. |
| Clear | Same quality as Clear, all heart, but contains some sapwood. |
| B Grade | Contains limited number of knots and other imperfections not allowed in Clear, all heart or Clear. |

Note: Additional grades are available but they are commonly used for structural purposes.

for color and grain continuity. Grade A is suitable for a smooth, painted finish. It is generally free of defects, and what minor defects are allowed are patched with fillers for a uniform, smooth surface. Grade B is generally not used for finished surfaces, except for utility shelving and similar uses. The surface is solid and free from open defects, but some knots, pitch streaks, and other minor imperfections are allowed.

When large, flat sheets are required for structural purposes instead of a finished surface, either plywood or particleboard is used. Particleboard is composed of small wood particles, fibers, or chips mixed together in a binder and formed under pressure into a panel. Like plywood, it is available in several thicknesses in 4 ft by 8 ft (1219 mm by 2438 mm) sheets. It is generally preferred for backing and framing of finish carpentry and architectural woodwork because it is less expensive and more dimensionally stable than plywood. Common thicknesses include ⅜, ½, ¾, and 1¼ in (10, 13, 19, and 32 mm).

**Figure 6.1**
Standard wood molding profiles

## Molding

Molding is trim used for decorative or functional purposes. For finish carpentry construction, standard profiles of molding are available in softwood and hardwood. A few representative profiles are shown in Fig. 6.1, although there are over a hundred available. In most cases, the standard molding profiles for base, casing trim, cornices, chair rails, handrails, and other applications are adequate. However, custom profiles can be detailed and specified when standard trim will not work. This is commonly done in commercial construction when molding made from a particular species of wood is

**Applicable standards for finish carpentry**

Hardwood Plywood and Veneer Association: ANSI/HPVA HP-1-2004, *American National Standard for Hardwood and Decorative Plywood*

Northeastern Lumber Manufacturers Association: *NeLMA Standard Grading Rules for Northeastern Lumber*

American Plywood Association: *US Product Standard PS 1-95 for Construction and Industrial Plywood*

Western Wood Products Association: *Western Lumber Grading Rules*

Wood Moulding and Millwork Producers Association: *WM Series Softwood Moulding Patterns Catalog*; *HWM Series Hardwood Moulding Patterns Catalog* not available. Refer to the section on standing and running trim for more information on custom wood molding.

## LUMBER [064000]

The raw material for architectural woodwork is broadly classified as either softwood or hardwood. Softwood refers to timber from evergreen trees, such as pine and fir; hardwood refers to timber from deciduous trees, such as oak and maple. The names are slightly misleading because many softwoods are physically quite hard and many hardwoods are actually soft.

Timber is manufactured into two forms for use in architectural woodwork: solid stock lumber and veneer. As the name implies, solid stock is a thick piece of lumber (generally ½ in [13 mm], or thicker) used alone to form some woodwork component. A veneer is a thin piece of wood (usually less than 1/16 in [1.6 mm]) sliced from a log and glued to some type of backing, usually particleboard.

### Lumber sources

Wood comes from a variety of locations throughout the world including North America, Central America, South America, Africa, Europe, India, Southeast Asia, Malaysia, Indonesia, and the Philippines. Most timber for architectural woodwork is manufactured into solid stock or veneer. However, as costs rise and availability decreases, other types of manufactured lumber products may be used in interior construction. Currently, products like oriented strand-board, glued-laminated timber, end-glued lumber, and composite wood beams are manufactured from wood products that were formerly considered waste.

The species of wood refers to the type of tree from which the lumber is taken. There are hundreds of species of wood that can be used for architectural woodwork and furniture, but only several dozen are used predominantly because of availability and cost. The designer's choice of a species depends on the availability and cost as well as how appropriate a species is for the intended use. Some species are so rare that they are only available as a veneer and not as solid stock. Local mill shops and lumber and veneer suppliers can provide information on availability and current costs. Table 6.4 lists some common hardwood species and their characteristics.

### Lumber cutting methods

The way lumber is cut from a log determines the final appearance of the grain pattern. There are three ways solid stock is cut from a log: plain sawing (also called flat sawing), quarter sawing, and rift sawing. These methods are illustrated in Fig. 6.2.

Because of the limited availability of some species of wood and the expense of making certain cuts, not all types of lumber cutting are available in all species. The availability of cuts in the desired species should be verified before specifications are written.

#### Plain sawing

Plain sawing makes the most efficient use of the log and is the least expensive of the three methods. Because the wood is cut with various orientations to the grain of the tree, plain sawing results in a finished surface with the characteristic cathedral pattern shown in Fig. 6.2(a).

#### Quarter sawing

Quarter sawing is produced by cutting the log into quarters and then sawing toward the center. Because the saw cut is nearly perpendicular to the grain, the resulting grain pattern is more uniformly vertical. See Fig. 6.2(b). Not only does this result in a different appearance than plain sawing, but quarter sawn boards also tend to twist and cup less, shrink less in width, hold paint better, and have fewer defects. Quarter sawing is more expensive than plain sawing.

**Table 6.4**
Comparative characteristics of selected hardwood species

| common name | common use | veneer availability | lumber availability | cost range | color |
|---|---|---|---|---|---|
| afrormosia | P, F | L | L | 3 | yellow to warm-brown; similar to teak |
| ash | | | | | |
| olive burl | F | A | L | 3 | white and brown burly pattern |
| white | T, C, F | A | A | 2 | cream to light brown |
| avodire | P, C, F | L | L | 3 | white to creamy gold |
| beech | F | A | A | 1 | white to reddish-brown |
| birch | | | | | |
| yellow birch | P, T, C, F | A | A | 1 | cream/light-brown tinged with red |
| select red | P, T, C, F | A | A | 2 | light-brown to reddish-brown |
| select white | P, T, C, F | A | A | 2 | creamy-white |
| bubinga | T, C | L | A | 3 | red with streaks of purple |
| butternut | P, T, C, F | L | L | 2 | warm buttery tan |
| cherry | P, T, C, F | A | A | 2 | reddish-brown |
| chestnut | P, T | R | R | 3 | light brown |
| cypress, yellow | P, F | L | A | 2 | yellowish-brown/red |
| ebony, macassar | P, F | A | L | 3 | dark-brown to black; streaked with yellowish-brown |
| elm | | | | | |
| American | P, F | A | A | 2 | light grayish-brown |
| slippery | P, F | A | A | 2 | reddish-brown heartwood; light brown sapwood |
| hickory, shagbark | F | A | A | 2 | creamy to reddish heartwood |
| lauan | | | | | |
| red | P, C, F | A | A | 1 | red to brown |
| white | C, F | A | A | 1 | light to grayish-brown to light reddish brown |
| limba | P, T, C, F | L | L | 2 | pale-yellow to light brown |
| mahogany | | | | | |
| African | P, T, C, F | L | L | 2 | reddish-brown to tannish-brown |
| Honduras | P, T, C, F | L | L | 2 | reddish-brown to tannish-brown |
| maple | | | | | |
| hard | C, F | L | A | 2 | cream to light reddish-brown |
| select white | C, F | L | A | 2 | creamy |
| birdseye | C, F | L | A | 3 | highly figured |
| soft | C, F | A | A | 1 | may contain dark streaks |
| oak | | | | | |
| red, northern | P, T, C, F | A | A | 2 | light-brown with reddish tinge |
| white | P, T, C, F | A | A | 2 | light-brown with shades of ochre |
| English brown | P, T, C | L | L | 3 | light-tan to deep brown |
| orientalwood | C, F | L | L | 3 | pinkish-gray to brown |
| paldao | P, T, C, F | L | L | 2 | gray to reddish-brown |
| pecan | P, F | A | A | 2 | reddish-brown heartwood, creamy sapwood |
| persimmon | F | L | L | 2 | light-brown with dark stripes |
| poplar, yellow | C | A | A | 1 | yellowish with slight greenish cast |
| rosewood | | | | | |
| Brazilian | P, T, C, F | L | R | 3 | dark-brown with black streaks |
| East Indian | P, F | L | L | 3 | dark-purple to ebony |
| sapele | C, F | A | A | 2 | dark red-brown |
| teak | P, C, F | A | L | 3 | tawny-yellow to light brown |
| tupelo | P | A | A | 1 | creamy to yellowish with brownish-streaked heartwood |
| walnut, black | P, T, C, F | A | A | 3 | gray-brown to dark brown |
| zebrawood | P | A | L | 3 | straw to dark-brown |

common uses:
P = paneling
T = trim
C = cabinetry
F = furniture

availability:
A = generally available
L = limited
R = rare

cost range:
1 = moderate
2 = high
3 = expensive

## Rift sawing

Rift sawing provides an even more consistent vertical grain because the saw cuts are always made radially to the center of the tree. Because the log must be shifted after each cut and because there is a great deal of waste, rift cutting is more expensive than quarter sawing and is seldom used, except for oak and a few other species.

## Lumber grading

Grading the quality of lumber for solid stock used in architectural woodwork is done differently from standard industry grading for shop lumber and plywood, which has been described in the previous section. The AWI has established three grades, Grades I, II, and III. The AWI standards establish the sizes of pieces that must be furnished free and clear of all natural or seasoning characteristics, which are considered defects. The standards also give the number of square inches per defect in boards larger than the required size that are free and clear of all defects. Although these three grades are not specified directly by the interior designer, the AWI *Quality Standards* do refer to them when defining the characteristics of a construction component under premium, custom, and economy grades that the designer does specify. For example, a premium grade handrail that is designed to have a transparent finish must be constructed of Grade I lumber, while Grade II lumber may be used to construct a custom grade handrail.

## Standard sizes

Because architectural woodwork is custom fabricated, almost any component can be detailed to whatever size is required without using standard sizes of boards as with finish carpentry. However, lumber for woodwork is manufactured in standard thicknesses, and it makes good economic sense to use these thicknesses to minimize waste, thereby reducing costs.

Lumber thickness for millwork is expressed in "quarters," which refers to quarter-inch increments. Thus, the thickness of a 5/4 piece of lumber is nominally 1¼ in (32 mm). However, this is the thickness before drying and surfacing. The actual finished thickness is less than the nominal thickness, and it is important to know the actual thicknesses to be able to economically detail woodwork. Table 6.5 gives the nominal and actual thicknesses of softwoods and hardwoods.

Although all the thicknesses may be available, for construction components that exceed 1 1/16 in (27 mm) for hardwoods and

**Figure 6.2**
Lumber cutting methods

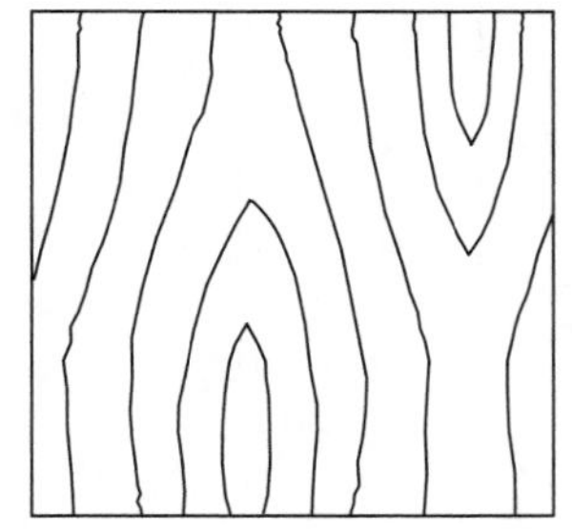
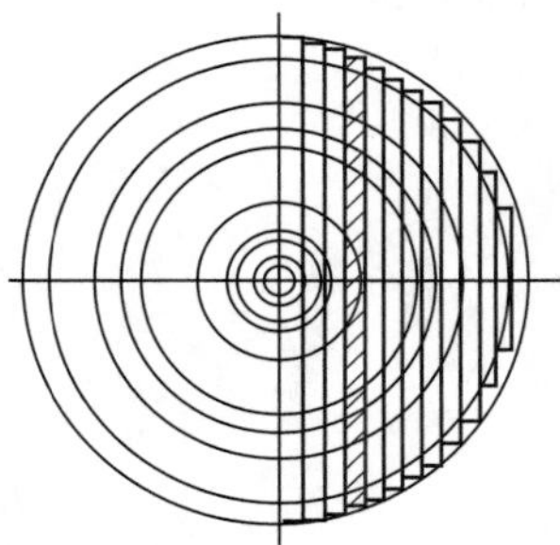

(a) plain sawing

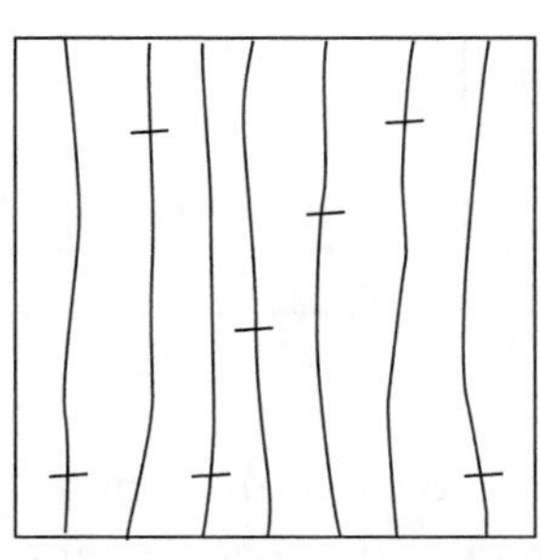
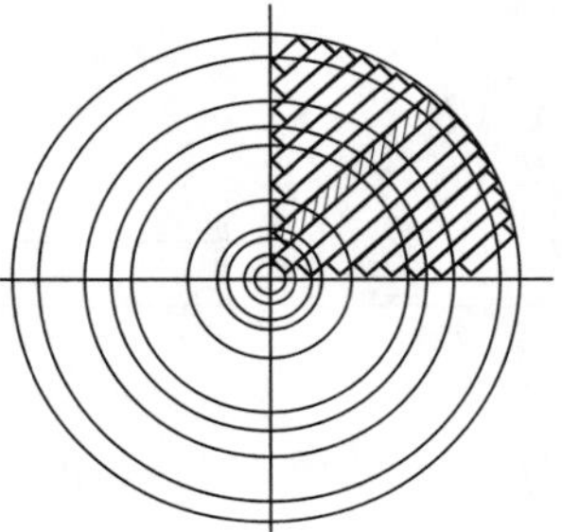

(b) quarter sawing

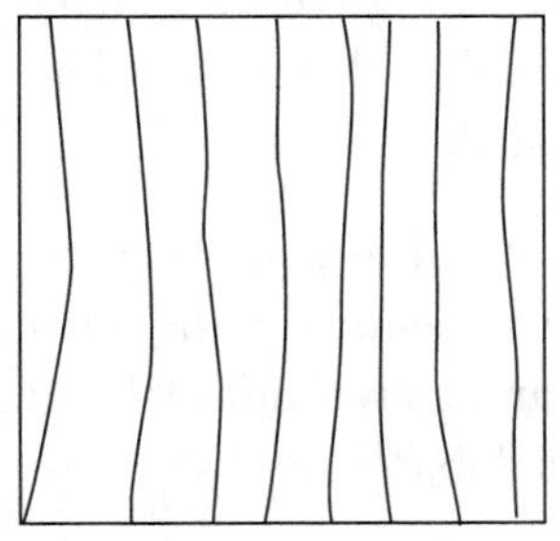
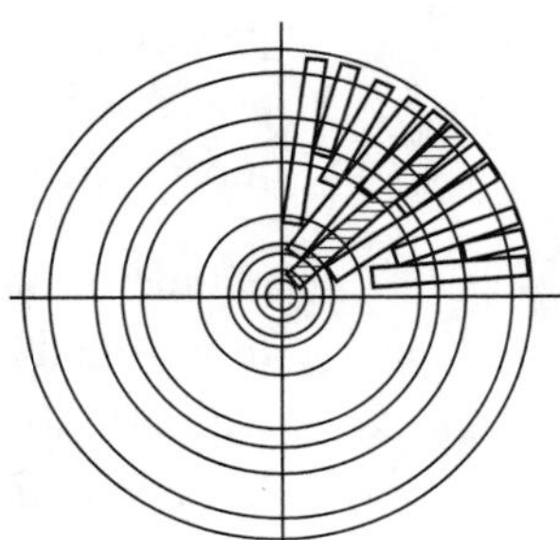

(c) rift sawing

**Table 6.5**
Standard sizes of hardwood lumber

| nominal thickness (in (mm)) | | finish thickness (in (mm)) | |
|---|---|---|---|
| quarters | thickness | hardwoods | softwoods |
| 4/4 | 1 (25) | 3/4 (19) | 3/4 (19) |
| 5/4 | 1 1/4 (32) | 1 1/16 (27) | 1 1/16 (27) |
| 6/4 | 1 1/2 (38) | 1 5/16 (33) | 1 3/8 (35) |
| 8/4 | 2 (51) | 1 1/2 (38) | 1 1/2 (38) |
| 10/4 | 2 1/2 (64) | 2 (51) | 2 1/4 (57) |
| 12/4 | 3 (76) | 2 1/2 (64) | 2 1/2 (64) |

1 1/2 in (38 mm) for softwoods, the architectural woodworker may glue two or more thinner pieces together, as described in the next section. One of the most common solid piece thicknesses is 3/4 in (19 mm), which is also the thickness of the substrate to which most veneer is applied.

Standard widths of woodwork lumber come in nominal 2 in increments, and the actual widths follow the same conventions as board lumber, as listed in Table 6.6.

## Built-up construction

Because fine hardwood is expensive and some species are in very short supply, most furniture and architectural woodwork are not constructed of large, solid pieces of wood as they once were. In some instances, this has actually improved the quality of furniture and woodwork. This is because contemporary veneered panels warp less and are more dimensionally stable than large pieces of solid wood. Instead of single pieces of solid wood, large expanses of flat panels or very thick trim are constructed by using veneer or gluing one or more smaller pieces of solid stock together.

### Gluing for width

When a wide board is required, one or more narrower boards are glued together. This not only minimizes the cost, it also minimizes possible warping and other lumber defects. When a board is glued for width, the mill shop selects boards with similar grain patterns to make the completed piece look like one piece as much as possible. The edges are tongue and grooved or splined for a better joint and glued in the shop. See Fig. 6.3.

### Gluing for thickness

Although thick pieces of solid stock are available for many species, 6/4 thickness is usually the thickest piece used alone. If thicker sections are required, 4/4 (3/4 in actual thickness) lumber is glued together and then cut or shaped to the required profile. Because this is done in the mill shop, only a fine hairline joint is visible, and after finishing even this is not noticeable if the wood grains have been well matched. See Fig. 6.4.

**Table 6.6**
Standard lumber widths

| nominal width (in (mm)) | finish width (in (mm)) |
|---|---|
| 2 (51) | 1½ (38) |
| 4 (102) | 3½ (89) |
| 6 (152) | 5½ (140) |
| 8 (203) | 7¼ (184) |
| 10 (254) | 9¼ (235) |
| 12 (305) | 11¼ (286) |

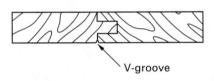

**Figure 6.3**
Gluing for width

V-groove

**Figure 6.4**
Gluing for thickness

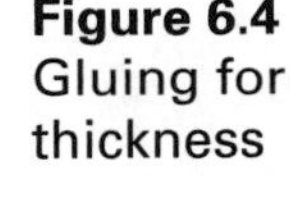


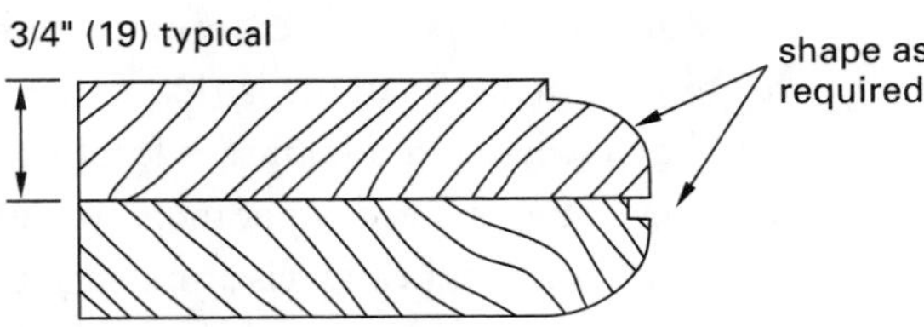


## Detailing suggestion

In order to prevent cupping and warping of wide boards, solid stock should not be detailed to a width of more than about six times its thickness. If a wider board is required, two or more pieces can be glued together or veneer construction can be used.

## Moisture content and shrinkage

Because all wood products shrink and swell with changes in moisture content in the air, all wood construction should be detailed to allow this movement to take place without putting undue stress on the wood joints. Shrinkage and swelling is not as much of a problem in architectural woodwork as it is for site-built finish carpentry. This is because of the improved manufacturing methods and the fact that solid stock and veneer can be dried or acclimated to a particular geographical region and its prevailing humidity.

However, there are some general guidelines that should be followed. In most of the United States, and in the Canadian provinces of Ontario and Quebec, the optimum moisture content of millwork for interior applications is from 5% to 10% with an average of 8%. The relative humidity necessary to maintain this optimum level is from 25% to 55%. In the more humid southern coastal areas of the U.S., in Newfoundland, and in the Canadian coastal provinces, the optimum moisture content is from 8% to 13% (11% average). The required relative humidity necessary to maintain this level is from 43% to 70%. In the dry southwestern regions of the U.S., and in the Canadian provinces of Alberta, Saskatchewan, and Manitoba, the corresponding values are from 4% to 9% (6% average). The relative humidity required is from 17% to 50%. See Fig. 6.5.

## Ecological concerns

The current concern about the deforestation of the world's tropical rain forests is causing many interior designers and architects to re-evaluate how they design and specify architectural woodwork. Because the problem is very complex and involves the supplying country's economic, political, and cultural milieu as well as worldwide economic factors, simply not specifying endangered species of timber may have very little effect on the problem. This is especially true because such a small percentage of endangered timber species is used for architectural woodwork.

**Figure 6.5** Recommended average moisture content for interior wood products

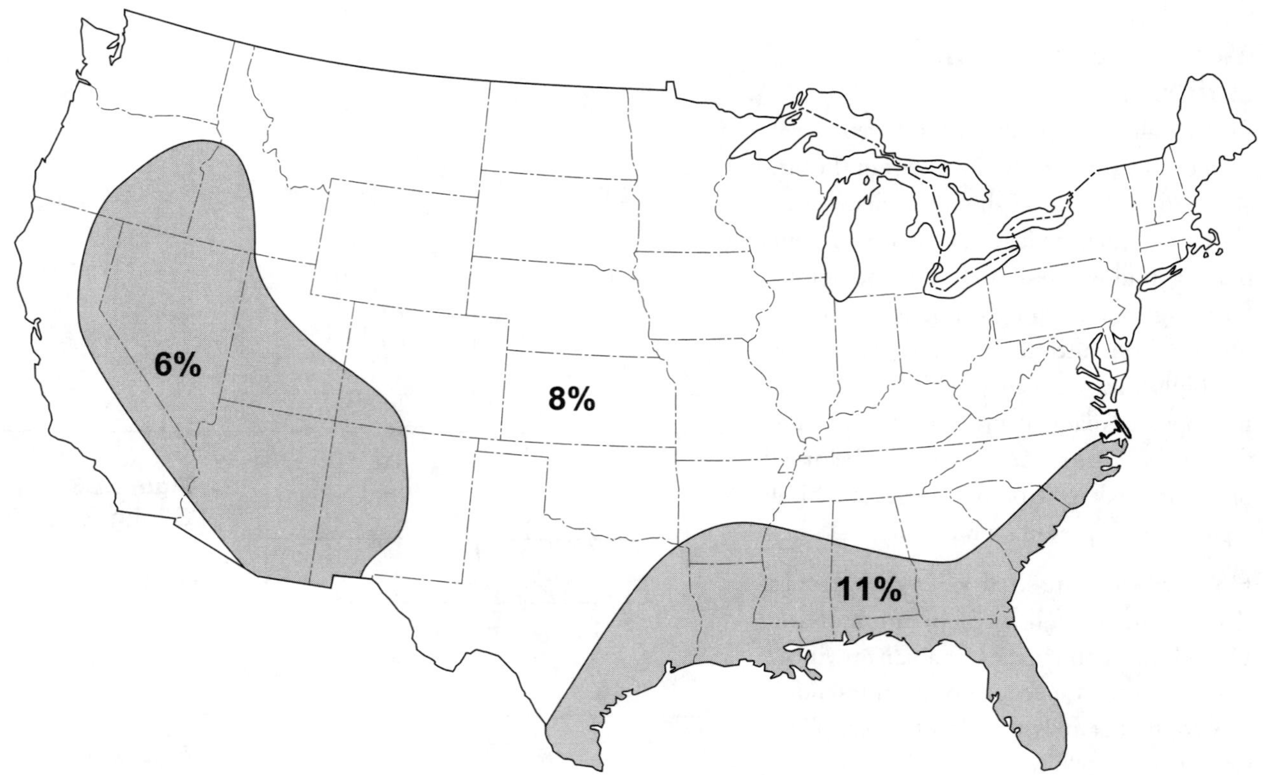


One position supported by many design and furniture associations is that conservation, harvesting, and a country's local economic development need not be incompatible if the timber comes from a wisely managed plantation or agro-forest to provide sustainable yield production. Unfortunately, less than 1% of the commercial timber trade is currently produced from sustainable yield forests.

Until more is known about the problem and more countries and timber suppliers begin to produce using sustained yield management, the designer can either choose to specify woods that can be shown to come from a sustainable yield forest or select one of the hundreds of alternative domestic species that are in plentiful supply.

In addition, the designer can choose to specify one of the many alternate products that are now available. For example, composite wood veneers give the designer a wide range of choices for decorative veneers for cabinets, paneling, custom furniture, and anywhere else standard veneers would be used. This product is manufactured by laminating plain or dyed veneers from sustainedly grown trees into an artificial "log." The composited log is then sliced to produce a wide variety of decorative veneers. The resulting veneers can look like standard wood veneer or have highly patterned, colorful, faces. Refer to Ch. 21 for more information on sustainable wood products.

## Dimensional changes due to moisture

Although detailing to allow for the expansion and contraction of wood is usually sufficient for most interior construction, when the amount of dimensional change must be known accurately, it can be calculated according to the following formula.

$$\Delta D = D_i\,(C_t\,(M_f - M_i))$$

| | | | |
|---|---|---|---|
| $\Delta D$ | change in dimension | – | – |
| $D_i$ | dimension at start of change | in | mm |
| $C_t$ | dimensional change coefficient ($C_t$ for shrinkage in tangential direction, $C_r$ for radial direction; radial shrinkage is shrinkage in the dimension perpendicular to the radial lines of tree growth.) See Table 6.7 for some representative coefficients. | – | – |
| $M_f$ | moisture content at end of change | % | % |
| $M_i$ | moisture content at start of change | % | % |

However, because of the many variables involved, the actual dimensional change based on this formula has a tolerance of 50% above or below the calculated distance. Any detailing based on this formula should take this into account.

**Table 6.7** Coefficients for dimensional change due to shrinkage or swelling within moisture content limits of 6% to 14%

| species | dimensional change coefficient[1] | | species | dimensional change coefficient[1] | |
|---|---|---|---|---|---|
| | radial, $C_r$ | tangential, $C_t$ | | radial, $C_r$ | tangential, $C_t$ |
| ash | | | iroko[2] | 0.00153 | 0.00205 |
| Oregon | 0.00141 | 0.00285 | lauan | | |
| white, green | 0.00169 | 0.00274 | dark red | 0.00133 | 0.00267 |
| avodire | 0.00126 | 0.00226 | light red | 0.00126 | 0.00241 |
| beech, American | 0.00190 | 0.00431 | mahogany[2] | 0.00172 | 0.00238 |
| birch | | | maple | | |
| paper | 0.00219 | 0.00304 | bigleaf | 0.00126 | 0.00248 |
| yellow, sweet | 0.00256 | 0.00338 | red | 0.00137 | 0.00289 |
| cativo | 0.00078 | 0.00183 | silver | 0.00102 | 0.00252 |
| cedar | | | persimmon, common | 0.00278 | 0.00403 |
| eastern red | 0.00106 | 0.00162 | red oak | | |
| western red[2] | 0.00111 | 0.00234 | commercial red | 0.00158 | 0.00369 |
| cherry, black | 0.00126 | 0.00248 | California black | 0.00123 | 0.00230 |
| douglas fir | | | redwood | | |
| coast-type | 0.00165 | 0.00267 | old growth[2] | 0.00120 | 0.00205 |
| interior north | 0.00130 | 0.00241 | second growth[2] | 0.00101 | 0.00229 |
| elm, American | 0.00144 | 0.00338 | sycamore, American | 0.00172 | 0.00296 |
| fir | | | teak[2] | 0.00101 | 0.00186 |
| California red | 0.00155 | 0.00278 | tupelo, black | 0.00176 | 0.00308 |
| Pacific silver | 0.00151 | 0.00327 | walnut, European | 0.00148 | 0.00223 |
| hickory | | | white oak | | |
| pecan | 0.00169 | 0.00315 | commercial | 0.00180 | 0.00365 |
| true hickory | 0.00259 | 0.00411 | yellow poplar | 0.00158 | 0.00289 |

Source: *Wood Handbook: Wood as an Engineering Material,* Forest Products Laboratory.

(1) Per 1% change in moisture content, based on dimension at 10% moisture content and a straight-line relationship between the moisture content at which shrinkage starts and total shrinkage. (Shrinkage is assumed to start at 30% for all species except those indicated by footnote 2.)

(2) Shrinkage is assumed to start at 22% moisture content.

**Figure 6.6** Veneer cutting methods

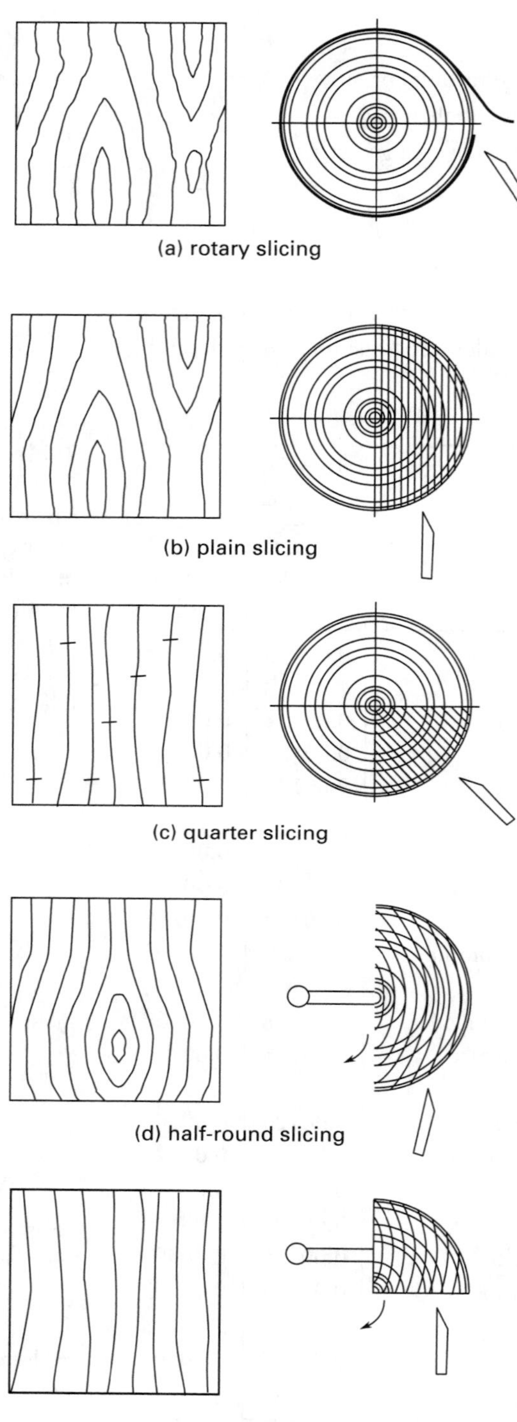


## VENEER [064216]

A veneer is a thin slice of wood. Veneer is glued to a backing material, most commonly particleboard, to hold it flat and provide a solid substrate for installation. Most veneers are cut about $1/28$ in (0.907 mm) thick, but thinner or thicker cuts can be specified to meet particular requirements. For example, a thick veneer can be specified to provide more durability or the ability to withstand the sanding and refinishing of minor nicks and scratches without showing the backing panel.

### Veneer sources

As with solid stock, veneers come from timber harvested worldwide. Because of the limited supply of some species, veneer cuts may be more readily available than solid stock in the same species because veneer provides a higher yield from a tree. Some of the veneers are listed in Table 6.4. Veneers are provided to woodwork shops by veneer suppliers who buy timber from around the world and cut it into veneers.

### Veneer cutting methods

Just as with solid stock, the way veneer is cut from a log affects its final appearance. There are five principal methods of cutting veneers, as shown in Figs. 6.6(a)–6.6(e). Plain slicing and quarter slicing are accomplished the same way as cutting solid stock, except the resulting pieces are much thinner. Quarter slicing produces a more straight-grained pattern than plain slicing because the cutting knife strikes the growth rings at an angle of approximately 90°.

In the *rotary slicing method*, the log is mounted on a lathe and turned against a knife, which peels off a continuous layer of veneer. This produces a very pronounced grain pattern that is often undesirable in fine quality wood finishes, although it does produce the most veneer with the least waste.

The *half-round slicing method* is similar to rotary slicing, but the log is cut in half, and the veneer is cut slightly across the annular growth rings. This results in a pronounced grain pattern, having characteristics of both rotary-sliced and plain-sliced veneers.

The *rift slicing method* consists of quartering a log and cutting at a slight angle to the growth rings. Rift slicing accentuates the vertical grain pattern and minimizes the horizontal "flake" that is caused by medullary rays. These are radial cells extending from the center of the tree to its circumference. They are most commonly found in oak; therefore, rift slicing is most often specified for oak to eliminate these medullary ray markings.

Because the width of a piece of veneer is limited by the diameter of the log or the portion of the log from which it is cut, several veneers must be put together on a backing panel to make up the needed size of a finished piece. The individual veneers come from the same piece of log, which is called a *flitch*. As the veneers are sliced from the log, they are kept in sequence so they can be matched later. The methods of matching veneers are discussed in the section on panel construction.

Because veneers are very thin, they must be glued to a solid backing to hold them flat and to provide the strength needed for constructing woodwork items. There are a number of products used for veneer backing, but the most common are particleboard and plywood, with particleboard being the panel of choice among most mill shops. The thickness of the backing panel depends on the use of the final panel product and its size, but the most common thickness is ¾ in (19 mm).

### Veneer grading

The Architectural Woodwork Institute (AWI) has established three grades of architectural woodwork: Premium, Custom, and Economy. These apply to cabinetwork, paneling, doors, trim, and all other types of architectural woodwork. Premium is the highest grade available in both material and manufacturing. It is intended for the finest work. It is the most expensive grade. Custom grade is intended for high-quality, conventional work. Economy grade is the lowest grade in both materials and manufacturing. It is intended for work where cost is more important than quality or in service areas where appearance is not critical. The AWI *Quality Standards* describe the level of material and manufacture for each of the three grades for every type of construction component. Architectural woodwork can be accurately and easily specified by referring to one of the three AWI grades.

As with lumber, the AWI defines four grades of veneers for panel surfacing. However, the designer does not specify these grades directly. Instead, the standard grades of Premium, Custom, and Economy are specified for each type of paneled product. The grade of veneer is automatically determined by the AWI *Quality Standards* according to which of these three quality level grades is specified. For example, Premium grade stile and rail paneling for transparent finish is constructed with Grade I face veneer (the highest), while Custom grade stile and rail paneling for opaque finish is constructed with Grade II face veneer.

## CABINETWORK [064100]

Cabinets include custom-manufactured built-in base and upper cabinets, freestanding fixtures, and open shelving cases designed and detailed for a particular project. Cabinetwork is built predominately of wood products, but it can also include other materials such as high-pressure decorative laminate, metal, glass, stone, leather, and other decorative and functional items built into the cabinet.

Various types of joints are used for millwork construction to increase the joint's strength and improve its appearance by eliminating mechanical fasteners, such as screws. With the availability of high-strength adhesives, screws, and other concealed fasteners, visible mechanical fasteners are seldom needed for the majority of work produced in the shop. Field attachment, however, often requires the use of blind nailing or other concealed fastening to maintain the quality look of the work. Some of the common joints used in millwork are shown in Fig. 6.7.

## Typical cabinet construction

Although architectural woodwork can be designed and built in an almost unlimited number of ways, certain standard methods of construction have been developed over time that satisfy the requirements of economy, strength, and stability. Upper and lower cabinets are common woodwork components with typical construction details. The basic construction techniques can be modified to suit individual project requirements. Fig. 6.8 shows the construction of a typical base cabinet. Countertops are included in cabinet construction.

### Countertop construction

Countertops are built separately from base cabinets and put in place in the field. This is because the countertops are built in single lengths that are much longer than any individual base cabinet. Building and installing the countertops separately also gives the installers the ability to precisely fit the countertop to the wall. This is most commonly done with a *scribe piece* on top of the backsplash or at the back of the countertop. A scribe piece is an oversized piece of plastic laminate or wood that can be trimmed in the field to follow any minor irregularities of the wall. As with other woodwork components, there are hundreds of possible configurations to countertops, including variations in width, materials, front edge shape and size, and backsplash size and shape. Some of the more common configurations are shown in Figs. 6.9(a)–6.9(d). (Figure 6.29 shows typical plastic laminate countertop edge treatments). See Fig. 7.5 for a countertop supported with steel angles.

### Drawer and door front construction

For both base and upper cabinets there are four basic categories of door and drawer front construction: flush, flush overlay, reveal overlay, and lipped overlay. These are shown in Figs. 6.10(a)–6.10(d).

**Figure 6.7**
Wood joints

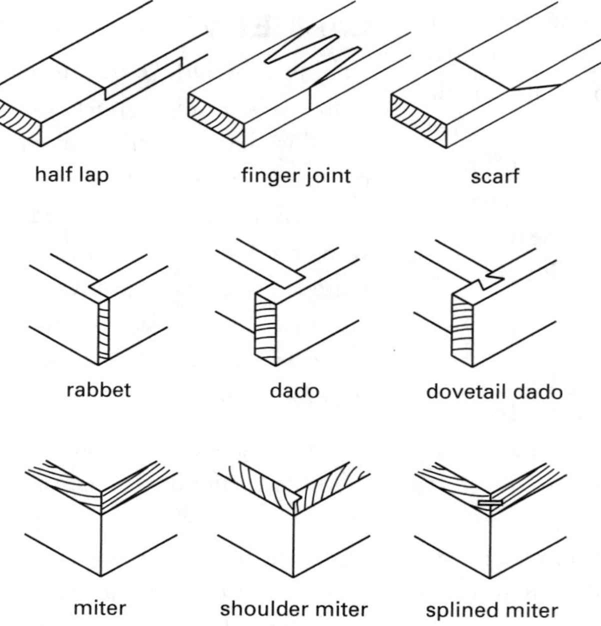

**Figure 6.8**
Typical base cabinet construction

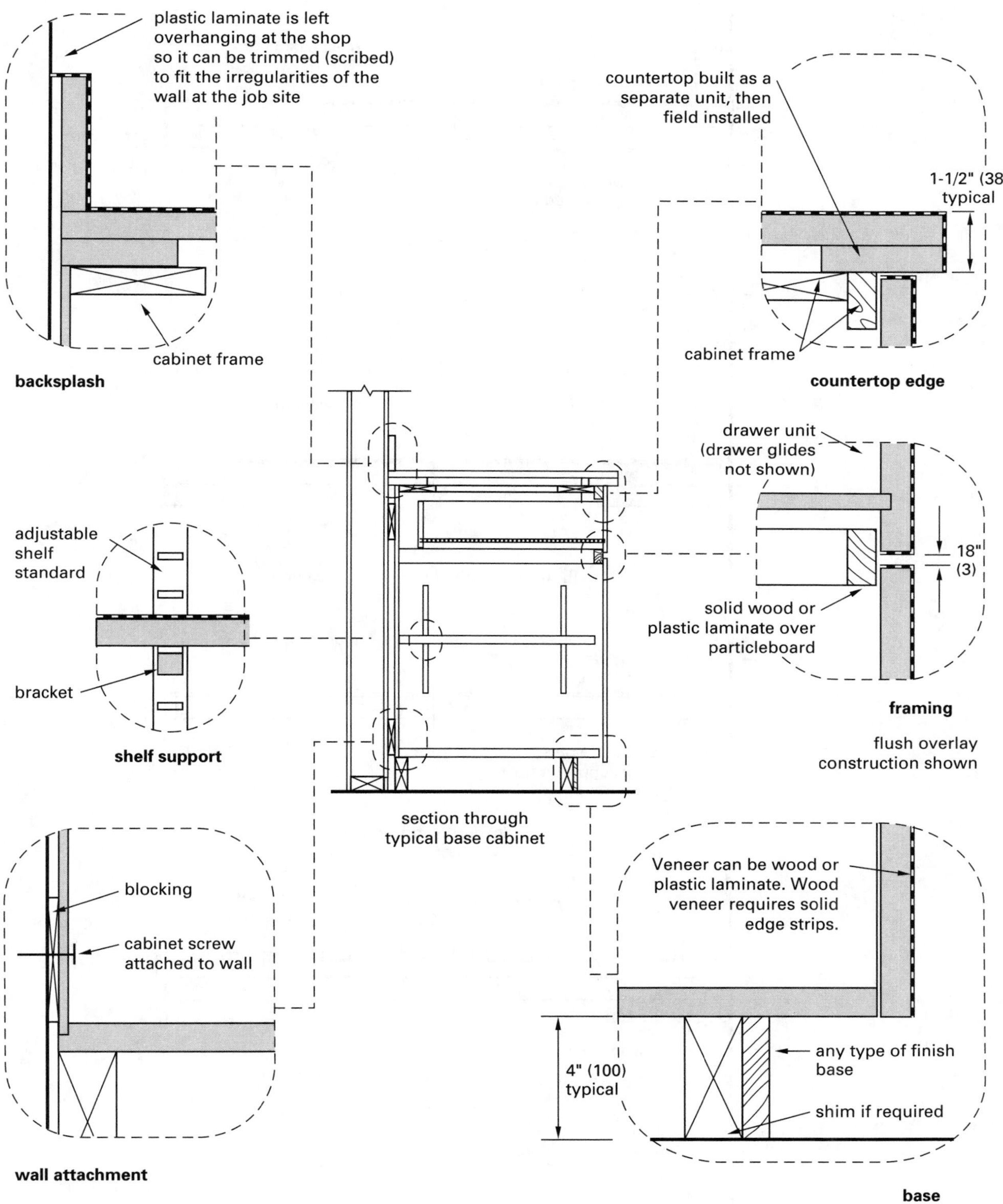
plastic laminate is left overhanging at the shop so it can be trimmed (scribed) to fit the irregularities of the wall at the job site
cabinet frame
backsplash
countertop built as a separate unit, then field installed
1-1/2" (38) typical
cabinet frame
countertop edge
adjustable shelf standard
bracket
shelf support
drawer unit (drawer glides not shown)
18" (3)
solid wood or plastic laminate over particleboard
framing
flush overlay construction shown
section through typical base cabinet
blocking
cabinet screw attached to wall
wall attachment
Veneer can be wood or plastic laminate. Wood veneer requires solid edge strips.
4" (100) typical
any type of finish base
shim if required
base

**Figure 6.9** Typical countertop details

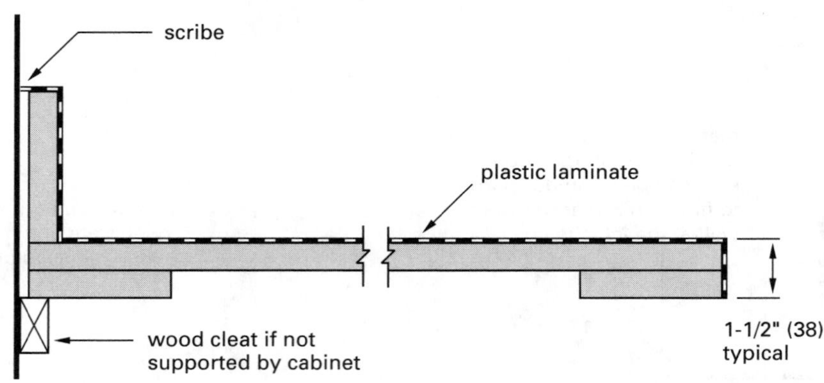


(a) plastic laminate

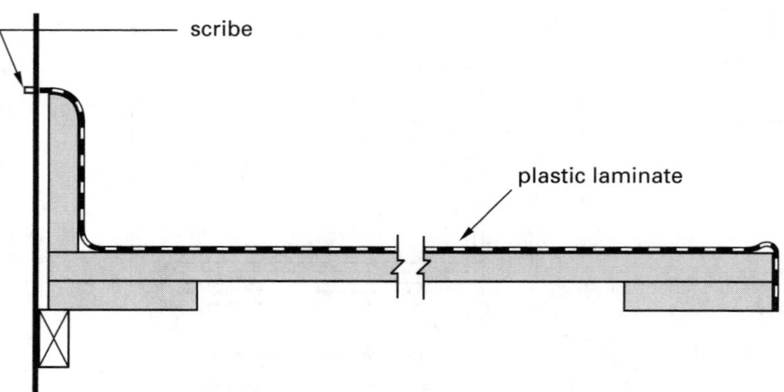


(b) plastic laminate with dripless edge

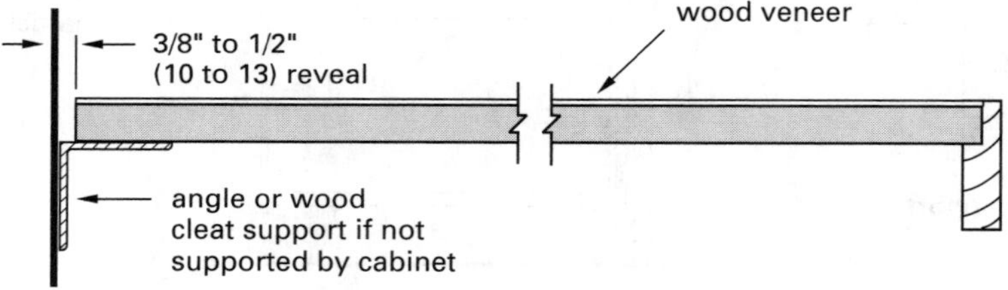


(c) hardwood veneer

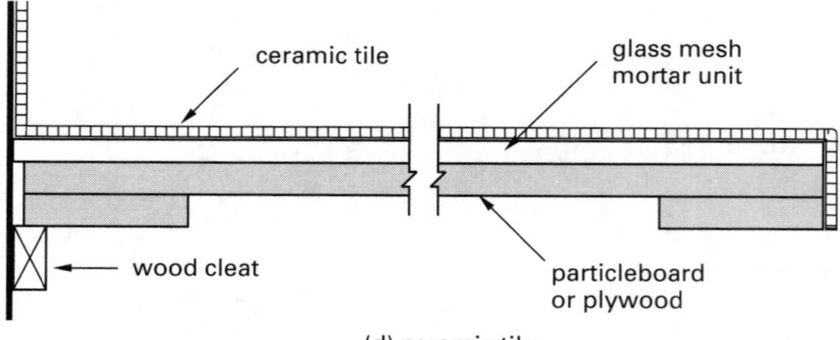


(d) ceramic tile

### Flush construction

In *flush construction,* the face of a drawer or door is installed flush with the face frame. The primary disadvantage of this type of construction is its expense because of the extra care required to fit and align doors and drawers within the frame. Another disadvantage is that, with use, the doors and drawers may sag. This results in nonuniform spacing between fronts and may cause some doors and drawers to bind against the frame.

A variation of flush construction is *lipped overlay construction,* in which part of the door or drawer overlaps the frame and covers the joint between the two pieces. See Fig. 6.10(d).

### Flush overlay

In *flush overlay construction,* the fronts of the doors and drawers overlap the face frame of the cabinet. Edges of adjacent door or drawer fronts are separated only enough to allow operation without touching, usually about ⅛ in (3 mm) or less. Only doors and drawers are visible and they are all flush with each other. As with flush construction, the mill shop must take great care in aligning and fitting the doors and drawers so that the gap between them is uniform; if the drawers and doors sag too much, problems arise. Flush overlay is typically used with high-pressure decorative laminate-clad cabinets.

### Reveal overlay

In *reveal overlay construction,* the edges of adjacent doors and door fronts are separated enough to reveal the face frame behind. The width of the reveal can be whatever the designer wants, subject to the width of the face frame. This construction is less expensive than flush overlay construction because minor misalignments and sagging are not as noticeable.

## Upper cabinet construction

Upper cabinets are very similar in construction to base cabinets. The most notable exceptions are that they are not as deep as base cabinets and some design and detailing consideration must be given to the underside because it is visible. In addition, there must be some way to securely anchor the cabinet to the wall. In residential construction, the cabinet is attached to the wall by screwing through the cabinet back and wall finish into the wood studs. In commercial construction where metal studs are used, wood *blocking* is required in the stud cavity

**Figure 6.10**
Types of cabinet door framing

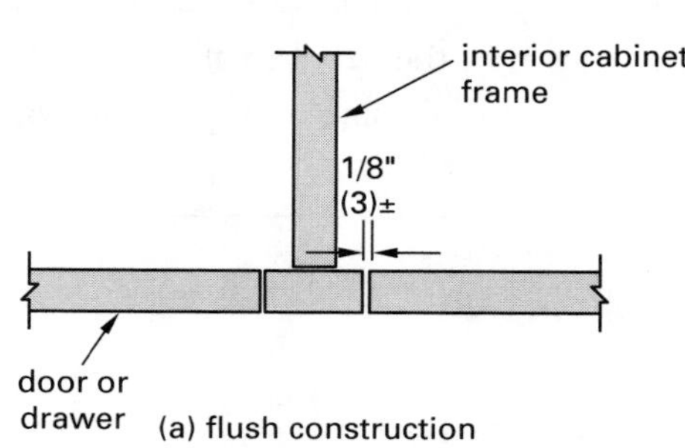

(a) flush construction

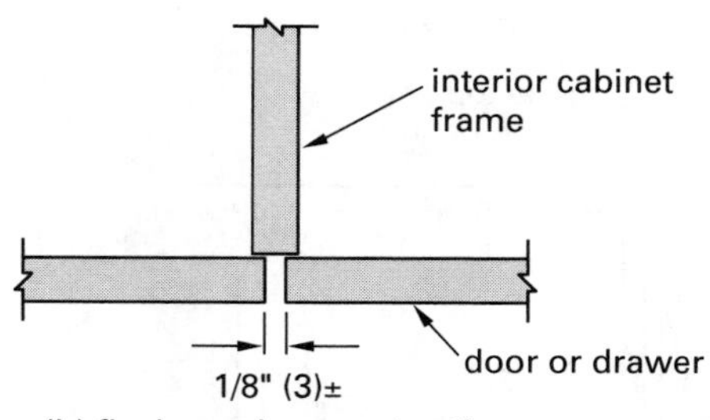

(b) flush overlay construction

interior cabinet frame and face frame

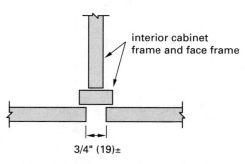

3/4" (19)±

(c) reveal overlay construction

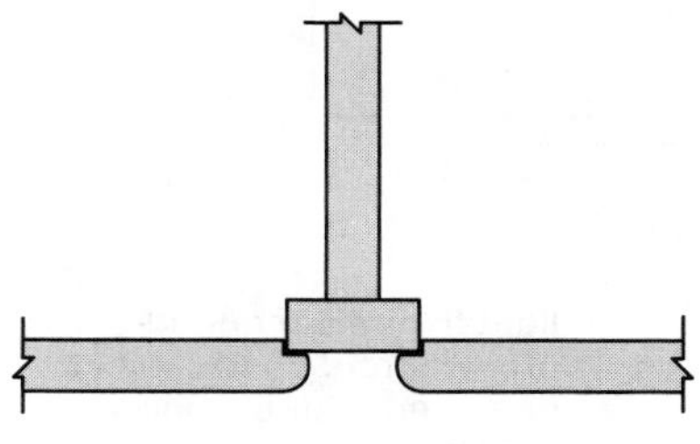
(d) lipped overlay construction

behind the wall finish. This blocking is installed as the studs are being erected and is attached to the studs with screws. The blocking provides a solid base for attaching the cabinets to the wall. Figure 6.11 shows a typical upper cabinet detail.

The top of the cabinet may be detailed against the ceiling or, as is common in residential construction, the cabinet may be placed below a dropped soffit. The space between the top of the cabinet and the ceiling may also be left open. The bottom edge of the doors may extend below the cabinet bottom as shown in the detail to allow for a finger pull instead of using door pull hardware.

**Figure 6.11**
Typical upper cabinet

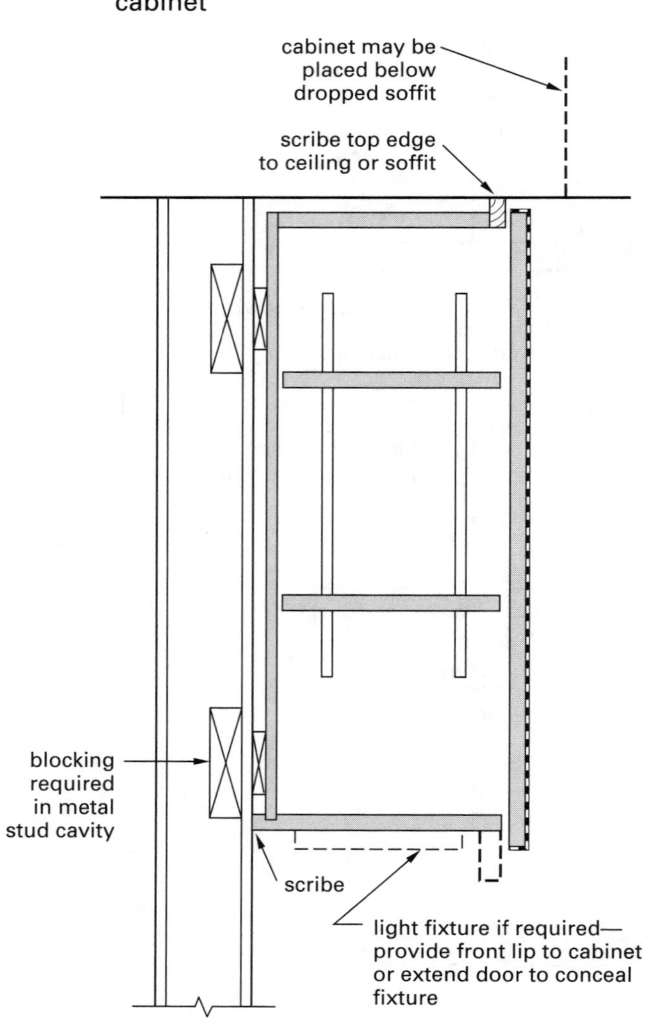


## Cabinet materials

Depending on the grade specified, AWI standards define the materials and minimum thicknesses for the various parts of a cabinet. These are summarized in Table 6.8.

## Shelving

Shelving may be mounted on adjustable metal standards attached to a partition, attached to floor-mounted cases, or built into enclosed, wall-hung cabinets. Figure 6.12 shows a common type of wall-hung shelving unit with an open front. Shelving cabinets may also be fitted with doors.

The shelves themselves may be trimmed on the front at the same thickness as the shelf, or a larger edge treatment can be applied. A few of these edge treatments are shown in Figs. 6.13(a)–6.13(c). The edges make the shelf appear thicker and give added strength for heavy loads.

When viewed from the front, the way the shelves intersect the supports depends on the quality of grade specified. For Premium grade and Custom grade shelving, stop dadoes or concealed, interlocking, fastening devices are used to attach fixed shelves to side supports. Economy grade shelving uses through dadoes. See Figs. 6.14(a)–6.14(b).

## Typical dimensions

Because architectural woodwork is custom designed and fabricated, any dimension of any component can be specified according to the needs of the job or the appearance desired. However, there are some standard dimensions that are common for cabinetwork and that have been found to work in most situations. Some of these are shown in Figs. 6.15(a)–6.15(c).

## Custom assemblies

A limitless number of designs can be developed with architectural woodwork. The details shown in this chapter are the most common and represent typical construction

**Table 6.8**
Materials and thicknesses for cabinet components

| component | material | minimum thickness (in (mm)) |
|---|---|---|
| body members—ends, divisions, bottoms and tops | panel product | 3/4 (19) |
| rails | lumber or panel product | 3/4 (19) |
| backs | panel product | 1/4 (6.4) |
| doors, up to 30 in wide by 80 in high (762 mm by 2032 mm) | medium density particleboard or medium density fiberboard core panel product | 3/4 (19) |
| drawer sides, backs and subfronts | lumber or panel product | 1/2 (12.7) |
| drawer bottoms | panel product | 1/4 (6.4) |
| drawer fronts | lumber or panel product | 3/4 (19) |
| wood shelves (minimum thicknesses given for spans listed) | lumber | 3/4 up to 36 (19 up to 914) 1 1/16 up to 48 (27 up to 1219) |
| wood shelves | veneer core plywood | 3/4 up to 36 (19 up to 914) 1 1/16 up to 48 (27 up to 1219) |
| plastic laminate clad shelves | medium density particleboard or fiberboard | 3/4 up to 32 (19 up to 813) 1 up to 42 (25.4 up to 1067) |

Source: Compiled from information in *Architectural Woodwork Quality Standards, 8th Edition, Version 1.0,* copyright 2003.

techniques. However, by modifying dimensions, configurations of components, trim shapes, and hardware, nearly any design concept can be realized.

Although architectural woodwork, by definition, is built from lumber products, other materials can be, and often are, incorporated into a woodwork design. Plastic laminate, metal, stone, fabric, leather, and other materials can be used to produce an endless variety of design detailing. For example, a stone top can be used on a custom reception desk, or metal strips can be inlaid into wall paneling. When such materials are incidental to the primary piece of architectural woodwork, they are sometimes fabricated and usually installed by the architectural mill shop as part of the contract.

**Figure 6.12** Typical shelving unit

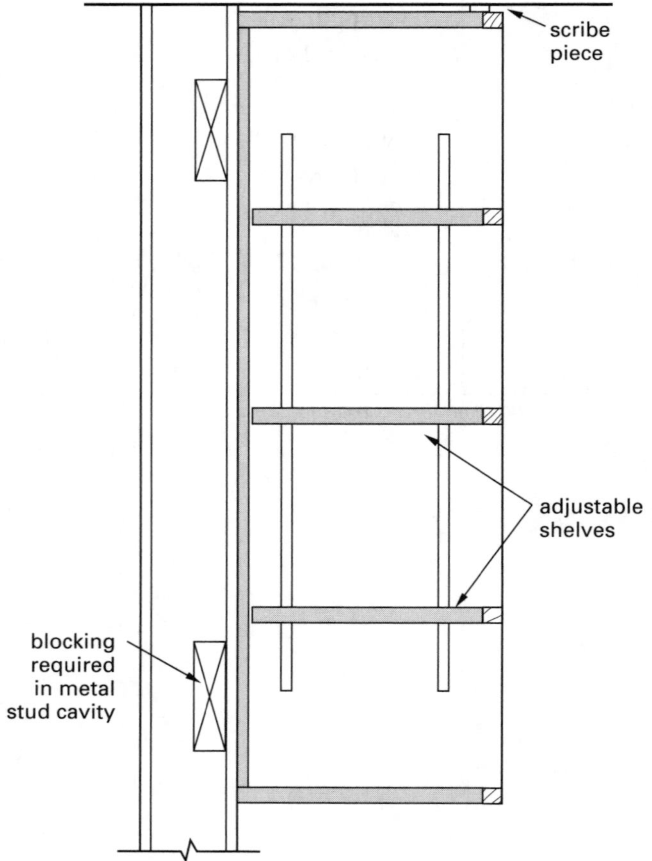


## Coordination

Because architectural woodwork is fabricated to very close tolerances in the mill shop and installed in the field on, against, or within construction that is not as precise, architectural woodwork design and detailing must account for the differences in both tolerances and construction quality. Designing scribe pieces as part of the woodwork, as described for countertops, is one way of doing this. Reveals between the woodwork and other construction can also be detailed to minimize the visibility of any minor irregularities. For paneling, cabinets, and other components that must be installed plumb, space must be provided for the installers to mount wood blocking and to shim portions of the woodwork. If this produces an irregular gap between the woodwork and the wall, some acceptable method of concealing the crack is necessary. Shimming may also be required to level cabinets on uneven floors. The shim space is then covered with the finished base.

Other coordination issues include the following: anticipating and detailing for minor building movement; making woodwork finishes compatible with free-standing furniture finishes; and designing components so that they can be fabricated in pieces, which can be fit within the doors, elevators, and other openings of a completed building. Additional coordination items include the following.

- Wood blocking should be shown within metal stud partitions to provide a solid method of attaching wall-hung woodwork.

- Unless the method for providing for adjustable shelves is specifically shown on the drawings, the woodworker has the option of using either multiple holes with plastic or metal pins to support the shelves, or metal or plastic shelf standards.

- Full extension drawer slides must be specified or shown on the drawings if they are required.

## Shelving deflection

Because one of the most common problems with shelving is excessive deflection under load, or outright collapse, the span and thickness of each shelf should be selected for minimum deflection. Shelves are simply thin, wide beams and obey the laws of statics. Therefore, any material of any size can be calculated using the standard beam equations. Table 6.9 summarizes these calculations for some common shelving materials, sizes, and spans based on a maximum deflection at the center of the shelf of ⅛ in (3.2 mm). The table gives the maximum total load before the deflection exceeds ⅛ in.

**Table 6.9** Maximum allowable total load in pounds (kg) for shelf deflection of ⅛ in (3.2 mm) for shelves of different materials, widths, and spans

| shelf length (in (mm)) | | 30 (760) | | | 36 (914) | | | 42 (1067) | | |
|---|---|---|---|---|---|---|---|---|---|---|
| shelf width (in (mm)) | | 8 (203) | 10 (254) | 12 (305) | 8 (203) | 10 (254) | 12 (305) | 8 (203) | 10 (254) | 12 (305) |
| component | shelf thickness (in (mm)) | lbm (kg) | lbm (kg) | lbm (kg) | lbm (kg) | lbm (kg) | lbm (kg) | lbm (kg) | lbm (kg) | lbm (kg) |
| medium-density particleboard faced with 0.05 in. plastic laminate | ¾ (19) | 58 (26) | 73 (33) | 87 (39) | 34 (15) | 42 (19) | 51 (23) | 21 (9) | 27 (12) | 32 (14) |
| | 1½ (38) | 388 (176) | 485 (220) | 583 (264) | 225 (102) | 281 (127) | 337 (153) | 142 (64) | 177 (80) | 212 (96) |
| high-density particle-board faced with 0.05 in plastic laminate | ¾ (19) | 146 (66) | 182 (83) | 218 (99) | 84 (38) | 105 (48) | 126 (57) | 53 (24) | 66 (30) | 80 (36) |
| birch-faced plywood with ¾ × ¾ softwood edge strip | ¾ (19) | 180 (81) | 225 (102) | 270 (122) | 104 (47) | 130 (59) | 156 (71) | 66 (30) | 82 (37) | 98 (44) |
| birch-faced plywood with ¾ × 1½ soft-wood dropped edge | ¾ (19) | 366 (166) | 412 (187) | 458 (207) | 212 (96) | 238 (108) | 265 (120) | 133 (60) | 150 (68) | 167 (76) |
| douglas fir, coast | ¾ (19) | 195 (88) | 244 (111) | 293 (133) | 113 (51) | 141 (64) | 169 (77) | 71 (32) | 89 (40) | 107 (48) |
| white oak | ¾ (19) | 178 (81) | 223 (101) | 267 (121) | 103 (47) | 129 (59) | 155 (70) | 65 (29) | 81 (37) | 97 (44) |
| red oak, black cherry | ¾ (19) | 149 (68) | 186 (84) | 224 (102) | 86 (39) | 108 (49) | 129 (59) | 54 (24) | 68 (31) | 81 (37) |
| walnut | ¾ (19) | 168 (76) | 210 (95) | 252 (114) | 97 (44) | 122 (55) | 146 (66) | 61 (28) | 77 (35) | 92 (42) |

For calculating total loads, books weigh about 65 lbm/ft$^3$ and paper weighs about 58 lbm/ft$^3$.
Note: These values are approximate. Actual allowable loads depend on quality of materials and craftwork.

**Figure 6.13** Alternate shelving edge treatments

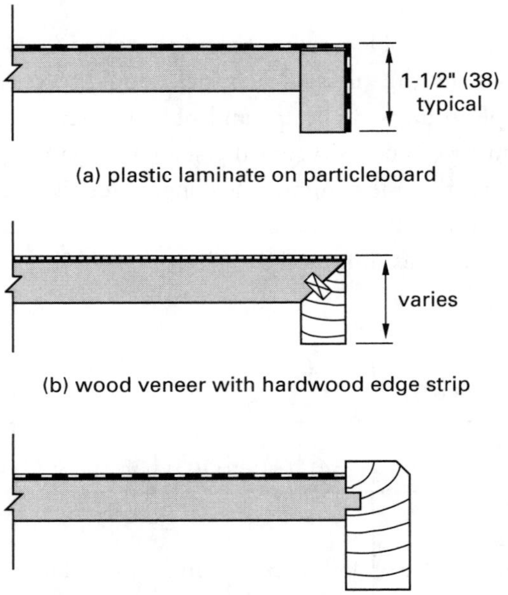

(a) plastic laminate on particleboard



(b) wood veneer with hardwood edge strip

(c) hardwood edge with raised lip

**Figure 6.14** Methods of shelving attachment

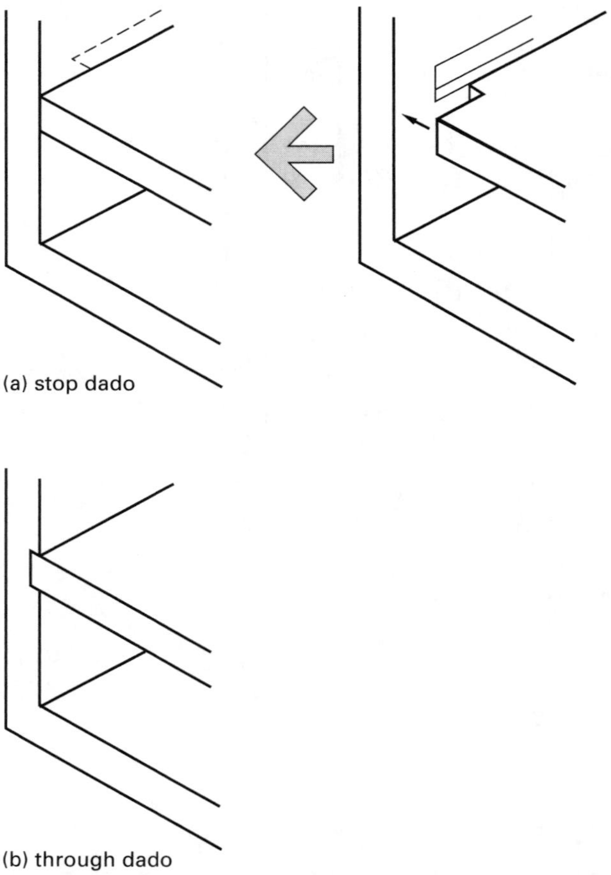

(a) stop dado

(b) through dado

• When under-cabinet lighting is provided, the exact height of the electrical conduit that connects to the fixture must be located so that it can be stubbed out accurately by the electrical contractor prior to wall finishing.

• Scribe pieces should be provided where the cabinet touches a wall to allow for out-of-plumb or out-of-line partitions.

## PANELING [064200]

### Panel types

Millwork paneling includes wood-clad and laminate-clad flush paneling and stile and rail paneling. Flush paneling is built up of thin wood veneers or laminate glued to backing panels of particleboard or plywood. Raised panel construction is the more traditional type, with separate panels built within borders of solid wood rails. Flush paneling has a single, smooth surface with very little trim. Other types of paneling include fabric-covered acoustical panels, grilles, and panels covered with metal or other materials.

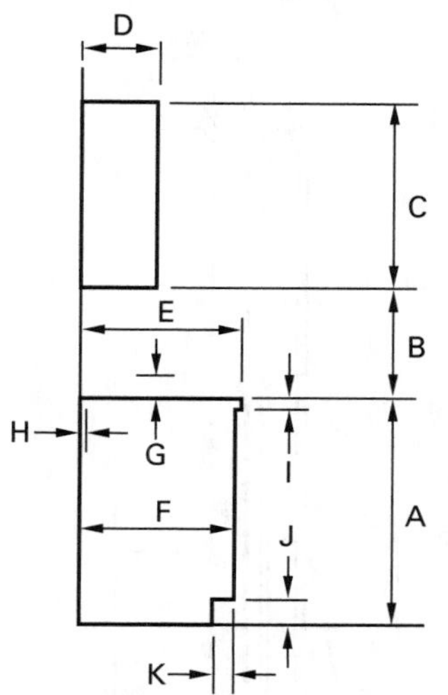


| | in | mm |
|---|---|---|
| A | 36 standup<br>31–33 vanity<br>29–30 sitdown | 914<br>787–838<br>737–762 |
| B | 18<br>21–24 above sink<br>24 above cooktop | 457<br>533–610<br>610 |
| C | 15, 18, 24, 30 | 381, 457,<br>610, 762 |
| D | 12 | 305 |
| E | 25 | 635 |
| F | 24 | 610 |
| G | 4 | 102 |
| H | 3/4 + scribe | 19 + scribe |
| I | 1-1/2 | 38 |
| J | 4 | 102 |
| K | 3 | 76 |

(a) standard kitchen cabinets

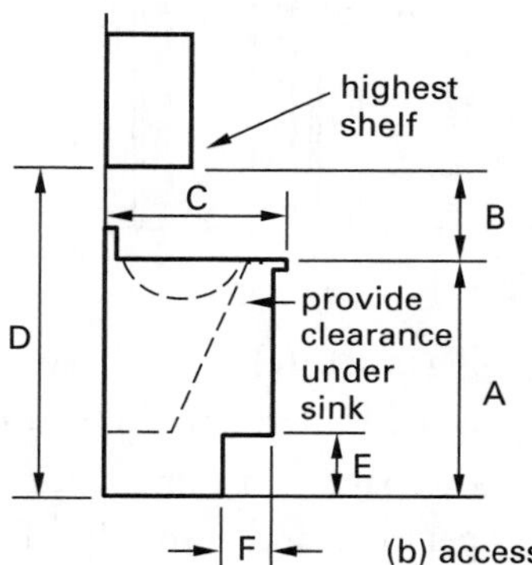

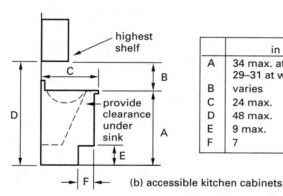

| | in | mm |
|---|---|---|
| A | 34 max. at sink<br>29–31 at work | 864<br>737–787 |
| B | varies | varies |
| C | 24 max. | 610 max. |
| D | 48 max. | 1219 max. |
| E | 9 max. | 229 min. |
| F | 7 | 178 |

(b) accessible kitchen cabinets

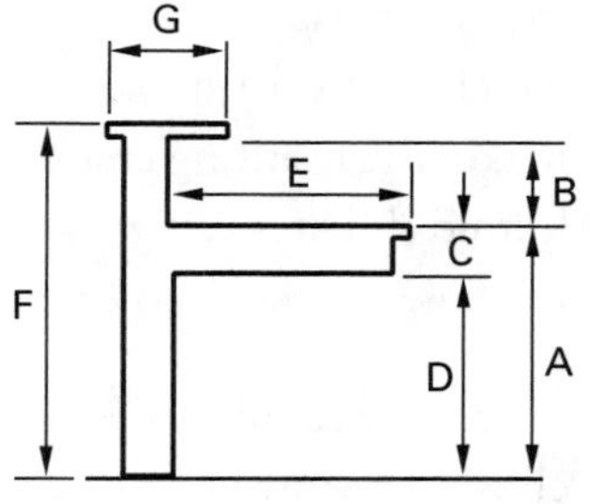


| | in | mm |
|---|---|---|
| A | 29–30 working<br>26 typing | 737–762<br>660 |
| B | 12 min. | 305 min. |
| C | varies | varies |
| D | 25 max. | 635 min. |
| E | 24–30 | 610–762 |
| F | 36–54 | 914–1372 |
| G | 6–15 | 152–381 |

(c) reception, work counter

**Figure 6.15**
Standard cabinet dimensions

## Typical panel construction

### Flush panel construction

Flush panels are built in the mill shop in large sections and are hung from walls with wood cleats or metal Z-clips, as shown in Figs. 6.16(a)–6.16(b). In some cases the panels can be directly screwed to the wall, as long as the fasteners are covered with additional trim or other decorative elements. In AWI Premium grade, veneer is applied to ¾ in (19 mm) backing panels; in Custom grade, it is applied to 7⁄16 in (11 mm) panels.

The edges of each panel can be tightly butted together to give a continuous appearance, or can be treated in a number of other ways, one of which is shown in Fig. 6.17(b). Likewise, inside and outside corners can be tightly joined or treated like field joints. See

**Figure 6.16**
Panel mounting methods

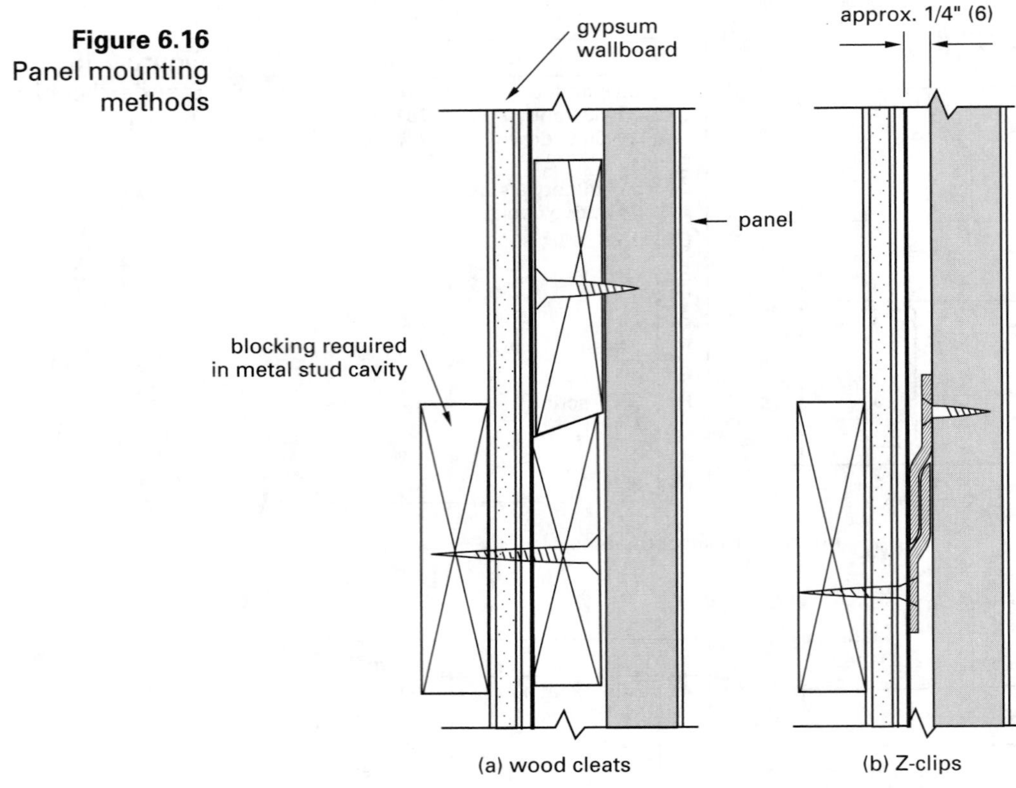


**Figure 6.17**
Panel edge connections

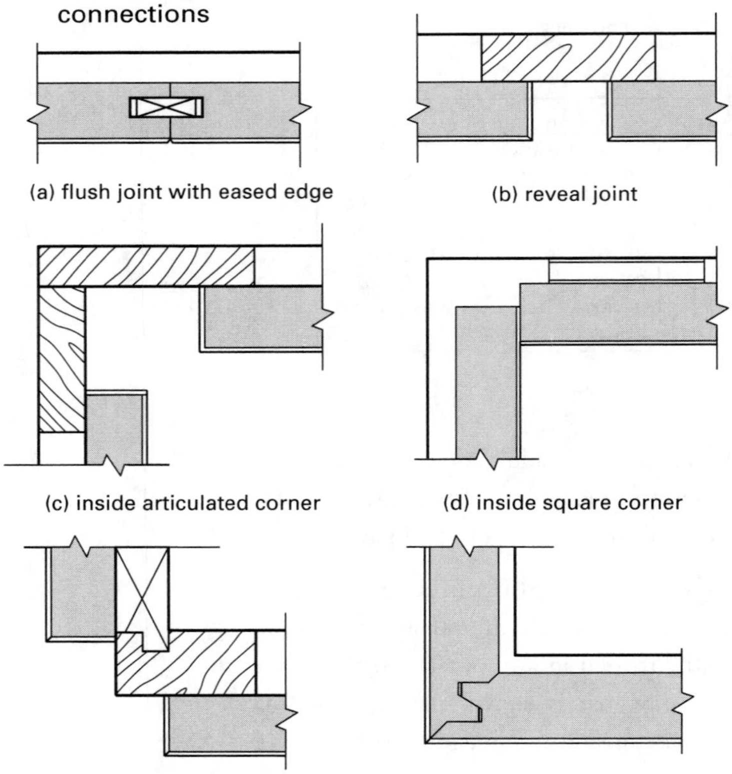

(a) flush joint with eased edge

(b) reveal joint

(c) inside articulated corner

(d) inside square corner

(e) outside articulated corner

(f) outside square corner

Figs. 6.17(c)–6.17(f). Whichever method is used, there should be some provision for the panels to move with changes in temperature and humidity. If a tight joint is used, as shown in Fig. 6.17(a), the edges of the veneer should be beveled slightly. If the panel shrinks or moves slightly, the V-joint makes the resulting crack less noticeable. In humid climates, a slight gap may be required to allow the panel to expand.

If panels are hung with wood cleats or Z-clips, there must be sufficient space near the ceiling for the panel to be lifted up and over the cleat or Z-clip and then lowered into place. This is usually a minimum of ¾ in (19 mm), but the exact dimension depends on the type of mounting clip used. The resulting gap may be left as a reveal or may be filled. It can also be covered with additional wood trim, as shown in Fig. 6.18.

The panel may extend to the floor or be held short of the floor so that a separate base can be installed. Several methods of doing this are illustrated in Figs. 6.19(a)–6.19(c).

## Curved paneling

Both flush paneling and stile and rail paneling can be fabricated for inside or outside curves. Several methods may be used to produce flush paneling. One method uses several thin layers of bendable plywood, which are laid against a curved form. The veneer is then applied to the backing. Another method uses several solid pieces of lumber, with edges beveled to form the desired curve, glued together. The finish face is sanded smooth and finished. A third method uses *kerfing*, which is a series of sawcuts in the back of the panel made perpendicular to the direction of the bend. Because the lines of the sawcut can telegraph through to the finished surface, this method is the least desirable.

Curved molding can also be produced in a number of ways. Solid pieces of wood can be cut with a band saw to the required radius out of a large piece of flat, solid stock. The pieces are then shaped to the desired profile. A second method uses several thin plies of material laminated to one another as they are formed into the required shape. A third method uses common lumber formed into the required shape and then covered with veneers of the finish wood. The method used is selected by the architectural woodworker based on the type of profile involved, the radius of the curve, and the particular fabricating methods the woodworker prefers to use.

### Stile and rail construction

Stile and rail panel construction consists of a frame of solid wood that contains individual panels. Along with various types of molding and matching doors, raised panel construction is used to detail traditional wood-paneled room interiors. See Fig. 6.20. Traditionally, the panels were also made from solid wood, but today it is more common for the panels to be veneered.

As shown in Fig. 6.21, the vertical frame pieces are called *stiles* and the horizontal members are called *rails*. The panels are held in place with grooves cut in the sides of the frames or with individual molding pieces, called *sticking*. Some of the various types of panels and methods of holding them in place are shown in Figs. 6.22(a)–6.22(c). Whichever method is used, there must be sufficient room allowed for expansion and contraction with changes in the moisture content.

Like flush paneling, stile and rail paneling may be hung on walls with wood cleats or metal Z-clips. If extensive molding is used, the panels can be screwed to wood blocking behind them and the fasteners can be concealed with molding. Individual panels are joined with dowels or splines to keep the edges flush.

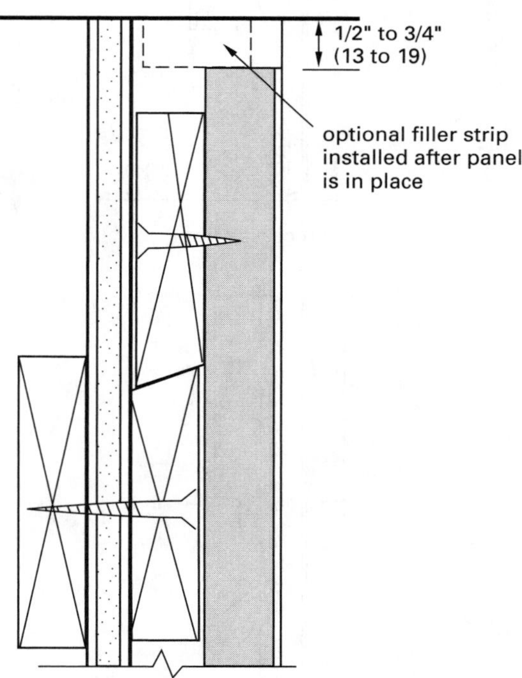


**Figure 6.18**
Panel detail at ceiling

**Figure 6.19**
Panel details
at base

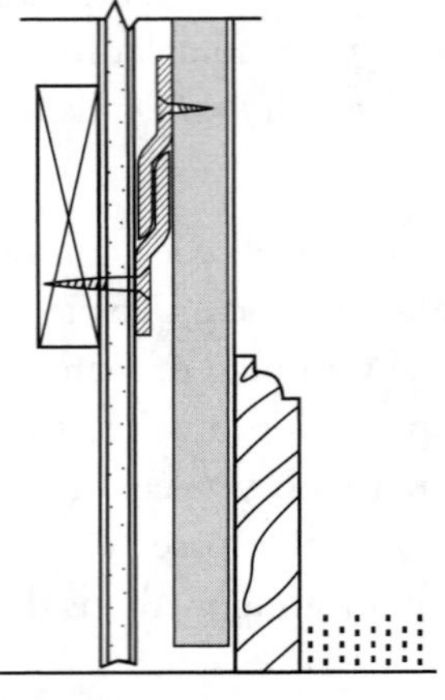

(a) applied base

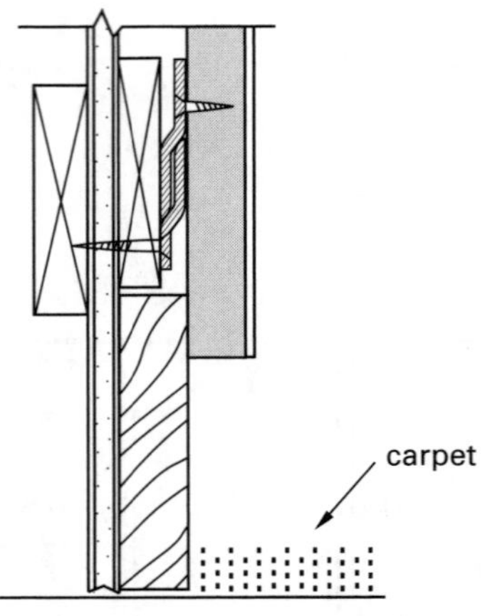


(b) recessed base

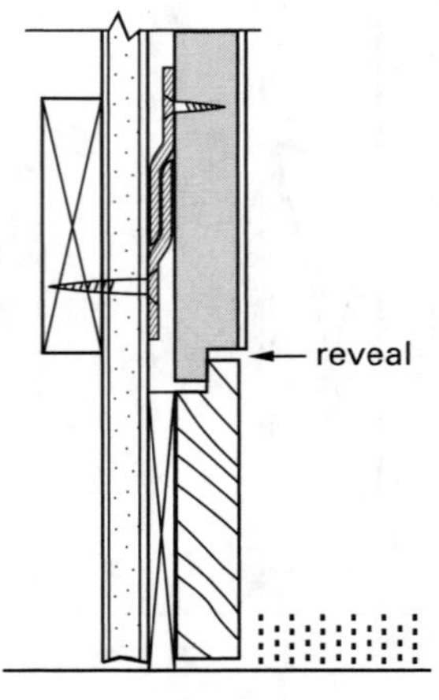


(c) flush base

## Matching wood veneer panels

When flush panels are finished with uniform materials such as plastic laminate of a single-color or fabric, matching adjacent panels is not a problem. However, when the flush panels are wood veneer, their matching is critical to the final appearance of the job. The methods of slicing a log to obtain veneers has been discussed in a previous section. This section discusses how those individual pieces of veneer are placed on a panel and how the panels are placed within a room. The three considerations, in increasing order of scale, are matching between adjacent veneer leaves, matching veneers within a panel, and matching panels within a room.

### Matching veneer leaves

Matching adjacent veneer leaves may be done in three ways, as shown in Figs. 6.23(a)–6.23(c). *Book matching* is the most common. As the veneers are sliced off the log, every other piece is turned over so that adjacent leaves form a symmetrical grain pattern. In *slip matching*, consecutive pieces are placed side by side with the same face sides being exposed. *Random matching* places veneers in random sequence, and even veneers from different flitches may be used.

Veneer leaves may be book-matched end to end as well as side to side if the length of the flitch is not long enough to cover the wall in a single piece. For rooms with high ceilings, the maximum length of flitch in the specified species should be determined so that the end conditions can be detailed accordingly.

Because book matching requires that every other leaf of veneer be turned over, the veneers may reflect light differently or accept stain and finishing differently depending on the species and flitch. The resulting color variations between veneers can be minimized by proper finishing techniques.

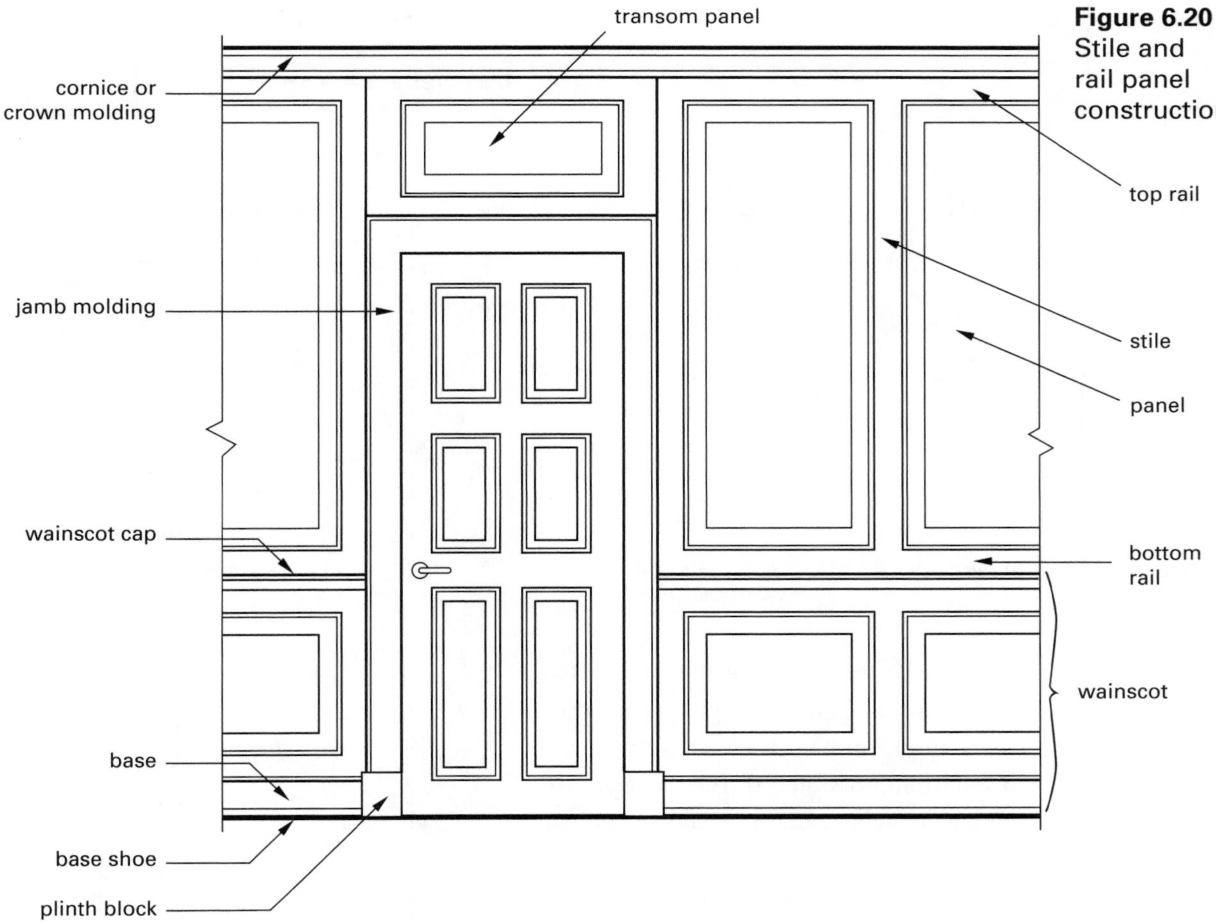

transom panel
cornice or
crown molding
top rail
jamb molding
stile
panel
wainscot cap
bottom
rail
wainscot
base
base shoe
plinth block

**Figure 6.20**
Stile and rail panel construction

face of partition
ground
panel
rim
stile
rail

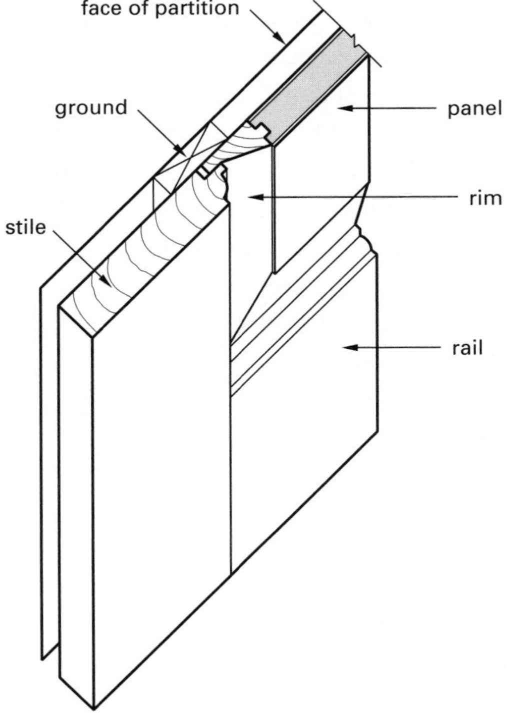

**Figure 6.21**
Stile and rail components

**Figure 6.22**
Panel details

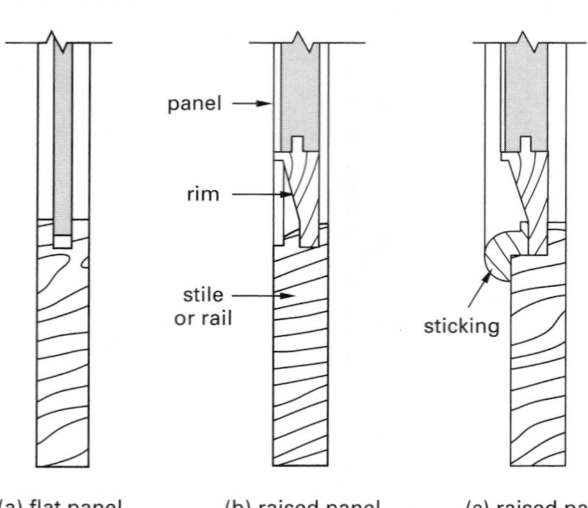


(a) flat panel

(b) raised panel

(c) raised panel with sticking

**Figure 6.23**
Matching veneer leaves

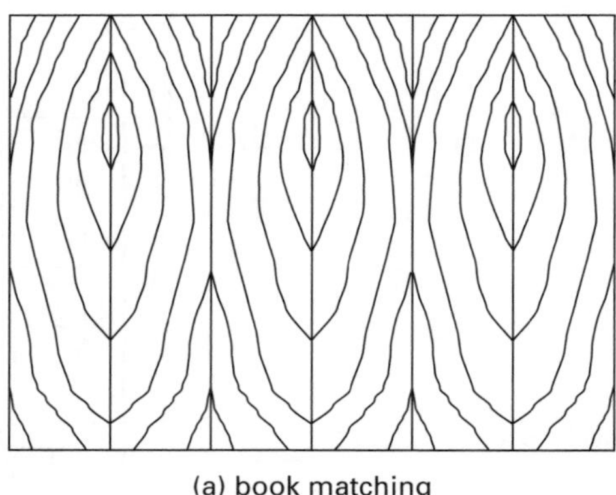

(a) book matching

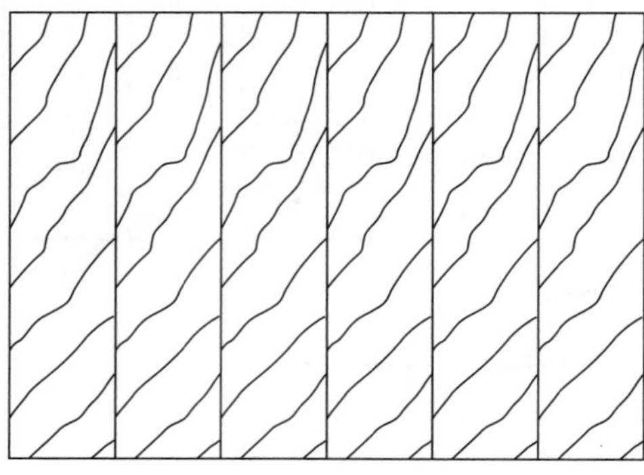

(b) slip matching

(c) random matching

## Matching veneers within a panel

Veneers must be glued to rigid panels (usually ¾ in (19 mm) particleboard) to make installation possible. If the veneers are random-matched, they are laid up in any sequence in any width. If the veneers are slip-matched, they are laid on the panels in whatever width they are as they are sliced off the log.

If the veneers are book-matched, there are three ways of matching veneers within a panel, as shown in Figs. 6.24(a)–6.24(c). A *running match* alternates book-matched veneer pieces regardless of their width or how many must be used to complete a panel. Any portion left over from the last leaf of one panel is used as the starting piece for the next. *Balance matching* uses veneer pieces trimmed to equal widths in each panel. There may be an even or odd number of individual leaves on each panel. In *center matching* there is an even number of veneer leaves of uniform width so that there is a veneer joint in the center of the panel. Center matching is the most expensive of the three methods. Balance matching is the most common type specified and produces the most pleasing assembly of veneers.

## Matching panels within a room

There are also three ways that panels can be assembled within a room to complete a project. Figures 6.25(a)–6.25(c) show these three methods by illustrating three sides of a room as though they were unfolded and the three walls laid flat.

The first and least expensive method of panel matching is called *warehouse matching*. Premanufactured panels, typically 4 ft wide by 8 ft or 10 ft long (1219 mm by 2438 or 3048 mm), are assembled from a single flitch that yields from six to twelve panels. They are field cut to fit around doors, windows, and other obstructions, resulting in some loss of grain continuity. If more than one set is required, matching the grain patterns between the two sets is not possible. Doors and cabinets cannot be matched with the paneling.

The second method, called *sequence matching*, uses panels of uniform width manufactured for a specific job and with the veneers arranged in sequence. If some panels must be trimmed to fit around doors and other obstructions, there is a moderate loss of grain continuity. Doors and cabinets cannot be matched with the paneling.

The third and most expensive method is *blueprint matching*. Here, the panels are manufactured to fit the room precisely and to line up with every obstruction so that grain continuity is uninterrupted. Veneers from the same flitch are matched over doors, cabinets, and other veneer-covered items.

## Coordination

As with cabinetwork, adequate provisions must be made in panel detailing for blocking, shim space, and scribe pieces, where the paneling is adjacent to other construction. Additional coordination items include the following.

• Wood blocking inside of partitions must be shown on the drawings for installation by other trades. If local construction

**Figure 6.24** Matching veneers within a panel

Note: adjacent panels shown slightly separated for clarity

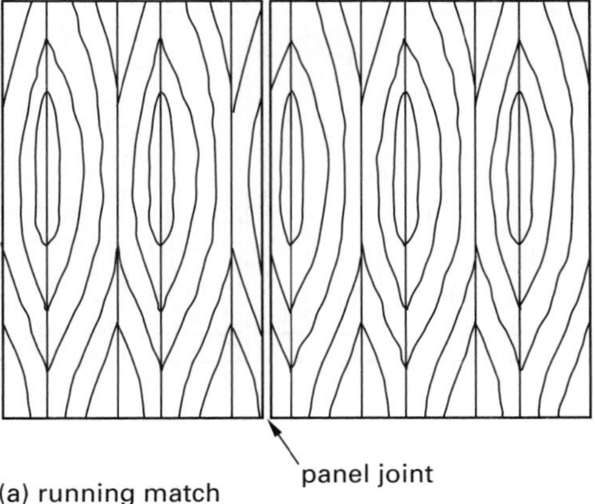


(a) running match

(b) balance match

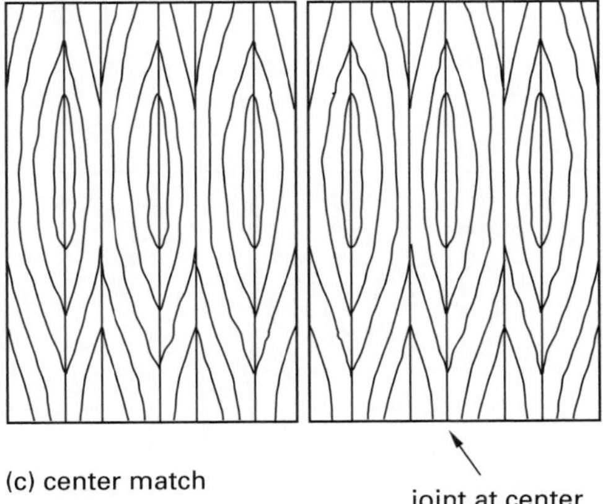


(c) center match

**Figure 6.25**
Matching panels within a room

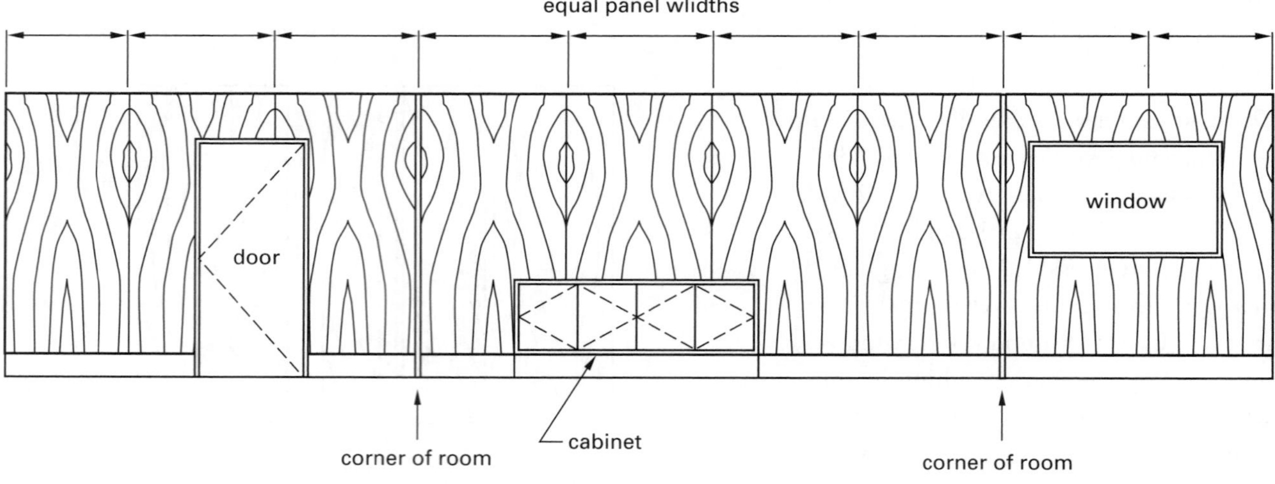


(a) warehouse match

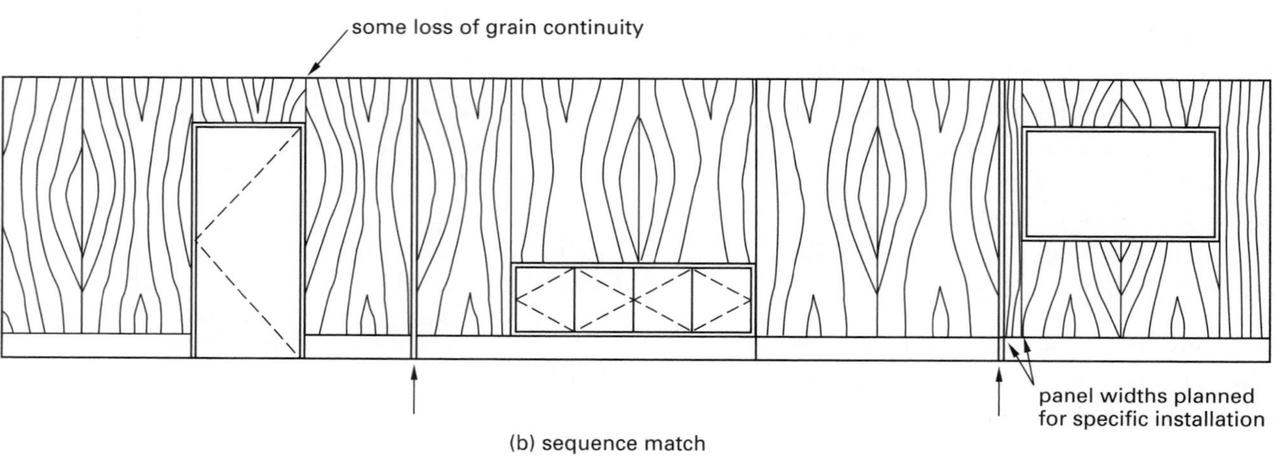


(b) sequence match

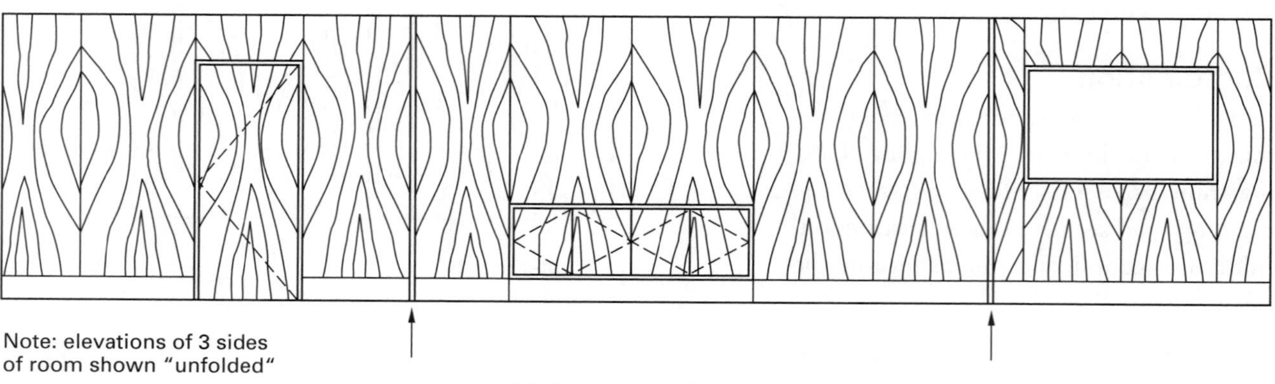

Note: elevations of 3 sides
of room shown "unfolded"


(c) blueprint match

practices require that surface backing be installed by trades other than the woodworker, the types and locations of these should be verified with the woodworker and shown on the drawings.

• The locations of all mechanical and electrical fixtures must be shown on the drawings so that the woodworker can make the necessary cutouts.

• Fire-retardant ratings of the finished paneling and wood blocking must be determined based on local codes and specifications. Refer to the section on fire ratings of architectural woodwork for more information.

## LAMINATES [064116]

### High-pressure decorative laminates

A common finishing material used with architectural woodwork is *high-pressure decorative laminate* (HPDL). This is a thin sheet material made by impregnating several layers of kraft paper with phenolic resins and overlaying the paper with a decorative melamine sheet and an alphacellulose overlay. The entire assembly is placed in a hot press under pressures as high as 1000 lbf/in.$^2$ (6895 kPa), or more where the various layers fuse together. Plastic laminates are used as finish surfaces for countertops, wall paneling, cabinets, doors, shelving, flooring, signs, and furniture.

Because laminates are very thin, they must be adhered to panel substrates, such as plywood or particleboard. However, special, thick laminates are available up to 1 in (25 mm) in thickness. Smaller pieces can be glued to solid pieces of lumber.

Several types of substrates are used for plastic laminate construction. These include particleboard, medium-density fiberboard (MDF), hardboard, and veneer core. Among these, 45 lbf density particleboard is one of the most commonly used. It is the most dimensionally stable, provides a smooth surface for laminating, has sufficient impact resistance, and provides enough strength for holding screws and for constructing panels and casework. In recent years, there has been some concern about the outgassing of formaldehyde from particleboard. With today's particleboard manufacturing techniques, the release of formaldehyde is negligible (0.3 parts per million or less). The laminate also provides a seal on the board, preventing most long-term emissions.

MDF is also a popular substrate for plastic laminate. MDF is made by breaking down

**Applicable standards for laminates**

**American National Standards Institute (ANSI):**

| | |
|---|---|
| ANSI A161.2 | *Decorative Laminate Countertops, Performance Standards for Fabricated High Pressure* |
| ANSI A208.1 | *Particleboard, Mat-Formed Wood* |
| ANSI A208.2 | *Medium Density Fiberboard for Interior Applications* |

**Architectural Woodwork Institute (AWI):**

| | |
|---|---|
| AWI | *Quality Standards,* Sections 300, 400, 500, and portions of 1300 |

**American Laminators Association (ALA):**

| | |
|---|---|
| ALA 1992 | *The Performance Standard for Thermoset Decorative Panels* |

**American Society for Testing and Materials (ASTM):**

| | |
|---|---|
| ASTM D1037 | *Standard Test Methods for Evaluating the Properties of Wood-Base Fiber and Particle Panel Materials* |

**National Electrical Manufacturers Association (NEMA):**

| | |
|---|---|
| LD 3 | *High-Pressure Decorative Laminates* |

wood fibers into very fine fluff no more than ⅛ in (3 mm) long and then mixing the fibers with glue and compressing them under high pressure. It is normally formed into 4 × 8 (1219 × 2438) sheets from ¼ in to 1¼ in (6 mm to 32 mm) thick. It can also be formed into molding from 16 ft to 24 ft (4877 mm to 7315 mm) long. Its density is from 44 lbf to 50 lbf (708 kg/m$^3$ to 800 kg/m$^3$) per cubic foot.

MDF has a smoother surface than particleboard, which reduces the potential for telegraphing through the laminate and makes this material suitable for gloss laminates. However, it is more expensive than particleboard and does not hold some types of screws as well.

In addition to being used as a substrate for laminates, MDF can be used for shelving, molding, and furniture, and as part of laminate flooring. Its dense, smooth composition allows routing and a flawless paint finish. It is dimensionally stable, so it does not warp, crack, or cup. Untreated MDF has the same fire rating as plywood, but special fire-resistant MDF is available. As with particleboard, MDF made with urea-based resins does emit formaldehyde (about 0.3 parts per million), but formaldehyde-free MDF with adhesives similar to those in polyurethane glues is available.

The last two substrates that can be used for plastic laminate, hardboard, and veneer core are not as widely used as particleboard and MDF. Like particleboard, hardboard has a smooth surface, but that can sometimes cause bonding problems. Veneer core is subject to warpage and other problems; therefore, its use is not recommended for interior applications.

Plastic laminate is available in a wide variety of finishes. The most common is the matte, or suede finish. It has a low light reflectance, is durable, and cleans easily. Another type is the mirror, or glossy, finish. This has a very high-gloss finish but should only be used for vertical applications where the potential for scratching is low. Other finishes include satin, embossed, and pebbly. Individual manufacturers should be consulted for the availability of colors and finishes.

There are several types and thicknesses of plastic laminate. The five most common are listed here.

- General purpose (GP50). This laminate is 0.050 in (1.27 mm) thick and is used for most horizontal applications.
- General purpose for vertical use (GP28). This is a thinner material manufactured for vertical applications that receive less wear and impact than horizontal surfaces. It is 0.028 in (0.71 mm) thick.
- Postforming (PF30, PF42). Although thin, general-purpose laminates can be bent to moderate radii (6 in to 8 in); a special postforming grade is required for tighter bends. Postforming grades of plastic laminate are heated in the shop, bent to the required form, and allowed to cool. Once this cooling takes place the laminate is set. PF30 laminate can be bent to an outside radius of ½ in (13 mm); PF42 can be bent to an outside radius of ⅝ in (16 mm). Inside radii of 3⁄16 in (5 mm) can also be formed.
- Cabinet liner (CL20). This laminate is 0.020 in (0.51 mm) thick and is intended for use where a decorative finish is required, but where the surface receives little wear, such as the vertical surfaces of cabinet and bookshelf interiors.
- Backing sheet (BK20). Whenever one side of a panel is faced with plastic laminate, a backing sheet must be placed on the opposite side to prevent warping and protect against dimensional instability. Backing sheets are thin, nondecorative laminates used for this purpose.

## Specialty laminates

There are several types of high-pressure decorative laminates manufactured for specific purposes. Although these generally cost more, they fill specific needs for interior construction.

• Colorthrough laminates. These laminates are manufactured with decorative papers throughout the thickness so that the resulting sheet is a solid color. This eliminates the dark line visible at the edge of sheets when they are trimmed. Colorthrough laminates are available in thickness of 0.050 in to 0.060 in (1.27 mm to 1.52 mm) and in postformed grades.

• Fire-rated laminates. These finishes comply with Class 1 or Class A ratings as long as the appropriate substrates and adhesives are selected. Their performance characteristics are the same as for standard laminates, but they cannot be postformed.

• Chemical-resistant laminates. Special formulation of the laminate materials gives these products additional resistance to strong chemicals found in laboratories, medical facilities, and photographic studios. They are available in horizontal as well as vertical thicknesses and can be postformed for curved surfaces.

• Static-dissipative laminates. For areas where static control is required, such as in hospital operating rooms, electronic manufacturing plants, and computer rooms, these laminates provide a conductive layer within the sheet. When connected to suitable grounding, they prevent the buildup of static charges and continuously channel such charges away.

• Thick laminates. Heavier, high-wear laminates are available where extra strength and impact resistance are required. Standard types include high-wear laminates, in thicknesses of 0.062, 0.080, and 0.120 in (1.58, 2.03, and 3.05 mm) (HW62, HW80, and HW120). SP125 is a specific-purpose grade with a thickness of 0.125 in (3.18 mm).

• Dimensional laminates. Dimensional laminates have deeply embossed finishes simulating textures, such as slate, woven fabrics, and leather. Because of the differences in high and low areas, they are a little more difficult to clean on horizontal surfaces, and the high points show wear more rapidly than the low points.

• Metal-faced laminates. A limited number of metal finishes is available. Metal finishes do not have the same wear resistance as real metal; therefore, metal-faced laminates should only be used on vertical surfaces subject to little abuse. They can be fabricated with standard woodworking equipment and cost much less than real metal. However, it is difficult to fabricate small, detailed items with finely crafted edges.

• Natural wood laminates. With this product, thin veneers of actual wood are bonded to the standard type of laminate kraft papers and resins. The laminate can be specified to provide untreated wood ready for finishing or with a protective layer of melamine resin.

• Flooring laminates. These are used for access flooring in computer rooms and other areas where individual panels of a raised flooring system are required. In most cases, the available colors and patterns are limited and are part of the access flooring manufacturer's standard product line, although custom orders are available.

• Tambours. Laminate-clad tambours are available from several manufacturers in colors and patterns that match other laminate sheets. Flat-sheet tambours, rounded surfaces, and other types are available.

• Engraving stock. For fabricating signs and nameplates, a special engraving stock is available with black, white, or red cores in a variety of surface colors and patterns.

For large orders and additional cost, custom patterns and colors can be specified, as can custom silk-screening of logos and other graphic designs.

## Thermoset decorative panels

Another type of laminate product is made by pressing a decorative overlay from a thermoset polyester or melamine, resin-impregnated, saturated sheet onto a cellulosic substrate, such as particleboard or medium-density fiberboard. This laminate type differs from high-pressure decorative laminates in that the decorative surface is fused to the substrate of particleboard, rather than being a thin veneer that must be adhesive bonded to another substrate. Because the process is usually done with pressures lower than HPDLs, these products are sometimes called low-pressure laminates, or melamine. The manufacturers that produce thermoset decorative panels form the American Laminators Association (ALA) and use the trade name Permalam® to identify these types of panels. The standard developed by the ALA requires that thermoset panels meet or, in some cases, exceed the minimum performance standards of HPDLs.

Because the decorative surface is part of the substrate, the potential problem of delamination is eliminated and the panels come ready to be fabricated. Generally, the cost of thermoset panels is less than that of HPDLs. However, there are currently several disadvantages to thermoset decorative panels: they come in a limited range of colors, textures, and grades; they cannot be postformed for curves; and they should not be used for high-wear horizontal surfaces, such as countertops. In addition, only a limited number of Class I or Class A fire-rated panels is available from a few manufacturers. Thermoset panels are typically used for furniture, fixtures, and kitchen cabinets, or where resistance to heavy use is not required.

Panels are available in thickness of 1/4, 3/8, 1/2, 5/8, 3/4, 1, and 1 1/8 in (6, 10, 13, 16, 19, 25, and 29 mm) in panel sizes from 4 ft to 5 ft wide (1219 mm to 1524 mm) and 6 ft to 18 ft long (1829 mm to 5486 mm).

## Detailing considerations

High-pressure decorative laminate is a very flexible material; an unlimited variety of built-in and free-standing construction can be designed. However, there are a few limitations to remember when detailing.

For panel applications, such as wall panels and cabinet fronts and sides, a balance sheet must be applied to the face opposite the finish face to prevent the panel from warping. Also, because the substrate is a wood product, panels will expand and contract with changes in temperature and humidity. There should be allowances from 1/64 in to 3/64 in (0.397 mm to 1.191 mm) between adjacent large panels to provide for dimensional changes. Wall panels are mounted to partitions in the same way as wood veneer panels, with wood cleats or Z-clips as shown in Fig. 6.16. As with wood panels, it is advisable to provide for slight misalignment between adjacent panels and to allow for dimensional changes. One way to do this is with a slight reveal joint, as shown in Fig. 6.26. Outside and inside corners can be detailed for a precise intersection as shown in Figs. 6.27(a) and 6.27(b).

Door and drawer fronts can be detailed with the faces and edges of HPDL, or two or more materials can be combined. Figures 6.28(a)–6.28(c) show some common methods of detailing cabinet door fronts.

Countertop edges are common in all types of construction. A variety of details is possible with HPDL; some samples of detailing are illustrated in Figs. 6.29(a)–6.29(d).

## STANDING AND RUNNING TRIM [064600]

Standing and running trim are items similar to standard molding sections applied as finish carpentry items. Unlike moldings, however, standing and running trim are custom fabricated to meet the requirements of a specific project.

*Standing trim* is woodwork of a fixed length intended to be installed as a single piece of wood. Examples include door frame trim, door stops, window casings, and similar items. *Running trim* is woodwork of a continuing length that must be installed in several pieces fitted end to end, such as base molding, cornices, chair rails, and soffits. *Rails* are gripping or protection surfaces on corridor walls of hospitals and the like and guard rails at glass openings.

The *profile* of trim, or its cross-sectional shape, can be identical to the many standard shapes available in premanufactured molding, or custom profiles can be milled. To create custom profiles, the mill shop makes a cutting blade with the desired profile, puts it on the molding machine, and runs solid stock through. If the profile is large or complex, more than one piece of molding may have to be run and then assembled to obtain the final trim.

When the size of hardwood handrails exceeds 1 1/16 in by 6 1/2 in (27 mm by 165 mm), the woodworking shop may glue for width or thickness to achieve the required size.

## Differences between grades of standing and running trim

Standing and running trim can be specified in any of the three AWI grades, but only Premium or Custom should be used for most quality woodwork. Premium grade provides a smoother finish for both transparent and opaque finishes. The differences between these two grades are summarized in Table 6.10.

## FIRE RATINGS OF ARCHITECTURAL WOODWORK

Although specific building code requirements for use of woodwork vary slightly across the United States and in Canada, there are many similarities among the codes. Refer to Ch. 19 for information on model building codes and a more complete discussion of occupancy and use areas.

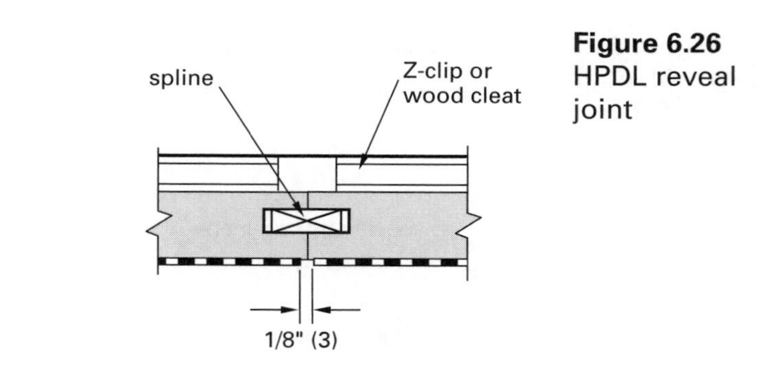


**Figure 6.26**
HPDL reveal joint

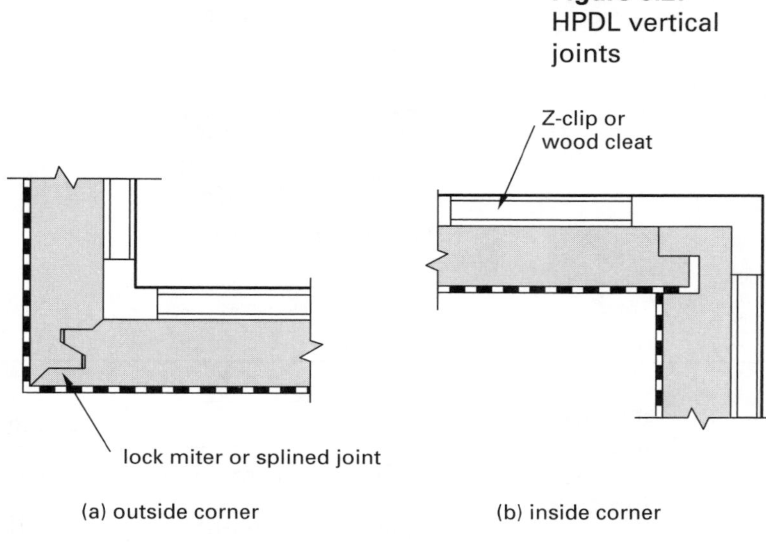


**Figure 6.27**
HPDL vertical joints

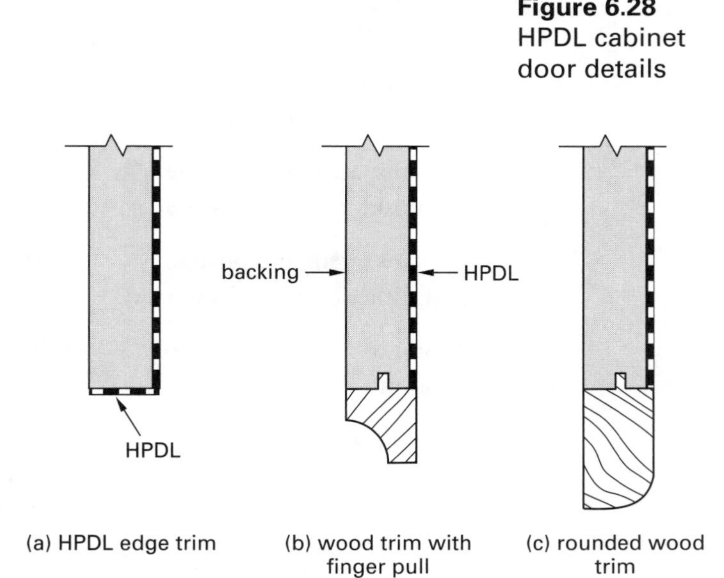


**Figure 6.28**
HPDL cabinet door details

**Figure 6.29**
HPDL edge treatments

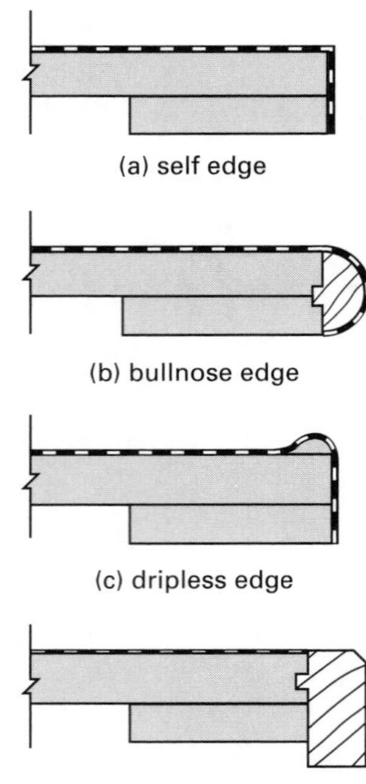


In general, most of the model building codes regulate the use of woodwork as a wall or ceiling finish but do not regulate the use of wood in furniture, cabinets, or trim. This includes cabinets attached to the structure.

Interior finish is defined in the International Building Code (IBC) (and similarly in other model codes) as wall and ceiling finish, including wainscoting, paneling, or other finish types applied structurally or for decoration, acoustical correction, surface insulation, or similar purposes. Requirements do not apply to trim (defined as picture molds, chair rails, baseboards, and handrails); to doors and windows or their frames; or to materials that are less than 1/28 in (0.9 mm) thick cemented to the surface of walls or ceilings.

The model building codes regulate the use of woodwork as a finish material by first

**Table 6.10**
Differences between premium and custom grades for standing and running trim

| item | premium grade | custom grade |
|---|---|---|
| material for transparent finish | Grade I | Grade II |
| material for opaque finish | Grade II | Grade II |
| smoothness of exposed surfaces | | |
| transparent and opaque finshes on flat surfaces | 150 grit sandpaper | 120 grit sandpaper |
| transparent and opaque finishes on molded surfaces | 120 grit sandpaper | 20 knife cuts per inch |
| transparent and opaque finishes on shaped surfaces | 120 grit sandpaper | 20 knife cuts per inch |
| transparent and opaque finishes on turned surfaces | 120 grit sandpaper | 100 grit sandpaper |
| flushness variation of factory joints | 0.015 in (0.38 mm) | 0.025 in (0.64 mm) |
| sanding cross scratches | none allowed for transparent finishes; not to exceed 0.25 in (6.4 mm) for opaque surfaces | none allowed for transparent finishes; not to exceed 0.25 in (6.4 mm) for opaque surfaces |

Source: Compiled from information in *Architectural Woodwork Quality Standards, 8th Edition, Version 1.0*, copyright 2003.

establishing different use areas in a building depending on their importance in relationship to the means of egress from the building. The three use areas include vertical exits and exit passageways, exit access corridors and other exitways, and rooms and enclosed spaces. Vertical exits (stairways) and dedicated exit passageways are protected escape routes and must have the most restrictive flame-spread classification for interior finishes. Exit access corridors and other exitways are not as protected and often have a lower flame-spread classification requirement. Rooms and enclosed spaces consist of all the remaining areas in a building and generally have the least-restrictive requirements.

The codes also divide buildings into categories, depending on their occupancy. While specific terms vary slightly from one code to the next, the general occupancy classifications include assembly, educational, mercantile, business, institutional, and residential.

For each use area in each occupancy group, the codes then limit the flammability of finish materials. For example, an exit stairway in a nursing home is inherently a more critical area than a living room of a single-family house, so its finishes must be less flammable.

Finish materials are placed in one of three classes depending on their flame-spread ratings. Flame-spread ratings indicate the flammability of a finish and are determined by subjecting the finish to a standardized laboratory test. Flame-spread ratings from 0 to 25 are considered Class A ratings (or Class I in certain codes); ratings from 26 to 75 are Class B ratings (or Class II); and ratings from 76 to 200 are Class C ratings (or Class III). Refer to Ch. 19 for more information.

All the model building codes have tables that indicate what flame-spread classification must be met, depending on the use area and occupancy group. Exits are always the most restrictive and require Class A (or Class I) finishes. Corridors generally require Class B finishes, and other areas typically require Class C finishes. See Table 19.3 for specific requirements in the IBC.

The model codes sometimes allow an increase of one category in the flame-spread classification of interior finishes when automatic sprinklers are installed throughout the building. For example, a corridor that requires a Class B finish in a nonsprinkler-fitted building may be allowed a Class C finish in a sprinkler-fitted building.

Most wood species without flame-retardant treatment have flame-spread ratings less than 200, and some even have ratings less than 75. This makes them appropriate for "other use" areas and some corridors without any special consideration.

The model codes do not regulate the use of wood for free-standing furniture or for cabinets and shelves attached to the building because they are not considered fixed construction. Although trim is not considered to be a wall or ceiling finish and is not regulated as such, it is regulated under a section on decoration and trim. The IBC states that material used as interior trim must have a minimum Class C flame spread index and smoke-developed index. Further, combustible trim, excluding handrails and guardrails, cannot exceed 10% of the aggregate wall or ceiling area in which it is located. Trim is not regulated in the National Building Code of Canada (NBCC) if it has a flame-spread rating less than 150 and its area does not exceed 10% of the area of the wall or ceiling on which it occurs.

The strictest regulation on the use of woodwork as an interior finish occurs when paneling is used on walls and ceilings. The paneling must meet the maximum flame-spread regulations of the code in force, based on occupancy and use area. However, because the codes generally do not regulate finishes less than 1⁄28 in (0.9 mm) thick, veneer less than this thickness with any flame-spread rating may be used if it is placed on fire-retardant-treated material, such as particleboard.

When high-pressure decorative laminate (HPDL) is used on paneling, it is not subject to regulation if it is less than 1⁄28 in (0.9 mm) thick. However, it should be applied to a substrate (usually particleboard) that is fire-retardant treated. Laminate for vertical use (GP28) is 0.028 in (0.71 mm) thick and, therefore, does not have to be treated. When thicker laminate is used and the flame- spread rating is critical, fire-rated laminate can be used on a fire-retardant treated substrate with the appropriate adhesive.

Blocking on the outside of the partition on which paneling is applied should also be fire-retardant-treated. In addition, some codes may require that blocking within the partition also be fire-retardant treated.

## SPECIAL WOODWORK ITEMS

Cabinets, shelving, paneling, and standing and running trim are some of the most common types of architectural woodwork; however, there are many other finish items that a mill shop can produce. These include custom doors and frames, upholstered wall systems, solid surfacing materials, stairwork, handrails, screens, shutters, and free-standing furniture.

### Doors

When a desired type, size, or finish of door is not available as a standard or custom order from a door manufacturer, an architectural woodworking shop can custom fabricate nearly any type of door, including flush doors as well as stile and rail doors. Usually, a custom door is required when an exotic species of wood is specified for the surface, when the door is part of a blueprint matching of interior paneling, or when additional materials are applied to the door. Custom-designed stile and rail doors, curved doors, blind doors, and oversized doors are also common items that require specialty work.

As with other custom woodwork items, doors are specified in any of the three AWI grades of Premium, Custom, or Economy. For wood veneer doors manufactured for a transparent finish, Premium grade requires that the vertical edges of the door be the same species as the face veneer and that the veneers for pairs of doors and doors with transoms be matched. These are not requirements for Custom grade doors. Refer to the AWI Quality Standards for other construction details based on these three grades.

For flush doors, various core and face constructions are available, but they are designated differently than stock doors using the WDMA I.S. 1 standards described in Ch. 3. A summary of these is shown in Table 6.11, and diagrams of common door constructions are shown in Fig. 3.6.

### Upholstered wall systems [097700]

There are several ways to cover walls with a fabric finish. Several of these, including those using proprietary track systems, are discussed in Ch. 10. Direct application of fabric and installation of proprietary systems are performed by separate contractors. However, when acoustic fabric-wrapped panels are detailed and specified, they are often fabricated and installed by the woodwork contractor.

Figure 6.30 illustrates one method of detailing a fabric-wrapped panel (showing two possible edge conditions) for fabrication by a woodwork contractor. As with other finish panels, the panel is hung on the wall using Z-clips or wood cleats. The panel is made from plywood or particleboard framed on all four sides with continuous wood blocking. The

**Table 6.11**
AWI door types

| AWI symbol | description |
|---|---|
| PC-5 ME | Particleboard core with crossband and face veneer on each side. Stiles and rails bonded to core. Vertical edge species matches face veneer species. |
| PC-5 CE | Particleboard core with crossband and face veneer on each side. Stiles and rails bonded to core. Vertical edge species compatible with face veneer species. |
| PC-7 ME | Particleboard core with two crossbands and face veneer on each side. Stiles and rails bonded to core. Vertical edge species matches face veneer species. |
| PC-7 CE | Particleboard core with two crossbands and face veneer on each side. Stiles and rails bonded to core. Vertical edge species compatible face veneer species. |
| PC-HPDL-3 | Particleboard core with nominal 0.048 in (1.22 mm) high-pressure decorative laminate each side. Stiles and rails bonded to core. |
| PC-HPDL-5 | Nominal 0.048 in (1.22 mm) high-pressure decorative laminate each side glued to hardwood crossbands on particleboard core assembly. Stiles and rails bonded to core. |
| SCLC-5 ME | Structural composite lumber core with crossband and face veneer on each side. Stiles and rails bonded to core. Vertical edge species matches face veneer species. |
| SCLC-5 CE | Structural composite lumber core with crossband and face veneer on each side. Stiles and rails bonded to core. Vertical edge species compatible with face veneer species. |
| SCLC -7 ME | Same as SLC-5 ME, but with seven-ply construction. |
| SCLC-7 CE | Same as SLC-5 CE, but with seven-ply construction. |
| SCLC-HPDL-5 | Nominal 0.048 in (1.22 mm) high-pressure decorative laminate each side glued to hardwood crossbands on structural composite lumber core assembly. Stiles and rails bonded to core. |
| | Note: particleboard core and SCLC core doors also available where the stiles and rails are NOT bonded to the core. Refer to AWI standards for a complete description. Stave lumber cores are also available but have commonly been replaced by SCLC cores. |
| FD 1½ | 1½-hour-rated and labeled fire door with either wood veneer or high-pressure decorative laminate face. |
| FD 1 | 1-hour-rated and labeled fire door with either wood veneer or high-pressure decorative laminate face. |
| FD ¾ | ¾-hour-rated and labeled fire door with either wood veneer or high-pressure decorative laminate face. |
| FD ⅓ | ⅓-hour-rated and labeled fire door with either wood veneer or high-pressure decorative laminate face. |
| SR | Sound retardant door manufactured to conform to STC ratings prescribed in ASTM E90. Available in thicknesses of 1¾, 2¼, 2½ in (44.4, 57.1, and 63.5 mm) and thicker as required. |
| LL | Lead-lined doors. Thickness of lead must be specified based on shielding rating required. May have either wood veneer or HPDL veneer and lead-lined vision panel. |
| ES | Electrostatic shielded door. Wire mesh embedded in center of core or between crossbanding and core. Mesh is grounded with braided wire pigtails through hinges. Number of pigtails must be specified. |
| IHC | Institutional hollow core. Stiles and rails wider than standard hollow core door. |
| SHC | Standard hollow core. Most economical door. |

Source: *Architectural Woodwork Quality Standards, 8th Edition, Version 1.0,* copyright 2003.

**Figure 6.30**
Fabric-wrapped panel

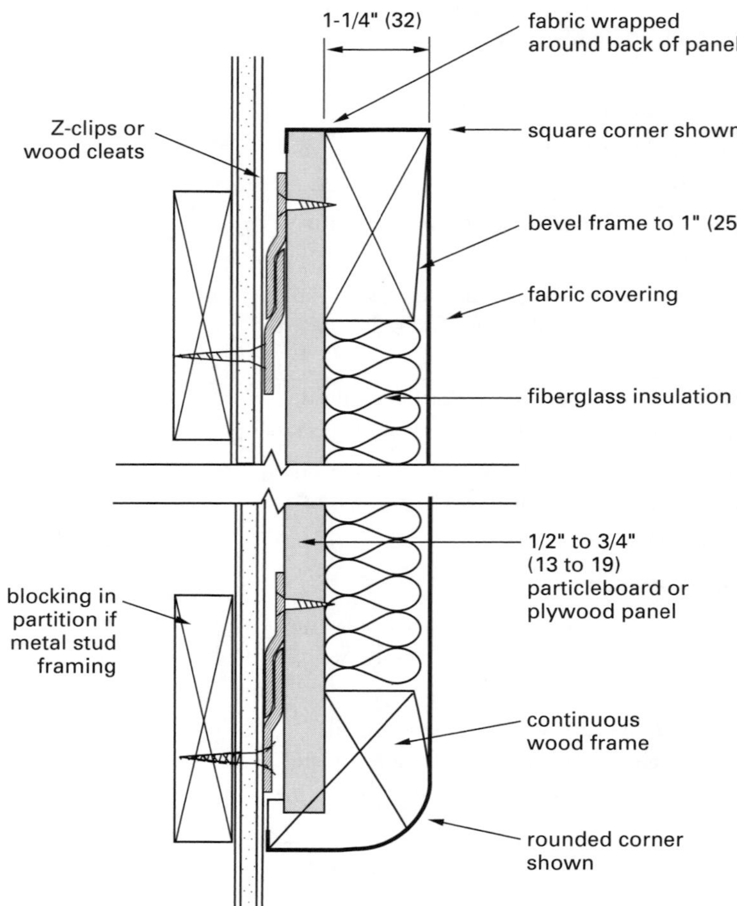


edges of the frame can be milled to any desired profile. The frame should be tapered slightly toward the interior of the panel to avoid having the concealed edge telegraph through the fabric. The interior of the panel is filled with fiberglass panels or fabric batting to act as the sound-absorbent material. If a hanging strip is required for artwork or other wall-suspended material, its size and location should be indicated on the drawings. Similar edge details can be used to create blind doors within the field of the partition.

It is usually best to limit woodworker-fabricated panels to simple shapes that can be covered with a single width of fabric. For walls with curves, angles, cutouts, and complex forms, and where continuous fabric is used, it is usually best to use one of the proprietary systems described in Ch. 10.

## Solid surfacing materials [066116]

Solid surfacing is a generic term for homogeneous, polymer-based surfacing materials. It is a combination of two ingredients—a filler, usually alumina trihydrate (ATH), and a clear resin binder, either acrylic or polyester—or a mixture of the two. Various colors and speckles can be added with pigments and small bits of the product itself. The material can be formed into flat sheets or into shapes such as kitchen sinks. Solid surfacing is most commonly used for kitchen and bath countertops, sinks, shower enclosures, toilet partitions, bars, and other areas where high-pressure plastic laminate might be used. However, it can also be used for furniture, flooring, and various consumer products.

Sheet goods used for countertops are normally ¾ in (19 mm) thick, but newer, lower-priced products are ½ in (12 mm) thick. There is even a ⅛ in (3 mm) thick product that is applied as a veneer; ¹⁄₁₆ in (2 mm) spray-on surfacing is also available. However, most fabricators still prefer to use the ¾ in material.

Because the color is integrated throughout the thickness of the material, scratches, dents, stains, and other types of minor damage can be sanded out or cleaned with a household abrasive cleanser. Because many of the available patterns resemble stone, solid surfacing is often used as a lightweight substitute for stone tops. One disadvantage to solid surfacing is its cost. It is about three times as expensive as high-pressure plastic laminate, but similar in cost to some granite or marble. The cost can be raised considerably if ornate inlays or decorative patterns are used.

Solid surfacing materials are easily fabricated and installed with normal woodworking tools. Edges can be routed for decorative effect. When two pieces must be butted together, a two-part epoxy or liquid form of the material is used for a seamless appearance.

## FINISHES [064000]

Finish is used on woodwork to protect it from moisture, chemicals, and contact, and to enhance its appearance. Woodwork can either be field finished or factory finished. Because it is more controllable, a factory finish is the preferred method, although minor cabinet and trim work is often field finished in single-family residential construction. For high-quality woodwork, field finishing is generally limited to minor touchup and repair.

Prior to finishing, the wood must be sanded properly and filled if desired. On many open-grained woods, such as oak, mahogany, and teak, a filler should be applied prior to finishing to give a more uniform appearance to the millwork; however, this is not required. Other types of surface preparation are also possible, depending on the aesthetic effect desired. The wood may be bleached to lighten it or to provide uniformity of color. Wood may also be mechanically or physically distressed to give it an antiqued or aged appearance. The color of the wood can also be changed in subsequent finishing operations by using shading or toning compounds.

### Opaque finishes

Opaque finishes include lacquer, varnish, polyurethane, and polyester. They should only be used on closed-grain woods where solid stock is required, and on medium-density fiberboard where sheet materials are required.

*Lacquer* is a coating material with a high nitrocellulose content modified with resins and plasticizers dissolved in a volatile solvent. Catalyzed lacquers contain an extra ingredient that speeds drying time and gives the finish additional hardness.

*Varnish* is a material consisting of various types of resinous material dissolved in one of several types of volatile liquids. Conversion varnish is produced with alkyd and urea formaldehyde resins. When a high solids content is specified, the finish becomes opaque.

*Polyurethane* is a synthetic finish that gives a very hard, durable finish. Although difficult to repair or refinish, polyurethane finishes offer superior resistance to water, many commercial and household chemicals, and abrasion. Opaque polyurethanes are available in sheens from dull satin to full gloss.

*Polyesters* are another type of synthetic finish that give the hardest, most durable finish possible. Opaque polyesters can be colored and are available only in a full gloss sheen. Like polyurethanes, polyester finishes are very difficult to repair and refinish outside the shop, but they give very durable finishes with as much as 80% of the hardness of glass.

### Transparent finishes

Transparent finishes include lacquer, varnish, vinyl, penetrating oils, polyurethane, and polyester.

#### Lacquer and varnish

Standard lacquers are easy to apply, easy to repair, and relatively low in cost. However, they do not provide the chemical and wear resistance that some of the other finishes provide. Catalyzed lacquers for transparent finishes are more difficult to repair and refinish, but are more durable and resistant to commercial and household chemicals. A special water-reducible acrylic lacquer is available if local regulations prohibit the use of other types of lacquers.

Conversion varnish has many of the same advantages of lacquer but can often be applied with fewer coats.

#### Vinyl

Catalyzed vinyl yields a surface that has the most chemical resistance of the standard lacquer, varnish, and vinyl finishes. Vinyl is also very resistant to scratching, abrasion, and other mechanical damage.

### Oils

Oil finishes are one of the traditional wood finishes. They are easily applied and give a rich look to wood, but they require re-oiling periodically and tend to darken with age. The look of an oil finish can be achieved with a catalyzed vinyl.

### Polyurethane and polyester

As with the opaque finishes, both polyurethane and polyester provide the most durable transparent finishes possible. They are the most expensive of the finishing systems and require skilled applicators. Transparent polyurethanes are available in sheens from dull to full gloss, while polyesters are available only in full gloss.

**Table 6.12**
AWI finish systems

| commonly available finishes | | |
|---|---|---|
| finish system | type | typical uses |
| nitrocellulose lacquer | transparent/opaque | interior trim, paneling, furniture, and ornamental work |
| pre-catalyzed lacquer | transparent/opaque | interior casework, paneling, furniture, ornamental work, frames, windows, blinds, shutters, and doors |
| post-catalyzed lacquer | transparent | interior casework, paneling, furniture, ornamental work, frames, windows, blinds, shutters, and doors |
| CAB[(1)] and water acrylic lacquer | transparent/opaque | interior casework, paneling, furniture, ornamental work, frames, windows, blinds, shutters, and doors |
| conversion varnish | transparent/opaque | interior casework, paneling, furniture, ornamental work, frames, windows, blinds, shutters, and doors |
| specialty finishes | | |
| finish system | type | typical uses |
| penetrating oil | transparent | interior use on furniture or trims with very low sheen |
| catalyzed vinyl | transparent/opaque | interior use on kitchen, bath, office furniture, and laboratory casework |
| catalyzed polyurethane | transparent/opaque | interior use for floors, stairs, high-impact areas and some doors |
| polyester | transparent/opaque | interior casework, paneling, furniture, ornamental work, windows, blinds, shutters, and some doors |
| UV curable epoxy polyester, urethane | transparent/opaque | interior doors, paneling, flooring, stair parts, and casework where applicable |

[(1)] cellulose acetate butyrate (CAB)

Source: *Architectural Woodwork Quality Standards, 8th Edition, Version 1.0*, copyright 2003.

### Stains

Prior to applying the final finish, wood may be stained to modify its color. The two types are water-based and solvent-based stains. Water-based stains yield a uniform color but raise the grain. Solvent-based stains dry quickly and do not raise the grain, but they are less uniform.

For shop-finished millwork, the Architectural Woodwork Institute lists 10 typical and specialty finishing systems, which include both transparent and opaque finishes. See Table 6.12. These are not the only finish systems available, but they make it easy to specify and provide a common standard. Refer to the AWI *Quality Standards* for more information on these finishes.

Whichever finish is selected, the specifications should include the requirement that finish samples be provided by the woodworker and approved prior to fabrication. If specific colors of stain or sheen must be matched, samples of these must be supplied by the designer to the mill shop so that finish samples can be made for approval.

## INSTALLATION OF ARCHITECTURAL WOODWORK [064000]

The mill shop is responsible for installing the woodwork they produce unless other contractual arrangements are made. Items are manufactured in sizes as large as practically possible and delivered to the job site when most of the other finish work has been completed. The mill shop is responsible for determining how to prefabricate the components and for assembling them in the field. However, problems should be anticipated, and very large units should be designed so that there are logical places where the woodworking shop can join units without compromising design intent. The shop drawings should show how the mill shop intends to break down the woodwork for shipment and install it. Potential problems should be discussed with the mill shop when the shop drawings are reviewed.

The AWI *Quality Standards* give the methods and allowable tolerances for installation of woodwork based on whether the wood is Premium or Custom grade.

# 7

# DECORATIVE METALS

Decorative metals include a wide variety of both functional and decorative products. These include spiral stairs, handrails, guardrails, and elevator interiors. Metal may also be used for custom doors and door facings, partition and millwork facings, building directories and kiosks, signs, custom light fixtures, ceilings, or as part of almost any construction assembly. The decorative options available to the designer are almost limitless. The most commonly used decorative metals include stainless steel, the copper alloys of bronze and brass, and aluminum. Carbon steel, copper, iron, zinc, and porcelain enamel are used less frequently.

In addition, steel or aluminum may be required strictly for utilitarian purposes to support or brace millwork, partitions, ceilings, and other construction.

## STAINLESS STEEL [057500]

### Types and uses

Stainless steel is an alloy of steel containing 12%, or more, of chromium. Additional elements, such as nickel, manganese, and molybdenum, are added to most types of stainless steel to impart particular qualities. Stainless steel is used for its corrosion resistance, strength, and appearance. In some alloys it is the strongest architectural metal available. For interior construction, common uses include wall and door coverings, railings, elevator finishes, lavatory and kitchen equipment, furniture, hardware, and concealed anchors and fasteners.

There are dozens of different types of stainless steels based on the composition of alloys, but only seven are commonly used for architectural purposes. They are referred to by number and include Types 201, 301, 302, 304, 316, 410, and 430, with Types 304 and 430 used the most for interior applications. The 200 series is also referred to as chromium-nickel-manganese stainless steel because of these added elements. The 300 series is chromium-nickel, and the 400 series is straight chromium. Table 7.1 summarizes the types, properties, and uses of stainless steel for interior design applications.

### Standard forms

Stainless steel is available in several stock forms that metal fabricators use to construct interior components. Knowing the availability of these forms when developing custom details can help reduce costs and simplify fabrication. These forms and their

## Alloy numbering systems

Stainless steel and other metals are commonly referred to by various names and numbers which, in the past, have been unique to each industry. Today, the Unified Numbering System (UNS) is used to designate all commercial metals and alloys. A typical UNS number consists of a letter prefix to designate the general type of metal and is followed by a five-digit number that identifies the specific alloy. The letter A represents aluminum; C, copper and copper alloys; N, nickel and nickel alloys; F, cast irons and cast steels; G, carbon and alloy steels; and S, stainless steel. For stainless steel and the copper alloys, the first three digits of the number are the same as the former alloy number type. For example, for Type 304 stainless steel, the UNS number is S30400. For copper alloy 280, which is also sometimes called by its previous trade name, muntz metal, the new number is C28000. The position of the old number designations in the new system makes it relatively easy to use both systems.

**Table 7.1**
Types and properties of stainless steel

| type | properties | uses |
|---|---|---|
| 201 | Similar to 301 and 302 but stronger and harder. | Where higher strength than 301 or 302 is required. |
| 301 | Can be cold rolled to very high tensile strengths; 300 series cannot be hardened by heat treatment; 300 series is nonmagnetic. | Structural members; roof drainage products. |
| 302 | Highly resistant to atmospheric corrosion; strong and hard. | Building exterior elements. |
| 304 | Similar to type 302 but is better for welding; most common type for architectural work and has largely replaced type 302. (302 and 304 are often referred to as 18-8 stainless because of the percentage of chromium and nickel.) | Store fronts, fascias, doors, railings, column covers, food preparation equipment, sinks, countertops; applications where welding is required. |
| 316 | Contains molybdenum for extra corrosion resistance for marine or extremely corrosive industrial environments. | Building elements where extreme corrosion is present or near saltwater locations. |
| 410 | Can be hardened by heat treatment; 400 series is magnetic. | Bolts, nuts, screws, and other fasteners in protected locations; special extruded shapes. |
| 430 | Less corrosion resistant than the 200 and 300 series; used primarily for interior applications; cannot be hardened by heat treatment. | Trim, column covers, appliances, railings, and other interior applications where lowest cost is required. |

standard nomenclature include sheet, plates, strips, bars, pipes, and tubing. See Fig. 7.1.

Sheet stock is considered any material less than 3/16 in (4.8 mm) thick and 24 in (610 mm) wide, or wider. Plates are pieces 3/16 in thick and thicker, and over 10 in (254 mm) wide. Strip stock is any material under 3/16 in thick and under 24 in. wide. Bar stock includes rounds, squares, flats, octagons, and hexagons. Flat bar stock is available in thicknesses from 1/8 in (3.2 mm) and thicker, and from 1/4 in up to 10 in wide (6.4 mm up to 254 mm). Round and square bar stock is available in diameters and sizes starting at 1/4 in (6.4 mm).

For larger round and rectangular sections pipe or tubing can be used. Round pipe is produced in standardized sizes and wall thicknesses and is used for many structural purposes as well as for pressure applications. It is subjected to several processes and mechanical tests at the mill. Round, square, and rectangular tubing is manufactured to exact outside diameter dimensions in a variety of diameters and wall thicknesses and is available in a wider variety of alloys and finishes not commonly available in pipe.

Both pipe and tubing are manufactured in either a welded or seamless form. Welded pipe and tubing are formed from coiled strip stock that is bent into shape and continuously welded. Seamless pipe and tubing are formed by extrusion. Tubing costs much less than pipe, and "ornamental" tubing (which is formed by welding) should be specified for most ornamental interior applications. Commonly available sizes of round, square, and rectangular tubing are shown in Figs. 7.2(a)–7.2(c).

Stainless steel is also available in other common shapes. Angles, channels, tees, and other structural shapes can be used in detailing; however, they are expensive because of their extra weight. Table 7.2 lists some typical sizes for small shapes used for interior detailing.

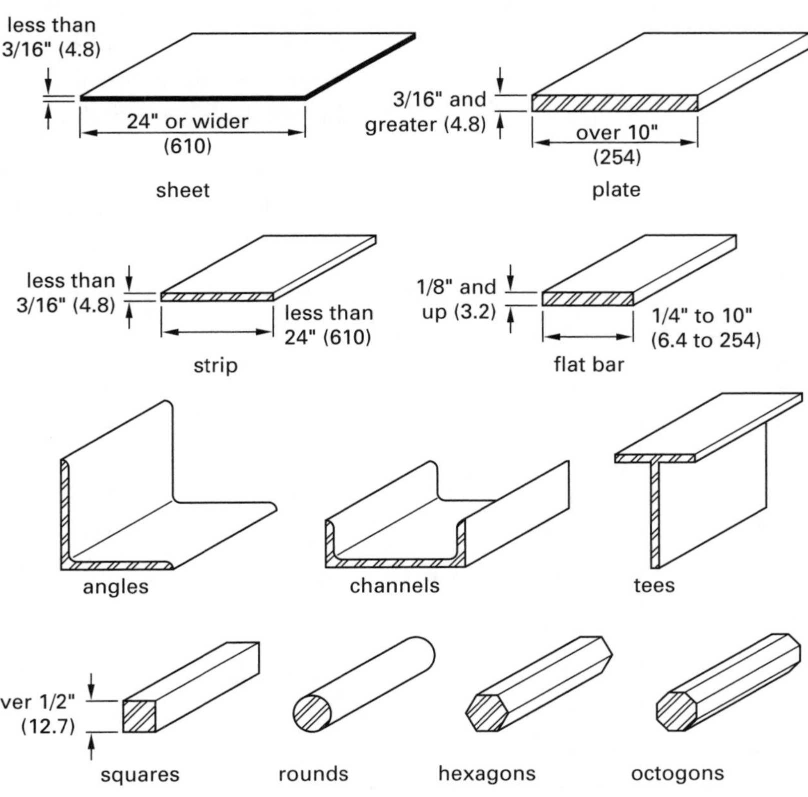


**Figure 7.1**
Stainless steel forms

**Figure 7.2**
Stainless steel ornamental tubing sizes

outside measurements

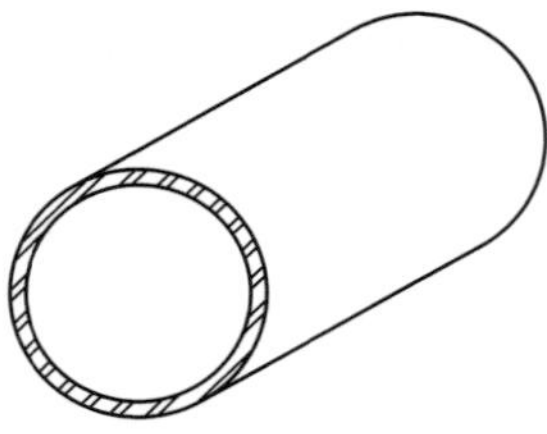

| in | mm |
|---|---|
| 1 | 25.4 |
| 1-1/2 | 38.1 |
| 2 | 50.8 |
| 2-1/2 | 63.5 |
| 3 | 76.2 |

(a) round tubing

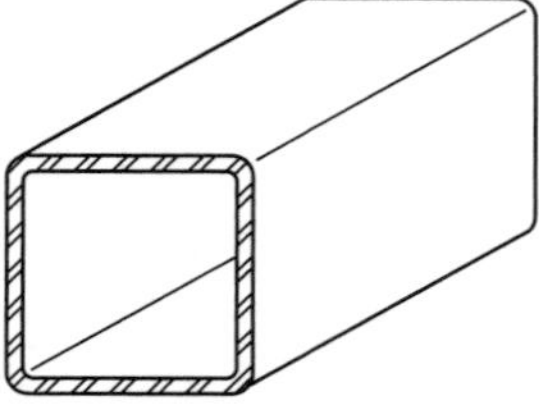

| in | mm |
|---|---|
| 3/4 | 19 |
| 1 | 25.4 |
| 1-1/4 | 31.8 |
| 1-1/2 | 38.1 |
| 1-3/4 | 44.5 |
| 2 | 50.8 |

(b) square tubing

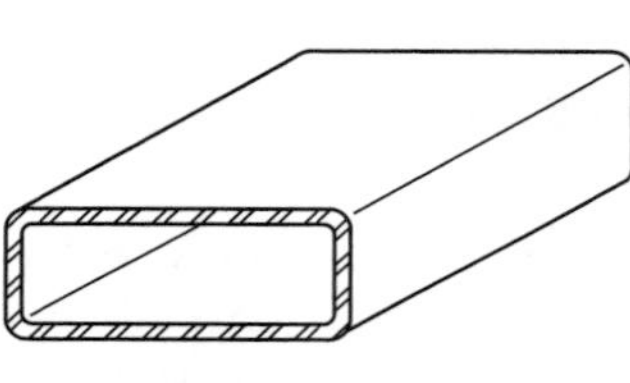

| in | mm |
|---|---|
| 1/2 x 1-1/2 | 12.7 x 38.1 |
| 3/4 x 1-1/4 | 19 x 31.8 |
| 3/4 x 1-1/2 | 19 x 38.1 |
| 1 x 1-1/2 | 25.4 x 38.1 |
| 1 x 2 | 25.4 x 50.8 |
| 1-1/4 x 2-1/2 | 31.8 x 63.5 |
| 1-3/4 x 3 | 44.5 x 76.2 |
| 1-3/4 x 4 | 44.5 x 101.6 |

(c) rectangular tubing

## Stainless steel finishes [057500]

Stainless steel is available in several finishes. These are produced either at the mill or by a metal fabricator and include rolled, polished, and etched finishes. Other types are available, but these are seldom used for architectural purposes.

Rolled finishes are produced on sheet material by passing the steel between rollers under pressure at the mill. The finish of the steel depends on the finish of the rollers and can range from a bright, reflective surface to a deeply embossed pattern. Each manufacturer produces its own set of proprietary rolled finishes and should be consulted concerning availability. Rolled finishes are the least expensive of all the finishes.

Polished finishes are the most common for architectural applications. These are produced by grinding, polishing, and sometimes buffing the metal until the desired surface is obtained. There are five industry-standard polished finishes for sheet and strip stock, which are described in Table 7.3. Generally, the more polished the finish, the higher the cost. Finishes for plates, bars, and tubing are specified a little differently, but all can be mechanically polished to match the sheet finishes described in Table 7.3.

Etched finishes are produced by dry or wet methods. Dry etching uses blasting with

**Table 7.2**
Standard sizes of stainless steel forms

| sizes | | thicknesses | |
|---|---|---|---|
| in | mm | in | mm |
| ¾ × ¾ | 19.1 × 19.1 | ⅛ | 3.2 |
| 1 × 1 | 25.4 × 25.4 | ⅛ and 3/16 | 3.2 and 4.8 |
| 1¼ × 1¼ | 31.8 × 31.8 | ⅛ and 3/16 | 3.2 and 4.8 |
| 1½ × 1½ | 38.1 × 38.1 | ⅛ and 3/16 | 3.2 and 4.8 |
| 2 × 2 | 50.8 × 50.8 | 3/16 and ¼ | 4.8 and 6.4 |
| 2½ × 2½ | 63.5 × 63.5 | 3/16 and ¼ | 4.8 and 6.4 |
| 3 × 3 | 76.2 × 76.2 | ¼, 5/16, and ⅜ | 4.8, 7.9, and 9.5 |

Table 7.3
Selected finishes of stainless steel

| finish no. | description | typical uses |
|---|---|---|
| 3 | Dull finish obtained by finishing with a 100-grit abrasive. | Institutional kitchen equipment; some architectural components where dull finish and low cost are required. |
| 4 | General-purpose polished finish obtained by finishing with a 120–150 mesh abrasive. It shows a visible grain that prevents mirror reflection. | Wall panels, column covers, restaurant equipment, hospital equipment, elevator interiors and doors, and furniture. |
| 6 | Dull satin finish with low luster. Has lower reflectivity than a no. 4 finish. | Wall panels, doors, and applications where contrasted with brighter finishes. |
| 7 | Highly reflective finish, almost mirrorlike. | One of the most common finishes for ornamental architectural components. |
| 8 | Most reflective finish. | Mirror and reflectors; not commonly used for interior applications. |

abrasive grit or glass beads to wear away a defined area. Stencils, metal templates, or adhesive materials are used to mask off portions of the metal. Wet etching uses acid to wear off some of the finish. Special masking must be used to maintain sharply defined areas and prevent the acid from undercutting the protected area.

## Detailing stainless steel

Custom details for stainless steel can be developed in the same way as for plain carbon steel or any other metal. Combinations of bar, plate, tubing, sheet stock, and other shapes can be detailed to nearly any configuration and in any combination. Stainless steel can be joined by welding, mechanical fasteners, and in some cases, with adhesives. For the smoothest joint, welding is preferred. However, the finish specified must make it possible to smooth and work the weld to match the adjacent finish. Some rolled and proprietary finishes cannot be matched after shop welding. When mechanical fasteners, such as screws, bolts, and rivets, are used, they should also be stainless steel to prevent galvanic action and rust stains caused by carbon steel fasteners. Adhesives are typically used to laminate sheet stock to other materials.

In order to simplify fabrication and minimize cost, it is best to use the smallest sizes and gages that satisfy the application. Table 7.5 gives some commonly used gages for various interior design applications. However, these are only guidelines; local fabricating shops should be consulted to determine the most readily available and appropriate size and gage for a particular use.

# BRONZE AND BRASS [057500]

## Types and uses

Bronze and brass are the terms commonly used to describe a range of copper alloys. There are three primary groups of copper alloys: those that are almost pure copper, those called architectural bronze or the common brasses, and the nickel-silver and silicon-bronze alloys. Technically, bronze is an alloy of copper and 2%, or more, of tin. Brass is an alloy of copper and zinc. In both metals, the predominant element is copper. In practical use, however, many of the alloys that are really brass are often referred to as bronze. In fact, none of the

## Spelling preferences for gage

Sometimes there is disagreement about whether the thickness of a metal should be spelled "gauge" or "gage." The correct spelling for technical use is "gage." This is supported by *The Random House Dictionary*, the Construction Specifications Institute, and various other industry sources, such as the *Recommended Standards on Production Procedures* published by the Northern California Chapter of the American Institute of Architects. It also has the practical value of being shorter to write and letter on drawings.

## Comparative metal gages

Gage sizing is commonly used to indicate the thickness of metal. Although most metal producers prefer to use decimal or metric measurements, gages are still used. Unfortunately, several different gage sizing systems have been developed throughout the history of the metals industry, with each gage number having a slightly different actual thickness and each system being used for different types of metal or the forms of metal produced. Table 7.4 shows four commonly used gage systems with the actual imperial and metric thickness of the gage number. When detailing and specifying metals, it is best to use the actual thickness required. Because not all thicknesses are available in all forms and from all suppliers, availability must be verified with a metal supplier or local ornamental metal shop prior to detailing.

**Table 7.4**
Comparative metal gages

| | aluminum, copper, brass, bronze sheets, strips, and wire; small copper and brass tubing | | stainless steel sheets | | stainless steel, aluminum, bronze, and large copper and brass tubing; stainless strip | | steel sheets | |
|---|---|---|---|---|---|---|---|---|
| | B&S & AWG | | USG | | BWG | | USG | |
| gage no. | in | mm | in | mm | in | mm | in | mm |
| 8 | 0.1285 | 3.264 | 0.1719 | 4.366 | 0.165 | 4.191 | 0.1644 | 4.176 |
| 10 | 0.1019 | 2.588 | 0.1406 | 3.571 | 0.134 | 3.404 | 0.1345 | 3.416 |
| 12 | 0.0808 | 2.052 | 0.1094 | 2.779 | 0.109 | 2.769 | 0.1046 | 2.657 |
| 14 | 0.0640 | 1.626 | 0.0781 | 1.984 | 0.083 | 2.108 | 0.0747 | 1.897 |
| 16 | 0.0508 | 1.290 | 0.0625 | 1.588 | 0.065 | 1.651 | 0.0598 | 1.519 |
| 18 | 0.0403 | 1.024 | 0.0500 | 1.270 | 0.049 | 1.245 | 0.0478 | 1.214 |
| 20 | 0.0320 | 0.813 | 0.0375 | 0.953 | 0.035 | 0.889 | 0.0359 | 0.912 |
| 22 | 0.0253 | 0.643 | 0.0312 | 0.792 | 0.028 | 0.711 | 0.0299 | 0.759 |
| 24 | 0.0201 | 0.511 | 0.0250 | 0.635 | 0.022 | 0.559 | 0.0239 | 0.607 |
| 26 | 0.0159 | 0.404 | 0.0187 | 0.475 | 0.018 | 0.457 | 0.0179 | 0.455 |
| 28 | 0.0126 | 0.320 | 0.0156 | 0.396 | 0.014 | 0.356 | 0.0149 | 0.378 |
| 30 | 0.0100 | 0.254 | 0.0125 | 0.318 | 0.012 | 0.305 | 0.0120 | 0.305 |

B & S = Brown and Sharp
USG = United States Standard Gage
AWG = American Wire Gage
BWG = Birmingham Wire Gage

**Table 7.5**
Applications of stainless steel sheet thicknesses

| gage | thickness in | thickness mm | typical applications |
|---|---|---|---|
| 11 | 0.1250 | 3.175 | door bumpers, thresholds, cover plates |
| 12 | 0.1094 | 2.779 | doors, kick plates, elevator panels, items subject to abuse and wear |
| 14 | 0.0781 | 1.984 | column covers, convector covers, large flush panels |
| 16 | 0.0625 | 1.588 | large mullions, unbacked fascia and panels |
| 18 | 0.0500 | 1.270 | corner guards, door sections, handrails |
| 20 | 0.0375 | 0.953 | window sills |
| 22 | 0.0312 | 0.792 | light mullions, stiffeners |
| 24 | 0.0250 | 0.635 | window framing, louvers |
| 26 | 0.0187 | 0.475 | cleats and clips, other fasteners |
| 28 | 0.0156 | 0.396 | laminated panels |
| 30 | 0.0125 | 0.318 | laminated panels |

Note: Verify appropriate gages with the metal fabricator.

most common copper alloys used in interior architectural work are true bronzes. To avoid confusion, copper alloys can be referred to by their alloy number. Table 7.6 lists the copper alloys commonly used for both interior and exterior architectural components.

For most interior design construction, any of the alloys listed in Table 7.6 can be specified subject to availability in the forms required. The choice is usually a matter of the final color and appearance required, along with the cost. However, the most commonly used alloys for interior construction include 220, 230, 260, 280, and 385. Table 7.7 summarizes the typical uses of the copper alloys. Because these alloys are true brasses and are the most frequently used alloys for interior applications, the word "brass" will be used for the remainder of this chapter even though the information applies to copper and most of the other alloys as well.

Although the copper alloys are corrosion resistant, they all change color with age and exposure to moisture in the air. After several years of weathering, those exposed to the exterior turn green or brown. For most interior use this is usually not a problem because the metal is protected from atmospheric moisture and chemicals. However, brass will tarnish and may show some color changes after several years, unless protected with some type of coating or refinished periodically.

## Standard forms

Brass is available in the standard forms of sheet, plate, bar stock, tubing, and pipe. As with stainless steel, these basic shapes are used to fabricate custom assemblies by various forming and fastening methods. Brass can also be extruded and cast. Extrusion is common for door and window frames, railings, and trim, while casting is used to manufacture hardware and plumbing fixtures. Custom extrusions can be designed and manufactured; however, this forming method is not economical unless the amount of extrusion required is very large.

Brass can be fabricated to any size required; however, it is more economical to design and detail ornamental brass using standard

**Table 7.6**
Types and properties of copper alloys

| alloy no. | UNS no. | common name | nominal composition | color |
|---|---|---|---|---|
| 110 | C11000 | copper | 99.9% copper | salmon-red |
| 122 | C12200 | copper | 99.9% copper<br>0.02% phosphorous | salmon-red |
| 220 | C22000 | commercial bronze | 90% copper<br>10% zinc | red-gold |
| 230 | C23000 | red brass | 85% copper<br>15% zinc | reddish-yellow |
| 260 | C26000 | cartridge brass | 70% brass<br>30% zinc | yellow |
| 280 | C28000 | Muntz metal | 60% copper<br>40% zinc | reddish-yellow |
| 385 | C38500 | architectural bronze | 57% copper<br>3% lead<br>40% zinc | reddish-yellow |
| 655 | C65500 | silicon bronze | 97% copper<br>3% silicone | reddish-gold |
| 745 | C74500 | nickel silver | 65% copper<br>25% zinc<br>10% nickel | warm silver |
| 796 | C79600 | leaded nickel silver | 45% copper<br>42% zinc<br>10% nickel<br>2% manganese<br>1% lead | warm silver |

Source: Copper Development Association, Inc., New York, NY.

shapes and sizes whenever possible. Figures 7.3(a)–7.3(d) illustrate some of these standard shapes. Tables 7.8–7.10 list standard sizes for these shapes. Hexagonal and octagonal tubing is also available on special order, as are some T-shapes, Z-shapes, and proprietary shapes. Note that square and rectangular tubing, channels, and angles have sharp corners, as contrasted with stainless steel and regular steel tubing, channels, and angles. While there are some standard shapes and sizes of ornamental brass available, several manufacturers use brass to fabricate proprietary shapes and products. These can be ordered from catalogs. For example, several manufacturers produce lines of brass railings for bars, guardrails, and handrails, including brackets and other accessories for a complete installation.

## Brass finishes [057500]

Brass is available in mechanical, chemical, and coated finishes. Mechanical finishing alters the surface of the metal by rolling or some other mechanical means. Chemical finishing alters the surface with chemical processes. Coatings are applied finishes that are formed from the metal itself through chemical or

**Table 7.7**
Uses of copper alloys for interior construction

| use | 110 | 122 | 220 | 230 | 260 | 280 | 385 | 655 | 745 | 796 |
|---|---|---|---|---|---|---|---|---|---|---|
| bank equipment | • | • | • | • | | • | • | | • | • |
| builders' hardware | | | • | • | • | | • | | • | • |
| ecclesiastical equipment | • | | • | • | • | • | | | | |
| elevators, escalators | | | • | • | | • | • | | • | • |
| food service equipment | • | • | | • | | • | | • | | |
| furniture | • | | • | • | • | • | | • | • | |
| grilles, screens | • | | • | • | • | | • | | • | • |
| lighting fixtures | • | • | • | | • | | • | | | |
| louvers | • | • | • | • | | | • | | | |
| plumbing fixtures | | | • | • | • | | | | | |
| railings | | • | • | • | • | • | • | | • | • |
| signs | • | • | • | • | • | • | • | | | |
| thresholds | | | | | | | • | | | • |
| toilet and bath accessories | | | • | • | • | | • | | | • |
| wall coverings | • | • | • | • | • | | | | | |
| wall panels | • | • | • | • | | • | | | | |

Source: Copper Development Association, Inc., New York, NY.

electrochemical conversion or by adding some other material. Combinations of these three basic finishing methods may be used.

Chemical conversion coatings can be used to change the color of brass or to give the appearance of natural weathering effects. Of all the conversion coatings, patinas (verde antiques) and statuary (oxidized) finishes are most often used for exterior applications. However, because chemical conversion coating processes are difficult to control, are expensive, and require a skilled finisher, they are not commonly used for interior applications.

The most commonly used mechanical and coating finishes for brass are summarized in Table 7.11. Where applicable, the standard number designations of these finishes assigned by the National Association of Architectural Metal Manufacturers (NAAMM) is given.

When specifying a brass finish, remember that the more highly polished a finish the more difficult it is to conceal scratches and to refinish. Also keep in mind that large, flat, highly polished surfaces tend to show variations in flatness (oil canning) more than textured or figured surfaces.

## DETAILING WITH BRASS [057500]

Brass can be formed into an unlimited number of shapes and sizes, and different pieces can be fastened to fabricate nearly any type of detail. Brass can also be combined with other materials, such as wood, plastic, and

**Figure 7.3**
Standard brass shapes

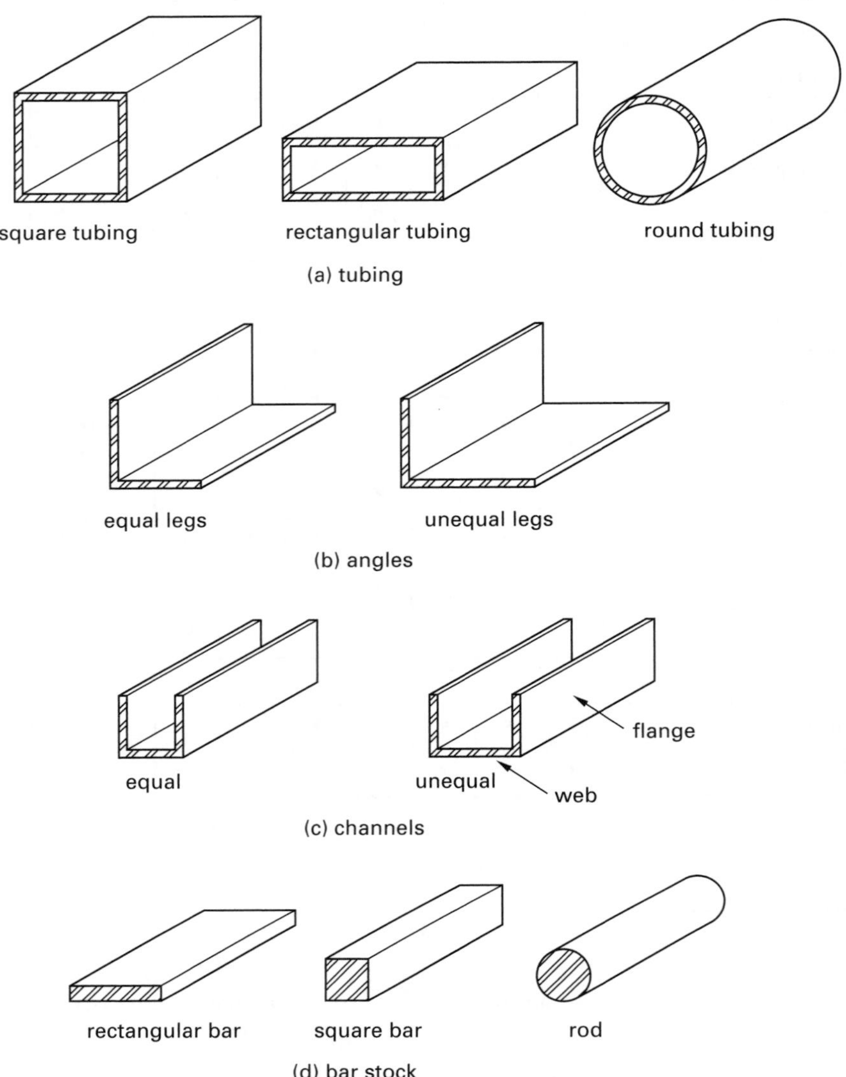


stone, to construct specialty items. However, standard shapes, sizes, and metal alloys should be used to minimize cost and fabrication difficulty. Following are some general guidelines for designing and detailing with brass.

## Standard sizes

Standard sizes and shapes of tubing, bar stock, and other shapes should be used whenever possible. The standard sizes given in the previous sections are some of the more commonly available. However, verify their availability with fabricators prior to developing details that use unusual shapes or sizes. Also verify the available alloys for the required shapes. The same alloy used for sheet stock may not be used for bar or tubing.

## Detailing with sheet stock

For details with large expanses of smooth, flat sheet stock, the metal gage must be thick enough to avoid oil canning or showing other surface imperfections. A minimum of 10-gage brass (0.1019 in [2.588 mm]) should be used when large areas are unsupported or unbacked. If the sheet has an embossed pattern, thinner material can be used because the patterning imparts stiffness to the sheet.

**Table 7.8**
Standard sizes of brass tube and pipe shapes

| square tubing(1) | | rectangular tubing(1) | | round tubing(1) | | pipe(2) | | | |
|---|---|---|---|---|---|---|---|---|---|
| | | | | | | nominal size | | actual outside diameter | |
| in | mm | in | mm | in | mm | in | mm | in | mm |
| ½ × ½ | 12.7 × 12.7 | ⅜ × 1 | 9.5 × 25.4 | ⅜ | 9.5 | 1 | 25.4 | 1.315 | 33.4 |
| ⅝ × ⅝ | 15.9 × 15.9 | ½ × 1 | 12.7 × 25.4 | ½ | 12.7 | 1¼ | 31.8 | 1.660 | 42.2 |
| ¾ × ¾ | 19.1 × 19.1 | ½ × 1¼ | 12.7 × 31.8 | ⅝ | 15.9 | 1½ | 38.1 | 1.900 | 48.3 |
| ⅞ × ⅞ | 22.2 × 22.2 | ½ × 1½ | 12.7 × 38.1 | ¾ | 19.1 | 2 | 50.8 | 2.375 | 60.3 |
| 1 × 1 | 25.4 × 25.4 | ½ × 2 | 12.7 × 50.8 | ⅞ | 22.2 | | | | |
| 1¼ × 1¼ | 31.8 × 31.8 | ⅝ × 1¼ | 15.9 × 31.8 | 1 | 25.4 | | | | |
| 1½ × 1½ | 38.1 × 38.1 | ¾ × 1 | 19.1 × 25.4 | 1¼ | 31.8 | | | | |
| 1¾ × 1¾ | 44.5 × 44.5 | ¾ × 1½ | 19.1 × 38.1 | 1½ | 38.1 | | | | |
| 2 × 2 | 50.8 × 50.8 | ¾ × 2 | 19.1 × 50.8 | 1¾ | 44.5 | | | | |
| 2½ × 2½ | 63.5 × 63.5 | 1 × 1½ | 25.4 × 38.1 | 2 | 50.8 | | | | |
| 3 × 3 | 76.2 × 76.2 | 1 × 2 | 25.4 × 50.8 | 2½ | 63.5 | | | | |
| 4 × 4 | 101.6 × 101.6 | 1 × 3 | 25.4 × 76.2 | 3 | 76.2 | | | | |
| | | 1¼ × 2 | 31.8 × 50.8 | 3½ | 88.9 | | | | |
| | | 1½ × 2 | 38.1 × 50.8 | 4 | 101.6 | | | | |
| | | 1½ × 3 | 38.1 × 76.2 | 5 | 127 | | | | |
| | | 1¾ × 3 | 44.5 × 76.2 | 6 | 152.4 | | | | |
| | | 1¾ × 4 | 44.5 × 101.6 | 8 | 203.2 | | | | |
| | | 2 × 3 | 50.8 × 76.2 | | | | | | |
| | | 2 × 4 | 50.8 × 101.6 | | | | | | |

(1) Tubing available in lengths up to 16 ft (4.8 m) and thicknesses from 0.016 in to 0.125 in (0.41 mm to 3.18 mm).
(2) Pipe available in lengths up to 20 ft (6.1 m).

Source: Manufacturers' catalogs.

When brass is laminated to particleboard or other backing, sheets as thin as 20-gage (0.032 in [0.813 mm]) can be used. Slightly thicker sheets of 18-gage, 16-gage, or 14-gage can also be used. Items that are fabricated of brake-formed brass should be from 14-gage or 12-gage metal (0.0640 in or 0.0808 in [1.626 mm or 2.052 mm]).

## Methods of fastening

Brass can be joined with mechanical fasteners or adhesives, or by brazing or soldering. Mechanical fasteners include screws, bolts, rivets, and various types of clips in compatible alloys. In most cases, the appearance of interior metalwork is improved if mechanical fasteners are concealed. If the installation makes it impossible to conceal fasteners,

**Table 7.9**
**Standard sizes of brass angles and channels[1]**

| angles[2] | | | | channels[3] | | | | | |
|---|---|---|---|---|---|---|---|---|---|
| equal legs | | unequal legs | | equal legs | | unequal legs | | | |
| | | | | | | in | | mm | |
| in | mm | in | mm | in | mm | flange | web | flange | web |
| ⅜ × ⅜ | 9.5 × 9.5 | ⅜ × ¾ | 9.5 × 19.1 | ¼ × ¼ | 6.4 × 6.4 | ½ | ⅜ | 12.7 | 9.5 |
| ½ × ½ | 12.7 × 12.7 | ½ × ¾ | 12.7 × 19.1 | ⅜ × ⅜ | 9.5 × 9.5 | ½ | ¾ | 12.7 | 19.1 |
| ⅝ × ⅝ | 15.9 × 15.9 | ½ × 1 | 12.7 × 25.4 | ½ × ½ | 12.7 × 12.7 | ½ | 1 | 12.7 | 25.4 |
| ¾ × ¾ | 19.1 × 19.1 | ½ × 1½ | 12.7 × 38.1 | ⅝ × ⅝ | 15.9 × 15.9 | ½ | 1¼ | 12.7 | 31.8 |
| 1 × 1 | 25.4 × 25.4 | ½ × 2 | 12.7 × 50.8 | ¾ × ¾ | 19.1 × 19.1 | ½ | 1½ | 12.7 | 38.1 |
| 1¼ × 1¼ | 31.8 × 31.8 | ¾ × 1 | 19.1 × 25.4 | 1 × 1 | 25.4 × 25.4 | ⅝ | 1¼ | 15.9 | 31.8 |
| 1½ × 1½ | 38.1 × 38.1 | ¾ × 1¼ | 19.1 × 31.8 | 1¼ × 1¼ | 31.8 × 31.8 | ⅝ | 1½ | 15.9 | 38.1 |
| 2 × 2 | 50.8 × 50.8 | ¾ × 1½ | 19.1 × 38.1 | 1½ × 1½ | 38.1 × 38.1 | ¾ | ½ | 19.1 | 12.7 |
| 2½ × 2½ | 63.5 × 63.5 | 1 × 1½ | 25.4 × 38.1 | 2 × 2 | 50.8 × 50.8 | ¾ | 1 | 19.1 | 25.4 |
| 3 × 3 | 76.2 × 76.2 | 1 × 2 | 25.4 × 50.8 | | | ¾ | 2 | 19.1 | 50.8 |
| | | | | | | 1 | ¾ | 25.4 | 19.1 |
| | | | | | | 1 | 1 ½ | 25.4 | 38.1 |
| | | | | | | 1 | 2 | 25.4 | 50.8 |
| | | | | | | 1 | 2 ½ | 25.4 | 63.5 |
| | | | | | | 1½ | 2½ | 38.1 | 63.5 |

(1) Verify availability of sizes and alloys with fabricator.
(2) Angles typically ⅛ in (3.2 mm) thick.
(3) Channel thickness varies with size ranging from 0.062 in to 0.125 in (1.58 mm to 3.18 mm).

Source: Manufacturers' catalogs.

their type, size, and location should be given careful consideration based on the final installed position.

Adhesives can be used for laminating sheets onto backing material or to join smaller pieces to other materials when exposed fasteners would be objectionable. Unless some additional mechanical fastening device can be incorporated into a detail, adhesive bonding should not be used alone where the metal must support forces other than its own weight. It is usually best to verify the advisability of using adhesives for a particular detail with an ornamental metal fabricator.

Brass can be joined by brazing, soldering, or welding. Brazing is the joining of two metals at an intermediate temperature above 800°F (438°C) using a nonferrous filler metal. Soldering is the joining of two metals using lead-based or tin-based alloy solder that melts below 500°F (260°C). Welding joins two metals by using high temperatures (much higher than brazing) to heat them above their melting points either with or without a filler metal. Of the

**Table 7.10**
Standard sizes of brass bar and rod stock

| rectangular bars | | | | square bars | rods | |
|---|---|---|---|---|---|---|
| in | mm | in | mm | in | in | mm |
| 1/8 × 1/4 | 3.2 × 6.4 | 3/8 × 1/2 | 9.5 × 12.7 | 1/4 | 1/4 | 6.4 |
| 1/8 × 1/2 | 3.2 × 12.7 | 3/8 × 3/4 | 9.5 × 19.1 | 5/16 | 5/16 | 7.9 |
| 1/8 × 5/8 | 3.2 × 15.9 | 3/8 × 1 | 9.5 × 25.4 | 3/8 | 3/8 | 9.5 |
| 1/8 × 3/4 | 3.2 × 19.1 | 3/8 × 1 1/2 | 9.5 × 38.1 | 1/2 | 1/2 | 12.7 |
| 1/8 × 1 | 3.2 × 25.4 | 3/8 × 2 | 9.5 × 50.8 | 5/8 | 5/8 | 15.9 |
| 1/8 × 1 1/4 | 3.2 × 31.8 | 1/2 × 3/4 | 12.7 × 19.1 | 3/4 | 3/4 | 19.1 |
| 1/8 × 1 1/2 | 3.2 × 38.1 | 1/2 × 1 | 12.7 × 25.4 | 1 | 1 | 25.4 |
| 1/8 × 2 | 3.2 × 50.8 | 1/2 × 1 1/4 | 12.7 × 31.8 | 1 1/4 | — | 31.8 |
| 3/16 × 3/8 | 4.8 × 9.5 | 1/2 × 1 1/2 | 12.7 × 38.1 | | | |
| 3/16 × 1/2 | 4.8 × 12.7 | 1/2 × 1 3/4 | 12.7 × 44.5 | | | |
| 3/16 × 3/4 | 4.8 × 19.1 | 1/2 × 2 | 12.7 × 50.8 | | | |
| 3/16 × 1 | 4.8 × 25.4 | 1/2 × 2 1/2 | 12.7 × 63.5 | | | |
| 1/4 × 1/2 | 6.4 × 12.7 | 1/2 × 3 | 12.7 × 76.2 | | | |
| 1/4 × 3/4 | 6.4 × 19.1 | 3/4 × 1 | 19.1 × 25.4 | | | |
| 1/4 × 1 | 6.4 × 25.4 | 3/4 × 1 1/2 | 19.1 × 38.1 | | | |
| 1/4 × 1 1/4 | 6.4 × 31.8 | 3/4 × 2 | 19.1 × 50.8 | | | |
| 1/4 × 1 1/2 | 6.4 × 38.1 | | | | | |
| 1/4 × 1 3/4 | 6.4 × 44.5 | | | | | |
| 1/4 × 2 | 6.4 × 50.8 | | | | | |

Source: Manufacturers' catalogs.

three methods, brazing is most often used for joining brass for architectural purposes. If possible, brazed joints should be concealed because the filler metal does not exactly match the brass.

## OTHER METALS

Although stainless and copper alloys are the most commonly used metals for interior ornamental metalwork, others are available. These include aluminum, monel metal, zinc, structural steel, and iron. Aluminum is used where existing door or interior glazing frames must be matched, or where metal is required but the color and finish of stainless steel or brass is not required. Aluminum is also used where light weight and low cost are needed. Structural steel is used where high strength is required for other construction elements and appearance is not a concern, or where a durable metal that can be refinished easily is required. Wrought iron is used in decorative work for components such as railings, balusters, and grilles.

### Aluminum [057500]

Aluminum is typically used in manufactured construction products, such as door and window frames, railings, screens and grilles, and cast fittings. However, aluminum is also available in the standard forms of bars, rods, tubes, and pipe that can be detailed

**Table 7.11**
Selected finishes of copper alloys

| NAAMM no. | name | description |
|---|---|---|
| buffed finishes: | | |
| M21 | smooth specular | Brightest mechanical finish available produced by grinding, polishing, and buffing to a mirrorlike surface. |
| M22 | specular | Bright finish produced by grinding, polishing, and only light buffing. |
| directional textured: | | |
| M31 | fine satin | Fine, velvety texture with tiny, nearly parallel scratches on the surface. |
| M32 | medium satin | Similar to fine satin but not as smooth. |
| M33 | coarse satin | Similar to medium satin but not as smooth. |
| M36 | uniform | Produced by a single pass of a no. 80 grit belt. |
| nondirectional textured: | | |
| M42 | fine matte | Texture produced by blasting metal with sand or metal shot. Use is limited to metal at least ¼ in (6 mm) thick. Texture shows fingerprints and holds dirt; protective organic coatings are required. |
| M43 | medium matte | Similar to fine matte but not as smooth. |
| | patterned | Produced by passing light-gage sheet stock between two engraved rollers or impressing patterns by stamping. Pattern varies with manufacturer. Patterning increases stiffness and eliminates distorted reflections. |
| clear organic coatings: | | |
| 06x | air-dry coatings | Most commonly used for interior ornamental metal. |
| 07x | thermoset | Used for hardware. |
| types of clear organic coatings: | | |
| | acrylic | Good color retention and resistance to impact and abrasion. Air-drying type used for architectural applications. Relatively high cost. |
| | cellulose acetate butyrate | Air-drying type. Used for interior applications because they tend to darken under exterior exposure. Moderate in cost and fair performance. |
| | epoxy | Used for interior applications where high resistance to impact and abrasion is required. Only available in thermosetting or two-part types. |
| | nitrocellulose | Used for interior applications where low cost is required. Air-drying type but must be stripped and reapplied frequently. |
| | urethane | Air-drying type used for interior applications where excellent resistance to abrasion and chemicals is required. Relatively high cost. |
| laminated: | | |
| L91 | clear polyvinyl-fluoride | A 1 mil sheet of polyvinylfluoride adhesively bonded to the brass. Resists abrasion, impact, and weathering. |
| | oils and waxes | Primarily used for maintenance by hand rubbing. |

Note: For a complete list of finishes, refer to the *Metal Finishes Manual* published by the National Association of Architectural Metal Manufacturers.

Reprinted with permission of the National Association of Architectural Metal Manufacturers (NAAMM), Chicago, IL.

to form custom fabrications. In addition, aluminum can be extruded from custom-designed dies into special shapes. However, the quantity required to make this economically feasible is usually greater than most interior design projects require. In most cases, standard extruded shapes are available as stock items that can be used for custom fabrication.

Aluminum is available in several finishes including mechanical, chemical, and anodic. Mechanical finishes include buffed, which produces a smooth specular surface; directional-textured; nondirectional-textured; and patterned. Directional-textured finishes can be specified as fine satin, medium satin, coarse satin, hand-rubbed, and brushed. Nondirectional-textured finishes, which cannot be used on material thinner than ¼ in (6 mm), include extra-fine matte, fine matte, medium matte, coarse matte, and fine shot blast. Heavier textured finishes are possible, but these are not typically used for interior design work.

A chemical finish is usually an intermediate process for some other final finish. Chemical finishes may be used to clean, etch, or prepare the metal for a coating.

The most common type of finish is the anodic, or anodized, which is an electrochemical process that forms an oxide coating on the metal surface when placed in a bath of chemicals with an electric current. The resulting coating can be clear or one of the common bronze or black colors. Aluminum can also be painted, electroplated, covered with porcelain enamel, and powder coated.

Aluminum can be joined by screwing, bolting, using concealed fasteners, welding, brazing, soldering, or adhesive bonding. Welding, brazing, and soldering should only be used when the joint is concealed, or prior to final finishing. Adhesive bonding should be limited to thin material in situations where high strength is not required. Verify the preferred joining methods with the fabricator prior to developing final details.

## Monel metal [057500]

Monel® metal, sometimes known as Benedict nickel, is an alloy of nickel and copper with other trace elements. It has a silver-gray color similar to stainless steel but with slightly more gray. Monel metal is highly resistive to salt spray and has a slightly lower coefficient of thermal expansion than stainless steel. However, it is about twice as expensive as stainless steel.

Monel is typically used in sheet form for roof panels, wall panels, and column covers. Standard sheet widths are 30, 36, and 48 in (760, 914, and 1220 mm), with a maximum sheet length of 144 in (3658 mm). Standard sheet thicknesses for interior design applications are 0.018, 0.021, and 0.031 in (0.457, 0.533, and 0.787 mm).

---

### Anodized color standards

One of the problems with anodized aluminum is matching colors from different products or fabricators or trying to match the color of a new component with that of an existing anodized product . The Architectural Anodizers Council (AAC) has established standards for six of the most commonly used colors that enable designers to specify these colors with the assurance that they will be uniform and match the same colors produced by other manufacturers. Additional colors will be added as they are developed and proven for production.

The colors, along with their AAC numbers, include champagne bronze (AAC-CB1), light bronze (AAC-LB2), medium bronze (AAC-MB3), dark bronze (AAC-DB4), deep bronze (AAC-DB5), and black (AAC-B6).

---

Monel is available in finishes ranging from a cold-rolled mill finish to mirror polish. It can also be textured and embossed, as can stainless steel. Outside, Monel weathers to a greenish-brown or a gray-green depending on the amount of salt in the air. Used for interior applications, Monel metal develops a light tarnish that can easily be removed with metal-polishing compounds.

## Zinc [057500]

Zinc is a metal that has been used throughout history for roofing, drainboards, and tabletops. For architectural uses, an alloy of zinc, with minor amounts of copper and titanium, is typically used. The copper reduces the brittleness of the base metal, and the titanium improves strength and grain structure. Other alloys are used for casting and extruding. Zinc naturally tarnishes and ages to an attractive, uniform gray-blue color. It costs about the same as stainless steel when used for countertops.

For interior applications, zinc is used in sheet form for countertops, backsplashes, and paneling. It is also available in extruded form and can be cast into ornamental grilles, hardware, and other art forms. Standard sheet widths are 20, 24, 28, and 39.4 in (508, 610, 711, and 1000 mm), with a maximum practical sheet length of 98 ft (30 m). Standard sheets are available in thicknesses from 0.012 in to 0.050 in (0.30 mm to 1.20 mm), with the standard thicknesses being 0.024, 0.026, and 0.028 in (0.60, 0.65, and 0.70 mm).

Zinc is available in a standard mill finish of reflective silver color or preweathered to a dull grayish-blue. The metal can also be embossed, hammered, polished, engraved, or colored using various techniques. However, most designers prefer the soft, gray color of the natural metal.

## Structural steel [051200]

Steel is used for construction where appearance is not a prime concern or where structural support is required for floor openings, bracing for heavy loads, long spans of unsupported millwork, partial height partitions, and other areas where high strength is required. Steel is also used for standard fabrications, such as industrial railings and spiral stairs. Where major structural work is required, a structural engineer must design and detail that portion of the construction. For minor bracing and support, simple standard shapes and sizes of steel can be specified by the designer. For example, Figs. 7.4 and 7.5 illustrate two situations where structural steel is used in conjunction with other interior construction. Figure 7.4 shows square steel tubing welded to a base plate, which is bolted to the floor to help support a low partition. Figure 7.5 shows one method to support lengths of countertop with open space below.

There are hundreds of standard shapes of structural steel. Like stainless steel, brass, and aluminum, steel is manufactured in sheets, plates, bars, rods, piping, square and rectangular tubing, angles, channels, and tees, as well as heavier H and I sections for structural columns and beams. For miscellaneous bracing and minor support, Table 7.12 gives some common sizes for the smaller sections. For a complete listing, refer to the *Manual of Steel Construction* published by the American Institute of Steel Construction. Note that unlike brass or aluminum, tubing, angles, channels, and other shapes have slightly rounded corners.

Steel forms can be bolted or welded together. When attached to concrete structural elements, steel is usually bolted with expansion anchors or power-actuated fasteners. Other materials, such as metal studs, wood blocking, plywood, and particleboard, are attached to steel with screws, bolts, or power-actuated fasteners.

## Iron [057600]

For ornamental work, iron is used in two forms, cast iron and wrought iron. Cast iron contains more than 1.7% carbon.

Wrought iron is almost pure iron, with from 0.03% to 0.05% carbon, although many blacksmiths use mild steel with carbon percentages in the range of 0.05% to 0.30%. Both alloys contain small amounts of other elements. Wrought iron and cast iron work are done by craftspersons using the historical techniques of forging, casting, stamping, and hammering to produce custom construction elements. Today, ironwork is used to fabricate railings, fences, grilles, screens, gates, lettering, room dividers, light fixtures, furniture, and other decorative elements. In many cases, wrought iron and cast iron fabrications are designed by the craftsperson or artist doing the work, with general design direction provided by the interior designer or architect.

Because of the unique nature of the material, ironwork is fabricated differently than other ornamental metals. Its finished appearance has a rough, hand-built look unique to the material. Ironwork is often left unfinished or painted black. Joining techniques are different as well; they usually emphasize the connection rather than try to conceal it. Wrought iron is joined by forge welding, riveting, collaring, and wrapping.

## OTHER SPECIALTY METALS

### Perforated metal [057500]

Perforated metal is sheet metal that has been punched with a regular pattern of holes. Standard perforations include round and square holes as well as slots in a wide range of patterns, hole sizes, and hole spacings. For interior applications, perforated metals are

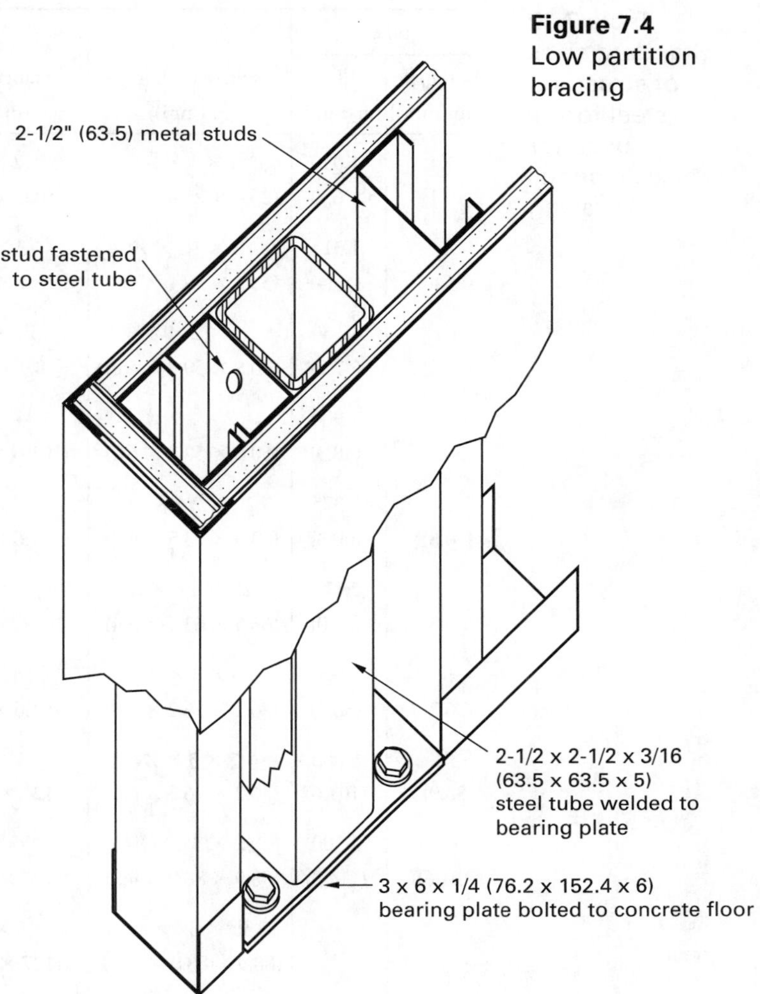


**Figure 7.4** Low partition bracing

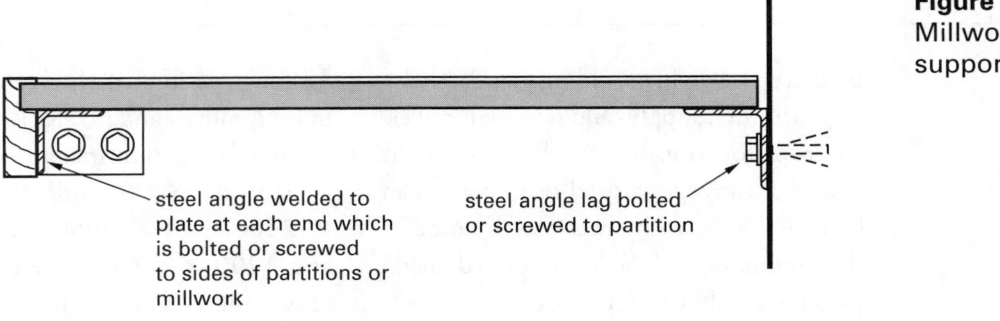


**Figure 7.5** Millwork support

**Table 7.12**
Standard sizes of structural steel forms used for miscellaneous bracing

| pipe[1] | | | | angles[3] | |
|---|---|---|---|---|---|
| nominal (in (mm)) | O.D., (in (mm)) | square tubing[2] (in (mm)) | rectangular tubing (in (mm)) | equal legs (in (mm)) | unequal legs (in (mm)) |
| ¾ (19.1) | 1.050 (26.7) | 1 × 1 × ⅛ (25.4 × 25.4 × 3.2) | 2 × 1 × ⅛ (50.8 × 25.4 × 3.2) | 1 × 1 × ⅛ (25.4 × 25.4 × 3.2) | 2½ × 2 × 3⁄16 (63.5 × 50.4 × 4.8) |
| 1 (25.4) | 1.315 (33.4) | 1½ × 1½ × 3⁄16 (38.1 × 38.1 × 4.8) | 3 × 2 × 3⁄16 (76.2 × 50.8 × 4.8) | 1¼ × 1¼ × 3⁄16 (31.8 × 31.8 × 4.8) | 2½ × 2 × ¼ (63.5 × 50.4 × 6.4) |
| 1¼ (31.8) | 1.660 (42.2) | 2 × 2 × 3⁄16 (50.8 × 50.8 × 4.8) | 3½ × 2½ × 3⁄16 (88.9 × 63.5 × 4.8) | 1½ × 1½ × 3⁄16 (38.1 × 38.1 × 4.8) | 3 × 2 × 3⁄16 (76.2 × 50.8 × 4.8) |
| 1½ (38.1) | 1.900 (48.3) | 2 × 2 × ¼ (50.8 × 50.8 × 6.4) | 4 × 2 × 3⁄16 (101.6 × 50.8 × 4.8) | 1½ × 1½ × ¼ (38.1 × 38.1 × 6.4) | 3 × 2 × ¼ (76.2 × 50.8 × 6.4) |
| 2 (50.8) | 2.375 (60.3) | 2½ × 2½ × 3⁄16 (63.5 × 63.5 × 4.8) | 4 × 2 × ¼ (101.6 × 50.8 × 6.4) | 1¾ × 1¾ × 3⁄16 (44.4 × 44.4 × 4.8) | 3 × 2 × 5⁄16 (76.2 × 50.8 × 7.9) |
| 2½ (63.5) | 2.875 (73.0) | 2½ × 2½ × ¼ (63.5 × 63.5 × 6.4) | 4 × 3 × 3⁄16 (101.6 × 76.2 × 4.8) | 1¾ × 1¾ × ¼ (44.4 × 44.4 × 6.4) | 3 × 2½ × 3⁄16 (76.2 × 63.5 × 4.8) |
| 3 (76.2) | 3.500 (88.9) | 3 × 3 × 3⁄16 (76.2 × 76.2 × 4.8) | 4 × 3 × ¼ (101.6 × 76.2 × 6.4) | 2 × 2 × 3⁄16 (50.8 × 50.8 × 4.8) | 3 × 2½ × ¼ (76.2 × 63.5 × 6.4) |
| 3½ (88.9) | 4.000 (101.6) | 3 × 3 × ¼ (76.2 × 76.2 × 6.4) | 5 × 2 × 3⁄16 (127 × 50.8 × 4.8) | 2 × 2 × ¼ (50.8 × 50.8 × 6.4) | 3 × 2½ × 5⁄16 (76.2 × 63.5 × 7.9) |
| 4 (101.6) | 4.500 (114.3) | 3½ × 3½ × 3⁄16 (88.9 × 88.9 × 4.8) | 5 × 2 × ¼ (127 × 50.8 × 6.4) | 2 × 2 × 5⁄16 (50.8 × 50.8 × 7.9) | 3½ × 2½ × ¼ (88.9 × 63.5 × 6.4) |
| | | 3½ × 3½ × ¼ (88.9 × 88.9 × 6.4) | 5 × 3 × 3⁄16 (127 × 76.2 × 4.8) | 2½ × 2½ × 3⁄16 (63.5 × 63.5 × 4.8) | 3½ × 2½ × 5⁄16 (88.9 × 63.5 × 7.9) |
| | | 4 × 4 × 3⁄16 (101.6 × 101.6 × 4.8) | 5 × 3 × ¼ (127 × 76.2 × 6.4) | 2½ × 2½ × ¼ (63.5 × 63.5 × 6.4) | 3½ × 3 × ¼ (88.9 × 76.2 × 6.4) |
| | | 4 × 4 × ¼ (101.6 × 101.6 × 6.4) | 5 × 4 × 3⁄16 (127 × 101.6 × 4.8) | 3 × 3 × ¼ (76.2 × 76.2 × 6.4) | 4 × 3 × ¼ (101.6 × 76.2 × 6.4) |
| | | | 5 × 4 × ¼ (127 × 101.6 × 6.4) | 3½ × 3½ × ¼ (88.9 × 88.9 × 6.4) | 4 × 3½ × ¼ (101.6 × 88.9 × 6.4) |

[1] Pipe is available in three weights. Standard weight is normally sufficient for miscellaneous interior detailing. The actual outside diameter (O.D.) is larger than the nominal size.
[2] Tubing is available in several wall thicknesses; the thinner ones are usually sufficient.
[3] Angles are designated by an L or ∠ symbol followed by the length of the legs, followed by the thickness.

Source: American Institute of Steel Construction, *Manual of Steel Construction,* 9th ed.

used as space dividers, railing guards, shelving, furniture, supply- and return air grilles, coverings for acoustical panels, custom light fixtures, or any specialty fabrication that can be constructed with sheet metal. Some of the commonly available perforated metal patterns are shown in Fig. 7.6.

Although perforated metal can be purchased in long rolls, standard stock sheet sizes for custom fabrication include 36 × 96, 36 × 120, 48 × 96, and 48 × 120 (900 × 2400, 900 × 3050, 1200 × 2400, and 1200 × 3050). There are hundreds of available hole shapes and sizes, but not all may be readily available. Availability and cost should be verified with a metal fabricator.

## Architectural mesh [057500]

Architectural mesh is a specialty metal that is most often used for elevator cab interiors, but it can be creatively applied in other interior applications, such as wall panels and door facings. Architectural mesh is formed by "weaving" thin strips of metal or heavy wire and then grinding off a portion of one face to reveal a highly textured, but relatively flat, surface. The final surface appearance depends on the type of weave, the type of metal used, and how much metal is ground off. Stainless steel and brass are the most commonly used materials.

## Spiral stairs [057113]

Spiral stairs are stairs having a closed circular form with wedge-shaped treads supported from a central, minimum diameter column (usually 4 in [100 mm]). Standard prefabricated spiral stairs are commonly made from steel. Treads can be exposed steel, hardwood over steel supports, recessed steel stair pans for infill with concrete or stone, or particleboard over a steel support that can be finished with carpet or resilient flooring. Handrails can be specified as wood, steel pipe, or some other ornamental metal. Custom spiral stairs can be fabricated of nearly any combination of wood, steel, or some other ornamental metal. Spiral stairs are available in standard diameters from 3 ft 6 in to 7 ft, in 6 in increments (1067 mm to 2134 mm, in 152 mm increments).

Spiral stairs can be fabricated with 22.5°, 27°, and 30° treads, with 30° treads being the most common. This means that there are 12 treads in a full 360° turn or three treads for each quarter circle of the stair. The riser height is set between 7½ in and 9½ in (191 mm and 241 mm) to make up the total floor-to-floor height, so each riser is the same and the headroom restriction is satisfied. When a square opening is used, a square landing at the top of the stairs makes

**Figure 7.6**
Perforated metal patterns

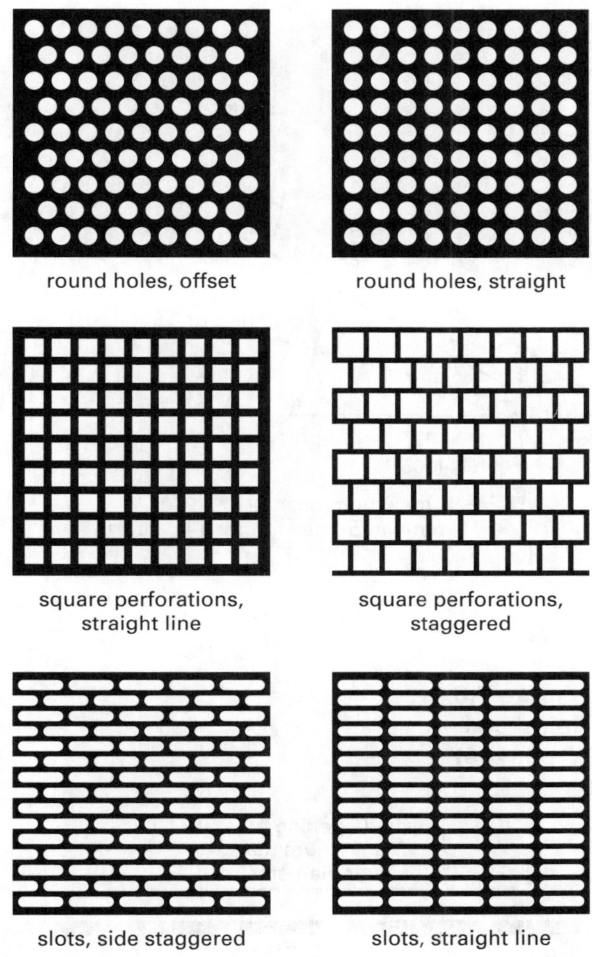


the transition between the stairs and the rest of the floor. Depending on the floor-to-floor dimension, circular stairs must be planned so that the first riser at the bottom and the last riser at the top are situated to allow people to enter and exit the stairway traveling in the right direction.

Most building codes allow spiral stairs to be used if certain size restrictions are met, as shown in Fig. 7.7. The minimum clear width must be 26 in (660 mm). The minimum tread width, measured perpendicular to the center line of the tread at a point 12 in (305 mm) from the support column, must be

**Figure 7.7**
Spiral stair building code requirements

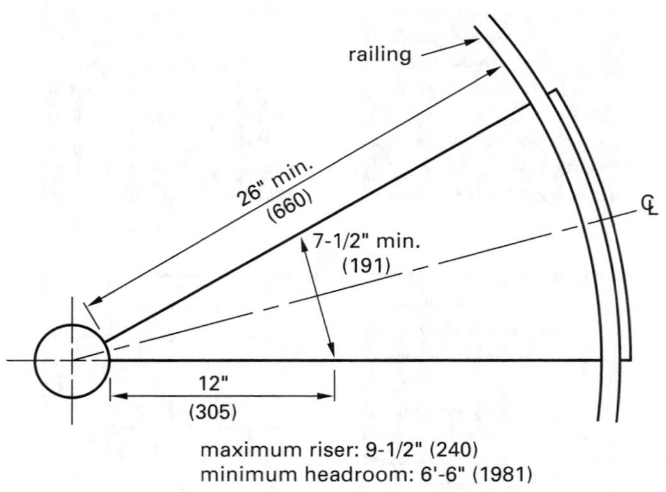


**Figure 7.8**
Spiral stair layout

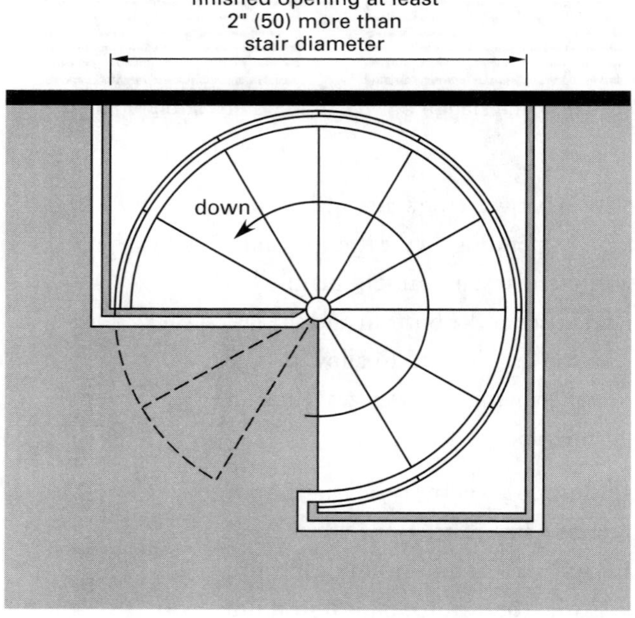


at least 7½ in (191 mm). The minimum amount of headroom is 6 ft 6 in (1981 mm), and the maximum riser height is 9½ in (241 mm). If these minimum dimensions are met, the International Building Code allows spiral stairs to be used in Group R, Division 3 occupancies (private homes) and from spaces serving not more than five occupants or from galleries, catwalks, and gridirons. These stairs can be used as required exits only if the area served is no more than 250 $ft^2$ (23 $m^2$).

Given these restrictions, spiral stairs must be at least 5 ft (1500 mm) in diameter, with about a minimum 8 in (200 mm) riser for a 27° tread and about a minimum 9 in (225 mm) riser for a 30° tread. This is based on having to achieve headroom clearance of 6 ft 6 in (1981 mm) plus about 2 in (50 mm) of upper landing thickness within a three-quarter circle turn. Using a 27° tread, there are 10 treads in a three-quarter circle; using a 30° tread, there are only 9 treads in the same turn.

Figure 7.8 shows one example of a 30° tread stair between two floors 9 ft (2743 mm) apart. If a full 360° turn was used, this would allow 13 risers (12 treads) to be used. If the floor-to-floor height is 9 ft (108 in [2743 mm]), then each riser would be 8.3 in (211 mm). However, calculating the headroom using nine risers in the three-quarter turn under the landing yields only 6 ft 3¾ in (1900 mm), which is too low to meet code requirements. If the riser height is increased to 9 in (229 mm), then sufficient headroom is provided as the stairs pass under the landing; however, only 12 risers are needed to make up the 108 in total height.

## GALVANIC ACTION

Galvanic action is the electrochemical process that occurs when dissimilar metals are in contact in the presence of an electrolyte, such as water. The result is the corrosion of one of the metals. Because most interior applications of metals are in relatively dry

**Table 7.13**
Galvanic series

zinc
galvanized steel
aluminum alloys: 5052, 3004, 3003, 1100, 6053
aluminum alloys: 2117, 2017, 2024
low-carbon steel
wrought iron
cast iron
Type 410 stainless steel, active
Type 304 stainless steel, active
Type 316 stainless steel, active
lead
copper alloy 280
copper alloy 675
copper alloys:
- 270
- 230
- 110
- 651, 655
- 923, cast

Type 410 stainless steel, passive
Type 304 stainless steel, passive
Type 316 stainless steel, passive

environments, galvanic action is not always a problem. However, detailing that puts dissimilar metals in contact should be avoided, especially in humid climates or where moisture may be present, either as vapor or in liquid form. Certain combinations of metals are more susceptible than others to galvanic action. Table 7.13 lists some of the metals used for interior applications. The farther apart the metals are from each other in the table, the greater the possibility of corrosion. The metals are listed from the most susceptible to corrosion to the least, from the top of the table down.

Galvanic action can be prevented by using the same, or compatible, metals and fasteners whenever possible. When two or more metals must be combined, they should be separated with isolators made from Teflon®, neoprene, or some other suitable material. Teflon-coated screws can also be used when necessary.

# 8

# FLOORING CONSTRUCTION

This chapter outlines some of the basic construction methods for flooring that is built on top of a structural floor and that is composed of several individual components. Chapter 9 discusses flooring finishes applied as a single thin material, such as resilient tile and carpet.

## WOOD FLOORING [096400]

### Types, uses, and grades

There are four basic types of wood flooring: strip flooring, plank flooring, block flooring, and solid block flooring. For all types of wood flooring, oak and maple are the most commonly used species. Oak and maple are hard, durable, and available. Other common hardwoods are beech and birch.

### Strip flooring

Strip flooring is one of the most common types of wood flooring. It consists of thin strips from 3⁄8 in (10 mm) to 25⁄32 in (20 mm) thick of varying lengths, with tongue-and-groove edges. See Fig. 8.1(a). Most strip flooring is 2¼ in (57 mm) wide, but 1½ in (38 mm) wide strips are also available. Strip flooring is used for residential and commercial wood floors for its appearance, warmth under foot, resiliency, and durability.

### Plank flooring

Plank flooring comes in the same thicknesses as strip flooring, but is from 3¼ in to 8 in (83 mm to 203 mm) wide. See Fig. 8.1(b). It is laid in random lengths with the end joints staggered. Plank flooring is used primarily in residential applications where a larger scale is desired. It is also used to simulate wider, authentic planking.

### Block flooring

Block flooring is made of preassembled wood flooring in three configurations. Unit block flooring is standard strip flooring assembled into a unit held together with steel or wood splines. Laminated block flooring is flooring made with from three to five plies of cross-laminated wood veneer. Both types of block flooring are from 5⁄16 in (8 mm) to 5⁄8 in (16 mm) thick and come in varying lengths depending on the manufacturer. Unit and laminated block flooring can be laid in any pattern, but herringbone is one of the most common.

Parquet flooring is made of preassembled units of several small, thin slats of wood in a variety of patterns. See Fig. 8.1(c). It is available either finished or unfinished. Some manufacturers make parquet with a cellular foam backing that is resilient and has a factory-applied adhesive for residential "peel-and-stick applications." Commercial applications use nonbacked units that are field finished. Parquet flooring is usually sold in 12 in squares that are $\frac{5}{16}$ in thick (300 mm squares, 8 mm thick) for mastic application, although some manufacturers make other sizes. Parquet flooring is easier and less expensive to install than other types of flooring. It also can be installed in a wide range of designs.

## Solid block flooring

Solid block flooring is made from solid *end grain blocks*. See Fig. 8.1(d). These are solid pieces of wood 2, 2½, 3, and 4 in thick (50, 64, 75, and 100 mm) laid on end with adhesive. Solid block floors are very durable and resistant to oils, mild chemicals, and indentation. They are used for industrial floors or other heavy-duty commercial applications.

## Special flooring

There are several variations of wood floors for special uses. These include resilient and relocatable floors. Resilient floors are wood strip floors laid on one of three types of systems described in the next section. They provide extra "spring" for uses like dance, gymnasium, and theater floors. Relocatable floors are systems of modular units, usually 4 $ft^2$ (1200.37 $m^2$), that can be quickly installed and dismantled. They are used for athletic and institutional floors, where the type of flooring needs to be changed frequently.

## Grades

Wood flooring is graded differently than other wood products. Grading rules are set by the various trade associations such as the Wood Flooring Manufacturers Association, known as NOFMA, and the Maple Flooring Manufacturers Association. Unfinished oak flooring is graded as Clear, Select, No. 1 Common, and No. 2 Common. Clear is the best grade with the most uniform color. Plain sawn is standard, but quarter sawn is available on special order. Piece lengths are 1¼ ft (381 mm) and longer, with an average length of 3¾ ft (1143 mm). Other species are graded as First, Second, and Third grades, along with some combination grades. First Grade corresponds to Select in oak, and Second Grade and Third Grade correspond to No. 1 Common and No. 2 Common, respectively. These are summarized in Tables 8.1–8.3.

## Additional flooring species

In addition to the commonly used maple, oak, birch, and beech, there are many other wood species, both domestic and imported, that can be used for flooring. Many are available in limited quantities, and some are expensive, but they all offer the designer a wide variety of colors, grain patterns, and figures

**Figure 8.1**
Types of wood flooring

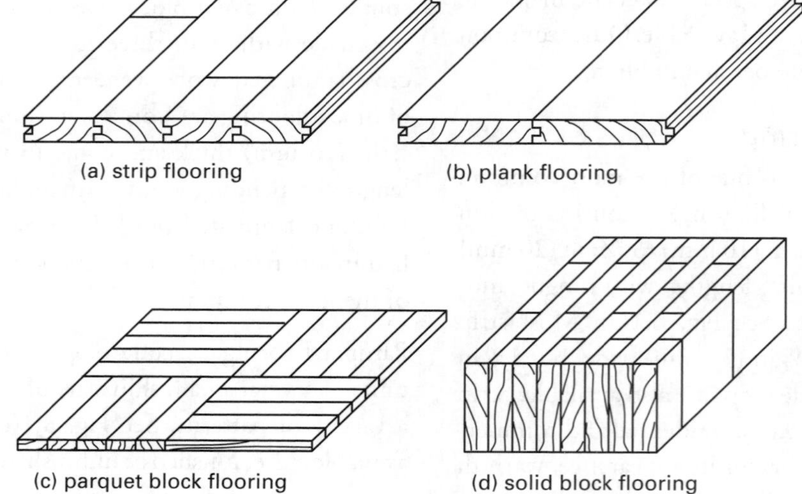

**Table 8.1**
Grades of unfinished oak flooring

| grade | bundled lengths | appearance description |
|---|---|---|
| Clear | 1¼ ft and up, average length 3¾ ft (380 mm and up, average length 1140 mm) | Best grade with the most uniform color. Plain sawn is standard with quarter sawn available on special order only. |
| Select | 1¼ ft and up, average length 3¼ ft (380 mm and up, average length 990 mm) | Limited character marks, unlimited sound sap. Plain sawn is standard with quarter sawn on special order only. |
| No. 1 Common | 1¼ ft and up, average length 2¾ ft (380 mm and up, average length 840 mm) | Variegated appearance, light and dark colors, knots, worm holes and other character marks. Imperfections are filled and finished. |
| No. 2 Common | 1¼ ft and up, average length 2¼ ft (380 mm and up, average length 686 mm) | Rustic appearance. Has all characteristics of the species. Red and white oak may be mixed. |

Combination grades: Select and Better (special order)
1¼ ft shorts (lengths of 9 in to 18 in [225 mm to 457 mm]) red and white oak mixed
No. 1 Common and Better

Source: NOFMA, the Wood Flooring Manufacturers Association.

**Table 8.2**
Grades of prefinished oak flooring

| grade | bundled lengths | appearance description |
|---|---|---|
| Prime | 1¼ ft and up, average length 3½ ft (380 mm and up, average length 1070 mm) | Excellent appearance with natural color variations permitted. Special order. |
| Standard | 1¼ ft and up, average length 2¾ ft (380 mm and up, average length 840 mm) | Variegated appearance with varying sound wood characteristics of species. |
| Tavern | 1¼ ft and up, average length 2¼ ft (380 mm and up, average length 690 mm) | Rustic appearance with all wood characteristics of species. Economical floor. |

Combination grades: Standard and Better, Tavern and Better

Source: NOFMA, the Wood Flooring Manufacturers Association.

**Table 8.3**
Grades of maple, beech, and birch flooring

| grade | bundled lengths | appearance description |
|---|---|---|
| First Grade | Bundles 1¼ ft and up (380 mm and up) | Best appearance. Natural color variation, limited character marks, unlimited sap. |
| Second Grade | Bundles 1¼ ft and up (380 mm and up) | Variegated appearance, varying sound wood characteristics of species. |
| Third Grade | Bundles 1¼ ft and up (380 mm and up) | Rustic appearance, all wood characteristics of species. Serviceable economical floor after filling. |
| Other grades: | Second and Better<br>First Grade white hard maple | Third and Better<br>First Grade red beech and birch |

Source: NOFMA, the Wood Flooring Manufacturers Association.

beyond what is available with maple and oak. Some of these available wood species are summarized in Table 8.4.

One newly introduced flooring material is bamboo, which can be used as an alternative to solid hardwood flooring as well as for veneer and paneling. Bamboo is not a tree, but a fast-growing grass that reaches maturity in three to four years. It can be obtained from managed forests where it is grown on steep slopes and hill lands where other forms of agriculture are difficult to propagate.

Bamboo flooring is available in ½ in (13 mm) and ¾ in (19 mm) thick strips about 3 in (76 mm) wide or wider, depending on the manufacturer. It is milled with tongue-and-groove edges, so it can be installed like standard wood flooring. It can be installed by nailing or with adhesive.

Bamboo is almost as hard (1130 psi on the Janka hardness scale) and twice as stable (0.00175) as red oak and maple. Refer to Table 8.4 for values of other flooring species. It is available in a natural color or a darker, amber color. It is prefinished with a durable polyurethane coating.

Another unusual flooring material comes from plantation-grown coconut palms. At commercial coconut plantations, palm wood can be harvested as a byproduct. Palm wood flooring is available in ¾ in by 3 in wide strips with tongue-and-groove edges like those of standard oak or maple flooring. It has a 1600 psi hardness on the Janka hardness scale and a stability of 0.00194. The flooring ranges from dark- to medium-red mahogany in color and is prefinished with polyurethane. Palm wood is also environmentally friendly in that palms produce for 60 to 80 years before becoming sterile, at which time they must be removed and replaced with new plants. Refer to Ch. 21 for more information on sustainable flooring products.

### Wood Floor Finishes

Several types of finishes are available for wood floors. One of the most common is water-based urethane. It produces a durable, quick-drying finish that satisfies environmental regulations for limited volatile organic compound (VOC) content. It dries clear and inhibits color changes in certain woods. In addition, water-based urethane is the best choice for some exotic woods that contain oils and chemical compounds that adversely react with some types of solvent-based finishes.

Oil-modified polyurethane also produces a durable finish, but it may be slower drying, contain an unacceptable VOC content, and darken some woods. However, some manufacturers have reformulated their oil-modified products to comply with VOC regulations.

Other finishes include moisture-cured urethanes and acid-cured (Swedish) finishes. Both provide an extremely durable cover but produce a strong, unpleasant odor during application.

## Typical installation details

Wood strip flooring must be installed over a suitable nailable base. Because wood swells when it becomes damp, provisions must be made to prevent moisture from seeping up from below and to allow for expansion of the completed floor. Strip flooring is installed by blind nailing through the tongue.

Figure 8.2 illustrates the typical installation method for residential floors on wood joists. The strip flooring is blind nailed to a suitable subfloor, either plywood or particleboard, typically ½ in (13 mm) minimum thickness. The subflooring should be laid with the long dimension perpendicular to the joists, with a ⅛ in (3 mm) gap between the panels and with the end joints staggered by 4 ft (1200 mm). A layer of 15 lbm asphalt felt may be laid to prevent squeaking and act as a vapor barrier.

Figure 8.3 shows two methods of installing wood flooring over a concrete subfloor in commercial construction. In Fig. 8.3(a), a sheet of ¾ in (19 mm) plywood is attached to the concrete to provide the nailable base. A layer of 6 mil polyethylene film is

**Table 8.4**
Wood flooring species

| species | availability | hardness | stability | common coloring |
|---|---|---|---|---|
| ash, white | M | 3 | 0.00274 | light color with heartwood light tan to dark brown |
| bamboo | M | 3 | 0.00175 | natural and amber |
| beech | L | 3 | 0.00431 | reddish-brown with sapwood pale white |
| birch | M | 3 | 0.00338 | light reddish-brown with white sapwood |
| cherry, black | M | 2 | 0.00248 | reddish-brown heartwood with light sapwood |
| cherry, Brazilian | C | 5 | 0.00300 | reddish-brown when seasoned; darkens in sunlight |
| cypress, Australian | L | 3 | 0.00162 | honey-gold to brown with darker knots |
| douglas fir | C | 1 | 0.00267 | yellowish-tan to light brown heartwood |
| hickory | L | 4 | 0.00411 | reddish-brown with dark brown stripes |
| jarrah | L | 4 | 0.00396 | dark brownish red heartwood with paler sapwood |
| mahogany, santos | M | 5 | 0.00238 | dark, reddish-brown |
| maple | C | 3 | 0.00353 | light color with creamy-white heartwood |
| merbau | L | 4 | 0.00158 | brown to dark red-brown |
| mesquite | L | 5 | 0.00129 | light brown to dark reddish-brown |
| oak, red | C | 3 | 0.00369 | reddish with lighter sapwood |
| oak, white | C | 3 | 0.00365 | grayish-brown heartwood with very light sapwood |
| padauk | M | 4 | 0.00180 | reddish to purple-brown with cream-colored sapwood |
| palm wood | M | 4 | 0.00194 | dark- to medium-red mahogany |
| pine, antique heart | L | 3 | 0.00263 | recycled pine of light tan to reddish-brown |
| pine, southern yellow | C | 2 | 0.00265 | light yellow to reddish- or yellowish-brown |
| purpleheart | L | 4 | 0.00212 | deep purple with cream-colored sapwood |
| teak | L | 2 | 0.00186 | yellow-brown to dark golden brown; cream sapwood |
| walnut | M | 2 | 0.00274 | chocolate brown heartwood with tan sapwood |
| wenge | L | 4 | 0.00201 | very dark brown with fine, black veins |

Availability: C = commonly available
M = moderately available
L = limited availability

Hardness: 1 = <700
2 = 700–1000
3 = 1000–1500
4 = 1500–2000
5 = 2000+

Stability: Listed values are the dimensional change coefficient. The lower the value, the more stable the wood.

Hardness based on the Janka hardness scale, which is the load required to embed an 11 mm steel ball to one-half its diameter in the wood. 5 = hardest; 1 = softest.

**Figure 8.2**
Wood strip flooring on wood framing

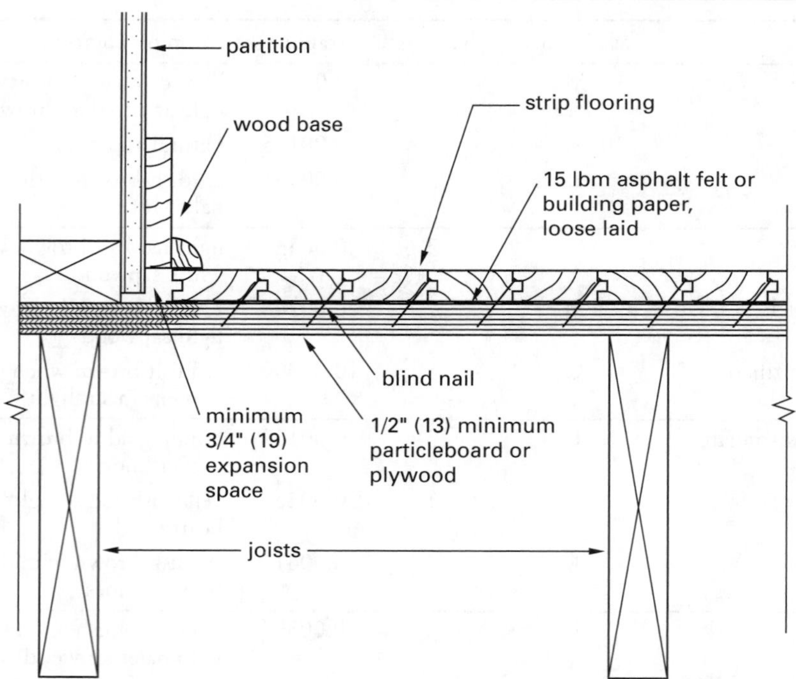


**Figure 8.3**
Wood strip flooring on concrete framing

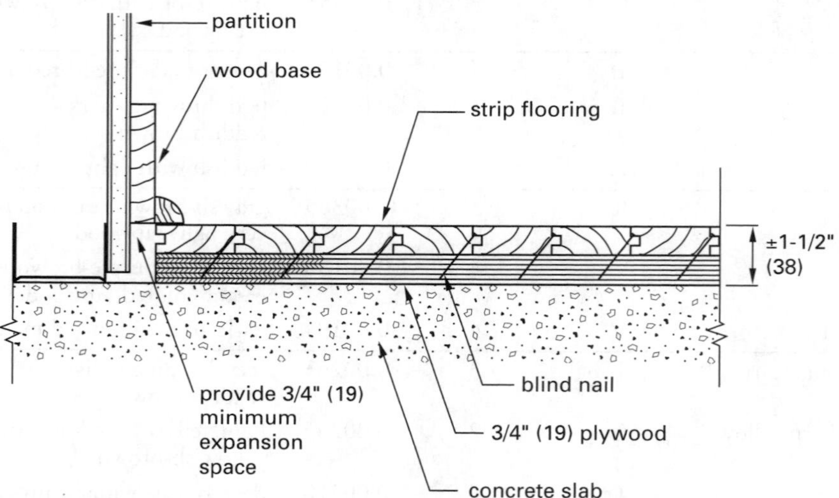


(a) wood strip flooring on plywood subfloor

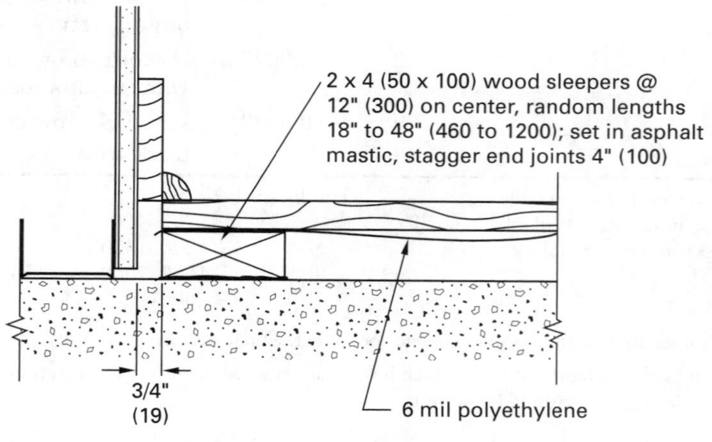


(b) wood strip flooring on sleepers

## Applicable standards for wood flooring

**American National Standards Institute (ANSI):**

ANSI/HPVA EF 2002 *American National Standard for Engineered Wood Flooring*

**American Society for Testing and Materials (ASTM):**

ASTM D2394 *Standard Methods for Simulated Service Testing of Wood and Wood-Base Finish Flooring*

**Maple Flooring Manufacturers Association (MFMA):**

*Grading Rules for Hard Maple*

**NOFMA, The Wood Flooring Manufacturers Association:**

*Official Flooring Grading Rules*

---

laid down first, if moisture may be a problem. The concrete subfloor should be level to within ¼ in in 10 ft (6.4 mm in 3050 mm) with no high spots or depressions.

In Fig. 8.3(b), the wood flooring is laid on wood sleepers. This method of installation not only results in a more resilient floor that is more comfortable under foot, but also provides an air space that allows excess moisture to escape. In both instances, a gap of about ⅜ in to ¾ in (10 mm to 19 mm) is left at the perimeter to allow for expansion. This gap is concealed with the wood base. If the size of the room exceeds 20 ft by 20 ft (6 m by 6 m), then additional expansion space may be required.

Resilient strip flooring systems can be installed in one of three ways. In the first, the flooring is nailed to wood sleepers that rest on resilient neoprene pads. See Fig. 8.4. The pads are spaced 12 in (300 mm) on center. The wood sleepers are nominal $2 \times 4$ ($50 \times 100$) pressure-treated wood 4 ft (1200 mm) long, spaced 9 in (225 mm) on center for $^{25}/_{32}$ in (20 mm) flooring, or spaced 12 in (300 mm) on center for $^{33}/_{32}$ in (26 mm) flooring. The sleepers should be laid end to end with a ¼ in (6 mm) gap between them and with the end joints staggered a minimum of 2 ft (600 mm).

The second system uses strip flooring locked into place and to each other with steel clips attached to a resiliently mounted anchor slot that is recessed into insulation board. See Fig. 8.5. Several variations are available from different manufacturers.

The third method uses spring-mounted isolation feet that support the wood sleepers to which the wood flooring is attached.

In all three methods of resiliently mounted wood flooring, the concrete subfloor must be depressed a distance sufficient enough to allow the finished floor to be level with the adjacent flooring. Because this distance can be anywhere from 1¼ in to 2½ in (32 mm to 64 mm), these methods are generally only used for new construction. To apply wood strip flooring over existing concrete floors, the method shown in Fig. 8.3(a) should be used because it minimizes the thickness required for the flooring. Even in this case, some provision for making the transition to a lower surface-applied flooring material must be made. If this is not possible, then thinner parquet flooring or block flooring can be used.

For most residential or commercial projects, laminated and parquet flooring are glued over a stable wood subfloor or directly onto a smooth concrete subfloor if moisture is not present. Figure 8.6 shows a typical residential application of parquet flooring. If the flooring is placed on a floor above a crawl

**Figure 8.4**
Resilient wood flooring system

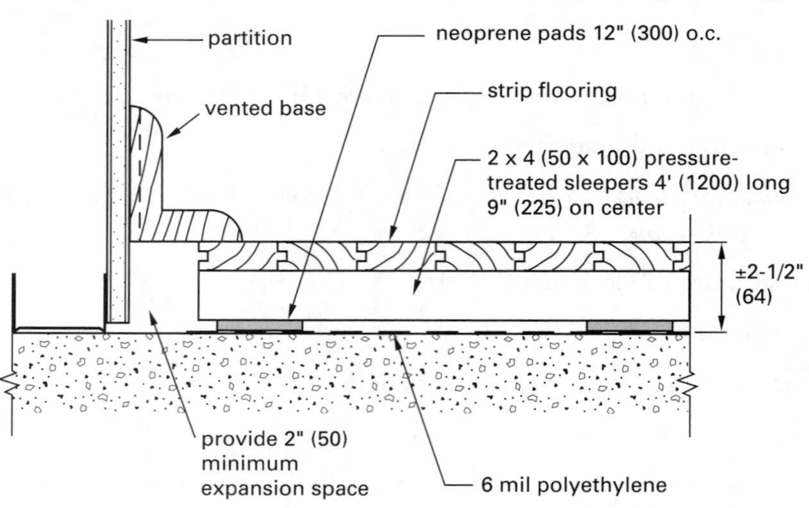


**Figure 8.5**
Strip flooring on resilient underlayment

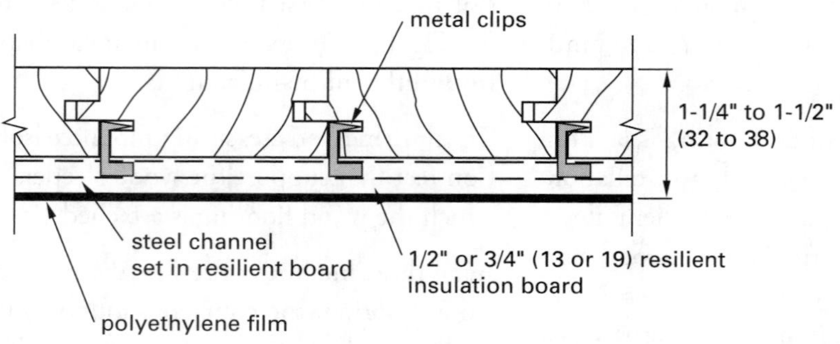


**Figure 8.6**
Wood parquet flooring

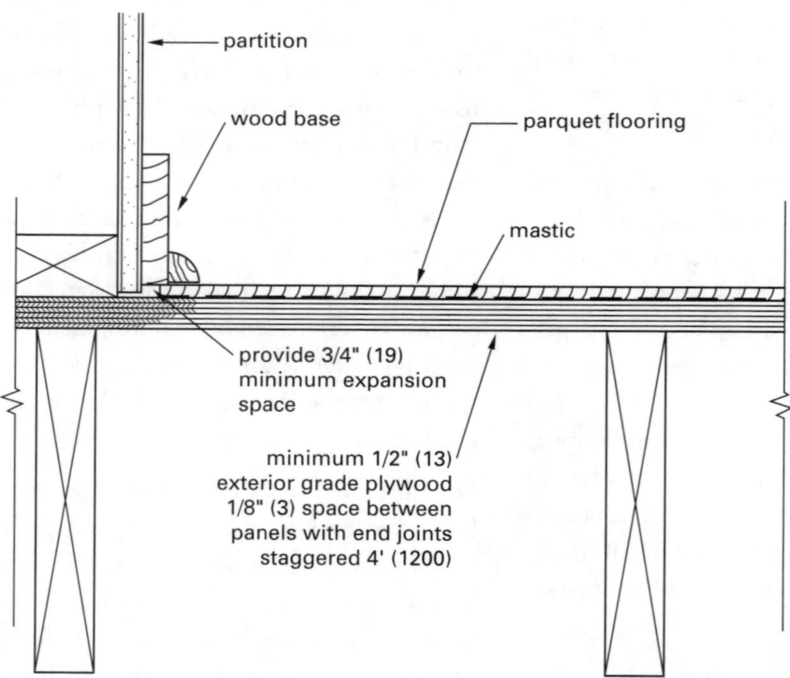

**Building code requirements for wood flooring**

Wood flooring is not regulated in Type III, IV, or V construction. For Type I and II construction, the applicable building code may require that the space between sleepers be filled with noncombustible material or fire-stopped so that no open space exceeds 100 $ft^2$ (9.3 $m^2$).

Additional code requirements apply to stage floors and conventional plank flooring.

space, the crawl space should be well-ventilated and the ground should be covered with 6 mil polyethylene.

### Coordination

- Areas below the floors on which wood flooring is installed should be ventilated to prevent passage of moisture from below.
- Concrete subfloors for parquet flooring must be level to within ¼ in in 10 ft (6 mm in 3050 mm).
- Concrete subfloors for resilient wood flooring systems must be level to within ⅛ in in 10 ft (3 mm in 3050 mm).

## LAMINATE FLOORING [096219]

Laminate flooring is a variation of plastic laminate material. It is composed of a clear-wearing sheet over a melamine-impregnated decorative printed sheet with core layers of phenolic-impregnated kraft paper. These sheets are laminated to a high-density fiberboard core under heat and pressure and covered with a water-resistant backing sheet.

The decorative printed sheet can be made to resemble natural wood, tile, or stone, or can be printed in solid colors or even have photographic-quality images in it. Laminate flooring is available in planks (similar to wood strip flooring but a little wider), square tiles, or rectangular blocks. It is about 5⁄16 in (8 mm) thick. It is normally laid on a cushioned foam underlayment with the tongue-and-groove edges glued together. A vapor barrier is normally required when it is laid over a concrete floor.

Laminate flooring is hard, durable, and resistant to staining. Because the decorative layer is printed, it can be made to resemble any material, including wood, and is relatively easy to install. It is gaining popularity where a less expensive alternative to wood or other types of flooring is required. It can be used in most locations but is not recommended for rest rooms or other wet areas.

## TILE [093000]

### Types and uses

Tiles are small, flat finishing units made of clay or clay mixtures. The advantages of tile include durability; water resistance (if glazed); ease of installation; ease of cleaning; a wide choice of colors, sizes, and patterns; fire resistance; fade resistance; and the ability to store heat for passive solar collection. The two primary types are ceramic tile and quarry tile.

*Ceramic tile* is a surfacing unit, usually relatively thin in relation to facial area, made from clay or a mixture of clay and other ceramic materials. It has either a glazed or an unglazed face and is fired above red heat during manufacture to a temperature sufficiently high to produce specific physical properties and characteristics.

*Quarry tile* is glazed or unglazed tile, usually with 6 $in^2$, or more, of facial area. It is made from natural clay or shale by extrusion.

Some of the other common types of tile include glazed wall tile, unglazed tile, ceramic mosaic tile, paver tile, quarry tile (glazed or unglazed), abrasive tile, and antistatic tile.

*Ceramic mosaic tile* is formed by either the dust-pressed or extrusion method, is ¼ in (6 mm) to ⅜ in (10 mm) thick, and has a facial area of less than 6 $in^2$ (3870 $mm^2$). Dust pressing uses large presses to shape the tile out of relatively dry clay. The extrusion process uses machines to cut tiles from a wetter and more malleable clay extruded through a die.

The United States tile industry classifies tile based on size: tile under 6 $in^2$ (3870 $mm^2$) is *mosaic tile*; tile over 6 $in^2$ is *wall tile*. Glazed and unglazed nonmosaic tile made by the extrusion method is *quarry tile*. Glazed and unglazed tile over 6 $in^2$ made by the dust-pressed method is called *paver tile*.

Tile is also classified according to its resistance to water absorption, with nonvitreous tile having a water absorption rate of more than 7.0%. Impervious tile has a water absorption rate of 0.5%, or less. In between

## Applicable standards for tile

**American National Standards Institute (ANSI):**

| | |
|---|---|
| ANSI A108.1 | *Installation of Ceramic Tile, a Collection (Includes the A108 and A118 Series)* |
| ANSI A108.1a | *Specifications for Installation of Ceramic Tile in the Wet-Set Method, with Portland Cement Mortar* |
| ANSI A108.1b | *Specifications for Installation of Ceramic Tile on a Cured Portland Cement Mortar Setting Bed with Dry-Set or Latex Portland Cement Mortar* |
| ANSI A108.1c | *Specifications for Contractors Option: Installation of Ceramic Tile in the Wet-Set Method with Portland Cement Mortar or Installation of Ceramic Tile on a Cured Portland Cement Mortar Bed with Dry-Set or Latex Portland Cement Mortar* |
| ANSI A108.4 | *Specifications for Installation of Ceramic Tile with Organic Adhesives or Water Cleanable Tile Setting Epoxy Adhesive* |
| ANSI A108.5 | *Installation of Ceramic Tile with Dry-Set Portland Cement Mortar or Latex-Portland Cement Mortar* |
| ANSI A108.6 | *Installation of Ceramic Tile with Chemical Resistant, Water Cleanable Tile-Setting and Grouting Epoxy* |
| ANSI A108.7 | *Installation of Electrically Conductive Ceramic Tile Installed with Conductive Dry-Set Portland Cement Mortar* |
| ANSI A108.8 | *Installation of Ceramic Tile with Chemical-Resistant Furan Mortar and Grout* |
| ANSI A108.9 | *Installation of Ceramic Tile with Modified Epoxy Emulsion Mortar/Grout* |
| ANSI A108.10 | *Installation of Grout in Tile Work* |
| ANSI A108.11 | *Interior Installations of Cementitious Backer Units* |
| ANSI A118.1 | *Specifications for Dry-Set Portland Cement Mortar* |
| ANSI A118.2 | *Specifications for Conductive Dry-Set Portland Cement Mortar* |
| ANSI A118.3 | *Specifications for Chemical Resistant Water Cleanable Tile-Setting and Grouting Epoxy* |
| ANSI A118.4 | *Specifications for Latex-Portland Cement Mortar* |
| ANSI A118.5 | *Specifications for Chemical-Resistant Furan Mortar and Grouts for Tile Installation* |
| ANSI A118.6 | *Specifications for Ceramic Tile Grouts* |
| ANSI A118.8 | *Specifications for Modified Epoxy Emulsion Mortar/Grout* |
| ANSI A136.1 | *Organic Adhesives for Installation of Ceramic Tile* |
| ANSI A137.1 | *Specifications for Ceramic Tile* |

**Tile Council of America, Inc. (TCA):**

*Ceramic Tile: The Installation Handbook*

these two tile types are semivitreous tile and vitreous tile.

Imported tile is classified differently than tile produced in the United States. European manufacturers classify tile according to its production method (either the dust-pressed or extrusion method), its degree of water absorption, its finish, and whether it is glazed or unglazed.

The classifications of abrasion resistance are Group I, light residential; Group II, moderate residential; Group III, maximum residential; and Group IV, commercial (having the highest abrasion resistance).

## Standard forms

Ceramic mosaic tile is available in standard nominal U.S. sizes of 1 × 1 and 2 × 2 (25 × 25 and 50 × 50) with a nominal thickness of ¼ in (6 mm). Some 2 × 1 tile, as well as small hexagonal shapes, are also available. Glazed wall tile is manufactured in standard nominal sizes of 4¼ × 4¼, 6 × 4½, and 6 × 6 (108 × 108, 152 × 114, and 152 × 152), with a nominal thickness of ¼ in or 5⁄16 in (6 mm or 8 mm). Individual manufacturers may produce other sizes as well.

Most manufacturers produce a complete line of trim pieces for ceramic tile installation. These include cove base, bull-nose, inside and outside corners, and other shapes that are most often required. The standard trim shapes are illustrated in Figs. 8.7(a) and 8.7(b). However, some manufacturers produce only a limited number of trim shapes; the availability of trim shapes should be verified prior to final selection.

Quarry tile is available in nominal flat sizes of 3 × 3, 4 × 4, 6 × 6, 8 × 8, 8 × 4, and 6 × 3 (75 × 75, 100 × 100, 150 × 150, 200 × 200, 200 × 100, and 150 × 75), with a nominal thickness of ½ in (13 mm). Trim pieces are similar to those of wall tile.

## Safety factors

Tile (and also terrazzo, stone, and other smooth surfaces) can be a potentially dangerous flooring surface, especially when wet or covered with grease or other slippery materials. To evaluate and specify the slip resistance of floor surfaces, the coefficient of friction (COF) is used. This is a measurement of the degree of slip resistance of a floor surface and ranges from 0 to 1. The higher the COF, the less slippery the surface. There are two basic measures of friction: the static coefficient of friction, and the dynamic coefficient of friction. The static coefficient of friction is measured from a resting position, while the dynamic coefficient is measured when the two surfaces are in relative motion. It is difficult to measure the dynamic COF; for accurate results, the measurement must be done in a laboratory. Most tests, in the laboratory and in the field, measure the static coefficient of friction.

Many variables affect slip resistance, including wet versus dry conditions, shoe material, a person's weight, the angle of impact, stride length, and floor contamination. Numerous tests have been developed to measure the COF accurately and consistently while accounting for slip-resistance variables. These tests include the following.

- ASTM D2047, *Standard Test Method for Static Coefficient of Friction of Polish-Coated Floor Surfaces as Measured by the James Machine.* This is one of the most common tests used and is considered by many to be the most accurate and reliable measurement of slip resistance. However, it can only be performed in the laboratory on smooth, dry surfaces. It should not be used for wet or rough surfaces.

- ASTM C1028, *Standard Test Method for Determining the Static Coefficient of Friction of Ceramic Tile and Other Like Surfaces by the Horizontal Dynamometer Pull-Meter Method.* This test measures COF in the field. It uses a Neolite heel assembly and can

**Figure 8.7** Ceramic tile shapes

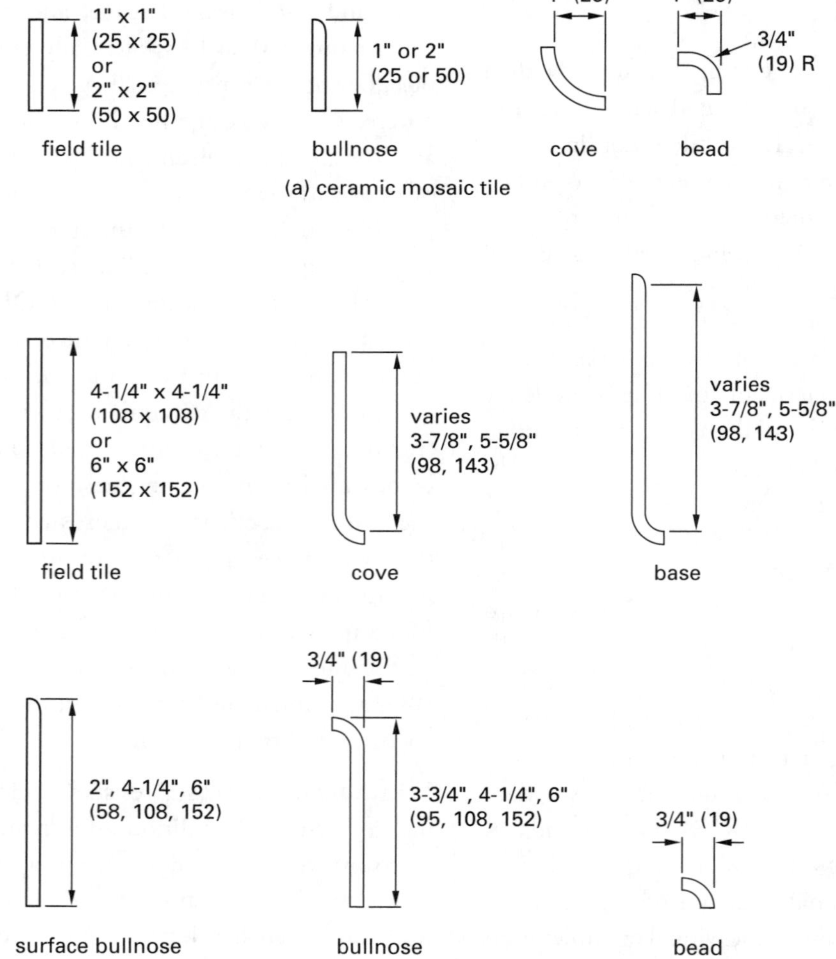


test both dry and wet surfaces, as well as smooth and rough floor surfaces. However, this test method produces inconsistent results from one surface to the next. The coefficients developed from this test cannot be compared with those from other tests.

- ASTM F1679, *Standard Test Method for Using a Variable Incidence Tribometer.* This test can be used either in the laboratory or in the field and can measure wet surfaces or surfaces contaminated with grease, oil, or similar substances.

- ASTM F1677, *Standard Test Method for Using a Portable Inclineable Articulated Strut Slip Tester.* Like the ASTM F1679 test, this test can be used either in the laboratory or in the field and can be used to measure wet surfaces or surfaces contaminated with grease, oil, or similar substances.

- ASTM F609, *Standard Test Method for Using a Horizontal Pull Slipmeter.* This test is also widely used in addition to the ASTM C1028 test. It measures static COF of footwear sole, heel, or related materials on walkway surfaces.

- ASTM F462, *Consumer Safety Specification for Slip-Resistant Bathing Facilities.* This test is used with soapy water for bathtubs and shower structures.

When using the ASTM D2047, the James Machine test, a COF of 0.5 has generally been considered the minimum required for a slip-resistant floor. Underwriters Laboratories requires a level of 0.5 or higher as a minimum safety level based on the ASTM C1028 standard. The Occupational Safety and Health Administration (OSHA) also recommends a COF of 0.5 as a minimum. Some have suggested a level of 0.6 for a good slip-resistant floor. In any case, when specifying slip resistance, the designer must refer to the specific test being used.

The Americans with Disabilities Act requires that a floor surface be slip resistant but does not give any specific test values. However, an appendix in a handbook to the ADA recommends a static coefficient of friction of 0.6 for accessible routes and 0.8 for ramps. This is based on a research project sponsored by the Architectural and Transportation Barriers Compliance Board (Access Board).

Until specific, uniform criteria are established, the designer should take into account the conditions under which floor tile and other flooring materials will be used before selecting a particular type of floor and specifying the minimum coefficient of friction. For example, a public lobby where snow and rain may be tracked in may need to be more slip resistant than a residential bathroom, where people are taking smaller strides without slippery shoe material.

## Typical details

Tile is laid on a suitable substrate using one of several formulations of mortar, or with adhesives. The joints are filled with grout. The particular type of mortar or adhesive and grout depends on the type of tile and the parameters of the job. The two most common methods of laying a tile floor are the thin-set method and the full mortar bed method.

### The thin-set method

Thin-set tile floors are laid on a suitable substrate, commonly a glass mesh mortar unit specifically manufactured for tile installation. This is a cementitious panel nailed to the subfloor. The tile is laid on a thin coating of dry-set or latex-portland cement mortar with latex-portland cement grout. See Fig. 8.8. A standard sand and portland cement grout can also be used. When using thin-set tile, the subfloor must be level, free from dirt and other contaminates, and able to support the extra weight of the tile. If a subfloor deflects or moves in some way, a thin-set tile installation will probably develop cracks. If movement or deflection of more than 1/360 of the span is expected, then a full mortar bed with a cleavage membrane should be used.

### The full mortar bed method

The full mortar bed method of laying ceramic tile floors is shown in Figs. 8.9(a) and 8.9(b). The tile and reinforced mortar bed are separated from the structural floor with a cleavage membrane (15 lbm roofing felt, or 4 mil polyethylene film) to allow the two floors to move independently. This system should be used on floors where excessive deflection is expected and on precast and posttensioned concrete floors. Because the mortar bed is reinforced with 2 × 2 (51 × 51), 16-gage

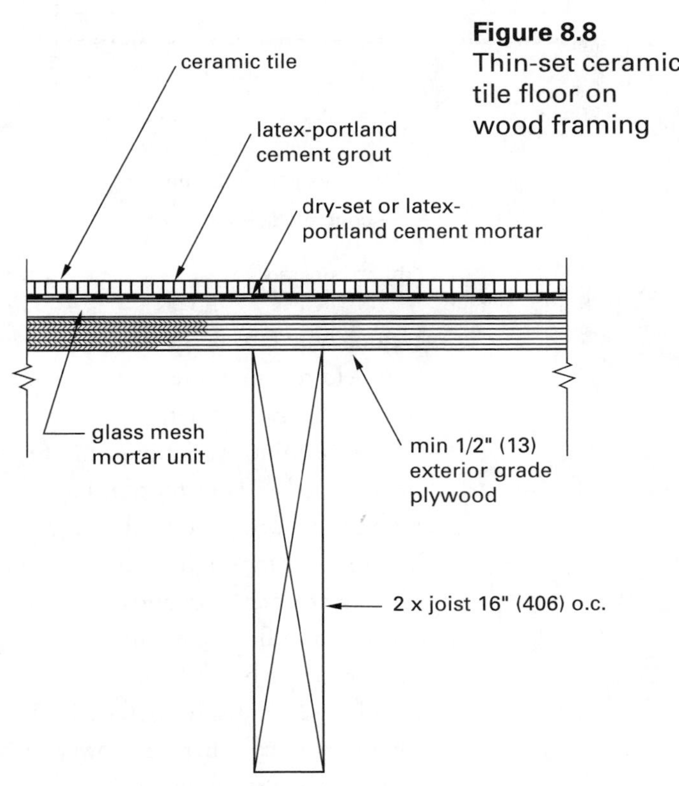


**Figure 8.8**
Thin-set ceramic tile floor on wood framing

**Figure 8.9**
Full mortar bed ceramic tile installations

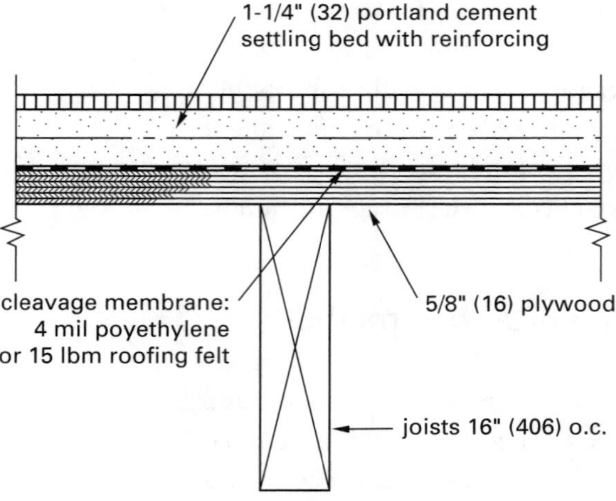


(a) on wood framing

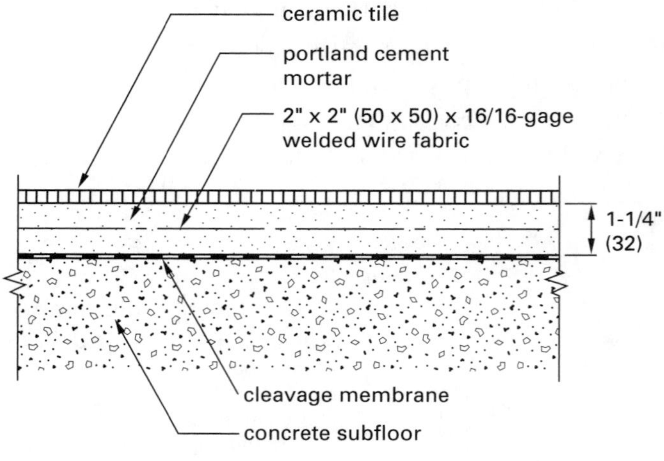


(b) on concrete

welded wire fabric, the tile and bed are rigidly held together as a unit. In addition to providing for movement, the full mortar bed allows for minor variations in floor level to be corrected with the mortar. The tile can be set on the mortar bed while it is still plastic or on a cured mortar bed using a second coat of dry-set or latex-portland cement mortar. If a waterproof floor is required, a waterproof membrane can be used in place of the cleavage membrane. This is the preferred method for tile floors in commercial showers or where continuous wetting will be present. Figure 8.9(b) shows the full mortar bed method over a concrete subfloor.

The full mortar bed method is not usually used in existing construction because of the required thickness of the mortar bed and the extra weight. Ideally, subfloors should be depressed about 1½ in (38.1 mm) so that the level of the floor matches adjacent flooring construction.

## Expansion joints

Some situations call for the use of expansion joints in ceramic tile floors. Expansion joints are required for large expanses of tile and where the tile abuts restraining surfaces, such as at columns, walls, and pipes. They are also required where backing materials change and where dissimilar floors occur. Expansion joints are not required in small rooms or corridors less than 12 ft (3.66 m) wide. If there are existing control, isolation, construction, or building expansions joints, the tile joints must coincide with them as well. Figures 8.10(a) and 8.10(b) show two tile expansion joint applications, and Table 8.5 gives the recommended sizes and spacing for expansion joints.

Expansion joints must be filled with sealant rather than grout. For joints where traffic is expected, a two-part polyurethane conforming to ASTM C920, Type M, Grade P, Class 25 should be used with a Shore A hardness of 35 or greater. Nontraffic areas can use a silicone, one-part polyurethane, or polysulfide sealant.

## Mortar for interior installations

There are several mortars and adhesives used for ceramic tile installation; each offers different characteristics for particular uses. These are summarized in Table 8.6. Compatible grouts are also available for each of the mortar types.

## Italian tile

The four types of Italian glazed tile and four types of unglazed tile are outlined as follows.

*Glazed*

Cottoforte: pink-red tile with good mechanical strength

Majolica: yellow-pink tile used for walls

White-body earthenware: used for walls and light residential floors

Monocottura: for interior and exterior floors

*Unglazed*

Red stoneware: commercial tile with high mechanical strength and excellent frost and abrasion resistance

Terra cotta: for interior and exterior floors

Fully vitrified stoneware: a nonporous porcelain or china tile

Clinker tile: similar to red stoneware for walls and floors

## Coordination

- For both thin-set and full mortar bed tile floors, verify the load-carrying capacity of the structural floor to support the extra weight of the tile.

- For thin-set tile floors, the maximum variation in the surface of the subfloor must not exceed ⅛ in in 10 ft (3 mm in 3050 mm).

- For full mortar bed tile floors, the maximum variation in the surface of the subfloor must not exceed ¼ in in 10 ft (6 mm in 3050 mm).

- If a floor must slope to a drain, the slope must be in the subfloor, not in the setting bed.

**Figure 8.10**
Ceramic tile expansion joints

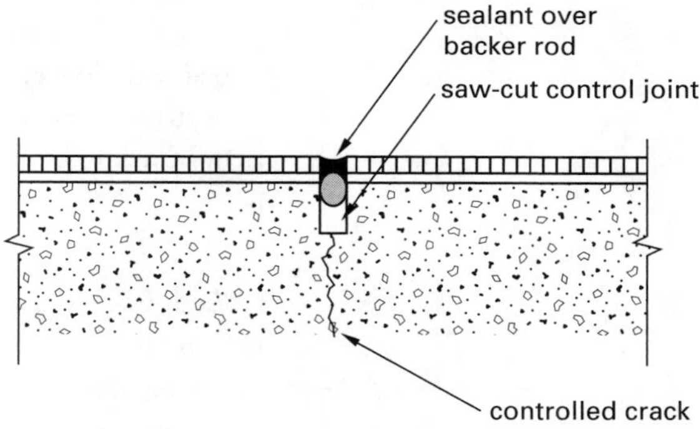


(a) expansion joint with thinset tile

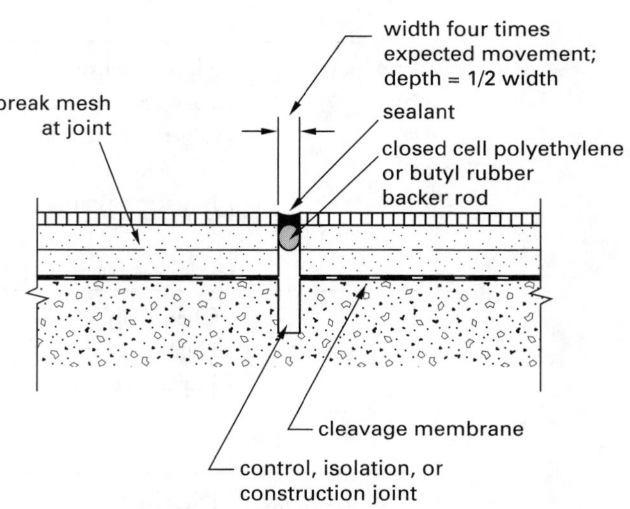


(b) expansion joint with full mortar bed tile

**Table 8.5**
Recommended ceramic tile expansion joint width and spacing

| | ceramic mosaic and glazed wall tile | quarry and paver tile | exposed to direct sunlight or moisture |
|---|---|---|---|
| spacing | 24 ft to 36 ft (7 m to 11 m) | 24 ft to 36 ft (7 m to 11 m) | 12 ft to 16 ft (3.5 m to 5 m) |
| width | ⅛ in to ¼ in[(1)] (3 mm to 6 mm) | ¼ in[(2)] (6 mm) | ¼ in (6 mm) |

[(1)] The preferred minimum is ¼ in, but the joint should never be less than ⅛ in.
[(2)] Same as the grout joint but not less than ¼ in.

**Table 8.6**
Mortar types and uses

| type | characteristics | use requirements and limitations | applications |
|---|---|---|---|
| portland cement | Strong, water resistant. Tile set while mortar in plastic state or on cured bed with dry-set or latex-portland cement mortar. Poor crack resistance. | Structurally sound substrate. Proper damp curing. | Only mortar used for full mortar bed installation on new or existing construction. Applied over substrates of concrete, masonry, wood, plaster, steel stud walls, etc. |
| dry set | Water resistant, impact resistant. Soaking of tiles not required. | Not a water barrier. Substrate must be true and level. Damp curing. | Thin-set applications. Applied over substrates of concrete, masonry, glass-mesh mortar units, portland cement mortar beds. |
| latex-portland cement | More water resistant than dry-set. Less rigid than portland cement mortar. Impact resistant. | Must dry out from 14 to 60 days for areas that may not dry out completely during use. Should not be used over plywood subfloors. Damp curing. | Thin-set applications where flexibility is required to accommodate minor floor movement. |
| epoxy | Chemically resistant. High bond strength. Impact resistant. | Level subfloor. Substrate must be clean and free of concrete curing compounds, oil, and sealers. | Thin-set on commercial floors where high impact and chemical resistance are needed. |
| modified epoxy emulsion | High bond strength. Shrinks less than other mortars. | Not chemically resistant. Modest resistance to cracking. | Thin-set applications. For light-duty or residential use only over plywood or concrete. |
| furan | Chemically resistant. High impact resistance. Excellent resistance to high temperatures. | Skilled applicators required. Expensive. Black in color. | For heavy use in commercial and industrial applications over all standard substrates, including existing tile and steel plate. |
| epoxy adhesive | High bond strength. Ease of application. | Little chemical resistance. | Thin-set for residential only on floors, walls, countertops. |
| organic adhesive | Ease of application. Economical. | Must have properly prepared backings for wet areas. | Thin-set for residential only on floors, walls, countertops. |

• Joint locations should coordinate with wall joints and other surrounding construction elements.

• Subflooring and underlayment for ceramic tile over wood joists must be installed dry, with closely spaced fasteners and with gaps between panels to allow for moisture-induced movement. The gaps must then be taped and filled prior to installing the tile.

## TERRAZZO [096600]

### Types and uses

Terrazzo is a composite material that is poured in place or precast. It is used for floors, stairs, and sometimes walls. Terrazzo consists of marble, quartz, granite, or other suitable stone chips in a matrix that is cementitious, modified cementitious, or resinous. Terrazzo is poured, cured, ground, and polished to produce a smooth surface.

The advantages of terrazzo include durability, water resistance, ease of cleaning, fire resistance, and a wide choice of patterns and colors. An unlimited number of terrazzo finishes can be achieved by specifying various combinations of chips and matrix colors.

There are four basic types of terrazzo. Standard terrazzo is the most common type, using small chips no larger than ⅜ in (9.5 mm). Venetian terrazzo uses chips larger than ⅜ in (9.5 mm). Palladian terrazzo uses thin, randomly fractured slabs of marble with standard terrazzo between. Rustic terrazzo has the matrix depressed to expose the chips. It is most commonly used for exterior applications where a rough surface is required.

The most commonly used matrix is cementitious, a mixture of white portland cement, sand, and water. Modified cementitious matrices, which consist of epoxy or polyacrylate mixed with the portland cement, are used when additional chemical resistance or conductivity is required or when the installation is thin-set. Resinous matrices of epoxy or polyester are used for thin-set applications. Conductive floors are used where static electricity buildup must be avoided. Conductive matrices are black due to their carbon content.

### Finishes

Terrazzo is generally finished to a smooth surface with an 80-grit stone grinder. However, to achieve a more textured surface, terrazzo can be ground with a rough, 24-grit grinder. Rustic terrazzo exposes some of the stone when the matrix is washed before it has set; however, this finish is usually not appropriate for interior flooring.

### Typical details

Terrazzo can be installed on walls as well as on floors. It can also be precast and poured into metal forms, such as stair pans. For floors, there are four methods of installation: sand cushion, bonded, monolithic, and thin-set. Each requires a different total thickness of material and different installation method. However, each method requires the use of divider strips placed at regular intervals to provide a controlled cracking point for the material, to facilitate leveling during installation, and for decorative purposes. Divider strips are most commonly a white alloy of zinc or brass in 12, 14, 16, or 18 (Brown and Sharp) gages (see Table 7.4). Strips ⅛, ¼, and ⅜ in (3, 6, and 10 mm) wide can also be used. They are available in T and L shapes in various depths appropriate for the installation method. Plastic and neoprene control strips are also used, with neoprene used over expansion joints in the concrete subfloor.

The sand cushion method, shown in Fig. 8.11, is the best way to avoid cracking the terrazzo. This is because the finish system is physically separated from the structural slab with a membrane, much the same as with a full mortar bed ceramic tile floor. Because the underbed is reinforced, the terrazzo system can move independently of the structure. The sand cushion method requires a total depth of 2½ in (64 mm) and weighs about 30 lbm/ft² (146 kg/m²); therefore, it is only appropriate for new construction where a structurally sound, depressed concrete floor slab can be provided. Divider strips should be located to provide areas of approximately 9 ft² to 36 ft² (0.8 m² to 3.3 m²). The length of each area should not exceed twice the width.

Bonded terrazzo reduces the total thickness and weight of the installation, but because the terrazzo is bonded to the concrete structural floor below, any deflection or other movement of the structure will cause the crack to telegraph through to the finished surface. See Fig. 8.12. Because bonded terrazzo requires a total depth of 1¾ in (45 mm) and weighs about 18 lbm/ft² (8.8 kg/m²), it is also only appropriate for new construction where a depressed concrete subfloor can be provided. Divider strips should be located to provide areas of approximately 16 ft² to 36 ft² (1.5 m² to 3.3 m²). The length of each area should not exceed twice the width. A bonded terrazzo base is illustrated in Fig. 8.13.

Monolithic terrazzo installations bond directly to the concrete structural floor without the use of a mortar underbed, as shown in Figs. 8.14 and 8.15. Like bonded installations, they will crack if the slab below deflects. However, they are only ½ in (13 mm) thick and weigh about 7 lbm/ft² (3.4 kg/m²). This makes them suitable for new construction, as well as for some types of remodeling, but only if the floor is structurally capable of supporting the extra weight without excessive deflection. The structural slab should also be level to within ⅛ in in 10 ft (3 mm in 3050 mm). Divider strips should be located to provide areas of approximately 200 ft² to 300 ft² (19 m² to 28 m²) in rectangular areas. The length of each area should not be more than 50% longer than the width. The divider strips should also be located at column center lines and over any control and construction joints in the concrete slab. When control joints in the concrete slab do not exist where divider strips are desired, the slab can be saw cut to no more than one third its thickness to create slab control joints. Saw cutting should be verified with the building architect and engineer to be sure that the structure is not weakened or that conduit and other items embedded in the slab are not damaged.

Thin-set terrazzo is similar to monolithic but only requires from ¼ in to ⅜ in (6 mm to 10 mm) thickness. It weights about 3 lbm/ft² (1.5 kg/m²). Epoxy, polyester, or polyacrylate matrices must be used for

**Figure 8.11**
Sand cushion terrazzo

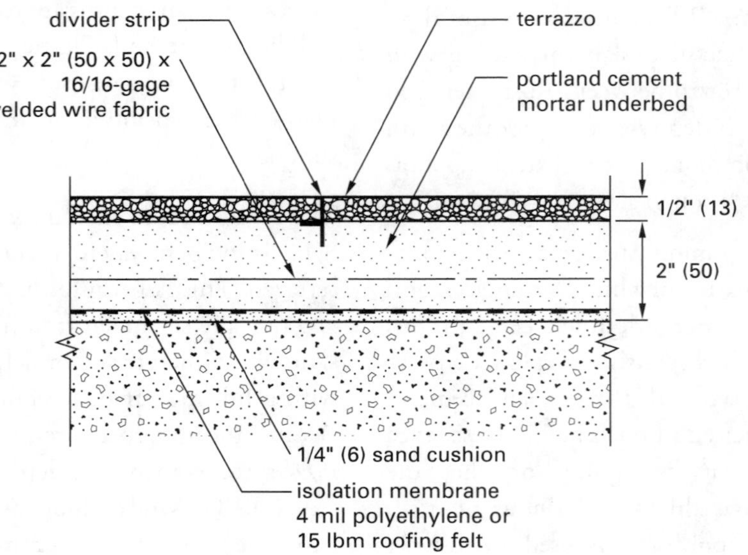

**Figure 8.12**
Bonded terrazzo

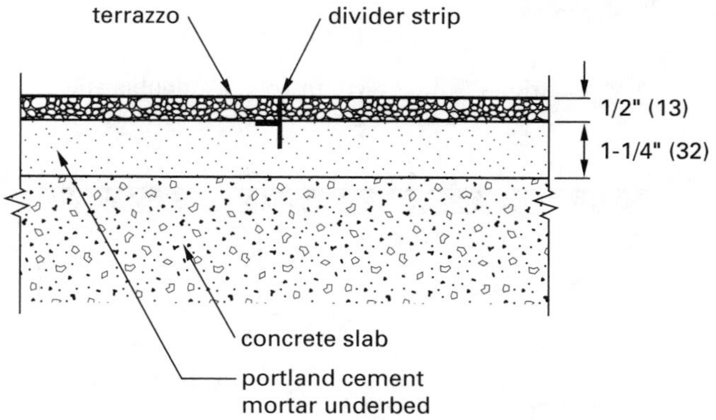

terrazzo
divider strip
1/2" (13)
1-1/4" (32)
concrete slab
portland cement mortar underbed

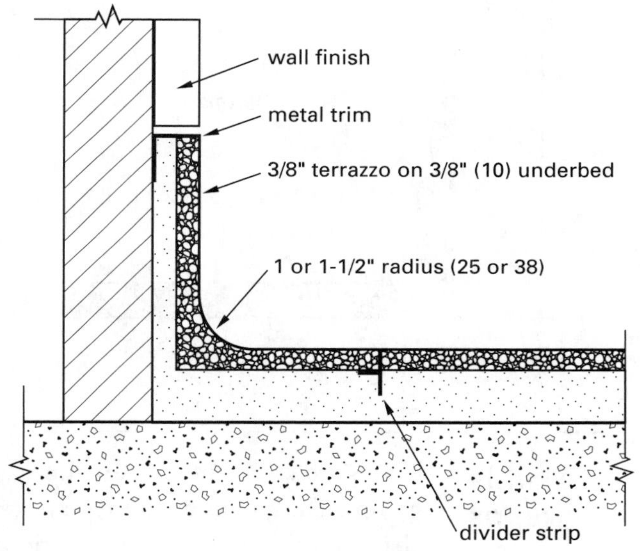


**Figure 8.13**
Terrazzo base

thin-set applications. Expansion strips with neoprene filler must be provided at all control joints in the structural slab, and divider strips should be located where a structural crack exists or can be anticipated. Divider strips are also used to create designs or patterns in the floor.

## Coordination

- Existing floors must be capable of supporting the extra weight of terrazzo.
- For sand cushion and bonded floors, the concrete subfloor must be level to within ¼ in in 10 ft (6 mm in 3050 mm).
- The design and installation of divider strips must coincide with the expansion and control joints of the concrete subfloor.
- For custom chip and matrix combinations, a minimum 6 × 6 (150 × 150) sample should be requested from the terrazzo contractor prior to installation.
- For bonded, monolithic, and thin-set installation, the subfloor must be free of compounds used to cure the concrete. It must also have the correct finish texture for the type of terrazzo installation: a troweled finish for bonded and a textured broom finish for monolithic floors.

# STONE FLOORING [096340]

Traditionally, stone flooring was laid in slabs about ¾ in (19 mm) thick on a thick mortar bed. While that method is still used today, new cutting and fabrication technology make it possible to use thin tiles of natural stone. Smaller sizes of thin tiles are usually not reinforced, but some manufacturers apply backings of fiberglass or other materials to add strength. Thin natural stone tiles not only reduce cost but simplify installation. They also make possible the use of stone flooring where it once was infeasible because of weight restrictions. Installation methods are similar to those for ceramic tile.

## Types and uses

There are five types of stone commonly used for flooring. These include granite, marble, limestone, slate, and sandstone. The same types of stone can be used for wall facing, as described in Ch. 10.

Granite is an igneous rock that has visible grains. It is available in a wide variety of colors, including gray, beige, white, pink, red, blue, green, and black. For interior use, there are five common finishes. A polished finish has a mirror gloss with sharp reflections. A honed finish has a dull sheen, without reflections. Fine-rubbed finishes produce a smooth surface that is free from scratches and has no sheen. A rubbed finish has a surface with occasional slight

**Figure 8.14**
Monolithic terrazzo

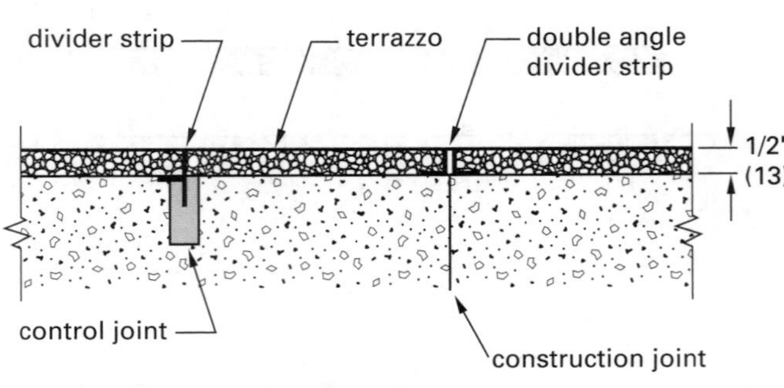


**Figure 8.15**
Monolithic terrazzo base

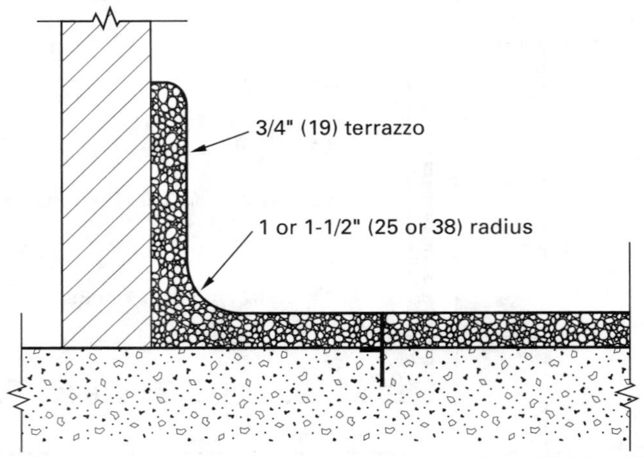


"trails" or scratches. Finally, a thermal, or flame, finish is coarse, with the exact amount of coarseness varying depending on the grain structure of the granite.

Marble is a metamorphic rock formed by layers of shells that, under heat and pressure, formed into a composition of crystalline grains of calcite and dolomite. Like granite, marble is available in a range of colors and patterns from uniform, pure white to vivid greens and reds with wild streaked patterns. The smoothest finish for marble is polished, which produces a glossy surface that brings out the full color and character of the marble. A honed finish has a satin-smooth surface with little or no gloss. An abrasive finish has a flat, nonreflective surface that is suitable for stair treads and other nonslip surfaces. A wet-sand finish yields a smooth surface that is also usable for nonslip floors.

Limestone is most commonly used for exterior surfaces, but a type of limestone, called *travertine*, is frequently used for interior flooring. Because of the way it is naturally formed, travertine has a network of holes in it. These must be filled with an epoxy resin (which can be colored to be

## Marble groups

The Marble Institute of America has developed a system that classifies marble into four groups. The groups do not represent the quality or value of the stone, but are based on the characteristics encountered in fabrication. Not all marbles in some of the groups are suitable for all applications, and the maximum size of available slabs varies depending on the group. Group C and Group D represent the most fragile stones, but with the proper finishing and fabricating techniques, these stones can still be used.

Group A: Sound marbles and stones, with uniform and favorable working qualities.

Group B: Marbles and stones similar in character to Group A, but with somewhat less favorable working qualities. They may have natural faults that require a limited amount of repair.

Group C: Stone with some geological flaws, voids, veins, and lines of separation. Some repair with filling, waxing, liners, and other kinds of reinforcing is done when necessary.

Group D: This group has the most variation in working qualities and contains more natural faults than Group C. It requires more repair and reinforcing than do Group C marbles.

compatible with the stone) to make a smooth surface. Travertine has a light, creamy color and is usually finished with a polished surface.

Slate is a fine-grained metamorphic rock that is easily split into thin slabs, making it ideal for flooring as well as roofing. Slate is available in color ranges of gray, black, green, brown, and deep red. A natural cleft finish shows the surface as it is when cleaved from the rock. The surface is rough, with levels ranging about 1/8 in (3.2 mm). A sand-rubbed finish gives an even plane and shows a slight grain. A honed finish is semipolished, without a sheen.

Sandstone is a sedimentary rock consisting of sand combined with other substances. When cleaved from the natural rock it is called *flagstone* and has a naturally rough surface. It can be used with irregular edges, just as it comes from the rock, or it can be cut into rectangular or square shapes.

### Standard forms

Thick stone for flooring is from 3/4 in to 1 in (19 mm to 25 mm) thick and varies in size depending on the stone type and availability of the specified color. Granite is available in sizes up to 4 × 10 (1200 × 3000); marble is available in sizes up to 5 × 7 (1500 × 2100) for Group A stone; and travertine is available up to about 3 × 4 (900 × 1200). Slate and sandstone come in smaller sizes, depending on the thickness and finish, but range from 8 × 16 to 24 × 36 (200 × 400 to 600 × 900). However, the practical maximum size for thick stone is about 36 in$^2$ (900 mm). Beyond this size, stone is difficult to lay and move around the interior of a building.

Stone tile is available in thicknesses of 3/16 in to 5/8 in (5 mm to 16 mm) in sizes of 1 × 1, 1 × 2, 2 × 2, 2 × 4, up to 5 × 10 (300 × 300, 300 × 600, 600 × 600, 600 × 1200, up to 1500 × 3000) depending on the manufacturer, thickness, and reinforcing method. Other stock sizes are available from some manufacturers, and all can be easily cut with standard carpentry or mason's tools.

### Composite stone flooring

Composite stone flooring is a class of manufactured materials that consists of stone chips mixed with a binder and formed into tiles. The stones used most often are quartz or marble. The binder most manufacturers use is a resin, but one manufacturer mixes the chips with a cement binding agent. The resin or other binder can be colored and, when combined with a variety of stone colors, yields a wide variety of colorations.

The material is used for flooring as well as for wall panels, countertops, column covers, and shower walls. It is hard, heat and stain resistant, noncombustible, and can be supplied with a polished, honed, textured, or sandblasted finish. It is installed like natural stone slabs, either in a mortar bed or with mastic.

The available sizes vary with each manufacturer, but common tile sizes include 12 × 12 and 24 × 24 (305 × 305 and 610 × 610). Slabs are available up to 53 × 120 (1346 × 3048) from one manufacturer. Thicknesses range from 3/8 in to 1 1/4 in (9.5 mm to 32 mm), depending on the size of the slab.

Composite stone is an environmentally friendly material because it uses recycled or waste material.

### Typical details

Stone flooring can be installed in two basic ways, using thin-set mortor or a full mortar bed. Full mortar bed applications are generally the best and must be used when the subfloor is uneven or when the stone varies in thickness, as with slate or sandstone. Thin-set applications are less expensive, add much less weight to the floor, and are faster to install. They are suitable for thin stone floors cut in uniform thicknesses in either residential or commercial construction.

**Figure 8.16**
Thin-set stone flooring

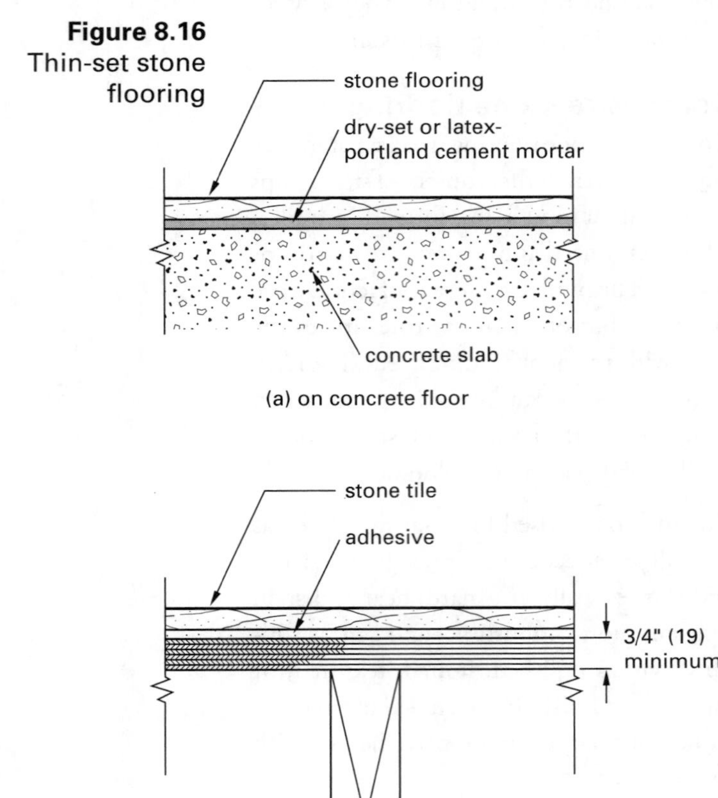


**Figure 8.17**
Full mortar bed stone flooring

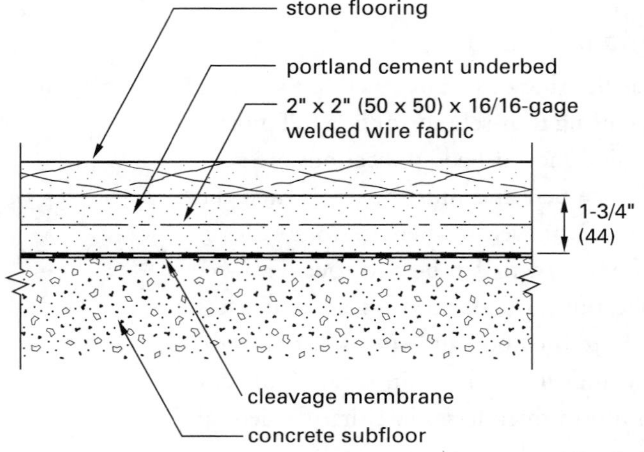


With thin-set installations, a uniform thickness of stone is set on the subfloor with a special thin-set mortar (about ⅛ in or less in thickness) or with an adhesive. Figure 8.16(a) shows a thin-set application on a concrete subfloor; Fig. 8.16(b) shows a thin-set application on a wood frame subfloor. Although the thin-set method is used primarily for thin stone, it can also be used for full-thickness slabs if required.

A full mortar bed installation requires that a layer of mortar from ¾ in to 1¼ in thick be applied to a suitably prepared, structurally sound subfloor. Then, either the stone is set in the semiwet mortar or the mortar is allowed to cure and the stone is set with another thin layer of dry-set mortar on top of the first. See Fig. 8.17. As with tile and terrazzo full mortar bed methods, a full mortar bed stone floor is usually restricted to new construction where the subfloor can be depressed enough so that the finish floor level aligns with adjacent construction.

With the full mortar bed method, the mortar can be bonded to the subfloor or separated from it with a cleavage membrane, usually 4 mil polyethylene. When a cleavage membrane is used, steel reinforcing mesh is placed in the mortar bed, allowing the finish floor to be structurally separate from the subfloor. If the subfloor deflects or moves slightly, the stone flooring is protected from cracking because it is not bonded to the structural floor.

Stone floors can be set with the joints tightly butted together or with spaces between joints. If there is a gap in the joint, it must be filled with grout or a portland cement/sand mixture that can be color-coordinated with the stone. Several special types of grout are available that are resistant to chemicals, fungi, and mildew. Latex grout is also available and provides some flexibility when slight movement in the floor is expected.

## Coordination

• Existing floors must be capable of supporting the extra weight of stone. Structural capacities should be verified with a structural engineer.

• For thin-set applications, concrete subfloors must be level to within ¼ in in 10 ft (6 mm in 3050 mm). Wood floors must be structurally sound and level to within 1/16 in in 3 ft (2 mm in 900 mm).

• Polished finishes should not be used in areas where the stone might get wet or on stairs because of the potential slippage problems. Flamed finishes with granite or an abrasive finish with marble are better choices in these applications and, in fact, are required by code in some applications.

• The edges of stone flooring adjacent to other materials should be protected from chipping with stone thresholds or metal strips. Figures 8.18(a) and 8.18(b) show two methods of making this transition.

## ACCESS FLOORING [096900]

Access flooring is a system of individual panels set on pedestals above a floor that allows electrical wiring, communications cabling, and small ducts to be placed between the structural floor and the raised flooring. Each panel can be removed individually to provide access to the services. Access flooring is typically used in large computer rooms where there is extensive cabling and where frequent access is needed. It is also used in recording studios, laboratories, communication centers, offices, and anywhere flexibility and accessibility to services are required.

Floor panels are 2 × 2 (600 × 600) and are set on adjustable steel or aluminum pedestals that support the panels at the corners. Some systems have stringers that connect the tops of the pedestals and provide additional lateral and gravity support. Pedestals can raise the flooring from 2½ in to 60 in (64 mm to 1525 mm) above the structural floor, depending on the space required for services. The panels are constructed of steel, aluminum, concrete, or particleboard, with finishes of plastic laminate, vinyl, or carpeting. Various types of pedestal systems are available from several manufacturers, depending on the loading requirements, size of installation, and height required. Perforated panels are used for air distribution, and special cutouts are used to bring cable and wiring through the panels. Accessories for ramps, closure panels, and handrails are also available.

**Figure 8.18**
Stone flooring edges

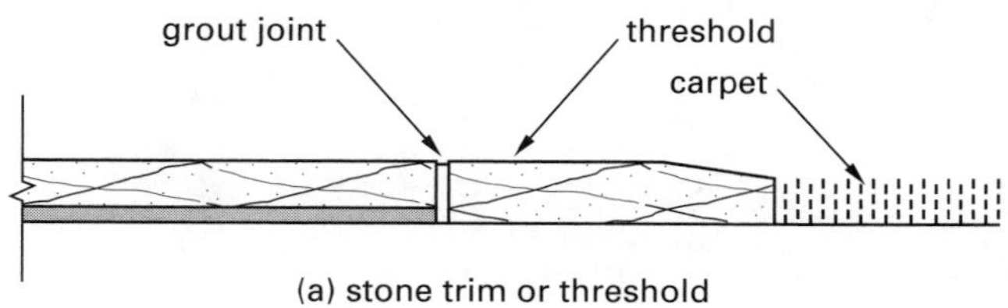

(a) stone trim or threshold

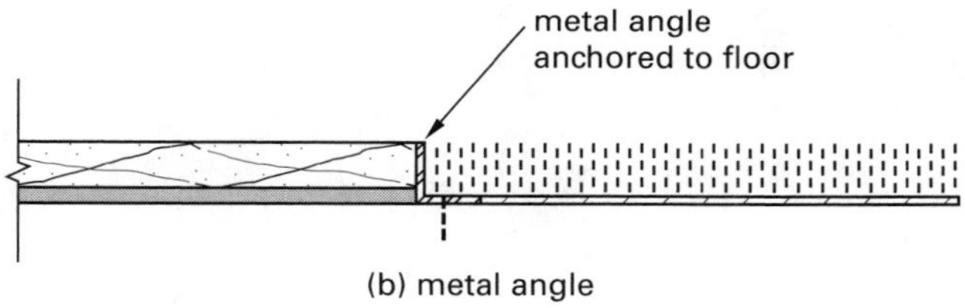

(b) metal angle

# 9 APPLIED FLOOR FINISHES

This section includes flooring that is applied as a single thin material, such as resilient tile and carpet. Refer to Ch. 8 for materials and construction techniques that involve several components applied to a structural floor. Refer to Ch. 21 for more information on sustainable floor finishes.

## CARPET [096800]

Carpet is one of the most commonly used flooring materials. If properly selected, it is attractive, durable, quiet, easy to install, and requires less maintenance than many other types of flooring. There are three basic forms of carpet: sheet carpet, carpet tiles, and rugs. Sheet carpet is available in rolls from 2 ft 3 in to 15 ft wide (690 mm to 4.6 m), depending on the manufacturing method, with 12 ft being a common width. Carpet tiles are individual squares of carpet. A rug is a soft floor covering, laid on the floor but not fastened to it, that does not cover the entire floor.

### Carpet fibers

Carpet is made from several fibers and combinations of fibers, including wool, nylon, acrylic, modacrylic, polyester, and olefin. The construction methods and properties of each of these fibers are summarized in Table 9.1.

#### Wool

Wool is a natural material and, overall, is one of the best materials for carpet. It is very durable and resilient, wears well, has superior appearance characteristics, is flame resistant, and is moderately easy to clean and maintain. Unfortunately, it is also one of the most expensive fibers for initial cost; however, in many situations the life-cycle cost can be lower than that of other carpet fibers.

#### Nylon

Nylon is an economical carpet material that is very strong and wear resistant. It has high stain resistance, excellent crush resistance, can be dyed with a wide variety of colors, and cleans easily. Some nylons create static problems and have a glossy sheen; however, these problems have generally been alleviated with improved fiber construction and by blending nylon with other fibers. New improvements in fiber construction also help to conceal dirt particles by increasing the light-scattering properties of individual filaments. Because of its many advantages, including cost, nylon is the most widely used fiber for both residential and commercial carpet.

**Table 9.1**
Carpet properties

| | fibers | | | | | |
|---|---|---|---|---|---|---|
| | wool | nylon | acrylic | modacrylic | polyester | olefin |
| manufacturing process: | | | | | | |
| tufted | • | • | • | | • | • |
| woven | • | • | • | • | | |
| needle punched | | • | | | | |
| fusion bonded | • | • | • | | | |
| typical construction | | | | | | |
| face weight, oz/yd | 30–55 | 20–40 | 25–42 | 40 | 32–55 | 26 |
| ($g/m^2$) | (1017–1865) | (680–1360) | (850–1420) | (1360) | (1080–1865) | (880) |
| total weight, oz/yd | 62–100 | 67–85 | 66–80 | 70–80 | 70–104 | – |
| ($g/m^2$) | (2100–33 900) | (2270–2880) | (2240–2710) | (2370–2710) | (2370–3520) | |
| pitch | 189 | 270 | 216 | 216 | 216 | 216 |
| stitches per inch | 8–9 | 7.5–11.25 | 8.75–11 | 7–9 | 7–9 | 12 |
| pile height (in (mm)) | 5/16–9/16 (8–14) | 1/8–5/8 (3–16) | 7/32–7/16 (5.5–11) | 3/16–15/64 (5–6) | 9/16–13/16 (14–21) | 5/16 (8) |
| surface: | | | | | | |
| level loop | • | • | • | | • | |
| cut pile | • | • | • | • | | • |
| cut/loop | | • | • | • | | |
| loop/random shear | | • | • | | | |
| flame spread | 55 | 35 | 25 | 20 | 20 | 80 |
| smoke developed, max. | 160 | 190 | 160 | 60 | 410 | – |
| resistance to: | | | | | | |
| abrasion | 4–5 | 5 | 3 | 2 | 3–4 | 4 |
| acids | 2 | 4–5 | 3 | 3 | 4 | 4 |
| alkalis | 2 | 4–5 | 4 | 3 | 4 | 4 |
| burns | 3 | 2 | 2 | 2 | 3 | 2 |
| crushing | 4–5 | 3 | 3 | 3 | 2–3 | 1–2 |
| insects and fungi | 2–5[1] | 4–5 | 4–5 | 4–5 | 4 | 4–5 |
| moisture | 2 | 2 | 3 | 3 | 3 | 5 |
| soiling | 3–4 | 3 | 3–4 | 3–4 | 4 | 4–5 |
| staining | 2–3 | 4 | 4 | 4 | 3 | 4–5 |
| static buildup | 2–4[1] | 1–4[1] | 3 | 3 | 3 | 4–5 |
| sunlight | 3–4 | 2 | 3 | 2–3 | 2–3 | 2–4 |
| properties | | | | | | |
| durability | 4–5 | 5 | 3–5 | 3–5 | 4 | 3 |
| ease of maintenance | 4–5 | 3 | 3–5 | 3–5 | 3–4 | 5 |
| resilience | 5 | 3 | 2 | 2 | 2 | 1 |
| appearance retention | 5 | 3–5 | 3–5 | 3–5 | 3–5 | 3 |

1 = poor 4 = very good [1] depends on treatment.
2 = fair 5 = excellent
3 = good

## Acrylic and modacrylic

Acrylic is a synthetic fiber that has moderate abrasion resistance, but has a more wool-like appearance than nylon. Like nylon, it can be dyed with a variety of colors, has good crush resistance, and is easy to maintain. It is also resistant to sunlight fading.

Modacrylic is a modified version of acrylic, containing a lower percentage of acrylonitrile units in its polymer base. It has a lower abrasion and alkali resistance.

## Polyester

Polyester carpet fiber is made from synthetic polymers and is highly abrasion resistant, cleans well, is mildew resistant, and is low in cost. It is sometimes used as a blend with nylon. However, it has only fair crushing resistance.

## Olefin

Olefin (polypropylene) is used primarily for indoor-outdoor carpet and as an alternate to jute for carpet backing. It is strong, very durable, stain resistant, and cleans easily. However, it is the least attractive of the artificial fibers and has low resilience as well as a low melting point.

# Manufacturing processes

Carpet is manufactured by weaving, tufting, needle punching, fusion bonding, and (less frequently) knitting and custom tufting.

## Weaving

Weaving is the traditional method of making carpet by interlacing warp and weft yarns. Warp is the yarn that runs lengthwise; weft is the yarn that runs crosswise. The number of warp lines of yarn in a 27 in (686 mm) width is called the *pitch*. The number of weft yarns per inch is referred to as the *wires* per inch. Weaving is a method that produces a very attractive, durable carpet, but it is the most expensive method of manufacturing carpet by machine. As shown in Figs. 9.1(a)–9.1(c) there are three primary methods of weaving.

Wilton carpet is produced on a jacquard loom that allows complex patterns and several types of surface textures—including level cut pile, level loop, cut/uncut, and multilevel loop—to be woven into the carpet. See Fig. 9.1(a). Different colors of yarn run beneath the surface of the carpet and are pulled up only when they are needed for the pattern. Therefore, Wiltons are generally heavier and more expensive that the other woven types for the same total weight.

Velvet carpet is the simplest form of weaving and places all the pile yarn on the face of the carpet. See Fig. 9.1(b). Velvet carpets are

**Figure 9.1**
Types of woven carpet

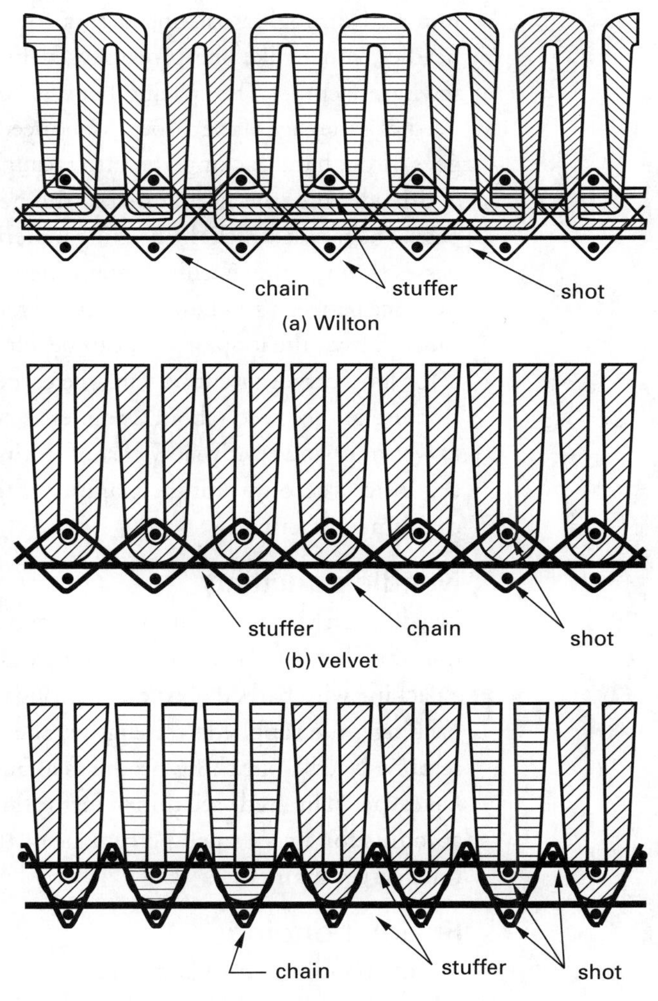

generally solid colors. However, multicolored yarns can also be used in a wide variety of surface textures, including plushes, loop pile, cut pile, multilevel loop, and cut-and-loop styles.

Axminster carpets are made on a modified jacquard loom that delivers different colors of yarn at different times according to the pattern desired. See Fig. 9.1(c). Because of the weaving process, Axminster carpets can be produced in a wide range of patterns and colors, from geometric to floral. Unlike the Wilton process, most of the pile yarn is placed on the surface. The carpet has an even, cut-pile surface with a heavily ribbed backing.

### Tufting

Tufting is a process in which pile yarn is punched through a backing with a row of needles, much like the process used by a sewing machine. The spacing between the needles is the gage of the carpet. As the needle goes through the backing, the yarn is caught and held while the needle makes the next pass. The rate at which the backing material passes through the machine determines the distance between stitches, or the stitch rate. Once tufted, the loop of yarn can be left as is for loop carpet or cut for cut-pile carpet. Because of the speed (about 25 times as fast as weaving) and relative low cost of tufting, this process accounts for the majority of the carpet manufactured.

### Needle punching

Needle punching is similar to tufting, except that the fiber is pushed and pulled through a backing with barbed needles. A secondary backing is then applied to strengthen the assembly. Needle punching produces a fairly flat carpet of limited variation in texture and accounts for a very small percentage of the total carpet market.

### Fusion bonding

Fusion bonding embeds the pile yarn in a backing of liquid vinyl. When the vinyl hardens, the tufts are permanently locked into the backing. Texture and pattern types are limited in fusion bonding, and it is used primarily for carpet tiles.

## Carpet properties

### Appearance and durability

The appearance and durability of a carpet are affected by the amount of yarn in a given area, how tightly that yarn is packed, and the height of the yarn. The pitch of a woven carpet is the number of ends of surface yarn in a 27 in (686 mm) width. For tufted carpet, this measurement is called the *gage*, which is the spacing, in fractions of an inch, between needles across the width of the carpet. Gages of $\frac{5}{64}$, $\frac{1}{10}$, and $\frac{1}{8}$ in (1.98, 2.54, and 3.2 mm) are common for contract carpet. The *stitch* (or stitch rate) is the number of lengthwise tufts in one inch. The wires per inch is the corresponding measurement in woven carpet. The higher the pitch or gage number and stitch numbers are, the denser the carpet is. The pile height is the height of the fiber from the surface of the backing to the top of the pile. Generally, shorter and more tightly packed fibers result in a more durable and more expensive carpet.

### Carpet flammability

There are two primary concerns related to the flammability of carpet: whether a carpet will ignite and sustain a fire if it is the first item ignited, and how flammable the carpet is when subjected to the heat and flame of a fully developed fire. To prevent carpet from igniting and spreading fire when exposed to something like a dropped match, current federal law requires that all carpet manufactured and sold in the United States meet the requirements of ASTM D2859, also known as the *Methenamine Pill Test.*

Regulations that address carpet flammability in fully developed fires are more varied. At the least, building codes regulate the maximum flame-spread rating of finish materials tested according to ASTM E84, *Standard Test Method for Surface*

*Burning Characteristics of Building Materials.* Also known as the *Steiner tunnel test,* this standard is not entirely appropriate for carpet, but it is still referenced in many codes. The Steiner tunnel test is also referred to as NFPA 255 and UL 723 by the National Fire Protection Association and Underwriters Laboratories, respectively. Refer to Ch. 19 for more information on finish flammability.

## Tuft density, average density, and weight density of carpet

One of the main determinants of carpet quality and durability is the density of the yarn that is exposed to wear. A carpet that has more yarn packed closer together will wear better than a looser constructed carpet. One measure of this density is the tuft density, which is the gage (or pitch for woven carpets) multiplied by the stitch (or wires per inch). This calculation gives the tufts per square inch. However, overall density is also dependent on the pile height, which is the distance from the top of the surface yarn to the top of the backing. Given two carpets with the same tuft density and face weight, the one with the lower pile height will wear better because the same amount of yarn is packed into a tighter space. The face weight is the number of ounces of yarn in the surface pile per square yard.

The average pile density, AD, takes into account the pile height and is calculated by the formula

$$AD = \frac{\text{face weight}_{\text{oz/yd}}(36)}{\text{pile height}}$$

This gives the amount of yarn per cubic yard. Generally, commercial carpet should have an average density of at least 3000.

The weight density is the average density multiplied by the face weight. This takes into account the value of pile weight on durability and resilience, because two carpets with different face weights and pile heights may have the same calculated average density, but the one with the higher weight density will wear better.

## Yarn weight and construction

Yarn weight refers to the thickness of the yarn and is called the yarn count. Construction is described in yarn plies and refers to the number of single yarns that are twisted together to make the yarn for tufting or weaving.

There are several methods of designating yarn count, depending on the manufacturing process and the country of manufacture. For tufted and fusion-bonded carpets two systems are used: the woolen count system and the denier system. The woolen count is the number of yards in 1 oz of finished yarn and also includes the number of plies. For example, a 3/80 count means 80 yd of three-ply yarn per ounce. The denier system is used for synthetic yarns and is measured in grams per 9000 m of yarn. For example, a yarn denier of 1250/4 means that 9000 m of a particular four-ply yarn weighs 1250 g.

Four systems are used for woven carpet, depending on the country: cotton count (United States), TEX (Europe, United Kingdom, New Zealand, Australia, and elsewhere), metric (Europe, United Kingdom, Japan), and Dewsbury. The cotton count and the TEX system are the most common. The cotton count is the number of 840 yard skeins (called hanks) in a pound of yarn. The TEX system is similar to the denier system but is a true metric count. A *tex* is the weight, in grams, of one kilometer of yarn. To keep the TEX system in the same order of magnitude as the denier system, the term *decitex* is sometimes used, which is the weight, in grams, of 10,000 m of yarn.

A more accurate test of carpet flammability is the *flooring radiant panel test,* ASTM E648 (also designated as NFPA 253 by the National Fire Protection Association). This test is required by all major federal agencies for their projects and by many other state and local jurisdictions. The amount of radiant energy needed to sustain flame is measured and defined as the *critical radiant flux.* It is measured in watts per square centimeter, and two classes, Class I and Class II, have been established. Corridors and exitways in hospitals and nursing homes must have a Class I rating (minimum of 0.45 W/cm$^2$). Corridors and exitways of all commercial buildings and hotels must have a Class II rating (0.22 W/cm$^2$); however, this test only applies to carpet in corridors, not in rooms and other areas. Refer to Ch. 19 for specific requirements for Class I and II finishes.

Other flammability tests that are required by some state and federal agencies include NFPA 258, *Recommended Practice for Determining Smoke Generation of Solid Materials.* The smoke density chamber test measures the smoke potential of burning materials and the amount of obscuration from that smoke. The chamber test measures flame spread as an alternate to the Steiner tunnel test.

## Carpet backing and cushioning

Carpet backing both provides support for and locks in the pile yarn. It also gives added strength and dimensional stability to carpets. In woven and knitted carpets the pile yarns and backing yarns are combined during the manufacturing process. Polypropylene yarn is the most common backing for woven carpet, but others include jute, cotton, and polyester. A coating of latex is often applied to woven carpet to provide additional dimensional stability and tuft bind.

Tufted carpet is manufactured by punching the yarns through a primary backing of woven or nonwoven polypropylene or woven jute. A secondary backing is then applied to hold the tufts in place and give added stability. This is usually a coating of latex, but a foam cushion or laminated fabric backing can also be applied. Needle-punched carpet is latex coated or foam backed.

An important part of carpet installation is the carpet cushion, sometimes called padding. Cushion is not appropriate for all carpet installation (such as direct glue-down installation), nor is it required; however, it is recommended. Cushioning increases the life of the carpet, provides increased resiliency and comfort, helps sound absorption, lessens impact noise, and improves thermal qualities in some situations. Common cushion materials include sponge rubber, felt, urethane, and foam rubber.

Sponge rubber is made from natural or synthetic rubber and other chemicals and fillers with a facing on the top side. It is available in flat sheets or a waffled configuration. Thicknesses range from ⅛ in to 5⁄16 in (3 mm to 8 mm), with weights from 41 oz/yd$^2$ to 120 oz/yd$^2$ (1390 g/m$^2$ to 4070 g/m$^2$).

Felt is available in four forms: hair, combination, fiber, and rubberized. Hair felt is composed of 100% animal hair. Combination felt is a mixture of animal hair and other fibers. Fiber felt is composed entirely of felt. Rubberized felt is any of the other three types with a rubberized coating on one side. Felt is available in thicknesses from ¼ in to 9⁄16 in (6 mm to 14 mm) and in weights from 32 oz/yd$^2$ to 86 oz/yd$^2$ (1080 g/m$^2$ to 2920 g/m$^2$).

Urethane is manufactured in three different ways to produce prime, densified, or bonded sheets. Its thickness ranges from ¼ in to ¾ in (6 mm to 19 mm). Prime urethane comes in densities from 1.3 lbm/ft$^3$ to 6 lbm/ft$^3$ (20.8 kg/m$^3$ to 96 kg/m$^3$). Densified urethane is available in densities from 2.7 lbm/ft$^3$ to 6 lbm/ft$^3$ (43 kg/m$^3$ to 96 kg/m$^3$). Bonded urethane can be specified in densities from 4 lbm/ft³ to 10 lbm/ft³ (64 kg/m³ to 160 kg/m³).

Foam rubber is commonly applied as an integral backing to some carpet. It is natural or synthetic latex rubber with additives and with a backing on one side. Its thickness ranges from ⅛ in to ⅝ in (3 mm to 16 mm), and its weight ranges from 28 oz/yd² to 65 oz/yd² (950 g/m² to 2200 g/m²).

All types of cushioning are available in widths of up to 12 ft (3.7 m).

## Installation

Carpet is installed in one of three ways: direct glue-down, stretched-in, or double glue-down. In direct glue-down installation, the carpet is attached to the floor with adhesive. The carpet may be installed with an integrated cushion. Direct glue-down installations resist shifting in heavy traffic areas and support wheeled traffic better than the stretched-in method. The direct glue-down method is also faster and less expensive to install. However, glue-down installation without cushioning does not last as long because of the increased wear on the carpet. It is also harder underfoot. Because direct glue-down installation requires a low-pile carpet, the choice of textures and construction methods is limited.

A stretched-in installation uses tackless strips attached around the perimeter of the room. These plywood strips have embedded sharp points that face toward the walls. Carpet cushion is either stapled to wood floors or glued to concrete floors after the tackless strips are in place. The carpet is then stretched against the strips, which hold the carpet in place. See Fig. 9.2.

Double glue-down uses a high-density cushion glued to the subfloor. The carpet is then glued to the cushion. This method combines the advantages of both stretched-in and direct glue-down installations. It is good for high traffic areas but is not as good as direct glue-down for rolling wheeled traffic.

Prior to installation, a seaming diagram should be submitted by the carpet installer for review. Carpet should be installed so that the nap runs in the same direction on all pieces. Whenever possible, seams should not run across heavy traffic areas or be placed where people tend to change walking directions, such as at corners of corridors, in front of elevators, or at doorways. Seams should also not run perpendicular to the width of a doorway. Although not ideal, seams across a door opening are acceptable and usually necessary for an economical installation.

## Carpet tile [096813]

Carpet tiles are individual pieces of carpet, typically 18 in², that are applied to the floor with pressure-sensitive adhesive. Because of their modular design, damaged or worn pieces can be replaced without removing the entire floor covering. They are generally specified for commercial installations where a frequent change in room layout is expected, where maintenance may be a problem, or where flat, undercarpet electrical and telephone cabling is used.

## Coordination

- Subflooring must be suitably prepared to receive carpet. Concrete floors must be

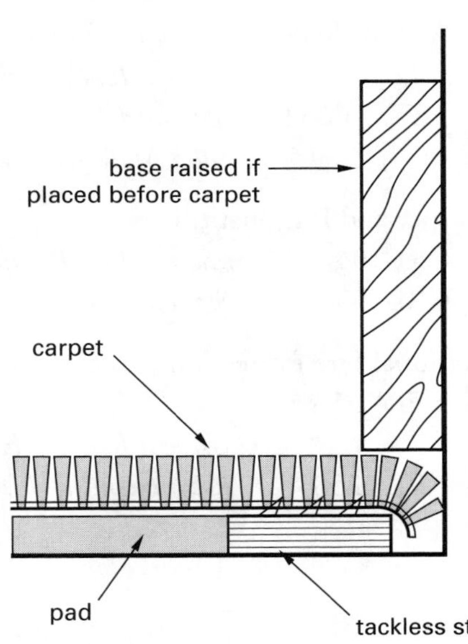


**Figure 9.2** Stretched-in carpet installation

smooth, with high points or ridges ground down and depressions and cracks filled.

• For direct glue-down applications, concrete floors must be free of moisture and curing agents.

• Wood subfloors must be flooring-grade plywood, particleboard, or hardboard, with joints filled and rough spots sanded smooth.

• Wood floors over crawl spaces or other damp locations should have ventilated space below with a vapor barrier placed over the earth in the crawl space.

• Edges of carpet adjacent to other flooring must be suitably terminated with standard binder bars, carpet grippers, or other custom details.

• Verify that the carpet installation meets ADA requirements. See Ch. 18.

## RESILIENT TILE FLOORING [096519]

Resilient flooring is a generic term that describes several types of composition materials made from various resins, fibers, plasticizers, and fillers. It is formed under heat and pressure to produce a thin material either in sheets or tiles. This sections describes the various types of resilient tile flooring, while the next section describes sheet flooring.

Resilient flooring is applied with mastic to a subfloor of concrete, plywood, or some other smooth underlayment. Some resilient floorings may only be installed on floors above grade, while others may be placed below, on, or above grade. Refer to the man-ufacturer's literature for specific recommendations. The types of resilient flooring used today include vinyl, vinyl composition, rubber, cork, vinyl-faced cork, and

**Applicable standards for carpet**

**American Society for Testing and Materials (ASTM):**

| | |
|---|---|
| ASTM D2859 | *Standard Test Method for Ignition Characteristics of Finished Textile Floor Covering Materials* |
| ASTM D4158 | *Standard Guide for Abrasion Resistance of Textile Fabrics (Uniform Abrasion)* |
| ASTM E84 | *Standard Test Method for Surface Burning Characteristics of Building Materials* |
| ASTM E162 | *Standard Test Method for Surface Flammability of Materials Using a Radiant Heat Energy Source* |
| ASTM E648 | *Standard Test Method for Critical Radiant Flux of Floor-Covering Systems Using a Radiant Heat Energy Source* (NFPA 253) |
| ASTM E662 | *Standard Test Method for Specific Optical Density of Smoke Generated by Solid Materials* (NFPA 258) |

**Carpet and Rug Institute:**

| | |
|---|---|
| CRI-104 | *Standard for Installation of Commercial Carpet* |
| CRI-105 | *Standard for Installation of Residential Carpet* |

**National Fire Protection Association (NFPA):**

| | |
|---|---|
| NFPA 253 | *Standard Method of Test for Critical Radiant Flux of Floor Covering Systems Using a Radiant Heat Energy Source* |
| NFPA 258 | *Recommended Practice for Determining Smoke Generation of Solid Materials* |

asphalt. Vinyl, vinyl composition, and rubber flooring are the most common. Resilient tile flooring properties are summarized in Table 9.2.

## Vinyl tile

Vinyl tile is the term commonly used to refer to flooring based on polyvinyl chloride (PVC). It is a good, durable, resilient flooring that is resistant to indentation, abrasion, grease, water, alkalis, and some acids. Vinyl comes in a variety of colors and patterns and is easy to install. It can be used below grade, on grade, or above grade. It must be installed over a clean, dry, and smooth surface. It is slightly more expensive than vinyl composition tile.

**Table 9.2**
Resilient tile flooring properties

| | vinyl | vinyl composition | rubber | cork | vinyl-faced cork | asphalt |
|---|---|---|---|---|---|---|
| common sizes (in (mm)) | 9 × 9, 12× 12, 24 × 24 (225 ×225, 300 × 300, 600 × 600) | 9 × 9, 12× 12, (225 × 225, 300 × 300) | 9 × 9, 12× 12, 18 × 18, 24 × 24 (225 × 225, 300 × 300, 450 × 450, 600 × 600) | 6 × 6, 9 × 9, 12 × 12 (150 × 150, 225 × 225, 300 × 300) | 9 × 9, 12 × 12 (225× 225, 300 × 300) | 9 × 9, 18 × 18 (225 × 225, 460 × 460) |
| thickness (in (mm)) | 1/16, 1/8 (1.6, 3.2) | 3/32–5/32 (2.4–4) | 3/32, 1/8, 3/16 (2.4, 3.2, 4.8) | 1/8–5/16 (3.2–8) | 1/8 (3.2) | 1/8 (3.2) |
| use[(1)] | B, O, A | B, O, A | B, O, A | A | A | A |
| load limit (psi (kg/cm$^2$)) | 200 (14) | 50–75 (3–5) | 200 (14) | 75 (5) | 75–150 (5–10.5) | 25 (2) |
| flame spread | 45–75 | 15–75 | 75 | – | – | 75 |
| smoke developed | 425 | 215–450 | 450 or less | – | 450 or less | – |
| resistance to: | | | | | | |
| alkalis | 4–5 | 4 | 4 | 1 | 4 | 1 |
| cigarette burns | 1–3 | 1–3 | 4 | 2 | 2 | 1 |
| grease/oil | 5 | 5 | 1 | 2 | 5 | 1 |
| indentation | 3–5 | 2–3 | 4 | 2 | 3 | 2 |
| stains | 2–5 | 2–5 | 4–5 | 1–2 | 2–4 | 2 |
| properties | | | | | | |
| durability | 4–5 | 3–4 | 4 | 1 | 2 | 2 |
| ease of maintenance | 3–4 | 3–4 | 2–3 | 1–2 | 3–4 | 2 |
| resilience | 1–4 | 1–4 | 4 | 5 | 3 | 1 |
| quietness | 2–5 | 1–4 | 5 | 5 | 3 | 1 |

1 = poor
2 = fair
3 = good
4 = very good
5 = excellent

(1) B = below grade. O = on grade. A = above grade.

Vinyl tiles are generally 12 in$^2$ (300 mm), although some are available in 9 in (225 mm) squares and larger sizes. Either 1/16 in or 1/8 in (1.6 mm or 3.2 mm) thicknesses are available; however, for commercial use and better residential floors, the 1/8 in thickness is preferred.

### Vinyl composition

Vinyl composition tile is similar to vinyl tile but includes various types of fillers that decrease the percentage of polyvinylchloride. While composition tile costs less than homogenous vinyl, it has less flexibility and abrasion resistance. Because of this, through-grain types should be specified. These are tiles where the color and pattern extend uniformly through the tile thickness. Normally, this tile is applied with mastic; however, peel-and-stick types are available for residential applications. Tile is also available with an attached foam backing for greater resilience.

### Rubber

Rubber flooring is made from synthetic rubber and offers excellent resistance to deformation under loads, providing a very comfortable, quiet, resilient floor. Rubber, however, is not very resistant to oils or grease, and it can be damaged if small objects on its surface cause indentations. This flooring is available with a smooth surface or with a patterned, raised surface that allows water and dirt to lie below the wearing surface, helping to prevent slipping or excessive abrasion. Rubber flooring is available in tiles or in sheet form in several thicknesses.

### Cork

Cork flooring is made of granulated pieces of bark from the cork oak tree that are bonded together under heat and pressure. By varying the heat or adding dyes, a variety of colors and patterns are produced—some with the characteristic straw color of cork and others as dark as walnut. Patterns range from standard, uniform flakes to alternating strips of dark and light material.

Cork is a renewable resource because after it is harvested, the tree grows a new skin in approximately nine years, which then can be harvested again. In addition, the cork industry helps preserve forests. Portugal, which produces about half of the world's cork, regulates harvesting and has made it illegal to cut down cork-producing trees.

Cork is available in tile and plank forms and is used where acoustical control or a high degree of resilience is desired. Tiles are commonly 12 in (305 mm) square and either 3/16 in (5 mm) or 5/16 in (8 mm) thick. Planks are 12 in (305 mm) wide and 3 ft (914 mm) long and consist of cork laminated to tongue-and-groove medium-density fiberboard.

Cork tile is installed using adhesive, while the plank form is edge-glued without being adhered to the subfloor. The entire floor then "floats" on the subfloor. In either case, the subfloor must be perfectly smooth so any unevenness does not telegraph through.

Cork flooring is available either unfinished or prefinished. Finishes include acrylic, polyurethane, and carnauba wax. Acrylic requires frequent reapplication—every four to six months. Polyurethane must be reapplied every three to seven years, and the old finish must be completely sanded off to ensure the new application will stick. Wax must be reapplied about once a year.

### Preparation of substrates

Preparation of the subfloor on which resilient tile or sheet flooring is placed is critical to a successful installation. Because moisture is the cause of most problems, concrete floors must be dry at the time of installation. For new concrete floors it may take from six to twelve weeks, or more, for the slab to thoroughly cure and dry. If there is any doubt, the slab should be tested for moisture. Below-grade and on-grade slabs should have a vapor barrier below them to prevent moisture from migrating from the earth. Concrete must be free of curing compounds, sealers, and hardeners that will interfere with the adhesive bonding. The slab must also be free of solvents, grease, oil, and similar compounds. The surface should be smooth and level to within ⅛ in in 10 ft (3 mm in 3050 mm), with no abrupt transitions or depressions. Construction and control joints should be filled and leveled with a latex patching compound.

Wood subflooring should be smooth, with all boards securely fastened. Generally, underlayment of plywood, hardboard, or particleboard is recommended. The board should be underlayment grade, at least ¼ in (6 mm) thick, and securely glued and nailed, with the joints staggered. The joints should be sanded and filled, if necessary, with all nails driven flush. Grade-level wood floors should be over a well-ventilated crawl space with a vapor barrier on the earth in the crawl space. Resilient floors may be installed over existing wood floors if they are smooth and tight and if all ridges are sanded. However, underlayment is preferred.

## RESILIENT SHEET FLOORING [096516]

Resilient flooring in sheet form has several advantages over tile. Although it is more difficult to install, it provides a floor with fewer seams. That makes the floor easier to clean, more hygienic, and more resistant to moisture spills. Some types of sheet flooring even allow the seams that do exist to be sealed. There are three primary types of sheet flooring: vinyl, rubber, and linoleum, with three variations of vinyl flooring. Conductive flooring and slip-retardant flooring are also available. The properties of the primary types of sheet flooring are shown in Table 9.3.

### Vinyl sheet flooring

Solid sheet vinyl, like solid vinyl tile, is a homogeneous, nonlayered construction of polyvinylchloride with color and pattern extending through the entire thickness. It is

**Applicable standards for resilient floor covering**

**American Society for Testing and Materials (ASTM):**

ASTM F693 *Standard Practice for Sealing Seams of Resilient Sheet Flooring Products by Use of Liquid Seam Sealers*

ASTM F710 *Standard Practice for Preparing Concrete Floors to Receive Resilient Flooring*

ASTM F1066 *Standard Specification for Vinyl Composition Floor Tile*

ASTM F1303 *Standard Specification for Sheet Vinyl Floor Covering With Backing*

ASTM F1344 *Standard Specification for Rubber Floor Tile*

ASTM F1516 *Standard Practice for Sealing Seams of Resilient Flooring Products by the Heat Weld Method*

ASTM F1700 *Standard Specification for Solid Vinyl Floor Tile*

ASTM F1859 *Standard Specification for Rubber Sheet Floor Covering Without Backing*

ASTM F1860 *Standard Specification for Rubber Sheet Floor Covering With Backing*

ASTM F1861 *Standard Specification for Resilient Wall Base*

**Table 9.3**
Resilient sheet flooring properties

| | solid sheet vinyl | inlaid vinyl | clear-coated rotogravure | rubber | linoleum |
|---|---|---|---|---|---|
| common widths (ft (mm)) | 4, 6 (1200, 1800) | 9, 12, 15 (2740, 3660, 4570) | 12, 15 (3660, 4570) | 3, 6 (900, 1800) | 6, 12 (1800, 3660) |
| thickness (in (mm)) | 0.08–0.1 (2, 2.5) | 0.071–0.10 (1.8–2.5) | 0.05–0.1 (1.3–2.5) | 3⁄32, 1⁄8, 3⁄16 (2.4, 3, 5) | 0.065–0.125 (1.6–3) |
| use[(1)] | B, O, A | B, O, A | B, O, A | B, O, A | A |
| load limit (psi (kg/cm$^2$)) | 200 (14) | 75–100 (5–7) | 75 (5) | 200 (14) | 75 (5) |
| flame spread | 45–75 | 45–75 | 45–75 | 75 | – |
| smoke developed | 450 or less | 450 or less | 450 or less | 100–450 | – |
| resistance to: | | | | | |
| alkalis | 4–5 | 4 | 3–4 | 4 | 2 |
| cigarette burns | 1–3 | 1–3 | 1–4 | 4 | 1–2 |
| grease/oil | 5 | 5 | 3–4 | 1 | 5 |
| indentation | 3–5 | 2–3 | 2 | 4 | 2 |
| stains | 2–5 | 2–5 | 2–5 | 4–5 | 4 |
| properties | | | | | |
| durability | 4–5 | 3–4 | 2 | 4 | 3 |
| ease of maintenance | 5 | 3–4 | 2–3 | 3–4 | 2 |
| resilience | 1–4 | 1–4 | 1–4 | 4 | 2 |
| quietness | 2–5 | 1–4 | 1–4 | 5 | 2 |

1 = poor
2 = fair
3 = good
4 = very good
5 = excellent

(1) B = below grade. O = on grade. A = above grade.

very durable and resistant to indentation and rolling wheeled traffic. Because the seams can be sealed with heat welding or solvent welding, it is an excellent floor for health care facilities, clean rooms, and industrial flooring.

Inlaid vinyl is one of the most commonly used sheet floorings. It includes various fillers and is manufactured with a felt backing. It is available in wider rolls than solid sheet vinyl, and the seams can be sealed with a two-part epoxy adhesive if necessary. It is also available with an integrated cushioned backing.

Clear-coated rotogravure vinyl is manufactured with colors and patterns printed on the surface, which is coated with clear vinyl. Because of the rotogravure printing process, an unlimited variety of patterns and colors can be applied. However, this flooring is not as durable and resistant to indentation and abrasion as the other vinyls; therefore, it is used primarily in the residential and light commercial market.

### Rubber sheet flooring

Rubber sheet flooring has the same properties as rubber tile, but with fewer seams. The decorative types of flooring with raised patterns are usually specified in sheet form.

### Linoleum

Linoleum is one of the traditional types of sheet flooring. It is composed of oxidized linseed oil or other binders, pigments, and fillers applied over a backing of burlap or asphalt-saturated felt. Linoleum is available as plain or battleship linoleum, which is a single color, or inlaid linoleum, which consists of multicolored patterns that extend through the thickness to the backing. Linoleum has very good abrasion and grease resistance but has limited resistance to alkalis. Light gage is used for residential floors, and heavy gage is used for commercial floors. Because it is composed of natural materials, linoleum is popular as a sustainable material.

## SEAMLESS FLOORING [096700]

Seamless flooring is a mixture of a resinous matrix, fillers, and decorative materials applied in a liquid or viscous form that cures to a hard, seamless surface. Depending on the type of matrix and the specific mixture, the flooring is either poured or troweled on a subfloor. Some products are self-leveling, while others must be worked to a level surface. Some products, such as epoxy terrazzo, are surface ground after they cure to produce a smooth surface.

Seamless flooring is high-performance flooring used where special characteristics, such as extreme hardness, severe stain and chemical resistance, high water resistance, and high standards for cleanliness and ease of cleaning, are required. It is used for industrial floors, commercial kitchens and food preparation plants, factories, clean rooms, laboratories, hospitals, correctional facilities, and parking garages.

The many materials used for seamless flooring are generally divided into thermosetting and thermoplastic products. Some of the more common thermosetting matrices are two-part epoxy, two-part polyurethane, polychloroprene (neoprene), and two-part polyesters. One-part mixtures are also available, but these are not as good as two-part mixtures. Common thermoplastic flooring includes acrylic and mastic products. Mastics are composed of asphalt emulsion, portland cement, and various types of sand or stone filler. Various proprietary mixtures are also on the market.

Seamless flooring is applied in thicknesses from 1/16 in to 1/2 in (2 mm to 13 mm), depending on the type of product. Mastics may be applied in thicknesses up to 1 1/2 in (38 mm). Seamless flooring is applied over a suitable base of concrete or wood subflooring, with the material turned up at the walls to form an integrated cove base.

# 10 WALL FINISHES

Wall finishes include those applied as a single, thin decorative covering, such as paint, wallpaper, and vinyl wall-covering, and those composed of several construction elements that add substantial thickness to a wall, such as ceramic tile or stone. In each case, the finish is not a structural part of the wall. However, some finishes require certain types of partition construction in order to be applied correctly. Refer to Ch. 1 for partition construction.

## PAINT [099100]

Paint is a generic term for a thin coating used to protect and decorate the surface to which it is applied. Paint is one of several types of coatings. Coatings are composed of a vehicle, which is the liquid part of the coating, and the body and pigments if the coating is opaque. The vehicle has a nonvolatile part, called the *binder*, and a volatile part, called the *solvent*. The binder, along with the body, forms the actual film of the coating, while the solvent dissolves the binder to allow for application of the coating. The solvent evaporates or dries, leaving the final finish. The body of most quality paints is titanium dioxide, which is white. Pigments give paint its color.

Paints are broadly classified into solvent-based and water-based types. Solvent-based paints have binders containing or dissolved in organic solvents; water-based paints have binders that are either soluble or dispersed in water. Epoxy, polyurethane, and other specialty coatings use special chemicals as binders, to impart unique qualities to the coating that are not found in standard solvent or water-based paints.

### Solvent-based paint

Clear, solvent-based coatings include varnishes, shellac, silicone, and urethane. When a small amount of pigment is added, the coating becomes a stain, which gives color to the surface but allows the appearance of the underlying material to show through. Stains are most often used on wood. Clear coatings can be used for interior applications because it is not necessary to have a pigment to protect the surface, as is usually required for exterior applications.

Oil paints use a drying or curing oil as a binder. In the past, linseed oil was the traditional oil, but other organic oils have been used. Today, synthetic, alkyd resin is used as the drying oil. Oil paints are durable but have a strong odor when applied and must be cleaned up with a solvent, such as mineral spirits. In addition, they cannot be painted on damp surfaces or on surfaces that may become damp from behind.

### Water-based paint

Latex paints are water-based paints that use either vinyl chloride or acrylic resins as binders. Acrylic latex is better than vinyl latex in its durability, hiding power, and resistance to bleeding of underlying stains. Both types are relatively free from odor, can be used indoors as well as outdoors, and can be thinned with water.

### Epoxy paint

Epoxy is used as a very durable binder for resistance to corrosion and chemicals. Epoxies also resist abrasion and strongly adhere to concrete, metal, and wood. Epoxy is considered a high-performance coating and requires skilled applicators. The fumes are noxious; therefore, special ventilation is usually required for on-site application.

### Polyurethane paint

Urethane is considered another high-performance coating. It is used for its superior resistance to abrasion, grease, alcohol, water, and fuels. Interior applications most often include clear coverings for wood floors and clear or pigmented paint for antigraffiti coatings. Polyurethane paint is sometimes used strictly for its aesthetic qualities because it can have a very high-gloss finish with an almost glasslike sheen.

**Table 10.1**
Standard paint gloss ranges

| common name | gloss range |
|---|---|
| flat | below 15 |
| eggshell | 5–20 |
| satin | 15–35 |
| semigloss | 30–65 |
| gloss | over 65 |

## Coordination

### Application

Successful application of coatings depends not only on the correct selection for the intended use, but also on the surface preparation of the substrate, the primer used, and the method of application. Surfaces must be clean, dry, and free from grease, oils, and other foreign materials. Application can be done by brushing, rolling, or spraying. The amount of coating material to be applied is typically specified as either wet or dry film thickness (WFT or DFT) in mils (thousandths of an inch) for each coat needed. The coating should be applied under dry conditions when the temperature is between 55°F and 85°F. If a semigloss or gloss paint is specified for gypsum wallboard partitions, the entire surface of the partition should receive a skim coat of joint compound to provide a uniform surface for the paint. If this is not done, the difference between the paper facing of the wallboard and the joint compound over joints and screws may become visible.

### Paint gloss

Most water- and solvent-based paints are available in several surface finishes, which are referred to as glosses. Gloss and semigloss paints are used for their washability and shiny appearance. However, gloss paints tend to show defects in the surfaces on which they are applied. Satin finish paints provide a dull luster while still retaining some washability. The type of gloss is determined by the amount of light reflected from a surface according to a standard test method. The common names and their gloss ranges are shown in Table 10.1.

## Environmental considerations

When recommending paint removal and specifying paint, the interior designer should be aware of two important environmental and safety considerations: the presence of lead-based paint and the use of volatile organic compounds.

Lead-based paint can be a problem in older homes and child-occupied facilities. In many remodeling projects, existing paint must be removed. If the building was constructed before 1978, it may have lead-based paint. Such paint is dangerous if it flakes off, is chewed on, or is released as dust during construction activities and ingested by children or other occupants.

Federal law requires that anyone conducting lead-based paint activities be certified and that lead-based paint be removed from some types of residential occupancies and child-occupied facilities by a certified company using approved methods for removal and disposal. This can considerably increase the cost of repainting. Sometimes, covering the wall with a new layer of gypsum wallboard or simply repainting is an acceptable alternative.

Volatile organic compounds (VOCs) are hydrocarbon solvents used in paints, stains, and other products. They are released into the air during the application of coatings and react with nitrous oxides and sunlight to form ozone, the same byproduct produced by automotive exhaust and other pollutants. As required by the Clean Air Act of 1972, the Environmental Protection Agency (EPA) issued a regulation in 1999 that requires the amount of VOCs in paint and other coatings to be reduced from previous levels. The amount of reduction depends on the coating and gloss types. For example, nonflat interior and exterior coatings must now have no more than 380 g/L of volatile organic compounds. The EPA regulation is applicable to all 50 states, the District of Columbia, and all U.S. territories. Some state and local jurisdictions, such as California, have VOC regulations even stricter than the federal rule.

For most interior projects, specifying VOC-compliant paint is not a problem because interior designers can require water-based products, which are generally environmentally friendly. In addition, manufacturers now offer flat, nonflat, and multicolor wall paints as well as many floor coverings, stains, and sealers with acceptable VOC levels. Refer to Ch. 21 for more information on sustainability and coatings.

## Applicable standards for interior paints and coatings

There are dozens of standards for all the available coatings and the many test procedures related to them. The standards listed here are for some of the more common paints and test methods.

**American Society for Testing and Materials (ASTM):**

- ASTM D1005 *Standard Test Method for Measurement of Dry Film Thickness of Organic Coatings Using Micrometers*
- ASTM D1212 *Standard Test Method for Measurement of Wet Film Thickness of Organic Coatings*
- ASTM D5146 *Standard Guide for Testing Solvent-Borne Architectural Coatings*
- ASTM D5324 *Standard Guide for Testing Water-Borne Architectural Coatings*

## WALLPAPER [097223]

Wallpaper is available in a range of colors, patterns, textures, and materials for direct application to plaster or gypsum wallboard partitions. Wallpaper is generally packaged in rolls 20½ in (520 mm) wide by 21 ft (6.4 m) long (about 36 $ft^2$ [3.3 $m^2$]) and may be all paper or paper backed with cotton fabric or some other material. Double and triple rolls are also available. Some wallpaper is available with a thin vinyl coating. Before application, a liquid sizing must be applied to the wall to seal the surface against alkali, reduce the absorption of the paste or adhesive used, and provide the proper surface for the wallpaper.

Most wallpaper is manufactured with a short pattern repeat, that is, the distance between one point to the next repeated same point. When one length of wallpaper is aligned with the next piece in a direct horizontal line it is called a *straight match*. If the next piece must be lowered to continue the pattern it is called a *drop match*. Some wallpapers have no repeat pattern because they are strictly for texture. However, some specialty mural or trompe l'oeil wallpapers are available that have no repeats because they are designed to be applied to form an overall image.

## VINYL WALLCOVERING [097216]

Vinyl wallcovering provides a durable, abrasion-resistant finish that is easy to clean and can satisfy most code requirements for flammability. It is available in a wide range of colors and patterns. Vinyl wallcovering typically comes in rolls 52 in or 54 in wide and 30 yd long. It can be specified either with or without an additional coating of polyvinylfluoride film, which provides added stain resistance and extra protection for the vinyl. Other types of protective films are also available, but they are not as stain resistant.

There are three grades of vinyl wallcovering: Type I is light duty, Type II is medium duty, and Type III is heavy duty. Type I has a total weight of 7 to 13 oz/$yd^2$ (237 to 440 g/$m^2$), Type II has a total weight of between 13 oz/$yd^2$ and 22 oz/$yd^2$ (440 g/$m^2$ and 745 g/$m^2$), and Type III has a weight of over 22 oz/$yd^2$ (745 g/$m^2$). Type I is used for residential and commercial applications where little or no abuse is expected. The vinyl serves as a substitute for paint while adding texture. Type II is used for residential, commercial, and institutional applications where a moderate amount of traffic and abrasion is expected, such as in offices, dining rooms, classrooms, and some corridors. Type III is used where extra heavy use is expected, such as public corridors, food-service areas, and hospitals.

Vinyl wallcovering is applied with mastic to properly prepared gypsum wallboard or smooth plaster walls. Primer should be used on new wallboard to prevent damage to the partition if the wallcovering is removed. Stripable adhesive is also available for use over unprimed gypsum wallboard. Two methods of seaming are used: double-cutting and butting. Double-cutting involves overlapping adjacent strips and then cutting through and removing both. This results in a very tight butt joint. Butting must be used for patterned wallcovering where matching is critical or with dark-colored or deeply

---

**Applicable standards for vinyl wallcovering**

American Society for Testing and Materials (ASTM):

| | |
|---|---|
| ASTM F793 | *Standard Classification of Wallcovering by Use Characteristics* |
| ASTM F1141 | *Standard Specification for Wallcovering* |

The Chemical Fabrics and Films Association (CFFA):

| | |
|---|---|
| CFFA-W-101-D | *Quality Standard for Vinyl-Coated Fabric Wallcovering* |

---

embossed material where removal of adhesive is difficult.

## FABRIC WALLCOVERING [097219]

Subject to flame-spread restrictions, several types of fabrics—including wool, silk, and synthetics—can be used for wallcovering. If the fabric is heavy enough, it can be applied directly to the wall with adhesives. Seams are butted together to give the appearance of a continuous wall surface. In most instances, the fabric must be backed with paper or some other material to prevent the adhesive from damaging the fabric and to give the fabric additional dimensional stability.

When fabric is applied as a single layer of material, the terminating edges are carefully cut against the ceiling, floor base, door molding, and other trim. The adhesive is usually sufficient to hold the fabric in place. A tuck joint should be provided in the following situations: where fabric abuts other finishes; where there is a danger of people brushing against the fabric edge; or where a neat and precise line is needed. This provides a small recess where the fabric can be tucked into a small crack. A tuck joint not only gives a neater edge but conceals any minor delamination of the fabric edges from the partition should it occur. Figures 10.1(a)–10.1(c) show some common tuck joints. Tuck joints can be used for both vinyl wallcovering and fabric wallcovering.

**Figure 10.1** Tuck joints for wallcoverings

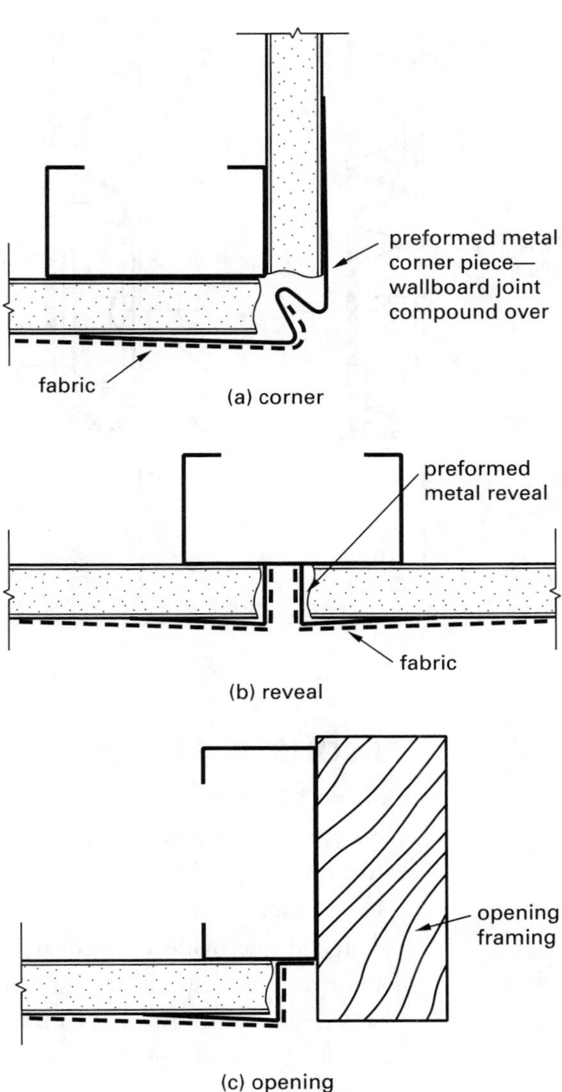


An alternate installation method is an upholstered wall, which is fabric stretched over a frame and secured into place. Two types of upholstered walls are shown in Fig. 10.2. Various proprietary stretch-fabric wall systems are available that allow fabric to be placed over inside and outside curved partitions as well as flat partitions. The edges can be straight or curved, and the fabric can be placed on doors as well. Some systems provide a fiberglass batting under the fabric for nominal sound absorption.

When the fabric is placed over a thick fiberglass batting the assembly becomes an acoustic panel, as described in the next section. In whatever way fabric wallcovering is applied, it must conform to the required fire rating for finishes either by being fire resistant itself or by being fire-retardant treated. Refer to Ch. 19 for flame-spread requirements of wall finishes.

**Figure 10.2** Types of upholstered walls

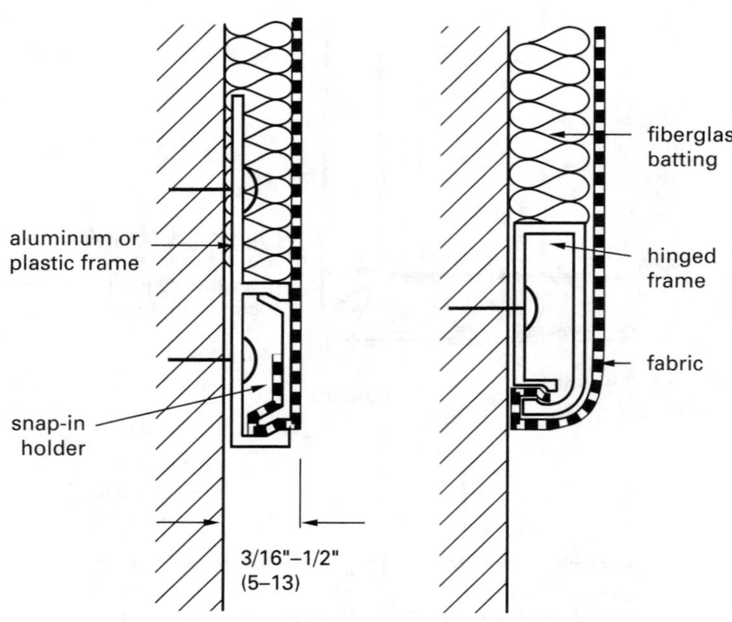


## ACOUSTIC PANELS [097700]

When a high degree of sound absorption is required, acoustic panels must be used. Although upholstered walls do provide some sound-absorbing qualities and can be designed to provide a high degree of sound absorption, acoustic panels differ in that they are designed as individual panels and have at least 1 in (25 mm) of sound-absorbing material. In addition, they are covered with a permeable material, such as a loose-weave fabric, so that the sound energy can pass through the fabric and be dissipated in the material underneath.

Acoustic panels can be purchased with a manufacturer's standard fabric or a customer's own material (COM), or they can be custom fabricated. Refer to Ch. 6 for information on how custom acoustic panels are constructed and attached to partitions. Refer to Ch. 11 for information on the fundamentals of acoustic control. When sound control is critical or when the room sounds will be either very high or low frequencies, an acoustical engineer should be consulted.

Two important decisions have to be made with regard to acoustic panels. The first concerns fabric type, and the second concerns core material. As mentioned, the fabric must be permeable to allow for sound energy to pass through. This also means that the fabric should not be backed. In addition, fabrics should be hydrophobic; that is, they must not absorb and hold moisture that could cause sagging and distortion. Hydrophobic fabrics include modacrylics, polyesters, cotton, linen, olefin, and wool. Hydrophilic fabrics (those that absorb and retain moisture) should be avoided or be limited to 25% of the fabric's content. These include silk, rayon, nylon, and acetate. Weaves that are balanced, such as jacquards and damasks, should be used; unbalanced weaves, such as satin, taffetas, and basket weaves, should be avoided.

Core material can be a loose material such as fiberglass or polyester batting, or a tackable material such as mineral fiberboard or tackable, acoustic fiberglass. Mineral fiberboard is a dimensionally stable composite of inorganic mineral fibers with a microperforated surface. Tackable acoustic fiberglass is noncombustible fibrous glass mat bonded with a resinous binder and formed into a rigid board with a finish face of thin, rigid fiberglass mesh. Avoid pressed, recycled paper products because these tend to absorb moisture and do not have good dimensional stability.

## STONE WALL FINISHES [097500]

### Types

As with flooring, stone commonly used for partition finishes includes granite, marble, limestone, slate, and sandstone. Because porosity is not a problem with interior vertical applications, travertine and other limestones are sometimes used for interior walls without being filled. In addition, cast stone and other artificial wall coverings are used and installed like stone. Cast stone is a mixture of cement, sand, and light aggregates cast in forms to look like stone. Refer to Ch. 8 for a description of the various types of natural stone and composite stone.

The maximum sizes of thick-cut stone depend on the type and thickness used. These are summarized in Table 10.2. Stone tile is discussed in the next section.

### Typical details

Like flooring, stone partition finishes can be constructed using thick slabs or thinly cut sheets. With the traditional, standard set method of applying stone, slabs about ¾ in to ⅞ in (19 mm to 22 mm) thick are attached to wall substrates (either masonry or gypsum wallboard) in large sheets with stainless steel wires or flat metal ties. Some stones, notably marble, have definite grain patterns, and because thick stone can be set using large slabs, the method of matching adjacent slabs must be specified. Like wood paneling, the grains can be matched in different ways. Figures 10.3(a)–10.3(f) show some of the common methods.

The wires or ties are attached to the stone at one end by being set in holes or slots cut into the back or sides of the panel. The other end is attached to the metal stud or masonry backup wall. See Fig. 10.4. Lumps of plaster of paris, called *spots*, are placed between the substrate and the back of the stone panel at each anchor. The spots hold the slab in place and allow for precise alignment before they harden. For rooms with normal ceiling heights, the stone rests on the floor and the anchors simply serve to hold each panel in place. The joints can be filled with nonstaining portland cement mortar, or sealant, or can be left open. As shown in Fig. 10.5, vertical joints show a slight gap and usually contain additional wire ties.

Where outside corners occur, a variety of details may be used. Some of these are illustrated in Fig. 10.6. When more than one level of stone is required in high spaces or where a horizontal joint is desired, one of the anchoring methods shown in Fig. 10.7(a)–10.7(c) can be used. If additional support is required, steel angles can be used as shown in Fig. 10.7(d).

With the new technology for cutting and laminating stone to various types of reinforcing backing, thin stone tiles are largely replacing the traditional thick slab construction. These tiles are about ⅜ in thick and come in sizes of 1 × 1, 1 × 2, and 2 × 2 (300 × 300, 300 × 600, and 600 × 600), although other sizes and thicknesses are available, depending on the manufacturer. In many cases the stone is simply mastic applied to a suitable substrate, usually gypsum wallboard on metal studs.

---

### Building code requirements for stone veneer

Most code requirements related to stone veneer are for exterior applications. However, the International Building Code provisions that commonly apply to interior stone include the following. Other codes have similar provisions.

- Stone veneer cannot support any load other than its own weight and the vertical dead load of the veneer above.
- Stone up to 2 in (50 mm) thick must be supported with corrosion-resistant ties no smaller in diameter than 0.148 in (3.76 mm) or 0.030 in by 1 in (0.76 mm by 25 mm) if they are sheet metal. Corrosion-resistant dowels may also be used.
- Individual veneer units adhered to backing with cement or mastic must have a shear adhesion of at least 50 psi (0.34 MPa) based on gross unit surface area.
- Additional anchoring or special details may be required in areas of high seismic risk.

---

**Table 10.2** Typical maximum sizes of building stone

| type | variety | maximum size (ft-in (mm)) |
|---|---|---|
| marble | Group A[(1)] | 5 ft by 7 ft<br>(1500 by 2130) |
| | Group B | 2 ft 6 in to 4 ft wide<br>4 ft to 7 ft long<br>(760 to 1200)<br>(1200 to 2130) |
| | Group C[(2)]<br>(for ¾ in and ⅞ in stone the smaller sizes should be used) | 2 ft 6 in to 4 ft wide<br>4 ft to 7 ft long<br>(760 to 1200)<br>(1200 to 2130) |
| | Group D[(2)] | 2 ft 6 in to 4 ft wide<br>4 ft to 7 ft long<br>(760 to 1200)<br>(1200 to 2130) |
| granite | | 4 ft by 10 ft<br>(1200 by 3050) |
| slate | panels | 4 ft by 6 ft 6 in<br>(1200 by 2000) |
| slate, natural finish | green or gray, ⅜ in thick (10 mm) | 8 in by 16 in (200 by 400) |
| | blue black | 18 in by 30 in (460 by 760) |
| | green or gray ¾ in thick (19 mm) | 15 in by 24 in (380 by 600) |
| slate | honed or sanded finish | 3 ft by 5 ft (900 by 1500) |
| limestone | 2 in thickness | 3 ft by 5 ft (900 by 1500) |

These dimensions are general guidelines only. Maximum sizes depend on the type of stone, the quarry, and the quantities needed. Check with the quarry and the local supplier before deciding on final sizes.

(1) Refer to Ch. 8 for a description of marble groups.

(2) A maximum size of 20 $ft^2$ (1.9 $m^2$) per piece is recommended for Groups C and D marble.

Source: Marble Institute of America; National Building Granite Quarries Association, Inc.; Indiana Limestone Institute of America, Inc.

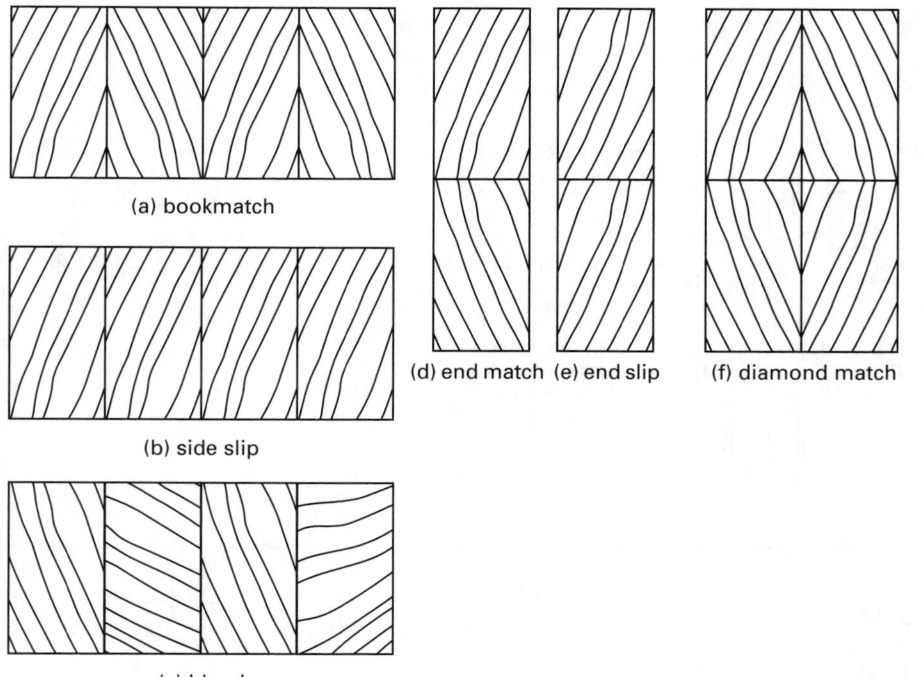


**Figure 10.3**
Stone grain matching

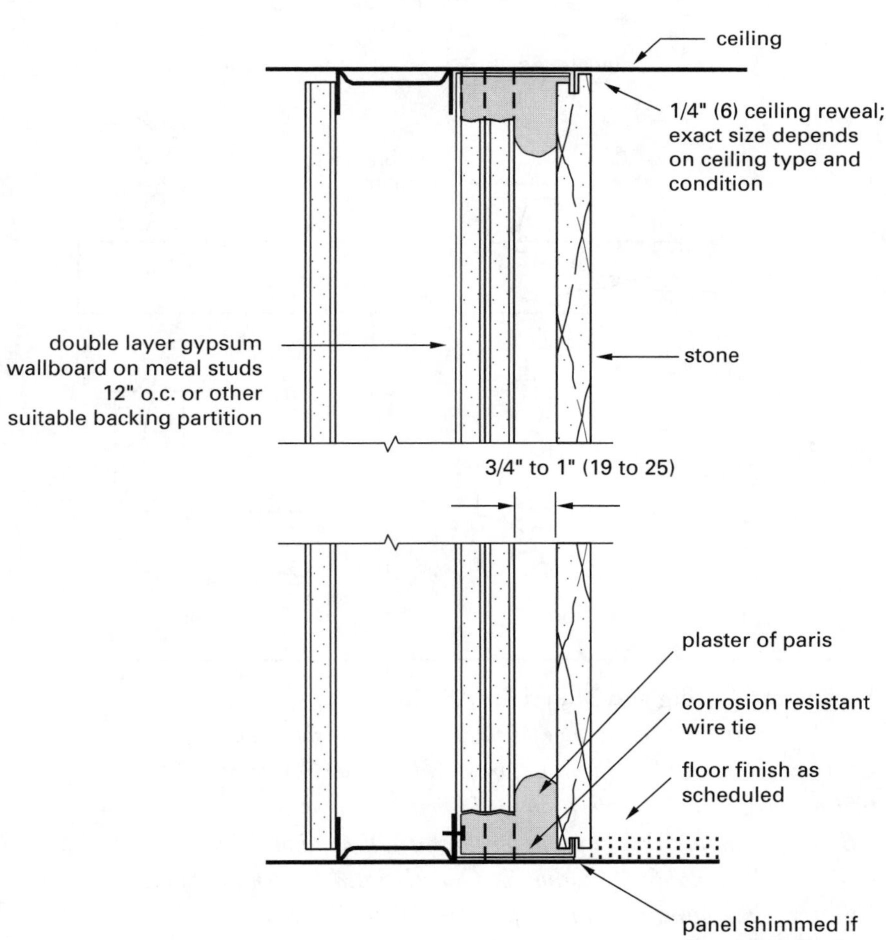


**Figure 10.4**
Interior stone veneer

**Figure 10.5**
Veneer at vertical joint

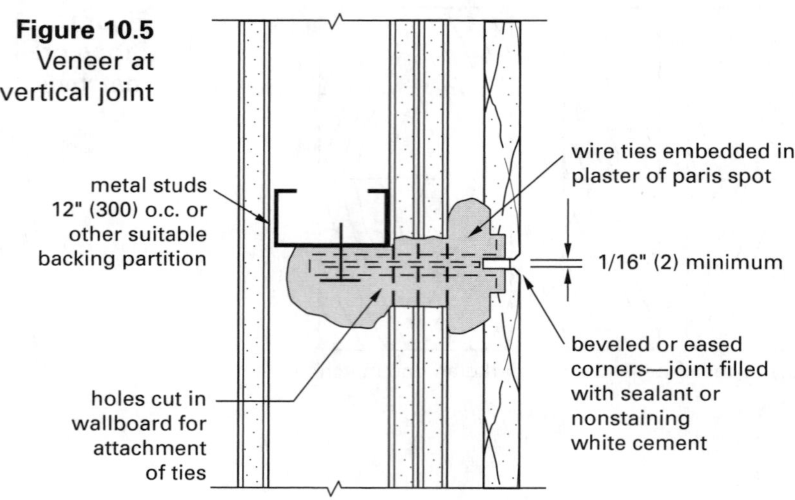


**Figure 10.6**
Vertical joint types for standard set stone

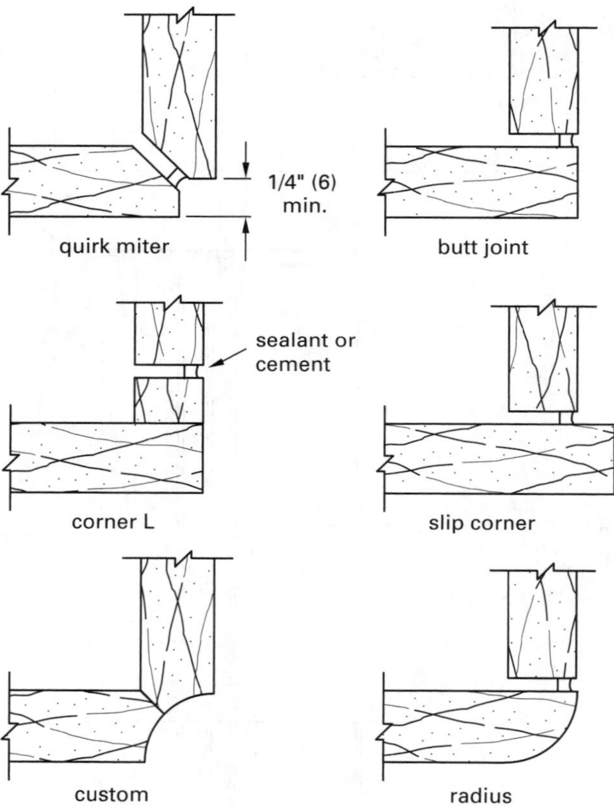


**Applicable standards for stone**

American Society for Testing and Materials (ASTM):

| | |
|---|---|
| ASTM C119 | *Standard Terminology Relating to Dimension Stone* |
| ASTM C503 | *Standard Specification for Marble Dimension Stone* |
| ASTM C568 | *Standard Specification for Limestone Dimension Stone* |
| ASTM C615 | *Standard Specification for Granite Dimension Stone* |
| ASTM C616 | *Standard Specification for Quartz-Based Dimension Stone* |
| ASTM C629 | *Standard Specification for Slate Dimension Stone* |

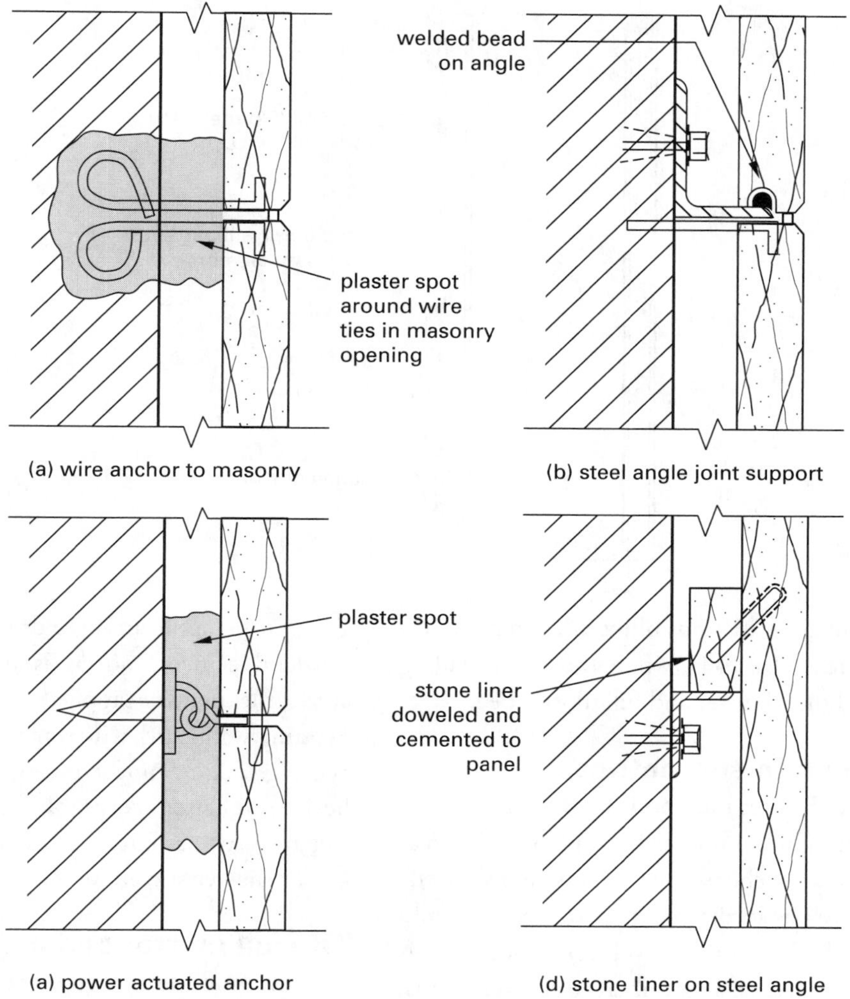


**Figure 10.7** Anchoring methods for horizontal joints

See Fig. 10.8. Some manufacturers provide special clips that hold the stone in place against the backup wall.

## Coordination

- The substrate must be sufficiently strong and stiff to carry the additional weight of stone. This is especially true of thick, standard-set stone.

- Because cutting and fitting for light switches, thermostats, and other wall-mounted items adds to the cost and interrupts the appearance of stone facings, these items should be given careful design consideration and, whenever possible, located where stone is not used.

- The size tolerances and squareness of surrounding construction must be sufficient to receive accurately cut stone.

- If stone is set to the floor without a base, the floor should be checked for level. The bottom of the stone may need to be cut to follow the floor line.

- If stone is placed on fire-rated partitions, anchoring requirements must be verified with the applicable building code.

- The maximum slab size for thick stone may be limited by the sizes of elevators, doors, and other limitations of the existing building.

## CERAMIC TILE WALL FINISHES [093000]

The types, sizes, and standards for ceramic wall tile and other vertical applications are the same as those described in Ch. 8 for floor construction. As with flooring, although there

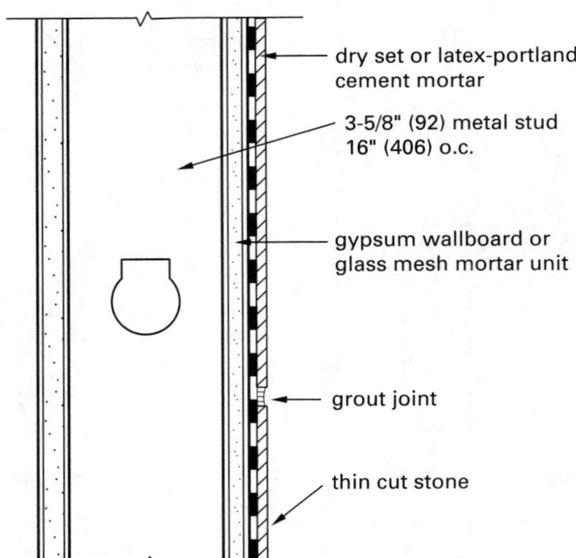


**Figure 10.8**
Thin-set stone partition finish

are many variations of installation methods, there are basically two methods of installing wall tile: thin-set and full mortar bed.

## The thin-set method

The thin-set method is used for residential and light commercial installations in areas such as kitchens, toilet rooms, and showers, as well as in dry areas. However, it should not be used in areas subject to continuous wetting, such as commercial shower rooms, pool areas, and the like. It is an appropriate application when weight and wall thickness must be kept to a minimum and where moderate cost is a consideration.

In the thin-set method, the supporting partition may be masonry or studs (wood or metal). If the tile will be subject to only occasional wetting, a water-resistant gypsum wallboard may be used over wood or metal studs. Such locations might include residential kitchens, powder rooms, or walls outside a residential tub or shower enclosure. If the tile will be subject to more-intense wet conditions, then glass mesh mortar units (or cement boards, as they are sometimes called) must be used on the studs. Areas where these backer boards are appropriate include residential tub and bath enclosures, gang showers, janitors' closets, and indoor pools.

For thin-set applications, a dry-set or latex-portland cement mortar is used. In dry areas, tile may be applied over standard gypsum wallboard with organic adhesive. See Fig. 10.9. Some types of organic adhesive are also acceptable for light-use wet areas such as kitchens and areas outside tub or shower surrounds.

## The full mortar bed method

Like ceramic tile flooring, the full mortar bed method is one of the most durable of the wall tile setting systems. It uses a thick bed of cured mortar as the base for the application of tile using a bond coat of dry-set or latex-portland cement mortar. It is typically used in commercial construction, either in dry or limited water-exposure areas or in continuously wet areas, such as gang showers, laundries, pools, and tubs. If the tile will be continuously wet, a waterproof membrane must be used. Although Fig. 10.10 shows an application over metal studs, a full mortar bed may also be used on masonry, concrete, or wood stud partitions as long as they can support the extra weight, which is approximately 18 $lbm/ft^2$ to 20 $lbm/ft^2$ (88 $kg/m^2$ to 98 $kg/m^2$).

**Figure 10.9**
Thin-set ceramic tile

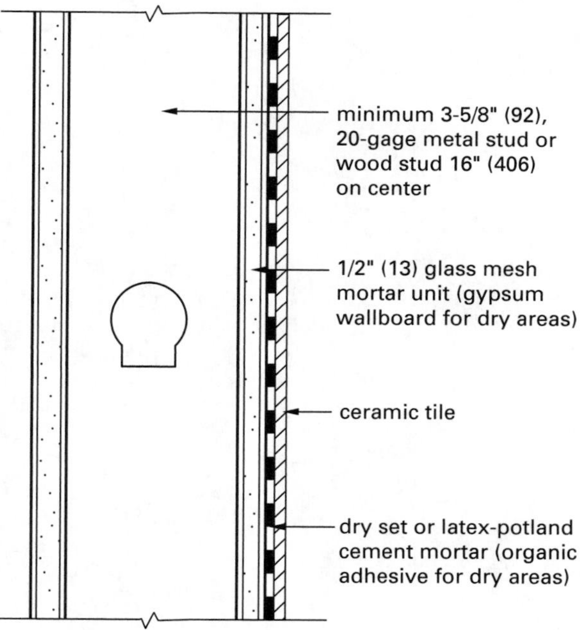


**Figure 10.10**
Full mortar bed ceramic tile

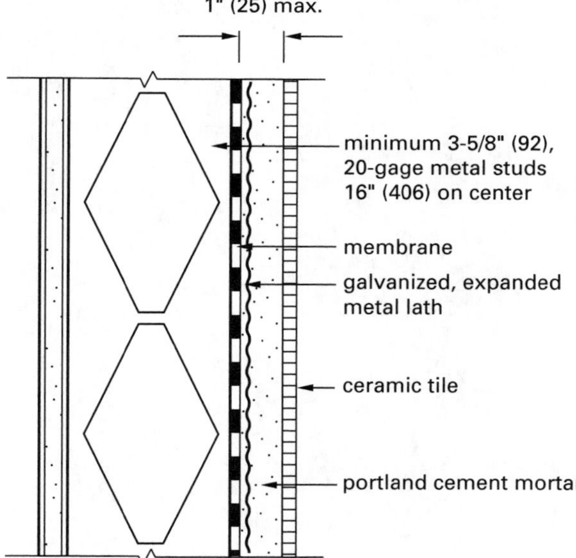

# 11

# ACOUSTICS

A room's acoustic quality can affect how it is used and perceived, as much as its furniture, finishes, colors, and shape can. Rooms or spaces that are too noisy or reverberant are distracting at best and unusable at worst. In some cases, such as in classrooms, inaudible sounds can be equally distracting.

There is a direct relationship between many interior construction design decisions and the resulting acoustic quality of a space. Room shapes and sizes, space planning, finish materials, construction techniques, and even furniture all influence the acoustic properties of a space, depending on the room's use and the sound sources within and adjacent to the room.

For most common situations, a basic knowledge of acoustics can help the interior designer make the best decisions. Complex designs, such as concert halls, recording studios, or locations where particularly troublesome noise sources exist, require the services of a qualified acoustical consultant.

## ACOUSTIC FUNDAMENTALS

### Qualities of sound

Sound travels in waves that consist of a high-pressure front followed by a low-pressure front. When the ear perceives a series of these pressure fronts of equal spacing, a tone is heard. Sound waves have four basic qualities: frequency, velocity, wavelength, and power.

Frequency is the number of successive pressure fronts that pass a given point in one second. It is measured in hertz (Hz) (one Hz equals one cycle per second). The sounds perceived as high notes or high-pitched sounds have high frequencies; base notes have low frequencies.

Velocity depends on the medium in which the sound is traveling and the temperature of the medium. In air at normal room temperature this is about 1130 ft/sec (345 m/s).

*Wavelength* is the distance between the pressure fronts measured in feet and inches (meters and millimeters). There is a direct relationship between frequency and wavelength based on the speed of sound. For sound in air at room temperature that relationship is given by

$$\lambda = \frac{1130}{f} \quad \text{[U.S.]} \quad \text{Eq. 11.1(a)}$$

$$\lambda = \frac{345}{f} \quad \text{[SI]} \quad \text{Eq. 11.1(b)}$$

$\lambda$ is the wavelength in feet (meters), and $f$ is the frequency in hertz. It is an inverse relationship; as the frequency increases the wavelength decreases, and as the frequency decreases the wavelength increases. This has a significant bearing on design because the size of architectural and finish components influences the behavior of sounds depending on their frequency.

Power is the quality of acoustic energy as measured in watts. It is this power that people perceive as loudness.

## Loudness

The human ear is sensitive to a large range of sound power, from about $10^{-16}$ W/cm$^2$ to $10^{-3}$ W/cm$^2$. Because of this and the fact that the sensation of hearing is proportional to the logarithm of the source intensity, the decibel (abbreviated dB) is used in acoustic descriptions and calculations. The decibel conveniently relates actual sound intensity to the way humans experience sound. By definition, 0 dB is the threshold of human hearing, and 130 dB is the threshold of pain. Some common sound intensity levels and their subjective evaluations are shown in Table 11.1.

Changes in loudness are subjective, but some common guidelines are shown in Table 11.2. These are useful for evaluating the effects of increased or decreased decibel levels in design situations. For example, spending money to modify a partition to increase its sound transmission class (defined later in this chapter) by 3 dB would not be worth the expense because the difference would hardly be noticeable.

**Table 11.1** Common sound intensity levels

| intensity level (dB) | example | subjective evaluation | intensity (W/cm$^2$) |
|---|---|---|---|
| 140 | jet plane takeoff | | $10^{-2}$ |
| 130 | gunfire | threshold of pain | $10^{-3}$ |
| 120 | hard rock band, siren at 100 ft | deafening | $10^{-4}$ |
| 110 | accelerating motorcycle | sound can be felt | $10^{-5}$ |
| 100 | auto horn at 10 ft | conversation difficult to hear | $10^{-6}$ |
| 90 | loud street noise, kitchen blender | very loud | $10^{-7}$ |
| 80 | noisy office, average factory | difficult to use phone | $10^{-8}$ |
| 70 | average street noise, quiet typewriter, average radio | loud | $10^{-9}$ |
| 60 | average office, noisy home | usual background | $10^{-10}$ |
| 50 | average conversation, quiet radio | moderate | $10^{-11}$ |
| 40 | quiet home, private office | noticeably quiet | $10^{-12}$ |
| 30 | quiet conversation | faint | $10^{-13}$ |
| 20 | whisper | | $10^{-14}$ |
| 10 | rustling leaves, soundproof room | very faint | $10^{-15}$ |
| 0 | threshold of hearing | | $10^{-16}$ |

### Human sensitivity to sound

Although human response to sound is subjective and varies with age, physical condition of the ear, and other factors, the following guidelines are useful.

- A healthy young person can hear sounds ranging from about 20 Hz to 20,000 Hz, while most adults hear sounds ranging from about 20 Hz to 16,000 Hz. People are most sensitive to frequencies in the 3000 Hz to 4000 Hz range. Speech is composed of sounds primarily ranging from 150 Hz to 5000 Hz, with most ranging from 500 Hz to 3000 Hz.

- The human ear is less sensitive to low frequencies than to middle and high frequencies, for sounds of equal energy.

- Most common sound sources contain energy over a wide range of frequencies. Because frequency is an important variable in how a sound is transmitted or absorbed (because of its wavelength), it must be taken into account in building acoustics. For convenience, measurement and analysis are often divided into eight octave frequency bands identified by their center frequency. These are 63, 125, 250, 500, 1000, 2000, 4000, and 8000 Hz. For detailed acoustic design, smaller bands are often used.

## SOUND TRANSMISSION

There are two basic problems in controlling noise (any unwanted sound): preventing or minimizing the transmission of sound from one space (or noise source) to another, and reducing the noise within a space. This section discusses sound transmission; the next section outlines the basics of sound absorption as the primary means of reducing noise in a space.

**Table 11.2** Subjective change in loudness based on decibel level change

| change in intensity level (dB) | change in apparent loudness |
|---|---|
| 1 | almost imperceptible |
| 3 | just perceptible |
| 5 | clearly noticeable |
| 6 | change when distance to source in a free field is doubled or halved |
| 10 | twice or half as loud |
| 18 | very much louder or quieter |
| 20 | four times or one-fourth as loud |

### Addition of decibels

When there are two or more sound sources in a space, it is often useful to know what the combined decibel level is. Because decibels are logarithmic, they cannot be added directly. There is a complex formula for adding two or more decibels, but for practical purposes the values in Table 11.3 can be used to give results accurate to within 1%. For three or more sources, first add two, then add the result to the third number, and so on.

**Table 11.3** Addition of decibels

| When difference between the two values is: | Add this value to the higher value |
|---|---|
| 0 or 1 dB | 3 dB |
| 2 or 3 dB | 2 dB |
| 4 to 8 dB | 1 dB |
| 9 dB or more | 0 dB |

## Transmission loss and noise reduction

Reducing sound transmission from one space to another to an acceptable level is one of the primary considerations in selecting construction elements and detailing barrier assemblies. Transmission of sound through a barrier is primarily retarded by the mass of the barrier. To a lesser extent the stiffness, or rigidity, of the barrier retards sound transmission. Given two barriers of the same weight per square foot, the one with less stiffness will perform better than the other. For construction, barriers may be partitions, floors, doors, glass, or anything that separates one room from another.

There are two important concepts in noise reduction: transmission loss and actual noise reduction between two spaces. Transmission loss only takes into account the loss through a barrier. Transmission loss is the difference, in decibels, between the sound power incident on a barrier in a source room and the sound power radiated into a receiving room on the opposite side of the barrier. This is a measurement typically derived in a testing laboratory from evaluation of a particular construction assembly or component at various octave band frequencies.

Noise reduction is the arithmetic difference, in decibels, between the intensity levels in two rooms separated by a barrier of a given

**Applicable standards for acoustics**

**Ceiling & Interior Systems Construction Association (CISCA):**

AMA I-II *Ceiling Sound Transmission Test by the Two-Room Method*

**American Society for Testing and Materials (ASTM):**

ASTM C423 *Standard Test Method for Sound Absorption and Sound Absorption Coefficients by the Reverberation Room Method*
ASTM E90 *Test Method for Laboratory Measurement of Airborne Sound Transmission Loss of Building Partitions and Elements*
ASTM E336 *Test Method for Measurement of Airborne Sound Insulation in Buildings*
ASTM E413 *Classification for Rating Sound Insulation*
ASTM E492 *Test Method for Laboratory Measurement of Impact Sound Transmission Through Floor-Ceiling Assemblies Using the Tapping Machine*
ASTM E497 *Standard Practice for Installing Sound-Isolating Lightweight Partitions*
ASTM E989 *Standard Classification for Determination of Impact Insulation Class*
ASTM E1007 *Standard Test Method for Field Measurement of Tapping Machine Impact Sound Transmission Through Floor-Ceiling Assemblies and Associated Support Structures*
ASTM E1110 *Standard Classification for Determination of Articulation Class*
ASTM E1111 *Test Method for Measuring the Interzone Attenuation of Open Office Components*
ASTM E1130 *Test Method for Objective Measurement of Speech Privacy in Open Offices Using Articulation Index*
ASTM E1264 *Classification for Acoustical Ceiling Products*
ASTM E1374 *Standard Guide to Open Office Acoustics and Applicable ASTM Standards*
ASTM E1408 *Standard Test Method for Laboratory Measurement of the Sound Transmission Loss of Door Panels and Door Systems*
ASTM E1414 *Standard Test Method for Airborne Sound Attenuation Between Rooms Sharing a Common Ceiling Plenum*

**American National Standards Institute (ANSI):**

ANSI S3.5 *Methods for the Calculation of the Speech Intelligibility Index*

transmission loss. Noise reduction depends not only on the transmission loss of the barrier but also on the area of the barrier separating the two rooms and the absorption of the surfaces in the "quiet" room. Noise reduction can be increased by increasing the transmission loss of the barrier, increasing the absorption in the "quiet" room (the one not producing the noise), decreasing the area of the barrier separating the rooms, or some combination of the three.

To simplify the selection of construction walls and other building components, a single-number rating system is often used to rate the transmission loss of the construction averaged across all octave band frequencies. This is the sound transmission class (STC) rating. The higher the STC rating, the better the barrier is (theoretically) at stopping sound. Table 11.4 shows some STC ratings and their effects on hearing.

STC ratings represent the ideal loss through a barrier under laboratory conditions. Partitions, floors, and other construction components built in the field are seldom constructed as well as those in the laboratory. Also, breaks in the barrier, such as cracks, electrical outlets, doors, and the like, significantly reduce the overall noise reduction.

In critical situations, transmission loss and selection of barriers should be calculated using the values for various frequencies rather than the single STC average value. Some materials may allow an acoustic "hole," stopping most frequencies but allowing transmission of a certain range of frequencies. However, for preliminary design purposes in noncritical situations, the STC value is adequate.

The transmission loss or noise reduction that a partition or floor/ceiling assembly should have depends on the use of the adjacent rooms, the expected noise sources, the sensitivity of the occupants, and the amount of money available to spend on sound control. In some situations, model building codes or local, state, or federal regulations set minimum criteria for sound isolation. Tables 11.5–11.7 give some suggested sound insulation criteria for common building uses. The U.S. Department of Housing and Urban Development (HUD) guidelines give minimum STC values for three grades, with Grade I having the best sound isolation.

## Noise criteria curves

All normally occupied spaces have some amount of background noise. This is undesirable because some noise is necessary to avoid the feeling of a "dead" space and to help mask other sounds. However, the acceptable amount of background noise varies with the type of space and the frequency of sound. For example, people are generally less tolerant of background noise in bedrooms than they are of noise in public lobbies, and they are generally more tolerant of higher levels of low-frequency sound than of high-frequency sound.

These variables have been consolidated into a set of noise criteria curves relating frequency in eight octave bands to noise level. See Fig. 11.1. Accompanying these curves are noise criteria ratings for various types of

**Table 11.4**
Effect of barrier STC on hearing

| STC | subjective effect |
|---|---|
| 25 | Normal speech can be clearly heard through the barrier. |
| 30 | Loud speech can be heard and understood fairly well. |
| 35 | Loud speech is not intelligible but can be heard. |
| 42–45 | Loud speech can only be faintly heard. Normal speech cannot be heard. |
| 46–50 | Loud speech not audible. Loud sounds other than speech can only be heard faintly if at all. |

**Table 11.5** Sound isolation criteria

| type of occupancy | area considered (source) | adjacent area (receiving room) | minimum STC[1] |
|---|---|---|---|
| single-family residential | bedrooms and living rooms | bedrooms | 40–48 |
| | | living rooms | 42–50 |
| | | bathrooms | 45–52 |
| | | kitchens | 45–52 |
| multifamily residential | see Tables 11.6 and 11.7 | | |
| offices—normal privacy | offices | adjacent offices | 45 |
| | | general office areas | 45 |
| | | conference rooms | 45 |
| | | toilets | 47 |
| | | corridors | 45 |
| | | kitchen/dining rooms | 47 |
| | | mechanical equipment | 52+[2] |
| offices—confidential, privacy required | offices | adjacent offices | 52 |
| | | conference rooms | 52 |
| | | other areas | 52 |
| offices—large general areas | general office areas | corridors, lobby | 37 |
| | | data processing | 42 |
| | | kitchen/dining areas | 42 |
| hotels/motels | bedrooms | adjacent bedrooms | 48+ |
| | | bathrooms | 52+ |
| | | corridor, public areas | 48+ |
| | | mechanical rooms | 52+[2] |
| apartments | see Tables 11.6 and 11.7 | | |
| schools | classrooms | adjacent classrooms | 42–48 |
| | | corridors/public area | 42 |
| | | shops | 52+ |
| | | music rooms | 52+ |
| | | toilets | 47 |
| | | kitchen/lunchroom | 47 |
| | music rooms | corridors | 52 |

(1) These are minimum values for actual in-field service. Assemblies with laboratory ratings should be higher.
(2) Some mechanical rooms may require special treatment, especially if there is large, commercial equipment or unusual noise producing situations.

Source: *Architect's Handbook of Formulas, Tables, and Mathematical Calculations.* David Kent Ballast. Englewood Cliffs, NJ: Prentice-Hall, 1988.

**Table 11.6**
**Sound isolation criteria of partitions between dwelling units**

| partition function between dwellings | | Grade I | Grade II | Grade III |
|---|---|---|---|---|
| apartment A | apartment B | STC | STC | STC |
| bedroom | bedroom | 55 | 52 | 48 |
| living room | bedroom(1, 2) | 57 | 54 | 50 |
| kitchen(3) | bedroom(1, 2) | 58 | 55 | 52 |
| bathroom | bedroom(1, 2) | 59 | 56 | 52 |
| corridor | bedroom(2, 4) | 55 | 52 | 48 |
| living room | living room | 55 | 52 | 48 |
| kitchen(3) | living room(1, 2) | 55 | 52 | 48 |
| bathroom | living room(1) | 57 | 54 | 50 |
| corridor | living room(2, 4, 5) | 55 | 52 | 48 |
| kitchen | kitchen(6, 7) | 52 | 50 | 46 |
| bathroom | kitchen(1,7) | 55 | 52 | 48 |
| corridor | kitchen(2, 4, 5) | 55 | 52 | 48 |
| bathroom | bathroom(7) | 52 | 50 | 46 |
| corridor | bathroom(2, 4) | 50 | 48 | 46 |

(1) The most desirable plan is to have the partition separating spaces with equivalent functions; for example, living room opposite living room. When this arrangement is not feasible, the partition must have greater sound-insulating properties.
(2) Whenever a partition wall might serve to separate several functional spaces, the highest criterion must prevail.
(3) Or dining, or family, or recreation room.
(4) Assuming there is no entrance door leading from corridor to living unit.
(5) If a door is part of the corridor partition, it must have the same rating as the corridor. The most desirable arrangement has the entrance door leading from the corridor to a partially enclosed vestibule or foyer in the living unit.
(6) Double-wall construction is recommended to provide, in addition to airborne sound insulation, isolation from impact noises generated by the placement of articles on pantry shelves and the slamming of cabinet doors.
(7) Special detailing is required for vibration isolation of plumbing in kitchens and bathrooms.

Source: *A Guide to Airborne, Impact, and Structureborne Noise Control in Multifamily Dwellings.* U.S. Dept. of Housing and Urban Development, HUD-TS-24 (1974).

**Table 11.7**
**Sound isolation criteria within a dwelling unit**

| partition function between dwellings | | Grade I STC | Grade II STC | Grade III STC |
|---|---|---|---|---|
| bedroom | bedroom(1, 2) | 48 | 44 | 40 |
| living room | bedroom(1, 2) | 50 | 46 | 42 |
| bathroom | bedroom(1, 2, 3) | 52 | 48 | 45 |
| kitchen | bedroom(1, 2, 3) | 52 | 48 | 45 |
| bathroom | living room(2, 3) | 52 | 48 | 45 |
| mechanical room | sensitive areas | 65 | 62 | 58 |
| mechanical room | less sensitive areas (kitchens, family rooms, etc.) | 60 | 58 | 54 |

(1) Closets may be profitably used as "buffer" zones, provided unlouvered doors are used.
(2) Doors leading to bedrooms and bathrooms preferably should be of solid-core construction and gasketed to ensure a comfortable degree of privacy.
(3) Special detailing is required for vibration isolation of plumbing in kitchens and bathrooms.

Source: *A Guide to Airborne, Impact, and Structureborne Noise Control in Multifamily Dwellings.* U.S. Dept. of Housing and Urban Development, HUD-TS-24 (1974).

**Figure 11.1**
Noise criteria (NC) curves

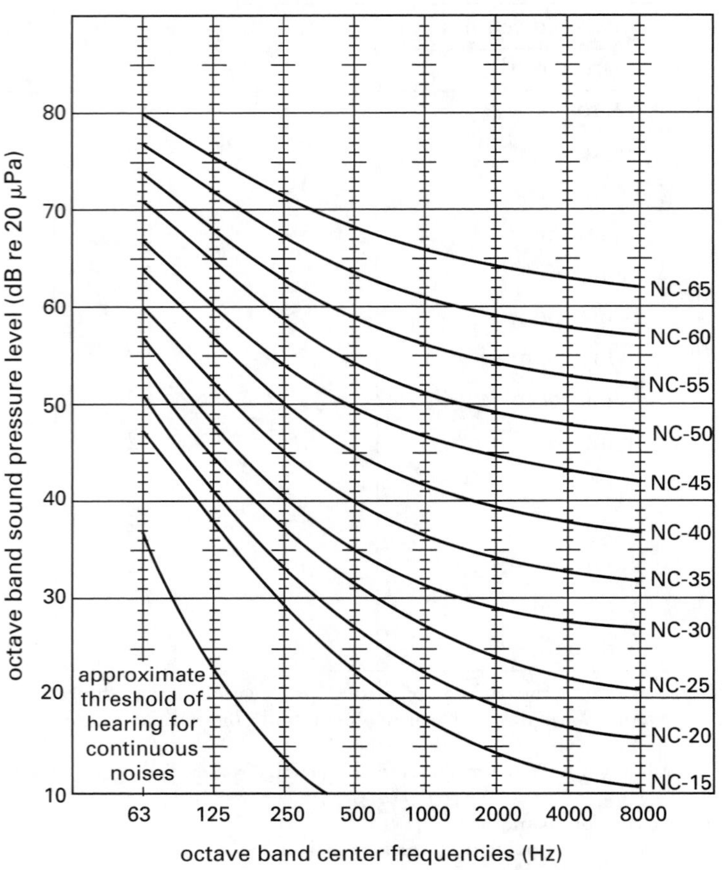


**Table 11.8**
Representative noise criteria

| type of space | preferred range of noise criteria (dB) |
|---|---|
| concert halls, opera houses, recording studios | 15–20 |
| bedrooms, apartments, hospitals | 20–30 |
| private offices, small conference rooms | 30–35 |
| large offices, retail stores, restaurants | 35–40 |
| lobbies, drafting rooms, laboratory work spaces | 40–45 |
| kitchens, computer rooms, light maintenance shops | 45–50 |

spaces and listening requirements. A representative sampling is shown in Table 11.8. Noise criteria (NC) curves can be used to specify the maximum amount of continuous background noise allowable in a space, to establish a minimum amount of noise desired to help mask sounds, and to evaluate an existing condition. When an NC rating is specified for a particular space it means that the noise in each of the eight octave bands cannot exceed the sound-pressure level shown on the left of the chart.

When background noise conforms to a noise criteria curve, it usually still contains too many low-frequency and high-frequency sounds to be comfortable. A modification of the NC curves, called the preferred noise criteria (PNC), has been established that has sound-pressure levels lower than the NC

**Building code requirements for sound transmission**

The International Building Code requires that walls and floor/ceiling assemblies separating dwelling units or guest rooms from each other and from public space provide airborne sound insulation for walls and both airborne and impact sound insulation for floor/ceiling assemblies. Walls and floor/ceiling assemblies must meet a sound transmission class (STC) rating of 50 if the assembly has been laboratory tested and 45 if the assembly is field tested. Floor/ceiling assemblies must meet an impact insulation class (IIC) rating of 50 if the assembly has been laboratory tested and 45 if the assembly is field tested. Dwelling unit entrance doors must be tight fitting to the frame and sill.

curves in the low- and high-frequency ends of the chart.

## SOUND ABSORPTION

Controlling sound transmission is only part of good acoustic design. The proper amount of sound absorption must also be considered. Although sound intensity levels decrease about 6 dB for each doubling of distance from the source in free space, this is not the case in a room. In a room, the sound level decreases very near the source, as it does in free space, but then it begins to reflect and levels out at a particular intensity. Of course, the *source* of the noise can be reduced, but this is not always possible. Sound absorption, then, is used to reduce the intensity level of sound within a space, to control unwanted sound reflections, improve speech privacy, and decrease reverberation.

### Fundamentals of sound absorption

The absorption of a material is defined by the coefficient of absorption, $\alpha$, which is the ratio of the sound intensity absorbed by the material to the total intensity reaching the material. Therefore, the maximum absorption possible is 1, that of free space, because no sound is reflected. Generally, a material with a coefficient below 0.2 is considered to be sound reflective and one with a coefficient above 0.2 is considered to be sound absorbing. These coefficients are published in the manufacturer's technical literature.

The three basic types of materials and construction components—porous materials, volume resonators, and vibrating panels—absorb sound in different ways.

Porous materials are the most common types and include items such as acoustic panels (described in Chs. 6 and 10) and acoustic ceiling tiles. In porous material, the sound energy is converted to heat by friction (absorbed) as it travels among the tiny fibers in the material.

Volume resonators (sometimes called Helmholtz resonators) are construction elements that have a small slot leading to a larger chamber. The chamber may be lined with porous material. A common commercial product of this type uses a concrete block with slits opening onto the cavity of the block. Volume resonators are designed to absorb low-frequency sound. The sound energy is converted to heat by friction at the opening and decreases in energy as it bounces around inside the cavity. If porous material is applied in the cavity, additional energy is lost as friction.

Vibrating panels are also designed to absorb low-frequency sound by converting sound energy to vibrational energy. They are usually designed with air space behind them, with or without porous material, depending on the frequencies they are designed to absorb.

The coefficient of absorption varies with the frequency of the sound, and some materials and construction elements are better than others at absorbing some frequencies. This is because of the varying wavelengths of all the frequencies according to Eq. 11.1. For example, a sound with a frequency of 3000 Hz has a wavelength of 0.38 ft (115 mm) while a sound with a frequency of 200 Hz has a wavelength of about 5.6 ft (1700 mm). This is a significant fact when selecting absorbing materials. For example, a 1 in (25 mm) layer of fiberglass covered with porous fabric has a coefficient of absorption of 0.99 for 1000 Hz frequencies but a coefficient of absorption of only 0.10 for 125 Hz frequencies. Because the wavelength of the higher frequency is closer to the small size of the fiberglass matrix, there is more opportunity for the sound to move against the absorbing material and be converted to heat. The longer wavelengths mostly travel right through the material without being absorbed and are reflected back into the room by the rigid partition behind. Volume resonators and vibrating panels are designed to overcome this inherent problem in thin porous materials.

Because of the relationship between absorption efficiency and frequency, in critical applications, the coefficient of absorption for a material should be reviewed in all the octave bands. However, for convenience, noncritical applications often use a single-number rating system. Previously, this was the noise reduction coefficient (NRC). The NRC is the average of a material's absorption coefficients at the four frequencies of 250, 500, 1000, and 2000 Hz, rounded to the nearest multiple of 0.05. Where low-frequency absorption is not critical, the NRC rating is a useful index for selecting materials. Some typical NRC ratings are shown in Table 11.9.

The NRC has been superseded by the sound absorption average (SAA), although both are similar and provide a single number rating. The SAA is the average of the absorption coefficients for the twelve one-third octave bands from 200 to 2500 Hz when tested in accordance with ASTM C423. Most product literature still gives the NRC ratings.

**Table 11.9**
Noise reduction coefficients

| material | NRC |
|---|---|
| vinyl tile on concrete | 0.05 |
| wood strip flooring | 0.10 |
| carpet, ½ in pile on concrete | 0.50 |
| carpet, direct glue to concrete | 0.30 |
| gypsum board walls | 0.05 |
| heavy plate glass | 0.05 |
| marble or glazed tile | 0.00 |
| fiberglass wall panel measuring 1 in with fabric cover | 0.80 |
| plywood paneling | 0.15 |
| heavy velour fabric (18 oz), draped to half area | 0.60 |
| suspended acoustic tile measuring ⅝ in | 0.60 |
| suspended acoustic tile measuring 1 in | 0.90 |

## Noise reduction within a space

The total absorption of a material depends on the material's coefficient of absorption and area. The unit used for this quantity is called the *sabin*, which is the absorption value of 1 $ft^2$ of material with a perfect absorption of 1.0. (An SI sabin equals 10.76 U.S. sabins.) Because most rooms have several materials with different areas, the total absorption in a room is the sum of the various individual material absorptions. Finishes and construction detailing should be balanced to provide the best overall room absorption. For example, depending on the use of the room, hard, nonabsorbing materials used on the floor and ceiling may have to be balanced with absorbing materials on the walls. Although noise reduction can be calculated with formulas in critical situations, most interior designs can follow these rules of thumb.

- Avoid designing rooms with hard, reflective surfaces on the walls, floor, and ceiling. The space could be too "live" and noisy.

• The average absorption coefficient of a room should be at least 0.20. An average absorption above 0.50 is usually neither desirable nor economically justified. A lower value is suitable for large rooms; larger values are suitable for small or noisy rooms.

• Each doubling of the amount of absorption in a room results in a noise reduction of only 3 dB, which is hardly noticeable. To make any difference, the total absorption must be increased by at least three times to reduce the noise by 5 dB, which is noticeable.

• Although absorptive materials can be placed anywhere, ceiling treatment for sound absorption is more effective in large rooms, while wall treatment is more effective in small rooms.

• Generally, absorption increases with an increase in thickness of a porous absorber, except for low-frequency sounds that require special design treatment.

• If a corridor is appreciably higher than its width, some absorptive material should be placed on the walls as well as the ceiling, especially if the floor is hard-surfaced. If the corridor is wider than it is high, ceiling treatment is usually enough.

• The amount of absorption of a porous type of sound absorber, such as fiberglass or mineral wool, depends on (1) material thickness, (2) material density, (3) material porosity, and (4) the orientation of the material's fibers. A porous sound absorber should be composed of open, interconnected voids.

## Calculating noise reduction within a space

In some situations, it may be necessary to increase noise reduction by increasing the sound absorption in a room. The effect of doing this can be calculated to see if the change is both sufficient and economically justified. To do this, calculate the total absorption of the room before the change. This is the sum of all the individual absorptions of the different materials. Then, calculate both the total absorption after the change and the noise reduction. Because of the logarithmic relationship of sounds, the formula includes using a common logarithm.

Calculate the total absorption of a material according to the equation

$$A = S\alpha \qquad \text{Eq. 11.2}$$

| | | | |
|---|---|---|---|
| $A$ | absorption | sabins | sabins |
| $S$ | area of the material | ft$^2$ | m$^2$ |
| $\alpha$ | coefficient of absorption | – | – |

Perform this calculation for each of the materials in the room, and sum the results.

Next, calculate the total absorption after the change, and compare it with the original value according to the equation

$$\text{NR} = 10 \log \frac{A_2}{A_1} \qquad \text{Eq. 11.3}$$

| | | | |
|---|---|---|---|
| NR | noise reduction | dB | dB |
| $A_1$ | total original room absorption | sabins | sabins |
| $A_2$ | total room absorption after the increase of absorption | – | – |

This formula relates to the overall reverberant noise level in a room and does not affect the noise level very near the source.

## Reverberation

Reverberation is the prolongation of sound as it repeatedly bounces off hard surfaces. It is an important part of the acoustic environment because it affects the intelligibility of speech and the quality of music. Technically, reverberation time is the time it takes the sound level to decrease 60 dB after the source has stopped producing the sound. It is a desirable quality if the reverberation time is appropriate for the use of the space. For example, the recommended time for offices and small rooms for speech is 0.3 sec to 0.6 sec, while for auditoriums it is 1.5 sec to 1.8 sec. Reverberation can be controlled by modifying the amount of

**Example: Calculating noise reduction**

A 15 ft by 20 ft room with a 9 ft ceiling has a carpeted floor with a 44 oz carpet on a pad ($\alpha = 0.40$), gypsum wallboard, and a gypsum board ceiling ($\alpha = 0.05$). What would be the noise reduction achieved by directly attaching acoustical tile with a given NRC of 0.70 to the ceiling?

Original total absorption of the room:

$$
\begin{aligned}
\text{floor:} \quad & (15\ \text{ft})(20\ \text{ft}) = (300\ \text{ft}^2)(0.40) = 120 \\
\text{walls:} \quad & (2\ \text{ft})(15\ \text{ft})(9\ \text{ft}) = (270\ \text{ft}^2)(0.05) = 14 \\
& (2\ \text{ft})(20\ \text{ft})(9\ \text{ft}) = (360\ \text{ft}^2)(0.05) = 18 \\
\text{ceiling:} \quad & (15\ \text{ft})(20\ \text{ft}) = (300\ \text{ft}^2)(0.05) = \underline{15} \\
& \text{Total} = 167\ \text{sabins}
\end{aligned}
$$

Absorption after treatment:

$$\text{ceiling} = (15\ \text{ft})(20\ \text{ft}) = (300\ \text{ft})(0.70) = 210\ \text{sabins}$$

Subtracting 15 from the old value and adding 210 as a new value, the net total is 362 sabins.

$$
\begin{aligned}
\text{NR} &= 10 \log \frac{362\ \text{sabins}}{167\ \text{sabins}} \\
&= 10 \log 2.17\ \text{sabins} \\
&= 3.4\ \text{dB}
\end{aligned}
$$

Increasing the absorption by this amount helps a little, but the difference is just perceptible (see Table 11.2). Tripling the absorption would be clearly noticeable.

absorptive or reflective finishes in a space. Each doubling of the absorption in a room reduces reverberation time by half.

## SOUND CONTROL

This section reviews some of the specific design and construction strategies that can be used to control sound and noise in various circumstances.

### Space planning for acoustic control

There are many ways the acoustic performance of a group of spaces or an individual room can be affected by floor plan layout and the size and shape of the room itself. In addition to designing walls and floors to retard sound transmission and proper use of sound absorption, there are several ways to help minimize acoustic problems with interior space planning. These are diagrammed in Fig. 11.2 and summarized below.

- Zone activities of similar noise levels and plan areas of similar use next to each other. See Fig. 11.2(a). For example, placing bedrooms next to each other is better than placing a bedroom next to a noisy space like the kitchen.

- Use quiet or semiquiet utility spaces as buffers between a noisy area and a quiet area. See Fig. 11.2(b).

- Use closets, bookshelves, and similar functions on a common wall to help separate two rooms. See Fig. 11.2(c). This not only helps add distance and mass to the common partition but also keeps furniture and other noise-producing objects away from the common wall. Using closets between bedrooms at a common wall is one example of this technique.

- Stagger doorways in halls and other areas to avoid providing a straight-line path for noise. See Fig. 11.2(d).

• Minimize the area of the common wall between two rooms where a reduction in sound transmission is desired. See Fig. 11.2(e). This is one of the variables of noise reduction discussed previously.

• Avoid room shapes that focus sound. See Fig. 11.2(f). Barrel vaulted hallways and circular rooms, for example, produce undesirable focused sounds. Rooms that focus sound in some places and not others may also deprive some listeners of useful reflections.

## Control of room noise

There are three ways sound can be controlled within a space: by reducing the loudness of the sound source, by modifying the absorption in the space, and by introducing nonintrusive background sound to mask the unwanted sound.

### Reducing loudness

Reducing the level of the sound source is not always possible if the sound is created by a fixed piece of machinery, people, or some similar situation. However, if the source is noise from the outside or an adjacent room, the transmission loss of the enclosing walls can be improved. If a machine is producing the noise, it can often be enclosed or modified to reduce its noise output.

### Modifying absorption

Modifying the absorption of the space can achieve some noise reduction. However, there are practical limits to adding absorptive materials. This approach is most useful when the problem room has a large percentage of hard, reflective surfaces.

**Figure 11.2** Acoustic control with space planning

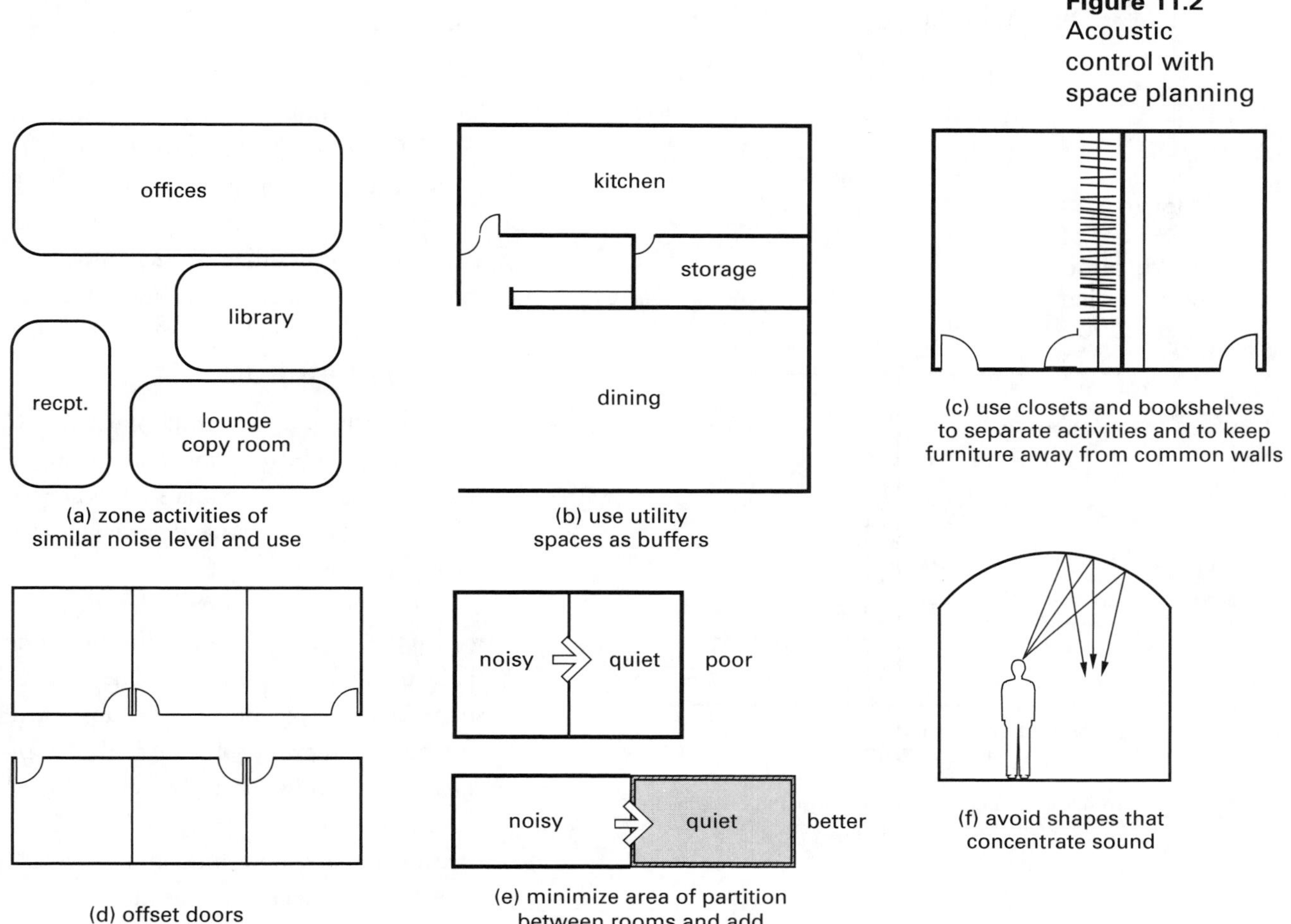


(a) zone activities of similar noise level and use

(b) use utility spaces as buffers

(c) use closets and bookshelves to separate activities and to keep furniture away from common walls

(d) offset doors

(e) minimize area of partition between rooms and add absorption to quiet room

(f) avoid shapes that concentrate sound

## Introducing background sound

In most cases, introducing nonintrusive background sound is desirable because it can mask unwanted noise. Some amount of background noise is always present. This may come from the steady hum of HVAC (heating, ventilating, and air conditioning) systems, business machines, traffic, conversation, or other sources. For example, if the sound level on one side (the noisy side) of a partition with an STC rating of 45 is 75 dB and the background noise on the quiet side of the partition is 35 dB, the noise coming through the partition will not be heard (theoretically) on the "quiet" side. See Fig. 11.3. The transmitted sound is 30 dB (75−45), which is below the background sound of 35 dB. If the background noise level is decreased to 25 dB, then transmitted sounds will be heard. Of course, this is only a general guideline; the frequency of the noise and the background sounds will affect what is actually heard.

The technique of introducing background sound is used to purposely introduce carefully controlled sound into a space rather than to rely only on random background noise. Speakers are placed in the ceiling of a space and connected to a sound generator, which produces a continuous, unnoticeable sound—often called white sound, random noise, or acoustic perfume—at particular levels across the frequency spectrum. The sound generator can be tuned to produce the frequencies and sound levels appropriate to mask the desired sounds. White sound is often used in open offices to provide speech privacy and to help mask office machine noise.

**Figure 11.3** Effect of background sound on noise perception

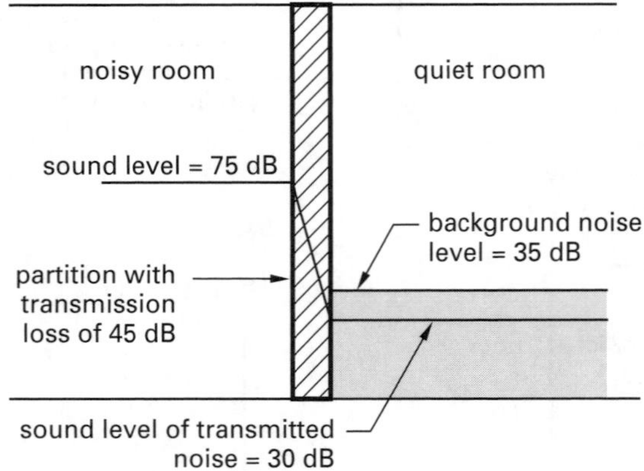


If transmitted sound level is below the background level, the sound is not perceptible.

## Speech privacy

In many spaces, the critical acoustic concern is not eliminating all noise or designing a room for music, but providing for a certain level of privacy while still allowing people to talk at a normal level. In many cases, speech privacy is regarded as a condition in which talking may be heard as a general background sound but not easily understood.

Speech privacy in areas divided by full-height partitions is usually achieved by sound loss through the partitions and, to a lesser extent, by the proper use of sound-absorbing surfaces. But in open areas, such as an open-plan office, speech privacy is more difficult to achieve. An open area with optimal acoustics will account for these five important design factors.

1. The ceiling must be highly absorptive. The ideal is to create, as much as possible, a "clear sky" condition so that sounds are not reflected from their sources to other parts of the space.

2. There must be space dividers that help reduce the transmission of sound from one space to the adjacent spaces. The dividers should have a combination of absorptive surfaces placed over a solid liner called a *septum*. The absorptive surfaces minimize sound reflections, and the septum reduces direct transmission of sound through the divider.

3. Other surfaces, such as the floor, furniture, windows, and light fixtures, must

be designed or arranged to minimize sound reflections. A window, for example, can provide a clear path for reflected noise around a partial height partition.

4. If possible, activities should be distanced to take advantage of the normal attenuation of sound with distance.

5. There should be a properly designed background masking system. If the right amount of sound-absorbing surfaces is provided, the surfaces absorb all sounds in the space, not just the unwanted sounds. Background sound must then be reintroduced to maintain the right balance between speech sound and the background masking sound.

## DETAILING FOR REDUCING SOUND TRANSMISSION

The control of sound transmission through a barrier depends primarily on the barrier's mass and, to a lesser extent, on its stiffness. Walls and floors are generally rated by their STC value; the higher the STC rating, the better the barrier is at reducing transmitted sound. Manufacturer's literature, testing

---

**Articulation index (AI) and articulation class (AC)**

Because speech privacy in open offices depends on the complex interaction of many variables, two measures are used to evaluate open office acoustics: the articulation class (AC) and the articulation index (AI). These test methods and rating systems have replaced the Speech Privacy Noise Isolation Class (NIC) and the Speech Privacy Potential (SPP) that were formerly used. The articulation class is determined by ASTM E1110, *Standard Classification for Determination of Articulation Class*, and the articulation index is determined by ASTM E1130, *Standard Test Method for Objective Measurement of Speech Privacy in Open Offices Using Articulation Index.*

The AC gives a rating of system component performance and does not account for masking sound. The AI measures the performance of all the elements of a particular configuration working together: ceiling absorption, space dividers, furniture, light fixtures, partitions, background masking systems, and HVAC systems. It is used to objectively test speech privacy of open office spaces, either in the actual space or in a laboratory mock-up of the space.

The articulation index can be used to (1) compare the relative privacy between different pairs of workstations or areas, (2) evaluate how changes in open office components affect speech privacy, and (3) measure speech privacy objectively for correlation with subjective responses. It has the potential for being a method to specify required levels of speech privacy; however, more research is needed in this area.

The articulation index predicts the intelligibility of speech for a group of talkers and listeners. The result of the test is a single-number rating. The AI rating can range from 0.00 to 1.00, with 0.00 being complete privacy and 1.00 being absolutely no privacy where all individual spoken words can be understood. Confidential speech privacy exists when speech cannot be understood and occurs when the articulation index is at or below 0.05. Normal speech privacy means concentrated effort is required to understand intruding speech and exists when the AI is from 0.05 to 0.20. Above an AI of 0.20, speech becomes readily understood. Unacceptable privacy exists when the AI is above 0.30.

Both the articulation index and the articulation class are intended only for open office situations where speech is the sound source of concern. However, the articulation index can be adapted for other open plans, such as in schools, and can be applied to measure speech privacy between enclosed and open spaces and between two enclosed rooms.

**Figure 11.4** Components of a partition resistant to sound transmission

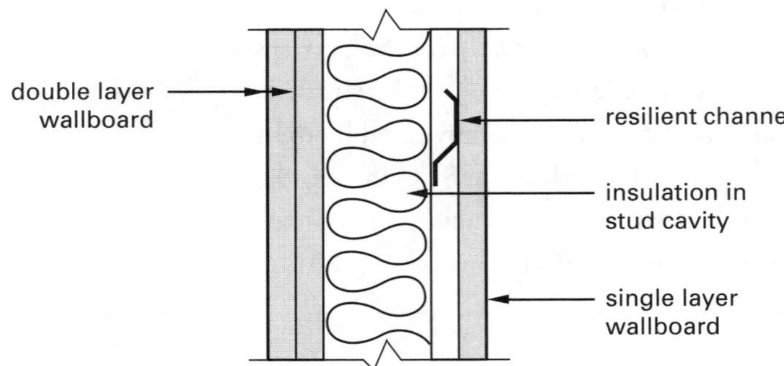


laboratories, and reference literature typically give the transmission loss at different frequencies. Some representative STC values for gypsum wallboard partitions are given in Fig. 1.21.

## Partitions

Several methods can be used to build a sound-resistant partition. These are diagrammed in Fig. 11.4. The first technique simply adds mass to the partition. This can be done by using a heavy material, such as masonry, for the partition or by using more than one layer of gypsum wallboard. Partitions with high STC ratings commonly have a double layer of wallboard on one or both sides of the stud. The second technique is to place insulation within the stud cavity. This absorbs sound (reduces its energy) that is transmitted through one layer of the partition before it reaches the other. Finally, resilient channels can be used as furring strips on one side of the partition. By design, only one leg of a resilient channel touches the stud, so that the wallboard "floats" and dampens sound striking it rather than transmitting it to the stud and through the partition.

Some representative STC ratings for various types of partitions are shown in Table 11.10.

However, constructing a partition with these elements is not enough. There are many ways sound can pass through, over, and around an otherwise well-built partition. These are shown in Fig. 11.5. Gaps in the partition must be sealed. Edges at the floor, ceiling, and intersecting walls must be caulked. (See Fig. 11.6.) Penetrations of the partition should be avoided; however, if they are absolutely necessary, they should also be sealed. For example, electrical outlets should be staggered in separate stud spaces and caulked, not placed back to back. See Fig. 11.7. Pipes, ducts, and similar penetrations provide a path for both airborne sound and mechanical vibration and, therefore, should not be rigidly connected to the partition. Any gaps between ducts or pipes and a partition should also be sealed and caulked.

It is critical to make sure that all cracks in a partition or other barrier are sealed. A hairline crack will decrease a partition's transmission loss by about 6 dB. A 1 $in^2$ (645 $mm^2$) opening in a 100 $ft^2$ (9.3 $m^2$) gypsum wallboard partition can transmit as much sound as the entire partition. A wall with 0.1% open area (from cracks, holes, undercut doors, and so on) can have only a maximum transmission loss of about 30 dB, no matter how solidly it is constructed. A wall with 1% open area can have only a maximum loss of about 20 dB.

Construction with a lower STC rating than the barrier itself should be avoided or given special treatment because it will decrease the overall rating of the barrier. Doors placed in an otherwise well-built sound wall are a common problem. For example, a partition 9 ft high by 15 ft long (2700 mm high by 4600 mm long) with an STC of 54 and a door in it measuring 3 ft by 7 ft (900 mm by 2100 mm) with an STC of 29 and sealed around its perimeter only has an overall STC of 37 dB.

However, the problem can be dealt with in several ways. The perimeter should be completely sealed with weather stripping specifically designed for sound sealing at the jamb

**Table 11.10** Transmission loss data for typical partition types

| construction description | STC |
|---|---|
| gypsum wallboard, ⅝ in (15.9 mm) thick, each side 3⅝ in (92.1 mm) metal studs | 42 |
| same as above with 3 in (75 mm) sound attenuation blankets in cavity | 48 |
| two layers ½ in (13 mm) gypsum wallboard, each side 2½ in (63.55 mm) metal studs with 1½ in (38 mm) sound attenuation blankets in cavity | 54 |
| same as above except only one layer drywall on one side of partitions | 50 |
| gypsum wallboard, ⅝ in (15.9 mm) thick, each side 2 × 4 (50 × 100) wood studs | 34 |
| same as above using resilient channels on wood studs | 45 |
| gypsum wallboard, ⅝ in (15.9 mm) thick, on 2 × 4 staggered wood studs on common 2 × 6 plate (50 × 150) with 2 in (50 mm) sound attenuation blanket in cavity | 45 |
| two layers ½ in gypsum wallboard each side 2 × 4 studs, gypsum wallboard mounted on one side on resilient clips, 3 in (75 mm) sound attenuation blanket in cavity | 59 |
| four-inch brick with ½ in (13 mm) plaster one side | 50 |
| lightweight concrete block measuring 4 in (100 mm) | 40 |
| standard weight concrete block measuring 4 in (100 mm) | 45 |
| standard concrete block measuring 4 in (100 mm), with ½ in (13 mm) gypsum wallboard on each side | 48 |
| lightweight concrete block measuring 8 in (200 mm) | 49 |

Note: Partition STC ratings include fully caulked perimeter and no flanking loss due to ceiling construction.

Source: *Architect's Handbook of Formulas, Tables, & Mathematical Calculations.* David Kent Ballast. Englewood Cliffs, NJ: Prentice-Hall, 1988.

and head and with a threshold or automatic door bottom at the sill. See Fig. 11.8. An automatic door bottom is a piece of hardware that drops a seal from the door to the floor or threshold as the door closes. Typical head and jamb seal details are shown in Figs. 4.12 and 4.13, while automatic door bottoms are illustrated in Fig. 4.14. The numbers in Table 11.11 illustrate the wide range of STC ratings for doors depending on the type of construction assembly. Refer to the manufacturer's literature for STC ratings for specific applications of the various types of available door seals.

The door itself should be as heavy as possible, preferably a solid core wood door or an insulated steel door. Solid core wood doors 1¾ in (44 mm) thick with correctly installed perimeter seals can achieve STC ratings in the low 30s. When higher STC ratings are required, insulated steel doors with double seals should be used. When an STC door rating over 49 is required, 2¼ in (57 mm) thick doors are used. Often, two sealed doors are used, separated by an air gap. For extremely critical installations, such as recording studios and concert halls, special prepackaged, sound-rated door assemblies should be used.

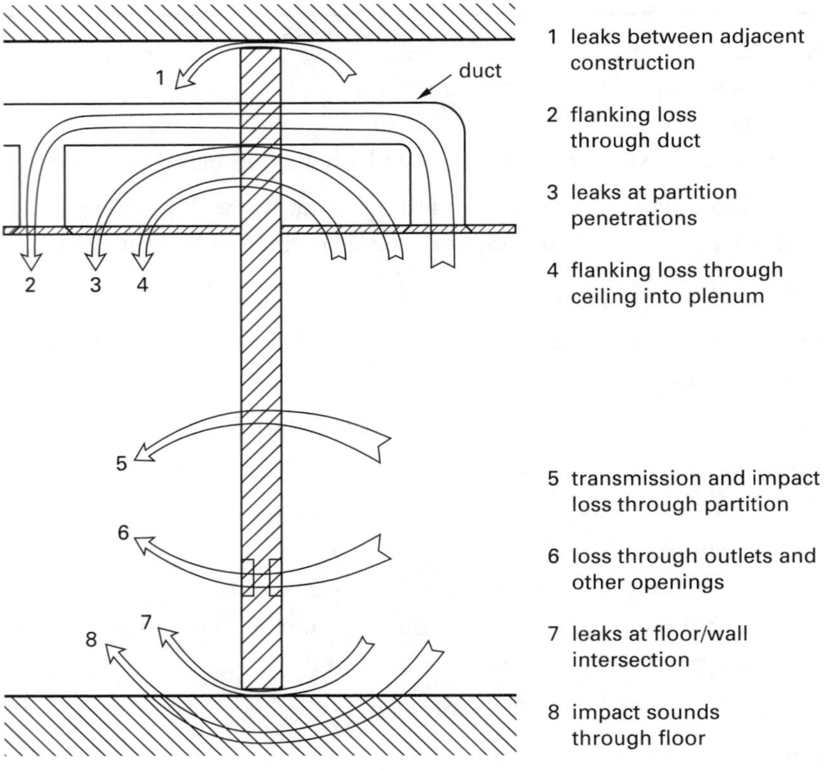


**Figure 11.5** Potential sources of sound leaks through partitions

Interior glass lights pose another problem for sound transmission. As shown in Table 11.12, single-thickness glass does not provide much sound attenuation. When higher ratings are required, laminated glass set in resilient framing should be used. See Fig. 11.9. Laminated glass provides more mass, and the plastic interlayer improves the damping characteristics of the barrier. Alternately, double- or triple-pane assemblies or double layers of laminated glass can be used.

In addition to correctly detailing doors and glazed openings in partitions, all flanking paths should be eliminated or treated appropriately. These include plenum spaces above ceilings, heating registers that pass from one room to the next, air conditioning ducts, pipes, and other penetrations. In many commercial projects, partitions extend only to the suspended ceiling, allowing sound to travel from one room, through the ceiling tile into the plenum, and into the adjacent room. Ideally, the partition should extend to the structural floor above. When this is not possible, some type of plenum barrier should be constructed. Two of these are illustrated in Figs. 11.10(a) and 11.10(b).

## Floor/ceiling assemblies

For floor/ceiling assemblies, a high STC rating is not enough to evaluate the effectiveness of transmission loss. Impact noise, or sound resulting from direct contact of an object with a sound barrier, can occur on any surface, but it generally occurs on a floor/ceiling assembly. It is usually caused by footfalls, shuffled furniture, and dropped objects on hard-surfaced floors, such as ceramic tile, hardwood, or resilient tile.

The result of impact noise caused by these kinds of activities is quantified by the impact insulation class (IIC) number, a single-number rating of a floor/ceiling assembly's impact sound performance. The higher the IIC rating, the better the floor performs at reducing impact sounds in the test frequency range.

**Figure 11.6**
Partition sealing detail

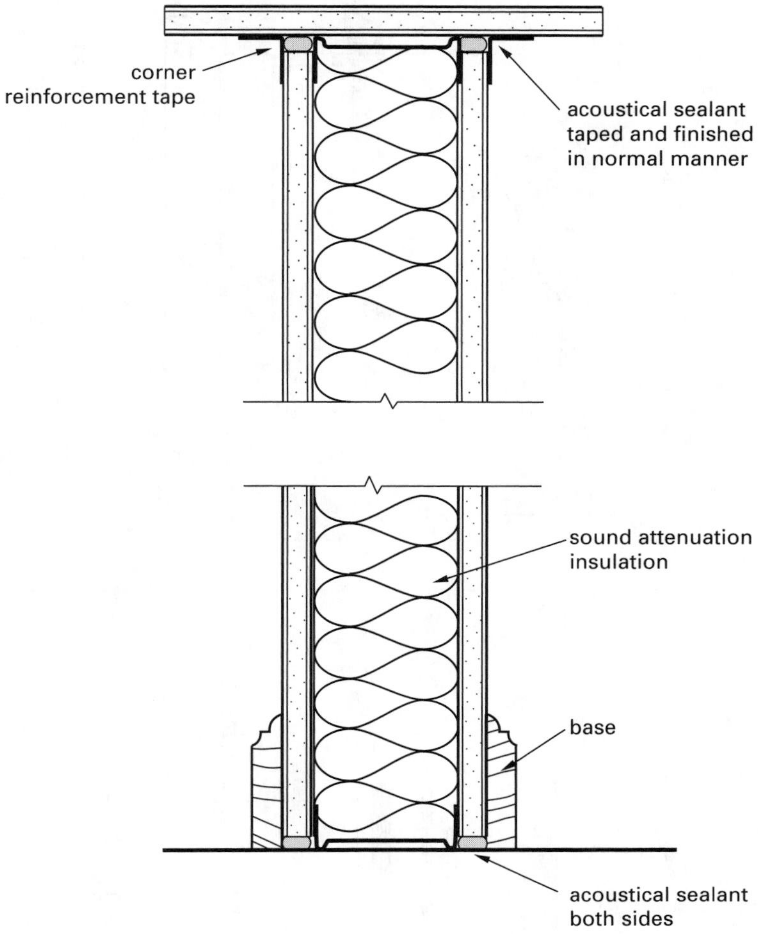

corner
reinforcement tape
acoustical sealant
taped and finished
in normal manner
sound attenuation
insulation
base
acoustical sealant
both sides

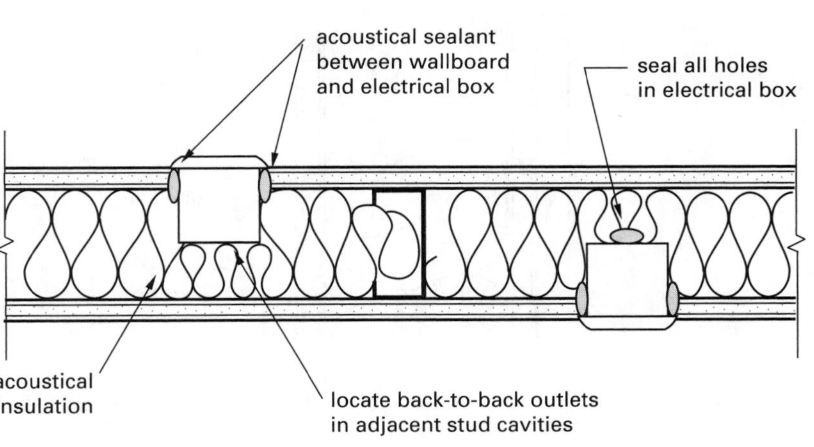

**Figure 11.7**
Placement of electrical outlets for acoustic control

acoustical sealant
between wallboard
and electrical box
seal all holes
in electrical box
acoustical
insulation
locate back-to-back outlets
in adjacent stud cavities

**Figure 11.8**
Principles of acoustic control for doors

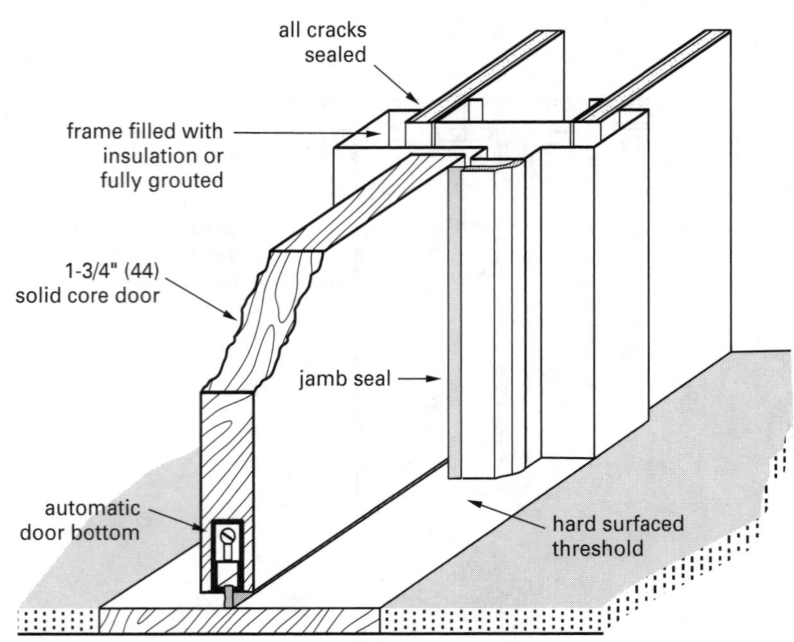


**Figure 11.9**
Glazing assembly for sound control

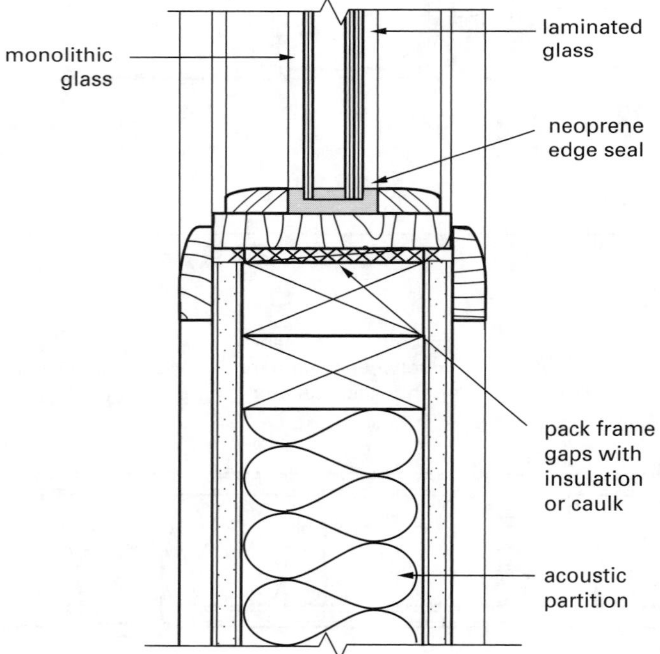

**Table 11.11** Transmission loss data for typical door assemblies

| door assembly | STC |
|---|---|
| hollow core 1¾ in (44 mm) thick with ¼ in (6 mm) gap at sill | 17 |
| solid core wood 1¾ in (44 mm) thick with no seal | 20 |
| solid core wood 1¾ in (44 mm) thick with perimeter seal and automatic door bottom | 29 |
| steel door 1¾ in (44 mm) thick with compressible perimeter seal and automatic door bottom | 44 |
| two 1¾ in (44 mm) solid core doors with full seals separated by 3 ft (900 mm) air space | 47 |

Note: These figures were compiled from various industry sources and represent typical ratings useful for preliminary design decisions. Refer to manufacturers' literature for more detailed data.

**Table 11.12** Transmission loss data for glass

| glazing assembly | STC |
|---|---|
| single strength float glass | 26 |
| float glass ¼ in (6 mm) thick | 29 |
| float glass ½ in (13 mm) thick | 33 |
| laminated glass ¼ in (6 mm) thick (0.030 in interlayer) | 35 |
| laminated glass ½ in (13 mm) thick (0.060 in interlayer) | 38 |
| laminated glass ¾ in (19 mm) thick (two, 0.060 in interlayers) | 41 |
| float glass ¼ in and ½ in thick with 2 in (50 mm) air space between | 39 |
| laminated glass ¼ in and ½ in thick with 6 in (150 mm) air space | 44 |

Note: In critical situations to achieve the above ratings, glass panels must be sealed at all edges. When using two layers of glass separated by an air space, the thicknesses of the glass lights should not be the same.

Source: *Architect's Handbook of Formulas, Tables, & Mathematical Calculations.* David Kent Ballast. Englewood Cliffs, NJ: Prentice-Hall, 1988.

In most cases, the construction of floors is already determined by the architectural design of a building, either existing or new. Fortunately, the IIC value of a floor depends mostly on its finish and can most easily be increased by adding carpeting. In critical situations, the ICC rating can also be improved by providing a resiliently suspended ceiling below, floating a finished floor on resilient pads over the structural floor, or providing sound-absorbing material (insulation) in the air space between the floor and the finished ceiling below.

## Structure-borne noise

Most problems with noise transmission occur when the source vibrates the air in the noisy space, which in turn strikes a partition or ceiling and travels through the construction assembly into another space. Noise can also be transmitted by a source directly through the structure of a building. Dropped objects and footfalls on hard-surfaced floors, as described previously, are one example. The most troublesome structure-borne noises are produced by machines, HVAC systems, plumbing fixtures, and water flowing through pipes.

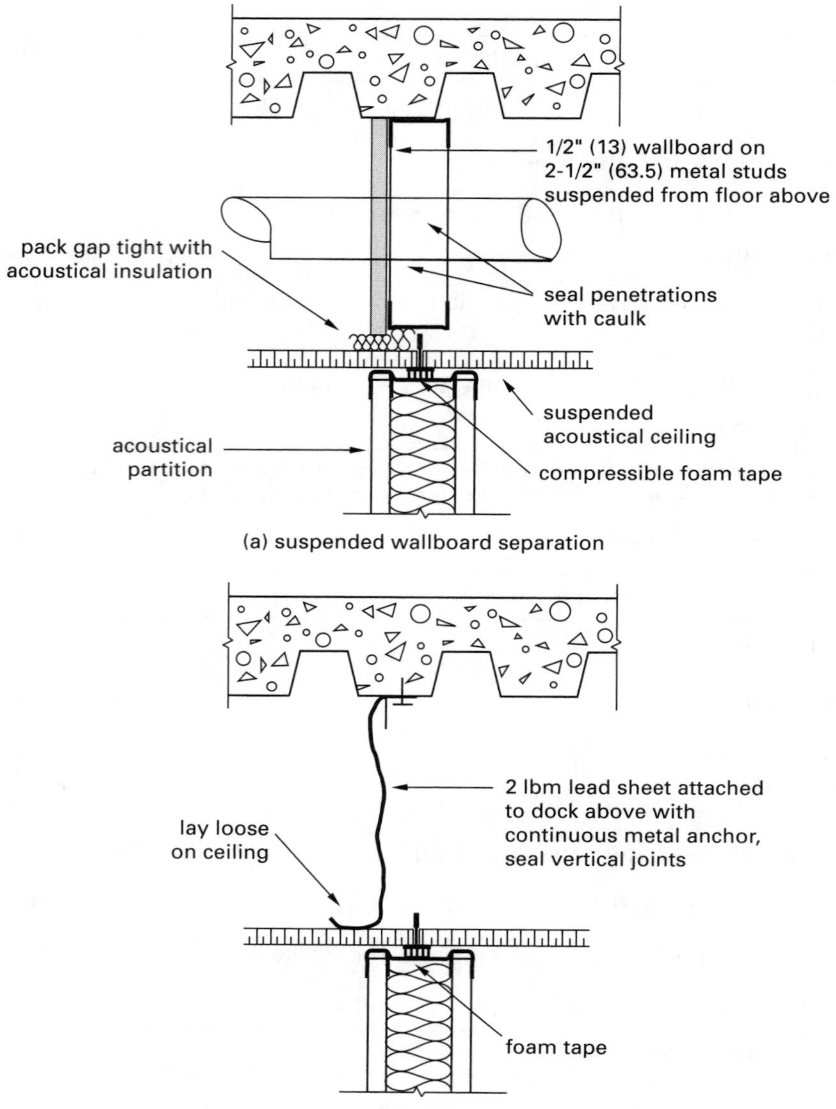


**Figure 11.10**
Plenum barriers

To control structure-borne noise, machines should be mounted on resilient pads or on special spring-supported mountings. Plumbing pipes should not be rigidly attached to studs, joists, or other structural elements. Instead, the pipe should be wrapped with insulation and then clamped to the supporting structure. Ducts should be lined with insulation, and connections between vibrating equipment and the ducts attached to it should not be rigid. Although it is nearly impossible to isolate plumbing fixtures from the structure, they can be planned so they are not adjacent to quiet areas. If this is not possible, insulated chase walls can separate areas with plumbing from other rooms.

## DETAILING FOR NOISE REDUCTION

As mentioned previously, there are three ways of controlling room noise, one of which is to increase the absorption. This is typically done with sound-absorbent finishes on walls, ceilings, and floors, although in large spaces, separate sound absorbers or reflectors can be suspended from the ceiling. In most situations acoustical ceiling tile,

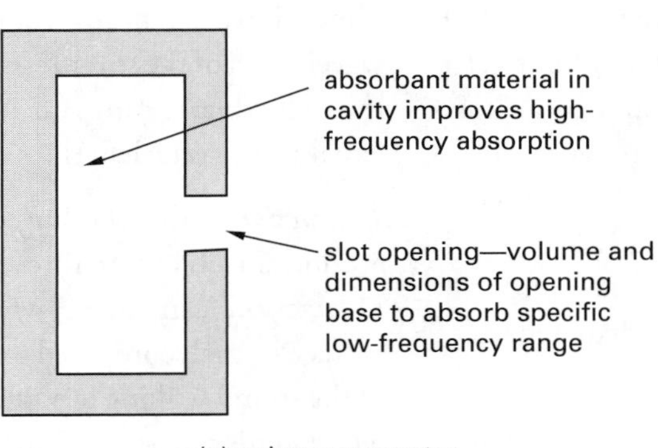

(a) volume resonator

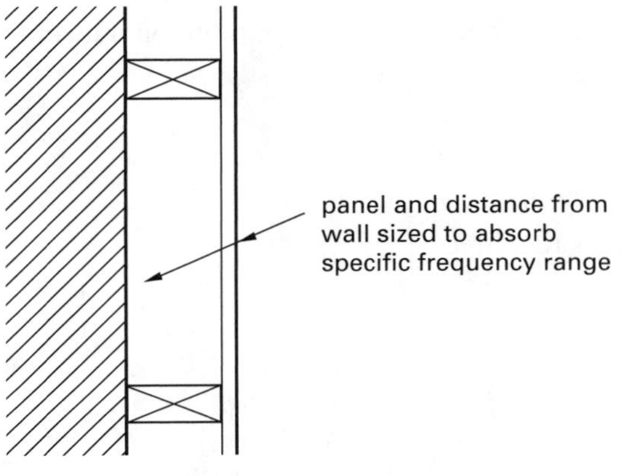


(b) vibrating panel

**Figure 11.11** Details for low-frequency sound absorption

carpeting, furniture, and other construction elements are usually sufficient to provide an adequate amount of absorption for typical residential and commercial uses. These include homes, offices, retail stores, restaurants, and the like.

If additional absorption is required, partitions are usually treated with acoustic panels or upholstered walls as shown in Figs. 6.30 and 10.2. Acoustical panels that are part of furniture systems can provide additional absorption. However, these types of panels are only effective for the higher frequencies and for speech. Controlling low-frequency and very high-frequency sounds within a room requires construction elements that can trap the longer, low-frequency wavelengths or control the very short high-frequency wavelengths. Low-frequency control usually requires an allowance for thicker partitions or more space to apply detailing that absorbs low-frequency sound. Various details can be developed to meet the particular requirements of the project and the specific frequencies that must be controlled. In critical situations, an acoustical consultant should assist in developing these types of details. Two typical methods for absorbing low-frequency sounds are shown in Figs. 11.11(a) and 11.11(b).

## REFLECTION, DIFFUSION, AND DIFFRACTION

*Reflection* is the return of sound waves from a surface. Sometimes, reflection rather than absorption is the goal, such as in concert halls, lecture auditoriums, and large conference rooms. A surface's reflectivity depends on its size, its smoothness, and the wavelengths of the sounds striking it. If the size of a surface is greater than or equal to four times the wavelength of a sound striking the surface, the angle of incidence equals the angle of reflection, just as with light. For example, in order to reflect a 1000 Hz sound with a wavelength of about 1.13 ft (344 mm), a reflector should be at least 4½ ft by 4½ ft (1.4 m by 1.4 m) wide. Similarly, if a surface has a rough texture and the individual surface variations are about equal to the wavelength striking it, the sound will tend to be scattered rather than reflected like a mirror.

Reflection can be useful for reinforcing sound in lecture rooms and similar spaces. It can also be annoying if it produces echoes, which occur when a reflected sound reaches a listener later than about 1/17 sec after the direct sound. Assuming a sound speed of 1130 ft/sec, an echo will occur whenever the reflected sound path exceeds the direct sound path by 70 ft or more.

*Diffusion* is the random distribution of sound from a surface. It occurs when the surface dimension of a reflector is about equal to the wavelength of the sound striking it, or when the individual textures on a large surface are equal to the wavelength.

*Diffraction* is the bending of sound waves around an object or through an opening. Diffraction can occur when a reflecting surface is small compared to the wavelength of the sound striking it. Diffraction explains why sounds can be heard around corners and why even small holes in partitions allow so much sound to be transmitted.

# 12

# STAIR DESIGN AND CONSTRUCTION

Stairways can be classified into two broad types: those used for strictly utilitarian purposes, such as exit stairs, and those designed to be a prominent design feature as well as provide vertical access, called monumental stairs. Interior design projects in both residential and commercial construction often require that new stairs be planned or that existing stairs be remodeled. For example, this can occur when a commercial tenant wants a private stairway connecting floors, when new mezzanines are planned, or when an existing stair configuration must be remodeled to meet current building codes.

This chapter discusses design guidelines for planning stairs and reviews construction requirements for common stair types. Although some code requirements are summarized in this chapter, refer to Ch. 20 for detailed building code requirements for exiting and stairway enclosure construction and to Ch. 18 for accessibility and Americans with Disabilities Act (ADA) requirements.

## STAIRWAY LAYOUT

### Configuration

The design and detailing of a stair begins with deciding on its basic configuration and shape, the approximate amount of space required, and the geometry of its layout. Some of the most common configurations are shown in Figs. 12.1(a)–12.1(h). Each of these types has many variations. For example, a simple straight run stair may be enclosed or partially open, may be interrupted with several landings, or may have landings that project from the face of the open side of the stair. L-shaped stairs can have equal or unequal legs. Monumental stairs can be designed in an unlimited number of configurations, sizes, and materials. The configuration of stairs is based on the space available and where the top and bottom of the stair must end.

### Horizontal layout

Once the basic configuration of a stairway has been determined, the width, total run, and landing depths and widths determine

**Figure 12.1**
Basic stair configurations

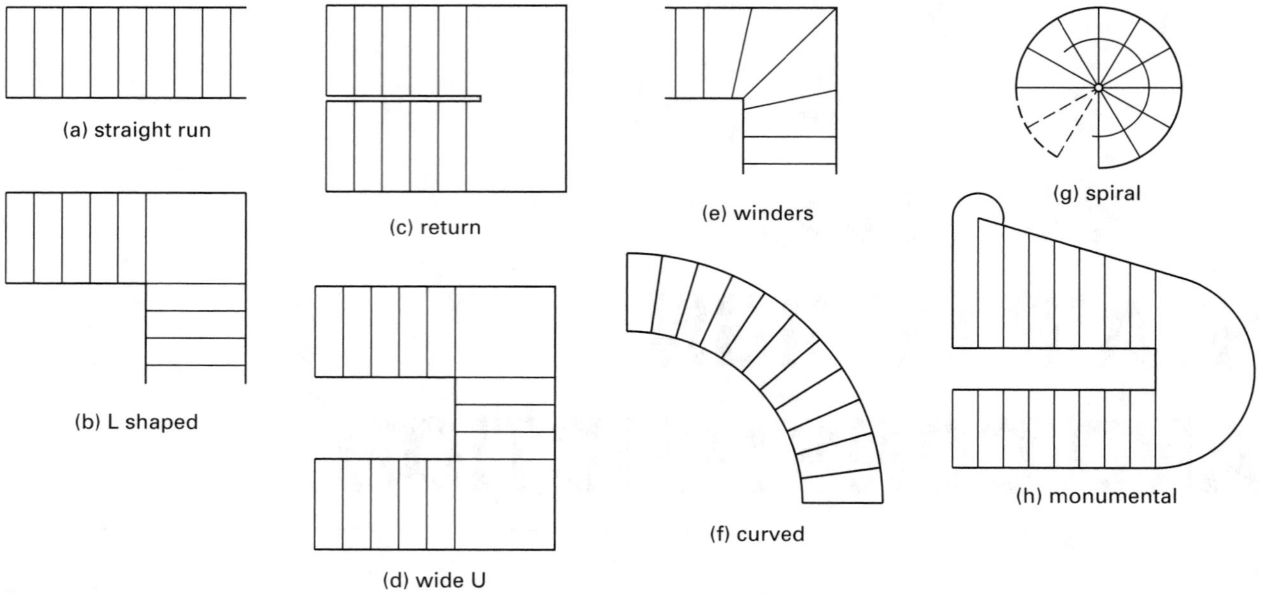

(a) straight run

(b) L shaped

(c) return

(d) wide U

(e) winders

(f) curved

(g) spiral

(h) monumental

**Figure 12.2**
Stair planning guidelines

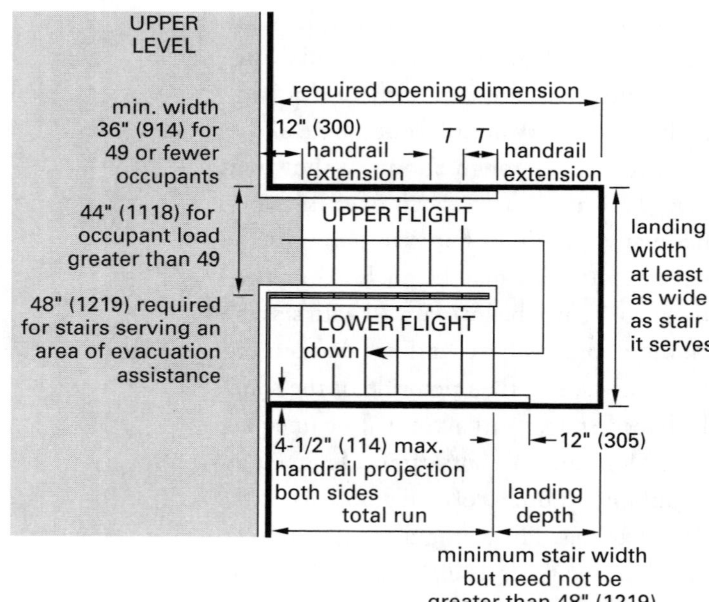


how much space is required. Figure 12.2 shows the minimum dimensions for laying out a stairway in plan view, including a landing. The total run depends on the depth of the treads and the number of risers and landings that will be used. Calculating stair risers and treads and total run is discussed in the next section.

The minimum width of any stair is 36 in (914 mm) and is 44 in (1118 mm) when the occupant load exceeds 49. Handrails may project a maximum of 4½ in (114 mm) on both sides of a stairway.

The layout of return stairs or wide U-shaped stairs requires a slight adjustment in the relationship between the lower flight and the upper flight in order for the center railing to make a smooth switchback. As shown in Fig. 12.3, the first riser of the upper flight of steps at the intermediate landing is offset from the last tread of the lower flight by one tread dimension. Because of the angular geometry, this allows the handrail to turn back at one point instead of jogging vertically at the landing.

This relationship is also shown in elevation view in Figs. 12.8 and 12.10.

If the last riser of the upper flight of steps ends one tread dimension short of the stairway opening, then the handrail can be extended the required 12 in (300 mm) without intruding into the upper level. Figure 12.11 shows a detailed schematic elevation view of this relationship.

## Vertical layout

The basic design and code requirements for vertical dimensions of stairs are shown in Fig. 12.6. Handrails must be provided on both sides of stairs (except for dwelling units) and must run continuously for the full length of the stair. Except for private stairways, handrails must extend horizontally beyond the upper riser by at least

**Figure 12.3**
Return stair plan layout

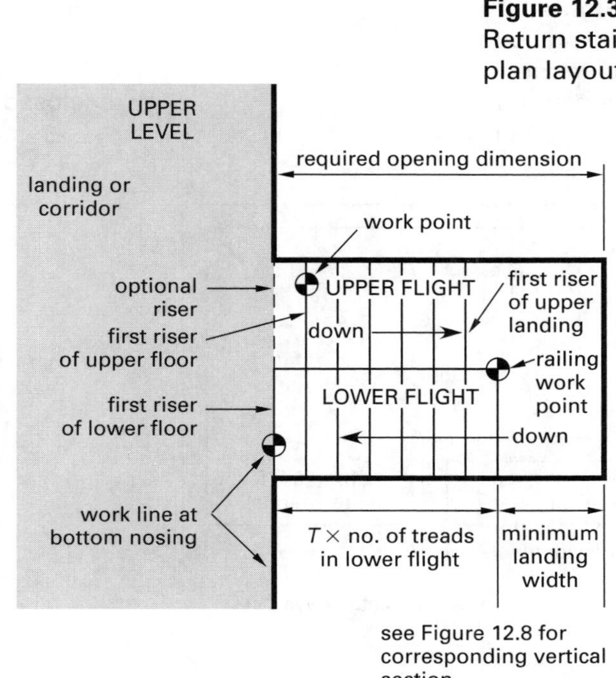


see Figure 12.8 for corresponding vertical section

## Building code requirements for horizontal layout

In addition to the requirements shown in Fig. 12.2, building codes limit the use of special types of stairs. These include winding, curved, and spiral stairways. They are only allowed as private stairways in homes, apartments, condominiums, and the like.

Winding stairways have tapered treads that are wider at one end than the other. See Fig. 12.4(a). When circular stairways have a smaller radius than required by code (see below), they are classified as winding stairways. When winders are used, they should all be the same shape and size, if possible. Winders are permitted as egress stairs only in dwelling units.

Curved stairways, previously called circular, have sides whose shape is a curve, most commonly a circular arc. The inside, or smaller arc, cannot be less than twice the required width of the stair. See Fig. 12.4(b). If it is, then it is considered a winding stairway. The International Building Code limits the least dimension of the tread at the smallest point to 10 in (254 mm).

Spiral stairs use wedge-shaped treads that radiate from a center support column. Spiral stairs are discussed in Ch. 7, but the code requirements are repeated in Fig. 12.4(c) for convenience. The allowable riser height is greater than for other stairs; it must be enough to provide a minimum headroom height of 6 ft 6 in (1981 mm) but cannot be greater than 9½ in (241 mm).

For enclosed exit stairways with doors adjacent to landings, the codes require that the door not encroach into the required exit path more than a certain distance, either as the door is opening or when the door is fully opened. IBC requirements are shown in Fig. 12.5. The dimensions in Fig. 12.5 do not include any allowance for evacuation assistance space, if it is required. However, these areas are normally provided in the building exit stairways.

**Figure 12.4**
Building code requirements for nonstraight stairs

12" (305)
11" (279) required width
min. 10" (254) at narrowest point (6" [152] for residential)
(10" [254] for residential)

(a) winding stairways

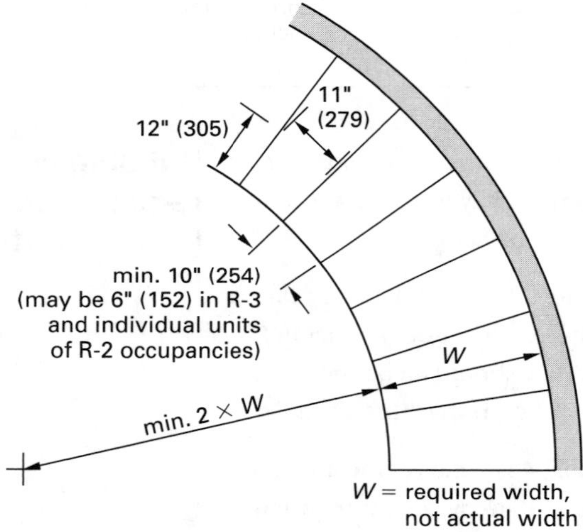


(b) curved stairways

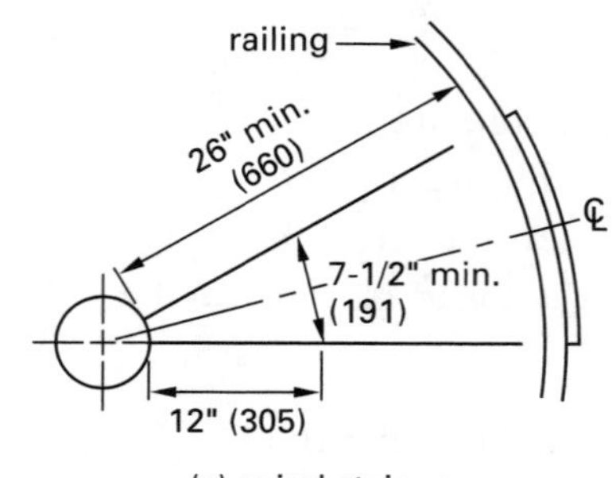


(c) spiral stairways

**Figure 12.5**
Planning guidelines for enclosed exit stairs

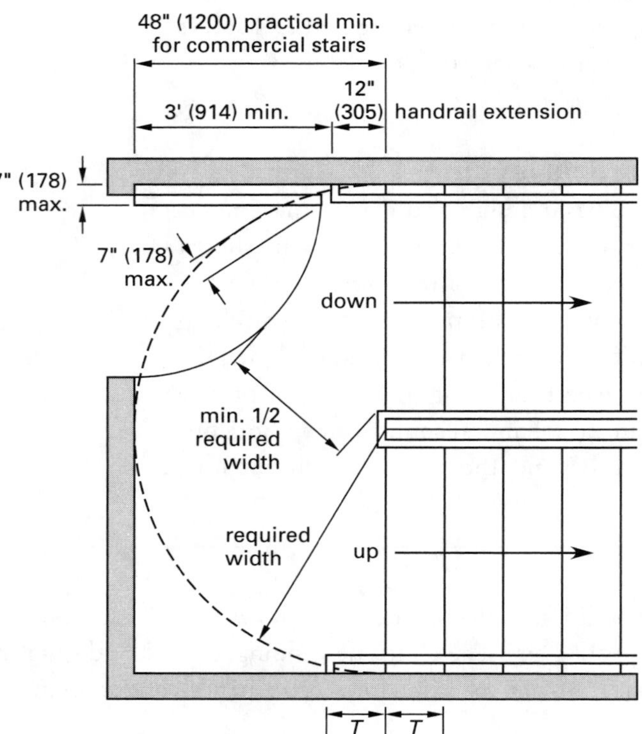


12 in (300 mm) and continue to slope for the depth of one tread beyond the bottom riser. For residential stairs the handrail may end at the top and bottom risers.

There has been extensive research into the best dimensions for the rise and treads of stairs and the safest and most comfortable proportion between the two. The maximum rise and minimum tread dimensions of 7 in and 11 in, respectively, represent some of the most current research, including considerations for the physically disabled. See Fig. 12.7. Some researchers recommend that treads should be even wider, from 12 in to 14 in. The tread of a stair is considered the horizontal projection of the distance from the edge of one nosing to the next. It does not include any part of the tread under the nosing.

Because stair dimensions are based on the normal stride of a person while ascending and descending a stair, various formulas have been used to determine one dimension based on the other. This is typically the case when the total rise is known and the number of risers must be a whole number without exceeding 7 in (178 mm) or 7¾ in (197 mm) on private stairways. Some of these equations include the following.

$$2R + T = 25 \text{ in} \quad \text{[U.S.] Eq. 12.1(a)}$$
$$2R + T = 635 \text{ mm} \quad \text{[SI] Eq. 12.1(b)}$$
$$RT = 75 \text{ in} \quad \text{[U.S.] Eq. 12.2(a)}$$
$$RT = 1905 \text{ mm} \quad \text{[SI] Eq. 12.2(b)}$$
$$R + T = 17 \text{ in} \quad \text{[U.S.] Eq. 12.3(a)}$$
$$R + T = 432 \text{ mm} \quad \text{[SI] Eq. 12.3(b)}$$
$$T = 20 \text{ in} - \frac{4R}{3} \quad \text{[U.S.] Eq. 12.4(a)}$$
$$T = 508 \text{ in} - \frac{4R}{3} \quad \text{[SI] Eq. 12.4(b)}$$

| | | | |
|---|---|---|---|
| $R$ | riser height | in | mm |
| $T$ | tread depth | in | mm |

Some of these formulas are rather old and represent proportions that were comfortable for people who, on average, were slightly smaller than the average size of people today. Equation 12.1, for example, was developed in the seventeenth century and originally stipulated that twice the riser plus the tread should be between 24 in and 25 in. Now the minimum should be 25 in and may be increased to 26 in. Of the four equations, Eq. 12.1 gives the widest tread based on a given riser height if the value of 25 in is used, and it can be used in most designs. A wider tread is generally safest, especially when descending stairs. When possible, a 12 in (305 mm) tread should be used.

Stairs consisting of just one or two risers are especially dangerous because people have a more difficult time recognizing the change in level. For these types of stairs the recommended minimum tread depth is 13 in (330 mm). In addition, there should be some means of making the level change more apparent, such as with riser lights or warning strips. Handrails must also be used as a visual cue to indicate that there is a level change and to give people something to hold onto as they traverse the steps.

The total run of a stair is calculated by taking the total rise in inches (millimeters) and dividing by an estimated riser height, usually 7 in (178 mm). If the result is not a round number, then the required number of risers is

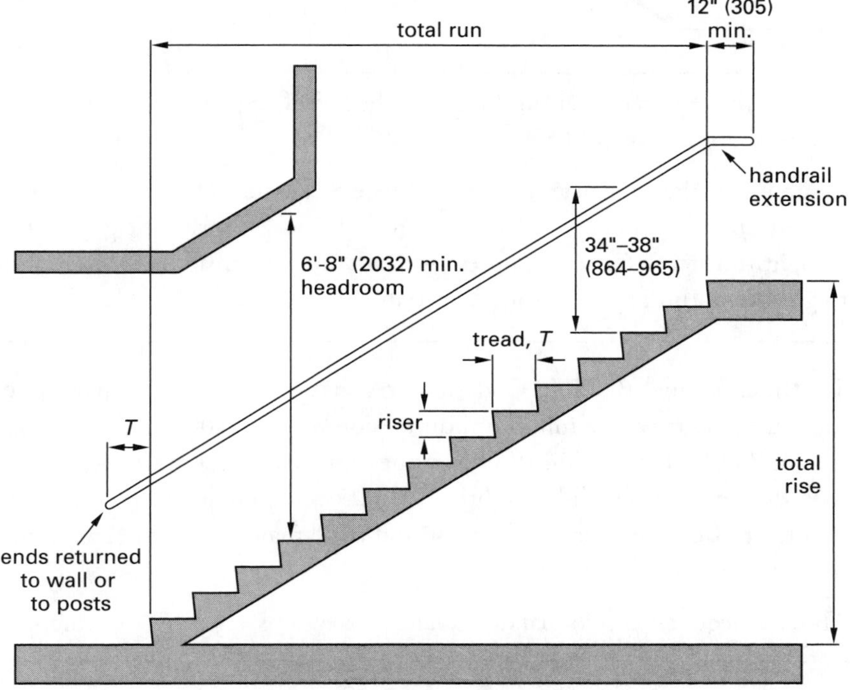


**Figure 12.6** Stair section design guidelines

the next highest full number. This is then divided into the total rise to obtain the actual required riser. The number of treads for a straight run stair is one less than the number of risers, and this number is multiplied by the tread dimension to obtain the total required run.

The maximum distance between landings is 12 ft (3660 mm); however, some research suggests that 9 ft (2740 mm) is a better dimension, especially for the physically disabled.

As noted in the previous section, the treads in return stairs or wide-U stairs should be set in a particular relationship so that the switchback of the center handrail occurs at a single point rather than being vertically offset. In addition, the top riser in the upper flight can be set back from the stair opening to allow for the required 12 in (305 mm) extension without interfering with the landing space, or to make the transition from handrail height to guardrail height (42 in). This geometry is illustrated in Fig. 12.8 and shown in more detail in Figs. 12.9–12.11.

The illustrations show the critical working points for designing a stair with any material and in any dimensions. For multiple-floor stair layouts, the upper flight in Fig. 12.8 should be increased by two risers. Then, the stairway can be stacked as many times as required, and the return flight will always lead the lower flight by one tread. For L-shaped stairways, the first riser of the upper flight should also begin one tread distance from the nosing of the last riser of the lower flight so that the handrail makes a direct 90° turn without a vertical offset rise.

As shown in Fig. 12.11, if the top of the handrail is placed 34 in (864 mm) above the nosing line, the railing will intersect a 42 in (1067 mm) guardrail in the location shown. Another method of making the transition from the handrail to the guardrail without the extra top tread is to locate the handrail at the required height and attach it to a separate railing that is higher than the handrail.

**Figure 12.7** Riser and tread dimensions

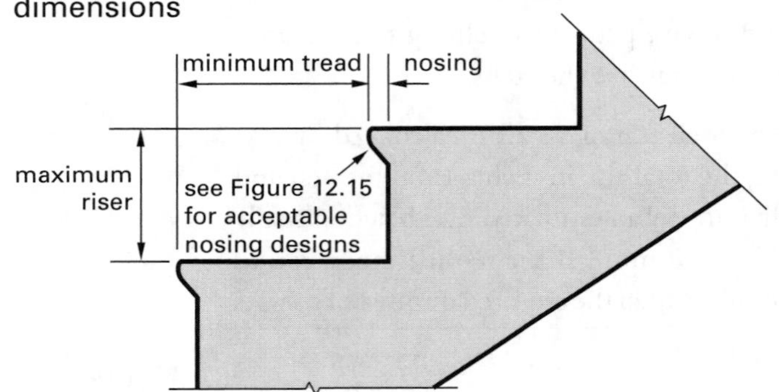


**Example: Calculating total straight stair run**

What is the required total run for a straight stair if the floor-to-floor height is 8 ft 6 in and the tread dimension is 11 in?

Assume that the riser height is 7 in. Divide 8 ft 6 in, or 102 in, by 7 to get 14.57 risers. Round up to 15 risers and divide 15 into 102 to get a riser height of about 6¾ in. In a straight run stair, 15 risers requires 14 treads. Using a tread of 11 in, multiply 14 times 11 to get a total run of 154 in, or 12 ft 10 in.

## Building code requirements for vertical layout

The International Building Code requires that every stairway having one or more risers must have risers with a minimum dimension of 4 in (100 mm) and a maximum dimension of 7 in (178 mm). Treads must be at least 11 in (279 mm) deep. These are consistent with the Americans with Disabilities Act (ADA) requirements. For private stairs serving an occupant load of less than 10, the rise and tread may be 7.75 in (197 mm) and 10 in (254 mm), respectively.

The code requirements for handrails, railing extensions, and headroom are shown in Fig. 12.6.

Under the International Building Code, stairways and ramps that are not adjacent to a wall and are more than 30 in (762 mm) above the floor must have guards as well as handrails. The guards must be a minimum of 42 in (1067 mm) above the leading edge of the tread as measured vertically. The handrails must be placed inside the guards, between 34 in and 38 in (864 mm and 965 mm) above the leading edge of the treads.

Refer to Ch. 20 for more information on code requirements for stairs.

## STAIR DESIGN AND CONSTRUCTION

### Wood stairs [064300]

Wood stairs can be constructed in an almost unlimited number of styles and details, from simple, utilitarian stairs to elaborate, custom-fabricated monumental staircases. Basic, straight run, U-shaped, and L-shaped stairs with little decorative features are normally site-built by finish carpenters. Decorative, prefabricated railings, balusters, and newel posts may be used in conjunction with the basic structure and the treads and risers of the stair. Open staircases with custom detailing, winding stairs, and spiral stairs are usually built in a mill shop and assembled on the site.

Figure 12.12 illustrates a typical site-built stairway and common construction components. An opening in the floor is framed with double joists. Wood carriages are cut out of 2 × 12 members to form the supports for the treads and risers. For narrow stairs

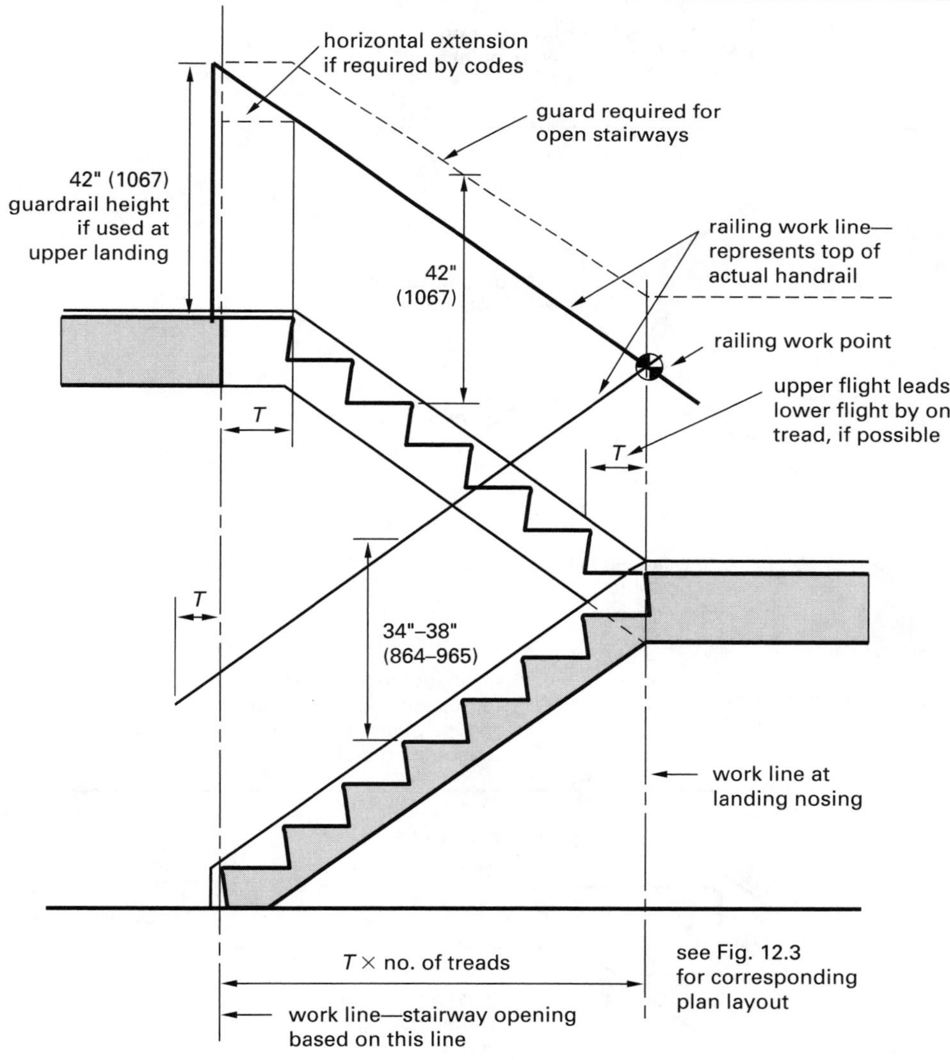


**Figure 12.8**
Return stair vertical layout

**Figure 12.9**
Stair layout at lower floor

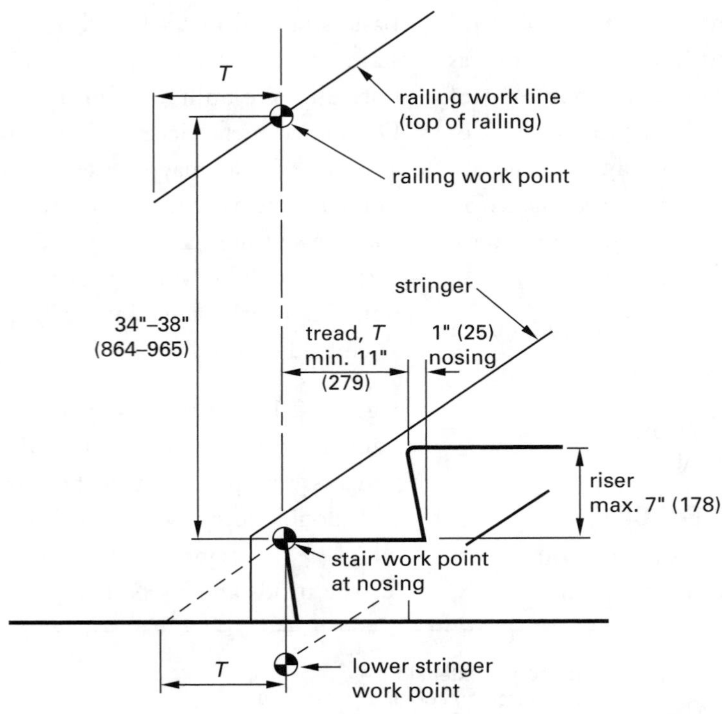


**Figure 12.10**
Stair layout at landing

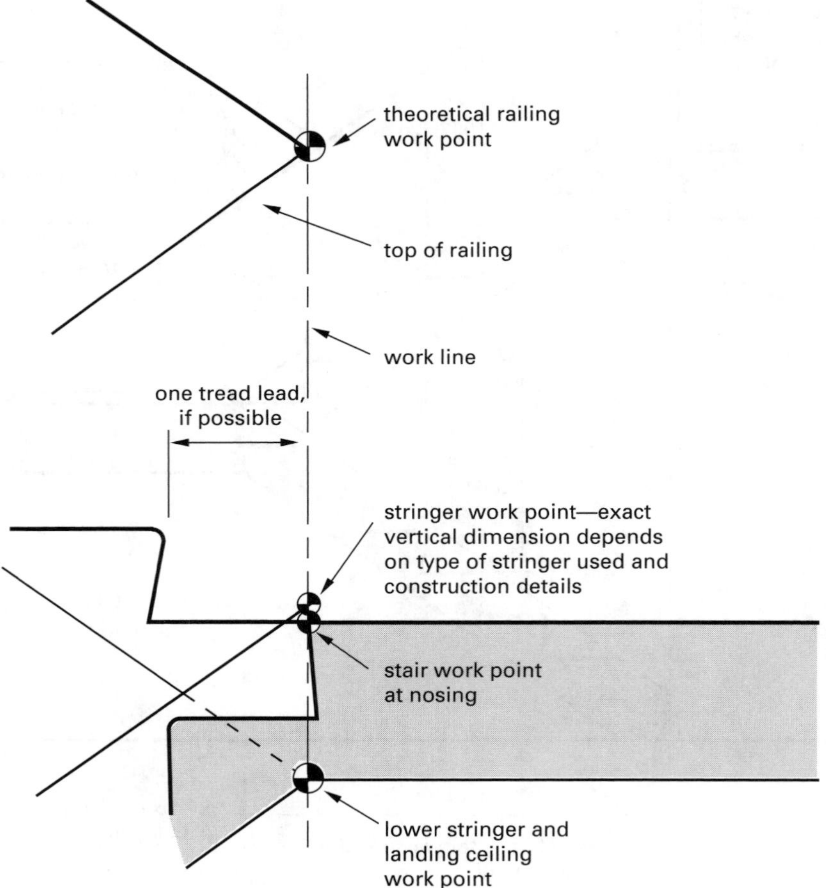

there are usually three carriages, one on each side and one in the center of the stair. If carpeting is used, the treads and risers are finished with plywood or particleboard. If exposed hardwood is used, either the treads can be finished with prebuilt treads with rounded nosings, or strip flooring can be applied over an underlayment of particleboard. Open stairs can have any type of railing and baluster configuration as long as minimum code requirements are satisfied.

## Steel and metal stairs [055100]

Steel stairs are prefabricated assemblies made to fit the dimensions required by the opening in which they are placed. As shown in Fig. 12.13, they are constructed of preformed steel risers and treads welded to a supporting framework of steel channels and angles. For utility stairs, the stringers are normally steel channels with the flanges of the channel on each side pointing away from the stairs. Landings are constructed of steel plate supported on channels and stiffening angles. The treads and landings are filled with 1½ in to 2 in (38 mm to 50 mm) of concrete. Any finish material used is applied over this supporting framework. If the underside of the stair needs to be finished,

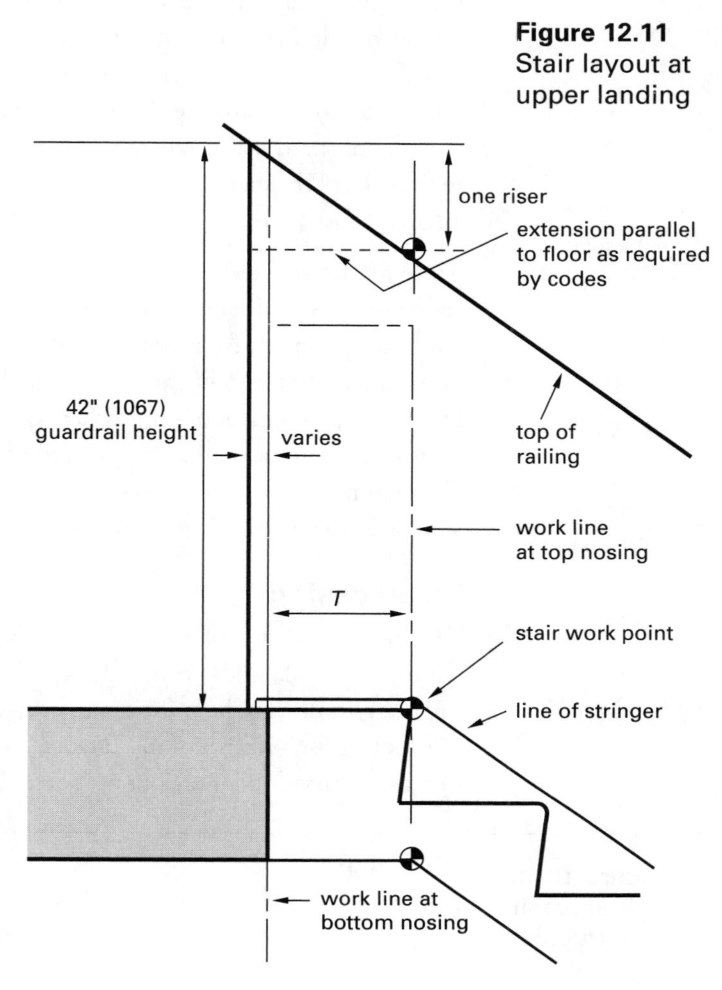


**Figure 12.11**
Stair layout at upper landing

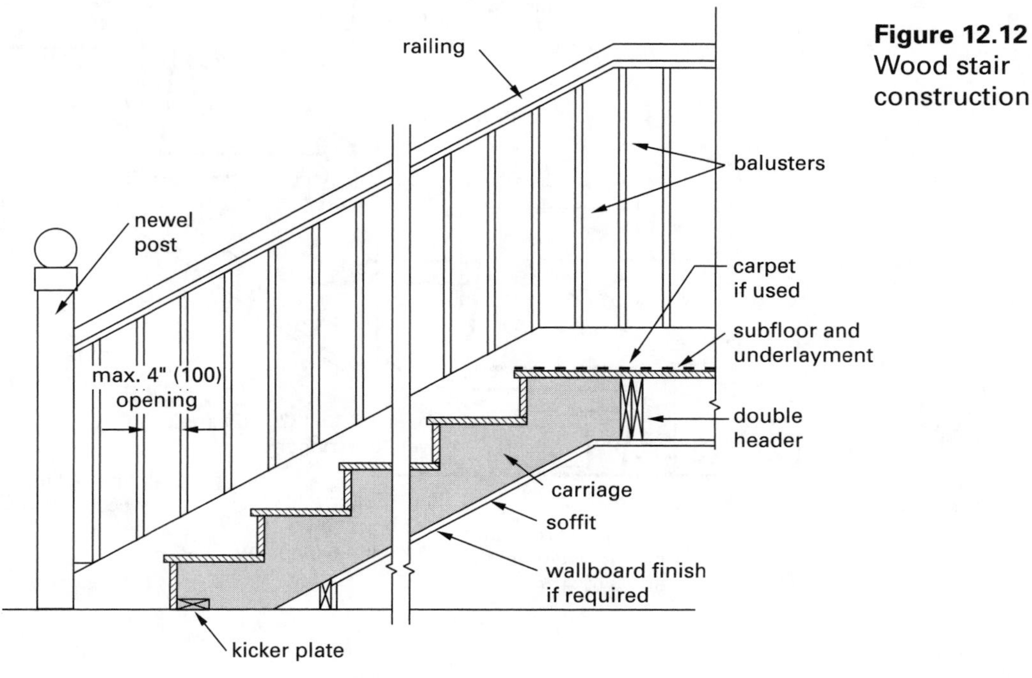


**Figure 12.12**
Wood stair construction

metal studs may be attached to the steel framework and covered with gypsum wallboard or some other material. Balusters and railings of utility stairs are also steel welded to each other and to the stringers or attached to the sides of the stairway opening. See Figs. 12.14(a) and 12.14(b).

More decorative steel or ornamental metal stairs are fabricated using similar techniques. The railing is made from ornamental metal or wood and the railing support can be metal, tempered glass, or some other type of custom-designed assembly. When tempered glass railing supports are specified, a detail similar to that shown in Fig. 12.19 is used.

## Tread design

The important parts of treads include their depth, material, and nosing design. The depth of treads must be sufficient to provide safe footing for both ascending and descending, as discussed in a previous section. The material should be a nonslip surface, but not so rough that feet may be caught on the nosing upon descending. Any nonslip material designed into the nosing should be level with the rest of the tread.

Traditionally, a coefficient of friction of 0.5 or greater has been a widely accepted standard for slip resistance. This number is developed in accordance with ASTM D2047, *Standard Test Method for Static Coefficient of Friction of Polish-Coated Floor Surfaces as Measured by the James Machine.* However, this test method is not applicable for wet surfaces and does not take into account other factors such as the type of shoe material, the type of contaminate on the stair, and the level of the surface. For wet surfaces two other ASTM test methods can be used: ASTM F1679, *Standard Test Method for Using a Variable Incidence Tribometer,* and ASTM F1677, *Standard Test Method for Using a Portable Inclineable Articulated*

**Figure 12.13**
Steel stair construction

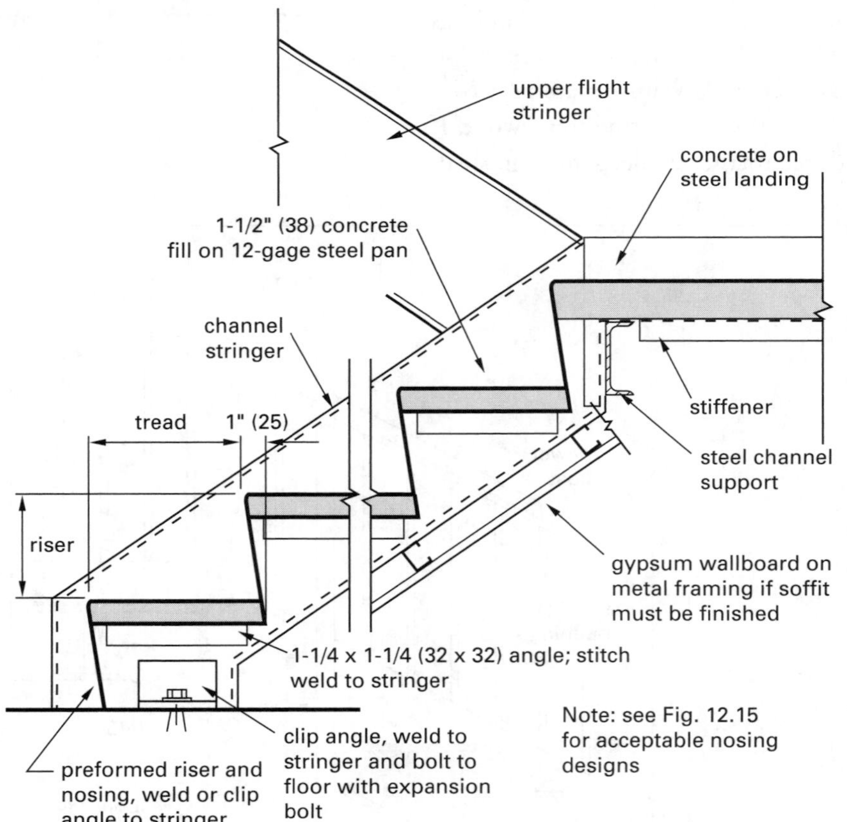

*Strut Slip Tester.* In some cases, a coefficient of 0.6 is a better minimum figure to use on stairways.

Safe and accessible design requires that nosings not be abrupt and have a maximum rounded edge of ½ in (13 mm). Figures 12.15(a)–12.15(c) show three possible nosing designs. Open risers should not be used.

Tread and riser finishes may include carpet, hardwood flooring, vinyl tile, concrete, ceramic tile, terrazzo, glass, special glass block pavers, or exposed steel plate. Ceramic tile and terrazzo stair finishes are illustrated in Figs. 12.16(a) and 12.16(b).

## Handrail design

Handrails are provided in stairways for many purposes: to help a user prevent loss of balance; to maintain stability in case of a

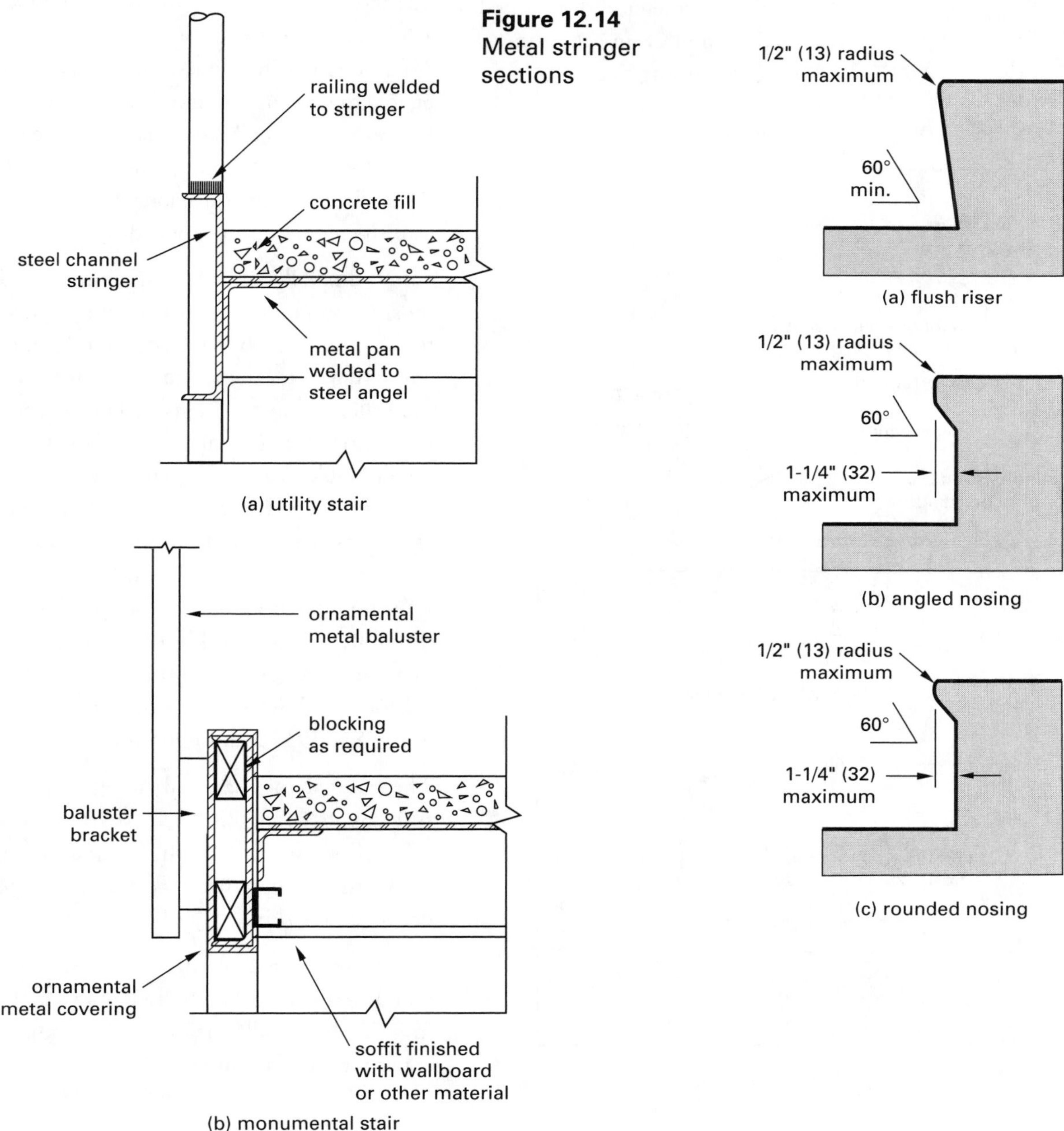


**Figure 12.14** Metal stringer sections

**Figure 12.15** Acceptable nosing shapes for safety and accessibility

fall; to guide people with visual or balance problems; and in some cases to help a user pull himself up when climbing a stair.

Because handrails help reduce the number of accidents and their severity, they are important design elements. Handrails should be designed so that people can both grip them with maximum effect and hold them by friction when pulling up or descending. Studies have shown that a circular shape is best for gripping and a 1½ in (38 mm) diameter is the best size. For children, an additional handrail should be about 1⅛ in to 1¼ in (29 mm to 32 mm) in diameter and mounted 22 in to a maximum of 28 in (560 mm to 710 mm) above the nosing line.

**Figure 12.16**
Ceramic tile and terrazzo stairs

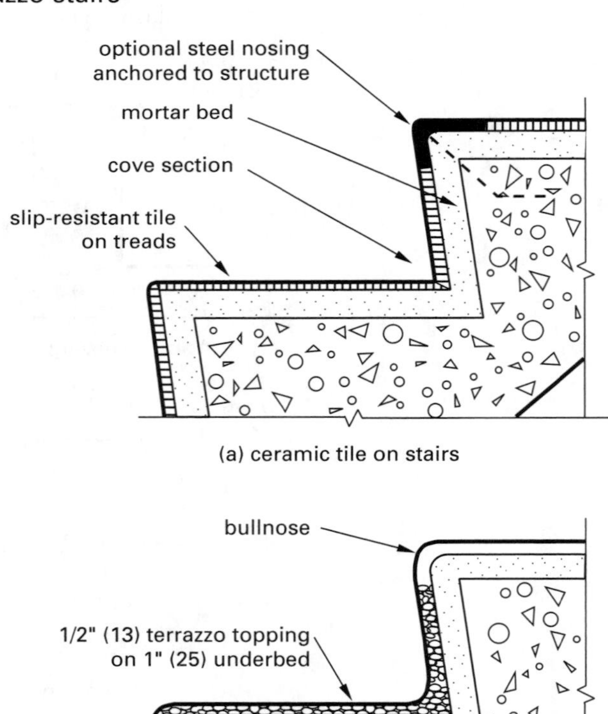


Building and accessibility codes require standard handrails to be mounted from 34 in to 38 in (865 mm to 965 mm) above the nosings. Some research studies have shown that the higher end of the range is best for safety, especially when descending. In open stairs, the International Building Code requires that a separate guard or low wall, in addition to the handrail, be provided at 42 in (1067 mm) above the height of the nosing.

By code there must be a space of at least 1½ in (38 mm) between the wall and the handrail. Some studies have suggested that this should be increased to anywhere from 1.6 in (41 mm) to 2¼ in (57 mm) to over 3½ in (89 mm), to allow sufficient space for people to grip the handrail in case of a slip. However, some codes do not allow a space larger than 1½ in (38 mm), and others limit the total maximum projection of the handrail into the required stairway width.

Combining all the code requirements and most current research, the best compromise for a handrail may be a 1½ in (38 mm) round handrail with a 2 in (51 mm) space between the wall and the rail. This makes the total projection 3½ in (89 mm), which is less than the allowable encroachment into the required exit stairway width. For monumental stairs and stairs that are not a minimum width, the space between the handrail and the wall should be increased, if not specifically prohibited by the local building code. The handrail should be mounted on the higher side of the allowable height range, from 36 in to 38 in (914 mm to 965 mm).

The materials for a handrail should provide a surface with enough coefficient of friction to allow gripping parallel to the handrail, while not being so rough that it would discourage use or abrade skin.

The International Building Code requires that intermediate handrails be within 30 in (762 mm) of all portions of the required egress width of a stairway.

## Building code requirements for handrails

The International Building Code requires handrails to be sized from 1¼ in to 2 in (32 mm to 51 mm) and have a shape that is easily gripped. There must be at least 1½ in between the inside of the handrail and the adjacent surface. Four acceptable designs are shown in Fig. 12.17. Handrails must be located from 34 in to 38 in above the nosing of the stairway. (See Fig. 12.6.) The Americans with Disabilities Act (ADA) also requires that handrails be sized between 1¼ in and 2 in (32 mm and 51 mm).

Because codes require that handrails be securely anchored, the partitions or rails adjacent to handrails should be detailed accordingly. For example, the IBC requires that guards be capable of withstanding a concentrated load of 200 lbm (90 kg) applied in any direction at any point along the handrail. This load is not in addition to the uniform load for guards. Wood stud partitions are usually sufficient to hold handrail brackets if they are attached directly to the studs. For metal stud partitions, solid wood blocking must be provided.

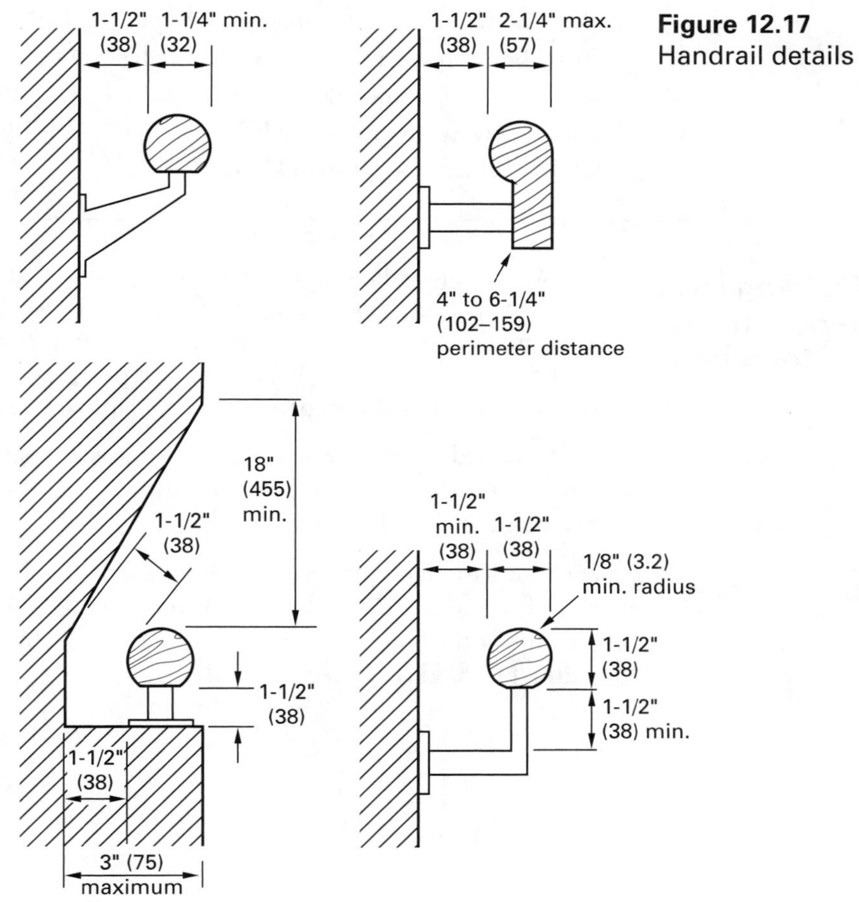


**Figure 12.17**
Handrail details

Note: The IBC requires handrails to have a gripping surface between 1-1/4" and 2" in diameter.
For noncircular cross sections, the perimeter dimension must be between 4 in and 6-1/4 in (102 mm to 160 mm) with a maximum cross-section dimension of 2-1/4 in (57 mm).

## Guard design [055200, 064316, 088100]

Guards protect people from falling into a floor opening. As such, they must be high enough to resist the center of gravity of the majority of people. This minimum height dimension is about 42 in (1067 mm) and is the height required by building codes. Although most codes do not require guards if the fall to the adjacent lower floor level is below a certain distance (30 in in the case of the IBC), even low areas should have guardrails for safety. Even a short fall can be dangerous.

In addition, the top portion of a guardrail should be designed to discourage people from sitting on it, in situations where this might be a likely occurrence. For example, high school students might be likely to sit on a handrail; elderly people would not.

When the space below the guardrail is open, it must be filled in some way to prevent small children from climbing through. Most codes now require a maximum spacing such that a sphere 4 in (102 mm) in diameter cannot pass through the rails. If there is a danger of objects falling off the floor, a toe board should also be provided. Bottom rails near the floor should be avoided if it is likely that people will climb on the rail, thus lowering the effective height of the guardrail.

Guards can be designed in a variety of ways, depending on the structure of the opening, the materials used, and the design style desired. Figure 12.18 shows a typical guardrail with steel balusters and a wood railing. Figure 12.19 illustrates a common method for supporting an ornamental metal rail with a tempered glass panel.

## Building code requirements for guards

Guards are required around unenclosed openings, landings, ramps, and balconies that are more than 30 in (760 mm) above the floor below. Guards must be no lower than 42 in (1067 mm) above the adjacent finished walking surface. A 34 in to 38 in (864 mm to 965 mm) height is allowed for guards in Group R-3 occupancies and interior guards in guest rooms of Group R-2 occupancies if the guards also serve as handrails for a stair.

The intermediate rails or ornamental patterns in open guards must be distanced such that a sphere 4 in (100 mm) in diameter cannot pass through. Refer to IBC Sec. 1013.3 for exceptions to the opening restrictions.

The International Building Code requires that guards be capable of withstanding a uniform load of 50 lbf/ft (0.73 kN/m) applied in any direction at the top and transferred to the structure at the bottom. Guards must also be capable of withstanding a concentrated load of 200 lbf (90 kN) applied in any direction at any point along the top.

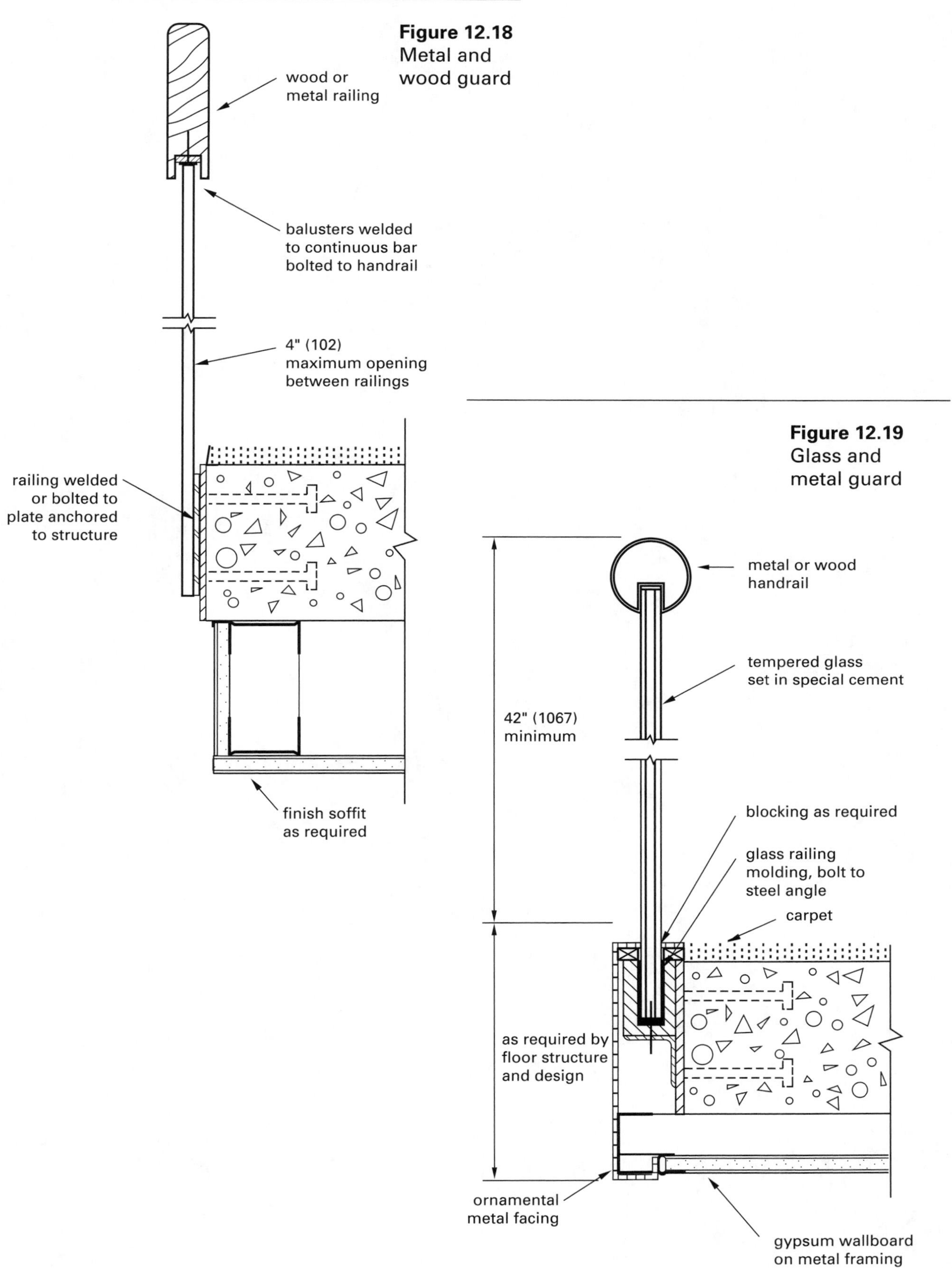


**Figure 12.18**
Metal and wood guard

**Figure 12.19**
Glass and metal guard

# 13

# SIGNAGE SYSTEMS

Signage system design includes planning the types of signs required, determining sign locations, designing and detailing custom signs, and specifying standard manufactured signs. For most commercial projects, a coherent and easily understood signage system is critical for identification, direction, and exiting. This is especially true for large, public buildings where users are not familiar with the layout. A discussion of the theory and implementation of wayfinding and signage system design is beyond the scope of this book. Rather, this chapter includes general information on signage system design that can affect the work of the interior designer or that must be coordinated with the interior construction.

There are many manufacturers that make complete lines of signage, from exterior signs to building directories to individual room plaques. In many instances, purchasing signs directly from a catalog is sufficient. A building owner or individual tenant may even assume the responsibility of providing signs themselves without any assistance from a designer. However, signage should be coordinated with the design and detailing of the space in which it is used, and this is often the responsibility of the interior designer. When custom signs are required or when special construction is needed for built-in signs provided by someone else, the designer must plan and develop appropriate details.

## PLANNING SIGNAGE

The design of a signage system actually begins with space planning and interior design. Space planning, circulation path layout, entry and exit locations, and visual clues and reference points are all critical to a coherent wayfinding and signage system.

A plan with a complicated layout of rooms, corridors, and spaces will require a more extensive system of signage to help people find their way and make sense of a confusing organization of space. In the worst case, no amount of signage may be able to completely overcome a poorly planned layout.

The three-dimensional form of a space and the colors, finishes, and furnishings used in the space can also provide reference points and visual clues to help people orient themselves and identify where they want to go.

The next step after designing a clearly organized space plan is to determine the types of signs required and their locations. There are four basic categories of interior signs: informational, directional, identification, and exit. Informational signs provide the building user with data about the building or space. These include building directories, kiosks, location maps, and how-to-use signs. Directional signs help people find their way around the building or space. Arrows, directional labels, and even stripes on the floor are examples of these signs. Identification signs label individual rooms, spaces, or components of a building, such as room names and numbers, toilet rooms, spaces where telephones are located, and accessible facilities. Exit signage includes the system for identifying the life-safety features of a building. In addition to exit signs, this may include stairway identification, locations of fire extinguishers and fire fighter telephones, and elevator lobby instructional signs.

The type, size, and complexity of the project determines the kinds of signs that are necessary. For example, a single-tenant office space will not need a directory, while a multifloor medical clinic will. A public space needs more directional signage than a private club.

Informational signs should be located where people are most likely to need the information the signs contain. Building directories, for example, should be near the entrances to the building or the elevators. Directional signs should be located where people need to make decisions about which way to go. Identification signs should be on or directly adjacent to the room, space, or element they identify and placed in a consistent relationship with that room, space, or element. For instance, all room names and numbers may be placed adjacent to the strike side of a door jamb. If this is the case, then some signs should not be placed on the door itself.

Next, a consistent method and position of mounting signs should be established. Signs can be mounted in a number of ways, as shown in Figs. 13.1(a)–13.1(d). In each case, once a placement has been established, the position, dimensions, and relationship to other building elements should be maintained so that people know where they can expect to find information.

For example, Fig. 13.2 shows suggested locations for the placement of room identification signs. In most cases it is preferable to place these types of signs within a horizontal band between 4 ft and 4 ft 4 in (1200 mm to 1300 mm) above the floor. This is about eye level for most people and is still easily accessible for children and persons in wheelchairs. Additional identification or information can be placed above the door if required.

Overhead signs are best located either in the center of the circulation path or directly over the room or object they identify. The lowest edge must be at least 80 in (2030 mm) above the floor. Projected signs and free-standing signs must also conform to accessibility guidelines, as described in Ch. 18.

## SIGNAGE MATERIALS [101400]

Almost any material can be used for interior signage because it does not have to resist temperature extremes, weathering, moisture, snow loading, and other abuse that exterior signs are subject to. However, some materials are used more frequently because of their availability, ease of fabrication, and coordination with existing premanufactured sign systems. This section briefly outlines some of the more common materials used.

### Plastics

Plastic is one of the most common materials for interior signage. It is durable, easy to fabricate, relatively inexpensive, can be formed in a variety of ways, and can be colored to produce an almost unlimited variety of sign types. Plastics are used by nearly every sign manufacturer to produce their lines of standard signage systems.

Several types of plastics are available for manufacturing signs; however, only a few

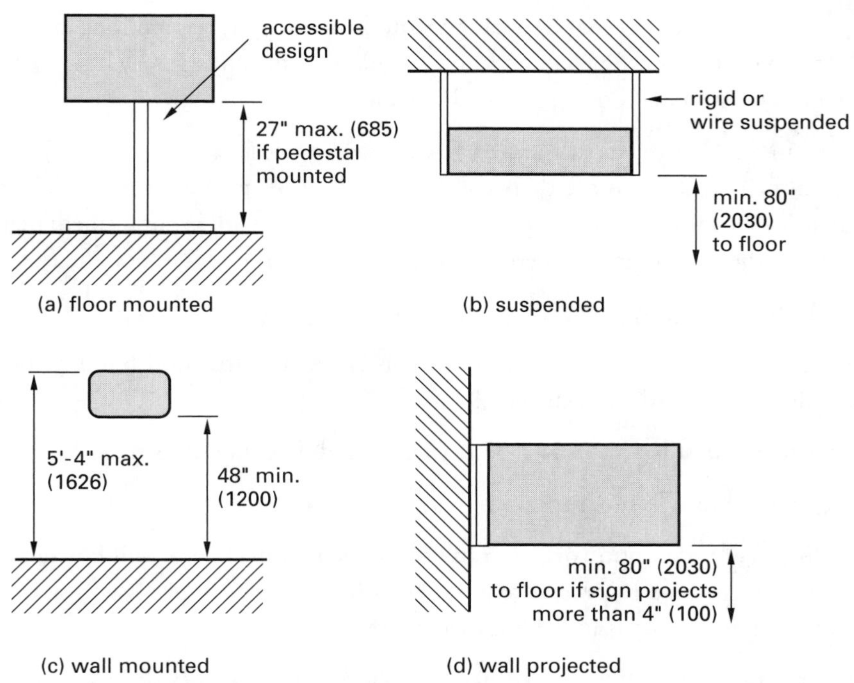


**Figure 13.1**
Sign mounting methods

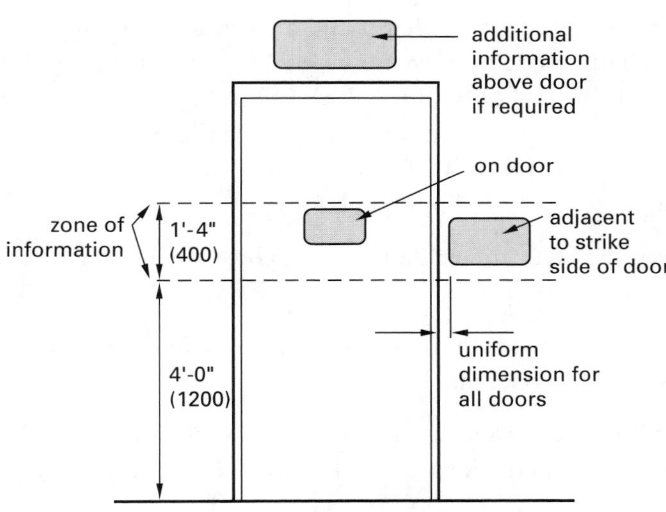


**Figure 13.2**
Placement of room identification signage

are commonly used. These include acrylic, polycarbonate, butyrate, fiber-reinforced polyester, and polyvinyl chloride (PVC).

Acrylic is the most commonly used type of plastic for signage. It is available clear or colored, in opaque or semi-opaque forms. Acrylic is easily formable and can be mounted in a number of ways. It can be scratched easily and will crack and shatter if struck hard enough. One type, called DR, has a higher impact strength than regular acrylic. Acrylics are available in a variety of thicknesses depending on the size of the sign and the rigidity required. Thicknesses of 1/16, 1/8, 3/16, and 1/4 in (1.6, 3, 5, and 6 mm) are common.

Polycarbonate has a very high impact resistance (in thicker, laminated constructions it is used for bullet-resistant glazing) and can be used where vandalism is a problem. Films are available from 0.005 in to 0.025 in (0.127 mm to 0.635 mm) thick, and sheets

## Building code requirements for signage

Most building code requirements referring to interior signage relate to exiting and accessibility. The International Building Code specifies regulations for exit signs, exiting, accessibility, stairway identification, and occupant load posting.

Exit signs must be located at exit and exit access doors and in exit access corridors so that no point in the corridor is more than 100 ft (30 480 m) from the nearest visible exit sign. They must also be located in access to exits where the exit or path is not immediately visible. Exceptions to these provisions, where exit signs are not required, include the following.

- locations where only one exit is required
- main entry doors where the exit is obvious and where the local building official has approved the omission of exit signage
- residences, guest rooms in R-1 occupancies, and dwelling units of R-2 occupancies
- sleeping rooms of I-3 occupancies

The exact number and location of exit signs often depends on the local building department's policy and what the field inspectors require. Usually, signs should be located so that people can always see two exit signs indicating two means of egress.

Exit signs are required to be illuminated and connected to an emergency power supply or be self-luminous and capable of remaining illuminated for a period of not less than 90 minutes.

When egress control devices (those that sound an alarm and do not unlatch for a given time delay) are used on exit doors, there must be an accompanying sign that reads: "PUSH UNTIL ALARM SOUNDS. DOOR CAN BE OPENED IN 15 SECONDS." If a door is permitted to have a key-operated lock from the egress side, it must have a sign that reads: "THIS DOOR TO REMAIN UNLOCKED WHEN BUILDING IS OCCUPIED." The letters in the sign must be 1 in (25 mm) high.

For assembly areas, the occupant load for the room or space must be posted near the main exit or at an exit access doorway.

In addition to the requirements for signage established by the Americans with Disabilities Act (ADA), the IBC has several mandates.

- Doors with access to areas of refuge must have a sign stating "AREA OF REFUGE," in conjunction with the international symbol of accessibility (see Fig. 18.16).
- When exit sign illumination is required, the "AREA OF REFUGE" sign must also be illuminated and a tactile sign complying with ICC/ANSI A117.1 must be provided.
- Exits and elevators not providing accessible means of egress must have signage indicating the locations of such exits.
- Elements such as door, seating, and stairways must have directional signage indicating the route to the nearest like accessible element. The signage must include the international symbol for accessibility.
- Doors to exit stairways must include a tactile sign with both raised letters and braille saying "EXIT."
- In assembly areas there must be a sign notifying the public of the availability of assisted listening devices.

**Building code requirements for signage (continued)**

- The international sign of accessibility is required at areas of refuge; unisex toilets; access to ADA-compliant entrances, dressing rooms, and locker rooms where not all in the building are compliant; and access to rooms where multiple single-user toilet or bathing rooms are clustered in a single location.

For more information on accessible signage, refer to Ch. 18 and to the ADA signage requirements sidebar in this chapter.

are available in thicknesses from 0.030 in to 0.500 in (0.762 mm to 13 mm). Clear polycarbonate is available, as is a limited range of colors.

Butyrate is used for vacuum-formed signs and letters because of its easy formability. It has a high impact resistance; however, it is only available in a limited range of transparent and translucent colors.

Fiber-reinforced polyester is also known as fiberglass. It has high impact strength but shows some graininess because of the glass fibers in the material. It is a durable material and has good light-diffusing properties.

Polyvinyl chloride (PVC) is seldom used for interior signage. Exceptions can be made where extreme moisture resistance is required or where there is no sunlight exposure.

## Metals

Although any type of metal can be used for signage, the most common materials are aluminum, stainless steel, brass, and bronze. Aluminum is lightweight, strong, durable, easily cut, and does not rust. It can be used in thin sheet form as a backing for applied lettering, or letters can be cut out of the sheet, leaving a negative image that can show other materials laminated beneath the aluminum. A cutout aluminum sheet is sometimes used for internally illuminated signs when backed with light-diffusing plastic. Individual letters can also be cut from thicker sheet stock and applied individually on other backing materials. Die stamping, embossing, and engraving can also be done on aluminum. Aluminum is available in natural mill finishes, anodized colors, baked enamel colors, or adhesive films.

Stainless steel can be fabricated in forms similar to aluminum. It can be used in thin sheet form as a backing for applied lettering, or letters can be cut out of the sheet. Stainless steel is also used for individual letters cut from thicker sheet stock, or as enclosures for large signs. In addition, die stamping, embossing, and engraving can be used with stainless steel.

Brass and bronze are most commonly used for either individual cut letters or cast plaques. Brass and bronze for signs are available in many of the alloys discussed in Ch. 7.

## Other materials

Some interior signs are made from adhesive film, photographic film, and direct painting. Other, less frequently used materials include wood, neon, and electronic signs, which are generally employed in special applications rather than for standard identification and directional signage.

### Adhesive films

Adhesive films are thin plastic or vinyl letters and symbols with an adhesive backing. Vinyl letters are die cut on a removable backing sheet. They are applied by removing the backing and placing the letters on a smooth, clean surface. Removable and permanent adhesives are available. Transfer lettering is a less expensive type in which the letters are printed on the back of a carrier sheet and then transferred to a surface by burnishing. These letters are very susceptible to damage

**Figure 13.3**
Photographic film signs

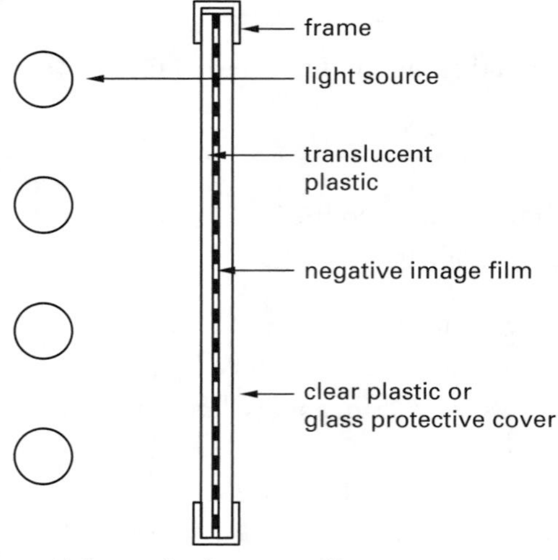


(a) negative image on film

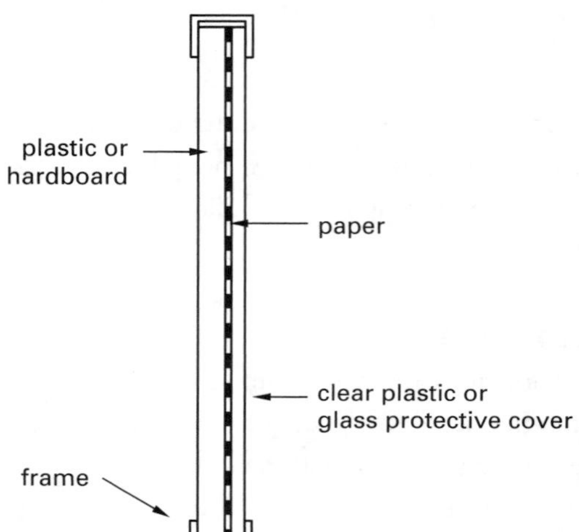


(b) positive image on paper

and must be protected with some type of transparent covering.

## Photographic films

Photographic films are produced by exposing artwork to light-sensitive photographic films and producing either a negative or positive image of the original artwork. The images may be printed on film or paper. Because of the photographic process, extremely accurate enlargements or reductions can be made of the original art. Negative film is often used for internally illuminated signs by sandwiching the negative film image between a clear outer covering of glass or plastic and an inner layer of light-diffusing plastic. See Fig. 13.3(a). Positive images printed on paper must be mounted on some other material, such as plastic, hardboard, or medium-density overlay plywood to keep them flat. See Fig. 13.3(b). For permanent signs, a protective outer covering should be added.

## Electronic signage

Electronic signs are being used more frequently for informational signage. Touch-screen video display units, for example, are used for building directories. These display units allow people to proceed through a menu-driven sequence of displays to find what they need. The displays can be reprogrammed as information changes.

# SIGN CONSTRUCTION [104400]

## Plastic signs

Plastic signs are available in a variety of forms, from simple, engraved plaques adhesively applied to walls, to large, three-dimensional custom fabrications. Most plastic signs for interior use are purchased as part of a manufacturer's standard product line with specific messages imprinted, engraved, or otherwise lettered as required by the job. Signs that need to be changed frequently are printed on inserts that are slipped into grooves on a carrier plaque or applied with a magnetic backing.

Signs are mounted to walls in a variety of ways, depending on the size, weight, and partition material. Several of the most common methods are shown in Figs. 13.4(a)–13.4(f). Small, lightweight signs are mounted with double-face tape, adhesive, or Velcro fasteners. Heavier signs must be mechanically fastened to the partition. The fasteners can be exposed, as shown in Fig. 13.4(d), or concealed. For signs thicker than $^3/_{16}$ in (5 mm), rods are fastened to the wall and fit within predrilled holes in the back of the sign. For very large or heavy signs,

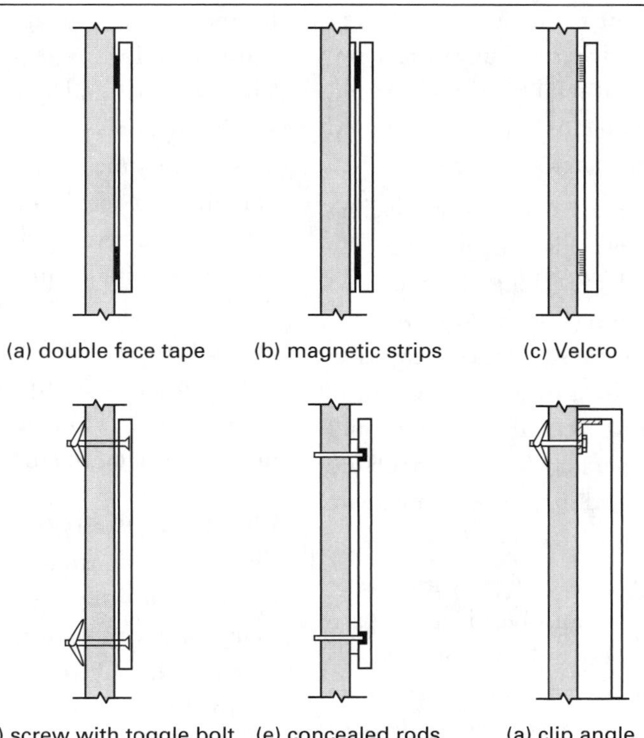


**Figure 13.4** Wall sign mounting methods

## ADA signage requirements

The Americans with Disabilities Act (ADA) requires that certain accessible rooms and features be clearly identified with the symbol for accessibility and that identification, directional, and informational signs meet certain specifications.

Permanent rooms and spaces must be identified with signs having raised lettering from ⅝ in to 2 in (16 mm to 51 mm) high, depending on the viewing distance and the height above the floor. Lettering must be uppercase, in sans serif or simple serif type, accompanied with Grade 2 braille. If pictograms are used, they must be at least 6 in (150 mm) high and accompanied by the equivalent verbal description placed directly below. Signs must be eggshell matte or use some other nonglare finish, and characters should contrast with their background. Permanent identification signs must be mounted on the wall adjacent to the latch side of the door such that there is a minimum clear floor space of 18 in by 18 in (455 mm by 455 mm) centered on the tactile characters and beyond the arc of the door swing. Mounting height to the baseline of the lowest tactile character must be 48 in (1220 mm) minimum and 60 in (1525 mm) maximum to the baseline of the highest tactile character.

Directional and informational signs must have lettering from ⅝ in to 3 in (16 mm to 75 mm) high, depending on the viewing distance and the height above the floor. Contrast and finish requirements are the same as for permanent room identification. Lettering can be uppercase or lowercase.

The international symbol for accessibility is required on parking spaces, passenger loading zones, accessible entrances, and toilet and bathing facilities when not all are accessible. Building directories and temporary signs do not have to comply with the requirements. In addition, the international telecommunications devices for the deaf (TDD) symbol is required to identify text telephones and volume control telephones. In assembly areas, permanently installed assistive listening systems must have the international symbol of access for hearing loss.

For more information and diagrams, see Ch. 18 and the building code requirements sidebar in this chapter. Verify additional requirements with the ADA Accessibility Guidelines (ADAAG).

separate hanger angles may have to be bolted to the partition and the sign hung from them. If necessary, metal stud partitions should have wood blocking installed so that a rigid attachment of the angles can be made.

Overhead signs are fastened to the ceiling with bolts or screws. Lightweight signs may be bolted through the ceiling tile or screwed directly to the ceiling grid. Heavy, overhead signs attached to a suspended acoustical ceiling may require a backing plate resting on the ceiling grid. Very heavy signs should be suspended separately from the structure above with threaded rods or other adequate support.

When detailing custom signs with plastic components, there must be adequate space for the plastic to expand and contract. Although interior temperature extremes are not great, large plastic panels need room to move.

## Metal signs

Custom metal signs can be fabricated in an unlimited number of ways. Lightweight metal signs are mounted using the same methods shown in Figs. 13.4(a)–13.4(f). For very large metal signs or plastic signs with a structural metal framework, such as wall-suspended signs, additional steel support may be required. Free-standing floor-mounted signs may need to be fastened to steel plates bolted into the structural floor.

**Figure 13.5** Metal letter mounting

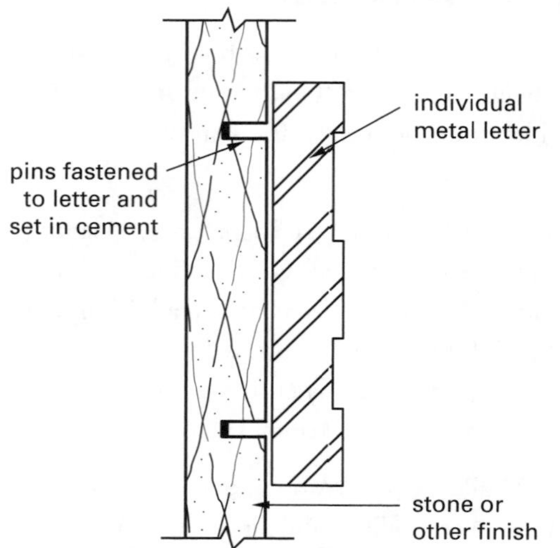


For most interior signage, metal signs usually consist of individual letters or symbols. If the letters are small and lightweight, they can be adhesively applied directly to the partition finish. Heavy metal letters have pins welded, brazed, or soldered to their backs. The letters are then cemented to the partition by setting the pins in predrilled holes in the finish material. See Fig. 13.5. This mounting method works well for applying letters or cast bronze plaques to hard materials, such as stone or tile. However, changing the sign means replacing the finish as well.

## Illuminated signs

Illuminated signs are used when ambient lighting is insufficient to provide clear visibility of a sign or when special emphasis is required. Signs can be lit in two ways: internally or externally. Internally illuminated signs either profile the letter forms with a bright background or show the letter forms themselves as bright against a dark background. In most cases, the letter forms and other symbols are cut out of other materials, such as metal or opaque plastic, and light shines through a translucent plastic face covering the cutout areas. Fluorescent lamps are typically used because they provide even illumination and are not as hot as other sources.

In order to achieve even illumination, the lamps must be placed a sufficient distance behind the sign face. See Fig. 13.6. This distance should be a minimum of 4 in (100 mm), and more if possible. The spacing between lamps should ideally be no more than the distance from the lamps to the sign face.

Illuminated signs must be ventilated and detailed and must be mounted so that lamps can be replaced and other routine maintenance can be performed. The interior designer must coordinate the location of the sign with the electrical engineer so that adequate power is available at the point required by the sign manufacturer.

Externally illuminated signs use ambient light, dedicated spotlights, or other light sources to provide highlighting. These signs are easier to fabricate and maintain than internally illuminated signs. In addition, the colors of signs illuminated from the exterior are usually truer than those of internally illuminated signs. However, if more than normal ambient light is required, a special fixture needs to be dedicated for the sign, and a clear line of sight should be maintained for uniform illumination. External lighting must be carefully designed to prevent glare, which can make it difficult, or even impossible, to read the sign.

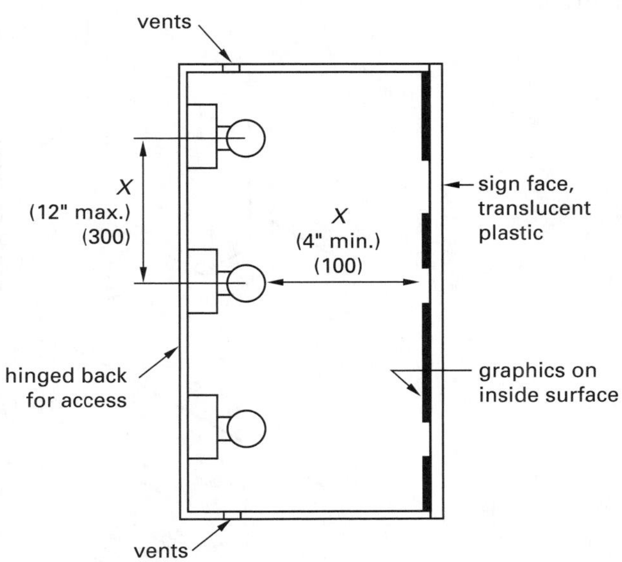


**Figure 13.6** Guidelines for internally illuminated signs

## SIGN TYPES

### Informational signs [101300]

The most common types of interior informational signs are building directories and floor directories. Building directories provide the names and locations of companies within a building and sometimes the names of people within each company. Floor directories provide the names and locations of offices or spaces on a specific floor or within a particular area on the floor.

Building or floor directories may be mounted flat on a wall, cantilevered from a wall, freestanding, or recessed into a wall. See Figs. 13.7(a)–13.7(d). In any case, adequate space must be provided in front of the sign so that people can refer to it without blocking other circulation or interfering with the required exit width. There must also be sufficient space for changing names, replacing lights, cleaning, and other maintenance.

Internally illuminated directories or those that use cathode ray tubes, such as touchscreen directories, need power and ventilation. They also must be mounted at a comfortable height.

### Directional signs [101400]

Because directional signs are so common to commercial interiors, a design should be planned to accommodate the variety of signs that are usually required. Directional signs are typically required at the entrance to a building or use area, at elevator lobbies and stairs, and at decision points in the circulation system. Several may be required at each point. Figures 13.8(a)–13.8(c) show the ideal locations for wall-mounted directional signage in some common plan configurations. Overhead signs can be used in some instances, but they still have to provide directions when viewed from any position and must have adequate clearance below.

### Identification signs [101400]

Identification signs must be placed on or near the room or object they identify. Room signs should be placed in a consistent location, as shown previously in Fig. 13.2. Signs identifying open areas or counters may need to be suspended or floor mounted when there is no partition for direct attachment. Identification signage is usually a combination of permanent signs, such as those identifying rest rooms, and temporary signs, such as those giving the name of an office occupant. As with directional signage, identification signage may require varied

**Figure 13.7**
Building or floor directory installations

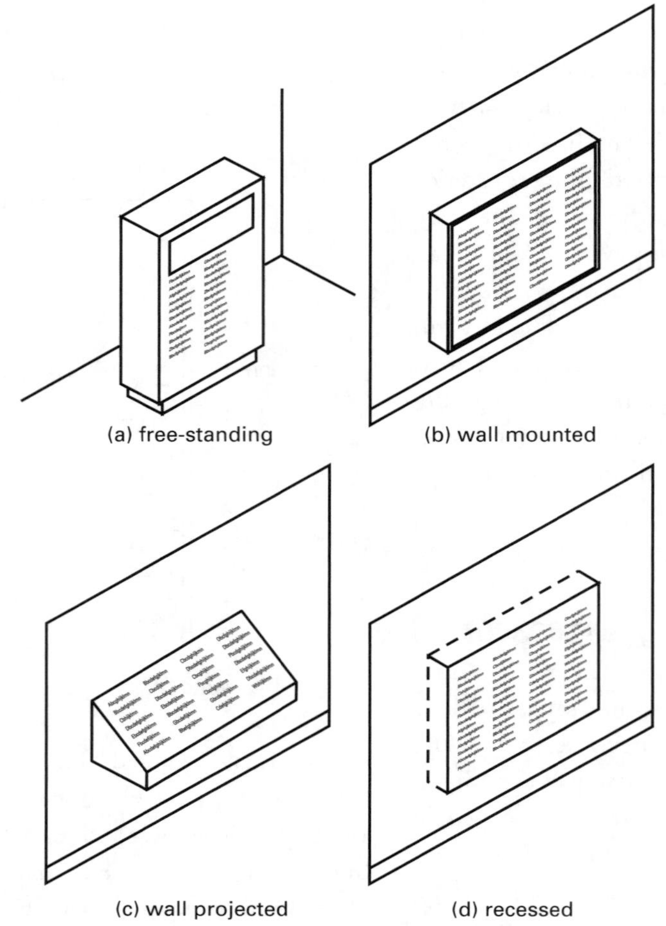


**Figure 13.8**
Preferred locations of corridor signs

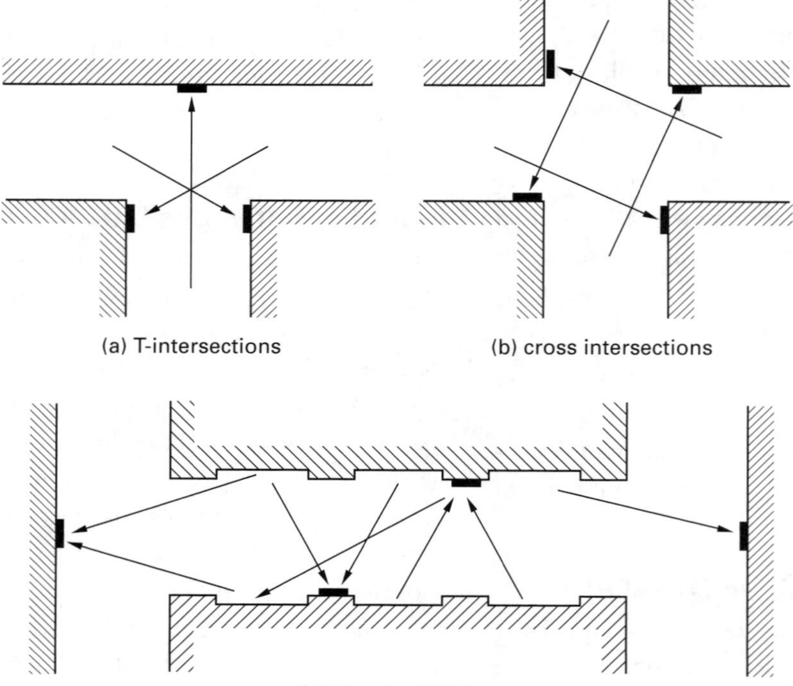

amounts of information on different signs. This need is usually accommodated by using a modular system of sign sizes mounted in a uniform position, as shown in Fig. 13.9, so that all signs are coordinated in their size, shape, and placement.

## Exit signs [101400, 265300]

The requirements for exit signs are determined by the applicable building code; however, the designer does have some choice of mounting styles and finishes. For example, an exit sign can be ceiling mounted or wall mounted, as long as its location satisfies the building code and provides sufficient headroom clearance. Figures 13.10(a)–13.10(d) illustrate some of the typical installation types and methods, and manufacturer's catalogs show specific types and styles.

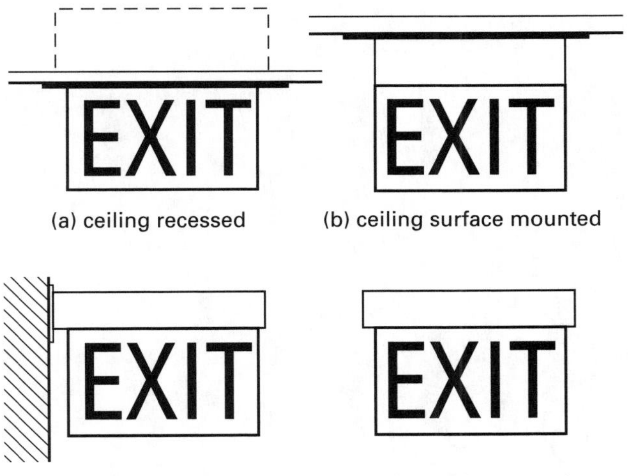

## Coordination with other design and construction features

Although a signage system may be developed by a signage company or graphic designer, the interior designer must coordinate design and construction features with the signage needs. These include the following.

- During initial space planning, keep circulation paths and room layouts as direct as possible to minimize the reliance on directional signs.

- Space planning and circulation paths should include distinct identifying landmarks so that people can get their bearings by using the landmarks in addition to referring to signage.

- Partitions must have sufficiently thick details when necessary, to accommodate recessed directories or other large, recessed signs.

- Wood blocking must be provided in metal stud partitions to facilitate the mounting of large or heavy signs. Extra bracing above suspended ceilings may also be required for suspended signs.

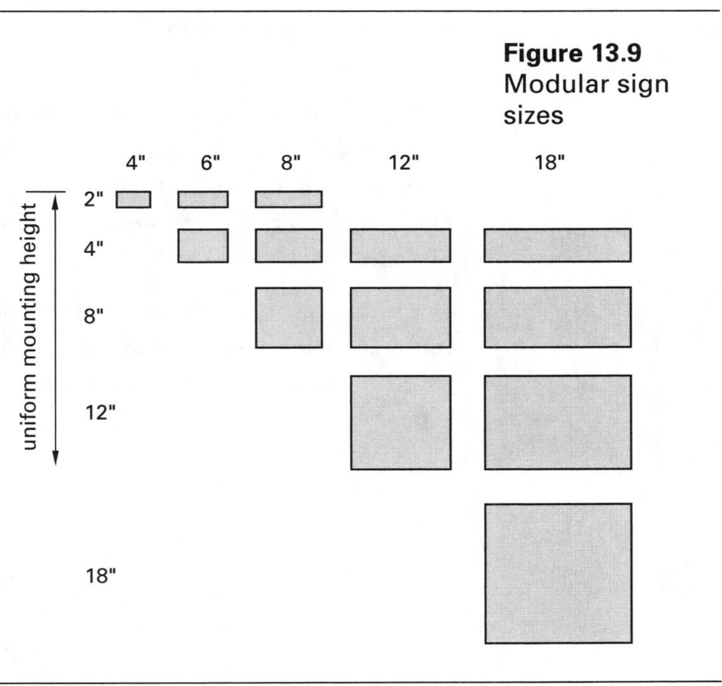


**Figure 13.9**
Modular sign sizes

**Figure 13.10**
Exit signs

EXIT
(a) ceiling recessed

EXIT
(b) ceiling surface mounted

EXIT
(c) wall projected

EXIT
(d) flat wall mounted

- No other fixtures, finishes, or furnishings (such as plants, furniture, or HVAC equipment) should be planned that might interfere with sign visibility.

- Extra space in front of a sign should be provided if it includes a tactile map for the blind.

- Light switches, thermostats, and other wall-mounted devices and equipment should be planned so that they do not interfere with standard locations for signage.

• Partition finishes should be specified and detailed in such a way that it is not impossible to mount signs. For example, fabric wallcovering may prevent adhesion of double-stick tape.

• Adequate space, power, and telecommunication lines must be provided for TDDs (telecommunications devices for the deaf) if they are used.

• The power supply for illuminated and electronic signs must be adequate for the requirements of the specified sign.

• Lighting must be controlled to avoid glare while still providing enough light for visibility, including that required for the elderly and visually impaired. In addition, ambient light should not conflict with illuminated signs.

# 14

# SECURITY SYSTEMS

Security is required for any type of interior design project. It may be as simple as a front door lock for a residence or as complex and sophisticated as a combination of physical barriers and an electronic surveillance, detection, and control system for a bank. Clients are demanding more security for their projects; therefore, interior designers must be aware of the types of systems and equipment that are available along with the kinds of coordination and support they, as designers, must provide. Common security problems include residential and commercial burglary, employee pilferage, vandalism, sabotage or theft of company records and property, confinement of prisoners, protection of personnel, safety and confinement in psychiatric wards, abduction, and in extreme instances, terrorism. Full security analysis, design of systems, and specification of equipment is beyond the scope of this book and must be performed by a knowledgeable security consultant or specialized vendor of security equipment. This chapter briefly outlines some of the basics of security planning for projects with low-level security needs and describes the typical areas where an interior designer must coordinate with the security specialist working on the job.

The interior designer should be a part of the team involved with security planning and specification. Depending on the complexity of the project, this team may include the building architect, a security consultant, equipment vendors, the client, the electrical engineer, and others. Lack of coordination and involvement on the part of the interior designer usually results in the security equipment appearing as though it were installed as an afterthought, without regard for the other materials and finishes. In some cases, poor coordination can result in additional construction time and costs for the client.

## SPACE PLANNING FOR SECURITY

Good security begins with a clear definition of the problem. Part of the programming document must include a clear statement by the client concerning the level of security required and a list of the potential threats. For some clients, such as large corporations and banks, security requirements are usually well defined. For others, such as small retail stores and offices, the client may not have given much thought to security beyond basic locks. The designer should raise the question and help these clients define security needs and possible responses. If the security problem is complex, the designer may suggest that a security specialist be included on the project team.

Good security involves physical as well as electronic barriers. The physical layout and construction of a space can have a profound effect on fundamental security as well as on how easy or difficult it is to plan and install monitoring and access devices.

During space planning, rooms, areas, and circulation paths should be designed to take advantage of proximity, line of sight, and location. Proximity refers to the location of one space near another. Line of sight allows either human or electronic surveillance of a given area. Location refers to where secure areas are planned in relation to the building perimeter, services, and other rooms. The following guidelines should be reviewed.

- Locate spaces together that have similar security requirements. This makes it easier to enclose the area with physical barriers, such as partitions and doors, provide monitoring, and minimize the number of electronic devices needed to control the area. This can reduce both construction complexity and costs.

- Plan for permanently stationed personnel to be in a central location with a clear line of sight to as many secure areas as possible. These may be security guards or other staff, such as secretaries, clerks, and nurses. This makes visual surveillance easier and can reduce the number and cost of electronic monitoring devices.

- Locate personnel at entries and other control points as a backup to locks and other electronic access and monitoring control devices.

- If required, lay out spaces and circulation to provide a clear line of sight for electronic surveillance, such as cameras and photoelectric, microwave, or infrared detection.

- Locate sensitive areas, such as computer rooms and private conference rooms, away from windows and the building's perimeter.

- If secure areas require service, locate them near separate entrances or the service elevator so that separation from public access can be maintained and travel distance is minimized.

- Plan for security areas to be near existing secure walls. These may be a building's concrete core wall or masonry walls. This can minimize construction costs if special, high-security partitions need to be built.

In addition to these basic space planning guidelines, a separate room may be required for a security control center. The size of the control center depends on the complexity of the building. A control center may be integrated with equipment for monitoring and controlling fire detection and suppression, mechanical systems, and communications systems. For small installations, the security equipment may be installed at the guard's desk or at a central control station. Large areas near entrances may also be required for X-ray or magnetic screening devices. In these instances, the client's security consultant will provide the required dimensions for space planning.

## SECURITY EQUIPMENT

In addition to physical barriers, security systems include methods for preventing entry, detecting intruders, controlling access to secure areas, and notifying security personnel or authorities in the event of unauthorized entry or other emergencies. The types of hardware and electronic devices used depend on the nature of the threat, the level of security desired, and the amount of money that can be devoted to the system. This section outlines some of the more common devices with which designers should be familiar.

## Intrusion detection [281600]

Security derived from intrusion detection devices can be classified into three types: perimeter protection, area or room protection, and object protection.

### Perimeter protection

Perimeter protection secures the entry points to a space or building. These include doors, windows, and skylights, and can also include ducts, tunnels, and other service entrances. Some of the more common types of perimeter protection include the following.

- Magnetic contacts. These are used on doors and windows to either sound an alarm when the contact is broken (the door or window is opened) or send a signal to a central monitoring and control station. These can be surface mounted, recessed into the door and frame, or concealed in special hinges. The hinges may only be available in certain sizes and finishes; therefore, the other hardware used on the job must be coordinated with them.

- Glass break detectors. These sense when a window has been broken or cut either by using metallic foil or with a small vibration detector mounted on the glass.

- Window screens. These screens have fine wires embedded in them that can be used to set off an alarm when they are cut or broken.

- Photoelectric cells. These cells detect when a beam of light has been broken, either by a door opening or by someone passing through an opening. These can be surface mounted but are more secure and look better if provisions are made to recess them in the partition or other construction.

### Area or room protection

Area or room protection devices sense when someone is in a room or an area within the field of coverage. These devices have the advantage of warning of unauthorized entry when perimeter sensors have not been activated. Area intrusion devices include the following.

- Photoelectric beams. These devices warn of intrusion by sending a pulsed infrared beam across a space. If the beam is broken the device either sounds an alarm or sends a signal to a monitoring station. Photoelectric beams can be focused in both large and small areas. The equipment is small and usually can be recessed or concealed.

- Infrared detectors. These detectors sense sources of infrared radiation, such as the human body, compared with the normal room radiation. They are unobtrusive but must have a clear field of view of the area they are protecting.

- Audio detectors. These detectors listen for unusual sounds in a space at levels above what is normally encountered. When that level is exceeded, an alarm is sounded. Microphones can also be used to continuously monitor all sounds in a space through a speaker at a central monitoring station.

- Pressure sensors. These sensors detect weight on a floor or other surface. Sensor mats can be separate fixtures laid over the existing floor finish or placed under carpet or other building materials.

- Ultrasonic detectors. These detectors emit a very high-frequency sound wave. When this is interrupted by an intruder, an alarm signal is activated. The range of ultrasonic detectors is limited to a space about 12 ft (3.7 m) high and 20 ft by 30 ft in area (6.1 m by 9.1 m).

- Microwave detectors. These detectors sense interruptions in the field of microwave radiation that they emit. Their use is limited in interior construction, however, because the microwave radiation can penetrate most building materials and can be reflected by metal.

### Object protection

Object protection is used to sense movement or tampering with individual objects, such as safes, artwork, file cabinets, or other equipment. Capacitance proximity detectors detect when metal objects are touched. Vibration detectors sense a disturbance of the object. Infrared motion detectors determine if the space around an object is violated.

### Electronic surveillance

Electronic surveillance is the interception of sound and electromagnetic signals with remote sensing devices. For example, with readily obtainable, relatively inexpensive technology it is possible to listen in on conversations from outside a building or pick up signals being emitted from a computer screen at a remote distance. For organizations that require security from this type of intrusion, special rooms are required that have electromagnetic or radio frequency shielding.

Sensitive government installations have used such shielding for some time. It is just recently that many companies are realizing they must protect themselves from corporate espionage as well as from other types of theft.

The basic principle behind electronic shielding involves building a "cage" of continuously conductive material that catches signals and conducts them to the ground. The type of cage depends on the amount of protection required and the bandwidth that must be shielded. The rating of protection is measured in decibels (dB) of attenuation. Many government and military facilities are designed for 100 dB attenuation across a broad bandwidth of signals. Theoretically, this level provides 100% protection. However, this level of protection requires heavy steel plate and expensive special construction. For most corporate needs, an attenuation of 60 dB stops more than 99.9% of the electronic signals coming from office computers and other sources.

To achieve acceptable levels of protection for most corporate uses, there are several products available. Copper foils can be used, but these are difficult to install and require soldered connections. There is also nonwoven fabric that is covered with an electronically conductive metallic coating. As with copper foil, this is placed behind the finished wall surface so it is not obtrusive. Other types of fabric material are also available as is metallic shielding paint. For windows, fine metal screens can be used, but special shielded glass is also available that looks like normal glass. Doors designed for radio frequency or electromagnetic shielding are also required. In addition to the conductive cage, filters must be provided for electrical, telephone, and computer cabling where they penetrate the shielding membrane.

In most cases, detailing rooms protected from electronic surveillance is straightforward and unobtrusive, but a security expert should be consulted for specific product specifications and detailing requirements.

## Access control [281300]

### Access control devices

Access to secure areas can be controlled with a number of devices. The simplest is the traditional mechanical lock. The various types of locksets are described in Ch. 4. High-security locksets are available that provide an additional level of security through the use of key types that are difficult to duplicate, special tumbler mechanisms, and long-throw dead bolts. There are also interlocking dead bolts that secure the door bolt to the strike so that the door jamb cannot be spread to disengage the bolt from the frame. To prevent knobs or lever handles from being torqued apart or otherwise opened by brute force or jimmying, most lock manufacturers provide security strikes, cover plates, cylinder guards, and other devices to make it more difficult to open a locked door.

Because access and duplication of keys can be a problem even for the most secure mechanical lock, various types of electronic locks are available. Not only can these selectively control access better than keys, but they can monitor who enters and exits a door and record the date and time of the access.

Card readers are common electronic access control devices. A plastic card containing a coded magnetic strip is used to unlock the door. Card readers can be connected to a central monitoring computer that keeps a log of which person's card was used to open which door and when that door was opened. The computer can be programmed to allow only certain cards to operate certain doors. Operation can be further limited to specific hours during the day and specific days of the week. If a card is lost or stolen, its access code can be quickly and easily removed from the system.

In most instances, card readers are mounted on the partition adjacent to the door. Proximity readers are also available that can be completely concealed behind a wall to prevent tampering and minimize the visual

## Ballistic threat levels

The security industry uses standard methods of referring to and specifying construction designed to resist ballistic attack. There are several test methods that use standard firearms and ammunition to test and rate products and construction assemblies, such as glazing and doors. Because not every installation requires the same amount of protection, it is useful to be aware of these standard protection levels so that construction is not over- or under-specified. Manufacturers of security equipment for interior construction refer to these protection levels in their literature. It is also good to be aware of the terms that clients and security consultants may use.

One of the most common standards is Underwriters Laboratories' ANSI/UL 752, *Standard for Safety for Bullet-Resisting Equipment*, which sets eight ballistic threat levels (from lowest to highest or UL-Level 1 to UL-Level 8, respectively). Construction can be listed based on what threat level it provides protection from. Ballistic threat Level 1, for example, provides protection from a 9 mm by 19 mm Parabellum round fired from a semi-automatic pistol with a 5 in barrel fired at a velocity of 1175 ft/sec. Ballistic threat Level 8 provides protection from a 7.62 mm NATO round fired from a combat rifle at a velocity of 2750 ft/sec.

Another common standard is the *Test Procedure for Transparent Materials for Use in Forced Entry or Containment Barriers* (HPW-TP-0500.02), developed by H. P. White Laboratory, Inc. This standard uses two test protocols: one to simulate ballistic attack and one to simulate forced entry. For the ballistic attack test, five threat levels are defined from A to E. A material designed to resist a threat Level A attack must pass a test that uses three shots of a .38 special bullet. Threat Level E must resist three shots of a .30-06 round.

A standard developed for the National Institute of Justice (NIJ Std. 0108.01) is more rigorous in the types of ballistics it uses. This standard defines six types of ballistic-resistant protective materials: Type I, Type II-A, Type II, Type III-A, Type III, and Type IV. Type I materials must protect against the standard round test using a .38 special and similar bullets. Type IV materials, at the extreme end of the scale, must protect against a standard test using a .30-06 round or an armor-piercing round.

Similar types of performance requirements have also been established by the U.S. Department of Defense, U.S. Department of State, and the Naval Civil Engineering Laboratory. The Naval Civil Engineering Laboratory, for example, has classifications for higher ballistic threats, including small arms multiple-impact threat (SAMIT) and small arms multiple-impact threat armor piercing (SAMITAP).

Specifics on the various standards and threat classification levels are listed later in this chapter.

impact of the reader. The user simply has to place the card near the reader for it to operate. Some readers will sense the card in a person's wallet or purse when it is within a few feet of the device.

Numbered keyboards operate in the same way by unlocking a door when the user enters the correct numerical code. However, numbered keyboards do not provide the same flexibility as magnetic cards. Numbered keypads can also be purchased integrated with a knob or lever handle. These are not connected to a central station, but do eliminate the problem with key control of standard locksets.

A variation on the magnetic card reader is the punched card access system used by many hotels. The key code can be changed each time a new person checks into a room; therefore, a previous occupant cannot copy or reuse a key.

New biometric devices are now available that can read individual biological features, such as the retina of the eye or a hand print, providing a counterfeit-proof method of identification. Although expensive, these devices are feasible when a very high level of security is required. Work is continuing on developing commercially available devices that can recognize voice prints and fingerprints.

### Locking mechanisms

Card readers and other devices control the operation of one of several types of locking mechanisms. One type is the electric lock, which retracts the bolt when activated from the secure side of the door. Unlatching from the inside is by a button or switch or by mechanical retraction of the bolt with the lever handle. Electric locks require an electric hinge or other power-transfer device to carry the low-voltage wiring from the control device to the door and then to the lock.

Electric strikes are also used. These replace the standard door strike and consist of a movable mechanism that is mortised into the frame. The latch bolt is fixed from the secure side of the door. On activation the electric strike retracts, allowing the door to be opened. On the inside, the latch bolt can be retracted by mechanical means with the lever handle.

Electric bolts are available that drop into a mortised fitting in the top or side of a door. On activation the bolt retracts, allowing normal operation of the door. A fail-safe feature retracts the bolt if there is a power failure or on activation of a fire alarm. Electric bolts are limited to use on nonexit doors because most building codes now require electronically controlled exit doors to be operable from the inside by purely mechanical means.

Doors can also be secured with electromagnetic locks. When activated, the lock holds the door closed with a powerful magnetic force. Card readers, keypads, buttons, or other devices deactivate the electromagnet. These can be designed to open on activation of a fire alarm or power failure.

### Notification systems [281600]

When intrusion is detected, an alarm signal is triggered. This signal can activate an alarm, such as a bell or horn, turn on lights, alert an attendant at a central control station, or be relayed over phone lines to a central security service. Combinations of all three notifications are also possible. If an office building has a central station, a building tenant may be able to connect special lease-space security with the central station. When a central station is notified, the alarms are automatically recorded in the system.

## DETAILING REQUIREMENTS

Interior construction design and detailing typically interfaces with security systems in four areas: physical barriers, such as partitions, doors, and glazing; hardware; millwork enclosures for security equipment; and miscellaneous support for wall- and ceiling-mounted equipment.

## Partitions

Standard interior partition, door, and glazing construction provide very little protection from someone determined to break into a building or room or from ballistic attack. For most interior projects, standard construction is used with intrusion alarms to discourage and impede unauthorized entry and to notify someone at a central monitoring station. If a higher level of security is required, gypsum wallboard partitions may need to be reinforced, or other partition types may need to be constructed. These are often reinforced and protected gypsum wallboard partitions, reinforced plaster, reinforced masonry, or concrete. Some common types of security partitions are shown in Figs. 14.1(a)–14.1(d).

If the threat is from ballistic attack rather than physical break in, ballistic armor can be used. This is a fiberglass-reinforced composite material available in rigid sheets like plywood. It is available in thicknesses from ¼ in to ½ in (6 mm to 12 mm). It is easily cut and applied to studs and can be covered with plastic laminate, wood veneer, vinyl wall covering, or wallpaper, or simply painted.

Very high-security partitions, such as vault enclosures, are beyond the scope of this

**Figure 14.1**
Security partitions

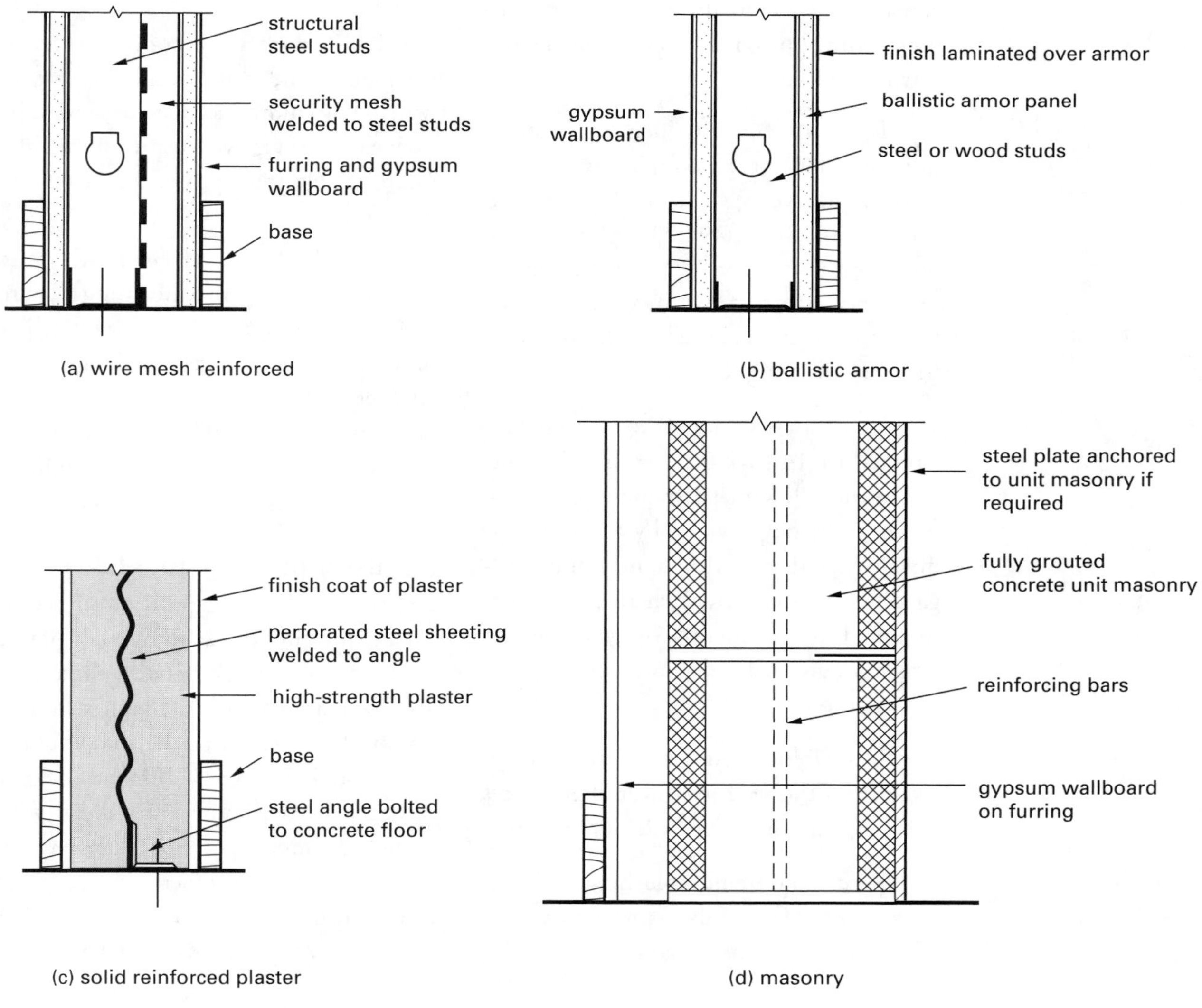

(a) wire mesh reinforced



(b) ballistic armor



(c) solid reinforced plaster



(d) masonry

book and are not typically encountered on most interior design projects. Regardless of what type of partition is constructed, it should be backed up with adequate intrusion alarms.

## Security doors [083453]

Doors are one of the weakest points in security construction. This is because they have several vulnerable components including the door itself, the attachment of the door to the frame, the frame, and the hardware. Any of these components can be compromised to gain entry. Although methods for detailing and specifying very high-security doors are beyond the scope of this chapter, the following suggestions can be used to increase the security of interior doors for most common applications. The construction of the door should be combined with appropriate access controls and intrusion alarms.

- For low-security residential construction, use solid core wood doors with heavy wood frames securely anchored to the partition. Mortise locksets with long-throw dead bolts (minimum 1 in [25 mm]) should be used that latch to a reinforced strike plate that is securely anchored to the partition framing with long screws.

- Moderate-security doors can be constructed of 14-gage steel with 2 in wide (51 mm) hollow metal frames. Additional security can be provided by using hollow metal steel doors with a minimum 12-gage face, with internal channel stiffeners mounted in a frame of 16-gage or heavier steel, fully grouted and securely anchored to the partition.

- If possible, plan doors so that they open away from the security threat. This places the hinges on the secure side of the door.

- Specify nonremovable hinge pins or hinges with safety studs to prevent removal of the door from the hinge side.

- Avoid the use of glazing. If necessary, use small lights of laminated glass or polycarbonate.

- Doors with electric locks or other types of electrical devices on the door leaf require a power-transfer connection. Security power transfers are mortised into the frame and hinge edge of the door and are only visible when the door is opened. A flexible, pivoting mechanism within the mortised enclosure boxes allows the door to be operated freely. Electric hinges are also available that completely conceal the wiring, even when the door is open.

- If louvers are required, they should be steel reinforced and covered with a strong wire mesh. Most manufacturers provide security louvers as part of their standard product line.

- For high-security doors, the locking mechanism and strike should be protected with ⅛ in (3 mm) steel plate to prevent jimmying and prying. Most hardware manufacturers supply these protective plates when specified.

- Most building codes require that exit doors be operable from the inside by purely mechanical motion without any reliance on electronics or power. There are electric latchsets and panic hardware devices that can be connected to a building's security system to serve as access control with monitoring signals while still allowing emergency exit.

## Security glazing [085653]

Depending on the application, security glazing for interior use must resist physical attack, ballistic attack, or both. Glazing may also be required to resist high winds and bomb blasts, which are beyond the scope of this book. There is a difference between physical-attack-resistant and bullet-resistant glazing. Laminated glass can prevent some small arms fire from penetrating, but can be broken through with various tools. Other types of glazing can resist both ballistic and forced-entry attack. As with any security design, the expected level of attack must be defined before the appropriate materials can be specified and detailed.

Security glazing includes many types of materials and products, depending on the level of security required. These include standard laminated glass, polycarbonate glazing, polycarbonate layered with glass, and polycarbonate and acrylic. Laminating materials include polyvinyl butyral (PVB), polyethylene, polyurethane, and polyvinyl films in several thicknesses.

The security industry uses several test standards and procedures to evaluate the effectiveness of glazing and other products to protect against attack. Three of these include ASTM F1233, *Standard Test Method for Security Glazing Materials and Systems*; UL 752, *Standard for Safety for Bullet-Resisting Equipment*; and HPW-TP-0500.02, *Test Procedure, Transparent Materials for Use in Forced-Entry or Containment Barriers*. The ASTM F1233 and HPW-TP-0500.02 standards include tests for both forced-entry and ballistic attack, while the UL 752 standard is limited to ballistic attack. During the forced-entry tests, both blunt instruments (such as sledgehammers) and sharp-impact weapons are used. The glazing is also subjected to thermal stress and chemical agents.

For theft-resistant glazing, many options are available. For storefronts and display cases that must resist simple "smash-and-grab" attacks, two plies of 1/8 in (3 mm) thick laminated glazing with a PVB interlayer may be sufficient. It takes at least one minute of loud, hard effort to break through this type of 1/4 in (6 mm) laminated-glass lite. A 1/2 in (13 mm) thick laminated glass lite may resist dozens of strikes with a sledgehammer before it is breached, outlasting an 8 in thick concrete block wall.

When additional strength and resistance to prolonged break-in attack are required, polycarbonate glazing should be used. This is

---

**Applicable standards for security glazing and doors**

**American Society for Testing and Materials (ASTM):**

| | |
|---|---|
| ASTM F476 | *Standard Test Methods for Security of Swinging Door Assemblies* |
| ASTM F571 | *Standard Practice for Installation of Exit Devices in Security Areas* |
| ASTM F588 | *Standard Test Methods for Measuring the Forced-Entry Resistance of Window Assemblies, Excluding Glazing Impact* |
| ASTM F1029 | *Guide for Selection of Physical Security Measures for a Facility* |
| ASTM F1233 | *Standard Test Method for Security Glazing Materials and Systems* |

**H.P. White Laboratory, Inc.:**

| | |
|---|---|
| HPW-TP-0500.02 | *Test Procedure, Transparent Materials for Use in Forced-Entry or Containment Barriers* |

**National Institute for Justice (NIJ):**

| | |
|---|---|
| NIJ Std. 0108.01 | *Ballistic-Resistant Protective Materials* |

**Underwriters Laboratories (UL):**

| | |
|---|---|
| UL 752 | *Standard for Safety for Bullet-Resisting Equipment* |
| UL 972 | *Burglary-Resisting Glazing Material* |
| UL 1034 | *Burglary-Resistant Electric Locking Machines* |

**U.S. Department of State**, standards SD-STD-01.01 and SD-STD-01.02

polycarbonate plastic sandwiched between outer protective layers of annealed, heat-strengthened, or tempered glass. The exact thickness and lamination construction depends on the degree of attack resistance required.

For ballistic-resistant glazing, there are three categories of materials.

- *All-glass security glazing.* This category is standard laminated glass that uses multiple layers of glass with PVB interlayers. This is the most affordable type of security glazing that can withstand lower levels of ballistic attack as well as common smash-and-grab attacks.
- *Glass-clad polycarbonates.* This category uses polycarbonate material with outer layers of glass that provide abrasion resistance as well as heat and chemical resistance. This type of glazing is more expensive than all-glass systems but can withstand higher levels of ballistic attack.
- *Laminated polycarbonates.* This category of glazing uses polycarbonate material with polyurethane interlayers. It prevents particles from flying off on the protected side of the glazing.

As with attack-resistant glazing, the expected threat level must be determined using one of the available standards, most commonly UL 752, ASTM F1233, or HPW-TP-0500.02. At a minimum, UL Level 3 should be specified. This will protect against an attack from a .44 magnum weapon. A security or glazing expert should be consulted to establish the correct threat level and help design the glazing installation.

The exact thickness and lamination construction depends on the size of the ballistic threat and the degree of attack resistance required, but ranges from about 1 in to 3 in (25 mm to 76 mm). This must be accommodated in the framing and partition detailing. In addition, the surrounding partition must have at least an equal amount of resistance. It does little good to have a high-security door or piece of glazing in a partition that can easily be broken through. See Fig. 14.2 for common security glazing details. Refer to manufacturers' literature and security consultants for more information and construction details.

Framed glass doors can also be fabricated with polycarbonate glazing.

**Figure 14.2**
Security glazing

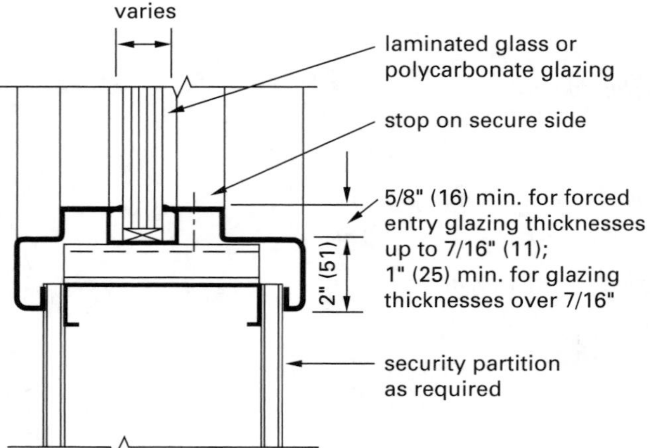


## Other detailing requirements

Additional areas of coordination required between interior construction and security systems design include hardware specification, millwork design, and support for recessed or surface-mounted equipment.

Because specialized security hardware often is not available in as many styles and finishes as standard hardware, the security types may dictate what styles and finishes are used in the remainder of a room or space, or on an entire project. Consultation with the client, architect, and security consultant should begin as soon as possible so that informed choices can be made as detailed interior design is progressing.

Millwork design for guard stations, security rooms, and equipment enclosures depends on the exact type, size, and weight of the equipment to be accommodated. This information is available from the equipment vendors or the security consultant. When the interior designer is the prime design consultant, the designer is usually the person who coordinates the millwork design with equipment requirements, client needs, and the work of the electrical consultant.

The type of physical support required for equipment also depends on the nature of the security system. The interior designer may need to show on the design drawings items such as blocking in partitions; hangers and support framing above ceilings; built-in enclosures in partitions and millwork; and precisely dimensioned openings for cameras, monitors, and other security equipment.

## COORDINATION WITH ELECTRICAL AND SIGNAL SYSTEMS

Although the security consultant, equipment vendor, electrical engineering consultant, and contractor are responsible for designing and installing security systems and the power they need to operate, the interior designer is often the person who must coordinate the efforts of these team members so that their work fits within the overall interior design and construction of the project. In most cases this involves making sure necessary information is transmitted between the members of the team and that all required data and details are shown on the final set of drawings. It also requires that the interior designer design and detail portions of the construction to accommodate the security equipment. Some of the important elements of electrical and signal system coordination include the following.

- Lighting required for surveillance and deterrence should be compatible with the general ambient lighting whenever possible.

- The closed circuit television (CCTV) vendor needs to know what type of lighting will be used to select the best type of camera tube. Conversely, the electrical engineer may need to provide a particular type of lighting for specific types of cameras.

- The interior designer must provide adequate space and support for video cameras, monitors, access devices, and control equipment. The electrical engineer needs to design power supply to these devices as well.

- Speakers may be required for public address and communication within secured areas and near doors. These should be coordinated with the other elements of the designer's reflected ceiling plan or partition detailing.

- Conduit must be shown on the electrical consultant's drawings to accommodate signal system wiring for remote-controlled locks, CCTV, and other security equipment.

- Power transfers for doors should be specified to meet the necessary level of security, but should be concealed whenever possible.

15

# DESIGNING FOR AUDIOVISUAL SPACES

Electronic display technology, including digital television, computer projection, and digital signage, is becoming a ubiquitous sight in all aspects of life. The technology is found in homes, conference rooms, training facilities, classrooms, building lobbies, entertainment venues, shopping centers, and elsewhere. As a result, the spaces in which these systems are used are becoming a more important part of interior design than ever before. The technology should be designed into spaces, rather than forced in as an afterthought.

This chapter provides basic guidelines for space planning and the design of rooms used for common types of audiovisual (AV) systems in commercial projects. However, this does not include the design of large auditoriums, nor does this chapter cover the specifics of equipment selection, acoustical and speaker design, wiring, or preparing AV presentations. If a project requires a sophisticated AV system, an AV consultant should be part of the design team. The technology is constantly changing as most presentation and display methods move to digital format from the former analog formats of slides and film.

## DISPLAY DEVICES [115200]

Because planning for an audiovisual room or other space depends greatly on the type of display or projector used, a basic understanding of the available equipment is important. This equipment includes digital displays, digital projectors, and projection screens.

Depending on the source, there are a variety of size formats, which must be known before detailed space planning can begin. These are summarized in Table 15.1.

### Digital displays

For small displays there are three types of display screens: the older cathode ray tube monitors, liquid crystal display screens, and plasma screens.

*Cathode ray tube* monitors (CRTs) are less expensive than liquid crystal display and plasma screens, and reproduce video well with good contrast and brightness. However, they are bulky and heavy. CRTs are increasingly being replaced by flat-panel displays, which are needed for widescreen television and motion picture formats.

**Table 15.1** Common projection formats

| | aspect ratios | | to calculate one factor if another is known | | | |
|---|---|---|---|---|---|---|
| source type | format designation ($W$:$H$) | ratio based on unit height | to find $D$ if $H$ is known | to find $D$ if $W$ is known | to find $H$ if $D$ is known | to find $W$ if $D$ is known |
| square slides, overheads | 1:1 | 1:1 | $H \times 1.41$ | $W \times 1.41$ | $D \times 0.707$ | $D \times 0.707$ |
| data graphics | 5:4 | 1.25:1 | $H \times 1.60$ | $W \times 1.28$ | $D \times 0.625$ | $D \times 0.781$ |
| standard television (NTSC) | 4:3 | 1.33:1 | $H \times 1.67$ | $W \times 1.25$ | $D \times 0.600$ | $D \times 0.800$ |
| horizontal 35 mm slides | 3:2 | 1.5:1 | $H \times 1.80$ | $W \times 1.20$ | $D \times 0.555$ | $D \times 0.832$ |
| HDTV | 16:9 | 1.78:1 | $H \times 2.04$ | $W \times 1.15$ | $D \times 0.490$ | $D \times 0.871$ |
| widescreen | 1.85:1 | 1.85:1 | $H \times 2.10$ | $W \times 1.14$ | $D \times 0.476$ | $D \times 0.881$ |
| CinemaScope® | 2.35:1 | 2.35:1 | $H \times 2.55$ | $W \times 1.09$ | $D \times 0.392$ | $D \times 0.920$ |

$W$ = screen width, $H$ = screen height, $D$ = screen diagonal

*Liquid crystal display* (LCD) screens have traditionally been better at showing more static displays of data, but newer models are available with faster refresh rates, making them about as good as plasma screens for fast-moving video. LCD screens also provide good viewing brightness in rooms with ambient light.

LCDs are generally not available in the larger sizes of plasma screens; common sizes range from 30 in to 45 in (762 mm to 1143 mm), although some larger sizes are available. As the technology develops, larger screen sizes will become available at lower costs.

*Plasma displays* are excellent for replicating the rich appearance of large-format film and are often used for full-motion widescreen video as well as for continuously moving computer text and graphics. Brightness and contrast are excellent under ideal conditions (no ambient light).

Plasma screens are available in common sizes of 42 in and 50 in (1067 mm and 1270 mm) up to about 63 in (1600 mm), but are more expensive than LCD screens. As the technology develops, larger screen sizes will become available but may be limited due to the difficulty of producing the glass required. Plasma screens are also heavier, run hotter, use more power, are more fragile, and are a little more difficult to install than LCD screens. Image burn—the retention of a ghost of an image that is left static on the screen for too long—can be more of a problem with plasma screens.

## Digital projectors

In addition to the older, three-lens CRT projectors, there are three main types of digital projection systems for normal business and commercial use: liquid crystal display, digital light processing, and liquid crystal on silicon.

*Liquid crystal display* (LCD) projectors have three separate glass panels—one each for red, green, and blue—through which light passes. Individual pixels can be controlled to allow different amounts of light through each screen, resulting in the final image. LCD projectors are a good choice for computer images.

*Digital light processing* (DLP) projectors are sometimes referred to as digital micromirror devices (DMDs). DLP projectors work by projecting light onto a DLP chip. This chip uses thousands of tiny mirrors to modulate the light going through the lens. Each mirror represents a single pixel. DLP technology provides a very high contrast ratio and less space between pixels, resulting in a smoother image. DLP is a good choice for projecting DVDs and VHS tapes.

*Liquid crystal on silicon* (LCOS) projectors use technology from both LCDs and DLPs. Liquid crystals applied to a mirrored surface open and close in response to the video signal, causing light to be reflected or blocked. This modulation of light creates the image. Currently, LCOS projectors are not as commonly used as LCD or DLP technology.

Brightness is an important factor for all projectors. A brighter projector allows a higher level of ambient light, which is good for classrooms, conference rooms, and public areas where light is required for note taking or other activities. Brightness is measured in lumens and ranges from 1000 to over 12,000 lumens. A common range is from 2000 to 4000 lumens for use in conference rooms. Portable units range from 1000 to 2000 lumens. If a room has exterior windows and the projector will have a low brightness, adjustable window coverings will be required.

Most digital projectors are provided with zoom lenses and many are available with a variety of lens types so placement within the room is not as critical as with CRT projectors. When permanent installation is required, even projectors without zoom lenses can be mounted from the ceiling at the correct distance from the screen. Most have built-in keystone correction, so that the projector can be mounted off center from the screen (near the ceiling, for example) and still provide an undistorted image. Some projectors have special mirror arrangements that allow the projector to be placed very close to the screen. For example, one manufacturer produces a unit that can project a 40 in (1016 mm) wide image while only 2.5 in (64 mm) from the screen. It can project a 100 in (2540 mm) image from less than 26 in (660 mm) away.

Projectors are available in a range of resolutions. Generally, higher resolutions result in sharper projected images. The resolution of the projector should match the resolution of the device driving it, whether that device is a computer, DVD player, or other source. However, most projectors have built-in compression and expansion software for automatic scaling between different resolutions. Table 15.2 shows some of the available resolutions.

In addition to affecting the sharpness and general appearance of the projected image, the projector resolution also affects the ideal viewing distances, as is described in the next section.

## Projection screens

Projection screens are available in a variety of types and sizes. To plan an AV room, the designer must know the size of the screen and the type of screen material to be used. Some screen materials, such as fiberglass matte white, diffuse light in all directions so the image can be seen from any angle up to about 60°. As shown in Fig. 15.1, this angle is measured from the initial angle of reflection and determines the ideal cutoff point for the position of viewers close to the screen.

While fiberglass matte white screens provide a wide viewing angle and enable more seating, they require projection sources with high brightness and control of ambient light. Other types of screens, such as glass beaded, reflect light better within a narrower range, often as small as 25° to 30°. These screens are better for situations with higher ambient light or less bright projection sources.

Screens are available in fixed configuration, motorized, manual pull-down, flat, and

**Table 15.2** Digital projector resolutions (in pixels)

| resolution | 4:3 aspect ratio | 16:9 aspect ratio | remarks |
|---|---|---|---|
| VGA | 640 × 480 | 854 × 480 | a WVGA is available for widescreen format; has been largely replaced by SVGA and higher resolution projectors |
| SVGA | 800 × 600 | 1024 × 576 | minimum required for PowerPoint®; a WSVGA is available for widescreen format |
| XGA | 1024 × 768 | | common resolution for portables and most common for general use; minimum required for video |
| WXGA | | 1366 × 768 | widescreen counterpart to XGA |
| SXGA | 1280 × 1024 | | used for critical graphic presentations; minimum for high-resolution graphics |
| SXGA+ | 1400 × 1050 | | |
| HD2 | | 1280 × 720 | |
| HDTV | | 1920 × 1080 | |
| UXGA | 1600 × 1200 | | |
| QXGA | 2048 × 1536 | | |
| QSXGA | 2560 × 2048 | | |

curved. Curved screens can improve the visibility for occupants of the front corner seats. Curved screens generally have a radius of one to two times the distance from the screen to the farthest viewer.

The size of the screen should match the aspect ratio of the projection media. The aspect ratio is the ratio of the length of an image to its height. These are shown in Table 15.1. The most common aspect ratios are 4:3 for standard television and computer projection and 16:9 for HDTV. If several types of media will be used, the screen size and shape should be planned for all types expected to be used. Black masking systems are available that can frame various aspect ratios as required.

## PLANNING GUIDELINES

Planning for AV spaces requires balancing several variables, including seating requirements, room size and shape, ceiling height, projection distance and method (front vs. rear), type of projection media, projection resolution, screen size and type, viewing angles, and seating layout.

In some cases, the existing physical limitations of the building and space planning dictate the basic size and shape of the AV space. In other cases, the client's audiovisual requirements, equipment, and audience size will be known in advance and the room configuration may be determined based on these criteria.

In most situations, the client's program defines the type of projection medium that will be used, the purpose of the presentations, and the size of the audience. The size and shape of the room, screen size, and specific equipment are then based on those parameters.

### Front projection guidelines

For most front projection methods, there are some common planning guidelines

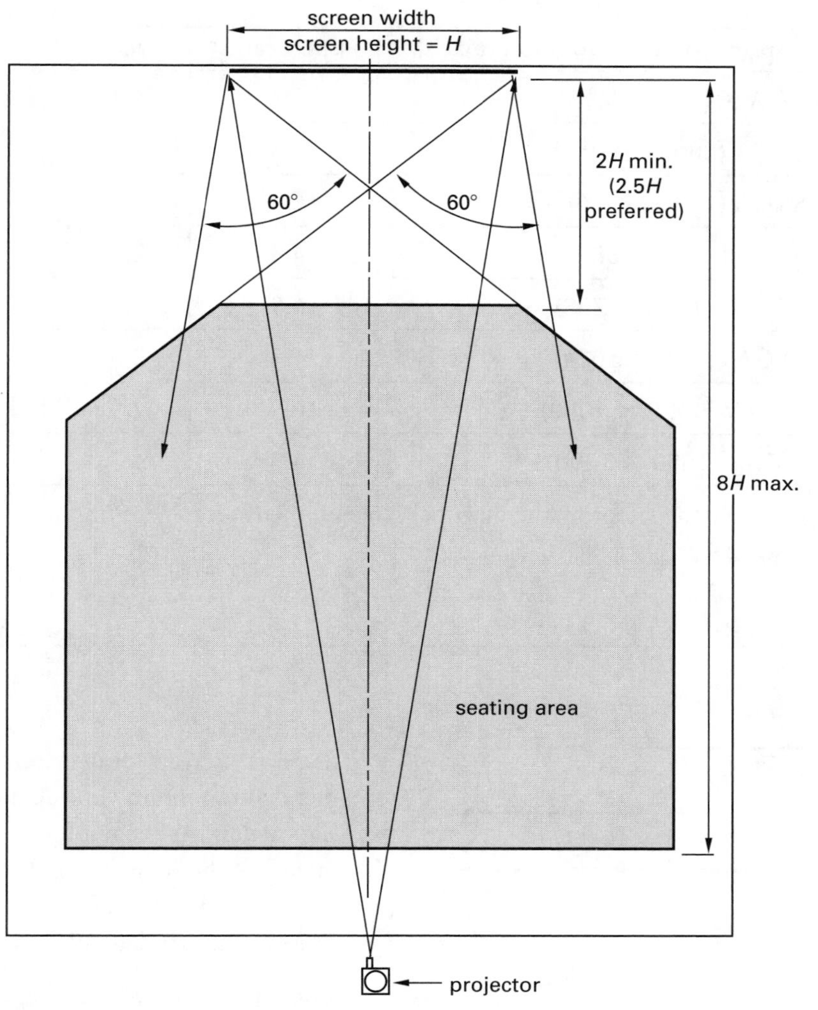


**Figure 15.1**
Seating guidelines for front projection

for arranging seating in relationship to the screen. These are illustrated in Fig. 15.1, and include guidelines for the closest viewer, the farthest viewer, and the angle of view of the screen. Guidelines for vertical dimensions are shown in Fig. 15.2.

Commonly used rules of thumb suggest that the closest viewer be no closer than two times the screen height. Two and a half times is preferred, but this is not always possible when space is limited.

However, these rules of thumb are based on larger screen sizes and older projection techniques and resolutions, such as occur with slide projection, motion pictures, and low-resolution video projection. For higher resolution computer monitors and television displays up to about 60 in (1524 mm)

**Figure 15.2**
Vertical screen dimension guidelines

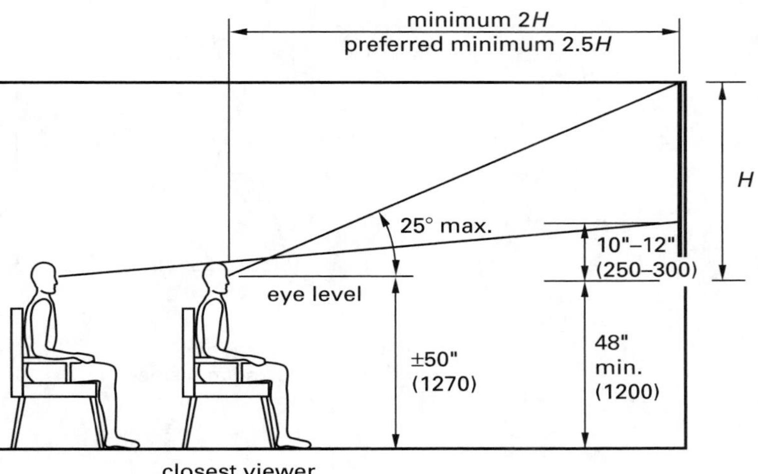

**Table 15.3** Factors for determining minimum viewing distances based on screen resolution

| display type and resolution (pixels) | aspect ratio | factor |
|---|---|---|
| VGA (640 × 480) | 4:3 | 4.3 |
| SVGA (800 × 600) | 4:3 | 3.45 |
| SVGA (1024 × 576) | 16:9 | 3.45 |
| XGA (1024 × 768) | 4:3 | 2.66 |
| WXGA (1366 × 768) | 16:9 | 2.66 |
| SXGA (1280 × 1024) | 4:3 | 2.0 |
| HDTV (1920 × 1080) | 16:9 | 1.9 |
| UXGA (1600 × 1200) | 4:3 | 1.7 |

Multiply the factor by the diagonal screen dimension to get minimum distance.

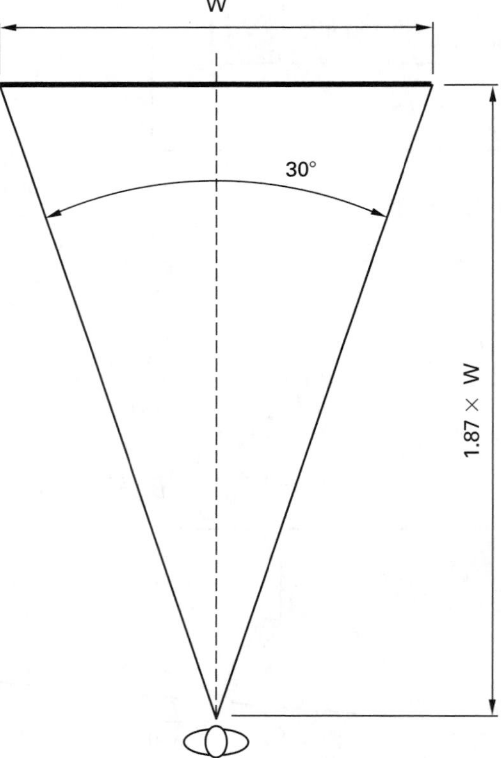


**Figure 15.3** Closest viewer based on minimum eye and head movement

diagonal screen dimension, the recommended minimum viewing dimensions are slightly less. As the resolution of the screen increases, the suggested minimum viewing dimension decreases. Refer to Table 15.3 for some recommended guidelines.

The factors listed in the table can be multiplied by the known diagonal screen dimension to get an approximate minimum viewing distance. To minimize head and eye movement in critical situations, such as in control rooms, the width of the display should ideally be within a 15° angle on each side of a centerline perpendicular to the screen, or 30° total. See Fig. 15.3. By applying basic trigonometry, this means that the closest viewer should be no less than the width of the screen multiplied by 1.87 (two times the arctangent of 15°).

The distance to the most distant viewer depends on the type of material being shown. Rules of thumb for maximum distances are six to eight times the image height for entertainment video, four to six times the image height for corporate or data presentations, and two to four times the image height for

**Example**
Calculating a minimum viewing distance

What is the approximate minimum viewing distance when using a 42 in (1067 mm) display with a resolution of 1024 × 768 pixels (XGA)?

The factor for this display, based on its diagonal dimension, is 2.66 as found in Table 15.3.

$$(2.66)(42 \text{ in}) = 112 \text{ in} \quad (9 \text{ ft } 4 \text{ in})$$

In SI units the solution is

$$(2.66)(1067 \text{ mm}) = 2838 \text{ mm}$$

critical applications such as control rooms, CAD drawings, and very fine detail.

Because ideal viewing distances (including the most distant viewer) depend on the screen height, they are dependent on the ceiling height of the room and the lowest edge of the screen. As shown in Fig. 15.2, in a room with a flat floor the lowest edge of the screen should be no less than 48 in (1220 mm) above the floor. However, the average eye level of a seated person is about 50 in (1270 mm). With head height added to this dimension, a screen with its lowest edge 48 in (1220 mm) above the floor will still cause viewing problems, especially for larger audiences. Depending on the seating layout, there will be about 10 in to 12 in (250 mm to 300 mm) of interference near the bottom of the screen. If there is sufficient ceiling height, the minimum distance from the floor to the bottom of the screen should be 54 in (1375 mm).

If there is enough vertical clearance, floors can be sloped or stepped with risers. Floors can be sloped up to a maximum of 1:8 for most seating as long as provisions are made for accessible access and seating according to ADA requirements. If risers are used, a step dimension from 4 in to 7 in (102 mm to 178 mm) provides for good sight lines over the person sitting in front.

The top of the screen should be no more than 30° above the closest viewer's horizontal line of sight, based on ergonomic guidelines that state that viewers should not have to rotate their heads more than 30° left or right or tilt them more than 25°. Thirty degrees above horizontal is often used as a general guideline.

The preferred viewing angle for a matte screen is 60° on both sides of the screen from lines representing the angles of reflection on each side of the screen. See Fig. 15.1. The preferred viewing angle for a beaded screen is 30° to 50° depending on the specific manufacturer's recommendations. Seating should be laid out within this ideal field of vision. The screen-viewing angle may suggest the ideal shape of the room. The viewing angles are based on the ability of the screen to scatter the projected light back to the audience as it is reflected. To minimize required head turn for the audience, especially in wide rooms, the seating can be laid out with curved rows.

Many business and educational AV spaces are planned in existing buildings or in new buildings where the ceiling height has already been established. In these cases, the ceiling height may dictate the screen size, which, in turn, will dictate the maximum number of viewers for the type of seating used. If the ceiling is a suspended acoustical ceiling, it is sometimes possible to relocate lights, conduits, and some mechanical ductwork to allow the ceiling to be raised in an AV room. If the screen size cannot be increased, multiple screens can be placed in the room to allow for adequate vision by a larger number of people.

## Rear projection guidelines

Rear projection screens are often used in permanent AV rooms. These screens have several advantages. The equipment is

**Example**
**Calculating a room shape and size**

A designer needs to determine the best size and shape for a briefing room. The room is planned to seat at least 24 people sitting at fixed tables 18 in (460 mm) deep. Assume a space between tables of 3 ft (910 mm) and a 30 in (760 mm) center-to-center spacing of people sitting at the tables. The client will be using computer projection with an aspect ratio of 4:3 to show video presentations and computer-generated information. The projection resolution will be XGA and the projector can be ceiling mounted 15 ft (4570 mm) from the screen. Because some ambient light will be required, the client will be using a beaded screen with a recommended viewing angle of 45°. A place for a presenter's lectern in the front of the room is required. The room has a flat floor and the ceiling height is 9 ft 6 in (2900 mm). What is the best size and shape for the room?

First determine the screen size. Because the floor is flat, assume that the bottom of the screen is 54 in (1375 mm) above the floor to minimize obstructed views. If the ceiling height is 9 ft 6 in (2900 mm), the maximum screen height can be 5 ft (1525 mm). If the format is 4:3, the screen width can be determined by multiplying the height by 1.33 as shown in Table 15.1. The screen should be 6 ft 8 in (2030 mm) wide. This screen width can be drawn on the front wall so the rest of the parameters and the seating can be laid out on a floor plan. See Fig. 15.4(a).

Knowing the projector will be mounted 15 ft (4570 mm) from the screen, the extreme lines of projection to the edges of the screen can be drawn with their equal lines of reflection. From these lines of reflection, the 45° bend angles can be drawn as shown in Fig. 15.4(a). These lines represent the ideal limits of viewing for the type of screen selected.

Assuming the closest viewer is within a 30° viewing angle, the closest distance can be calculated by multiplying the screen width of 80 in (2030 mm) by 1.87 to give approximately 150 in (3810 mm) or 12 ft 6 in. The maximum recommended viewing distance for video and data projection for business situations is between four and six times the height of the screen. Taking an average of five times and multiplying by 5 ft (1525 mm) gives an approximate maximum viewing distance of 25 ft (7620 mm).

Using the seat spacing and table size and spacing given in the problem, 26 seats can be laid out as shown in Fig. 15.4(a) such that the viewers are within the ideal angle of vision of the beaded screen stated in the problem. The distance to the farthest row is only slightly more than the 25 ft (7620 mm) distance calculated, but well within the maximum recommended six times screen height of 30 ft (9145 mm).

Assuming a rectangular shape and allowing for a circulation space of about 5 ft (1525 mm) behind the last row and on either side of the longest rows, the resulting shape is nearly square and approximately 28 ft (8535 mm) on a side.

The maximum angle of view above horizontal for the closest viewer can be checked, knowing the distance from the screen and the height of the average eye level of 50 in (1270 mm) above the floor. In this example, as shown in Figure 15.4(b), the closest viewer is 12 ft 6 in (3810 mm) away with a vertical distance from horizontal to the top of the screen of 5 ft 4 in (1625 mm).

$$\theta = \arctan\frac{\text{height}}{\text{distance}} = \arctan\frac{64\text{ in}}{150\text{ in}} = 23.1°$$

The resulting angle is 23°, about the recommended angle and well below the maximum recommended angle of 30°.

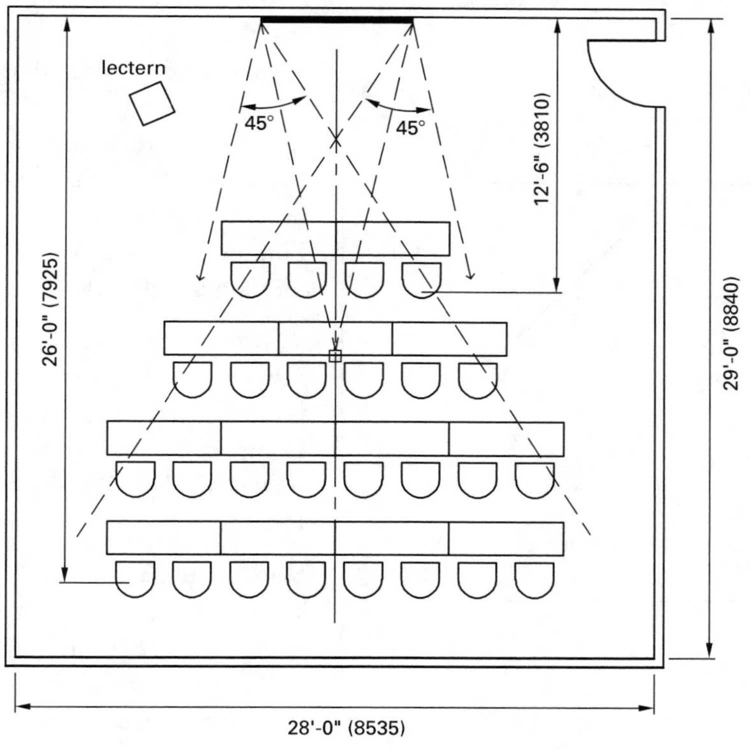


(a) plan layout

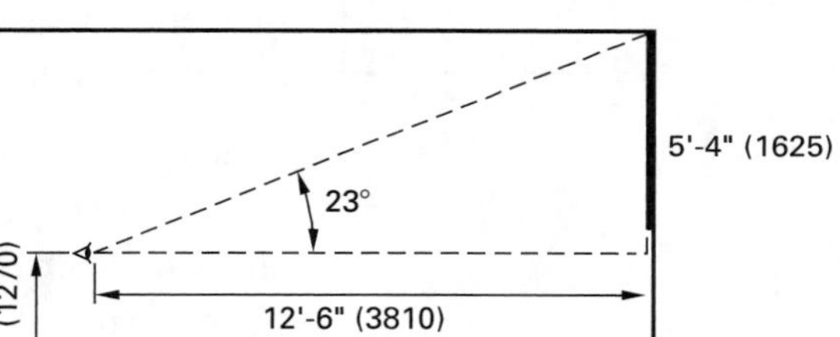


(b) vertical layout

**Figure 15.4** Determining room size based on projection criteria

concealed, providing security and reducing noise, there is no interference with the projection beam from fixed obstructions or the audience, and the amount of space required behind the audience is reduced. Rear projection screens tend to reflect less ambient light than front projection screens, so they are also preferable where there will be a relatively high level of ambient light in the audience. For business and educational purposes, some ambient light is desirable so that the audience can take notes, read text, or see the speaker. In contrast, front projection AV rooms require a lower ambient light level so that the image on the screen is not degraded.

The major disadvantage of rear projection is that an extra room is required behind the screen. A basic rule of thumb is that the projection room needs to be about as deep as the width of the screen. However, using short focal length lenses and mirrors can minimize the required depth of the room, as illustrated in Fig. 15.5. Some projectors have very short throw lengths, so a rear projection room need not be very large.

**Figure 15.5**
Use of mirrors for rear screen projection

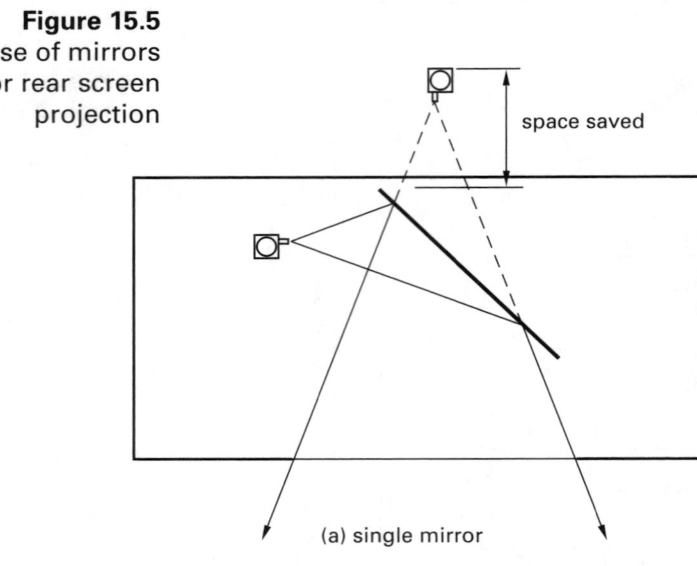


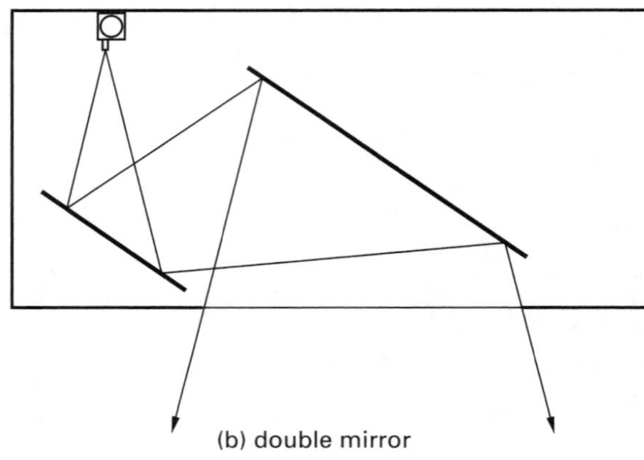


**Figure 15.6**
Diffusion of light through rear projection screen

Another disadvantage of rear projection is that the ideal audience seating area is generally smaller than with front projection. This is because the light is transmitted through a screen rather than being reflected, and the effective angle within which the screen can bend the light to viewers is smaller than for front projection screens. Figure 15.6 shows this optical principle.

When applied to an entire rear projection screen for the full width of an audience, the geometry appears as shown in Fig. 15.7. Compare this with the projection lines shown in Fig. 15.1 and superimposed in Fig. 15.7.

Some manufacturers of rear projection screens also produce screens with fresnel lenses on the back and special coatings that increase the bend angle. These improve the uniformity of the projected image and widen the acceptable viewing area. Individual manufacturers should be consulted for the types of screens and exact bend angles available.

Where exactly to locate the edges of the seating area depends on two things: first, the angle at which the image strikes the screen (which in turn depends on the focal length or throw distance of the lens used), and second, the type of screen used, which determines how far the light is bent (the bend angle shown in Fig. 15.6). For very preliminary planning, seating should be limited to an area within a 45° line on either side of a line perpendicular to the screen. Note that if two screens are used side by side for multiple projector presentations, the desirable seating area decreases for both rear and front projection because of this effect.

## VIDEO [115200]

The use of video images in AV presentations has increased greatly in recent years, primarily because program material previously on videotape is now available in DVD format. Videotapes and DVDs have largely replaced standard movie film. Many types of

**Figure 15.7** Seating guidelines for rear projection

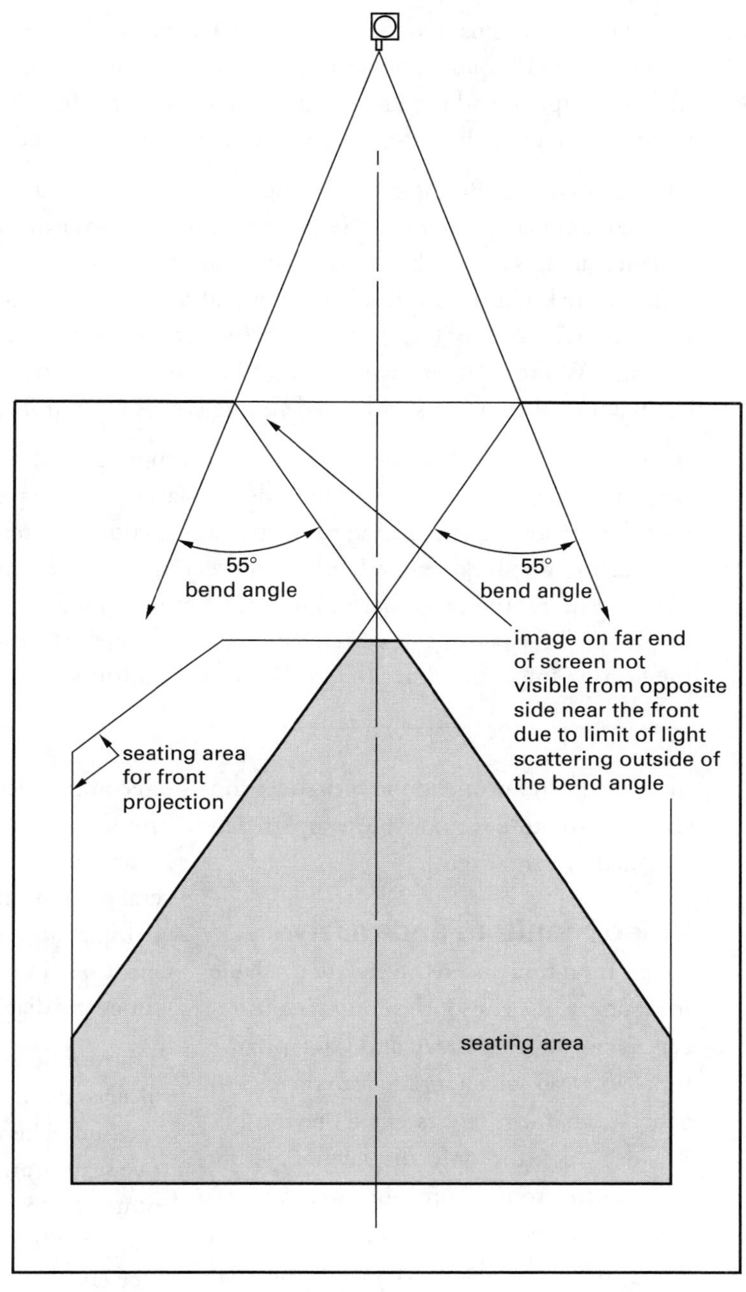

## Building code requirements for auditoriums

Most dedicated auditoriums for audiovisual (AV) purposes are designed as part of the architecture of a building. However, large-capacity rooms are sometimes designed as part of the interior design work in new construction or remodeling. Depending on their exact use, these AV rooms may be classified as business, educational, or assembly occupancies. (Refer to Ch. 19 for a discussion of occupancy groups.) Regardless of the classification, the higher occupant load requires a minimum of two exits from the room. These exits must be separated by some distance, as dictated by the prevailing code.

The International Building Code (IBC), for example, requires that any assembly area with an occupant load greater than 49 must have at least two exits. These must be separated by a distance not less than half the diagonal dimension of the room, or one-third that dimension if the entire building is sprinklered. For auditoriums and other rooms with a concentrated use, the IBC occupant load factor is 7 $ft^2$/person for rooms without fixed seating. This means that any AV room larger than 343 $ft^2$ (49 persons $\times$ 7 $ft^2$/person) must have two exits. The occupant load for rooms with fixed seating equals the number of seats.

If a large AV room is classified as an assembly occupancy, additional code requirements apply. If fixed seats are used, then main and side exits, aisle widths, ramp slopes, steps, and handrails must be constructed according to the prevailing code requirements. Assembly occupancies also require the use of panic hardware on exit doors. The Americans with Disabilities Act (ADA) requires that, whether or not fixed seating is used, a certain number of spaces must be provided for persons in wheelchairs. Assisted listening devices may also be required for the hearing impaired. Refer to Ch. 18 for more information on ADA requirements.

multimedia shows once done with slides and recorded sound have now been superseded by video presentations.

### Video monitors and receivers

Video monitors and receivers are available in a variety of sizes. Both monitors and receivers use either a screen and CRT picture tube, an LCD screen, or a plasma screen to generate an image (as described previously). A video monitor only displays a picture from an electronic source such as a camera, a video tape recorder, or a receiver tuned to an off-the-air broadcast. A receiver equipped with a tuner can select one of the on-the-air channels or cable transmission of television broadcasts. The screen size is referred to by its diagonal dimension.

The viewing distances and angles of video monitors depend on the resolution of the screen (the number of lines per inch) and the distance from the screen to the viewer. Recommended viewing angles and distances are shown in Fig. 15.8 for standard video monitors and receivers used for viewing general programming images. When the screen is displaying detailed text or graphics, viewers must be closer, in the range of three to six times the diagonal screen dimension.

The number of people who can view a screen of a given dimension depends on the seating method. The variation in audience size for two seating arrangements using a 20 in (508 mm) screen is illustrated in Figs. 15.9(a) and 15.9(b). The approximate number of viewers that can be accommodated with various sizes of screens is listed in Table 15.4. Figure 15.10 illustrates some guidelines for the mounting heights of monitors. When larger audiences must be accommodated, multiple displays can be distributed along the length of the room.

For viewing HDTV images, the recommended minimum seating distance is

**Figure 15.8** Viewing area for video monitors and receivers

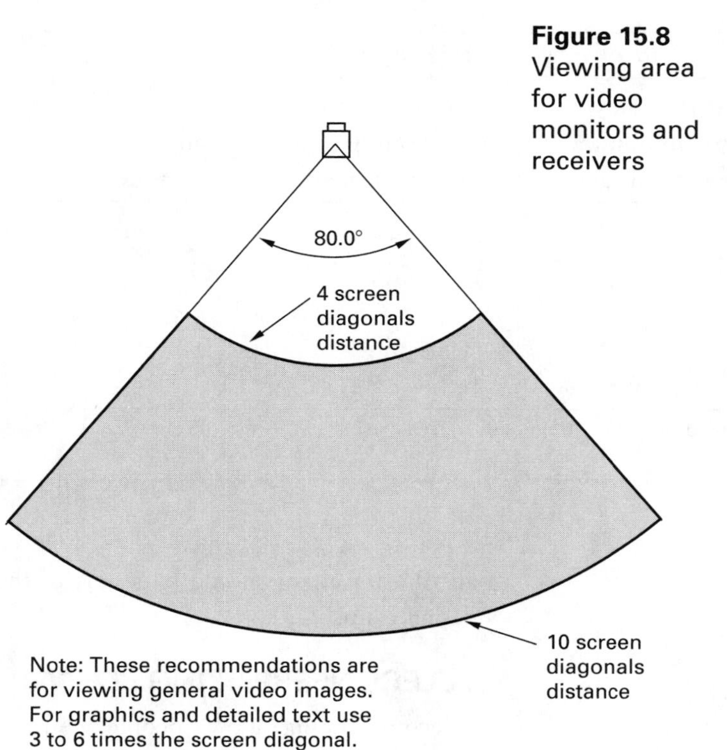


**Figure 15.9** Seating capacities for a 20 in (510 mm) screen

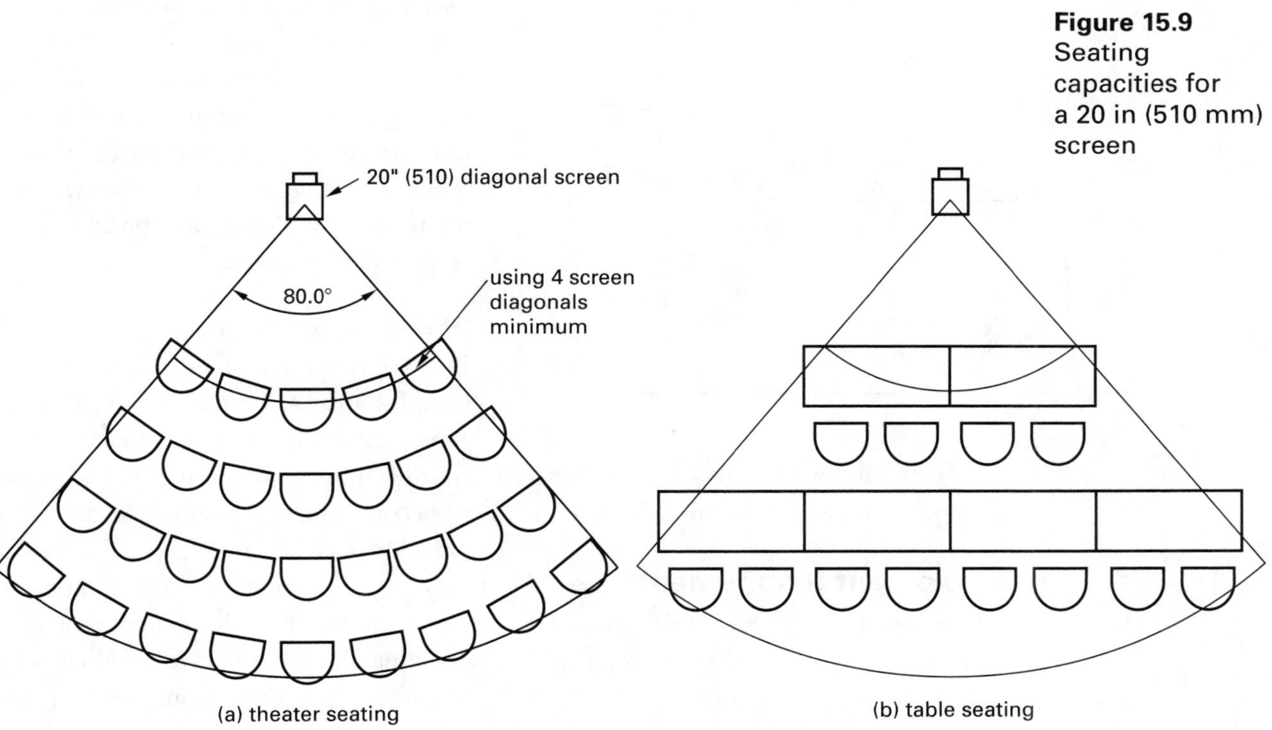

**Table 15.4** Number of viewers of a single video screen

| screen size | | no. of viewers, theater style | | |
|---|---|---|---|---|
| in | mm | 8 $ft^2$/person with 5$D$ minimum seating distance | 6 $ft^2$/person with 4$D$ minimum seating distance | no. of viewers at desks |
| 12 | 305 | 7 | 12 | 4 |
| 20 | 508 | 18 | 30 | 12 |
| 25 | 635 | 28 | 54 | 20 |
| 35 | 890 | 45 | 84 | 44 |

Note: Based on maximum viewing distances of 10 times the screen diagonal.

**Figure 15.10** Video monitor mounting heights

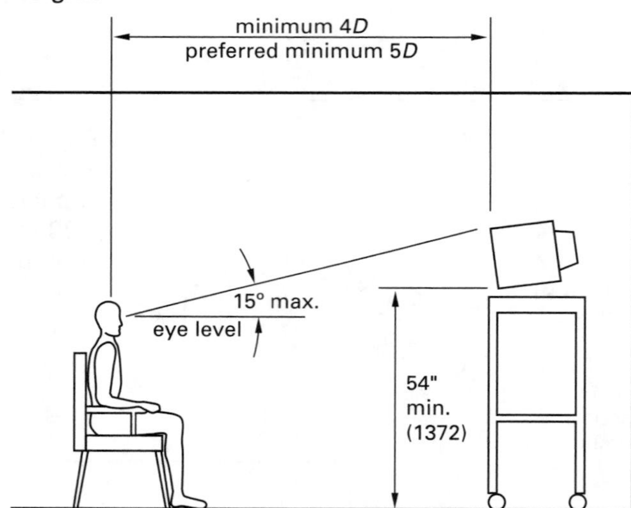


approximately two times the diagonal dimension of the screen, as shown in Table 15.3.

## Equipment requirements

The equipment required for video presentations varies widely. The simplest setup needs only a single monitor and a DVD player. Complex video presentation rooms require large projectors, monitors, a sound system, control equipment, and possibly cameras and special lighting. For these installations, an AV consultant should be a part of the design team.

# TELECONFERENCING [274000]

Teleconferencing allows people who are geographically separated to meet and communicate. The communication can be as simple as a standard conference call over telephone lines, or as complex as a satellite linkup of full-motion video conferencing with additional communication of computer graphics and facsimile. This section discusses preliminary planning for video teleconferencing using video cameras and monitors with sound, and possibly other graphic display devices.

## Planning guidelines

Because video teleconferencing requires a complex mix of communications equipment, cameras, monitors, microphones, control equipment, lighting, and acoustics, a teleconferencing consultant is needed to provide detailed design and specifications for the equipment and final layout of the space. However, much of the preliminary space planning and construction detailing is the responsibility of the interior designer.

Video teleconferencing is expensive to install and operate. Its use is usually limited to larger companies that can afford the initial installation cost and for whom the savings in travel expenses justifies the cost. However, video teleconferencing is becoming more affordable due to technical advances in hardware design and signal compression, the use of digital information on dial-up and broadband digital circuits (instead of satellite transmission and dedicated phone lines), and the standardization of transmission protocols.

A teleconferencing facility requires a dedicated space large enough to contain the conference table, cameras, and monitors; the equipment and control room; space for other equipment, such as facsimile units and graphic display screens; additional seating; and possibly a coffee bar. The relationship of the conference table to the cameras and monitors is especially important and determines the basic size and shape of the room. The simplest setup, for very small groups, uses just one camera and one monitor. However, it is more common to use two or more cameras and two or more monitors so that overall views of larger groups can be shown as well as close shots of individual participants.

Figures 15.11(a) through 15.11(c) show some common table shapes used for video teleconferencing. Each has its disadvantages and advantages. The straight table arrangement is simple and requires little space; however, it is only good for very small groups of three or four people, each of whom must lean forward to see the others in the room. The semicircular table allows each person to be equidistant from the cameras and monitors, but often appears too formal. The wedge-shaped table looks more like a conference table and allows eye contact across the table. However, it makes camera placement difficult and requires people to lean forward to see someone on the same side of the table.

The conference table usually contains microphones and controls and establishes each participant's chair location in relation to the cameras, monitors, and lighting. Therefore, it

**Figure 15.11**
Table shapes for video teleconferencing

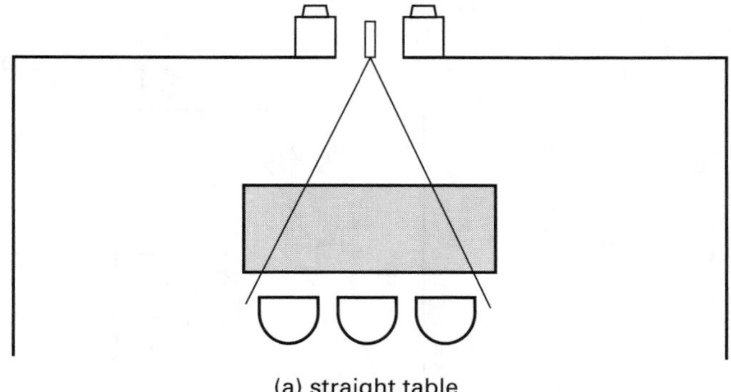

(a) straight table

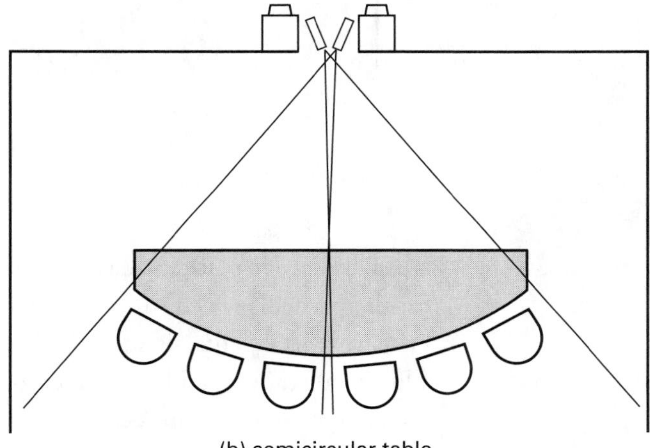

(b) semicircular table

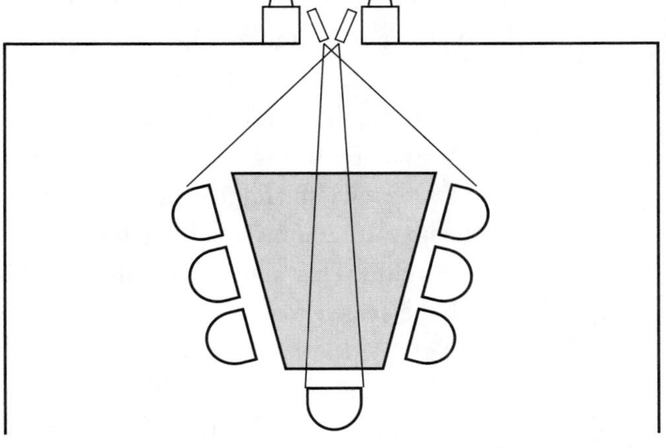

(c) wedge-shaped table

**Figure 15.12**
Seating distances for video teleconferencing

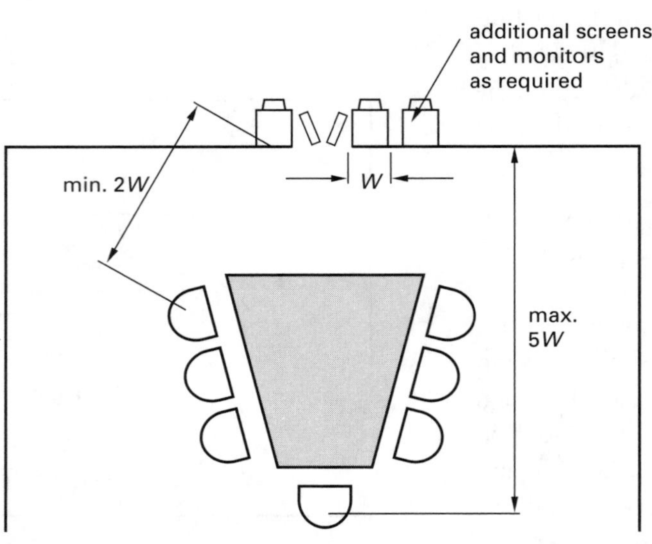


is usually fixed in place and custom designed for the particular needs of the facility. The primary participants sit at the table, but additional seating can be included behind the table if larger groups occasionally need to be accommodated.

As with standard television monitor viewing, there is a limit to the maximum viewing distance for visibility. See Fig. 15.12. Rules of thumb require that the closest viewer be no closer to the screen than two times the screen width and that the farthest viewer be no farther away than five times the screen width. This allows type and graphics on the screen to be visible. General views of people can be seen from greater distances. For example, a 21 in (533 mm) diagonal monitor has a width of about 15 in (381 mm); therefore, the maximum viewing distance would only be about 74 in or 6 ft 2 in (1880 mm). Because of these visibility requirements, large monitors are usually required for groups over five or six.

The number of cameras needed depends on the number of people. One camera is sufficient for up to four people. When there are more than four people, at least two cameras are required so images of individuals are large enough to see. Additional cameras may be required in the ceiling or elsewhere for viewing documents.

## Room requirements

Regardless of the type of equipment used and the size of the table, video teleconferencing rooms must always be designed and detailed for optimal acoustics, lighting, and comfort. The perimeter partitions must be detailed to control sound transmission from surrounding spaces. This requires partitions that extend from the floor to the ceiling with all cracks sealed, including penetrations such as electrical receptacles. If partitions are constructed of wallboard, a double layer on each side can be used with acoustical insulation in the stud cavity. Refer to Chs. 1 and 11 for more information on acoustics and partition construction. HVAC equipment and ductwork should also be separated or insulated to control sound transmission and structure-borne sound from other spaces. The room finishes must also limit reverberation that could interfere with speech intelligibility. This is easily done by using absorptive finishes, such as carpeted floors and acoustical ceilings. Acoustic wall panels can also be used if additional absorption is needed.

Lighting should consist of general room illumination with additional spotlighting on the faces of the participants and some backlighting to visually separate the participants from the background. A teleconferencing consultant or lighting consultant can recommend specific lighting types and positions for best visibility and picture quality.

Good colors to use include grays and blues. White walls should be avoided, as they tend to be too bright. The table color should not be very dark or very light. Dark tables absorb too much light, while light tables reflect too much unflattering light under the faces of the participants. Also, avoid patterned wall finishes; these can produce an annoying moiré effect on the screen.

# 16

# MECHANICAL & ELECTRICAL SYSTEMS COORDINATION

This chapter reviews construction design and detailing that must be coordinated with mechanical and electrical systems. Although the interior designer is not responsible for designing building systems or producing construction drawings for them, he or she must often coordinate with consulting engineers and the architect concerning the locations of plumbing fixtures, air diffusers, sprinklers, and other mechanical and electrical elements.

In many cases, existing mechanical and electrical services are fixed, thereby dictating the locations of interior design elements. In other cases, the interior designer has some flexibility in suggesting the locations of certain mechanical fixtures. For new construction, the interior designer often works with an architect or engineer to coordinate the desired locations of mechanical and electrical equipment based on space planning requirements. Refer to Ch. 21 for more information on sustainability related to mechanical and electrical systems.

## HVAC EQUIPMENT [230000]

HVAC is the acronym for *heating, ventilating, and air conditioning* and includes all the equipment used for these purposes. One system may combine all three, or there may be two or more systems used to heat, ventilate, and cool a building.

### Types of systems

HVAC systems are often classified by the medium used to heat or cool the building. The two primary methods of heating and cooling use air or water. In some parts of the country, electricity is also used for heating. Some systems use a combination of media.

#### All-air systems

All-air systems cool or heat spaces by conditioned air alone. Heat or cool air is transported to the space with supply and return air ducts. A common example of an all-air system is a residential forced hot air furnace. A boiler powered by oil or gas heats air that is distributed throughout the house in ductwork. In each room there are also return air ducts that collect the cooled air and return it to the furnace for reheating. If necessary, an air conditioning unit is connected to the same ductwork to provide cooled and humidified or dehumidified air.

For commercial buildings, there are several variations of HVAC systems available, including variable air volume, high-velocity dual duct, constant volume with reheat, and multizone systems. Each type requires supply air ductwork, registers, and return air grilles in all spaces. Registers are connected to the supply air ductwork and can be adjusted to control the direction of air flow and the volume of air coming through them. In many instances, separate ductwork is not used for return air; rather, grilles are placed in the suspended ceiling to collect return air. The space above the suspended ceiling and the structural floor above is called the *plenum*. The mechanical system draws the return air back through the plenum to a central collecting point on each floor, where it is then directed through ducts to the building's heating plant on another floor.

In commercial construction, if fire-rated partitions extend through the suspended ceiling, supply air ducts and openings for return air must penetrate the partitions. At the locations where the penetrations occur, fire dampers are required that automatically close in the event of a fire.

Supply air registers are often connected to the main ductwork with flexible ducting. This allows some adjustability in the exact location of an air register if its location conflicts with some other ceiling-mounted item, such as a light fixture. Because return air grilles are generally not connected to ducts in commercial construction, they may also be relocated if overall air circulation is maintained. The mechanical engineer should be consulted to determine how much the registers can be moved.

**Figure 16.1**
Convectors

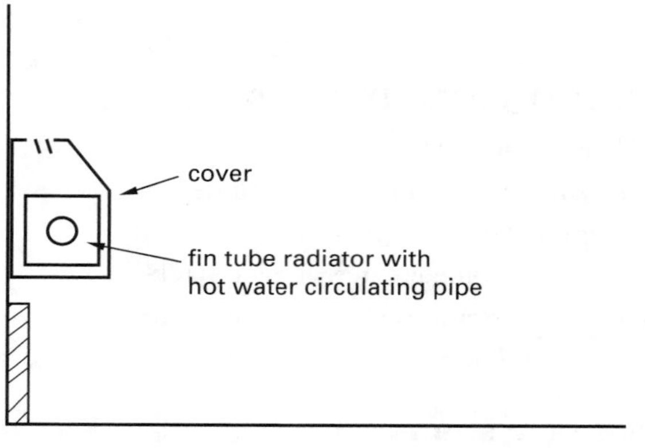


(a) residential baseboard convector

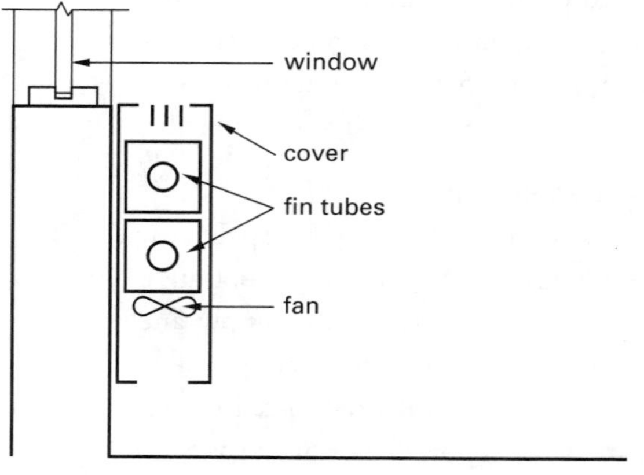


(b) commercial wall-mounted convector

## All-water systems

All-water heating systems use a convector in each space through which hot water is circulated. The hot water heats the fins of the convector. As air is drawn over the fins, it is heated. The air may be circulated by convection, as with most residential baseboard fin-tube radiators, or by forced circulation created with a fan. Figures 16.1(a) and 16.1(b) illustrate two common types of convectors. When commercial convectors are used for heating there is usually an additional forced air system with diffusers in the ceiling to provide conditioned air.

There are also combination systems that use ductwork for supplying fresh air, but also use water to heat or cool the air before it is introduced into the conditioned space. These are called *terminal reheat systems*, and the equipment is located in the plenum. Other installations use an all-water system for heating and a separate duct system for ventilation and cooling. In geographical areas where electric heat is economical, radiant panels can be used. They are mounted in the walls or created by running cables in the ceiling. Sometimes electric panels are used to overcome localized drafts.

## System Requirements

HVAC systems can affect interior construction detailing related to space planning, ceiling design and layout, and remodeling in several ways, as described in the following sections.

### Space for ducts, pipes, and mixing boxes

In residential construction, small ducts and plumbing pipes are typically run within the walls and floor joists or in crawl spaces or attics. Occasionally, larger horizontal ducts in a house must be run below the floor joists and a dropped ceiling or furred-down space must be built to conceal them.

In commercial construction, horizontal ducts are normally run in the plenum, and vertical ducts are normally run within their own chases. A *chase* is a fully enclosed shaft containing nothing except ducts or piping. Large, horizontal ducts may occupy most of the vertical distance between a suspended ceiling and the structure above, making it difficult if not impossible to recess light fixtures. This is particularly true with standard line-voltage recessed incandescent downlights, which can be deep. Sometimes it is possible to substitute smaller, low-voltage or low-clearance light fixtures to fit within the low space below a duct. Refer to Fig. 16.2 for some typical clearances required of various types of recessed luminaires.

Another consideration when planning a ceiling layout is the locations of mixing boxes, which are also located in the plenum. A *mixing box* adjusts the quantity or temperature of air going into a space from the main air supply line(s), reduces the velocity of air, and attenuates noise. Lines from thermostats are connected to the mixing boxes. With variable air volume systems, the *VAV*

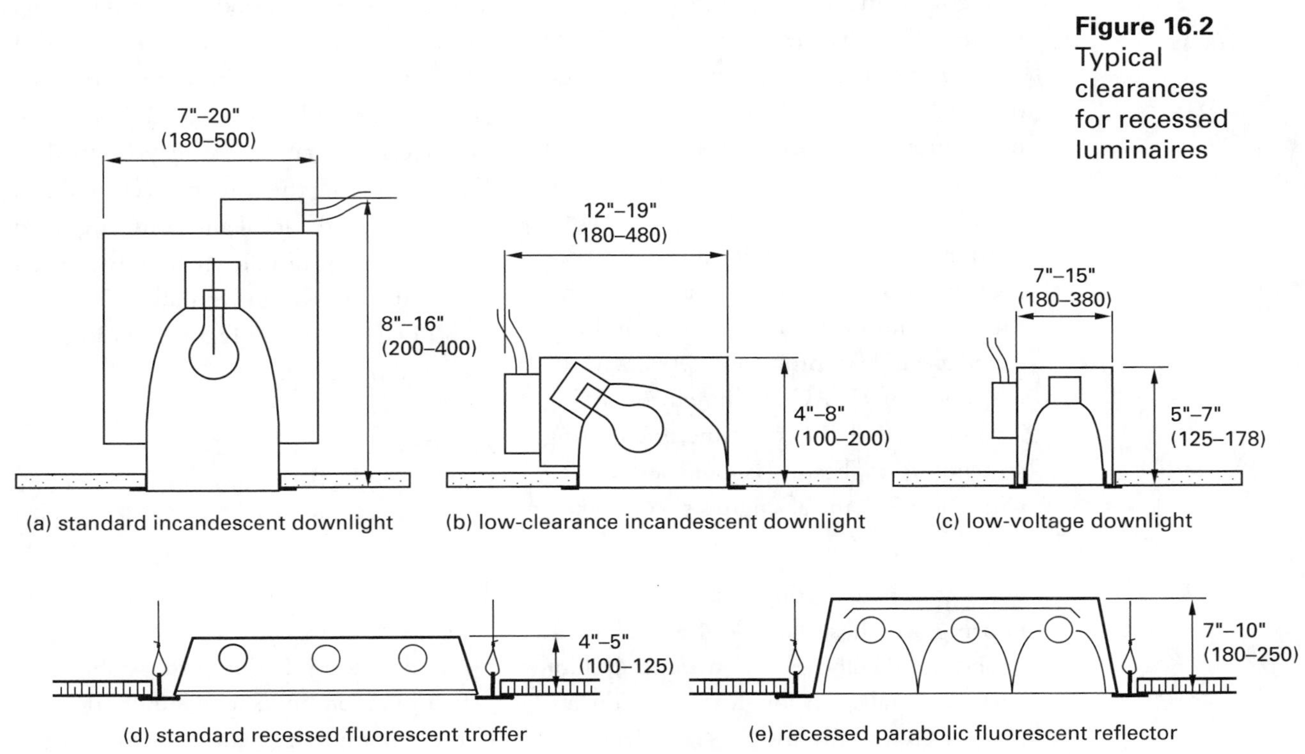


**Figure 16.2** Typical clearances for recessed luminaires

*box*, as it is called, varies the quantity of air. One duct leads in and one or more lead out and are attached to registers mounted in the ceiling. A VAV box is typically placed above the ceiling within or near the space it serves. With dual-duct systems, the mixing box mixes cool and hot air coming into it from two separate ducts and distributes the mixed air to ducts serving individual rooms or spaces. With terminal reheat systems, the box contains a hot water coil that provides additional heat to the air stream. Terminal reheat systems can easily be identified by air ducts and copper pipes leading into them.

Depending on the type and capacity of the system, mixing boxes can range in size from 6 in to 18 in high, 24 in to 60 in long, and 14 in to 66 in wide (150 mm to 450 mm high, 600 mm to 1500 mm long, and 350 mm to 1700 mm wide). Mixing boxes may interfere with light fixture placement and other recessed ceiling items. But because of their size and connection with ductwork and thermostats, mixing boxes are often expensive and difficult to move.

It is advisable to verify the size and location of ductwork, mixing boxes, and piping before locating light fixtures and other recessed ceiling items. This information can be found on HVAC plans, by consulting with the mechanical engineer, or by visual inspection on the job site. However, remember that actual construction seldom exactly follows the drawings, so on-site viewing of the space above the ceiling is the best way to confirm the location of existing HVAC, plumbing, electrical, and fire protection services. If the relocation of HVAC equipment or piping is contemplated, the cost, time, and heating and cooling implications should be discussed with the mechanical engineer, contractor, and client.

Some commercial construction uses access flooring, which is a false floor of individual panels raised above the structural floor with pedestals. Although access flooring is most commonly used to run electrical, communication, and computer wiring, it can be used for some types of HVAC ductwork that serve individual workstations. Refer to Ch. 8 for more information on access flooring.

Small pipes can be run within standard partitions in commercial construction, but larger pipes need to be placed in deeper walls or in chase walls. A chase wall consists of two runs of studs separated by several inches, the exact dimension being determined by the largest pipe or duct that has to be concealed. Only the finish side of each run of studs is covered with wallboard. Chase walls are commonly used between back-to-back commercial toilet rooms where extensive plumbing work and toilet carriers are required. A toilet carrier is a steel framework that is bolted to the floor inside a pipe chase and that carries the weight of wall-hung toilets. Figs. 16.3(a) and 16.3(b) illustrate some of the types and sizes of pipes and the minimum partition space required.

## Plenum requirements

In commercial construction where the plenum is used as a return air space, building codes prohibit the use of combustible materials, such as wood or exposed wire, within the space. However, some types of telephone and communication wiring are plenum rated (Teflon coated) for use in such locations, and these may be used in place of running the wires in steel conduits. If required by the local authority, fire-rated dividers must be installed to limit the spread of fire and smoke horizontally. Normally, such dividers are simply an extension of a fire-rated partition.

## Access

Building codes (and common sense) require that access be provided to certain components of mechanical and electrical systems. These include such things as valves, fire dampers, heating coils, mechanical equipment, electrical junction boxes, communication junction boxes, and similar devices. If these components are located above a suspended acoustical ceiling, access is provided by simply removing a ceiling tile. In other locations, such as gypsum wallboard ceilings or partitions, access doors are required for anything that might need to be inspected, adjusted, or repaired. Access doors are small steel doors with frames that are opened by turning a thumb turn or using a key. If required, access doors are available as a fire-rated assembly.

## Thermostats

The locations of thermostats are normally determined by the mechanical engineer so they are away from exterior walls, heat sources, or other areas that may adversely affect their operation. They are normally located 48 in (1200 mm) above the floor, but this should be coordinated with light switches and other nearby wall-mounted control devices. The mounting height must also be coordinated with the maximum allowable reach distances for accessibility, which may lower the thermostat heights to 44 in (1120 mm) for an obstructed forward reach.

## Coordination with other ceiling items

The interior designer should coordinate the location of supply and return air diffusers with other ceiling items, such as lights, sprinkler heads, smoke detectors, and speakers, so that the ceiling is as well planned as possible. However, the mechanical engineer must be consulted to verify that the desired locations do not adversely affect the operation of the HVAC system. Generally speaking, air supply registers should be placed near windows and other sources of heat loss or heat gain, while return air grilles should be placed away from the supply points to provide good heat and air circulation throughout the space.

## Window coverings

Because window coverings can affect the heating and air conditioning load in a space and may interfere with supply air diffusers or other heating units near the window, the interior designer should have the mechanical engineer or architect check the proposed type, size, and mounting of window coverings to verify that they will not create a problem with the HVAC system. In commercial construction, for example, there should be at least 2 in (50 mm) between the glass and any window covering to avoid excessive heat buildup, which might cause the glass to crack or break. Refer to Fig. 5.14.

**Figure 16.3**
Pipe chases and partitions

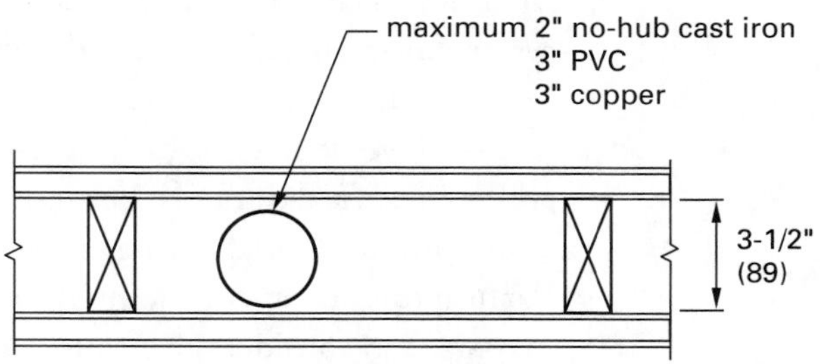


(a) typical residential wood stud partition

| | stud size | | | |
|---|---|---|---|---|
| type of pipe | 2-1/2" (64) | 3-5/8" (92) | 4" (102) | 6" (152) |
| cast iron | — | — | 2" (51) | 3" (76) |
| PVC | 2" (51) | 2-1/2" (64) | 3" (76) | 4" (102) |
| copper | 2" (51) | 3" (76) | 3-1/2" (89) | 5" (127) |

maximum sizes of pipes in partitions of varying depths

(b) commercial metal stud partition

## Space planning and furniture placement

In residential construction, the existing locations of ductwork and air registers may not work if remodeling is extensive. A mechanical contractor or mechanical engineer should be consulted to determine if the existing furnace has adequate capacity to change or add onto a residence, and whether and how ducts and registers need to be relocated.

In commercial construction, most HVAC systems are designed to work independently of partition relocation and furniture placement. However, in some cases HVAC zones are designed for only one layout and may not work with the desired zoning of a new plan. For furniture placement, the interior designer may want to consider the locations of floor registers, fin-tube baseboard radiators, and other equipment as it affects the placement of furniture and built-in woodwork.

### Acoustic separation

Mechanical and electrical services often pose problems with maintaining acoustic separation, especially in office spaces where ducts, convectors, and piping run continuously along an exterior wall while partitions intersect the exterior wall at regular intervals. Special detailing or construction may be required to create a continuous sound seal around the floor and ceiling, above the ceiling, and along the perimeter wall. For example, the cracks between the wallboard and all pipe and duct penetrations must be sealed with acoustic sealant.

A common problem exists where an office wall intersects an exterior wall with a convector running near the floor. The openings in the convector that allow warm air to circulate also allow sound to penetrate and travel inside the convector, past the partition, and out the openings on the other side. The convector must be modified in some way to prevent this, either by cutting the convector and piping (a difficult and expensive option) or by sealing inside the convector while still allowing the hot water pipe to run continuously.

### Air supply options [233000]

There are several types of air supply diffusers available, depending on the requirements of the HVAC system, the type of wall or ceiling in which they are mounted, and the appearance desired. Some of the more common types are shown in Figs. 16.4(a)–16.4(c).

Air diffusers 1 ft or 2 ft (300 mm or 600 mm) square are commonly used in suspended acoustical ceilings because they fit within standard ceiling grids, are easy to install, and are inexpensive. They simply lay onto the gridlike ceiling tile as shown in Fig. 16.4(a). Similar types are available for gypsum wallboard and plaster ceilings. These usually have a trim flange that snaps onto the diffuser and covers the rough cut opening in the ceiling, as shown in Fig. 16.4(b).

## Circuit protection

In addition to the protection provided by circuit breakers in the panel boxes that trip off if the circuit is overloaded, there are two other types of protection provided in electrical wiring. The first is grounding, which is a separate wire in addition to the two that provide power. The grounding of an electrical system prevents a dangerous shock if someone touches an appliance with a short circuit and simultaneously touches a ground path, such as a water pipe. The ground wire provides a path for the fault.

A ground fault, however, can create other problems, because the current required to trip a circuit breaker is high and small leaks of current can continue unnoticed until someone receives a dangerous shock or a fire develops. Ground fault interrupters (GFIs) are devices that detect small current leaks and disconnect the power to the circuit or appliance. GFIs can be a part of a circuit breaker or installed as part of an outlet. Ground fault interrupters are required for outdoor outlets and in bathrooms and kitchens as well as other locations specified in the National Electrical Code.

Slot air diffusers can be used when the appearance of the air distribution device needs to be minimized or when the available space does not allow a square diffuser. As shown in Fig. 16.4(c), these diffusers are long and narrow and contain from two to eight slots, resulting in a finished opening of about 3 in to 8 in (75 mm to 200 mm) in width. They can be purchased in any length and used for either supply or return air. There is a box above that is as long as the slots. Air is supplied by a flexible round duct attached to the side of the box. Slot air diffusers are available for either suspended acoustical ceilings or gypsum wallboard and plaster ceilings. However, they are usually used with wallboard ceilings to provide a trim, unobtrusive method of distributing air.

## POWER AND COMMUNICATION

### Power system requirements [262000]

Electrical systems include power for lighting (discussed in the next section), convenience outlets, and fixed equipment. As with lighting, the electrical engineer (or electrical contractor on some residential work) designs and specifies the exact type of circuiting, wire sizes, and other technical aspects of the electrical systems. The interior designer, however, is often responsible for schematically showing the desired locations of outlets and switches, where power is required for special built-in equipment, and the appearance of cover plates and other visible electrical devices.

There are several types of conductors that supply power throughout a building. These extend from the electrical service entrance to the circuit breaker boxes to the individual switches, lights, and outlets. Nonmetallic sheathed cable, sometimes referred to by the trade name Romex®, consists of two or more plastic-insulated conductors and ground wire surrounded by a moisture-resistant plastic

**Figure 16.4** Ceiling details for air distribution

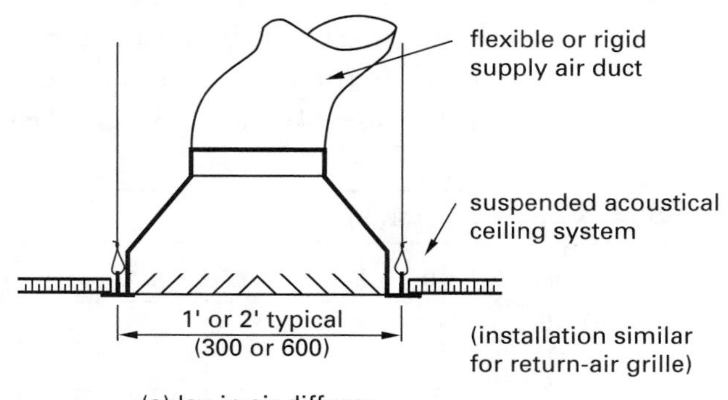


(a) lay-in air diffuser

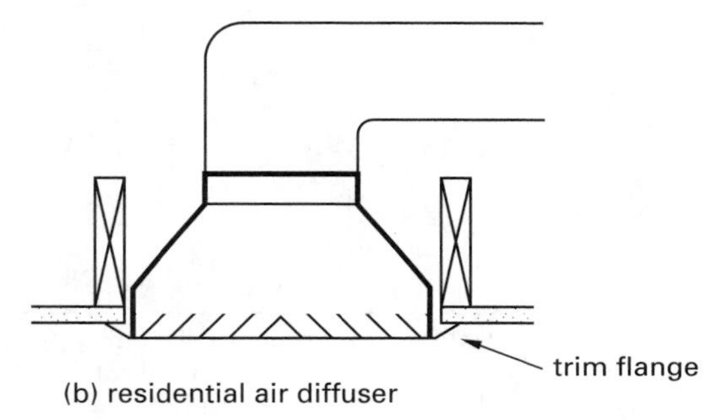


(b) residential air diffuser

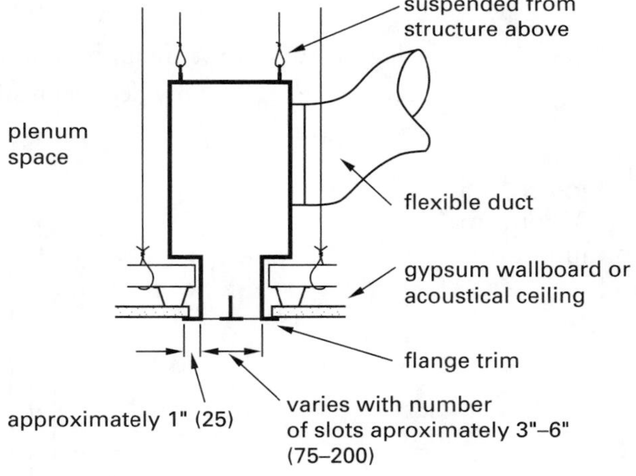


(c) slot air diffuser

## Steel conduit types and sizes

There are three types of steel conduit: electrical metallic tubing (EMT), intermediate metal conduit (IMC), and rigid steel conduit (RS). EMT is the most commonly used because it is lightweight and can be easily bent on the job site.

For some detailing where electrical service is required and space is limited, it is necessary to know the outside diameter of the conduit and what the minimum bend can be for a given size of conduit. The size of the conduit depends on the number of conductors within it, which is regulated by the National Electrical Code. Conduit size can be determined by referring to the electrical engineer's drawings. Table 16.1 gives the outside diameters of some of the smaller sizes of conduit that are likely to be encountered in interior construction work.

**Table 16.1** Outside diameters of conduit

| nominal size | | EMT | | IMC | | RS | |
|---|---|---|---|---|---|---|---|
| in | mm | in | mm | in | mm | in | mm |
| ½ | 13 | 0.71 | 18 | 0.82 | 21 | 0.84 | 21 |
| ¾ | 19 | 0.92 | 23 | 1.03 | 26 | 1.05 | 27 |
| 1 | 25 | 1.16 | 30 | 1.29 | 33 | 1.32 | 33 |
| 1¼ | 32 | 1.51 | 38 | 1.64 | 42 | 1.66 | 42 |
| 1½ | 38 | 1.74 | 44 | 1.89 | 48 | 1.90 | 48 |
| 2 | 50 | 2.20 | 56 | 2.37 | 60 | 2.38 | 60 |
| 2½ | 64 | 2.88 | 73 | 2.87 | 73 | 2.88 | 73 |

EMT electrical metallic tubing
IMC intermediate metal conduit
RS rigid steel conduit
Source: ANSI C80.1, C80.3, and C80.6.

Figure 16.5 shows the minimum field bends for smaller sizes of conduit so that adequate clearance can be provided when space is limited.

**Figure 16.5** Minimum conduit bends

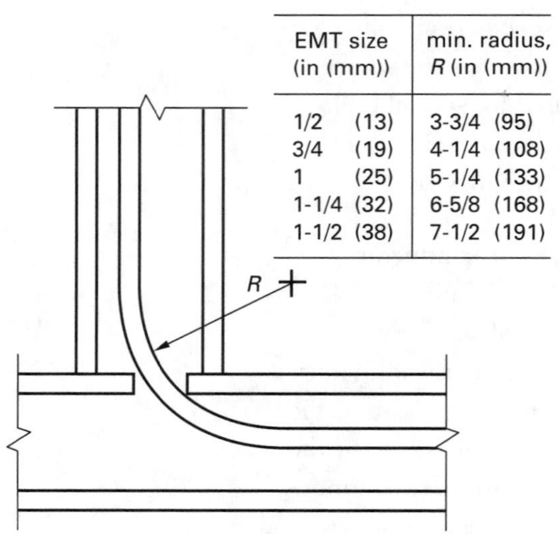


| EMT size (in (mm)) | min. radius, *R* (in (mm)) |
|---|---|
| 1/2 (13) | 3-3/4 (95) |
| 3/4 (19) | 4-1/4 (108) |
| 1 (25) | 5-1/4 (133) |
| 1-1/4 (32) | 6-5/8 (168) |
| 1-1/2 (38) | 7-1/2 (191) |

jacket. This type of cable can be used in wood or metal-stud residential buildings and those not exceeding three floors, as long as it is used with wood studs (or metal studs with holes through which the cable passes, protected by bushings or grommets) and is protected from damage by being concealed behind walls and ceilings.

Flexible metalclad cable, also known as armored or BX cable (or the common term "flex"), consists of two or more plastic-insulated conductors encased in a continuous spiral-wound strip of steel tape. It is often used in remodeling work because it can be pulled through existing spaces within a building. It is also used to connect commercial light fixtures to junction boxes so that the fixtures can be easily relocated in a suspended acoustical ceiling.

For commercial construction and large multifamily residential construction, individual plastic-insulated conductors must be placed in metal conduit or other approved carriers. Conduit supports and protects the wiring, serves as a system ground, and protects surrounding construction from fire if the wire overheats or shorts. Another type of cabling is under-carpet wiring. This is thin, flat, protected wire that can be laid under carpet without protruding. Cable for both 120 V circuits and telephone lines is available; however, it must be used with carpet tiles so it is readily accessible. Under-carpet wiring connects pedestals in the middle of the room that contain electrical outlets and telephone connections to junction boxes in nearby walls, where the wiring is connected to standard conduit-enclosed cable.

For some remodeling work, it may be very difficult or impossible to install new conduit or armored cable. In such cases, surface-mounted metal raceways can be used. These are thin conduits, usually rectangular in shape, that are fastened to the wall or ceiling. Plastic-sheathed cable is installed, and then a protective cap that encloses the conduit is applied. Outlet and switch boxes are available as part of each manufacturer's system.

Outlets, switches, and other types of connections to the power supply must be made in junction boxes. For single switches and duplex outlets, they measure about 2 × 4 (50 × 100). Larger boxes are 4 in$^2$ or 4½ in$^2$. (100 mm or 114 mm). Longer boxes are available, or several can be connected if there are more than two switches or two duplex outlets. Boxes are about 1½ in or 2⅛ in deep (38 mm or 54 mm). Junction boxes are also required where light fixtures are connected to the electrical system.

The National Electrical Code (NEC), International Residential Code (IRC), and ICC Electrical Code specify the minimum spacing of outlets. For residential construction, convenience receptacle outlets must be provided in every kitchen, family room, dining room, living room, library, den, sunroom, bedroom, recreation room, and similar rooms according to the requirements in the code. Receptacles must be installed so that no point along the floor line in any wall space is more than 6 ft (1829 mm) from an outlet. In a long run of wall (corners included), outlets cannot be spaced farther than 12 ft (3658 mm) apart. If a wall space is shorter than 6 ft (1829 mm) long but longer than 2 ft (610 mm) and is unbroken by doorways, fireplaces, and similar openings, it must also have an outlet.

Receptacles for kitchen countertops must be ground-fault circuit interrupters and must be installed so that no point along the wall line is more than 24 in (610 mm) from a receptacle. A receptacle outlet must be installed at each wall counter space that is 12 in (305 mm) wide or wider. Island counters must have at least one receptacle if they have a long dimension of 24 in (610 mm) or greater and a short dimension of 12 in (305 mm) or greater.

Refer to the IRC or NEC for additional outlet location requirements.

## Telephone and communication system requirements [273000]

Interior design drawings usually show telephone and communication systems on the same plan as the power outlets. The interior designer is responsible for indicating the locations of such items as telephones, intercommunication systems, public address speakers, buzzers, and computer terminals. The locations are also shown on the electrical engineer's drawings. As with power outlets, the actual circuiting, wire sizes, and connections to central equipment are usually determined by the electrical engineer or the contractor responsible for installing the equipment.

Because telephone and communication systems are low-voltage systems, the requirements for conduit and other protection are not quite as stringent as those for standard voltage power. In many cases, an outlet box is provided at the connection in the wall and the wire is run within the walls and ceiling spaces without conduit. However, in some commercial construction, all cable is required to be protected in conduit. As previously described, special plenum-rated cable is available that does not require conduit; however, it is more expensive than standard cable.

# LIGHTING

## Light sources [265100]

Light sources can affect construction detailing because of their size, weight, location, method of mounting, and heat output. For example, cove lighting requires a continuous piece of construction that is large enough and strong enough to support and conceal the luminaires. Recessed downlights require coordination with other mechanical and electrical systems to ensure that sufficient clearance is available above the ceiling. The following briefly describes some of the typical light sources.

### Incandescent

An incandescent lamp consists of a tungsten filament placed within a sealed bulb containing an inert gas. Several types and shapes are used in surface-mounted lights, recessed downlights, and other types of fixtures.

Common incandescent lamps are used in many types of luminaires. Depending on the wattage and size of the lamp, the housing can be fairly large, sometimes requiring substantial clearance above the ceiling for recessed downlights. Reflector lamps, such as types R, ER, and PAR, require similar large clearances and may require separation from combustible materials because of their heat output if the luminaire is not specially designed and rated for use near combustible materials.

When space is limited, miniature, low-voltage MR lamps and housings can be used. They not only require less space but also produce less heat than standard line voltage lamps, although their operating temperature near the lamp can be high.

Tungsten halogen is one type of incandescent lamp. Light is produced by the incandescence of the filament, but there is a small amount of a halogen, such as iodine or bromine, in the bulb with the inert gas. Through a recurring cycle, part of the tungsten filament is burned off as the lamp operates, but the burnoff mixes with the halogen and is redeposited on the filament instead of on the wall of the bulb as in standard incandescent lamps. This results in longer lamp life, low lumen depreciation over the life of the lamp, and a uniform light color. Because the filament burns under higher pressure and temperature, the bulb is made from quartz and is much smaller than standard incandescent lamps. These lamps are often referred to as quartz-halogen. Both standard-voltage (120 V) and low-voltage tungsten halogen lamps are available.

In addition to their other advantages, tungsten halogen lamps have a greater efficacy than standard incandescents, are compact, and give more light in the blue end of the spectrum due to their higher operating temperature, resulting in a light that looks whiter.

However, because they operate at high temperatures and pressures, failures result in an explosive shattering of the lamp. For this reason, halogen lamps are enclosed in another bulb or are covered with a piece of glass or a screen.

Low-voltage lamps are another class of incandescent. In addition to tungsten halogen lamps, standard filament types are available. As the name implies, these lamps operate at less than 120 V, usually 12 V. However, since they operate at higher current (amperage), their filaments have to be thicker to carry the added current. Because the filaments are thicker they are also more compact, resulting in smaller lamps and lamps with better beam control than standard incandescents.

Due to their smaller filaments and better beam control, low-voltage lamps are often used where small luminaires are required or where a narrow beam spread is needed. Because of their narrow beam spread, low-voltage lamps are energy efficient when lighting small objects or larger objects at a distance. The main disadvantage to these lamps is that a transformer is required to step down the line voltage. This results in a bulkier luminaire and higher initial cost.

Incandescent lamps are used in many standard and custom installations because they are inexpensive, compact, easy to dim, can be repeatedly started without a decrease in lamp life, and have a warm color rendition. In addition, their light output can be easily controlled with reflectors and lenses. Their disadvantages include low efficacy, short lamp life, and high heat output.

## Fluorescent

Fluorescent lamps are used where a more efficient source than incandescent lamps is required, or where a linear source of light is needed. Because fluorescent lamps are larger than incandescent lamps, it is more difficult to control their light output precisely; therefore, they are usually more suitable for general illumination. Compact fluorescents are available that fit within a reflector housing similar to incandescent downlights and wall washers. However, these types of luminaires still require more space than small incandescent lamps or low-voltage reflector lamps. Fluorescent lamps are ideal for continuous lighting, such as cove lighting used to illuminate a ceiling, or downlighting used to uniformly wash a partition with light.

Today, many of the standard T12, straight fluorescent lamps are being replaced by smaller and lower wattage T8 and T5 lamps, and incandescent lamps are being replaced by compact fluorescent lamps. The primary advantage to both is the energy savings realized by getting the same light level for less power input (wattage). In fact, many of the popular, older T12 lamps are no longer manufactured as mandated by the Energy Policy Act of 1992 (EPACT).

The T8 and T5 lamps (with 1 in and ⅝ in diameters, respectively) have become more popular because of their higher efficacy and better color rendition. The smaller-diameter lamps also make it possible to design smaller luminaires and more efficiently control the light.

Compact fluorescent (CF) lamps consist of T4 or T5 tubes bent in a U-shape, with the pins in one end of the lamp. Various configurations are available using tubes clustered in two, three, or four bends. In addition to providing energy savings, these lamps have a much longer life (10,000 hours) than the standard incandescent lamps they can replace. Most compact fluorescent lamps are designed to work in a fixture specifically designed for them, although some have a built-in ballast and a medium screw base so they can be used in older fixtures and floor and table lamps.

All fluorescent lamps have a ballast, a device that supplies the proper starting and operating voltages to the lamp. When detailing custom fluorescent installations or fixtures (as well as low-voltage incandescent installations), the detail must provide a space for the ballast, either near the lamp or remotely located.

### High-intensity discharge

High-intensity discharge (HID) lamps produce light by passing an electric current through a gas or vapor under high pressure. HID lamps include mercury vapor, metal halide, and high-pressure sodium (HPS).

In the *mercury vapor lamp*, an electric arc is passed through high-pressure mercury vapor to produce both ultraviolet light and visible light, primarily in the blue-green spectral band. For improved color rendition, various phosphors can be applied to the inside of the lamp to produce more light in the yellow and red bands. Mercury vapor lamps have a long life but poor color rendering.

*Metal halide lamps* are similar to mercury vapor lamps except that halides of metals are added to the arc tube. This increases efficacy and improves color rendition but decreases lamp life. Metal halide lamps provide the best combination of features of the high-intensity discharge lamps. They have good color rendering properties, high efficacy, and relatively long life. The main disadvantage is that metal halide lamps experience a large shift in apparent color temperature over their life. Like all HID lamps, metal halide lights have an outer bulb to protect the arc tube and to protect people from dangerous ultraviolet light. There are three types of outer bulbs: clear, phosphor-coated, and diffuse. Clear bulbs are used when optical control is required. Phosphor-coated lamps are used for better color rendition. Diffuse bulbs are specified in recessed downlight fixtures installed in low ceilings.

*HPS lamps* produce light by passing an electric arc through hot sodium vapor. The arc tube must be made of a special ceramic material to resist attack by the hot sodium. High-pressure sodium lamps have efficacies from 80 lm/W to 140 lm/W, making them among the most efficient lamps available. They also have an extremely long life: about 10,000 hours for the improved-color lamps, and up to 24,000 hours for other types. Unfortunately, standard high-pressure sodium lamps produce a very yellow

## Emergency lighting

The International Building Code, the National Electrical Code, the Life Safety Code, and Canadian codes include provisions for emergency lighting in commercial buildings. Because each jurisdiction differs slightly in its requirements, the local codes in force must be reviewed. Generally, however, all codes require that in the event of a power failure, sufficient lighting must be available to safely evacuate building occupants.

Emergency lighting is required in exit stairs and corridors as well as in such occupancies as places of assembly, educational facilities, hazardous locations, and other places where occupancy loads exceed a given number. The usual minimum lighting level required is 1 fc (10.8 lux) at floor level. Illuminated exit signs are also required in most commercial buildings. There must be an exit sign at each exit door and at each door leading to an exit-way. There also must be directional exit signs at corridor intersections and where a corridor changes direction. Emergency lighting circuits and exit lights are usually a part of the original architectural design of a building. However, extensive remodeling must also include proper connection to the emergency circuits and installation or relocation of exit signs. It must always be evident to the occupants where the exits are.

light. However, with available color correction versions, color rendition is acceptable for some interior applications.

Although HID lamps are very efficient, their use in interior applications is usually limited to general illumination of large spaces such as gymnasiums, parking garages, and industrial settings.

### Neon and cold-cathode

In addition to the three basic types of lamps, there are also neon and cold-cathode lamps. Neon lamps can be formed into an unlimited number of shapes and are used for signs and specialty accent lighting. By varying the gases within the tube, a variety of colors can be produced. Cold-cathode lamps are similar to neon in that they can be produced in long runs of thin tubing bent to shape. They have a higher efficacy than neon lamps, are slightly larger (about 1 in (25 mm) in diameter), and can produce several shades of white as well as many colors. Both types require small metal brackets to hold the lamp in place. Both types also require a transformer.

## Lighting systems

The type of lighting system selected determines the required construction detailing. For recessed lighting there must be sufficient clear space above the ceiling to install the specified fixtures. For most standard recessed fluorescent troffers used in commercial construction this is not a problem. For some large, recessed incandescent downlights, it may be necessary to relocate HVAC ductwork, conduit, and plumbing pipes to accommodate the locations and spacing of fixtures. Because relocation usually increases construction cost, it should be avoided when possible. An alternate is to select low-clearance fixtures.

Before design begins, the available clearances should be verified by reviewing the architectural and mechanical drawings and by viewing the actual installation of the above-ceiling construction. Although exact sizes depend on the particular luminaire used, Figs. 16.2(a)–16.2(e) show some typical size ranges of various recessed fixtures.

For cove lighting, the exact configuration of the supporting construction depends on the size of the luminaire, the sight lines to conceal the fixture, the particular photometric characteristics of the lamp, and the desired design of the cove strip. If a luminaire specifically built for cove lighting is used, the manufacturer's catalogue should be consulted for any critical placement dimensions. Figures 16.6(a)–16.6(d) show some of the common shapes for cove lighting and the important dimensions for detailing.

For all lighting, the ability to easily relamp fixtures should be considered when developing details. Clear access should be maintained around the lamp. Sufficient clearance also should be provided for removal of the lamps, especially large lamps such as fluorescent tubes.

## Control devices

The interior designer should decide how the lights in a space will be switched. This decision is based on the function of the lighting, how much individual control is required, where the switches are best located, energy conservation needs, and the maximum electrical load requirements on any one circuit.

The function of a space may simply require one on/off switch for all the lights in the space. In a lecture room, for example, it may be necessary to provide several circuits and switches so that some lights can be turned off while some remain on. Multiple switching also gives users the flexibility of saving energy by turning off some lights when they are not required.

Switches should be located at the door that is primarily used to enter a space so that they can easily be turned on and off as people

**Figure 16.6**
Types of cove lighting

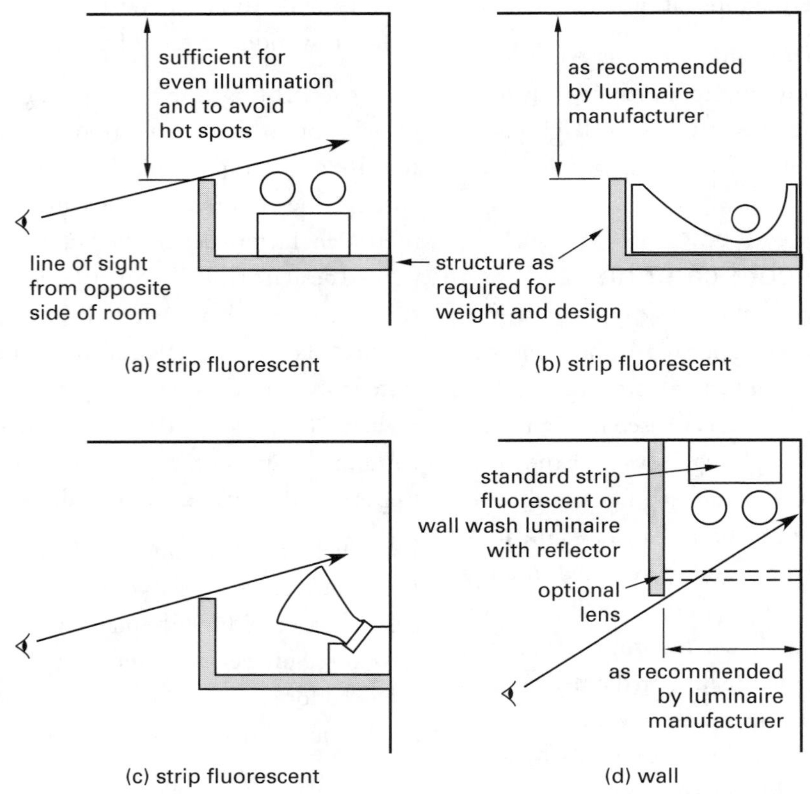


enter or leave the room. If there are two doors or the space is very large, three- or four-way switches can be used. These allow a light to be switched at two or three different locations, respectively.

The circuiting of lights also depends on the type of control required. A group of lights connected to a dimmer switch must be on its own circuit. Both incandescent and fluorescent lights can be dimmed. However, fluorescent dimmers are more expensive, and special fixtures are required to minimize flicker as they are dimmed. Incandescent lights should be on a circuit separate from fluorescent lights. In commercial installations this is often mandatory because incandescent lights are on 120 V circuits and fluorescent lights are usually connected to 277 V circuits. Large commercial installations use 277 V circuits because they are more efficient. Lights can also be switched by low-voltage relay switching, automatic time clocks, and proximity devices that sense when people enter or leave a room.

Finally, the number of switches depends on electrical load limitations. This is determined by the electrical engineering consultant or, on small projects, by the electrical contractor. Electrical codes limit the total wattage that can be connected to any one circuit; therefore, a large space with a great deal of lighting will have several switches. Wall space near doors and other detailing should make provisions for multiple switches, if necessary.

## Custom detailing for lighting

For many projects, the light fixtures available from manufacturers' catalogues may not be appropriate for a particular design. In these cases, custom fixtures can be designed and fabricated. Although the interior designer may develop the general design parameters for size, shape, and finishes, a qualified lighting designer should develop the actual details for fabrication. If Underwriters Laboratories (UL)-approved components are used in a custom fixture, the unit can usually be installed without further approvals. If custom components are designed, the entire custom luminaire may have to undergo lengthy and expensive testing before it is approved by code officials for use.

## PLUMBING

### Plumbing system requirements [221000]

Plumbing systems consist of two major components: hot and cold water supply, and drainage. In all plumbing installations, residential or commercial, water is supplied under pressure to individual plumbing fixtures. Because of this and because the pipes are generally small, it is relatively easy to locate pipes within wall cavities, ceiling structures, and other areas in order to supply a fixture, even if the fixture is some distance from the main source of water. However, the closer the fixture is to the source, the less costly it is to run piping to it.

Drainage systems present a more difficult problem. Because they work by gravity, drain pipes must be sloped downward to carry away wastes. In addition, vent pipes are required. Figure 16.7 shows a simplified diagram of the several components of a typical drainage and vent system.

The first component attached to the fixture is the trap. With a few exceptions, traps are located at every fixture and are designed to catch and hold a quantity of water to provide a seal that prevents sewage system gases from entering the building. The locations where traps are not installed include fixtures that have traps as an integral part of their design (for example, toilets) and where two or three adjacent fixtures are connected (for example, a double kitchen sink).

Traps are connected to the actual drainage piping and must also be connected to vents. Vents are pipes connected to the drainage system at various locations, open to outside air, and designed to serve two purposes. First, they allow built-up sewage gases to escape, instead of bubbling through the water in the traps. Second, they allow pressure in the system to equalize so that discharging waste does not create a siphon that would drain the water out of the traps.

From the trap, sewage travels to a vertical stack via fixture branch lines. If the stack carries human waste from toilets, it is called a *soil stack.* If the stack only carries wastes other than human waste, it is known as a *waste stack.*

Vents from individual fixtures are connected above the fixtures in two ways. If a vent connects to a soil or waste stack above the highest fixture in the system, the portion of the stack above this point is known as a *stack vent.* The stack vent extends through the roof. Multistory buildings use a separate pipe for venting, called a *vent stack.* It either extends through the roof or connects with the stack vent above the highest fixture, as shown in Fig. 16.7.

### Locating plumbing fixtures

Because of the cost of plumbing and the necessity of sloping drainage pipes, fixtures should be located as close to existing plumbing lines as possible. These include horizontal lines or vertical risers that run continuously through a multistory building. Drains must be sloped a minimum of ¼ in/ft (6 mm /300 mm) (although ⅛ in/ft is allowed for pipes larger than 3 in). Therefore, if a pipe must be concealed within a floor space, the slope and the size of the pipe itself will limit the distance from the fixture to a connection with a riser. Figure 16.8 illustrates these principles.

The maximum distance from a fixture and a vertical or horizontal waste line usually depends on the space available to maintain

**Figure 16.7**
Drainage system components

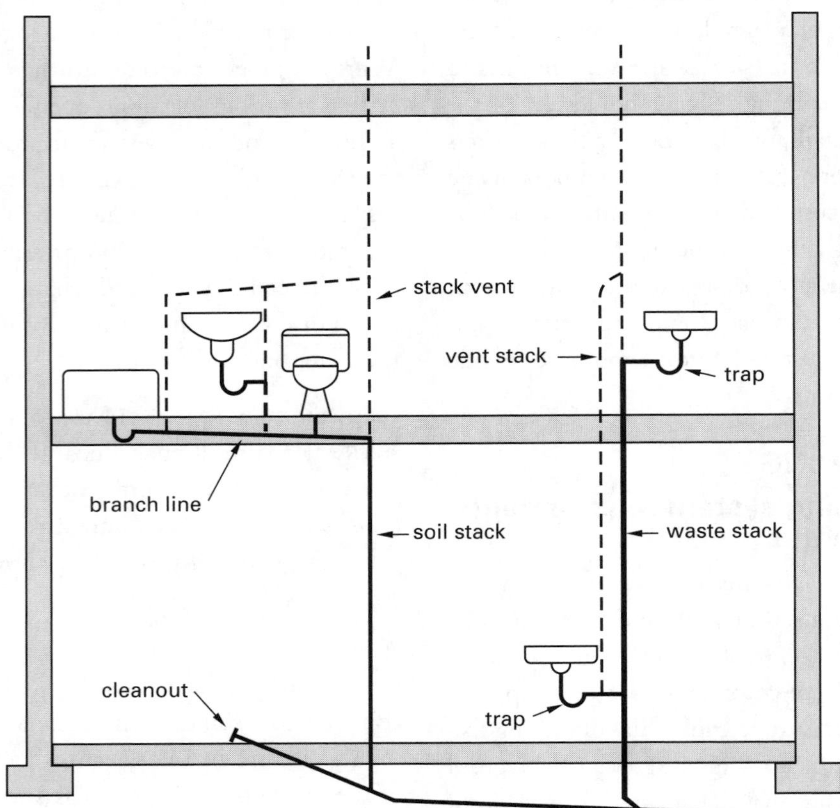


**Figure 16.8**
Planning for drainage lines

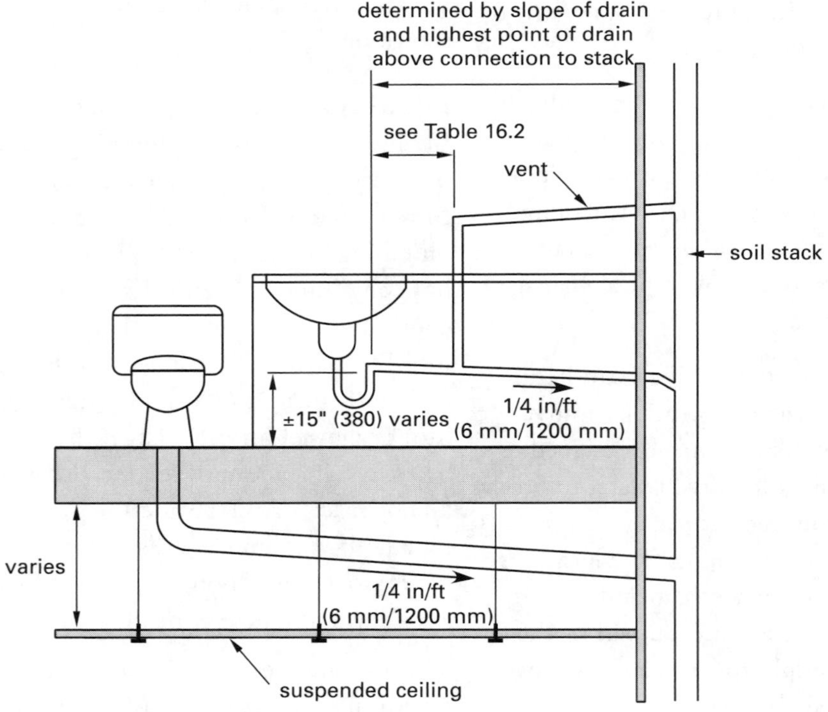

a ¼ in (6 mm) slope. This is the case when the vent is located adjacent to the fixture. However, there are some instances when there is no wall or other construction directly behind the fixture in which to conceal vertical piping (for example, a sink in a peninsula cabinet). The vent must be located some distance away from the fixture's trap. Plumbing codes limit the maximum distance from a trap to the nearest vent. This depends on the size of the pipe. Table 16.2 gives the maximum distances allowed by the Uniform Plumbing Code.

In commercial buildings, most plumbing is concentrated in one area near the core where it serves the toilet rooms, drinking fountains, and similar fixtures. To provide service to sinks, private toilets, and the like, wet columns are sometimes included in the building. These are areas, usually at a structural column location, where hot and cold supply and drainage risers are located. Individual tenants can easily tap into these lines, if desired, without having to connect to more remote plumbing.

If extensive plumbing work is required, the necessary pipes may not fit within the space provided by standard partitions. A soil stack from a toilet, for example, requires a 3 in (76 mm) diameter pipe that has an actual outside diameter somewhat larger than 3 in. In some instances, a 4 in (100 mm) pipe is required. In this case, either thicker partitions or plumbing chases are required. Some common pipe sizes and partitions required to accommodate them are shown in Fig. 16.2. Chase walls are used to conceal very large pipes or groups of pipes, such as between two back-to-back toilet rooms. Chase walls are constructed with two sets of studs with a space between large enough for the pipes. Figure 1.13 illustrates typical chase wall construction.

## FIRE PROTECTION [211000]

Fire protection systems include detection devices, such as smoke and heat detectors; alarm, communication, and annunciation equipment; and fire suppression systems. Sometimes only one or two of these components are used, such as smoke detectors in homes. In commercial construction, all of these components are present and interconnected into a complete fire protection system.

The most common component of a fire protection system that the interior designer may need to coordinate with is the sprinkler system. Although the designer does not design sprinkler systems, the locations of sprinkler heads may be suggested by the designer to coordinate with other ceiling-mounted items.

**Table 16.2**
Horizontal distance of trap arms to vents

| trap drain size (in) | maximum distance to trap (ft-in) | trap drain size (mm) | maximum distance to trap (mm) |
|---|---|---|---|
| 1¼ | 2 ft 6 in | 32 | 762 |
| 1½ | 3 ft 6 in | 38 | 1067 |
| 2 | 5 ft | 51 | 1524 |
| 3 | 6 ft | 76 | 1829 |
| 4+ | 10 ft | 102+ | 3048 |

¼ in/ft (20.9 mm/m)

Reproduced from the 1997 edition of the *Uniform Plumbing Code*, copyright 1997, with the permission of the publishers, the International Association of Plumbing and Mechanical Officials.

## Sprinkler locations [211313]

The design and installation of sprinkler systems are governed by local building codes. However, most codes refer to the standard published by the National Fire Protection Association, NFPA-13, which classifies the relative fire hazard of buildings into three groups: light, ordinary, and extra hazard. Light hazard occupancies include the type of uses most interior designers deal with. They include residences, offices, hospitals, schools, other institutions, museums, retail space, auditoriums, and restaurants.

The hazard classification and other requirements determine the required spacing of sprinklers. When designing reflected ceiling plans for most occupancies, the following guidelines can be used.

In light hazard occupancies there must be one sprinkler for each 200 $ft^2$ (18.6 $m^2$) if the system is not hydraulically designed, or 225 $ft^2$ (20.9 $m^2$) if the system is hydraulically designed. Most sprinkler systems for commercial buildings are hydraulically designed either by the fire protection engineer or the fire protection contractor, so that the maximum coverage of 225 $ft^2$ is typically used in light hazard occupancies. However, for open wood joist ceilings, the maximum area drops to 130 $ft^2$ (12.1 $m^2$).

The maximum spacing between sprinkler heads is 15 ft (4570 mm) for the 225 $ft^2$ coverage requirement, with the maximum distance from a wall being half the required spacing, or 7½ ft (2285 mm). The minimum distance from partitions to the nearest sprinkler is 4 in (100 mm). Sprinklers near vertical obstructions (such as columns) over 4 in (100 mm) wide up to 24 in (609 mm) must be located at a distance at least three times the maximum distance of the obstruction. See Fig. 16.9.

There is also the small room rule. A small room is defined as a room with a smooth ceiling area, not exceeding 800 $ft^2$ (74 $m^2$), and of the light hazard occupancy classification. Within a small room, sprinklers may be located not more than 9 ft (2740 mm) from any single wall, as long as the sprinkler spacing and area limitations are not exceeded.

When beams, dropped ceilings, or other obstructions project below the main ceiling where the sprinklers are located, they must be located a certain distance away from the projection so that the water stream is not deflected. See Fig. 16.10(a). Table 16.3 gives the maximum distance above the bottom of the beam or obstruction based on the distance from the sprinkler to the obstruction, as shown in Figs. 16.10(a) and 16.10(b).

When sprinklers are installed in rooms with furniture systems, free-standing partitions, privacy curtains, or room dividers, there must be a minimum distance between the sprinkler and the top of the obstruction. This is diagrammed in Fig. 16.10(b), and the minimum distances are given in Table 16.4.

## Sprinkler heads [211313]

In most construction, only the sprinkler heads are visible, and several styles are available, including recessed, upright, pendent, and sidewall. Recessed types have a smooth cover that is flush with the ceiling. When there is a fire, the cover falls away and the sprinkler head activates. Upright heads are used where there is exposed plumbing and high, unfinished ceilings. Pendent sprinklers are the traditional types for finished ceilings, where the head extends a few inches below the ceiling. Sidewall heads are used for corridors and small rooms when one row of sprinklers will provide adequate coverage for narrow spaces. Horizontal sidewall sprinklers also can be plumbed from the walls instead of from the ceiling, which makes them useful for remodeling work.

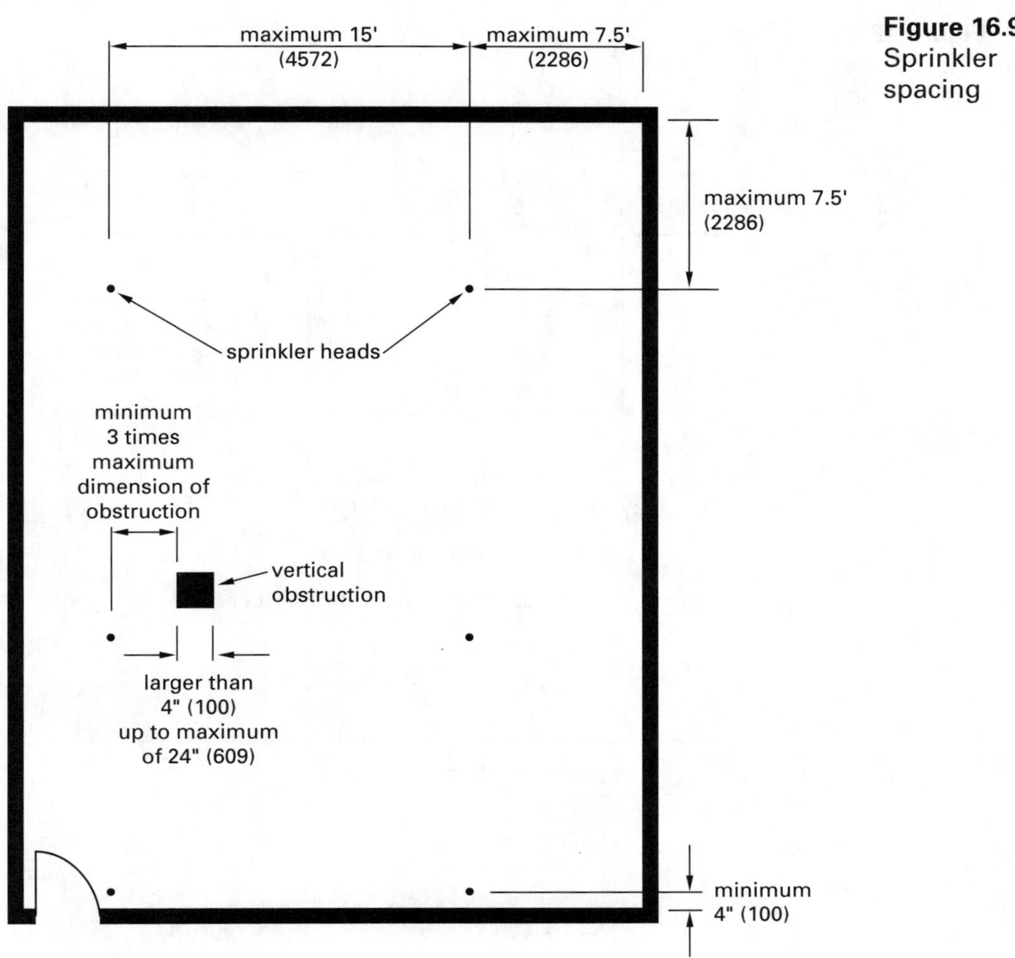


**Figure 16.9**
Sprinkler spacing

**Figure 16.10**
Sprinklers near obstructions

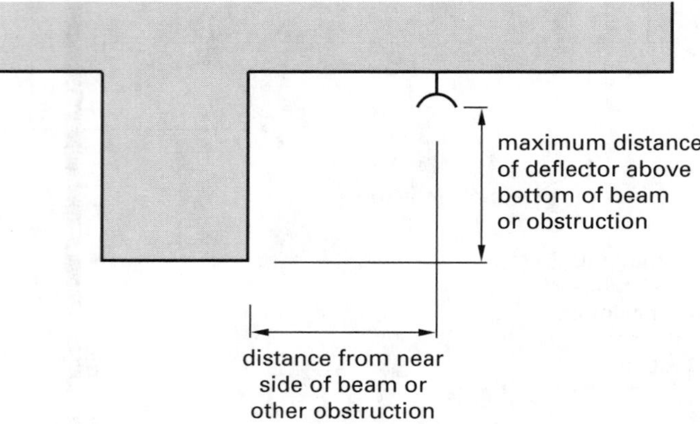


(a) sprinklers next to obstructions

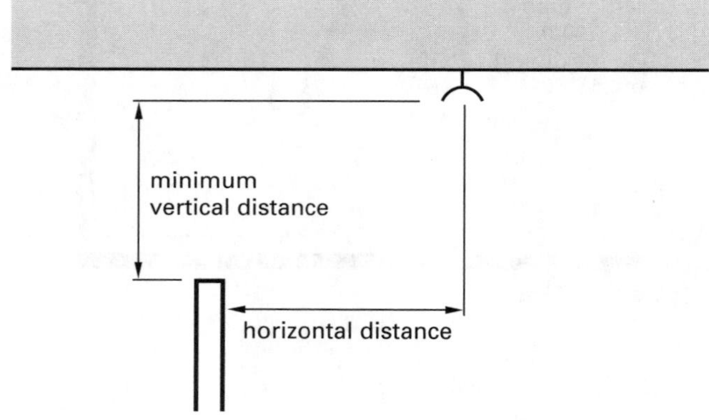


(b) sprinklers above obstructions

**Table 16.3** Position of sprinkler near beams or dropped ceilings

| distance from sprinkler to side of beam or obstruction (ft-in) | maximum allowable distance from deflector to bottom of beam or obstruction (in) | distance from sprinkler to side of beam or obstruction (mm) | maximum allowable distance from deflector to bottom of beam or obstruction (mm) |
|---|---|---|---|
| less than 1 ft | 0 | less than 305 | 0 |
| 1 ft to less than 1 ft 6 in | 2½ | 305 to less than 457 | 64 |
| 1 ft 6 in to less than 2 ft | 3½ | 457 to less than 610 | 89 |
| 2 ft to less than 2 ft 6 in | 5½ | 610 to less than 762 | 140 |
| 2 ft 6 in to less than 3 ft | 7½ | 762 to less than 914 | 190 |
| 3 ft to less than 3 ft 6 in | 9½ | 914 to less than 1067 | 241 |
| 3 ft 6 in to less than 4 ft | 12 | 1067 to less than 1219 | 305 |
| 4 ft to less than 4 ft 6 in | 14 | 1219 to less than 1372 | 356 |
| 4 ft 6 in to less than 5 ft | 16½ | 1372 to less than 1524 | 419 |
| 5 ft to less than 5 ft 6 in | 18 | 1524 to less than 1676 | 457 |
| 5 ft 6 in to less than 6 ft | 20 | 1676 to less than 1827 | 508 |
| 6 ft to less than 6 ft 6 in | 24 | 1827 to less than 1981 | 610 |
| 6 ft 6 in to less than 7 ft | 30 | 1981 to less than 2134 | 762 |
| 7 ft to less than 7 ft 6 in | 35 | 2134 to less than 2286 | 889 |

**Table 16.4**
Position of sprinkler near room dividers and similar obstructions

| horizontal distance from sprinkler to obstruction (in) | minimum vertical distance (in) | horizontal distance from sprinkler to obstruction (mm) | minimum vertical distance (mm) |
|---|---|---|---|
| 6 or less | 3 | 152 or less | 76 |
| more than 6 to 9 | 4 | more than 152 to 229 | 102 |
| more than 9 to 12 | 6 | more than 229 to 305 | 152 |
| more than 12 to 15 | 8 | more than 305 to 381 | 203 |
| more than 15 to 18 | 9.5 | more than 381 to 457 | 241 |
| more than 18 to 24 | 12.5 | more than 457 to 610 | 318 |
| more than 24 to 30 | 15.5 | more than 610 to 762 | 394 |
| more than 30 | 18 | more than 762 | 457 |

# 17

# STRUCTURAL COORDINATION

This chapter discusses some of the common structural systems and structural issues with which the interior designer should be familiar. As with mechanical and electrical systems, the designer should have a basic working knowledge of building structure and be able to read architects' and engineers' plans in order to make informed decisions about a variety of questions. These questions include the following.

- Is an element structural, and is it feasible to modify it?
- Can floor penetrations be made?
- Is building movement expected, and how can it be accommodated?
- Is a structural review necessary for the proposed new floor loading?
- How should new interior construction elements interface with existing structural elements?
- Will fire protection of structural elements need to be repaired, or should new protection be included in the design?

In addition to providing information about these kinds of questions, this chapter reviews the basic vocabulary and graphic representation of structural elements the interior designer should know when reviewing drawings and working on the job site.

The majority of this chapter covers commercial construction. Refer to the section near the end of the chapter for a discussion of residential and small commercial structural systems that use wood framing.

## STRUCTURAL SYSTEMS

This section briefly describes the most common types of structural systems. The interior designer will most likely encounter these systems when modifications are proposed or required because of interior design decisions.

### Steel [051200]

Steel is one of the most commonly used structural materials because of its high strength, availability, and ability to adapt to a wide variety of structural conditions. Steel is particularly suited to multifloor construction because of its strength and structural continuity.

Two of the most common steel structural systems are the beam-and-girder system and the open-web steel joist system. See Figs. 17.1(a) and 17.1(b).

In the beam-and-girder system, large members span between columns, and smaller beams are framed into them. The girders span the shorter distance, while the beams span the longer distances. Typical spans for this system are from 25 ft to 40 ft (7.6 m to 12 m), with the beams spaced about 8 ft to 10 ft on center (2440 mm to 3050 mm). The steel framing is usually covered with steel decking (see Fig. 17.13), which spans between the beams. A concrete top is poured over the decking to complete the floor slab. This type of construction is commonly found in mid- to high-rise office buildings.

When this type of structural system is encountered, there is usually limited space between the bottom of the girders and the suspended ceiling. The possibility of adding new mechanical ductwork or installing large recessed light fixtures should be reviewed before final decisions are made about the reflected ceiling plan.

Open-web steel joists span between beams or bearing walls as shown in Fig. 17.1(b). The various types of open-web joists can span from 20 ft (6.1 m) up to 144 ft (44 m). Depths range from 8 in to 72 in (200 mm to 1830 mm). Open-web joists are typically spaced 2 ft to 6 ft on center (600 mm to 1800 mm). As with the beam-and-girder system, steel decking spans between the joists, and a concrete slab is poured on top of the decking. A detailed view of one end of an open-web steel joist is shown in Fig. 17.2.

Interior designers usually encounter open-web steel joists in one-story or low-rise buildings with wide column spacing. Because the webs are open, mechanical and electrical service ducts, pipes, and conduit can easily be run between the web members. Suspended ceilings and other lightweight interior elements can also easily be hung from the bottoms of the joists.

## Concrete [033100]

There are many variations of concrete structural systems, but the two primary types are cast-in-place and precast. With cast-in-place buildings, concrete is poured into forms where it hardens before the forms are removed. Precast components are usually formed in a plant and shipped to the job site where they are set in place and rigidly connected to form the structure.

The majority of cast-in-place concrete systems utilize only mild steel reinforcing set in the formwork before the concrete is placed. However, in some instances with long-span structures, cast-in-place concrete is post-tensioned. This means that steel cables are tightened after the concrete sets, creating extra compression forces in the beam or slab. If a slab is post-tensioned, it should not be penetrated for pipes or conduit.

There are five basic types of cast-in-place systems. These are shown in Fig. 17.3. The beam-and-girder system shown in Fig. 17.3(a) functions in a manner similar to a steel system in which the slab is supported by intermediate beams, which are carried by larger girders. Typical spans are in the range of 15 ft to 30 ft (4.6 m to 9.1 m). The slab is poured integrally with the beams.

A concrete joist system (see Fig. 17.3(b)) is comprised of concrete members spaced 24 in or 36 in (610 mm or 914 mm) apart, run-ning in one direction, which frame into larger beams. The slab is also poured integrally with the joists. Because the joists are close together, it is more difficult to drill holes for small pipes and conduit.

With flat plate construction, shown in Fig. 17.3(c), the floor slab is designed and

**Figure 17.1**
Common steel structural systems

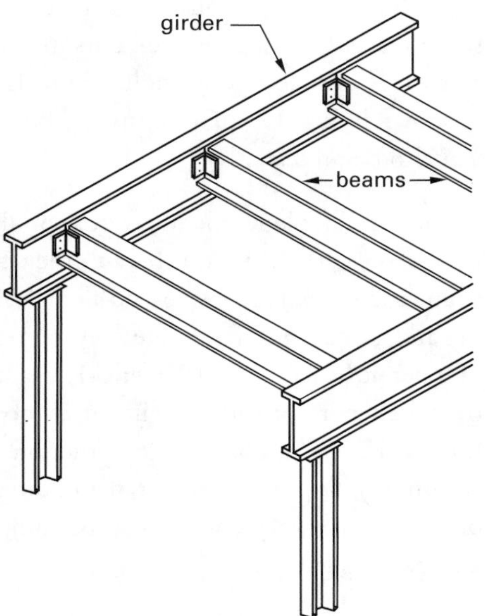


(a) beam-and-girder system

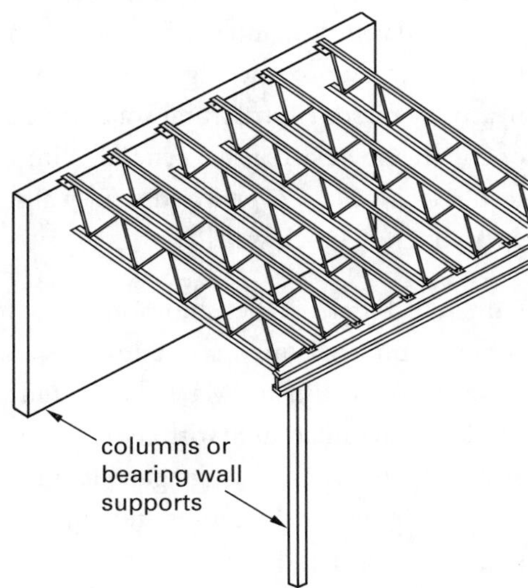


(b) open-web steel joist system

**Figure 17.2**
Open-web steel joist

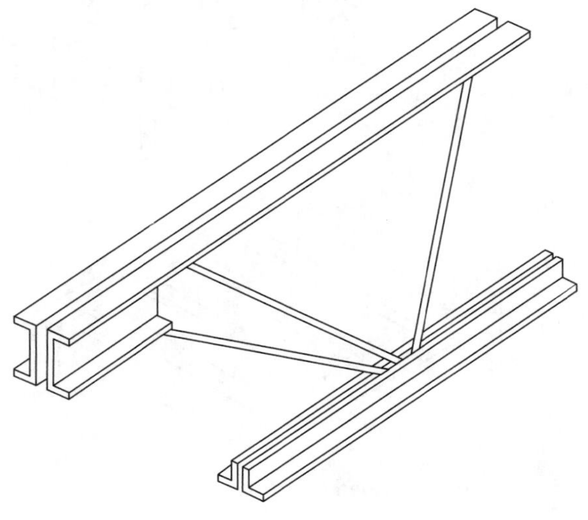

reinforced to transfer loads directly to the columns, which generally do not exceed 25 ft (7.6 m) spacing. Flat plate construction is commonly used in situations where floor-to-floor height must be kept to a minimum. Because of the closely spaced reinforcing required, it is often difficult to drill these types of floors for electrical service or small pipes.

Flat slab construction, shown in Fig. 17.3(d), is similar to flat plate, except that drop panels (increased slab thickness around the columns) are used to increase strength. Sometimes the truncated pyramids or cones are used instead of drop panels.

A waffle slab system (more technically, a two-way joist system), shown in Fig. 17.3(e), can provide support for heavier loads at slightly longer spans than the flat slab system. Waffle slabs are often left unexposed, with lighting integrated into the coffers.

Precast concrete consists of factory-made pieces. High-strength steel cables are

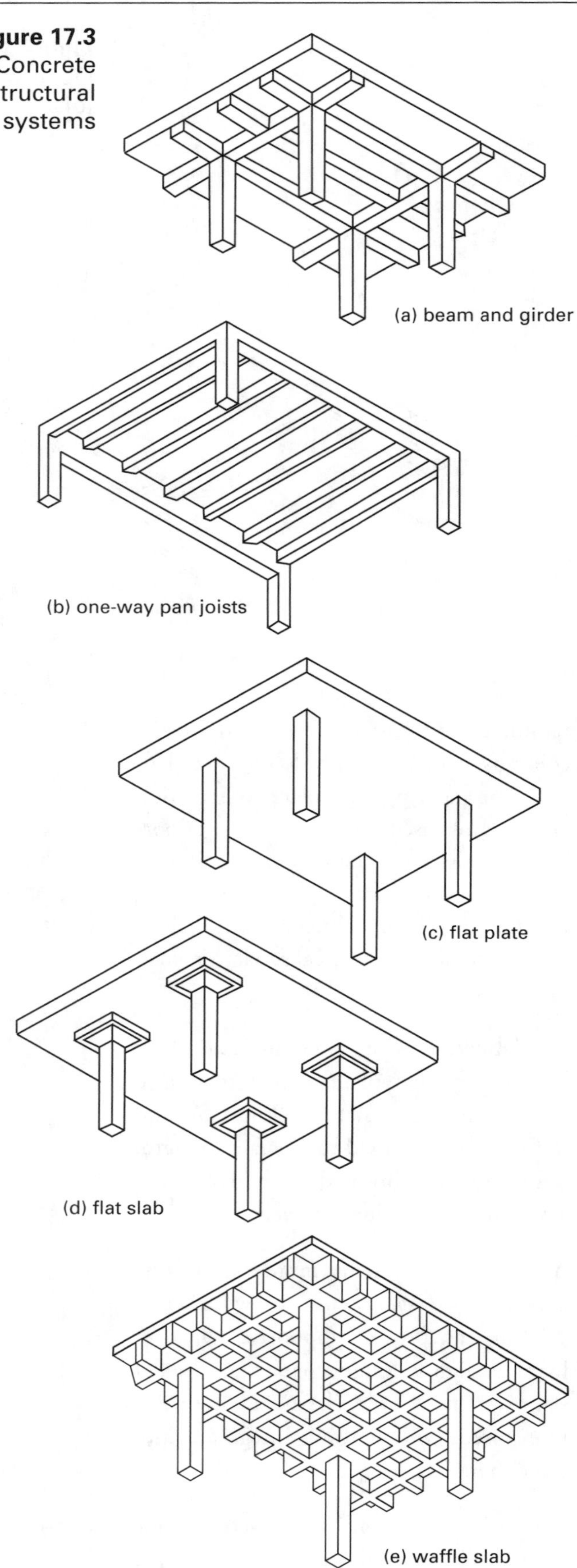


**Figure 17.3** Concrete structural systems

stretched in the precasting forms before the concrete is poured. After the concrete attains a certain minimum strength, the cables are released, and they transfer compressive stresses to the concrete. The members are then shipped to the construction site and set in place. Precast concrete floors include single tees, double tees, and hollow core slabs as shown in Fig. 17.4. Columns and beams can also be precast.

Single- and double-tee members are a popular form of precast construction because they can simultaneously serve as beam-and-floor decking and are easy and fast to erect. A topping of concrete (usually about 2 in thick) is placed over the tees to provide a uniform, smooth floor surface. Double-tee construction is commonly found in industrial buildings, one- and two-story commercial buildings, and parking garages.

## Masonry [042200]

As a structural system in contemporary construction, masonry is generally limited to bearing walls, discussed in the following section. Masonry includes brick and concrete block, but due to the high cost of brick, nearly all masonry structural walls are built of concrete block. Brick is generally limited to use as a veneer over wood stud walls or over concrete block walls.

Concrete block is the common term for concrete unit masonry, also known as concrete masonry units (CMU). This building product is manufactured with cement, water, and various types of aggregate including gravel, expanded shale or slate, expanded slag or pumice, and limestone cinders.

CMU dimensions are based on a nominal 4 in module, with actual dimensions being ⅜ in less than the nominal dimension to allow for mortar joints. Unit dimensions are referred to by width, height, and then length. One of the most common sizes is an 8 × 8 × 16 unit, which is actually 7⅝ in wide and high and 15⅝ in long. (A metric block is 190 × 190 × 390 with 10 mm joints.) Concrete block is manufactured in a wide variety of shapes to suit particular applications.

Concrete block is manufactured with two open cells. The cells in the block may be left open when loading is light, or reinforced and filled with grout if more strength is needed. Figure 17.5 shows the construction of a typical reinforced, grouted concrete masonry wall. If an opening is required in a concrete block wall, a structural engineer should be consulted to design the required support for the opening. Creating a small opening for a door or small window is usually not a difficult procedure. Interior design elements can be suspended from masonry walls by using the appropriate type of fastener.

## Bearing walls

Bearing walls support loads from above. These include live loads, such as people and furniture, and dead loads, such as the weight of the structure itself. A bearing wall may be concrete, masonry, or wood framing. Because of their nature as structural supports, bearing walls cannot be removed and can only be pierced for doors and other openings if the top of the opening is framed with an adequately engineered lintel or beam.

Interior designers should be able to recognize common instances of bearing walls, either from the architect's drawings or from field observations. When it is not clear if a wall is loadbearing or not, an architect or structural engineer should be consulted if any modifications are contemplated.

In residential construction, exterior walls (the walls under the eaves of a roof) are usually bearing walls, and some interior partitions may also be bearing. The first-story exterior walls of a two-story house are nearly always loadbearing. If a wall needs to be cut for a moderately sized opening (a doorway, for example), it is a relatively simple

**Figure 17.4**
Precast concrete shapes

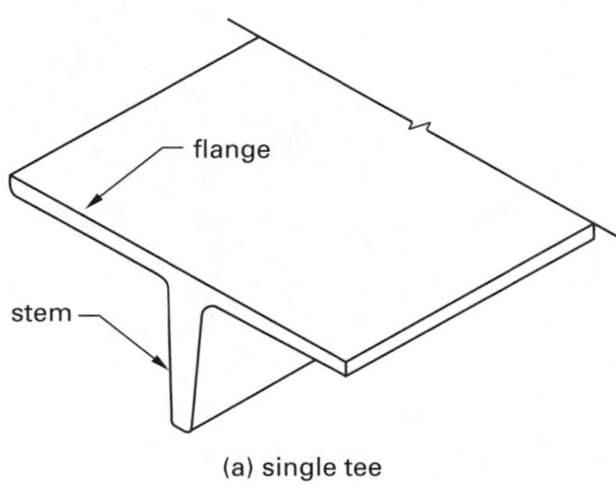


(a) single tee

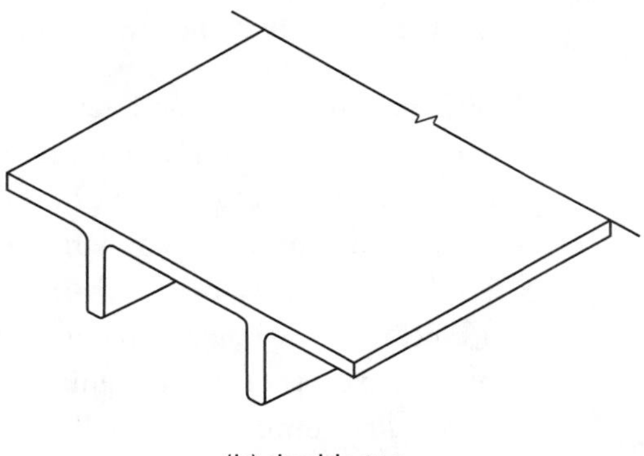

(b) double tee

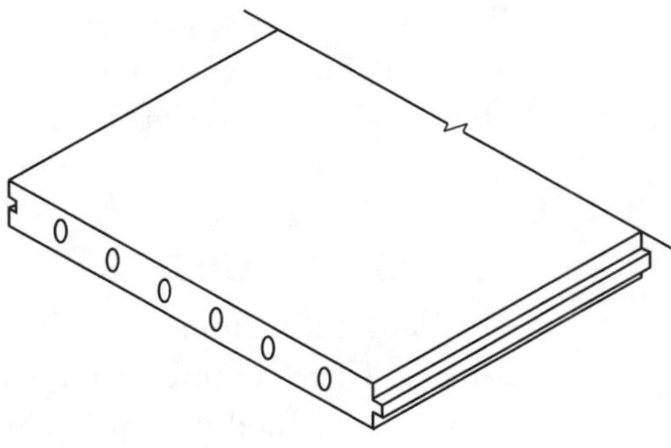

(c) hollow-core slab

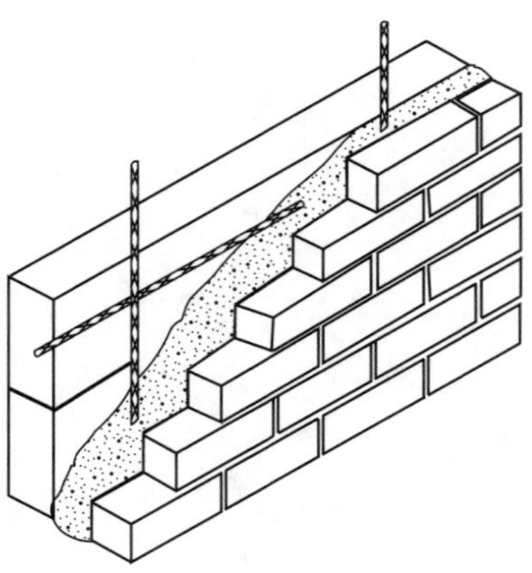

**Figure 17.5** Reinforced, grouted concrete masonry wall

matter to have additional studs installed with a double header or some other type of lintel.

In commercial construction, fewer bearing walls are used than in residential construction; most structures are some form of column-and-beam system with nonbearing infill. The core walls of high-rise buildings are nearly always structural and cannot be pierced except for small openings for pipes. In smaller commercial buildings, concrete walls and many masonry walls are bearing.

In all cases, a structural engineer should be consulted if the interior designer is not sure whether a wall is bearing or not and if an opening needs to be created in the wall.

## LOADS ON BUILDINGS

A building load is a force acting on a building element. There are three major load types: gravity, lateral, and dynamic. This section discusses these loads and how they affect interior design.

### Gravity loads

Gravity loads include dead loads and live loads.

Dead loads are the vertical loads due to the weight of the building and any permanent equipment. These include such things as columns, beams, exterior and interior walls, floors, and mechanical equipment. Building structures are designed initially to support all the dead loads. Even though the interior designer will plan interior partitioning and other construction elements that change the dead loads, the original design of the building considers these normal dead loads on an average square-foot basis; that is, in the initial design, an allowance is made for interior partitioning. The only time an interior designer should consult a structural engineer is if plans call for the installation of unusually heavy partitioning (such as a masonry wall) or heavy equipment.

Live loads include the weight of people, furniture, and other moveable equipment. Buildings are originally designed to accommodate a particular amount of uniform live load, which is established by building codes for different occupancies. For example, the structure of residential floors is designed for a live load of 40 lbf/ft$^2$ (0.18 kN/m$^2$), while offices are designed for 50 lbf/ft$^2$ (0.22 kN/m$^2$).

Codes also require that floors be designed to support concentrated loads if the specified load on an otherwise unloaded floor would produce stresses greater than those caused by the uniform load. The concentrated load is assumed to be located on any space 2½ ft$^2$ (0.232 m$^2$).

If a space is being designed for a use other than its original purpose and the floor loading will be increased (for heavy equipment, book stacks, or files, for example), the designer should consult with a structural engineer to determine if the floor is capable of carrying the additional load. If it is not capable, the designer should have additional structural reinforcement engineered. In some high-rise buildings, the structural bays near the center of the building were originally designed for heavier loading. File rooms and book stacks should be located in such spaces in the early planning stages.

### Lateral loads

Lateral loads include wind loads and earthquake loads. As with dead loads these are provided for in the original design of the building. However, they may need to be taken into account if interior construction elements will be attached to the structure of the building or are required by code to resist earthquake loads.

The instances when the interior designer needs to consider the effects of wind on a building are discussed in the section on building movement.

For earthquake loading, the International Building Code and other model codes divide the United States into different zones, representing the potential severity of seismic activity. In the least severe zones, no special detailing needs to be included by the interior designer. In high-risk areas, the designer must ascertain the requirements for the particular geographical area in which the project is located.

Interior construction elements that may need to be detailed to resist earthquake forces include partitions that are tied to the ceiling or are over 6 ft (1829 mm) high, suspended ceilings, HVAC ductwork, light fixtures, sprinkler and other piping, bookcases, storage cabinets and laboratory equipment, and access floors. Some common details for ceiling bracing are shown in Ch. 2.

### Dynamic loads

When a load is applied suddenly or changes rapidly, it is called a *dynamic load.* When a force is only applied suddenly, it is often called an *impact load.* Examples of dynamic loads are automobiles moving in a parking garage, elevators traveling in a shaft, or a helicopter landing on the roof of a building. Interior designers seldom encounter situations where dynamic loads are imposed by the interior use of the building. However, if such a condition may exist, the designer should consult with a structural engineer.

## BUILDING MOVEMENT

All buildings move to some extent. Movement can be caused by shrinkage of materials (like wood), compression of materials over time, deflection of materials under load (like floors), ground settling or heaving, earthquakes, swaying caused by wind, and expansion and contraction caused by temperature differentials.

Interior construction must take into account the possible movement of the building structure. For example, interior partitions in commercial construction that attach to the structural floors above and to the perimeter of the building should be designed with slip joints to allow the building to move slightly without putting pressure on the partitions. Movement at the top of the partition can be caused by structural deflection of the floor above, and movement at the perimeter can be caused by wind sway. Partitions rigidly attached to the structure may buckle and crack if slip joints are not used.

Figures 1.9, 1.10, and 1.11 illustrate some common methods of detailing slip joints. Similar types of slip joints should be used whenever minor building movement is expected. Large movements are accommodated by building expansion joints, but these are usually already in place as part of the design of the building.

In large buildings, provisions have to be made to allow parts of the building to move separately. To enable this movement, the structure of each part is entirely separated during design and construction. The large joints are covered inside the building with expansion joint covers (from 2 in to 8 in wide) that can slide back and forth as the building moves. Two of the common conditions are shown in Fig. 17.6. If these conditions are encountered during interior design, they cannot be covered up with other finish materials.

## FLOOR PENETRATIONS

In addition to determining the maximum allowable loads, floor construction may limit the number and type of floor penetrations, if any are possible at all. Floor penetrations range from minor items, such as a core drill for an electrical conduit, to major reconstructions, such as for stairways.

**Figure 17.6** Expansion joint cover assemblies

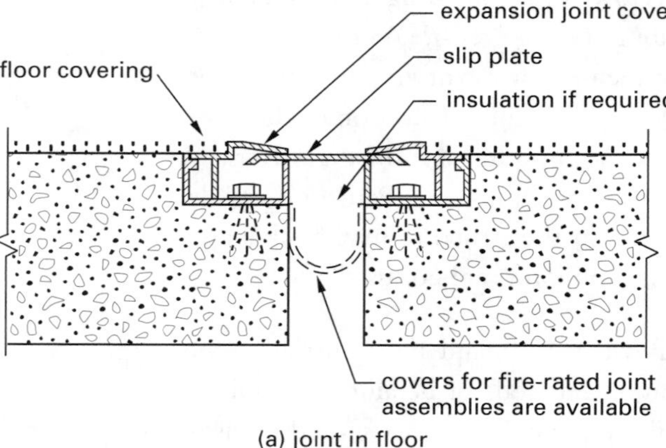


(a) joint in floor

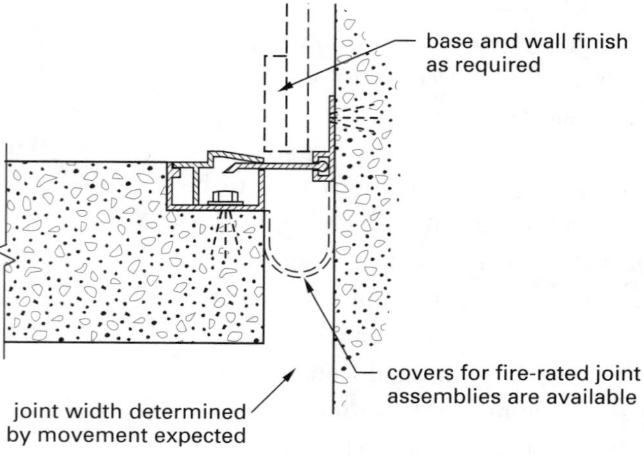


(b) joint at wall

Floors in commercial buildings are constructed primarily of poured-in-place concrete, precast concrete, or concrete-on-metal decking. Poured-in-place concrete framing types include those shown in Fig. 17.3. All of the cast-in-place concrete structural systems are difficult to cut through easily, but of the five types shown in Fig. 17.3, the beam-and-girder system and one-way pan joist system are the easiest to penetrate with small core drilling for pipes and poke-through electrical outlets. This is because there is less reinforcing in these systems.

Cast-in-place concrete floor systems can be pierced for small openings such as a floor-mounted electrical box. However, holes cannot be cut where the columns intersect the floor or where beams are located. For larger openings, the easiest types of concrete floors to cut are flat plates and flat slabs. However, for large openings, these floors still require additional structural support around the opening, which must be designed by a structural engineer. The ribs of waffle slabs can be cut for large openings, such as stairways, but this task is difficult and also requires additional support around the cut.

Because the stems of tee sections are deep and contain prestressed cable they cannot be cut, so openings are limited to the areas between the tee sections. For hollow core slabs, small openings can be cut through the existing cores but should not be cut through the solid portion where the prestressing cables are located.

Post-tensioned concrete is another concrete structural system that is sometimes found in buildings. In this system, the post-tensioning steel strands (called *tendons*) are stressed after the concrete has been poured in place and cured. Because they are stressed under high pressure and keep this stress during the life of the building, the slabs in which they are located cannot be cut.

One of the most common types of floor and roof construction is concrete-on-metal decking. Corrugated sheet steel is supported by steel beams and columns, and serves as a working platform, the form for the concrete, and part of the structural system. Concrete is poured over the decking and leveled to create the final rough floor. Because of the nature of this structural system, it is easy to have small and moderately sized holes cut for conduit, ductwork, and the like. If larger penetrations are required for stairways or elevators, steel angles or beams can be placed around the perimeter of the cut to provide the necessary support.

Whenever a cut in a concrete floor is proposed, reinforcing bars and other embedded items can be located by having the floor X-rayed near the proposed cut.

## FIRE-RESISTIVE RATINGS

As described in Ch. 19, all buildings are classified by the building code as a certain type based on the fire-resistance ratings of various major components such as structure, exterior walls, and shaft enclosures. In commercial construction, the structural frame of a building may be protected with fire-resistant construction rated from 1 hour to 3 hours. The rating and method of protection is part of the original architect's building design. However, there are instances where the interior designer may want to remove the existing covering and replace it with something else. The new covering must provide the same amount of fire protection as the existing covering. Common examples of this include replacing a column or beam cover with another size or shape of cover, or enclosing a new vertical shaft (such as a stairway or dumbwaiter).

If steel is protected with spray-on fireproofing, there may be some damage when other construction elements are attached. However, the fireproofing can easily be repaired to maintain the fire-resistant rating of the member.

## RESIDENTIAL AND SMALL COMMERCIAL STRUCTURAL SYSTEMS

Structural systems for single-family residential construction and small commercial construction typically use wood and wood products as the primary material.

Wood is one of the oldest and most common structural materials. It is plentiful, inexpensive, relatively strong in both compression and tension, and easy to work with and fasten. In contemporary construction, wood may be used either directly as it is cut from a tree or as a hybrid wood product where pieces of wood are manufactured into a larger structural element.

Figure 17.7 shows typical residential construction. In addition to showing how the joists and exterior stud wall are constructed, this drawing shows how the joists are set on a sill plate, which is anchored to the concrete foundation wall.

In this type of construction, bearing walls are typically made with small, repetitive elements called *studs*. For residential construction, the most common type of stud wall consists of 2 × 4 (actual size of 1½ in by 3½ in [38 mm by 89 mm]) studs placed 16 in (406 mm) on center. Occasionally, 6 in (152 mm) deep studs will be used. Studs of this size are adequate to support a one-story or two-story house. The same stud size and spacing are used for nonbearing walls and interior partitions.

*Joists* are horizontal repetitive members used to support the floor. They are made from nominal 2 in thick wood and their depth is determined by the distance they are required to span. Common depths are 8 in, 10 in, and 12 in. The actual size of an 8 in joist is

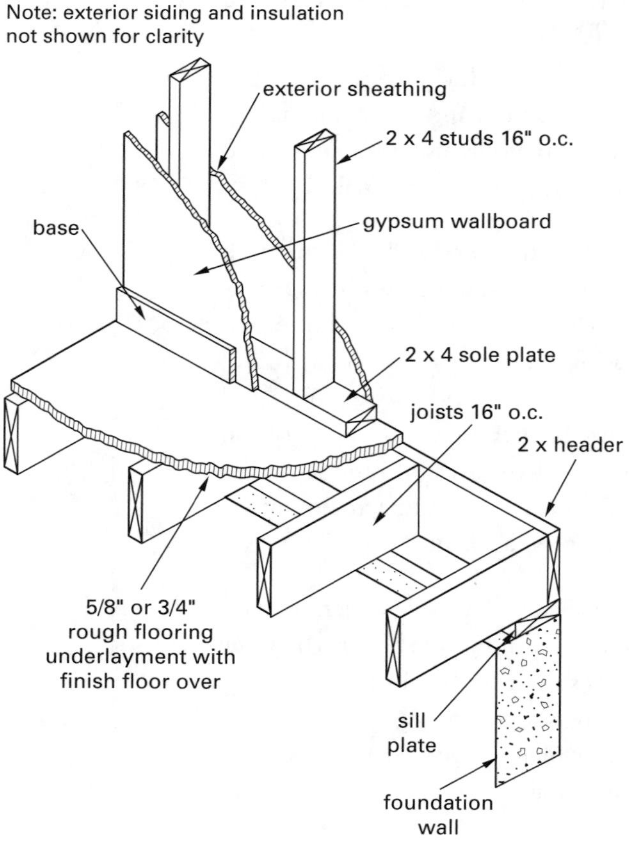

**Figure 17.7**
Residential framing

Note: exterior siding and insulation not shown for clarity

7¼ in. The actual sizes of 10 in and 12 in joists are 9¼ in and 11¼ in, respectively.

The space between joists is spanned with plywood or particleboard subflooring on which underlayment is placed in preparation for finish flooring. Sometimes, a single sheet of ¾ in (19 mm) subfloor/under-layment is used, although it is not as desirable.

Sheathing is nailed to the outside of the stud wall to stiffen it and provide a nailing base for the exterior finish material. If brick veneer is used, the brick is held to the sheathing with corrugated metal strips. On the inside of the wall, ½ in gypsum wallboard is nailed or screwed to the studs. Insulation is placed between the studs and joists in thicknesses as required by the climate of the region.

When openings for doors and small windows are required, they are framed at the top with lintels (also called headers). These are usually double 2 × 4, 2 × 6, or 2 × 8 members oriented vertically to act as a beam to carry the loads. See Fig. 17.8.

When large openings are required, framing methods other than double two-by members must be used. These may include using stronger laminated veneer lumber (as described in the next section), glued laminated beams, or small steel beams.

**Figure 17.8**
Open framing

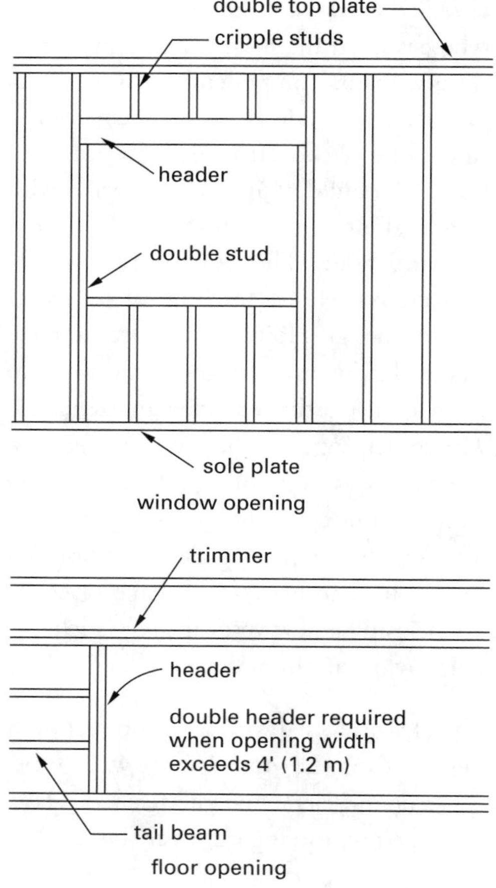

**Figure 17.9**
Platform construction

rafter
double top plate
stud
header - continuous
floor sheathing
joist
exterior sheathing
stud
sole plate
sill plate

Joists can normally span up to about 20 ft (6100 mm). When longer spans are required or a beam is needed to support several joists, steel or manufactured wood products must be used.

For two-story construction, a technique called *platform framing* is used, as illustrated in Fig. 17.9. With this method, wood studs one story high are placed on a sole plate at the bottom and spanned with a double top plate at the ceiling level. The second-floor joists bear on the top plate and, when the second-floor sheathing is in place, serve as a platform on which to erect the second-story stud walls and roof.

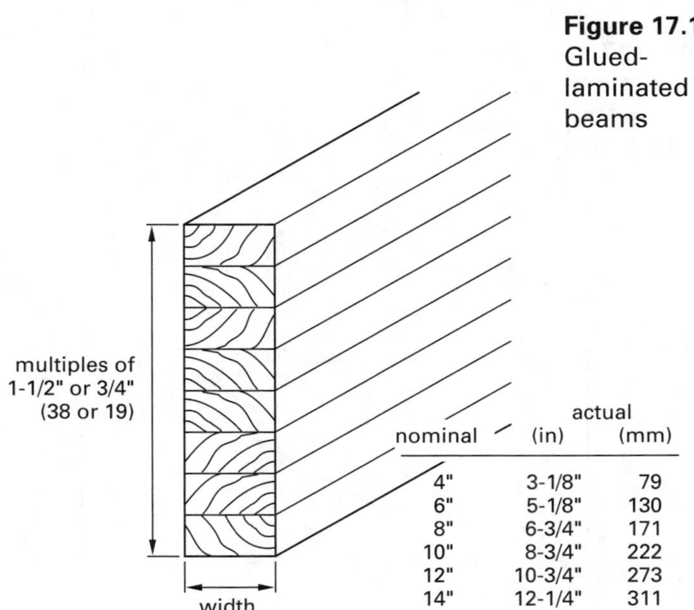


| nominal | actual (in) | actual (mm) |
|---|---|---|
| 4" | 3-1/8" | 79 |
| 6" | 5-1/8" | 130 |
| 8" | 6-3/4" | 171 |
| 10" | 8-3/4" | 222 |
| 12" | 10-3/4" | 273 |
| 14" | 12-1/4" | 311 |

**Figure 17.10**
Glued-laminated beams

When stronger members are required in small commercial construction and some residential construction, glued-laminated members may be used. See Fig. 17.10. Glued-laminated wood members are built up from a number of individual pieces of lumber glued together and finished under factory conditions for use as beams, columns, purlins, and other structural components. Glulams, as they are usually called, are used where larger wood members are required for heavy loads or long spans and simple sawn timber pieces are not available or cannot meet the strength requirements. Glulam construction is also used where unusual structural shapes are required and appearance is a consideration. In addition to being fabricated in simple rectangular shapes, glulam members can be formed into arches, tapered forms, and pitched shapes.

Glulam members are manufactured in standard widths and depths as shown in Fig. 17.10. If necessary, interior design components may be framed into glulam beams using simple wood fasteners.

**Figure 17.11** Manufactured lumber products

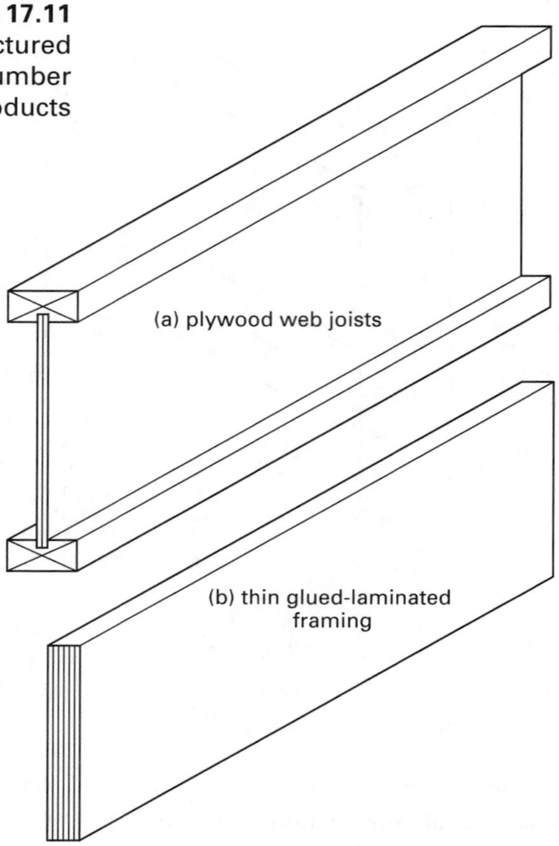

## Alternative structural materials

In an effort to employ the many structural advantages of wood and increase utilization of forest products while minimizing the problems of defects and limited strength in solid wood members, several manufactured products have been developed.

One is a lightweight I-shaped joist consisting of a top and bottom chord of solid or laminated construction separated by a plywood web. See Fig. 17.11(a). This type of joist is used in residential and light commercial construction and allows longer spans than are possible with a solid wood joist system. It has a very efficient structural shape, like a steel wide-flange beam, and because it is manufactured in a factory, problems such as warping, splits, checks, and other common wood defects are eliminated. This product is stronger and stiffer than a standard wood joist. Its use is increasing because straight, good-quality solid joists are becoming more expensive and difficult to find. Within limits, holes can be drilled in the web to accommodate small pipes and electrical wiring.

Another manufactured product is a wood member manufactured with individual layers of thin veneer glued together. See Fig. 17.11(b). Often referred to as laminated veneer lumber (LVL), it is used primarily for headers over large openings, either singly or built-up for beams. It is stronger than solid lumber of the same dimensions.

# GRAPHIC REPRESENTATION OF STRUCTURAL ELEMENTS

Existing structural supports generally cannot be removed and can only be relocated with great effort and expense. The interior designer must know how to identify structural elements on plans and sections in order to plan spaces and locate other interior elements intelligently. Fig. 17.12 shows some common symbols and drafting conventions that indicate various types of structural elements.

Sometimes the same symbol represents different elements depending on whether the view of the drawing is plan or section. For example, the H-shaped section in Fig. 17.12 represents a steel column if seen on a floor plan, but it (or a similar H-shaped section) represents a wide-flange beam if viewed in a vertical cross section.

# DEFINITIONS

*Core drill:* a machine used to cut a small opening in a concrete floor for conduit or poke-through electrical outlets

*Core wall:* in a high-rise building, the wall generally used as part of the structure of the building and surrounding the common building services such as elevator and stairway shafts, toilet rooms, mechanical rooms, and the like

*Cripple stud:* a stud above a door opening or below a windowsill

*Decking:* light-gage sheets of steel that are ribbed, fluted, or otherwise stiffened by shape for use in constructing a floor or roof. See Fig. 17.13.

**Figure 17.13**
Steel decking

**Figure 17.12**
Structural symbols

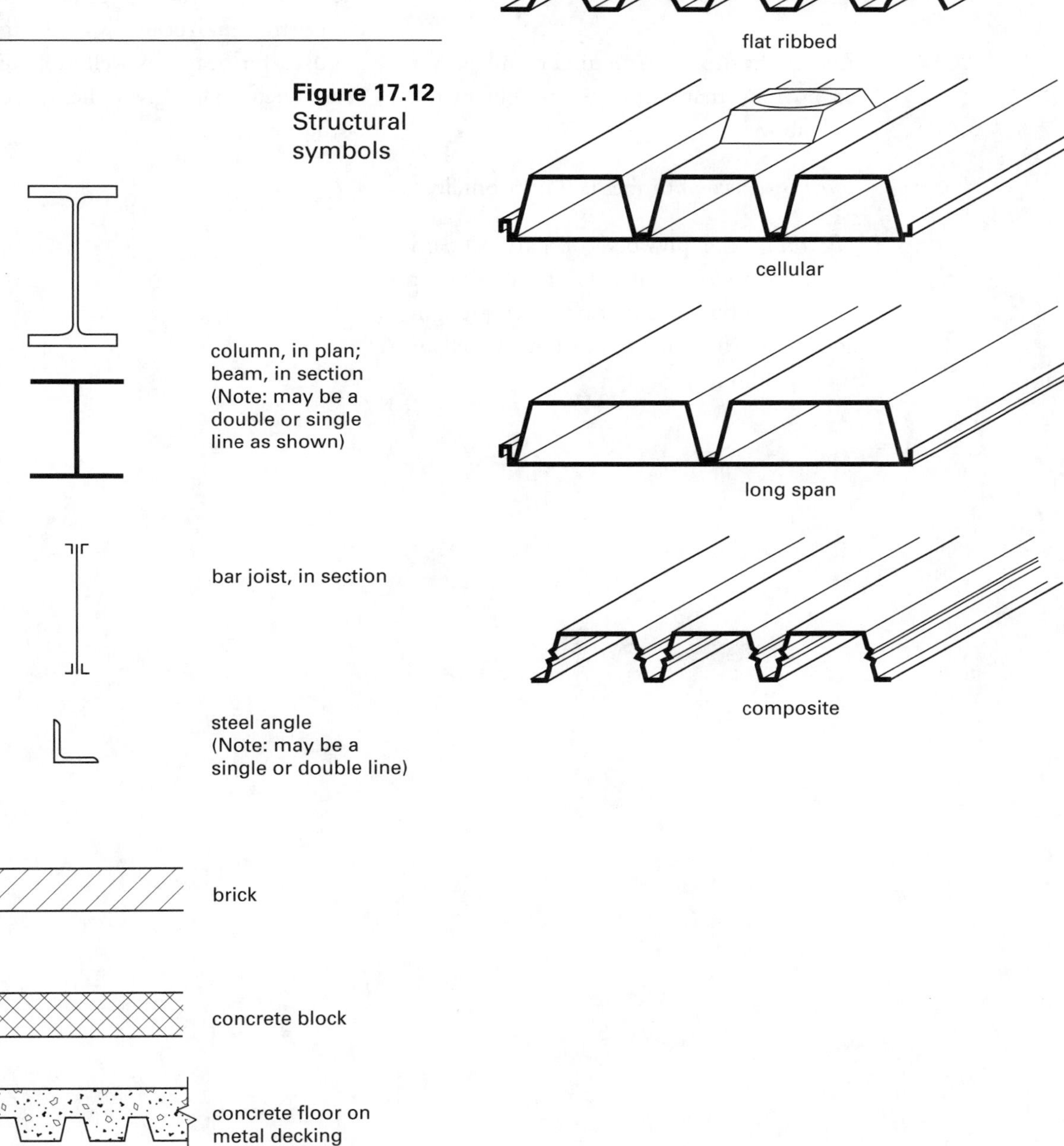

*Grout:* a mixture of portland cement, water, and sand, containing enough water to allow it to be poured or pumped into joints, spaces, and cracks within masonry walls

*Header:* a framing member that crosses and supports the ends of joists, transferring the weight of the joist to parallel joists. Headers are used to form openings in wood-framed floors.

*Lintel:* a horizontal structural member over an opening that carries the weight of the wall above it

*Purlin:* a piece of timber laid horizontally

*Sheathing:* the plywood or particleboard covering placed over exterior studding or rafters of a building that provides strength and a base for the application of wall or roof cladding

*Sole plate:* a horizontal wood member that serves as the base for the studs in a stud partition

*Trimmer:* a wood member in a floor or roof used to support a header

*Wide-flange beam:* a structural beam of steel having a shape whose cross section resembles the letter H. A wide-flange beam has wider flanges than an I-beam. Wide-flange beams are used for beams as well as columns because their shape gives them strength in both directions.

# 18

# BARRIER-FREE DESIGN

Barrier-free design, or *universal design,* should be an integral part of every building and interior space. Although building codes and many federal and state agencies require accessibility, the overriding regulation today is the Americans with Disabilities Act (ADA). This federal law requires, among other things, that all commercial and public accommodations be accessible to people with disabilities. Although the ADA is not a national building code and does not depend on inspection for its enforcement, building owners must either comply with the requirements or be liable for civil suits.

The ADA is a complex, four-title civil rights law. Title III, Public Accommodations, is the part that most affects designers. The current design requirements for construction are mainly found in the ADA Accessibility Guidelines (ADAAG), 1991, which is technically Appendix A to 28 CFR 36, the Code of Fed-eral Regulations rule that implements Title III of the Act. When designers refer to the ADA, they are usually referring to the design criteria contained in the ADAAG.

At the time of this writing, a revision of the ADAAG had been issued (in July 2004) by the Architectural and Transportation Barriers Compliance Board (commonly called the Access Board). However, this revision had not yet been adopted or implemented by any of the various agencies that actually enforce standards based on the Access Board's guidelines. Changes to the ADA must be formally adopted by the Department of Justice, and that body will write the final rules that the public must follow. The Board's guidelines will also serve as the basis for standards used to enforce the Architectural Barriers Act (ABA) of 1968. The ABA covers facilities that are designed, built, altered, or leased with federal funds. In addition, the ADAAG will serve as the basis for standards issued by four other standard-setting Federal agencies: the General Services Administration, the Department of Defense, the Department of Housing and Urban Development, and the U.S. Postal Service. Previously, the standard used by these agencies was the Uniform Federal Accessibility Standards (UFAS). At the time of this writing, the General Services Administration and the Postal Service have adopted the new ADAAG 2004 while the Department of Defense and the Department of Housing and Urban Development have not. Because the Justice Department, as well as other federal agencies, is expected to adopt the new ADAAG, the information contained in this chapter is based on the revised ADAAG (2004).

One of the most significant changes to the 2004 version of the ADAAG is the degree to which it coordinates with other model building codes and standards. Specifically, the Access Board has made its guidelines more consistent with the International Building Code (IBC), industry standards, and ICC/ANSI A117.1-2003, *Accessible and Usable Buildings and Facilities.* In some cases, the ADAAG references provisions of the IBC and other industry standards. This coordination effort is meant to facilitate compliance.

Additionally, the 2004 ADAAG has expanded scoping provisions. *Scoping provisions* are requirements that dictate when and how many accessible elements must be provided. For example, scoping provisions tell the designer how many seats a restaurant must allow for wheelchair access or what types of drinking fountains must be provided. Many additional types of facilities are now covered, such as play areas, swimming pools, amusement rides, detention facilities, and others. Refer to the ADAAG for all the scoping requirements.

The ADAAG has also been reorganized with a new numbering system consisting of three parts. The first part deals with the ADA application and scoping, the second part covers the ABA application and scoping, and the last part gives the technical requirements intended to be used by both the ADA and ABA. The technical requirements consist of the detailed provisions for accessible elements, many of which are covered in this chapter.

Other local and federal laws and regulations also govern accessibility. For example, the ADA does not cover single- or multi-family housing. Multi-family housing is regulated mainly by the federal Fair Housing Act and by some state laws.

In order to design according to the most recent rules, the designer must first determine which accessibility law applies to the project (ADA, the Fair Housing Act, or the Architectural Barriers Act) and then determine what the applicable guidelines are. To verify the most current regulations, contact the Department of Justice, Civil Rights Division, Disability Rights Section (**www.usdoj.gov/crt/ada**) and the Access Board (**www.access-board.gov**).

**Figure 18.1** Maneuvering clearances

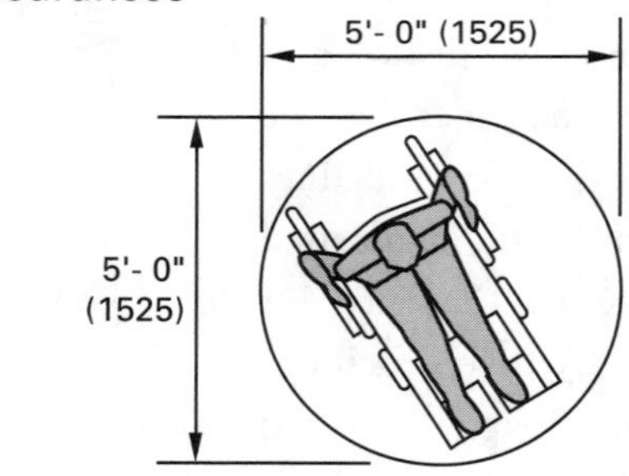


(a) turning diameter

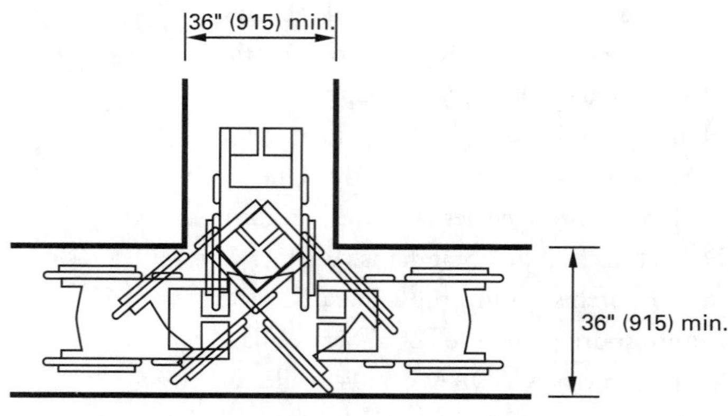


(b) T-shaped space for 180° turns

## ACCESSIBLE ROUTES

An *accessible route* is a continuous unobstructed path connecting all accessible elements and spaces in a building or facility. (For the purposes of this book, exterior requirements are not covered.) It includes corridors, doorways, floors, ramps, elevators, lifts, and clear floor space at fixtures. The standards for accessible routes are designed to accommodate persons with severe disabilities using wheelchairs, but are also intended to provide ease of use for people with other disabilities.

Accessible routes and other clearances are based on basic dimensional requirements of wheelchairs. The minimum clear floor space required to accommodate one stationary wheelchair is 30 in by 48 in (760 mm by 1220 mm). For maneuverability, a minimum 60 in (1525 mm) diameter circle is required for a wheelchair to make a 180° turn, as shown in Fig. 18.1(a). In place of this, a T-shaped space may be provided, as shown in Fig. 18.1(b).

The minimum clear width for an accessible route is 36 in (915 mm) continuously and 32 in (815 mm) at a passage point, such as a doorway. The passage point cannot be more than 24 in (610 mm) long. The minimum passage width for two wheelchairs is 60 in (1525 mm). If an accessible route is less than 60 in wide, then passing spaces at least 60 in by 60 in (1525 mm by 1525 mm) must be provided at intervals not to exceed 200 ft (61 m). These requirements are shown in Figs. 18.2(a) and 18.2(b).

In toilet rooms the turning space may overlap with the required clear floor space at fixtures and controls and with the accessible route. The minimum dimensions for turns in corridors or around obstructions are shown in Figs. 18.3(a) and 18.3(b).

An accessible route may have a slope of up to 1:20 [1 in rise for every 20 in of distance (25.4 in for 508 mm)]. Slopes any greater than this are classified as ramps and must meet the requirements given later in this chapter.

## DOORWAYS

### Width and arrangement

Doors must have a minimum clear opening width of 32 in (815 mm) when the door is opened at 90°. The maximum depth of a doorway 32 in (813 mm) wide is 24 in

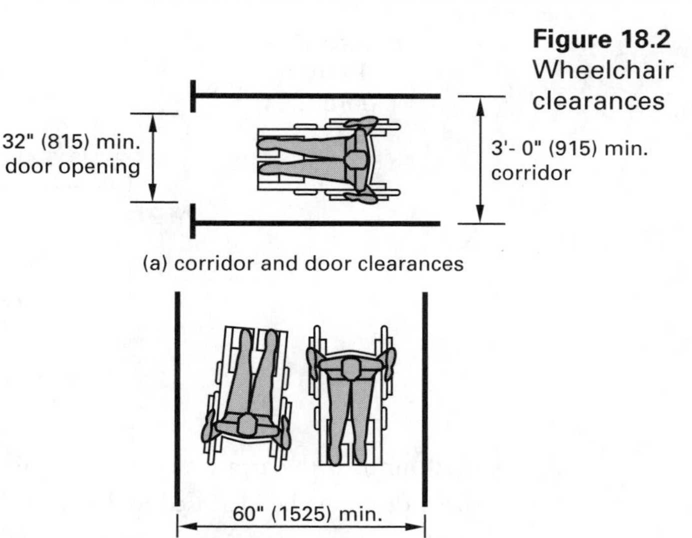


**Figure 18.2**
Wheelchair clearances

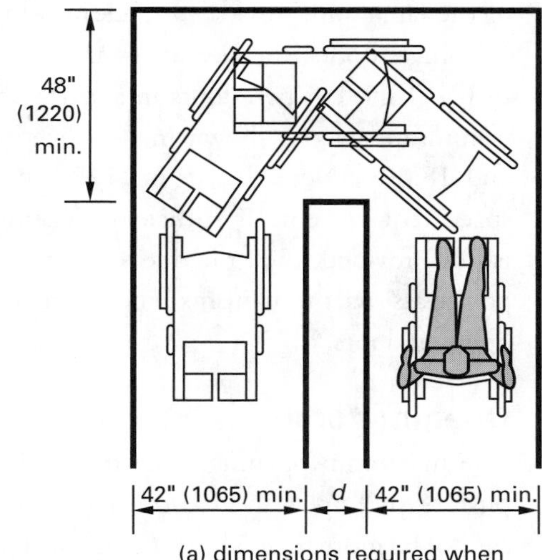


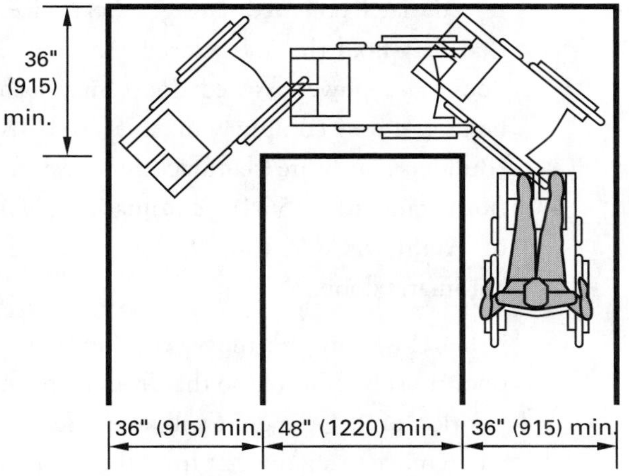


**Figure 18.3**
Turn in corridors or around obstructions

**Figure 18.4** Doorway clearances

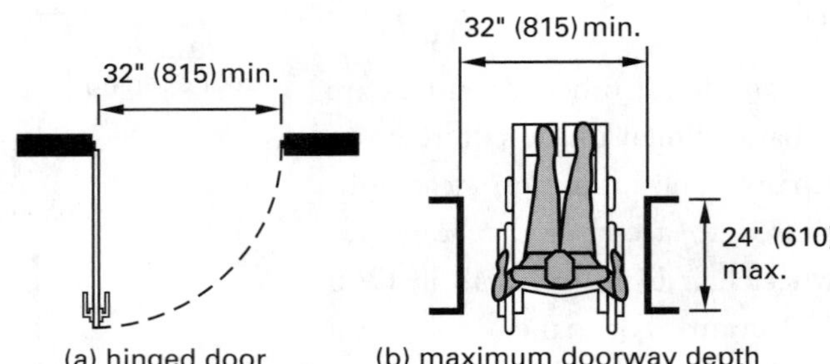


(610 mm). If the area is deeper than this, the width must be increased to 36 in (915 mm). See Figs. 18.4(a) and 18.4(b).

Maneuvering clearances are required at standard swinging doors to allow easy operation of the latch and provide for a clear swing. For single doors, the clearances are shown in Fig. 18.5. For two doors in a series, the minimum space is shown in Figs. 18.6(a) and 18.6(b). Note the 48 in (1220 mm) space requirement. If sufficient clearance is not provided, then the doors must have power-assisted mechanisms or be automatic-opening doors.

### Opening force

The maximum opening force required to push or pull open an interior hinged door cannot be more than 5 lbf-ft (22.2 N). This force does not include the force required to retract the latch bolts or disengage other devices that may hold the door closed. Automatic doors and power-assisted doors may also be used if they comply with ANSI/BHMA (Builders Hardware Manufacturers Association) standard A156.10 (automatic doors) or ANSI/BHMA 156.19 (low-powered, automatic doors).

When closers are used the sweep period of the door must be adjusted so that from an open position of 90°, the door will take at least 5 sec to move to a point 12° from the latch, as measured to the leading edge of the door.

### Hardware

Thresholds at doorways cannot exceed ½ in (13 mm) in height and must be beveled so that no slope of the threshold is greater than 1:2. Operating devices must have a shape that is easy to grasp. This includes lever handles, push-type mechanisms, and U-shaped handles. Round-shaped door knobs should not be used. If door closers are provided, they must be adjusted to slow the closing time. Hardware for accessible doors cannot be mounted less than 34 in (865 mm) or more than 48 in (1220 mm) above the finished floor.

## PLUMBING FIXTURES AND TOILET ROOMS

ICC/ANSI A117.1 and the ADA govern the design of the components of toilet rooms as well as individual elements, such as drinking fountains, bathtubs, and showers. As mentioned in a previous section, toilet rooms must have a minimum clear turning space of a 5 ft (1525 mm) diameter circle in addition to the minimum access areas required at each type of fixture. The 5 ft circle can overlap with required access at controls and fixtures and with the accessible route. Doors can swing into the turning space but cannot swing into the clear space at fixtures.

### Toilet stalls

There are several acceptable layouts for toilet stalls. Minimum clearances for two

**Figure 18.5** Maneuvering clearances at doors

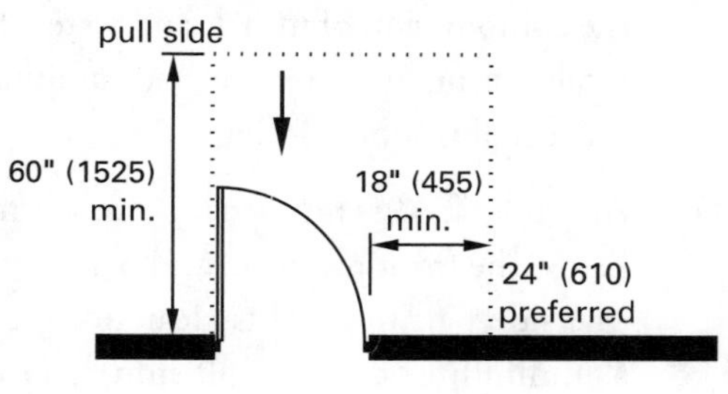


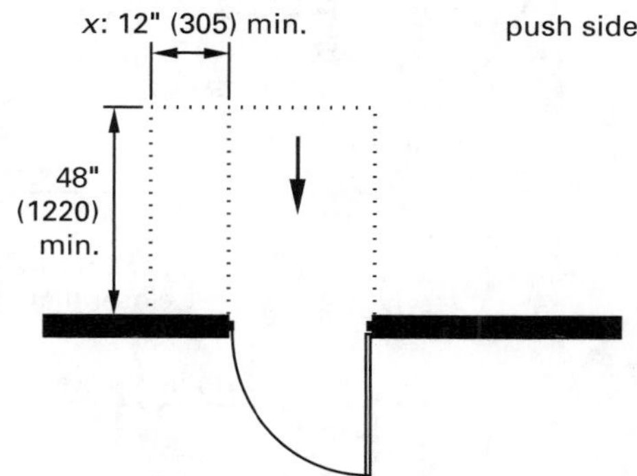


(a) front approaches—swinging doors

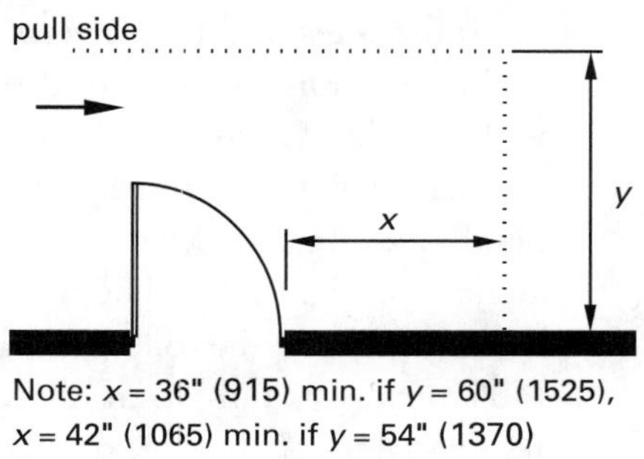


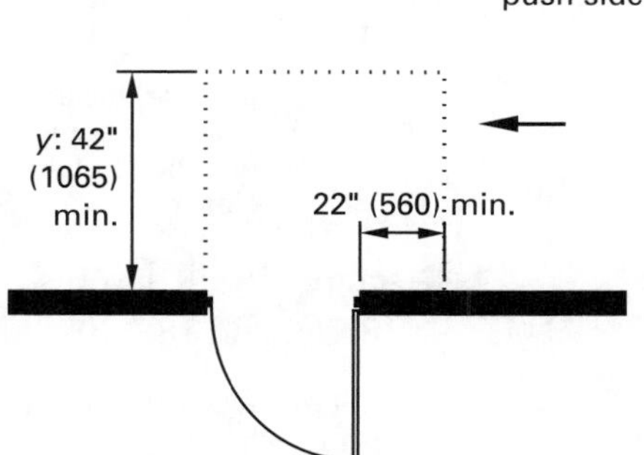


(b) hinge side approaches—swinging doors

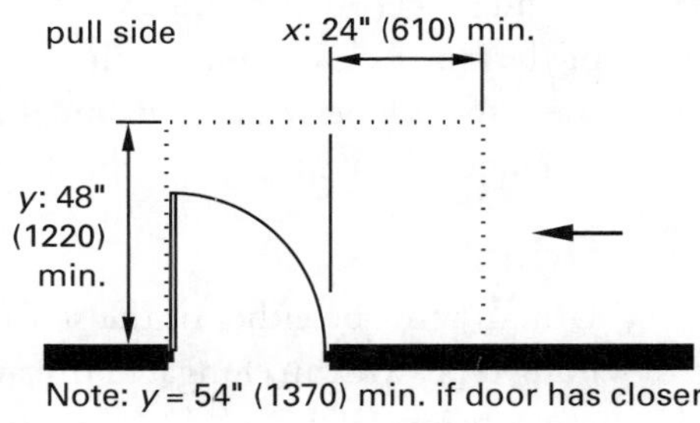


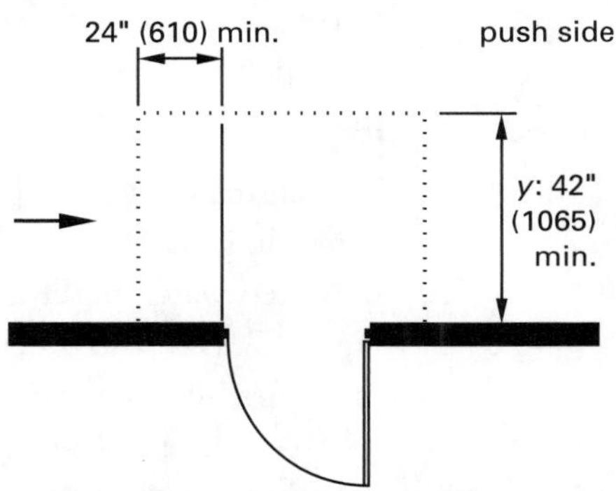


(c) latch side approaches—swinging doors

**Figure 18.6**
Double door clearances

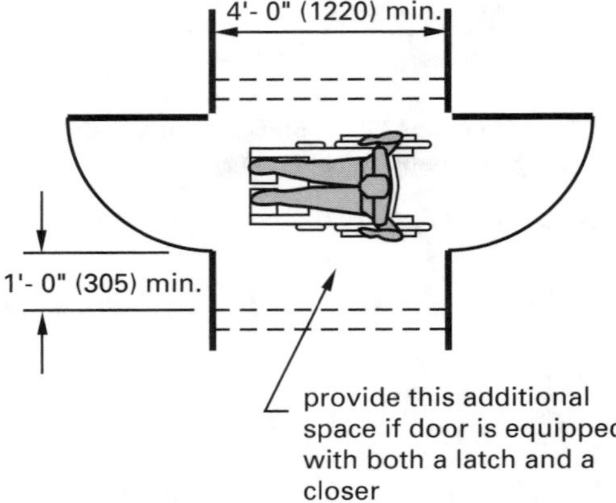


standard stall layouts are shown in Figs. 18.7(a) and 18.7(b).

Exceptions to the toilet room requirements may be allowed if alterations to a qualified historic building would threaten or destroy the historic significance of the building and the State Historic Preservation Officer agrees to the exception. Still, either one ADAAG-compliant toilet room for each sex or one unisex toilet room must be provided.

The clearance depth of a toilet stall varies depending on whether a wall-hung or floor-mounted water closet is used, as shown in Fig. 18.7. Doors to toilet stalls that have the minimum required compartment area must swing out and must be located in the front partition or in the side wall farthest from the water closet. Doors may swing in as shown in Fig. 18.7(a) only if they do not swing into the minimum required area. Doors must have a minimum clear width of 32 in (815 mm). Grab bars must also be provided as illustrated, mounted from 33 in to 36 in (840 mm to 915 mm) above the floor.

In addition to the dimensional requirements shown in Fig. 18.7, the ADAAG requires that at least one ambulatory toilet stall be provided where there are six or more toilet stalls or where the combination of urinals and water closets totals six or more fixtures. An ambulatory toilet stall is shown in Fig. 18.8.

All toilet stalls must have toe clearance below the front partition and below at least one side partition. This clearance must be a minimum of 9 in (230 mm) above the floor and extend a minimum of 6 in (150 mm) beyond the compartment-side face of the partition. Refer to the full text of the ADAAG for additional requirements for children's toilets and toilet stalls.

If toilet stalls are not used, the centerline of the toilet must still be between 16 in and 18 in (405 mm and 455 mm) from a wall with grab bars at both the back and side of the water closet. A clear space in front of and beside open water closets should be provided, as shown in Fig. 18.9(a). The dimension from the centerline of the toilet is 16 in to 18 in (405 mm to 457 mm) to an adjacent wall. In residential units, the edge of a lavatory may be located a minimum of 18 in (455 mm) from the centerline of the toilet as shown in Fig. 18.9(b). Toilet paper dispensers must be installed with the centerline between 7 in and 9 in (180 mm and 230 mm) in front of the water closet, and with the outlet of the dispenser between 15 in and 48 in (380 mm and 1220 mm) above the floor.

## Urinals

Urinals must be either of the stall- or wall-hung type, with an elongated rim at a maximum height of 17 in (430 mm) above the floor. A clear floor space of 30 in by 48 in (760 mm by 1220 mm) must be provided in front of the urinal, which may adjoin or overlap an accessible route. Urinal shields that do not extend beyond the front edge of the rim may be provided with 29 in (735 mm) clearance between them.

**Figure 18.7**
Toilet stall dimensions

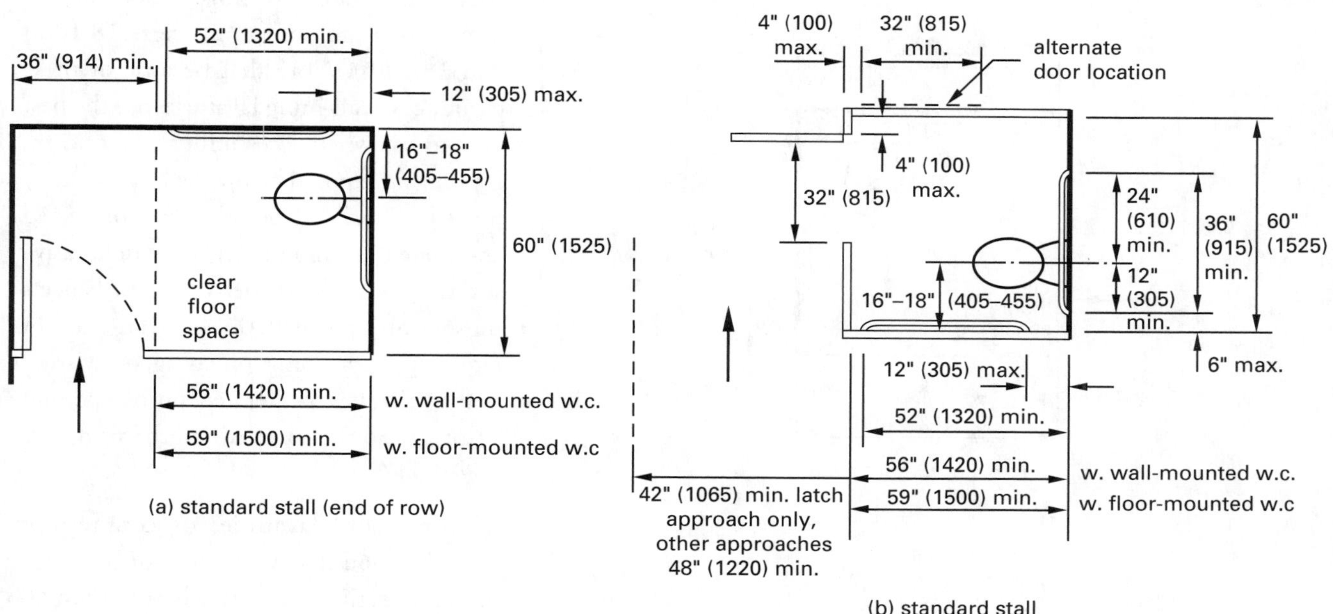


**Figure 18.8**
Ambulatory toilet stall dimensions

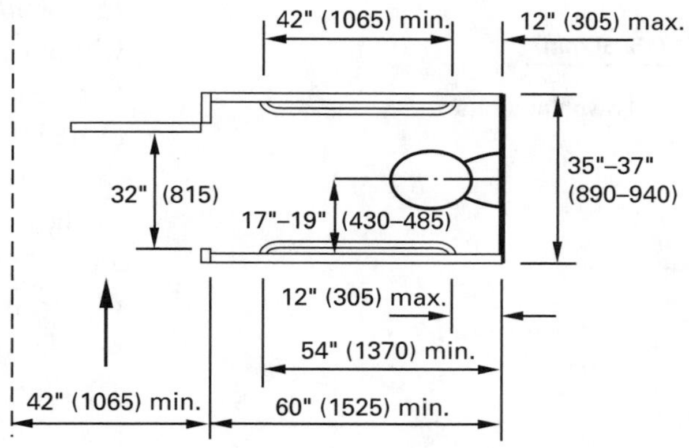

**Figure 18.9**
Clear floor space at water closets

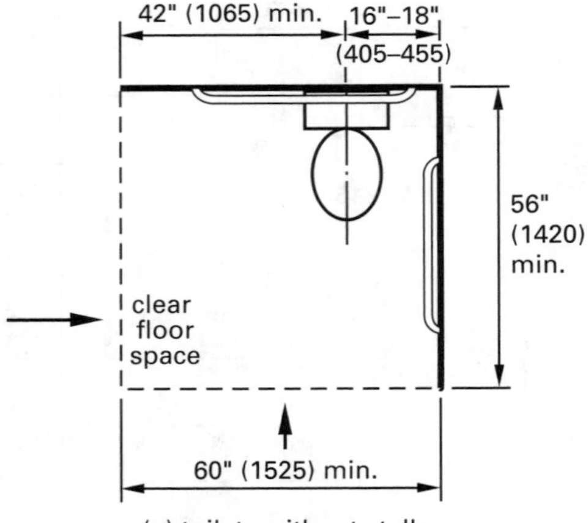


(a) toilets without stalls

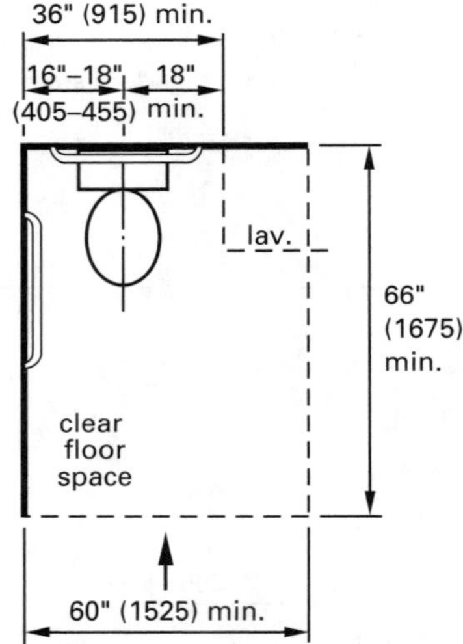


(b) residential dwelling units

## Lavatories and sinks

Lavatories and sinks must be designed to allow someone in a wheelchair to move under the fixture to allow easy use of the basin and water controls. The required dimensions are shown in Figs. 18.10(a) and 18.10(b). Note that because of these clearances, wall-hung lavatories are the best type to use when accessibility is a concern. If pipes are exposed below the lavatory, they must be insulated or otherwise protected and there must not be any sharp or abrasive surfaces under lavatories or sinks. Faucets must be operable with one hand and cannot require tight grasping, pinching, or twisting of the wrist. Lever-operated, push-type, and automatically controlled mechanisms are acceptable types.

Mirrors above lavatories or countertops must be mounted with the bottom edge of the reflecting surface no higher than 40 in (1015 mm) from the floor. The bottom edge of other mirrors must be no higher than 35 in (890 mm) from the floor.

The maximum height of a lavatory or sink above the floor is 34 in (865 mm).

## Drinking fountains

Requirements for drinking fountains are shown in Figs. 18.11(a) and 18.11(b). Free-standing or built-in drinking fountains without clear space below must have a clear floor space in front of them at least 30 in deep by 48 in wide (760 mm by 1220 mm), with the long dimension parallel to the fountain, to allow a person in a wheelchair to make a parallel approach. The IBC requires that two drinking fountains be provided, one for wheelchair users and one for persons who are standing. In lieu of two separate fountains, a combination unit that provides for both may be provided.

## Bathtubs

Bathtubs must be configured as shown in Figs. 18.12(a) and 18.12(b). An in-tub seat or a seat at the head of the tub must be

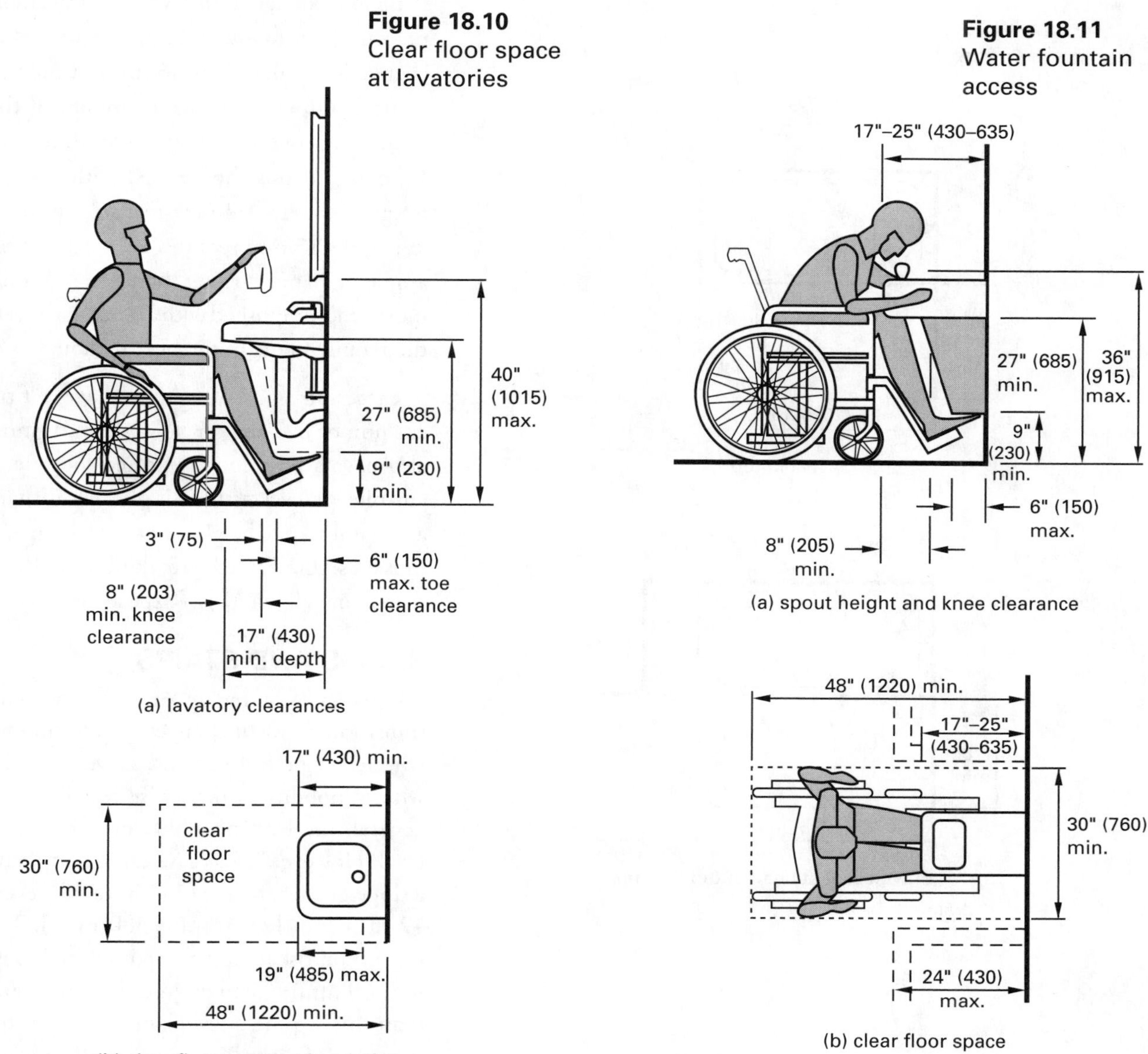


**Figure 18.10**
Clear floor space at lavatories

(b) clear floor space at lavatories

**Figure 18.11**
Water fountain access

(b) clear floor space

provided, as shown in the drawing. Grab bars must be provided. If an enclosure is provided, it cannot obstruct the controls or transfer from wheelchairs onto seats or into the tub. Enclosure tracks cannot be mounted on the rim of the tub.

### Showers

Shower stalls may be one of two basic types, as shown in Figs. 18.14(a) and 18.14(b). When facilities with accessible sleeping rooms or suites are provided, a minimum number of rooms that have roll-in showers, as specified by the ADA, is required. A seat is required in the smaller shower stall configuration, while a folding seat is required in the larger configuration if a permanent seat is provided. Grab bars must be provided and mounted from 33 in to 36 in (840 mm to 915 mm) above the floor. Because there are so many variations and scoping requirements for showers, refer to the ADAAG for a complete description.

## FLOOR SURFACES

Floor surfaces must be stable, firm, and slip resistant. See Ch. 8 for a discussion of slip resistance and ADA recommendations.

**Figure 18.12**
Clear floor space at bathtubs

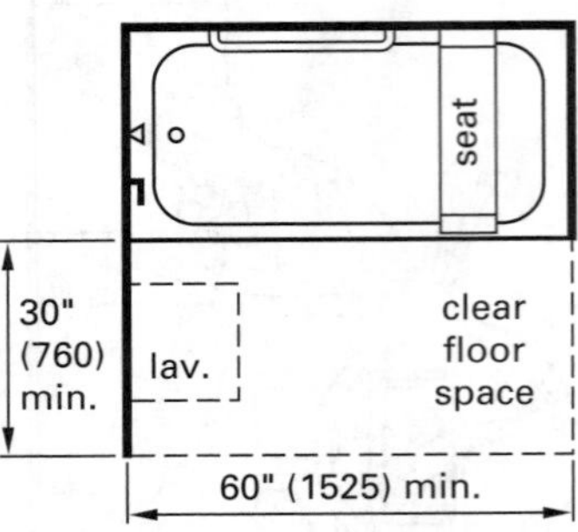


(a) with seat in tub

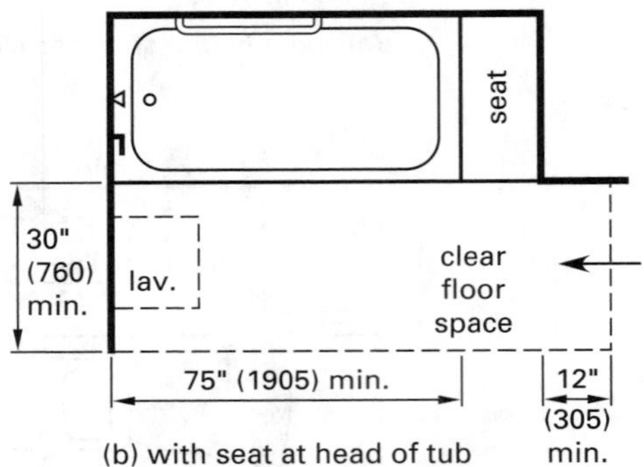


(b) with seat at head of tub

o drain
◁ shower head
┓ shower controls

If there is a change in level, the transition must meet the following requirements. If the change is less than ¼ in (6 mm), it may be vertical and without edge treatment. If the change is between ¼ in and ½ in (6 mm to 13 mm), it must be beveled with a slope no greater than 1:2 (a ½ in rise requires 1 in length [13 mm requires 26 mm], for example). Changes greater than ½ in (13 mm) must be accomplished with a ramp that meets the requirements in the next section.

If carpeting is used, it must have a firm cushion or backing, or no cushion. It must also have a level loop, textured loop, level cut-pile, or level cut/uncut pile texture with a maximum pile height of ½ in (13 mm). It must be securely attached to the floor and have trim along all lengths of exposed edges.

## RAMPS AND STAIRS

Ramps are required to provide a smooth transition between changes in elevation for wheelchair-bound persons, as well as those whose mobility is otherwise restricted. In general, the least possible slope should be used. However, in no case can a ramp have a slope greater than 1:12 (1 in rise for every 12 in of run [25 mm for 300 mm]). The maximum rise for any ramp is limited to 30 in (760 mm). Changes in elevation greater than this require a level landing before the next run of ramp is encountered. In some cases where existing conditions prevent the 1:12 slope, a 1:10 slope is permitted if the maximum rise does not exceed 6 in (150 mm) and a 1:8 slope is permitted if the maximum rise does not exceed 3 in (75 mm).

The minimum clear ramp width is 36 in (915 mm), with landings at least as wide as the widest ramp leading to them. Landing lengths must be a minimum of 60 in (1525 mm). If ramps change direction at a landing, then the landing must be at least 60 in square.

Ramps with rises greater than 6 in (150 mm) or lengths greater than 72 in (1830 mm) must have handrails on both sides,

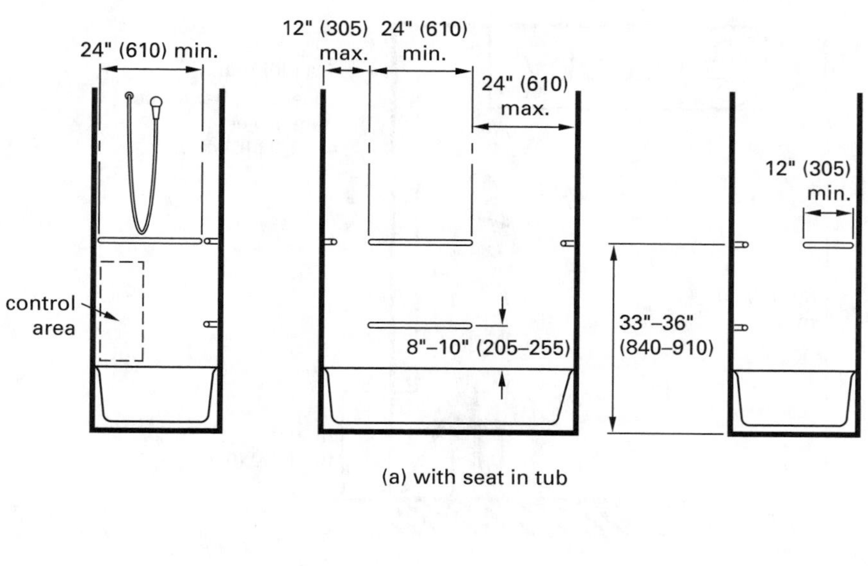


(a) with seat in tub

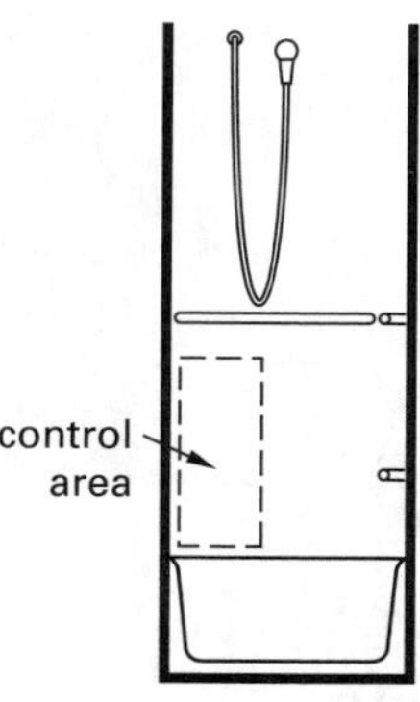


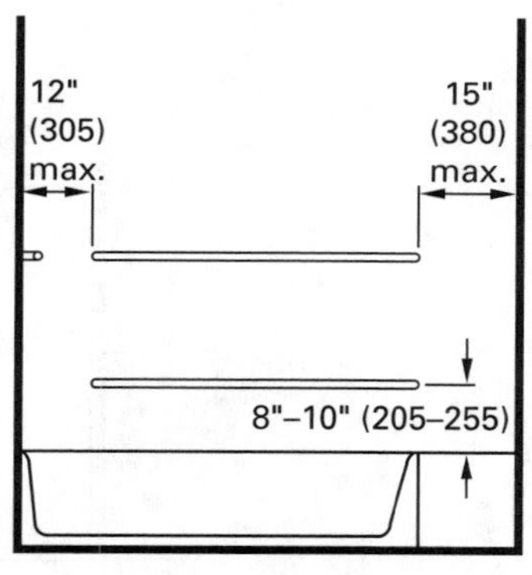


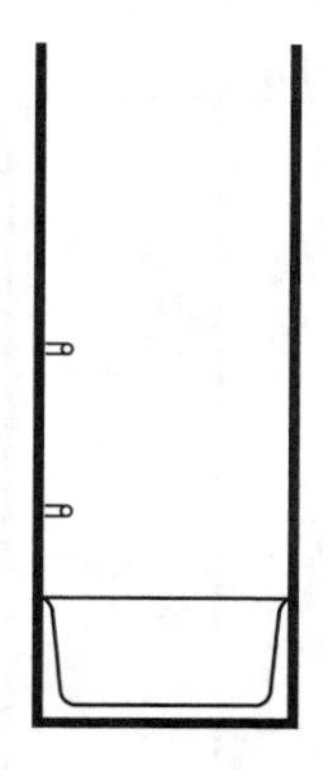

(b) with seat at head of tub

**Figure 18.13**
Grab bars at bathtubs

with the top of the handrail from 34 in to 38 in (865 mm to 965 mm) above the ramp surface. Where handrails are not continuous between runs they must extend horizontally at least 12 in (305 mm) beyond the top and bottom of the ramp segment and have a gripping surface diameter from 1¼ in to 2 in (32 mm to 51 mm). Handrails are not required for ramps adjacent to seating in assembly areas. Refer to the ADAAG for design requirements for noncircular handrail cross sections.

Stairs that are required as a means of egress and stairs between floors not connected by an elevator must be designed according to certain standards specifying the configurations of treads, risers, nosings, and handrails. The maximum riser height is 7 in (180 mm), and the treads must be a minimum

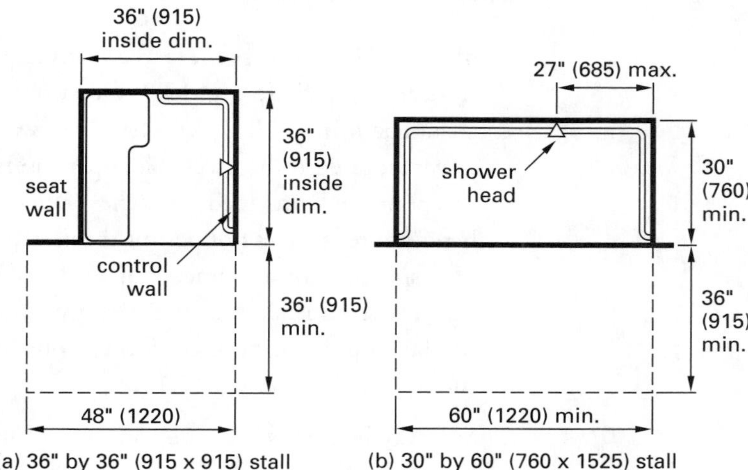


(a) 36" by 36" (915 x 915) stall

(b) 30" by 60" (760 x 1525) stall

**Figure 18.14**
Accessible shower stalls

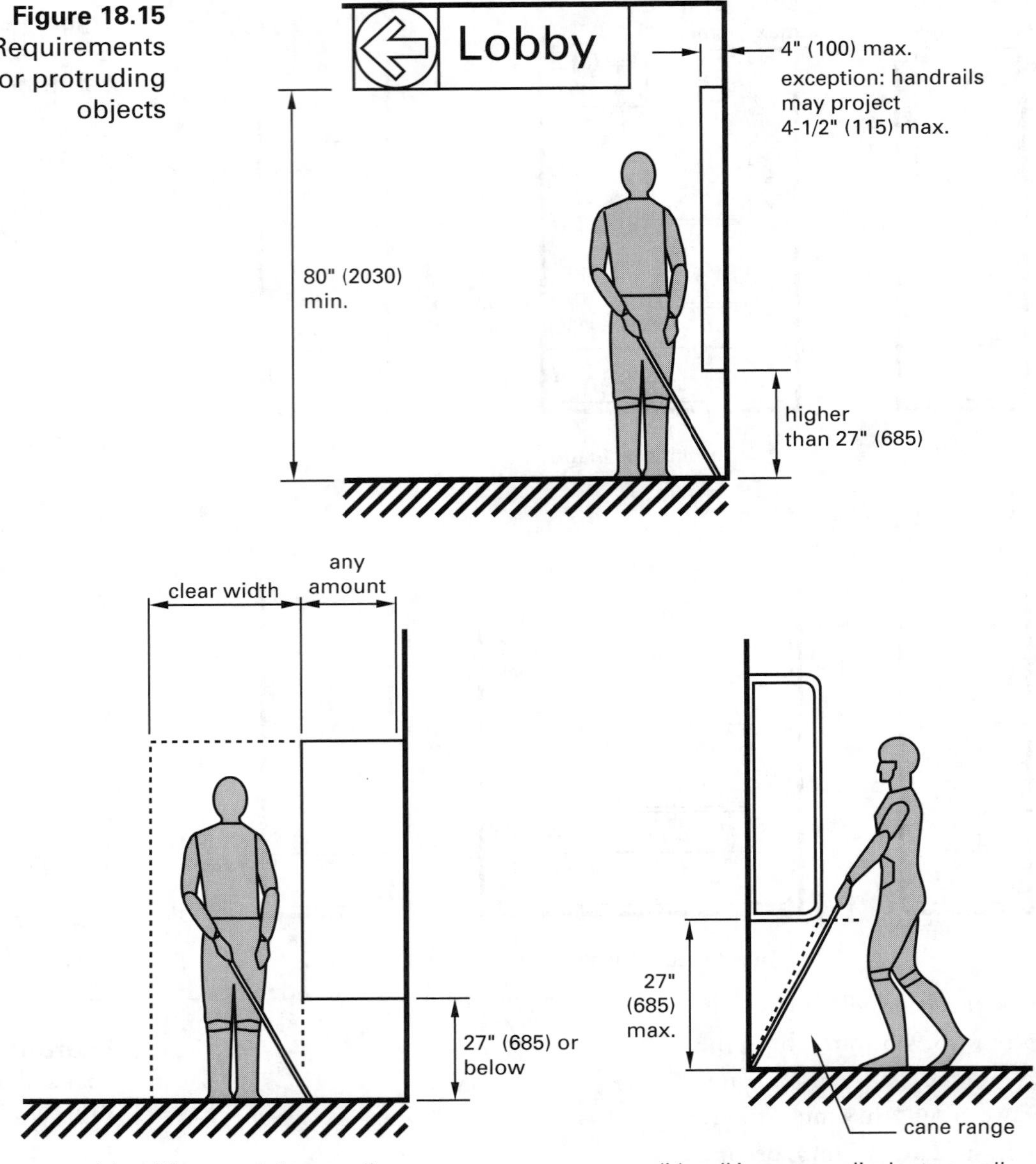


**Figure 18.15** Requirements for protruding objects

(a) walking parallel to a wall

(b) walking perpendicular to a wall

of 11 in (280 mm) as measured from riser to riser, as shown in Fig. 12.9. Open risers are not permitted. However, when a stairway is *not* required to be accessible, open risers are permitted provided that the opening between treads does not permit the passage of a sphere with a diameter of 4 in (102 mm). The undersides of the nosings must not be abrupt and must conform to one of the styles shown in Fig. 12.15.

Stairway handrails must be continuous on both sides of the stairs. The inside handrail on switchback or dogleg stairs must always be continuous as it changes direction. Other handrails must extend beyond the top and bottom riser, as shown in Fig. 12.6. The top of the gripping surface must be between 34 in and 38 in (865 mm to 965 mm) above stair nosings. The handrail must have a gripping surface diameter from 1¼ in to 2 in (32 mm to 51 mm). There must be a clear space between the handrail and the wall of at least 1½ in (38 mm). Some acceptable handrail configurations are shown in Fig. 12.17.

When an exit stairway is part of an accessible route in an unsprinklered building (not including houses), there must be a clear width of 48 in (1220 mm) between handrails.

## PROTRUDING OBJECTS

There are restrictions on the size and configuration of objects and building elements that project into corridors and other walkways because they present hazards for the visually impaired. These restrictions are shown in Figs. 18.15(a) and 18.15(b); they are based on the use of a cane by someone with severe vision impairment. A protruding object with a lower edge less than 27 in (685 mm) above the floor can be detected, therefore it may project by any amount.

Regardless of the situation, protruding objects cannot reduce the clear width required for an accessible route or maneuvering space. In addition, if the vertical clearance of an area adjacent to an accessible route is reduced to less than 80 in (2030 mm), a guardrail or other barrier must be provided.

## DETECTABLE WARNINGS

Detectable warning surfaces are required on walking surfaces in front of stairs, hazardous vehicular areas, and other places where a hazard may exist without a guardrail or other method of warning. The surfaces must consist of truncated domes as specified in the ADAAG. At the time of this writing, the detectable warning provisions of the ADA only applied to boarding platforms in transportation facilities.

Door handles are also required to have textured surfaces if they are part of a door that leads to an area that might prove dangerous to a blind person, such as doors to loading platforms, boiler rooms, or stages.

## SIGNAGE AND ALARMS

Signage for visually impaired people must be provided that gives emergency information and general circulation directions. Signage is also required for elevators.

Emergency warning systems are required that provide both a visual and audible alarm. Audible alarms must produce a sound that exceeds the prevailing sound level in the room or space by at least 15 dB. Visual alarms must be flashing lights that have a flashing frequency of about one cycle per second. Alarms must comply with NFPA 72.

The Americans with Disabilities Act requires that certain accessible rooms and features be clearly identified with the symbol for accessibility. The ADA also requires that identification, directional, and informational signs meet certain specifications.

Permanent rooms and spaces must be identified with signs having raised lettering from ⅝ in to 2 in (16 mm to 51 mm) high, depending on the viewing distance. Lettering must be uppercase, in sans serif or simple serif type accompanied with Grade 2 braille. If pictograms are used, they must be at least 6 in (150 mm) high, and must be accompanied with the equivalent verbal description placed directly below the pictogram. Signs must be eggshell matte or some other nonglare finish with characters and symbols contrasting with their background. Permanent identification signs must be wall-mounted adjacent to the latch side of the door such that there is a minimum clear floor space of 18 in by 18 in (455 mm by 455 mm) centered on the tactile characters and beyond the arc of the door swing. The mounting height to the baseline of the lowest tactile character must be 48 in (1220 mm) minimum and 60 in (1525 mm) maximum to the baseline of the highest tactile character. When there is no wallspace to the latch side of the door, including double-leaf doors, the sign must be placed to the right of the right-hand door.

Directional and informational signs must have lettering from ⅝ in to 3 in (16 mm to 75 mm) high, depending on the viewing distance, which is detailed in a table in ADAAG. Contrast and finish requirements are the same as for permanent room identification. Lettering can be uppercase or lowercase.

**Figure 18.16** International symbol for accessibility

The international symbol for accessibility is required on parking spaces, passenger loading zones, accessible entrances, and toilet and bathing facilities when not all are accessible. See Fig. 18.16. Building directories and signs that are temporary do not have to comply with the requirements.

Refer to the ADAAG for the detailed requirements for signage.

## TELEPHONES

If public telephones are provided, then there must be at least one telephone per floor conforming to the requirements as shown in Figs. 18.17(a) and 18.17(b) and as specified

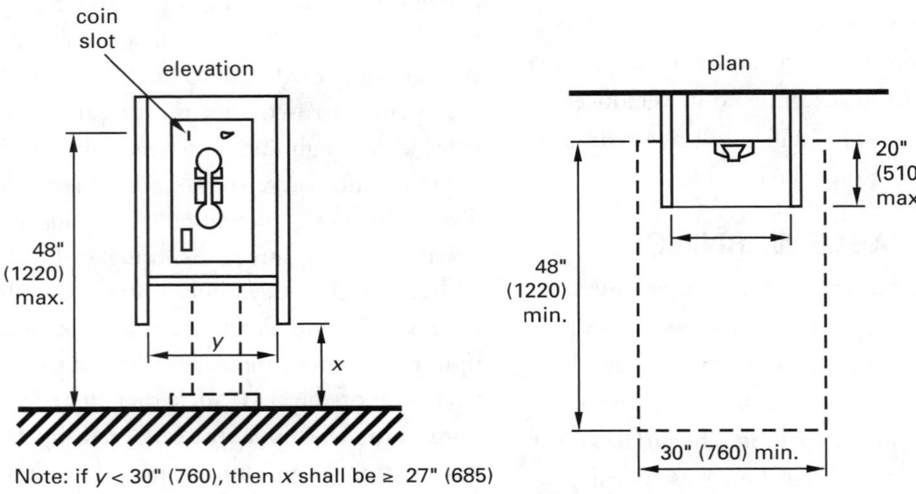


(a) forward reach possible

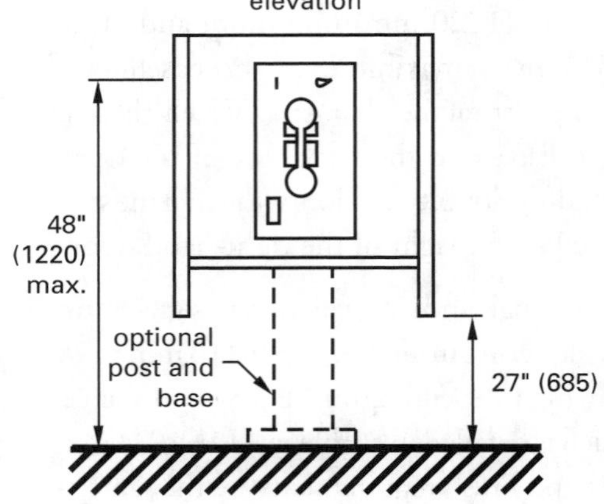


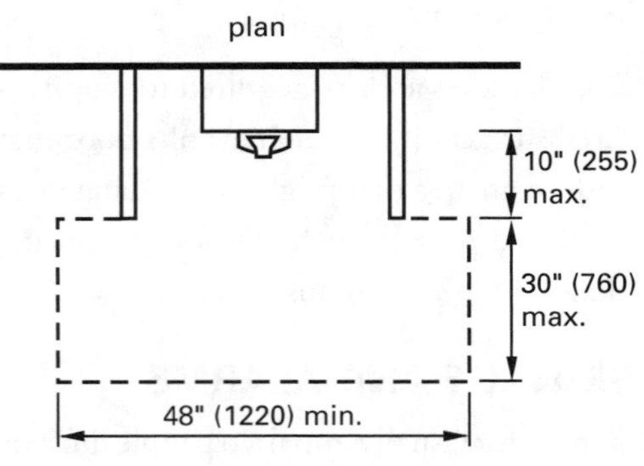


(b) side reach possible

**Figure 18.17** Telephone access

in the ADA requirements. If there are two or more banks of telephones, there must be at least one conforming telephone per bank. When four or more public pay telephones are provided, at least one interior public text telephone (TTY) is required. Refer to the ADAAG for other TTY requirements in various building types.

Accessible telephones may be designed for either front or side access. The dimensions required for both of these types are shown in Figs. 18.17(a) and 18.17(b). In either case, a clear floor space of at least 30 in by 48 in (760 mm by 1220 mm) must be provided. The telephones should have pushbutton controls and telephone directories within reach of a person in a wheelchair.

The international TTY (teletypewriter) is required to identify the locations of those phones, and volume control telephones must have a sign depicting a telephone handset with radiating sound waves. In assembly areas, permanently installed assistive listening systems must have the international symbol of access for hearing loss. See Figs. 18.18(a) and 18.18(b).

Refer to the ADA requirements and local codes for detailed rules on telephone types and installation requirements.

(a) TTY symbol

(b) access for hearing loss symbol

**Figure 18.18** International TTY and hearing loss symbols

## SEATING

If fixed or built-in seating or tables are provided in accessible public- or common-use areas, then at least 5%, but not less than one, of the seating areas must be accessible. This includes such facilities as restaurants, nightclubs, and similar spaces. In new construction and when possible in remodeling, the number of tables should be dispersed throughout the facility. If smoking and nonsmoking areas are provided, the required number of seating spaces must be proportioned among the smoking and nonsmoking areas. The area for this type of seating must comply with the dimensions shown in Fig. 18.19.

**Table 18.1** Minimum number of wheelchair spaces for assembly areas

| capacity of seating in assembly areas | number of required wheelchair locations |
|---|---|
| 4 to 25 | 1 |
| 26 to 50 | 2 |
| 51 to 150 | 4 |
| 151 to 300 | 5 |
| 301 to 500 | 6 |
| 501 to 5000 | 6, plus 1 for each 150, or fraction thereof, from 501 through 5000 |
| 5001 and over | 36, plus 1 for each 200, or fraction thereof, over 5000 |

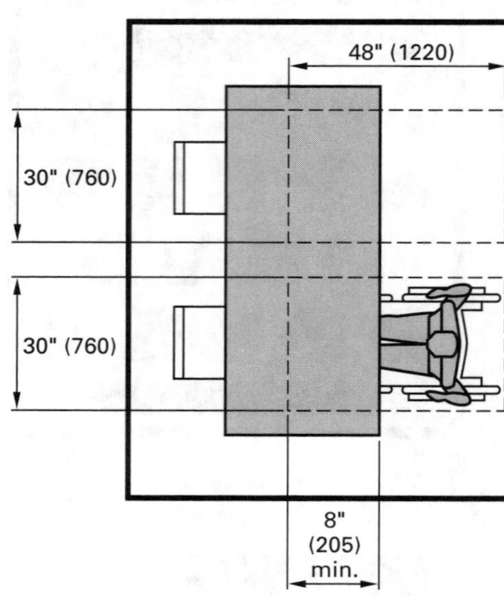


**Figure 18.19** Minimum clearances for seating and tables

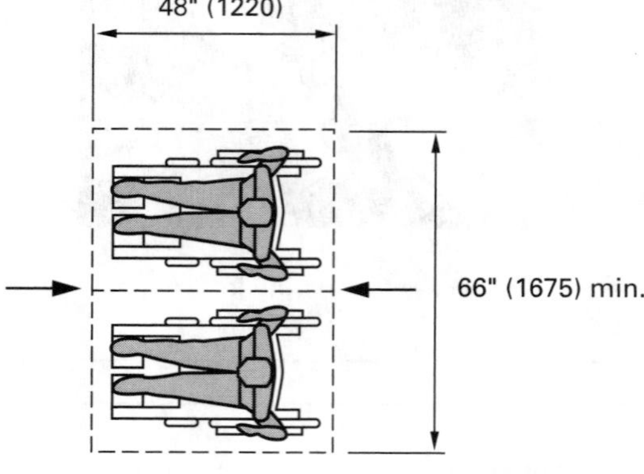


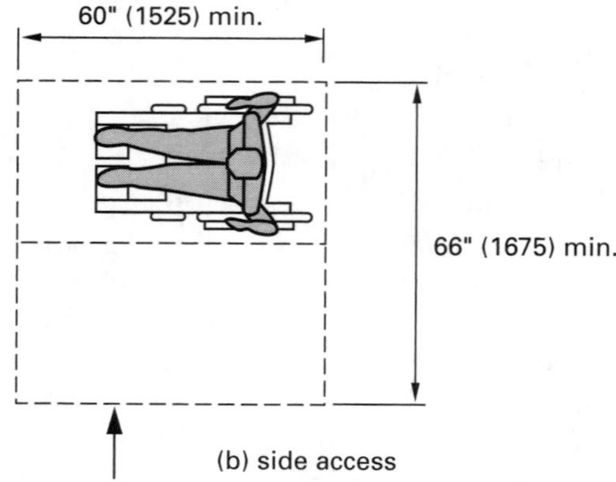


**Figure 18.20** Wheelchair seating spaces

In places of assembly with fixed seating, the minimum number of wheelchair locations is given in Table 18.1. At least 5% of all fixed aisle seats must be aisle seats with no armrests on the aisle side, or with removable or folding armrests on the aisle side. Signs notifying people of the availability of these seats must be posted at the ticket office. The wheelchair areas must be an integral part of the overall seating plan and must be provided so that people have a choice of admission prices and lines of sight comparable to those available for members of the general public. At least one companion seat must be provided next to each wheelchair area. Wheelchair areas must adjoin an accessible route that also serves as a means of emergency egress. Space for wheelchair areas must conform to Figs. 18.20(a) and 18.20(b).

When assembly areas are part of a remodeling project and it is not feasible to disperse the seating areas throughout, the accessible seating areas may be clustered. These clustered areas must have provisions for companion seating and must be located on an accessible route that also serves as a means of emergency egress.

Refer to the complete text of the ADA for requirements for audio-amplification systems and assisted listening devices and signage required for assembly areas.

## CONSTRUCTION TOLERANCES AND THE ADA

In the construction industry, buildings and portions of buildings are not, and cannot be, built to perfection. Construction components are manufactured and installed according to generally accepted tolerances. For example, a floor plan may show a wall at a single, specific distance from another wall, but in reality the wall may be ¼ in (6 mm) on one side or the other of the theoretical position shown on the drawings. This is normal and accepted in the construction industry. There are different tolerances for different building elements, but all construction components have acceptable tolerances. For example, the positional tolerance for the placement of concrete is much greater than the manufacturing tolerance for millwork produced in a factory.

Because many of the dimensions given in the ADA are a single dimension stating a minimum or maximum, compliance problems can arise when a dimension is taken directly from the ADAAG and placed on the designer's drawings. If the contractor builds an element that does not conform exactly to the dimensions given on the drawings but is within industry standard tolerances, the element can be considered to be installed correctly, but not in compliance according to the ADA.

For example, if the height of multiple sinks in a cabinet must be a maximum of 34 in (865 mm) above the floor, this dimension is often copied directly to the designer's drawings. The contractor may install the cabinet and sinks measuring from one point on the floor and be within acceptable limits. However, if the floor is not level and slopes down along the length of the cabinet, another sink may be ¼ in to ½ in higher than the maximum. Although the floor, cabinet, and sink installation may be within industry standard tolerances, they may exceed ADA dimensions.

Although the discrepancies can be minor, they can be the basis for legal action and expensive remediation work.

Both the ADAAG and ICC/ANSI A117.1-2003 state that all dimensions are subject to conventional industry tolerances except where the requirement is stated as a range with specific minimum and maximum end points. However, they also state that dimensions that are not marked as a minimum or maximum are absolute.

In order to avoid potential problems and accommodate the reality of imperfection in building construction, the designer should follow a few simple recommendations. First, when an accessible dimension is given as a minimum or maximum, the drawings should give a dimension a little more than the minimum or a little less than the maximum to allow for minor manufacturing or installation inaccuracies. How much allowance to give depends on the construction element and specific circumstances, but around ¼ in to ½ in is usually sufficient. Second, when a dimension is given as a range, the drawings should show the midpoint of that range or be well within the limits of the range; they should not show one of the limits themselves. Third, if a specific, single dimension must be taken directly from an accessibility dimension and placed on the drawing, take extra care to highlight the fact that the contractor *must* meet the dimension exactly. This can be done by making a note on the drawing that is obvious to the contractor and emphasizes the importance of holding to an exact dimension.

# 19

# BUILDING CODES AND REGULATIONS

This chapter and Ch. 20 on means of egress discuss the major provisions common to most building codes as they affect interior construction. This chapter also reviews some of the more common regulations other than building codes that pertain to building. However, because each jurisdiction has its own requirements and amendments to model codes, the applicable code specific to each jurisdiction must be reviewed to determine complete requirements for a specific project. In addition to the information in this chapter, refer to individual sidebars in previous chapters, which discuss building code requirements as they pertain to the topic of each chapter. Ch. 18 summarizes the requirements for barrier-free design.

This chapter is based on the International Building Code (IBC), which was first published in 2000. Many local and state jurisdictions around the country have adopted the IBC or will adopt it soon, replacing their use of the Uniform Building Code, the Standard Building Code, or the BOCA National Building Code.

## BUILDING REGULATIONS

Building codes are only one type of regulation affecting the design and construction of buildings, along with interior construction. Additional requirements that may be applicable include legal and administrative regulations at the federal, state, and local levels. For example, a state may enforce flammability regulations for furniture, while the building code used in that state will not regulate furniture at all.

### State and federal regulations

Most states have agencies that regulate building in some way. In addition to a state building code, state government may enforce energy codes, environmental regulations, fabric flammability standards, and specific rules relating to state government buildings, institutions, and other facilities.

At the national level, several federal agencies may regulate a construction project, such as military construction or federal prison construction. Certain federal agencies may also regulate or issue rules covering a specific part of construction, such as the safety-glazing requirement issued by the Consumer Product Safety Commission (CPSC).

For interior designers, the most notable national federal-level law is the Americans with Disabilities Act (ADA), which regulates, among other things, the removal of barriers for the physically disabled. The ADA requirements are based on the American National Standard Institute's (ANSI) ICC/ANSI A117.1, *Accessible and Usable Buildings and Facilities.* However, additional provisions are given in the ADA regulations. Although very similar to the ICC/ANSI A117.1 standard, the ADA is not a code or standard, but a piece of civil rights legislation. However, designers must adhere to its provisions when designing the facilities covered by the law. Ch. 18 covers requirements for barrier-free design.

## Local regulations

Local codes may include amendments to the model building code in use. These amendments usually pertain to specific concerns or needs of a geographical region or are provisions designed to alleviate local problems that are not addressed in the model codes. For example, a local amendment in a mountainous area might require a higher snow load factor for roof design based on the local climate.

Local regulations may also include requirements of agencies that govern hospitals, nursing homes, restaurants, schools, and similar institutions, as well as rules of local fire departments.

## Model building codes

Local jurisdictions (including states) may write their own building codes, but in most cases a model code is adopted into law by reference. A model code is one that has been written by a group comprised of experts knowledgeable in the field, without reference to any particular geographical area. Adopting a model code allows a city, county, or district to have a complete, workable building code without the difficulty and expense of writing its own. If certain provisions need to be added or changed to suit the particular requirements of a municipality, the model code is enacted with modification. Even when a city or state writes its own code, it is usually based on a model code. Exceptions include some large cities, such as New York and Chicago, and a few states that have adopted the Life Safety Code or have their own.

Today, the primary model code is the International Building Code (IBC) produced by the International Code Council and first published in 2000. It is a consolidation of the three model codes previously published in the United States, developed by three code-writing groups. The IBC combines provisions of all three of the previous model codes and is organized in the same format that the three code-writing groups used in the most recent editions of their codes. At the time of this writing, many jurisdictions had adopted the IBC, and others were in the process of adopting it. Some jurisdictions are still using the most recent edition of one of the three previous model codes. The intent is for the IBC to bring uniformity to code practices across the country and in other countries, and eventually to replace the other three model codes.

The three model codes previously used throughout the United States and still used by some jurisdictions are

- The Uniform Building Code (UBC), used in the western and central regions of the United States and published by the International Conference of Building Officials (ICBO)

- The BOCA National Building Code, used in the northeastern part of the country and published by the Building Officials and Code Administrators International (BOCA)

- The Standard Building Code (SBC), used in much of the southeastern United States and published by the Southern Building Code Congress International (SBCCI)

The primary code for Canadian provinces is the National Building Code of Canada (NBC). Other Canadian codes regulate plumbing, housing, fire safety, and other specific areas of construction.

In 2003 the three code groups merged to form the International Code Council (ICC).

The eventual use of one model code throughout the majority of the country will bring consistency and make it easier for designers and architects to work across the United States. About the same time the ICC was developing the International Building Code, the National Fire Protection Association (NFPA) developed its own building code, NFPA 5000. However, this code has largely been rejected by local and state jurisdictions in favor of the IBC. The material in this chapter is based on the International Building Code, which will most likely become the most commonly used model code in the United States.

## Adjuncts to building codes

In addition to a building code, there are companion codes that govern other aspects of construction. The same groups that publish the model building codes publish these. For example, the International Code Council also publishes the International Residential Code, the International Fire Code, the International Mechanical Code, the International Plumbing Code, and the International Zoning Code, among others.

The electrical code used by all jurisdictions is the National Electrical Code (NEC), published by the National Fire Protection Association (NFPA). In order to maintain greater uniformity in building regulations, the International Code Council does not publish an electrical code, but relies on the NEC. The ICC only publishes administrative text necessary to administer and enforce the NEC.

Model codes also make extensive use of industry standards that are developed by trade associations such as the Gypsum Association, government agencies, standards-writing organizations such as the American Society for Testing and Materials (ASTM) and the National Fire Protection Association (NFPA), and standards-approving groups such as the American National Standards Institute (ANSI). Standards are made a part of a building code by reference name and number and date of latest revision. For example, most codes adopt by reference the American National Standard ICC/ANSI A117.1-1998, *Accessible and Usable Buildings and Facilities.* This standard was developed by the International Code Council based on previous ANSI accessibility standards and is approved by ANSI.

## Legal basis of codes

In the United States, the authority for adopting and enforcing building codes is one of the police powers given to the states by the Tenth Amendment to the United States Constitution. Each state, in turn, may retain those powers or delegate some of them to lower levels of government, such as counties or cities. Because of this division of power, the authority for adopting and enforcing building codes varies among the states.

Building codes are usually adopted and enforced by local governments, either by a municipality or, in the case of sparsely populated areas, a county or district. A few states write their own codes or adopt a model code statewide. Regulation in Canada is the responsibility of provincial and territorial governments.

Codes are enacted as laws just as any other local regulation. Before construction, a building code is enforced through the permit process, which requires that builders submit plans and specifications for checking and approval before a building permit is issued. During construction, the department responsible for enforcement conducts inspections to verify that building is proceeding according to the approved plans. However, the design professional is ultimately responsible for making sure that the design meets all applicable codes and regulations.

## TESTING AND MATERIAL STANDARDS

All approved materials and construction assemblies referred to in building codes are required to be manufactured according to accepted methods or tested by approved agencies according to standardized testing procedures, or both. There are hundreds of standardized tests and product standards for building materials and constructions. Some of the more common ones are listed in this section.

As previously stated, standards are developed by trade associations, standards-writing organizations, and government agencies. By themselves, standards have no legal standing. Only when they are referred to in a building code and that code is adopted by a governmental jurisdiction do standards become law.

### Standards-writing organizations

The American Society for Testing and Materials (ASTM) is one organization that publishes thousands of test procedures that prescribe, in detail, such things as how the test apparatus must be set up, how materials must be prepared for the test, the length of the test, and other requirements. If a product manufacturer has one of its materials successfully tested, it will indicate what tests the material has passed in its product literature. Standards are developed through the work of committees of experts in a particular field. Although ASTM does not actually perform tests, its procedures and standards are used by testing agencies.

The National Fire Protection Association (NFPA) is another private, voluntary organization that develops standards related to the causes and prevention of destructive fires. NFPA publishes hundreds of codes and standards in a multivolume set that covers the entire scope of fire prevention including sprinkler systems, fire extinguishers, hazardous materials, fire fighting, and many others. As mentioned earlier in this chapter, NFPA is also publishing its own building code.

Other standards-writing organizations are typically industry trade groups that have an interest in a particular material, product, or field of expertise. Examples of such trade groups include the American Society of Heating, Refrigerating, and Air-Conditioning Engineers (ASHRAE); the Illuminating Engineering Society (IES); the Gypsum Association (GA); and the Tile Council of America (TCA). There are hundreds of these construction trade organizations.

The American National Standards Institute (ANSI) is a well-known organization in the field, but unlike the other standards groups, ANSI does not develop or write standards. Instead, it approves standards developed by other organizations and works to avoid duplications between different standards. For example, ANSI 108, *Specifications for Installation of Ceramic Tile*, was developed by the Tile Council of America and reviewed by a large committee of widely varying industry representatives. Although the ANSI approval process does not necessarily represent unanimity among committee members, it requires much more than a simple majority and mandates that all views and objections be considered and that a concerted effort be made toward their resolution.

### Testing laboratories

When a standard describes a test procedure or requires one or more tests in its description of a material or product, a testing laboratory must perform the test. A standards-writing organization may also provide testing, but in most cases a Nationally Recognized Testing Laboratory (NRTL) must perform the test. An NRTL is an independent laboratory recognized by the Occupational Safety and Health Administration to test products to the specifications of applicable product safety standards. The two most widely known are described as follows.

One of the most well known testing laboratories is Underwriters Laboratories (UL). Among other activities, UL develops standards and tests products for safety. When a product successfully passes the prescribed test, it is given a UL label. There are several types of UL labels, and each means something different. When a complete and total product is successfully tested, it receives a *listed label.* This means that the product passed the safety test and is manufactured under the UL follow-up services program.

Another type of label is the *classified label.* This means that samples of the product were tested for certain types of uses only. In addition to the classified label, the product must also carry a statement specifying the conditions that were tested for. This allows field inspectors and others to determine if the product is being used correctly.

One of the most common uses of UL testing procedures is for doors and other opening protections. For example, fire doors are required to be tested in accordance with UL 10B, *Fire Tests of Door Assemblies,* and they must carry a UL label. Fire ratings for doors are discussed in Ch. 3. UL 263, *Fire Tests for Building Construction and Materials,* is the same as the ASTM E119 test and is used to test partitions, floor assemblies, column covers, and similar construction assemblies.

The results of UL tests and products that are listed are published in UL's *Building Materials Directory.*

Another well-known testing laboratory is ETL Semko, which is a division of Intertek Testing Services. Like UL, ETL Semko tests a wide variety of products and applies labels to indicate compliance with testing standards. It also performs periodic follow-up inspections of manufacturers to verify continued compliance with manufacturing requirements. It includes the products bearing the ETL Listed Mark in its *Directory of Listed Products.*

## Types of tests and standards

There are hundreds of types of tests and standards for building materials and assemblies that examine a wide range of properties, from fire resistance to structural integrity to durability to stain resistance. Building codes indicate what tests or standards a particular type of material must satisfy in order to be considered acceptable for a particular use. For example, gypsum wallboard must meet the standards of ASTM C36, *Standard Specification for Gypsum Wallboard.*

The most important types of tests for interior design components are those that rate the ability of a construction assembly to prevent the passage of fire and smoke from one space to another, and those that rate the degree of flammability of a finish material. The following summaries include fire testing for building products and finishes. Flammability standards for carpet are described in Ch. 9. Standards for individual products are listed in sidebars in the chapters covering those products.

Several tests are commonly used for fire-resistive assembly ratings and surface flammability. Details on these tests follow.

### ASTM E119

One of the most commonly used tests for fire resistance of construction assemblies is ASTM E119, *Standard Methods of Fire Tests of Building Construction and Materials.* This test involves building a sample of the wall or floor/ceiling assembly in the laboratory and setting a standard fire on one side of it (actually, controlled gas burners). Monitoring devices measure temperature and other aspects of the test as it proceeds.

There are two parts to the E119 test. The first measures heat transfer through the assembly. The goal of this test is to determine the temperature at which the surface or adjacent materials on the side of the assembly not exposed to the heat source will combust. The second is the "hose stream" test and uses a high-pressure hose stream to simulate how well the assembly stands up to an impact from falling debris and the cooling and eroding effects of water. Overall, the test evaluates an assembly's ability to prevent the passage of fire, heat, and hot gases for a given amount of time.

For construction assemblies testing according to ASTM E119, a time-based rating is given to the assembly. In general terms, this rating is the amount of time an assembly can resist a standard test fire without failing. The ratings are 1 hour, 2 hours, 3 hours, and 4 hours. Doors and other opening assemblies can also be given 20-minute, 30-minute, and 45-minute ratings.

## NFPA 252

NFPA 252, *Fire Tests of Door Assemblies*, evaluates the ability of a door assembly to resist the passage of flame, heat, and gases. It establishes a time-endurance rating for the door assembly, and the hose stream part of the test determines if the door will stay within its frame when subjected to a standard blast from a fire hose after the door has been subjected to the fire-endurance part of the test. This standard also describes a procedure for measuring the unexposed surface temperature of the door, often called the maximum transmitted temperature rise. For doors in exit enclosures and exit passageways in buildings without sprinklers, the IBC limits the maximum surface temperature on the unexposed side of the door to 450° F (250° C). This is so that excessive radiant heat will not prevent people from using the exits. Similar tests include UL10B, UL10C, and UBC 7-2.

## NFPA 257

NFPA 257, *Standard on Fire Test for Window and Glass Block Assemblies*, prescribes specific fire and hose stream test procedures to establish a degree of fire protection in units of time for window openings in fire-resistive walls. It determines the degree of protection from the spread of fire, including flame, heat, and hot gasses.

Flammability tests for building and finish materials determine the following.

- whether a material is flammable, and if so, if it simply burns with applied heat or if it supports combustion (adds fuel to the fire)
- the degree of flammability (how fast fire spreads across the material)
- how much smoke and toxic gas the material produces when ignited

The following six tests are typically used for building and interior construction, although not all of them may be in any one building code. Refer to the section on furniture and flammability later in this chapter for tests related to fabrics and furniture.

## ASTM E84

ASTM E84, *Standard Test Method for Surface Burning Characteristics of Building Materials*, is one of the most common fire testing standards. It is also known as the *Steiner tunnel test* and rates the surface burning characteristics of interior finishes and other building materials by testing, in a narrow test chamber, a sample piece with a controlled flame at one end. The primary result is a material's flame-spread rating compared to glass-reinforced cement board (with a rating of 0) and red oak flooring (with an arbitrary rating of 100). ASTM E84 can also be used to generate a "smoke developed" index.

With this test, materials are classified into one of three groups based on their tested flame-spread characteristics. These groups and their flame-spread indexes are given in Table 19.1.

Class A is the most fire resistant. Product literature generally indicates the flame spread of the material, either by class (letter or Roman numeral) or by numerical value. Building codes then specify the minimum flame-spread requirement for various occupancies in specific areas of the building (see Table 19.3). These are discussed in the next section, under Finishes.

### ASTM E662

The *Standard Test Method for Specific Optical Density of Smoke Generated by Solid Materials* measures the amount of smoke given off by a flaming or smoldering material or finish. During this test, the material is tested when it first smolders and then when a flame source is added. A smoke density value from 0 to 800 is developed. Most codes require a smoke density of 450 or less for finish materials. This is the same test as NFPA 258.

### NFPA 265

The *Room Corner Test*, NFPA 265, is sometimes required in addition to or instead of an ASTM E84 rating for interior finishes. This test determines the contribution of interior wall and ceiling coverings to room fire growth. It attempts to simulate real-world conditions by testing the material in the corner of a full-sized test room. It was developed as an alternate to the E84 Steiner tunnel test. For the test, the textile wall covering is applied to three sides of an 8 ft by 12 ft by 8 ft high room. An ignition source is placed in the room and provides a heat output of 40 kW for 5 minutes and then 150 kW for 10 minutes. Rating is based on whether (1) the flame does not spread to the ceiling during the 40 kW exposure and (2) other conditions are met during the 150 kW exposure, including no flashover and no spread of flame to the outer extremity of the 8 ft by 12 ft wall. A rating is either pass or fail.

### NFPA 253

NFPA 253 is the *Flooring Radiant Panel Test* used for floor coverings. It is discussed in more detail in Ch. 9, under the Carpet section, and in the next section of this chapter.

| class | flame-spread index |
|---|---|
| I (A) | 0–25 |
| II (B) | 26–75 |
| III (C) | 76–200 |

**Table 19.1** Flame-spread ratings

### NFPA 286

NFPA 286 is the *Standard Methods of Fire Tests for Evaluating Contribution of Wall and Ceiling Interior Finish to Room Fire Growth, 2000 Edition.* This standard was developed to address concerns with interior finishes that do not remain in place during testing according to the E84 tunnel test. It evaluates materials other than textiles. It is similar to NFPA 265 in that materials are mounted on the walls or ceilings inside a room, but more of the test room wall surfaces are covered, and ceiling materials can be tested. This test evaluates the extent to which finishes contribute to fire growth in a room, assessing factors such as heat and smoke released, combustion products released, and the potential for fire spread beyond the room.

### NFPA 701

NFPA 701 is the *Standard Methods of Fire Tests for Flame-Resistant Textiles and Films.* This test establishes two procedures for testing the flammability of draperies, curtains, or other window treatments. Test 1 provides a procedure for assessing the response of fabrics lighter than 21 oz/yd$^2$ individually and in multilayer composites used as curtains, draperies, and other window treatments. Test 2 is for fabrics weighing more than 21 oz/yd$^2$, such as fabric blackout linings, awnings, and similar architectural fabric structures and banners. NFPA 701 is appropriate for testing materials that are exposed to air on both sides. A sample either passes or fails the test.

## FIRE-RESISTIVE STANDARDS

Building codes recognize that there is no such thing as a fireproof building; there are only degrees of fire resistance. Because of this, building codes specify requirements for two broad classifications of fire resistance as mentioned in the previous section: resistance of materials and assemblies, and surface burning characteristics of finish materials.

## Construction materials and assemblies

In the first type of classification, the amount of fire resistance that a material or construction assembly must have is specified in terms of an hourly rating as determined by ASTM E119 for walls, ceiling/floor assemblies, columns, beam enclosures, and similar building elements. Codes also specify what time rating doors and glazing must have as determined by NFPA 252 or NFPA 257, respectively. For example, exit-access corridors are often required to have at least a 1-hour rating, and the door assemblies in such a corridor may be required to have a 20-minute rating.

Building codes typically have tables indicating what kinds of construction meet various hourly ratings. Other sources of information for acceptable construction assemblies include Underwriters Laboratories' *Building Materials Directory*, ETL Semko's *Directory of Listed Products*, manufacturers' proprietary product literature, and other reference sources.

The assemblies that interior designers are most often concerned with include permanent partitions, doors, glazed openings, and portions of floor/ceiling constructions. Occasionally, if a project involves build-out of two or more floors, shaft enclosures, such as stairways, must also be detailed to meet the applicable fire-resistive requirements.

The fire-resistive ratings of existing building components are important in determining the construction type of the building. This is discussed in greater detail in the section of this chapter titled Classification Based on Construction Type.

It is important to note that many materials by themselves do not create a fire-rated barrier. It is the construction assembly of which they are a part that is fire resistant. A 1-hour-rated suspended ceiling, for example, must use rated ceiling tile, but it is the assembly of tile, the suspension system, and the structural floor above that carries the 1-hour rating. In a similar way, a 1-hour-rated partition may consist of a layer of ⅝ in (15.9 mm) Type-X gypsum board attached to both sides of a wood or metal stud according to certain conditions. A single piece of gypsum board cannot have a fire-resistance rating by itself, except under special circumstances defined by the new International Building Code.

## Types of fire-resistance-rated walls and partitions

One of the most common types of construction assemblies the interior designer details is a partition. The new IBC makes important distinctions between various types of fire-resistance-rated walls and partitions. These include fire partitions, fire barriers, fire walls, and smoke barriers. Fire partitions are one of the most common fire-resistance-rated partitions used by interior designers.

A *fire partition* is a wall assembly with a fire-resistance rating of 1 hour used in the following designated locations.

- walls separating dwelling units such as rooms in apartments, dormitories, and assisted living facilities
- walls separating guest rooms in Group R-1 occupancies, such as hotels, and R-2 and I-1 occupancies
- walls separating tenant spaces in covered mall buildings
- corridor walls

The exceptions include (1) corridor walls permitted to be nonrated by Table 1017.1 and (2) dwelling and guest room separations in Type IIB, IIIB, and VB buildings equipped with automatic sprinkler systems. In these construction types, separation walls may be ½-hour rated.

In most cases, fire partitions must provide a continuous barrier. This means that they must extend from the floor to the underside of the floor or roof slab above *or* to the ceiling of a fire-resistance-rated floor/ceiling or roof/ceiling assembly. They must be securely attached at the top and bottom and extend continuously through concealed spaces, except where permitted to terminate below a fire-resistance-rated floor/ceiling or roof/ceiling assembly. There are several exceptions. Some of the more commonly used options for fire partitions are shown in Fig. 19.1. Refer to Sec. 708 of the IBC for complete information.

Openings in fire partitions must be a minimum of ¾ hour except for corridors, which must be protected by 20-minute fire-protection assemblies.

Although two options are available to separate rooms with fire partitions (as shown in options (a) and (b) in Fig. 19.1) and four options are available for corridor separation, using continuous slab-to-slab partitions is usually the best option for commercial construction. It provides the best passive control of smoke and fire without relying on the integrity of a ceiling assembly. Slab-to-slab partitions are also often the easiest and least costly for contractors to construct, although there could be instances where other methods may be preferred.

A *fire barrier* is a vertical or horizontal assembly that is fire-resistance rated and is designed to restrict the spread of fire, confine it to limited areas, and/or afford safe passage for protected egress. In general terms, a fire barrier offers more protection than a fire partition. Fire barriers are used for the following purposes.

- to enclose vertical exit enclosures (stairways), exit passageways, horizontal exits, and incidental use areas

- to separate different occupancies in a mixed-occupancy situation

**Figure 19.1**
Options for fire-partition construction

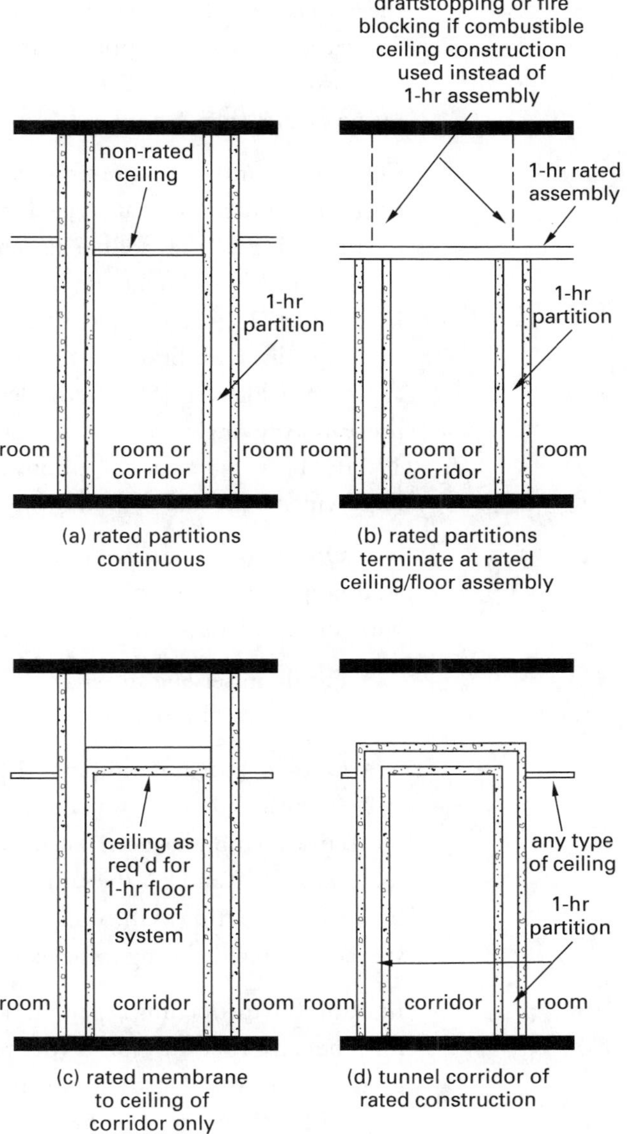

- to separate single occupancies into different fire areas
- to otherwise provide a fire barrier where specifically required by code provisions in the IBC as well as the other international codes

Unlike fire partitions, fire barriers must always be continuous from the floor slab to the underside of the floor or roof slab above. There are only a few exceptions. Fire barriers may also be required to have a fire-resistance rating greater than 1 hour.

Openings in fire barriers are required to have a degree of protection that varies depending on the rating of the fire barrier and may range from ¾ hour to 3 hours according to IBC Table 715.4 (see Table 19.2). In any case, openings are limited to a maximum aggregate width of 25% of the length of the wall. Any single opening cannot exceed 120 $ft^2$ (11 $m^2$) in area. Exceptions to these requirements include the following.

- Openings can be greater than 120 $ft^2$ if adjoining fire areas are equipped throughout with an automatic sprinkler system.
- Fire doors serving an exit enclosure can exceed the above limitation.
- Openings are not limited to 120 $ft^2$ or 25% of the length of the wall if the opening protective assembly has been tested according to ASTM E119 and has the same or greater fire-resistance rating as the wall. This allows special, fire-rated glazing to be used.

In addition to openings, penetrations (as for pipes and conduit), joints (between the partition and other construction), ducts, and air transfer openings must be protected as specified in the code.

A *fire wall* is a fire-resistance-rated wall that is used to separate a single structure into separate construction types or to provide for allowable area increases by creating what amounts to separate buildings, even though they are attached. As such, they are wall assemblies that are seldom, if ever, designed by interior designers; they are typically part of the original architecture of a building. The unique thing about fire walls is that, in addition to providing fire-resistance ratings from 2 to 4 hours, they must extend continuously from the foundation to or through the roof and they must be designed and constructed such that under fire conditions, the structure on one side can collapse without affecting the structural stability of the adjacent building.

A *smoke barrier* is a continuous vertical or horizontal membrane with a minimum fire-resistance rating of 1 hour, designed and constructed to restrict the movement of smoke. It is a passive form of smoke control. Openings in smoke barriers must have at least a 20-minute rating.

## Finishes

In the second type of fire-resistive classification, single layers of finish material are rated according to ASTM E84 and their use is restricted to certain areas of buildings based on their rating and whether or not the building is sprinklered. See Table 19.3. The purposes of this type of regulation are to control the flame-spread rate along the surface of a material and to limit the amount of combustible material in a building.

The materials tested and rated according to surface burning characteristics include finishes such as wainscoting, paneling, heavy wall covering, or other finishes applied structurally or for decoration, acoustical correction, surface insulation, or similar purposes. In most cases, the restrictions do not apply to trim such as chair rails, baseboards, and handrails; or to doors, windows, or their frames; or to materials that are less than 1/28 in (0.9 mm) thick cemented to the surface of noncombustible walls or ceilings.

Traditionally, the E84 test was used exclusively for interior finishes, but the IBC also allows the use of finish materials other than textiles if they meet requirements set forth

**Table 19.2** Fire-protection ratings of openings

Fire Door and Fire Shutter Fire Protection Ratings

(IBC Table 715.4)

| type of assembly | required assembly rating (hr) | minimum fire door and fire shutter assembly rating (hr) |
|---|---|---|
| fire walls and fire barriers having a required fire-resistance rating greater than 1 hour | 4 | 3 |
| | 3 | 3[(1)] |
| | 2 | 1½ |
| | 1½ | 1½ |
| fire barriers having a required fire-resistance rating of 1 hour: | | |
| shaft exit enclosure and passageway walls | 1 | 1 |
| other fire barriers | 1 | ¾ |
| fire partitions: | | |
| corridor walls | 1 | ⅓[(2)] |
| | 0.5 | ⅓[(2)] |
| other fire partitions | 1 | ¾ |
| | 0.5 | ⅓ |
| exterior walls | 3 | 1½ |
| | 2 | 1½ |
| | 1 | ¾ |
| smoke barriers | 1 | ⅓[(2)] |

[(1)] Two doors, each with a fire protection rating of 1½ hours, installed on opposite sides of the same opening in a fire wall, shall be deemed equivalent in fire protection rating to one 3-hour fire door.
[(2)] For testing requirements, see Sec. 715.3.3.



in the IBC when tested in accordance with NFPA 286 and when a Class A finish would otherwise be required.

Refer to Ch. 9 for a discussion of carpet flammability and tests specifically related to carpet.

The Uniform Building Code had a table similar to Table 19.3 except it used the Roman numerals I, II, and III instead of letters and discusses the different requirements for sprinklered and unsprinklered buildings in the text rather than in the table. It set requirements for three areas of a building, but the most restrictive was enclosed vertical exitways, the next most restrictive included other exitways, and the least restrictive included rooms or areas.

If textile wall coverings are used, they must comply with one of three conditions. They must be rated as Class A according to ASTM E84 and be protected by an automatic sprinkler system, or they must meet the requirements the Method B test protocol of NFPA 265, or they must meet the requirements of

**Table 19.3**
Maximum flame-spread classes for occupancy groups

Interior Wall and Ceiling Finish Requirements by Occupancy[11]

(IBC Table 803.5)

| | sprinklered[12] | | | nonsprinklered | | |
|---|---|---|---|---|---|---|
| group | exit enclosures and exit passage-ways[1,2] | corridors | rooms and enclosed spaces[3] | exit enclosures and exit passage-ways[1,2] | corridors | rooms and enclosed spaces[3] |
| A-1 & A-2 | B | B | C | A | A[4] | B[5] |
| A-3[6], A-4, A-5 | B | B | C | A | A[4] | C |
| B, E, M, R-1, R-4 | B | C | C | A | B | C |
| F | C | C | C | B | C | C |
| H | B | B | C[7] | A | A | B |
| I-1 | B | C | C | A | B | B |
| I-2 | B | B | B[8,9] | A | A | B |
| I-3 | A | A[10] | C | A | A | B |
| I-4 | B | B | B[8,9] | A | A | B |
| R-2 | C | C | C | B | B | C |
| R-3 | C | C | C | C | C | C |
| S | C | C | C | B | B | C |
| U | | no restrictions | | | no restrictions | |

For SI: 1 inch = 25.4 mm, 1 square foot = 0.0929 m².

(1) Class C interior finish materials shall be permitted for wainscotting or paneling of not more than 1000 square feet of applied surface area in the grade lobby where applied directly to a noncombustible base or over furring strips applied to a noncombustible base and fireblocked as required by Sec. 803.4.1.

(2) In exit enclosures of buildings less than three stories in height of other than Group I-3, Class B interior finish for nonsprinklered buildings and Class C interior finish for sprinklered buildings shall be permitted.

(3) Requirements for rooms and enclosed spaces shall be based upon spaces enclosed by partitions. Where a fire-resistance rating is required for structural elements, the enclosing partitions shall extend from the floor to the ceiling. Partitions that do not comply with this shall be considered enclosing spaces and the rooms or spaces on both sides shall be considered one. In determining the applicable requirements for rooms and enclosed spaces, the specific occupancy thereof shall be the governing factor regardless of the group classification of the building or structure.

(4) Lobby areas in Group A-1, A-2 and A-3 occupancies shall not be less than Class B materials.

(5) Class C interior finish materials shall be permitted in places of assembly with an occupant load of 300 persons or less.

(6) For churches and places of worship, wood used for ornamental purposes, trusses, paneling, or chancel furnishing shall be permitted.

(7) Class B material is required where the building exceeds two stories.

(8) Class C interior finish materials shall be permitted in administrative spaces.

(9) Class C interior finish materials shall be permitted in rooms with a capacity of four persons or less.

(10) Class B materials shall be permitted as wainscotting extending not more than 48 inches above the finished floor in corridors.

(11) Finish materials as provided for in other sections of this code.

(12) Applies when the exit enclosures, exit passageways, corridors, or rooms and enclosed spaces are protected by a sprinkler system installed in accordance with Sec. 903.3.1.1 or Sec. 903.3.1.2.

NFPA 286. These tests are described earlier in this chapter. For *ceilings*, textile finishes must either meet the requirements ASTM E84 with sprinklers or NFPA 286.

The IBC now regulates the ratings of some floor coverings. These include textile coverings or those comprised of fibers—in other words, carpet. It specifically excludes traditional flooring types such as wood, vinyl, linoleum, and terrazzo.

The IBC requires textile or fiber floor coverings to be of one of two classes as defined by NFPA 253, the *flooring radiant panel test*. In this test the amount of radiant energy needed to sustain flame is measured and defined as the critical radiant flux.

Two classes are defined by the flooring radiant panel test, Class I and Class II. Class I materials have a critical radiant flux of not less than 0.45 W/cm$^2$, and Class II materials have a critical radiant flux of not less than 0.22 W/cm$^2$. Class I materials are more resistant to flame spread than Class II materials. Class I finishes are typically required in vertical exits, exit passageways, and exit access corridors in Group I-2 and I-3 occupancies (hospitals, nursing homes, and detention facilities). Class II flooring is typically required in the same areas of Groups A, B, E, H, I-4, M, R-1, R-2, and S occupancies. In other areas carpet must conform to DOC FF-1 (ASTM D2859), the pill test. Refer to Ch. 9 for more information on the pill test.

The exception to the requirements stated in the paragraph above is that if the building is equipped with an automatic sprinkler system, Class II materials are permitted in any area where Class I materials would otherwise be required. Also, materials complying with DOC FF-1 may be used in other areas.

### Decorations and trim

Curtains, draperies, hangings, and other decorative materials suspended from walls or ceilings in occupancies of Groups A, E, I, and R-1, and dormitories in Group R-2, must be flame resistant and pass the NFPA 701 test or must be noncombustible. In Group I-1 and I-2 occupancies, combustible decoration must be flame retardant unless quantities are so limited as to present no hazard. The amount of noncombustible decorative materials is not limited, but the amount of flame-resistant materials is limited to 10% of the aggregate area of walls and ceilings, except in A occupancies, where it is limited to 50% if the building is fully sprinklered.

Material used as interior trim must have a minimum Class C flame-spread index and smoke-developed index. Combustible trim (such as wood trim), excluding handrails and guardrails, cannot exceed 10% of the aggregate wall or ceiling area in which it is located.

For an explanation of the terms used in this section, refer to the definitions at the end of this chapter.

## CLASSIFICATION BASED ON OCCUPANCY

Occupancy refers to the type of use assigned to a building or interior space such as an office, restaurant, private residence, or school. Buildings and spaces are grouped by occupancy classifications based on similar life safety characteristics, the presence of fire hazards, and combustible contents.

The philosophy behind occupancy classification is that some uses are more hazardous than others. For example, a building where flammable liquids are present is more dangerous than a single-family residence. Also, residents of a nursing home will have more trouble exiting than young school children who have participated in fire drills. In order to achieve equivalent safety in building design, each occupancy group therefore varies by fire protection requirements, area and height limitations, type of construction restrictions (as described in the next section), and means of egress elements.

## Occupancy groups

Every building or portion of a building is classified according to its use and is assigned an occupancy group. This is true of the IBC as well as Canadian model codes and the three former U.S. model codes still used in some jurisdictions. The IBC classifies occupancies into ten major groups.

| | |
|---|---|
| A | assembly |
| B | business |
| E | educational |
| F | factory and industrial |
| H | hazardous |
| I | institutional |
| M | mercantile |
| R | residential |
| S | storage |
| U | utility |

Six of these groups are further divided to distinguish subgroups that define the relative hazard of the occupancy. For example, in the assembly group, an A-1 occupancy includes assembly places, usually with fixed seats, used to view performing arts or motion pictures, while an A-2 occupancy includes places designed for food and/or drink consumption. Table 19.4 shows a brief summary of the occupancy groups and subgroups and gives some examples of each. This table is not complete, and the IBC should be consulted for specific requirements.

If a particular project doesn't seem to fit any of the categories, the local building official should be consulted for a determination of the occupancy classification of that project.

Knowing the occupancy classification is important in determining other building requirements, many of which relate to the architectural design of a building, such as the maximum area, the number of floors allowed, and how the building is separated from other structures. For interior design, occupancy classification affects the following.

- calculation of occupant load
- egress design
- interior finish requirements
- use of fire partitions and fire barriers
- fire detection and suppression systems
- ventilation and sanitation requirements
- other special restrictions particular to any given classification

## Mixed occupancy and occupancy separation

When a building or area of a building contains two or more occupancies, it is considered to be of mixed occupancy. Mixed occupancies are common in architectural and interior design. For instance, the design of a large office space can include an office occupancy (B occupancy) adjacent to an auditorium used for training, which would be an assembly occupancy (A occupancy) if it had an occupant load over 49. Commercial interior design often involves planning a new space of one occupancy that is next to an existing space of another occupancy. Each occupancy must be separated from other occupancies with a fire barrier of the hourly rating as defined by the particular code that applies. The required hourly rating determines the specific design and detailing of the partition separating the two spaces. The IBC shows required occupancy separations with a matrix table with hourly separations ranging from 1 hour to 4 hours. When the building is equipped with an automated sprinkler system, the required hourly ratings may be reduced by 1 hour. The other model codes have similar tables.

## Accessory and incidental uses

In the IBC there are two variations of the concept of mixed occupancies that have their own particular requirements: accessory occupancies and incidental use areas.

**Table 19.4** Occupancy groups summary

| occupancy group | description | examples |
|---|---|---|
| A-1 | assembly with fixed seats for viewing of performances or movies | movie theaters, live performance theaters |
| A-2 | assembly for food and drink consumption | bars, restaurants, clubs |
| A-3 | assembly for worship, recreation, etc., not classified elsewhere | libraries, art museums, conference rooms > 49 occupant load |
| A-4 | assembly for viewing of indoor sports | arenas |
| A-5 | assembly for outdoor sports | stadiums |
| B | business for office or service transactions | offices, banks, educational above the 12th grade, post office |
| E | educational by more than 5 people through 12th grade | grade schools, high schools, daycare if > 5 children and > 2.5 years old |
| F-1 | factory moderate hazard | see code |
| F-2 | factory low hazard | see code |
| H | hazardous—see code | see code |
| I-1 | more than 16 ambulatory people on 24-hour basis | assisted living, group home, convalescent facilities |
| I-2 | medical care on 24-hour basis | hospitals, skilled care nursing |
| I-3 | more than 5 people restrained | jails, prisons, reformatories |
| I-4 | daycare for > 5 adults or infants (< 2.5 years) | daycare for infants |
| M | mercantile | department stores, markets, retail stores, drugstores, sales rooms |
| R-1 | residential for transient lodging | hotels and motels |
| R-2 | residential with 3 or more adults | apartments, dormitories, condominiums, convents |
| R-3 | one- or two-dwelling units with attached uses or childcare less than 6 years old and less than 24-hour care | bed and breakfast, small childcare |
| R-4 | residential assisted living where number of occupants exceeds 5 but less than 16 | small assisting living |
| dwellings | must use International Residential Code | |
| S | storage—see code | see code |
| U | utility—see code | see code |

Note: This is just a quick summary of the groups and examples of occupancy groups. Refer to the IBC for a complete list, or check with local building officials when a use is not clearly stated or described in the code.

An *accessory occupancy*, formerly called an accessory use area, is a space or room that is used in conjunction with the main occupancy but does not exceed 10% of the floor area of the main occupancy. Accessory occupancies do not need to be separated from the main occupancy with a fire barrier. For example, a small gift shop in a hospital would be considered an accessory occupancy and therefore not require the 2-hour occupancy separation normally required between an M occupancy and an I-2 occupancy. The two exceptions to this provision are Group H occupancies or incidental use areas.

The 2006 IBC has renamed *accessory use areas* as *accessory occupancies*, and the requirements have been moved from chapter 3 of the code to chapter 5. Some additional requirements have also been added. The first limits the area and height of the accessory occupancy to the tabular values in Table 503 of the IBC used by architects to determine the maximum size and height of a building based on its occupancy and construction type. These are generally not a significant factor for interior design, as the 10% limitation usually does not exceed the tabular values. The second requirement clarifies that the accessory occupancy is to be classified individually on the basis of its use, and not simply given the occupancy classification of the building's major use.

An *incidental use area* is an area that is incidental to the main occupancy and has the same classification as the nearest main occupancy but, by code, must be separated from the main occupancy by a fire barrier. The incidental rooms or areas and the separations required are given in Table 508.2 of the IBC. See Table 19.5.

When the table allows a sprinkler system to substitute for a fire barrier, the incidental use area must be separated by a smoke barrier and the sprinklers only have to be in the incidental use area. Doors must be self-closing or automatic-closing.

## Allowable area based on occupancy group

The International Building Code and other codes limit a building's area, height, and number of stories based on its occupancy and construction type. (Refer to the next section for a brief discussion of construction type.) The concept is that the more hazardous a building is the smaller it should be, making it easier to fight a fire and easier for occupants to exit in an emergency.

In most cases, a building's area and height are determined by its original architectural design. Occasionally, a client will ask an interior designer to design an existing building for an occupancy different than the original occupancy. If the existing building is not large enough to accommodate the new occupancy, the project may be infeasible, or other significant steps may need to be taken to make the project work.

For example, consider a 12,000 $ft^2$ (1115 $m^2$), Type V building formerly used as a low-hazard factory (F-2 occupancy) proposed to be remodeled into a nightclub (A-2 occupancy). The IBC states the basic maximum allowable floor area as 13,000 $ft^2$ (1208 $m^2$) for the F-2 occupancy and 6000 $ft^2$ (557 $m^2$) for the A-2 occupancy (see Table 503 of the IBC). While the building would work as a factory, the entire area could not be used as a nightclub unless other steps were taken. Even though the client's program called for a 10,000 $ft^2$ (929 $m^2$) nightclub, the IBC states that only 6000 $ft^2$ (558 $m^2$) of the building could be used.

It is beyond the scope of this book to describe how such problems could be solved, but the interior designer should be aware of the potential problem when existing building occupancies are changed. Specific requirements for maximum allowable area and height are given in Ch. 5 of the IBC.

**Table 19.5** Incidental use areas

Incidental Use Areas
IBC Table 508.2

| room or area | separation[1] |
|---|---|
| furnace room where largest piece of equipment is over 400,000 Btu/hr input | 1-hour or provide automatic fire-extinguishing system |
| rooms with boilers where the largest piece of equipment is over 15 psi and 10 hp | 1-hour or provide automatic fire-extinguishing system |
| refrigerant machinery rooms | 1-hour or provide automatic fire-extinguishing system |
| parking garage (Section 406.2) | 2 hours, or 1-hour and provide automatic fire-extinguishing system |
| hydrogen cut-off rooms, not classified as Group H | 1-hour in Group B, F, H, M, S, and U occupancies, 2-hour in Group A, E, I, and R occupancies |
| incinerator rooms | 2 hours and automatic sprinkler system |
| paint shops, not classified as a Group H, located in occupancies other than Group F | 2 hours, or 1-hour and provide automatic fire-extinguishing systems |
| laboratories and vocational shops, not classified as Group H, located in Group E and I-2 occupancies | 1-hour or provide automatic fire-extinguishing system |
| laundry rooms over 100 $ft^2$ | 1-hour or provide automatic fire-extinguishing system |
| storage rooms over 100 $ft^2$ | 1-hour or provide automatic fire-extinguishing system |
| Group I-3 cells equipped with padded surfaces | 1-hour |
| Group I-2 waste and linen collection rooms | 1-hour or provide automatic fire-extinguishing system |
| waste and linen collection rooms over 100 $ft^2$ | 1-hour or provide automatic fire-extinguishing system |
| stationary lead-acid battery systems having a liquid capacity of more than 100 gal (380 L) used for facility standby power, emergency power, or uninterrupted power supplies | 1-hour in Group B, F, M, S, and U occupancies, 2-hour in Group A, E, I, and R occupancies |

For SI: 1 $ft^2$ = 0.0929 $m^2$

[1] Where an automatic fire-extinguishing system is provided, it need only be provided in the incidental use room or area.

## CLASSIFICATION BASED ON CONSTRUCTION TYPE

Every building is classified into one of five major types of construction based on the fire resistance of certain building components. Under the IBC, these components include the structural frame, interior and exterior bearing walls, and floor and roof construction. Under the UBC, components also included shaft enclosures, permanent partitions, and exterior doors and windows. The five types of construction are Types I, II, III, IV, and V. Type I buildings are the most fire resistive, while Type V are the least fire resistive. For example, the structural frame of a Type I building must have a 3-hour rating, while the frame in a Type III building must only have a 1-hour rating. Type I and II buildings are noncombustible, while Types III, IV, and V are considered combustible. In four of the types there are two subgroups designated with an A or B suffix, which indicates whether the construction is fire protected or not. In the IBC there are now Types I-A, I-B, II-A, II-B, III-A, III-B, IV, V-A, and V-B. Specific requirements for each of the building elements are given in Tables 601 and 602 of the IBC.

The purposes of designing buildings to a certain classification are to protect the structural elements from fire and collapse and to prevent fire from spreading from one building to another. In combination with occupancy groups, building type limits the area and height of buildings. For example, a Type I building of any occupancy (except certain hazardous occupancies) can be of unlimited area and height, while a Type V building is limited to only a few thousand square feet in area and one or two stories in height, depending on its occupancy. Limiting height and area based on construction type and occupancy recognizes that it becomes more difficult to fight fires, provide time for egress, and rescue people as buildings get larger and higher. It also recognizes that the type and amount of combustibles existing due to the building's use and construction affect its safety.

There are several interrelated variables concerning construction type, most of which are determined by the architect when designing the building. For existing buildings, the construction type is already established. To determine the construction type of a project, ask the local building official, or check with the building's architect if it is currently being designed or has recently been constructed.

Interior designers must know the construction type if major changes are being made. For example, if the occupancy of a building or portion of a building is being changed from a B (business) to an A (assembly) occupancy, the interior designer must know the construction type to verify that the maximum area is not exceeded. If it is, it may be necessary to construct a fire wall or add sprinklers. This is a similar situation to that described in the previous example concerning allowable area based on occupancy group. In addition, construction type can affect the required fire ratings of coverings of structural elements, floor/ceiling assemblies, and openings in rated walls. For example, during a remodeling, the required fire rating of a protected beam may be changed to accommodate new construction, and the interior designer would have to detail or specify repairs or new construction to return the assembly to its original rating.

## GLAZING

Code requirements for interior glazing focus on two basic issues: (1) its use in hazardous locations and (2) its use in fire-rated assemblies such as partitions and doors.

When glass is installed in hazardous locations—that is, where it is subject to human impact—it must be safety glazing (i.e., tempered glass or laminated glass). The exact locations where safety glazing is required are discussed in Ch. 5 and shown in Fig. 5.13.

The requirements for glass used in fire-rated doors are discussed in Ch. 20.

For glass used in fire-resistance-rated partitions, the IBC differentiates between two types of glazing: fire-protection-rated glazing and fire-resistance-rated glazing.

*Fire-protection-rated glazing* is ¼ in thick wired glass in steel frames or other types of glazing that meet the requirements of NFPA 252, *Standard Methods of Fire Tests of Door Assemblies*, or NFPA 257, *Standard for Fire Test for Window and Glass Block Assemblies.* Such glazing must have a 45-minute rating and is limited to 1-hour-rated fire partitions or fire barriers when the fire barrier is used to separate occupancies or to separate incidental use areas. The amount of such glazing is limited to 25% of the area of the common wall within any room using the glazing. This limitation applies to partitions separating two rooms as well as to a partition separating a room and a corridor. Individual lights of fire-protection-rated glazing cannot exceed 1296 $in^2$ in area (9 $ft^2$ [0.84 $m^2$]), and any one dimension cannot be more than 54 in (1372 mm). The IBC accepts ¼ in wired glass as meeting the requirements for a 45-minute rating without specific testing, but other glazing must meet the NFPA 252 or NFPA 257 test requirements for a 45-minute rating.

As stated in Ch. 5, new requirements in the 2006 edition of the IBC only allow the use of wired glass in hazardous locations if the glass can meet the requirements of 16 CFR 1201. This has the effect of precluding its use in doors, sidelights, and similar situations. As described in Ch. 5, one of the newer glazing products must be used, such as fire-resistance-rated glazing that also is classified for impact resistance.

*Fire-resistance-rated glazing* is glass or other glazing material that has been tested as part of a fire-resistance-rated wall assembly according to ASTM E119. This glazing definition allows the use of special fire-rated glazing that can have fire-resistive ratings up to 2 hours. Refer to Ch. 5 for a discussion of these types of glazing products. This type of glazing may be used in partitions that must have a rating higher than 1 hour, although the glazing must have the same rating as the partition in which it is used. There are no area limitations.

For additional code requirements of glazing and a discussion of topics, including fire-rated glazing, wired glass, and safety glazing, refer to Ch. 5.

## FIRE DETECTION AND SUPPRESSION

Fire detection, alarm, and suppression systems have become important parts of a building's overall life safety and fire protection strategies. Almost all new buildings are now required to have some type of detections device, even if it is a single smoke detector in a residence. Other occupancies, such as high-rise buildings and hotels, must have elaborate detection and alarm systems, including communication devices on each floor to allow firefighters to talk with each other and with occupants in the event of an emergency.

The term *fire protection system* is used to describe any fire alarm or fire-extinguishing device or system that is designed and installed to detect, control, or extinguish a fire, or to alert the occupants or the fire department that a fire has occurred, or any combination of these. Most systems are designed to be automatic, which means they provide an emergency function without human intervention and are activated by the detection of one or a combination of the following.

- smoke or other products of combustion
- a rise in temperature to a predetermined level
- a rate of rise of temperature to a predetermined rate of change

For large or complex buildings, a complete fire protection system may include many elements such as smoke and heat detectors, sprinklers, alternate fire-extinguishing systems (halon, for example), portable fire extinguishers, standpipes, smoke control systems, and smoke and heat vents.

Sprinklers are the most common type of suppression system and are required in nearly all new high-rise buildings and hotels. They are also becoming commonplace in many other types of commercial buildings. One of the major changes from the UBC to the IBC is that sprinklers are either mandated in occupancies where they were not before, or the code gives generous tradeoffs for using sprinklers. For example, in a non-sprinklered building of A, B, E, F, M, S, or U occupancy, corridors must have a 1-hour rating. In a sprinklered building of the same occupancy, the corridors need not be rated. The intent of the new code is to encourage designers, developers, and builders to install sprinkler systems, recognizing their value as a part of the entire life safety system of a building.

The design and layout of a sprinkler system are the responsibility of the mechanical engineer or fire protection contractor, but the interior designer should be aware of sprinkler system requirements, most notably the spacing of sprinkler heads and the types of heads available. Some of these requirements are given in Ch. 16.

The National Fire Protection Association has developed standards that are followed by most building departments for the design of sprinkler systems. These are NFPA-13 for commercial buildings and NFPA-13R for residential construction. The NFPA standards are required by reference by the model codes and the IBC.

## OTHER REQUIREMENTS

In addition to the provisions mentioned in the previous sections, the IBC and the other model building codes regulate many other aspects of construction. These include, among many others, the use and structural design of individual materials, excavations, demolition, and elevators. In addition to the model codes, there are local, state, and federal regulations that may govern the design of a particular project. Specific requirements for barrier-free design and means of egress are discussed in Chs. 18 and 20, respectively.

### Guards (guardrails)

A *guard* is a component whose function is to prevent falls from an elevated area. For example, an opening on the second floor that overlooks the first floor must be protected with a guard. In the UBC, guards were called guardrails. Guards are required along open-sided walking surfaces, mezzanines, industrial equipment platforms, stairways, ramps, and landings that are more than 30 in (762 mm) above the floor below. There are several exceptions, including stages and raised platforms.

Guards must be a minimum of 42 in (1067 mm) high and designed such that a sphere with a 4 in (102 mm) diameter cannot pass through any opening up to a height of 34 in (864 mm). Guards must be designed to resist a load of 50 lbf/ft (0.73 kN/m) applied in any direction at the top of the guard. Other design requirements and exceptions are detailed in Sec. 1013 of the IBC.

### Mechanical systems

The International Mechanical Code, companion to the IBC, details the requirements for materials and design of systems for heating, ventilating, and air-conditioning systems. Most of these do not directly affect the interior designer except where mechanical elements, such as supply air-diffusers and return air grilles, are visible in the finished space. Refer to Ch. 16 for information on coordinating with mechanical systems.

### Plumbing systems

The IBC and other model codes specify in great detail how a plumbing system must be designed. They also specify the number of sanitary fixtures required based on the type of occupancy. In most cases, satisfying the requirements is the responsibility of the mechanical engineer and architect. However, in some cases, the interior designer may be involved with remodeling toilet rooms in commercial buildings. In this case, it is helpful to know how many fixtures are required when preliminary design layouts are being developed. For example, the International Plumbing Code, which is a companion volume to the IBC, gives the minimum number of toilets, lavatories, drinking fountains, and other fixtures required in a building. For convenience, these provisions are also given in Ch. 29 of the IBC.

### Electrical systems

The IBC and the other three former model codes reference the National Electrical Code, published by the National Fire Protection Association. As with other companion codes, the NEC details the requirements for materials and design of the power supply and lighting systems of buildings. Most of these do not directly affect the interior designer except where electrical elements, such as outlets, are visible in the finished space. The NEC, for example, specifies the maximum spacing for outlets and the requirement for ground fault interrupter outlets. Refer to Ch. 16 for more information on coordinating with electrical systems.

### Sound ratings

The IBC requires that wall and floor/ceiling assemblies in residential occupancies separating dwelling units or guest rooms from each other and from public spaces be designed and constructed to provide for sound-transmission control. The code specifies a minimum sound transmission class (STC) of 50 (45 if field tested) for walls. The requirement does not apply to dwelling unit entrance doors. However, these doors must be tight-fitting to the frame and sill. The minimum impact insulation class (IIC) for floors must be 50 (45 if field tested). Construction details that satisfy these requirements must be selected. Refer to Ch. 11 for more information on acoustics.

## FURNITURE FLAMMABILITY

Although the IBC and other model codes do not regulate furniture flammability, some local or state jurisdictions do include furniture flammability standards as part of their purview. The following standards describe the more commonly used tests that furniture must meet when required by either the local authority having jurisdiction or state laws. These standards define limits on a material's flammability in terms of one or more of the following characteristics: resistance to ignition, resistance to flame spread, resistance to smoldering, prevention of smoke development, prevention of heat contribution to the growth of a fire, and prevention of toxic gas release.

### ASTM E1352 (CA TB 116)

ASTM E1352 (CA TB 116) is the *Standard Test Method for Cigarette Ignition Resistance of Mock-Up Upholstered Furniture Assemblies.* It is similar to CA TB 116 (California Technical Bulletin), NFPA 261, and BIFMA X5.7 (Business and Institutional Manufacturers Association). It determines how a composite material (padding and covering) reacts to a lighted cigarette. The mock-up includes vertical and horizontal surfaces meeting at a 90° angle. The cushion fails the test if it breaks into flames or if a char more than 2 in (55 mm) long develops. The BIFMA standard allows a 3 in char length before the sample fails, and it classifies fabrics into class A, B, C, or D, with class A being the most resistant to charring.

### ASTM E1353 (CA TB 117)

ASTM E1353 (CA TB 117) is the *Standard Test Methods for Cigarette Ignition Resistance of Components of Upholstered Furniture.* It is similar to CA TB 117 and NFPA 260. It tests the resistance of individual components (fabric and fillings) of upholstered furniture to cigarette ignition as well as flame. Separate fill materials such as expanded polystyrene beads, cellular materials, feathers, nonartificial filling, and artificial fiber filling are tested separately for a variety of characteristics.

## ASTM E1537 (CA TB 133)

ASTM E1537 (CA TB 133) is the *Standard Test Method for Fire Testing of Upholstered Seating Furniture.* It is similar to CA TB 133, NFPA 266, BFD IX-10 (Boston Fire Department), and UL 1056. This is the most accurate of the three test mentioned here because it evaluates the response to an open flame of an actual sample of furniture. During the test several measurements are made, including the rate of heat and smoke released, total amount of heat and smoke released, concentration of carbon oxides, and others. The most important measurement is the rate of heat release, which quantifies the intensity of the fire generated. It is one of the strictest tests for furniture and is required in many states.

## DEFINITIONS

The following terms are frequently used by building codes to precisely communicate meaning. Although the differences between terms are sometimes subtle, they are important. Refer to Ch. 20 for definitions related to means of egress.

*Combustible:* material that will ignite and burn, either as a flame or glow, and that undergoes this process in air at pressures and temperatures that might occur during a fire in a building

*Fire assembly:* an assembly of a fire door, fire window, or fire damper, including all required anchorage, frames, sills, and hardware

*Fire barrier:* a new term in the 2000 IBC meaning a fire-resistance-rated vertical or horizontal assembly of materials designed to restrict the spread of fire in which openings are protected

*Fire partition:* a new term in the 2000 IBC meaning a fire-resistive component used to separate dwelling units in R-2 construction, guest rooms in Group R-1 construction, and tenant spaces in covered mall buildings, and also used as corridor walls. Fire partitions generally are required to have a minimum 1-hour fire-protection-rated construction except in certain circumstances. They are similar to fire barriers, but the requirements for support are not as strict.

*Fire-protection rating:* the period of time an opening assembly, such as a door or window, can confine a fire or maintain its integrity, or both, when tested in accordance with NFPA 252, UL 10B, or UL 10C for doors, and NFPA 257 for windows. An assembly that requires a fire-protection rating must withstand fire exposure and thermal shock as with a fire-resistance rating, but not heat transmission as walls, columns, and floors do.

*Fire-rated:* use "fire-protection rating"

*Fire resistance:* the property of a material or assembly to withstand or resist the spread of fire or give protection from it

*Fire-resistance rating:* the period of time a building component such as a wall, floor, roof, beam, or column can confine a fire or maintain its structural integrity, or both, when tested in accordance with ASTM E119, *Standard Methods for Fire Tests of Building Construction and Materials.* This is different from a fire-protection rating, which involves protected opening assemblies.

*Fire-resistive construction:* same as "fire resistance"

*Fire retardant:* should not be used as a noun. As an adjective it should only be used as a modifier with defined compound terms such as fire-retardant-treated wood.

*Flame resistance:* the ability to withstand flame impingement or give protection from it. This applies to individual materials as well as combinations of components when tested in accordance to NFPA 701, *Standard Methods of Fire Tests for Flame-Resistant Textiles and Films* (see Ch. 10).

*Flame retardant:* should not be used as a noun. As an adjective it should only be used as a modifier with defined compound terms such as flame-retardant treatment.

*Flame spread:* the propagation of flame over a surface

*Flame-spread index:* the numerical value assigned to a material tested in accordance with ASTM E84, *Standard Test Method for Surface Burning Characteristics of Building Materials*

*Flammable:* capable of burning with a flame and subject to easy ignition and rapid flaming combustion

*Noncombustible:* material that will not ignite and burn when subjected to a fire. The IBC and UBC classify a material as noncombustible only if it is tested in accordance with ASTM E136, *Noncombustible Material—Tests,* or if it has a structural base of noncombustible material with a surfacing not more than ⅛ in (3.18 mm) thick that has a flame-spread index no greater than 50.

*Trim:* includes picture molds, chair rails, baseboards, handrails, door and window frames, and similar decorative or protective materials used in fixed applications

# 20

# MEANS OF EGRESS

Although provisions for means of egress in the model building codes and specific state and local codes vary in details, they are all based on similar concepts. The information in this chapter is based on the International Building Code (IBC). Exact egress requirements should be reviewed for designs regulated by the local applicable code or by amendments to the model code being used.

## EXITING

Exiting, or "means of egress" as it is called in the codes, is one of the most important requirements of any building code. This chapter covers the basic concepts and requirements of exiting. Many jurisdictions have adopted or are in the process of adopting the IBC, but many others are still using one of the three model codes or their own state or city code. However, even these older codes are based on the same principles discussed in this chapter.

The majority of this chapter covers means of egress as it applies to commercial construction. Refer to the separate section on residential exiting for requirements related to one- and two-family houses.

### The egress system

The IBC, UBC, and other codes define *means of egress* as a continuous and unobstructed path of vertical and horizontal egress travel from any point in a building or structure to a public way. The means of egress consists of three parts: the exit access, the exit, and the exit discharge. These must lead to a public way. A public way is any street, alley, or similar parcel of land essentially unobstructed from the ground to the sky that is permanently appropriated to the public for public use and has a clear width of not less than 10 ft. See Fig. 20.1.

The *exit access* is that portion of the means of egress that leads to the entrance to an exit. Exit access areas may or may not be protected, depending on the specific requirements of the code based on occupancy and construction type. They may include components such as rooms, spaces, aisles, intervening rooms, hallways, corridors, ramps, and doorways. In concept, exit access does not provide a protected path of travel. In the IBC, even fire-protection-rated corridors are considered exit access. The exit access is the portion of the building where travel distance

**Figure 20.1**
Egress system

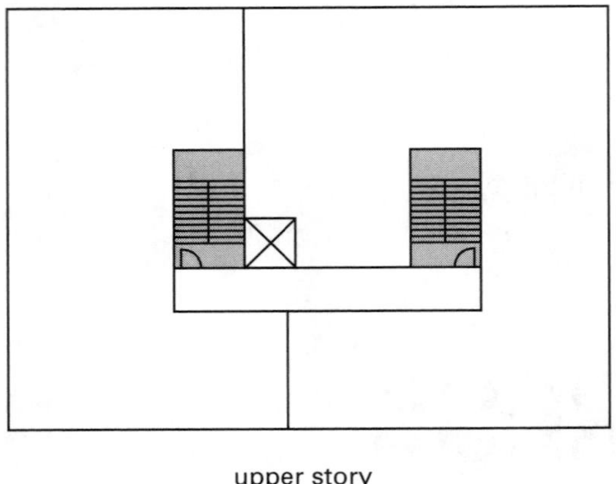


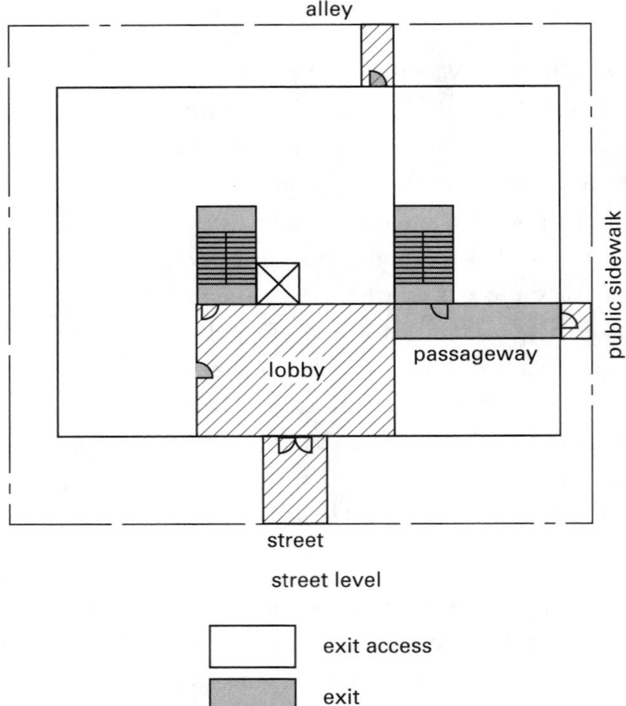


is measured and regulated (see the section on Maximum Travel Distance in this chapter).

The *exit* is the portion of the egress system that provides a protected path of egress between the exit access and the exit discharge. Exits are fully enclosed and protected from all other interior spaces by fire-resistance-rated construction with protected openings (doors, glass, etc.). Exits may be as simple as an exterior exit door at ground level or may include exit enclosures for stairs, exit passageways, and horizontal exits. In the IBC, exits may also include exterior exit stairways and ramps. Depending on building height, construction type, and passageway length, exits must have either a 1-hour or 2-hour rating. Travel distance is not an issue once the exit has been reached.

The *exit discharge* is the portion of the egress system between the termination of an exit and a public way. Exit discharge areas typically include portions outside the exterior walls such as exterior exit balconies, exterior exit stairways, and exit courts. Exit discharge may also include building lobbies of multistory buildings if one of the exit stairways opens onto the lobby and certain conditions are met. These conditions require that the exit door in the lobby is clearly visible, that the level of discharge is sprinklered, and that the entire area of discharge is separated from areas below by the same fire-resistance rating as for the exit enclosure that opens onto it. In the IBC, exterior exit stairways and ramps are considered to be exits, not exit discharge areas.

## Occupant load

The occupant load is the number of people that a building code assumes will occupy a given building or portion of a building. It is based on the occupancy classification as discussed in Ch. 19, including assembly, business, educational, and the other categories. Occupant load assumes that certain types of use will be more densely packed with people than others, and that exiting provisions should respond accordingly. For example, an auditorium needs more exits to allow safe evacuation than does an office space with the same floor area.

The IBC requires the occupant load to be established by using one of two methods:

counting the number of fixed seats if fixed seating is provided, or consulting an IBC table.

In the first method, the actual number of fixed seats becomes the occupant load. For example, the occupant load for an auditorium with fixed seating could be calculated by counting the number of seats. If the fixed seating area also has areas in which fixed seating is not installed, such as waiting spaces, designated standing room, and wheelchair spaces, the occupant load for these spaces is determined using the IBC table and added to the number of fixed seats. Aisles are not to be considered for additional occupant load.

In the second method, the occupant load is determined by taking the area in square feet (or square meters) assigned to a particular use and dividing by an *occupant load factor* as given in the code. In the IBC, the occupant load factor (or floor area in square feet per occupant) is given in Table 1004.1.1. The IBC table is reproduced here as Table 20.1. This is the most common method of calculating occupant load.

The occupant load factor is the amount of floor area presumed to be occupied by one person. It is based on the generic function of building spaces and is not the same as the occupancy groups discussed in Ch. 19. The occupant load factors, over time, have been found to consistently represent the densities found in various uses. IBC Table 1004.1.1 also shows whether the occupant load must be calculated based on net or gross area. The *gross floor area* includes stairs, corridors, toilet rooms, mechanical rooms, closets, and interior partition thickness. *Net floor area* includes just the space actually used. Most common uses are included in the table, but the IBC gives the local building official the power to establish occupant load factors in cases where a use is not specifically listed.

The previous codes have tables similar to Table 20.1, although the exact factors may vary slightly.

Also, when an occupant load from an accessory space exits through a primary space, the egress facilities from the primary space occupant load must include their own occupant load plus the occupant load of the accessory space. This provision simply requires that the occupant loads be cumulative as occupants exit through intervening spaces to an ultimate exit.

In determining the occupant load, all portions of the building are presumed to be occupied at the same time. However, the local building official may reduce the occupant load if the official determines that one area of a building would not normally be occupied while another area is occupied. An example of this would be the lunchroom of a factory area where the factory workers are either in the work area or the lunchroom, but not in both at the same time.

If there are mixed occupancies or uses, each area is calculated with its respective occupant load factor and then all loads are added together.

## Required number of exits

The number of exits or exit access doorways from a space, a group of spaces, or an entire building is determined based on several factors. These include the occupant load and occupancy of a space, the limitations on the "common path of egress travel" (which is described in the next section), and specific requirements when large occupant loads are encountered.

All buildings or portions of a building must, of course, have at least one exit. When the number of occupants of a space exceeds the number given in the code, then at least two exits must be provided. The idea is to have an alternate way out of a room, group of rooms, or building if one exit is blocked. The IBC requires two exits when the occupant load of a space exceeds the numbers given in IBC Table No. 1015.1. This is reproduced

**Table 20.1**
Maximum floor area allowances per occupant

| function of space | floor area (ft$^2$ per occupant) |
|---|---|
| agricultural buildings | 300 gross |
| aircraft hangars | 500 gross |
| airport terminals | |
| concourse | 100 gross |
| waiting areas | 15 gross |
| baggage claim | 20 gross |
| baggage handling | 300 gross |
| assembly | |
| gaming floors (keno, slots, etc.) | 11 gross |
| assembly with fixed seats | see 1003.2.2.9 |
| assembly without fixed seats | |
| concentrated (chair only—not fixed) | 7 net |
| standing space | 5 net |
| unconcentrated (tables and chairs) | 15 net |
| bowling centers, allow 5 persons for each lane including 15 ft of runway, and for additional areas | 7 net |
| business areas | 100 gross |
| courtrooms—other than fixed seating areas | 40 net |
| day care | 35 net |
| dormitories | 50 gross |
| educational | |
| classroom areas | 20 net |
| shops and other vocational rooms | 50 net |
| exercise rooms | 50 gross |
| H-5 fabrication and manufacturing areas | 200 gross |
| industrial areas | 100 gross |
| institutional areas | |
| inpatient treatment areas | 240 gross |
| outpatient areas | 100 gross |
| sleeping areas | 120 gross |
| kitchens, commercial | 200 gross |
| libraries | |
| reading rooms | 50 net |
| stack areas | 100 gross |
| locker rooms | 50 gross |
| mercantile, basement and grade floor areas | 30 gross |
| areas on other floors | 60 gross |
| storage, stock, and shipping areas | 300 gross |
| parking garages | 200 gross |
| residential | 200 gross |
| skating rinks, swimming pools | |
| rinks and pools | 50 gross |
| decks | 15 gross |
| stages and platforms | 15 net |
| accessory storage areas, mechanical equipment rooms | 300 gross |
| warehouses | 500 gross |

For SI: 1 ft$^2$ = 0.0929 m$^2$

**Example 1**
Calculating a restaurant occupant load

What is the occupant load for a restaurant dining room that is 2500 ft$^2$ (232.25 m$^2$) in area?

In Table 20.1, dining rooms are included under the use of "Assembly without fixed seats, unconcentrated," with an occupant load factor of 15 ft$^2$ (1.39 m$^2$). Dividing 15 (139) into 2500 (232.25) gives an occupant load of 167 persons (166.67 rounded up to 167).

**Example 2**
Calculating an office occupant load

What is the occupant load for an office with a gross area of 3700 ft$^2$ (343.73 m$^2$) that also has two training classrooms of 1200 ft$^2$ (111.48 m$^2$) each?

An office, as a business area, has an occupant load factor of 100 (9.29) gross, so 3700 (343.73) divided by 100 (9.29) gives an occupant load of 37 persons. Classrooms have an occupant load factor of 20 (1.86). Two classrooms of 1200 (111.48) give a total of 2400 ft$^2$ (222.96 m$^2$). 2400 ft$^2$ (222.96 m$^2$) divided by 20 (1.86) gives an occupant load for the classrooms of 120. The total occupant load of all the spaces, therefore, is 37 plus 120, or 157 persons.

in Table 20.2.

There are several exceptions where the life-safety risk is so minimal that it is acceptable to have only one exit. Two of these exceptions include the second story of an apartment with only four units and a maximum travel distance of 50 ft, and a business occupancy in a one-story building with a maximum occupant load of 50 and a maximum travel distance of 75 ft. Other exceptions are given in IBC Table 1019.2.

Three exits are required when the occupant load is between 501 and 1000, and at least four exits are required when the occupant load is greater than 1000.

## Common path of egress travel

Even if the occupant load of a space or a building is less than that shown in Table 20.2, two exits are still required if the common path of egress travel exceeds limits given in the code. The *common path of egress travel* is that portion of an exit access that the occupants are required to traverse before two separate and distinct paths of egress travel to two exits become available. See Fig. 20.2. Even if two exits are not required based on occupant load, if the common path of travel exceeds 75 ft (32 m) for all except H-1, H-2, and H-3 occupancies, then two exits from a space are required. The distance is increased to 100 ft (30.5 m) in some occupancies if certain conditions are met. For example, in B, F, and S occupancies, if the building is fully sprinklered, the maximum length of common path of egress travel is increased to 100 ft (30.5 m).

## Maximum travel distance

*Exit access travel distance* is the distance that an occupant must travel from the most remote point in the occupied portions of the exit access to the entrance to the nearest exit. Because exit access areas are not protected,

**Table 20.2**
Occupant load triggering requirement for two exits

Spaces with One Means of Egress
(IBC Table 1015.1)

| occupancy | maximum occupant load |
|---|---|
| A, B, E[(1)], F, M, U | 49 |
| H-1, H-2, H-3 | 3 |
| H-4, H-5, I-1, I-3, I-4, R | 10 |
| S | 29 |

[(1)] Day care maximum occupant load is 10.

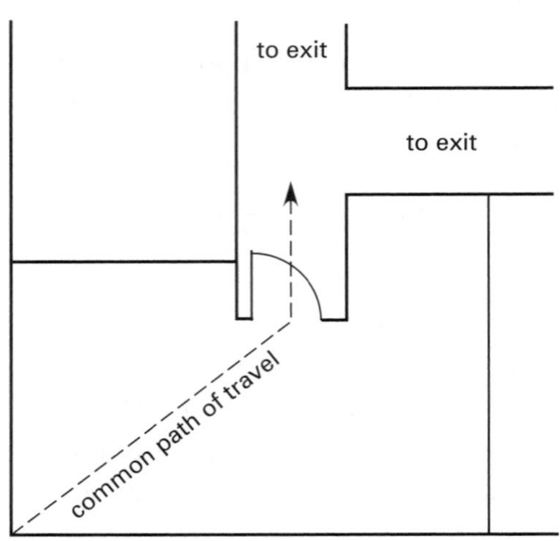


**Figure 20.2** Common path of egress travel

the code limits how far someone must travel to safety. Once a person is safely in an exit, travel distance is not an issue. Maximum travel distances are based on the occupancy of the building and whether or not the building is sprinklered. There are special requirements in the IBC as well as the older model codes that decrease the allowable travel distances in some occupancies and situations such as malls, atria, hazardous locations, educational uses, and assembly seating.

The maximum exit access travel distances are given in IBC Table 1016.1. (See Table 20.3.) The footnotes to this table refer to other sections of the code for specific occupancy requirements.

## Separation of exits

Once the number of exits or exit access doorways required for each room, space, or group of rooms is known, the arrangement of those exits can be determined. When two exits are required, they must be placed a distance apart equal to not less than one-half the length of the maximum overall diagonal dimension of the building or area to be served, as measured in a straight line between the exits or exit access doorways. This rule is shown diagrammatically in Figs. 20.3(a) and 20.3(b). This requirement is intended to prevent a fire or other emergency from blocking both exits because they have been positioned too close together.

If three or more exits are required, two must conform to the one-half or one-third diagonal distance rule. The 2006 version of the IBC eliminated all mention of where any additional exit doors or exit access doorways beyond two must be located.

In the IBC, there is a provision that reduces the minimum separation distance to one-third the maximum diagonal dimension of the room or area to be served if the building is fully sprinklered.

Exits or exit access doorways must also be located so that their availability is obvious.

## Exit Widths

The required minimum width of an exit is determined by multiplying the occupant load by the appropriate factor given in Table 1005.1 of the IBC. The resulting number is the minimum total width in inches (or millimeters). Other codes have similar methods of calculating total exit width. In occupancies other than H-1, H-2, H-3, H-4, and I-2, the factor is 0.3 for stairways and 0.2 for egress components other than stairways in unsprinklered buildings. In sprinklered buildings, the factors are 0.2 for stairways and 0.15 for other egress components. The factors are higher for the H and I occupancies because of the increased risk these occupancies present. If a greater width is specified elsewhere in the code, the larger number must be used.

For example, consider the calculated office occupant load of 157 determined in Ex. 2, calculating an office occupant load. To determine the minimum width of a corridor in this office in an unsprinklered building, multiply 157 by 0.2 to get a required width of 31.4 in (798 mm). However, elsewhere in the code the minimum width of a corridor serving an occupant load greater

**Table 20.3**
Exit access travel distances

Exit Access Travel Distance[1]

(IBC Table 1016.1)

| occupancy | without sprinkler system (ft) | with sprinkler system (ft) |
|---|---|---|
| A, E, F-1, I-1, M, R, S-1 | 200 | 250[2] |
| B | 200 | 300[3] |
| F-2, S-2, U | 300 | 400[2] |
| H-1 | not permitted | 75[3] |
| H-2 | not permitted | 100[3] |
| H-3 | not permitted | 150[3] |
| H-4 | not permitted | 175[3] |
| H-5 | not permitted | 200[3] |
| I-2, I-3, I-4 | 150 | 200[3] |

For SI: 1 foot = 304.8 mm

[1] See the following sections for modifications to exit access travel distance requirements:
Section 402: for the distance limitation in malls.
Section 404: For the distance limitation through an atrium space.
Section 1016.2: For increased limitation in Groups F-1 and S-1.
Section 1025.7: For increased limitation in assembly seating.
Section 1025.7: For increased limitation for assembly open-air seating.
Section 1019.2: For buildings with one exit.
Chapter 31: For the limitation in temporary structures.

[2] Buildings equipped throughout with an automatic sprinkler system in accordance with Sec. 903.3.1.1 or 903.3.1.2. See Sec. 903 for occupancies where sprinkler systems according to Sec. 903.3.1.2 are permitted.

[3] Buildings equipped throughout with an automatic sprinkler system in accordance with Sec. 903.3.1.1.



than 50 is given as 44 in (1118 mm). Because 44 in is the larger of the two, it must be used as the minimum width.

If two or more exits are required, the total width must be divided such that the loss of any one means of egress does not reduce the available capacity to less than 50% of the required capacity.

The IBC also requires that if doors are part of the required egress width, their clear width must be used, not the width of the door. For example, a 36 in door actually provides about 33 in of clear width when the thickness of the door in the 90° open position and the width of the stop are subtracted from the full width.

## Exiting through intervening spaces

Normally, building codes intend that means of egress from a room or space should lead directly to a corridor, exit enclosure, exterior door, or some other type of exit

**Figure 20.3**
Arrangement of exits

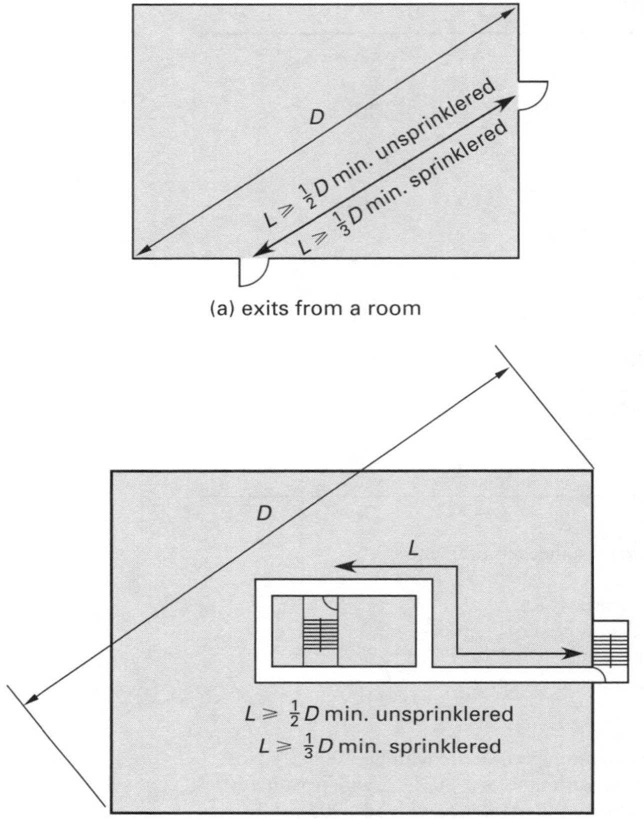


(a) exits from a room

(b) exits from a building or group of rooms

element. However, egress can pass through an adjoining room provided that the room is accessory to the area served and is not an H occupancy. Additionally, there must be a discernible path of egress travel to an exit. For example, the door to a private office could lead into a larger general office area, which then leads into a corridor.

The code specifically states that egress cannot pass through kitchens, storerooms, closets, or spaces used for similar purposes. Exit access also cannot pass through a room that can be locked to prevent egress.

However, an exception new to the 2006 IBC allows egress to pass through a stockroom serving a Group M occupancy if the following four conditions are met. First, the stockroom must be of the same hazard classification as that found in the main retail area. Second, not more than 50% of the exit access can be through the stockroom. Third, the stockroom cannot be subject to locking from the egress side. Fourth, there must be a demarcated, minimum 44 in (1118 mm) wide aisle defined by full or partial height fixed walls or similar construction that will maintain the required width and lead directly from the retail area to the exit without obstruction.

## CORRIDORS

A *corridor* is a fully enclosed portion of an exit access that defines and provides a path of egress travel to an exit. The purpose of a corridor is to provide a space where occupants have limited choices as to paths or directions of travel. When two exits are required, corridors must be laid out so that it is possible to travel in two directions to an exit. This ensures that occupants have an alternate way out if one path is blocked.

As part of the exit access portion of the egress system, corridors may or may not be made of fire-resistive construction depending on the occupancy, the occupant load, and whether or not the building is fully sprinklered. This is discussed in the corridor construction section.

As outlined in the previous section titled Exit Widths, corridors must be sized using the method of multiplying the occupant load by the appropriate factor. However, the width of an exit cannot be less than 44 in (1118 mm), with the following exceptions.

- 24 in (610 mm)—access to electrical, mechanical, and plumbing equipment
- 36 in (914 mm)—all occupancies where occupant load is less than 50

• 36 in (914 mm)—within a dwelling unit

• 72 in (1829 mm)—Group E occupancies serving occupant load of 100 or more

• 72 in (1829 mm)—Group I occupancy corridors serving health care centers for ambulatory patients incapable of self-preservation

• 96 in (2438 mm)—Group I-2 occupancies where bed movement is required. One of the major differences between the IBC and the previous UBC is that corridors in buildings with a sprinkler system in occupancy groups A, B, E, F, M, S, and U do not have to have a fire-resistive rating of 1 hour.

The width of a corridor cannot be encroached upon, with the following exceptions (see Fig. 20.4).

• Doors opening into the path of egress travel can reduce the required width up to one-half during the course of the swing, but when fully open the door cannot project more than 7 in (178 mm) into the required width.

• Horizontal projections such as handrails, trim, fixtures, and lights can project horizontally from either side up to a maximum of 4 in (102 mm). However, horizontal projections cannot reduce the minimum clear widths of accessible routes.

## Corridor construction

Corridors must be fire-resistance rated according to IBC Table 1017.1 (see Table 20.4), and they must be constructed as fire partitions, as described in Sec. 708 of the IBC. This means that the corridor walls must extend from the floor to the underside of the structural slab above *or* to the underside of a fire-resistive-rated ceiling. Some of the options are diagrammed in Fig. 19.1.

There are four exceptions when corridors do not have to be fire-resistance rated. These include

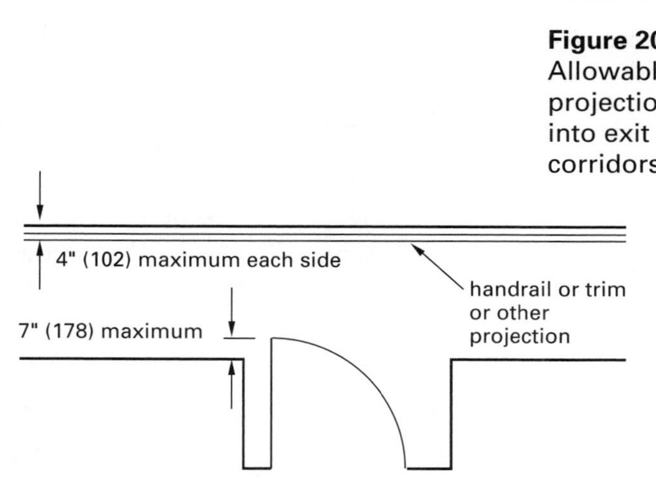


**Figure 20.4** Allowable projections into exit corridors

• Group E occupancies where classrooms and assembly rooms have half of their required egress leading directly to the exterior at ground level

• corridors in a dwelling unit or a guest room in a Group R occupancy

• corridors in open parking garages

• Group B occupancies that only require one exit by other provisions in the code

## Openings in corridors

Openings in corridors include doors, glazing, and fire shutters. These are required to have a minimum opening protection assembly rating of 20 minutes as prescribed in Sec. 715 of the IBC. (Normally, glazing in fire partitions is required to be rated at 45 minutes.) When interior windows are used between rooms and corridors, the total area of fire-protection-rated glazing (tested in accordance with NFPA 257) cannot exceed 25% of the area of the common wall between the corridor and the room. However, if fire-resistance-rated glazing (tested in accordance with ASTM E119) is used, the 25% area limitation does not apply. Glazing in fire partitions is discussed in more detail in Ch. 19. Doors are discussed in a following section.

**Table 20.4** Corridor fire-resistance ratings

Corridor Fire-Resistance Rating

(IBC Table 1017.1)

| occupancy | occupancy load served by corridor | required fire-resistance rating (hr): without sprinkler system | required fire-resistance rating (hr): with sprinkler system[3] |
|---|---|---|---|
| H-1, H-2, H-3 | all | not permitted | 1 |
| H-4, H-5 | greater than 30 | not permitted | 1 |
| A, B, E, F, M, S, U | greater than 30 | 1 | 0 |
| R | greater than 10 | 1 | 0.5 |
| I-2[1], I-4 | all | not permitted | 0 |
| I-1, I-3 | all | not permitted | 1[2] |

[1] For requirements for occupancies in Group I-2, see Sec. 407.3.
[2] For a reduction in the fire-resistance rating for occupancies in Group I-3, see Sec. 408.7.
[3] Buildings equipped throughout with an automatic sprinkler system in accordance with Sec. 903.3.1.1 or 903.3.1.2, where allowed.



## Corridor continuity

When a corridor is required to be fire-resistance-rated, it must be continuous to an exit and not pass through intervening rooms. The concept is based on the idea that once an occupant reaches a certain level of safety in the egress path, that level should not be reduced as the occupant progresses through the remainder of the egress system. As with most requirements of the code, there are a few exceptions.

First, corridors may pass through foyers, lobbies, and receptions rooms as long as these spaces are constructed as required for the corridors. In essence, these spaces become enlarged portions of the corridor.

The second exception allows corridors in fully sprinklered Group B buildings to pass through enclosed elevator lobbies if all areas of the building have access to at least one required exit without passing through the lobby.

## Dead ends

A dead end is a condition where the occupant of a building has only one choice of direction leading to an exit access doorway or an exit. When corridors are required to lead to two or more exits, the occupant should always have at least two choices of direction. The code does allow dead ends in corridors if the corridors do not exceed 20 ft (6096 mm) in length. There are three exceptions in the IBC where longer dead-end corridors are allowed.

- Dead ends are not limited in length where the length of the corridor is less than 2.5 times the narrowest part of the dead-end corridor.
- B and F occupancies may have 50 ft (15 240 mm) dead-end corridors if the entire building is equipped with an automatic sprinkler system.
- Dead-end corridors may be 50 ft long in Group I-3 occupancies of Conditions 2,

3, or 4. These condition numbers refer to the specific security arrangements in detention facilities and are seldom encountered by interior designers.

## DOORS

Because doors present a potential obstruction to egress throughout the egress system, they are highly regulated by building codes. A means of egress door must meet the following design criteria.

- It must be readily distinguishable from the adjacent construction.
- It must be readily recognizable as a means of egress door.
- It cannot be covered with mirrors or other reflective material.
- It cannot be concealed with curtains, drapes, decorations, or similar materials.

Doors that are provided in excess of the minimum required must meet the same requirements as those of required doors.

### Size of doors

The minimum width of egress door openings must be sufficient for the occupant load served, but the clear width must be at least 32 in (813 mm). The clear opening width must be measured between the face of the door and the doorstop when the door is open 90°. In practical terms this means that 36 in doors must be used as egress doors. The maximum width of swinging egress doors is 48 in (1219 mm). The minimum height of egress doors must be 80 in (2032 mm).

There are several exceptions to the size requirements, including doors in residential occupancies, sleeping room in I-3 occupancies, and others. Refer to Sec. 1008.1.1 of the IBC for details on these exceptions.

### Door swing

Egress doors must be pivoted or side-hinged. This is to ensure that the egress door is familiar to the user and easy to operate. There are some exceptions to the requirement for side-swinging doors, including private garages; office areas; factory and storage areas with an occupant load of 10 or less; individual dwelling units of R-2, R-3, and R-4 occupancies; power-operated doors; and a few others. Refer to Sec. 1008.1.2 in the IBC for all of the exceptions allowed.

In most cases, special doors (such as revolving, sliding, and overhead doors) are not considered to be required exits. Power-operated doors and revolving doors are sometimes allowed if they meet certain requirements. Revolving doors, for example, must have leaves that collapse under opposing pressure and must have a diameter such that at least 36 in (914 mm) of exit width is provided when the leaves are collapsed. There must also be at least one conforming egress door in close proximity. For additional requirements for special doors, refer to Sec. 1008.1.3 in the IBC.

Further, egress doors must swing in the direction of travel when the area served has an occupant load of 50 or more. This is to prevent a door from being blocked when people are trying to get out in a panic. See Fig. 20.5(a). Doors also must not swing into a required travel path such as a corridor. In many instances, to meet this requirement, exit doors must be recessed as shown in Fig. 20.5(b).

Doors without closers must have a maximum opening force of 5 lbf (22 N), and doors with closers must have a maximum opening force of 15 lbf (67 N). The maximum allowable force to set the door in motion is 30 lbf (133 N). The door must swing to a full-open position when subjected to a 15 lbf (67 N) force. All of these required maximum forces are measured on the latch side of the door.

### Fire-resistive rating requirements

Egress doors in fire-resistance-rated partitions are required to have a fire rating. The specific fire rating varies depending on the

**Figure 20.5**
Exit door swing

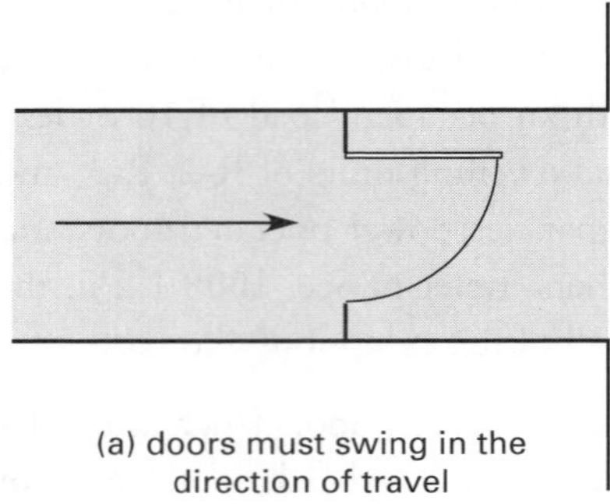

(a) doors must swing in the direction of travel

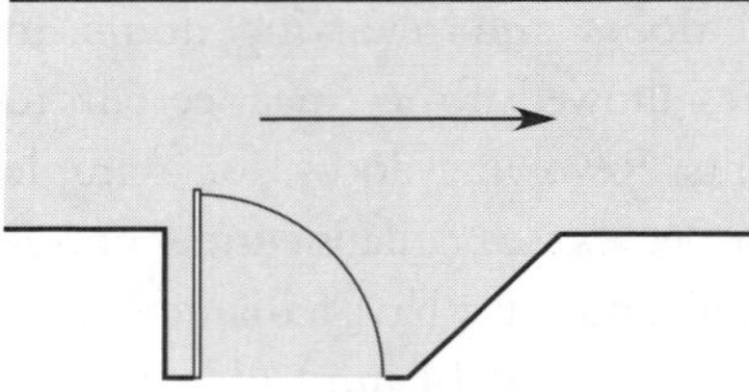

(b) doors must not swing into the required exit path more than 7" (178)

rating of the partition. These ratings are shown in IBC Table 715.4, which is reproduced in Table 19.2. For most interior design applications, four door assembly ratings are commonly encountered. These are summarized in Table 20.5. A more complete table of fire-door classifications and additional information on fire-protection-rated doors is given in Table 3.3 and in Ch. 3. Remember that under the IBC, if a building is fully sprinklered, corridors in A, B, E, F, M, S, and U occupancies (and in some other situations) do not have to have a fire rating, so fire-protection-rated doors are not required.

In addition to having a 20-minute fire rating, doors in corridors and smoke barriers must meet the requirements for positive-pressure fire testing (NFPA 252 or UL 10C, but without the hose stream test) as discussed in Ch. 3. These doors must also meet the requirements for smoke and draft control tested in accordance with UL 1784, *Standard for Safety for Air Leakage Tests for Door Assemblies*, with an artificial bottom seal installed across the full width of the bottom of the door. These may need to carry an "S" label if required by the local authority having jurisdiction. Smoke barriers are commonly used to separate health care and detention facilities into separate zones. They are also required in vertical shafts, vestibules to stairways, and areas of refuge.

All hardware on fire doors must be tested and approved for use in fire exits. Fire doors must be operable from the inside without the use of any special knowledge or effort. This provision is intended to prohibit devices such as combination locks, thumb turn locks, and multiple locks. Some occupants in a building may not be familiar with these or similar devices and may find them too difficult to operate during panic conditions or when visibility is low. The code does provide for some exceptions such as in residential

**Table 20.5**
Required ratings of doors based on partition type

| use of partition | rating of partition | required door assembly rating |
|---|---|---|
| corridors | 1 hour or less | 20 minute |
| smoke barriers | 1 hour | 20 minute |
| fire partitions | 1 hour | ¾ hour |
| exit passageways | 1 hour | 1 hour |
| exit stairs | 1 hour | 1 hour |
| occupancy separations | 1 hour | ¾ hour |
| exit stairs | 2 hours | 1½ hour |
| occupancy separations | 2 hours | 1½ hour |

units, places of detention, and a few other situations.

For certain occupancies, such as educational and assembly spaces with an occupant load of 50 or more, panic hardware is required. This is hardware that unlatches the door when pressure is applied against a horizontal bar rather than requiring a turning motion as with a level handle or doorknob.

Fire doors must be self-closing or automatic-closing. *Self-closing* simply means that there is a closer or other device on the door that returns the door to the closed position after someone passes through it. *Automatic-closing* doors are those that are normally held open but that automatically close upon activation of a smoke detector, fire-alarm system, or other approved device.

When fire doors are closed, they must be secured with an active latch bolt. This is to secure the door during a fire, preventing fire and gas pressure from pushing the door open.

Operating devices, including door handles, pulls, latches, and locks, must be installed on the door a minimum of 34 in (864 mm) and a maximum of 48 in (1219 mm) above the finished floor. The only exception is that locks used only for security purposes and not for normal operation can be installed at any height.

Additional requirements for power-operated doors, horizontal sliding doors, and revolving and access-control doors, as well as for delayed-egress locks, gates, thresholds, floor elevations, and door arrangements, are given in Sec. 1008.1 of the IBC.

### Glazing in fire-protection-rated doors

The requirements for glazing in fire-door assemblies vary depending on what type of partition the door is located in.

Because standard wired glass is no longer permitted in hazardous locations, including doors, other types of fire-protection-rated glazing and fire-resistance-rated glazing must now be used, as discussed in Ch. 5. In nonhazardous locations, wired glass can still be used subject to the size limitations shown in Table 20.6.

When clear fire-resistance-rated glazing is used in doors, the manufacturer should be consulted to determine the most appropriate type and any area limitations based on the required fire rating of the door. Additional area limitations may be found in NFPA 80, *Standard for Fire Doors, Fire Windows.*

## STAIRWAYS

A *stair* is defined by the IBC as a change in elevation accomplished by one or more risers. A *stairway* is one or more flights of stairs, with the necessary landings and platforms connecting them, that form a continuous passage from one level to another. As such, interior designers often design stairways as part of their work.

Less frequently, interior designers are involved with the design and detailing of exit stairways for buildings. However, there are occasions when a new, private stairway is installed as part of the design for a multifloor tenant, or existing exit stairways are modified as part of a remodeling project.

### Exit stairways

Because vertical shafts provide the most readily available path for fire and smoke spreading upward from floor to floor, interior exit stairways must be completely enclosed. In buildings four or more stories high, the stairways must be enclosed with 2-hour-rated walls; in buildings less than four stories high, 1-hour-rated construction is required. Doors into 2-hour stairways must be rated as 1½-hour doors, and doors into 1-hour stairways must have a 1-hour rating.

There are nine exceptions to the hourly rating requirements found in Sec. 1020.1 of the IBC. Three are commonly encountered in interior design work: The first states that

**Table 20.6** Maximum size of wired glass panels

| opening fire protection rating | size of glass allowed | | |
|---|---|---|---|
| | area | width | height |
| 20 minute | no limit | no limit | no limit |
| ¾ hour | 1296 in$^2$ (0.84 m$^2$) | 54 in (1372 mm) | 54 in (1372 mm) |
| 1 hour | 100 in$^2$ (0.065 m$^2$) | 10 in (254 mm) | 33 in (838 mm) |
| 1½ hour | 100 in$^2$ (0.065 m$^2$) | 10 in (254 mm) | 33 in (838 mm) |

in other than Groups H and I occupancies, a stairway serving an occupant load less than 10 stories and not more than 1 story above the level of exit discharge does not have to be enclosed. The second states that stairways serving and contained within a single residential dwelling unit in Groups R-2 and R-3 occupancies and guest rooms in R-1 occupancies are not required to be enclosed. The third states that in other than Groups H and I occupancies, up to 50% of the number of egress stairways serving only one adjacent floor do not have to be enclosed. For interior designers, this means that a private stairway serving only one floor above or below could be open and designed as a monumental stairway.

## Requirements for all stairways

Stairways serving an occupant load of 50 or more must be at least 44 in (1118 mm) wide or as wide as determined by multiplying the occupant load by 0.3, 0.2, or some other factor as discussed previously. Those serving an occupant load of less than 50 must not be less than 36 in (914 mm) wide. Handrails may project 4½ in (114 mm) into the required width.

Stair risers cannot measure less than 4 in (102 mm) or more than 7 in (178 mm), and treads must not be less than 11 in (279 mm). Risers for barrier-free stairs cannot exceed 7 in (178 mm). Treads must have an acceptable nosing design as discussed in Chs. 12 and 18. For residential occupancies and private stairways in R-2 occupancies, the maximum riser may be 7¾ in (197 mm), and the minimum tread may be 10 in (254 mm).

There are other requirements for curved stairways, winders, spiral stairways, and stairs serving as aisles in assembly seating areas. Winding, curved, and spiral stairways may be used as exits in R-3 occupancies and in private stairways of R-1 occupancies only if they meet certain design conditions as described in Ch. 12.

Landings must be provided at the top and bottom of every stairway, and the minimum dimension in the direction of travel must not be less than the width of the stair, but need not be more than 48 in (1219 mm) if the stair is a straight run.

Handrails must be provided on both sides of the stair. Intermediate handrails are required so that all portions of the stairway width required for egress capacity are within 30 in (762 mm) of a handrail. Another way of stating this is that stairways wider than 5 ft (1524 mm) must have intermediate handrails.

The exceptions to the requirement that handrails be provided on both sides include the following.

• aisle stairs with a center handrail

• stairs within dwelling units, spiral stairways, and aisle stairs serving seating only on one side

• decks, patios, and walkways that have a single change in elevation where the landing depth on each side is greater than what is required for landings

• single risers in Group R-3 occupancies at an entrance or egress door

• single risers within dwelling units of R-2 and R-3 occupancies

The tops of handrails must be between 34 in and 38 in (864 mm and 962 mm) above the nosing of the treads and must extend horizontally not less than 12 in (305 mm) beyond the top riser and not less than the depth of one tread beyond the bottom riser. Refer to Fig. 12.6. The ends must be returned or terminate in a newel post. The size and graspability dimensions of handrails are shown in Fig. 12.17. There must be a space at least 1½ in (38 mm) wide between the wall and the handrail.

Refer to Ch. 12 for additional discussion of building code requirements for stairway layout, handrails, and guardrails, as well as for diagrams of the code requirements described here. Refer to Ch. 18 for accessibility requirements.

## RESIDENTIAL EXITING

Exiting requirements for individual dwelling units and single-family houses are not as stringent as those for commercial occupancies. Some provisions are given in the IBC, but all are found in the International Residential Code (IRC).

Only one exit is required from the basement or second story of a house. However, basements with habitable space and every sleeping room must have an exterior door or an escape and rescue window with the minimum dimensions as shown in Fig. 20.6. These emergency and escape windows are also required in Group R and I-1 occupancies under the IBC. If the escape and rescue opening is below grade level it must lead to a window well that conforms to certain requirements given in the IRC. Bars, grills, covers, and screens are permitted to be placed over emergency escape openings only if the coverings can be released or removed from the inside without the use of a key, tool, or force greater than that which is required for normal operation.

The one required exit door must be at least 3 ft (914 mm) wide and 80 in (2032 mm) high. The lock or latch must be readily operable from the inside without the use of a key or special knowledge or effort. However, unlike commercial construction, a night latch or dead bolt may be used in addition to the main lock, provided its operation does not require the use of a key or tool.

Unlike most commercial construction, residential exits may pass through kitchens, storerooms, and similar spaces. However, the IBC does not allow exiting from a sleeping area through other sleeping areas or toilet rooms. Hallways must be a minimum of 3 ft (914 mm) wide.

**Figure 20.6** Emergency escape and rescue window

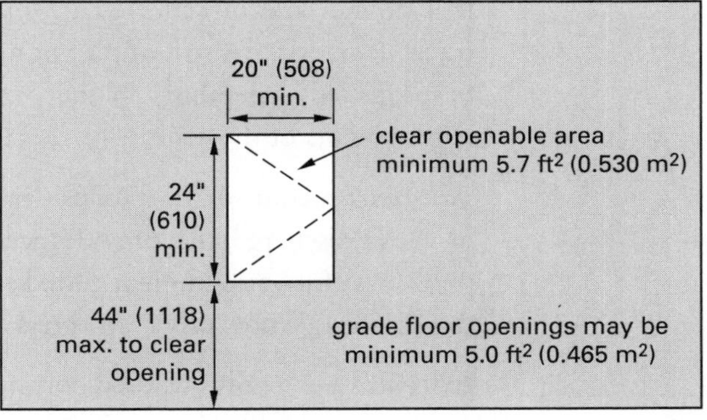

Stairways must also be at least 3 ft (914 mm) wide, and handrails cannot project more than 4½ in on both sides. Handrails must be mounted between 34 in and 38 in (864 mm and 965 mm) above the nosing of the tread, and there must be at least one handrail. The maximum riser height is 7¾ in (196 mm), and the minimum tread depth is 10 in (254 mm).

Refer to the International Residential Code for One- and Two-Family Dwellings for more information.

## DEFINITIONS

The following terms are frequently used by building codes to precisely communicate meaning. Additional terms are defined in the main text of this chapter. Although the differences between terms are sometimes subtle, the interior designer should be familiar with them.

*Area of refuge:* an area where persons unable to use stairways can remain temporarily while waiting for assistance

*Automatic-closing:* as applied to a door, automatic-closing means that a door is normally held in the open position but is released to close upon activation by a smoke detector or other type of fire alarm system. Automatic-closing doors must be self closing.

*Common path of egress travel:* that portion of exit access that occupants must travel before two separate and distinct paths of egress to two exits become available

*Corridor:* an enclosed exit access component that defines and provides a path of egress travel to an exit. A corridor may or may not be protected depending on the particular requirements of the code.

*Exit court:* a court or yard (considered part of an exit discharge) that provides access to a public way for one or more required exits. In the IBC this is now called an egress court.

*Exit enclosure:* a fully enclosed portion of an exit that is only used as a means of egress and that provides for a protected path of egress either in a vertical or horizontal direction. Depending on construction type, height, and building occupancy, an exit enclosure must have either a 1-hour or 2-hour rating, and all openings must be protected. An exit enclosure must lead to an exit discharge or a public way.

*Exit passageway:* a horizontal, fully enclosed portion of an exit that is only used as a means of egress. An exit passageway leads from an exit doorway to an exit discharge or a public way. A common example of an exit passageway is an exit from the door at the ground level of an interior stairway that leads through the building to an outside door.

*Fire assembly:* an assembly of a fire door, fire window, or fire damper, including all required anchorage, frames, sills, and hardware

*Fire-door assembly:* any combination of a fire door and its frame, hardware, and other accessories that provides a specific degree of fire protection to an opening

*Fire exit hardware:* panic hardware that is listed for use on fire-door assemblies

*Horizontal exit:* an exit through a minimum 2-hour-rated wall that divides a building into two or more separate exit access areas to afford safety from fire and smoke

*Occupant load:* the number of persons for which the means of egress of a building or part of a building is designed

*Panic hardware:* a door latching assembly that includes a device that releases the latch when a force is applied in the direction of egress travel

*Self-closing:* as applied to a door, self-closing means that the door is equipped with a device (most commonly a door closer) that will ensure closing after the door has been opened

*Stair:* a change in elevation consisting of one or more risers

*Stairway:* one or more flights of stairs, either exterior or interior, with the necessary landings and platforms connecting them to form a continuous and uninterrupted passage from one level to another

*Travel distance:* the measurement of the distance between the most remote, occupied point of an area or room to the entrance of the nearest exit that serves it. It is part of the exit access and is measured along the natural and unobstructed path of egress travel.

# 21 SUSTAINABLE DESIGN

Sustainable building design (also known as "green" building design) is an increasingly important part of interior design. Sustainable design encompasses a wide range of concerns including the environmental impact of an interior design project, wise use of materials, energy conservation, use of alternative energy sources, adaptive reuse, indoor air quality, recycling, reuse, and other strategies to achieve a balance between the consumption of environmental resources and the renewal of those resources. Sustainable design considers the full life cycles of a building and the materials that comprise it. This includes considering the impact of raw material extraction through its fabrication, installation, operation, maintenance, and disposal.

Although an architect addresses many sustainability issues during the design of a building, there are many steps the interior designer can take to minimize the environmental impact of interior build-out.

## BUILDING RATING SYSTEMS

Several organizations have emerged that provide industry-recognized ratings of the relative sustainability of a building or interior build-out. These organizations develop objective criteria that designers must follow in order to receive particular types of ratings. Although conforming to these criteria is not mandatory by any building code, some governmental entities and large corporations may require their designers to follow a particular organization's guidelines. The following are the major rating systems in the United States, Canada, and Britain.

### Leadership in Energy and Environmental Design (LEED®) Certification

The Leadership in Energy and Environmental Design Green Building Rating System is a national consensus-based building rating system designed to accelerate the development and implementation of green building practices. The rating system was developed by the U.S. Green Building Council, which is a national coalition of leaders from all aspects of the building industry, working to promote buildings that are environmentally responsible and profitable and that provide healthy places to live and work. In addition to the rating system, the full LEED program offers training workshops, professional accreditation, resource support, and third-party certification of building performance. In order for a building to be certified, certain prerequisites must be achieved and enough points must be earned to meet or exceed the program's technical requirements. Points add up to a final score that relates to one of four possible levels of certification: certified, silver, gold, and platinum. LEED is one of the primary building rating systems in the United States.

There are several rating systems for different building types. LEED-NC for new construction was the first rating system. The LEED program now also offers rating systems for commercial interiors, existing buildings, core and shell development, homes, and neighborhood development.

### Leadership in Energy and Environmental Design BC

The Canada Green Building Council (CaGBC) has adopted the United States' LEED program for use across Canada. The requirements are essentially the same except that SI units are used, reference is made to Canadian standards and regulations, protection of fish habitats is recognized, a few definitions are changed, and a few other minor modifications are made to tailor the requirements for Canada.

### Building Research Establishment Environmental Assessment Method

The Building Research Establishment (BRE) is a British organization that provides research-based consultancy, testing, and certification services covering all aspects of the built environment and associated industries. The BRE Environmental Assessment Method (BREEAM) is a method of reviewing and improving the environmental performance of buildings. There are methods to review offices, industrial buildings, retail buildings, and homes.

BREEAM evaluates the performance of buildings in the areas of management, energy use, health and well-being, pollution, transportation, land use, ecology, materials, and water use. Credits are awarded in each area and added to produce a total score. The building is then given a rating (pass, good, very good, or excellent) and awarded a certificate.

The BRE also runs a certified environmental profiling system that provides a measurement of the environmental performance of building materials and products.

## PRODUCT CERTIFICATION

As with buildings, there are organizations that certify products as being environmentally sound. The following are the most notable.

### Green Seal

Green Seal® is an independent, nonprofit organization that strives to achieve a more sustainable world by promoting environmentally responsible production, purchasing, and products. Among other programs, Green Seal develops environmental standards for products in specific categories and certifies products that meet them. The organization meets the criteria of the International Organization for Standardization (ISO) 14020 and 14024 for ecolabeling. Green Seal's product evaluations are conducted using a life-cycle approach considering energy, resource use, emissions to air, water, and land, and health impacts of the product. The Green Seal is awarded to products that have a low impact on the environment and also work well.

### Greenguard

The Greenguard Environmental Institute is a nonprofit, industry-independent organization that oversees the Greenguard Certification Program. This program tests indoor products for emissions to ensure that they meet acceptable indoor air quality (IAQ) pollutant guidelines and standards. Products are tested for total volatile organic compounds (VOCs), formaldehyde, total aldehydes, respirable particles, carbon monoxide, nitrogen oxide, and carbon dioxide emissions.

Products that meet the standards of Greenguard are added to the Greenguard Registry. Products include building materials, furnishings, furniture, cleaning and maintenance products, electronic equipment, and personal care products. Greenguard also sets allowable emission levels for their testing, using the lesser value of levels established by the Environmental Protection Agency's procurement specifications, the state of Washington's indoor air quality program, the World Health Organization, and Germany's Blue Angel Program for electronic equipment.

### Scientific Certification Systems

Scientific Certification Systems (SCS) is a private scientific organization established to advance both public and private sectors toward more environmentally sustainable policies. Under its Environmental Claims Certification program, SCS certifies specific product attributes such as biodegradability and recycled content. It also certifies environmentally preferable products, which are products that can have a smaller environmental impact than similar products performing the same function. Building products that can be certified include carpet, nonwoven flooring, composite panel products, adhesives and sealants, furniture, paints, and other wall coverings.

SCS also certifies forests if they are well managed under their Forest Certification Program, as mentioned later in this chapter under the section on wood and plastic products.

### ISO 14000

The International Standards Organization (ISO) is a nongovernmental organization comprised of national standards bodies from over 120 countries. ISO 14000 is a collection of standards and guidelines covering issues such as performance, product standards, labeling, environmental management, and life-cycle assessment as they relate to the environment. Several of the individual standards and guidelines are applicable to building products.

ISO 14020 presents a set of principles to be followed by practitioners of environmental labeling. ISO 14024 covers labeling programs and specifies the procedures and principles that third-party certifiers, or "ecolabelers", must follow. These principles include that an organization may not have any financial interest in the products it certifies, must conduct scientific evaluations using internationally accepted methodologies, and must use a life-cycle approach when evaluating products. The ISO 14040 series of standards covers requirements for life-cycle assessments.

## MATERIALS

The selection, use, and detailing of materials in a building represent a significant part of the total sustainability of an interiors project. As with energy consumption and other sustainability issues, material selection and detailing must be done taking into consideration the entire life cycle of the interior design. Traditional concerns of function, cost, appearance, and performance must also be considered.

### Life-cycle assessment

A *life-cycle assessment* (LCA) is an evaluation of the environmental impact from the use of a particular material or product in a building. An LCA commonly includes four phases. These are

- the definition of the goals and scope of the study
- an inventory analysis
- an impact assessment
- an improvement analysis or interpretation

The first step in the process is to determine the purpose and goals of doing the study. Limits of the study and the units for study must also be established so alternatives can be compared and the framework for data acquisition can be developed.

The *inventory analysis* is often the most difficult part because it involves determining and quantifying all of the inputs and outputs of the product under study. These might include the energy required to obtain the raw materials and process or manufacture them, the energy of transportation, the need for ancillary materials, and the pollution or amount of waste involved in the manufacturing, use, and disposal processes. The ability to recycle the material is also considered. Some of the criteria used for evaluating building materials are given in the next section.

The *impact assessment* attempts to characterize the effects of the processes found in the inventory analysis in terms of their impacts on the environment. The analysis may include such things as resource depletion, generation of pollution, health impacts, or effects on social welfare. For example, the energy required to produce a product may necessitate the addition of electrical generating capacity, which in turn may produce both waterborne and airborne pollution.

Finally, the results of the study are reported in the *improvement analysis* phase. Suggestions are given for reducing the environmental impact of all the raw materials, energy, and processing required to produce the product or construction activity.

There are four main stages in a product's life cycle. These are raw-material acquisition, manufacturing, use in the building, and disposal or reuse. The potential individual elements of each stage are as follows.

**Figure 21.1**
Life-cycle inventory model

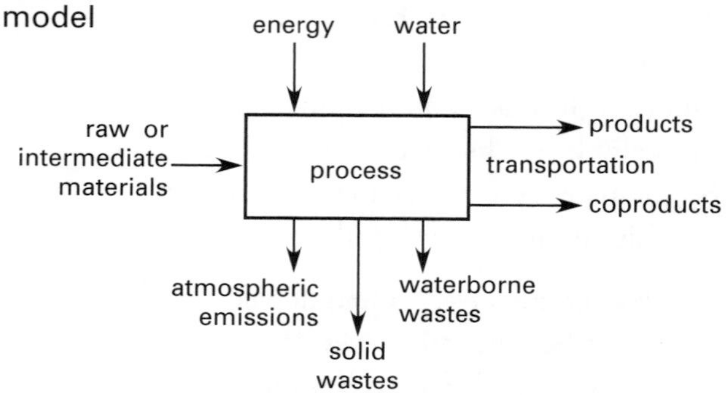

energy
water
raw or intermediate materials
process
products
transportation
coproducts
atmospheric emissions
solid wastes
waterborne wastes

*Raw-material acquisition*:

- acquisition of raw materials and energy from mining, drilling, or other activities
- processing of raw materials
- transportation of raw materials to processing points

*Manufacturing*:

- conversion of processed raw materials into a useful product
- manufacturing or fabrication of materials into the final product
- packaging of the product
- transportation of the finished product to the job site

*Use and maintenance*:

- installation or construction of the product into the building
- long-term use of the product throughout its life or the life of the building
- maintenance and repair of the product throughout its life

*Disposal or reuse*:

- demolition of the product used in the building
- conversion of waste into other useful products
- waste disposal of the product
- reuse or recycling of the product if not disposed or converted

At least once during the life cycle (at any point, but most commonly during inventory analysis), consideration must be given to all the inputs and outputs of the system or product under study. These include what energy and other raw materials are required to acquire, process, and use the product and what releases to the air, water, and land are produced. A useful model for doing this is shown in Fig. 21.1.

Using this model is helpful in directing the required collection of data. Inputs for energy are typically in units such as British thermal units or megajoules, inputs for raw materials are in pounds or kilograms, and water is commonly in gallons or liters. Output is typically given by weight in pounds or kilograms.

## Criteria for evaluating building materials

The following are some criteria for evaluating how sustainable a product or construction process is. Of course, not all these criteria apply to every product.

• *Embodied energy.* The material or product should require as little energy as possible for its extraction as a raw material, initial processing, and subsequent manufacture or fabrication into a finished building product. This includes the energy required for transportating the raw materials and finished products during their life cycles. The production of the material should also generate as little waste and pollution as possible.

• *Renewable materials.* A material is sustainable if it comes from sources that can renew themselves within a fairly short time. LEED credits are given for using rapidly renewable building materials and products for 5% of the total value of all building materials and products used in the project. Rapidly renewable products are typically those made from plants that are harvested within a cycle of 10 years or less. Products that meet this criterion include wool carpets, bamboo flooring and paneling, straw board, cotton batt insulation, linoleum flooring, poplar OSB, sunflower seed board, and wheatgrass cabinetry.

• *Recycled content.* The more recycled content a material has, the less raw material is used and the less energy is required to process the raw materials into a final product. Each of the three types of recycled content should be considered: post-consumer material, post-industrial material, and recovered materials. These terms are defined at the end of this chapter.

• *Energy efficiency.* Materials, products, and assemblies should reduce the energy consumption in a building.

• *Use of local materials.* Using locally produced materials reduces transportation costs and can add to the regional character of a design. A building can receive LEED credit if 20% of the building materials and products it uses are manufactured within a radius of 500 mi (804 km). Additional credit is available if 10% or more of its materials and products are also extracted, harvested, or recovered, as well as manufactured, within 500 mi (804 km) of the project.

• *Durability.* Durable materials will last longer and generally require less maintenance over the life of a product or building. Even though initial costs may be higher, the life-cycle costs may be less.

• *Low volatile organic compounds* (VOC) *content.* LEED credits are given for using low-emitting materials, including adhesives and sealants, paints and coatings, carpet systems, composite wood and laminate adhesives, and systems furniture and seating. The standards that must be met vary with the material. Refer to the LEED program for exact requirements and standards.

• *Low toxicity.* Selected materials should emit little or no harmful gases such as chlorofluorocarbons (CFCs), formaldehyde, and others listed on the Environmental Protection Agency's list of hazardous substances.

• *Moisture problems.* If possible, materials should be selected that resist or prevent the growth of biological contaminants.

• *Water conservation.* Products should reduce water consumption in buildings and landscaping.

• *Maintainability.* Materials and products should be cleanable and otherwise maintainable with only nontoxic or low-VOC substances.

• *Potential for reuse and recycling.* Some materials and products are more readily recycled than others. Steel, for example, can usually be separated and melted down to make new steel products. On the other hand, plastics used in construction are difficult to remove and separate.

• *Reusability.* A product should be reusable after it has served its purpose in the original building. Careful detailing of assemblies is one way to accomplish this. A reusable product becomes a salvaged material in the life cycle of another building.

## Salvaged materials

Salvaged materials should be used as much as possible. This includes items such as doors, window units, cabinetry, furnishings, and equipment. There may be extra costs involved in preparing salvaged materials for reuse, but these costs can be offset by savings on new materials and the costs associated with their production or disposal. Reused materials, such as brick or timber from old buildings, can even add to the aesthetic appeal of a new building.

## Metals

Although metals require large amounts of embodied energy for their production, they have a high potential for recycling. Steel is the most common metal used in buildings and is commonly recycled as scrap to produce more steel. Steel with a recycled content up to 30% or more is readily available. Aluminum is also widely used and is available with a recycled content of 20% or more. Copper has great value as a recycled material, and brass, bronze, and stainless steel can also be recycled if separated.

Problems can arise with some metals that are plated or coated with chemicals. Electroplating processes produce high levels of pollution and by-products. Alternatives to these processes include powder coatings and plastic polymer coatings. Whatever finish is applied, it should be readily removable to facilitate recycling.

## Wood

Lumber and wood products represent a large portion of both residential and commercial construction, from rough framing to furniture. This includes both softwoods and hardwoods from domestic and foreign sources. Deforestation, processing, and the manufacture of wood products represent a large ecological problem, but interior designers can minimize this by applying three sustainable strategies: using reclaimed wood, specifying sustainable or alternative materials, and using certified wood products.

*Reclaimed wood* is wood salvaged from old buildings or structures and prepared for a new use. Preparation may include removing nails and other fasteners, drying, and cutting or planing. In addition to being ecologically sound, reclaimed wood members have a unique visual character that many interior designers and clients find desirable.

*Sustainable or alternative materials* encompass a wide range of products. Standard solid-wood framing products can be replaced with engineered wood products such as wood I-joists or laminated veneer lumber. Panel products that use waste material, such as particleboard and medium-density fiberboard (MDF), are good sustainable products but often require adhesives and resins that emit urea formaldehyde and other polluting gases. However, formaldehyde-free MDF and low-emission panels that use phenol-formaldehyde or urethane adhesives are available. These have a formaldehyde level of 0.04 ppm (parts per million) or less, which is below the commonly accepted level of 0.05 ppm. Another alternative to urea formaldehyde is methylene-diphenyl isocyanate (MDI). This resin does not emit toxic gases during use, and it requires less dryer energy and lower press temperatures than traditional binders.

Other innovative products can be used in some instances to replace rough lumber. *Straw particleboard*, for example, is made from wheat straw, a waste product from farming. The straw is milled into fine particles and hot-pressed together with formaldehyde-free resins. It can be used for both construction and furniture making. Other agricultural products used in particleboard are rice straw and bagasse, which is residue from the processing of sugar cane. Post-consumer recycled waste paper can be used for making building panels. A building can receive a LEED credit for using low-emitting materials such as wood and agrifiber products that contain no added urea-formaldehyde resins.

Many alternative products exist for finish carpentry and architectural woodwork. Molding can be made from medium-density fiberboard or molded high-density polyurethane foam. Composite wood veneers are manufactured from readily available and fast-growing trees by slicing veneers, dyeing them, and gluing them back into an artificial "log," which is then sliced. By varying the dye colors and how the log is cut, a wide variety of veneers are possible, from those that look like standard wood to highly figured and colored products.

*Certified wood products* are those that use wood obtained through sustainable forest management practices. While there are many forest certification groups in North America, the most well known is the Forest Stewardship Council (FSC). This international body oversees the development of national and regional standards based on basic forest management principles and criteria. It accredits certifying organizations that comply with its principles. The three groups currently accredited by the FSC in the United States are the SmartWood program of the Rainforest Alliance, the Forest Conservation program of Scientific Certification Systems (SCS), and SGS Systems and Services Certification, Inc.

The FSC has 10 basic principles and 56 individual criteria by which it evaluates organizations for accreditation. It has also established additional regional criteria for different parts of the United States. The 10 principles are these.

- Forest management must respect all applicable laws of the country in which activities occur and must comply with FSC principles and criteria.

- Long-term tenure and use rights to the land and forests must be defined, documented, and legally established.

- The rights of indigenous peoples to own, use, and manage their land must be recognized and respected.

- Forest management practices and operations must maintain or enhance the long-term social and economic well-being of workers and local communities.

- Forest management must encourage the efficient use of the forest's products to ensure economic viability and environmental and social benefits.

- Forest management must conserve biological diversity, water resources, soils, ecosystems, and landscapes to maintain the ecological functions of the forest.

- A management plan must be written, implemented, and maintained.

- Monitoring must be conducted to assess the condition of the forest, yields, chain of custody, and management activities and their social and environmental impacts.

- Management activities in high-conservation-value forests must maintain or enhance the attributes that define such forests.

- Plantations must follow the first nine principles and the criteria that apply to plantations. Plantations should complement the management of, reduce pressures on, and promote the restoration and conservation of natural forests.

A building can receive a LEED credit if a minimum of 50% of wood-based materials and products it uses are certified in accordance with the FSC's principles and criteria. Only a very small fraction of forests comply with FSC criteria, but there are many other well-managed forests in North America and elsewhere.

## Plastic

Plastics used in interiors projects should include those that are marked to identify them for recycling. If possible, compostable plastics should be specified. Polyethylene terephthalate (PET) from soft-drink containers, for example, can be used to manufacture carpet with properties similar to polyesters.

Two new developments in plastic may improve the sustainability of this material type. First, *bioplastics* are biodegradable plastics derived from plant sources instead of from petroleum. In particular, *polylactide acid* (PLA) is a bioplastic made from harvested corn and currently used in fibers for carpet manufacture. Second, the development of *metallocene polyolefins* has allowed polyolefins to be precisely manufactured with specific properties. Metallocene polyolefins can replace PVC and other plastics that are more harmful to the environment, and may be used for window frames, membrane roofing, siding, and wire sheathing.

## Finishes

Selecting interior finish materials can be a primary method of improving a building's sustainability because these materials are one of the main potential sources of indoor air pollution and are typically replaced several times over the life of a building. Finishes fall into the categories of adhesives, flooring, wall finishes, and ceiling finishes. The following sections give some of the more traditional finish materials as well as some alternative sustainable materials that are being used more frequently for both residential and commercial construction.

### Adhesives

The adhesives and coatings used with many types of finishes are a potential problem. Most adhesives contain plastic resins and other materials that can emit gases. Three types of low-emission and zero-VOC adhesives can be used for installing carpet, resilient flooring, plastic laminates, sheet metal, wood veneers, and some types of wall coverings. These three types are dry adhesives containing resins and stored in capsules released by pressure, water-based adhesives containing latex or polyvinyl acetate, and natural adhesives containing plant resins in a water dispersion system. A building can receive a LEED credit for using adhesives and sealants with a VOC content less than that defined in the California South Coast Air Quality Management District (SCAQMD) Rule 1168, which is among the lowest VOC content standards in the country.

### Flooring

When selecting *carpet*, there are three major considerations for sustainability: raw-material use, raw-material disposal, and indoor air quality. Good raw materials include recycled soft-drink containers (PET) and wool. Although wool has a higher initial cost, it is a renewable resource, wears well, and may have a lower life-cycle cost than a less expensive carpet that typically needs to be replaced more frequently. Carpet cushion made from recycled materials should also be selected. These materials can include tire rubber and synthetic and natural fiber from textile mill waste.

Disposing of carpet is a problem. Much used carpet is discarded in landfills, and it does not decompose easily. But separating the various components for recycling is difficult, and recycling is generally more expensive than landfill disposal. Nylon 6, a type of nylon fiber, can be recycled easily. Although some manufacturers have made efforts to recycle used carpet, the amount of carpet recycled is just a fraction of the amount disposed.

Carpet tiles are generally more sustainable than broadloom carpet. This is because only a small number need to be replaced when they are damaged or worn. Also, the adhesives used with them tend to emit less gas than broadloom adhesives. Several manufacturers have instituted programs to recycle the tiles.

Carpet can affect indoor air quality (IAQ) because of its construction and the adhesives used in direct-glue applications. Most carpet is made by bonding the face fiber to a backing with a synthetic latex resin. The latex can be replaced with fusion bonding, in which the face fiber is heat-welded to a sponge plastic backing. Carpets made with a needlepunching process also avoid the use of latex bonding. The Carpet and Rug Institute (CRI) has a voluntary testing program under which manufacturers have their carpets tested by an independent agency for four emissions: total VOC, styrene, formaldehyde, and 4-phenylcyclohexene (4-PC). Carpet that passes the test criteria is allowed to carry the CRI IAQ carpet testing program label, known as the "Green Label." The CRI also recommends that the ventilation system should be operated at maximum capacity during installation and for 48 to 72 hours after. An interior build-out can receive a LEED credit for using carpet systems that meet or exceed the requirements of the CRI IAQ carpet testing program.

*Vinyl flooring* provides many benefits, including durability, easy cleaning, a wide choice of patterns and colors, and relatively low cost. However, it requires highly refined petrochemicals for its manufacture and contains a large percentage of polyvinyl chloride (PVC) that can cause environmental problems during manufacture and disposal. Because of the high concentration of chloride in the tile, hazardous substances can be given off if vinyl flooring is incinerated. Some vinyl tile is manufactured from recycled PVC, and one brand is made without chlorine. As with carpet, low-VOC adhesives should be specified for laying vinyl flooring.

*Rubber flooring* made from recycled tires is also available, both as tile and as sheet goods. This flooring is durable, slip resistant, and resilient. However, because of the methods of manufacture and the binders that are used, recycled rubber flooring may give off indoor pollutants. This type of flooring should only be used where there is adequate ventilation, as in outdoor sports areas, locker rooms, and other utility spaces.

*Linoleum* is available in tile or sheet form and can also be used for wall base. Linoleum is made from natural, renewable products including linseed oil, rosin, cork powder, and pigments. It is a durable floor material, does not generate static electricity, and is biodegradable, waterproof, fire resistant, and naturally antibacterial. When used with low-VOC adhesives it emits only low levels of contaminants, less than vinyl flooring.

*Cork flooring* is made from a renewable resource, the bark of cork oak trees, which regenerates every 9 to 10 years. Cork forests are well managed and protected by the countries that have them. The only disadvantage to using cork as a natural material is that it must be imported from Mediterranean countries, increasing the transportation energy required. Although cork requires binders to hold the individual pieces together, the binders in use today are phenol-formaldehyde, polyurethane, and all-natural protein products. Cork flooring using urea formaldehyde should not be used. Cork can be finished with water-based urethanes with very low VOCs that provide durability along with water and chemical resistance. Cork should be installed with a water-based, low-VOC latex adhesive. Cork flooring is also an excellent absorber of sound.

*Wood flooring* offers many options for sustainable use. First, wood originating from well-managed forests can be selected. Both domestic and tropical hardwood is available from sustainable, FSC-accredited, certified sources. Second, veneered and laminated products using a plywood or MDF core can be used. Finally, salvaged solid-wood flooring is available. Whenever possible, prefinished flooring should be used to eliminate the need for sanding and finishing on the job site, which could create indoor air quality problems. If adhesives are required, they should be low-VOC content types. On-site finishing should use only water-dispersed urethanes. Varnishes, acid-cured varnishes, and hardening oils for on-site finishing should be avoided.

As an alternative to standard wood floors, bamboo or palm wood can be used. *Bamboo* is a fast-growing grass that reaches maturity in three to four years. It is almost as hard and twice as stable as red oak or maple, and is sold in tongue-and-groove strips prefinished with a durable polyurethane coating. *Palm wood* is harvested as a by-product of commercial coconut plantations. It is harder than maple or oak and is also sold in tongue-and-groove strips and prefinished with polyurethane.

*Ceramic tile* is generally considered a sustainable material in spite of the high embodied energy required to produce it and the transportation costs to get it from the factory to the job site. It uses readily available natural materials, is very durable, produces practically no harmful emissions, and requires very little maintenance. Some tile is made from post-consumer or post-industrial waste products using from 25% to 100% recycled material. Cement mortars and grouts are also environmentally friendly and produce very few emissions. Avoid epoxy-modified grout, plastic adhesives with solvents, and sealers that contain VOCs.

## Wall finishes

*Gypsum wallboard* is manufactured with 100% recycled content for its paper faces and with some recycled content for the core. Some manufacturers mix recycled newspaper with gypsum as the core material. In addition, about 7% of the gypsum used in the industry is synthetic. Synthetic gypsum is chemically identical to natural, mined gypsum, but is a by-product of various manufacturing, industrial, and chemical processes. The main source of synthetic gypsum in North America is *flue-gas desulfurization.* This is the process whereby power-generating and similar plants remove polluting gases from their stacks to reduce the emission of harmful materials into the atmosphere. Synthetic gypsum represents an efficient application for refuse material. By itself, gypsum wallboard does not contribute in any significant degree to indoor air pollution. However, adhesives, paints, and calking can be pollution sources and should be specified carefully.

Disposal of gypsum wallboard is problematic because wallboard cannot be reused when taken out of an old building. Some gypsum wallboard plants are recycling old wallboard. However, the wallboard must be separated from other materials and be free of screws, nails, and lead paint. Currently, the cost of collecting and transporting the old wallboard is a disincentive for recycling. If the wallboard can be recycled, it is pulverized and can be worked into the ground as a soil additive.

*Sisal wallcovering* is a natural material made from the fiber of the henequen plant. The branches are harvested and the fiber is extracted, dyed, and spun into yarn. Although fairly rough and not suitable for wet areas, sisal wallcovering and floor covering is durable, requires low maintenance, and reduces sound reflection and transmission. It should be applied with a zero-VOC adhesive and detailed to allow slight expansion and contraction as it absorbs and releases humidity.

Paints and other coatings require careful consideration in their selection and use. Although federal, state, and local regulations have eliminated most coatings that contain dangerous components such as lead and cadmium and have limited the use of VOCs, some commercial coatings may still contain these components. Generally, paint sold now must comply with the VOC limits set by the Environmental Protection Agency (EPA) as required by the Clean Air Act. The limits are set in the National Volatile Organic Compound Emission Standards for Architectural Coatings, 40 CFR Part 59. Many types of coatings are listed in this standard. For example, the VOC content of flat interior paint cannot exceed 250 g/L (2.1 lbm/gal) while non-flat interior paint cannot exceed 380 g/L (3.2 lbm/gal). (Enforcement of the rule is based on SI units.) California has stricter standards, limiting flat paint to 100 g/L (0.84 lbm/gal) and non-flat coatings to 150 g/L (1.3 lbm/gal). In the future, California will further reduce these limits.

A building can receive a LEED credit for the use of interior paints and coatings that comply with the VOC and chemical component limits of the Green Seal Standard GS-11. Green Seal standards for flat paint are stricter than EPA standards, as they state that flat interior paint cannot exceed 50 g/L (0.42 lbm/gal).

### Ceilings

Acoustical ceiling tile that uses recycled content from old tiles, newsprint, or perlite is available. Other materials, such as clay and wood fibers, may also be used. Fiberglass ceiling panels are also available with recycled content. Recycled content varies but can be up to 95%, depending on the manufacturer and the product type. Old tile can be repainted if the correct procedures and type of paint are used. One manufacturer offers a recycling program that allows customers to ship old tile to its plant if the manufacturer's own tile is specified as the replacement. The cost of recycling ceiling tile is typically less than the cost of sending the material to a landfill. Even the grid that holds the tile can be recycled as scrap steel.

However, tile may shed fiber as it ages or if it is damaged. This loose fiber can be collected by the HVAC system if the plenum is used as a return air space. The use of separate ducts for return air or the regular vacuuming of the plenum can alleviate some of the problem.

### Furnishings

In addition to their other sustainability issues, furnishings in residential and commercial settings can be a significant source of formaldehyde because of the particleboard, MDF, and coatings used in their construction. The following strategies can be used to improve sustainability through the selection and specification of furnishings.

- Use refurbished or reused office furniture.
- Consider furniture made from steel, solid wood, and glass, all readily recycled materials.
- Specify that furnishings be fabricated with reclaimed wood or with wood certified under standards established by the Forest Stewardship Council (FSC).
- Require that furnishings be fabricated with formaldehyde-free medium-density fiberboard or strawboard.
- Use furniture with cushions, workstation panels, and fabrics made with recycled PET (polyethylene terephthalate) from soda bottles.
- Look for fabrics with biodegradable and nontoxic dyes.
- For furniture, use finish coverings made of cotton, wool, ramie, blends, or other natural materials. Use chemical-free organic cotton fabrics.
- Use low-VOC finishes.
- Use powder coatings for finishes instead of standard paint.
- Require that cushions be foamed with CO2-injected foam or other environmentally friendly materials.

## ENERGY EFFICIENCY

Although much of the energy efficiency of a building is determined by the original architecture and mechanical system design, there are many strategies that the interior designer can use to reduce energy use. These can be grouped into four broad categories: building commissioning, mechanical systems, electricity use, and plumbing. Refer to Ch. 16 for a review of mechanical and electrical systems and lighting.

### Building commissioning

Building commissioning is the process of inspecting, testing, starting up, and adjusting building systems and then verifying and documenting that they are operating as intended and that they meet the design criteria of the contract documents. Commissioning is an expansion of the traditional testing, adjusting, and balancing (TAB) that is commonly performed on mechanical systems, but with greatly broadened scope over a longer time period.

Which building systems require commissioning depends on the complexity of the building and the needs of the owner. These systems may include some or all of the following.

- mechanical systems, including heating and cooling equipment, air handling equipment, distribution system, pumps, sensors and controls, dampers, and cooling tower operation
- electrical systems, including switchgear, controls, emergency generators, fire management, and safety systems
- plumbing systems, including tanks, pumps, water heaters, compressors, and fixtures
- sprinkler systems, including standpipes, alarms, hose cabinets, and controls
- fire management and life-safety systems, including alarms and detectors, air handling equipment, smoke dampers, and building communications
- vertical transportation, including elevator controls and escalators
- telecommunication and computer networks

Most building commissioning occurs during the design and initial occupancy of the building. During this time the architect, owner, mechanical engineer, electrical engineer, contractors, and others as required perform the main building commissioning.

**Figure 21.2** Displacement ventilation

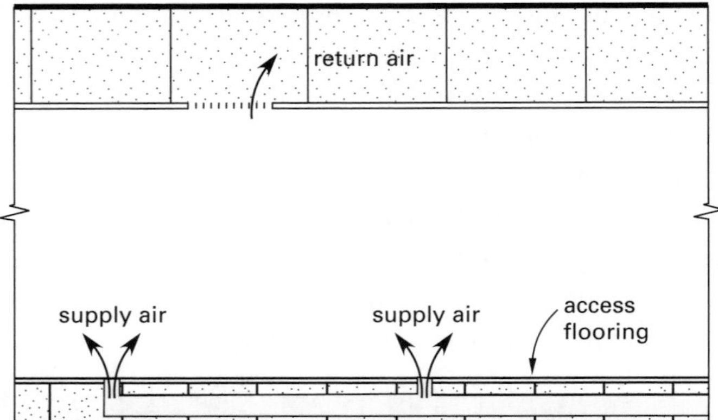


For an interior design project, commissioning involves verifying and ensuring that the building elements are designed, installed, and calibrated to operate as intended for the tenant's scope of work. For an interior design project to receive LEED credit, following the guidelines is mandatory. For LEED certification, the commissioning team must not include individuals directly responsible for the project design or construction management.

## Mechanical systems

The interior designer can take a variety of actions to reduce energy consumption by mechanical systems. These include the following.

- Specify that the tenant's portion of the HVAC system must conform to ASHRAE/IESNA Standard 90.1, *Energy Standard for Buildings Except Low-Rise Residential Buildings*, or to the local energy code, whichever is more stringent. (The ASHRAE/IESNA standard is described later in this chapter.) This is a mandatory requirement for LEED certification. If energy use is reduced beyond this minimum amount, a project can receive LEED credit.
- Do not use any mechanical system components for the tenant space that include CFC-based refrigerants. This is a mandatory requirement for LEED certification.
- If possible, use displacement ventilation. Displacement ventilation is an air distribution system in which supply air originates at floor level and rises to return air grilles in the ceiling, as shown in Fig. 21.2. Because supply air is delivered close to users, it does not have to be cooled as much, resulting in energy savings. It is also a good system for improving indoor air quality, because these systems typically use a high percentage of outdoor air, and for removing heat generated by ceiling-level lights. This system can also be used in conjunction with personal temperature control and flexible underfloor wiring.

Most displacement ventilation systems use an access flooring system to provide space for underfloor ducting and to allow rearrangement of air supply outlets as the space layout changes. However, this makes displacement ventilation appropriate only for new construction, where the additional floor-to-floor height can be set to accommodate the 12 in (305 mm) or more that is required for ductwork along with coordination of stairways and elevators.

A variation of this system uses supply air outlets located low on exterior walls, but this only works for spaces within about 16 ft (5 m) of the exterior wall.

### Electricity use

• Reduce the amount of power needed for lighting by designing task/ambient systems or by other means, such as the use of daylighting. A project can receive LEED credit if the lighting power density is reduced a certain amount below the ASHRAE/IESNA Standard 90.1 level.

• Specify automatic occupancy lighting controls in all spaces that are not regularly occupied, such as copy rooms, storage rooms, restrooms, and the like.

• Have the electrical engineer set up nonemergency lighting on a programmable timer that turns lighting off after business hours and that includes a manual override capability. Of course, this requires the approval of the building owner.

• Specify daylight-responsive controls in all occupied spaces within 15 ft (4570 mm) of windows and under skylights.

• Specify finishes with high reflectance to improve daylighting.

• Specify energy-efficient appliances and equipment. A project can receive LEED credit if minimum standards are surpassed.

• If the building owner approves, specify submetering equipment to measure and record energy uses within a tenant space. Along with this, arrange for the energy costs to be paid by the tenant and not to be included in the base rent. Of course, this also requires the approval of the building owner.

### Plumbing

• Specify low-flow fixtures and other strategies to reduce water consumption. A project can receive LEED credit if at least 50% of the tenant occupancy requirements include strategies for using 20% less water than the baseline amount calculated for the tenant space *after* meeting the fixture performance requirements of the Energy Policy Act of 1992. Additional credit is available if these percentages are increased.

## INDOOR AIR QUALITY

Indoor air quality (IAQ) is an important aspect of sustainable design and many of the decisions made by the interior designer regarding interior materials and construction can affect IAQ. In addition to simply maintaining health, the quality of indoor air affects people's sense of well-being and can affect absenteeism, productivity, creativity, and motivation. Indoor air quality is a complex subject because there are hundreds of different contaminants, dozens of causes of poor IAQ, many possible symptoms that building occupants may experience, and a wide variety of potential strategies for maintaining good IAQ. This section outlines some of the more important areas of knowledge with which you should be familiar. Because IAQ has become such an important topic in building design, there is no shortage of laws and standards devoted to regulating it. Some of these are given at the end of this section.

### Indoor air contaminants

Indoor air contaminants can be broadly classified into two groups: chemical contaminants and biological contaminants. Chemical contaminants include things such as volatile organic compounds, inorganic chemicals, tobacco smoke, and dozens of others, while biological contaminants include mold, pollen, bacteria, and viruses.

#### Chemical Contaminants

*Volatile organic compounds* (VOCs) are chemicals that contain carbon and hydrogen and that vaporize at room temperature and pressure. They are found in many indoor sources, including building materials and common household products. Common sources of VOCs in building materials include paint, stains, adhesives, sealants, water repellents and sealers, particleboard, furniture, upholstery, and carpeting. Other sources include copy machines, cleaning agents, and pesticides.

The EPA has established regulations for VOCs in coatings. The final regulation on VOCs in architectural, industrial, and maintenance coatings was issued on September 13, 1998. This regulation listed the maximum content of VOCs in the various types of coatings. The maximum VOC levels of some common coatings were listed in the previous section. However, state laws also regulate VOCs, and each state may permit a different level. For example, the California South Coast Air Quality Management District has very strict limits on the volatile organic content of paints.

*Formaldehyde* is a colorless gas with a pungent odor. It is used in the preparation of resins and adhesives that are most commonly found in particleboard, wall paneling, furniture, carpet adhesives, and other glues used in the construction and furnishings industry. Formaldehyde is designated as a probable human carcinogen and has irritant effects on the eyes and respiratory tract.

The maximum suggested or allowable exposure rates vary by agency. ASHRAE recommends a maximum continuous indoor air concentration of 0.1 parts per million (ppm). OSHA specifies that concentrations should not exceed 0.75 ppm in an 8-hour period with a maximum 15-minute short-term exposure of 2 ppm. In order to qualify as Greenguard certified, a product cannot emit more than 0.05 ppm.

The problems associated with formaldehyde can most easily be solved by minimizing the sources of formaldehyde within a space, using two or three coats of sealants, or airing out the building before occupancy.

There are potentially hundreds of organic and inorganic chemicals that may be harmful to humans. The California Office of Environmental Health Hazard Assessment has a list of 76 chemicals (at this writing) that the state regulates. The list includes the chronic inhalation reference exposure level (REL) for each in micrograms per cubic meter ($\mu g/m^3$). These levels were developed as a result of California's Proposition 65, which was passed in 1986. Proposition 65 requires businesses to provide a clear and reasonable warning before knowingly and intentionally exposing anyone to a listed chemical.

The Greenguard Environmental Institute also produces a list of products, chemicals in those products, and allowable maximum emission levels. Some of the common chemicals include VOCs, formaldehyde, aldehydes, 4-phenylcyclohexene, and styrene, as well as particulates and biological contaminates. In order to be certified by Greenguard, a product must meet these standards after being tested according to ASTM D5116 and D6670, the state of Washington's protocol for interior furnishings and construction materials, and the EPA's testing protocol for furniture.

*Secondhand smoke*, also called environmental tobacco smoke (ETS), is a mixture of the smoke given off by the burning ends of cigarettes, pipes, and cigars and the smoke exhaled from the lungs of smokers. Secondhand smoke has been found to contain over 4000 substances, more than 40 of which are known to cause cancer in humans and many of which are strong irritants. The EPA and the California EPA have found that exposure to secondhand smoke increases risk for cancer and other serious health effects. To improve indoor air quality, either smoking should be banned completely from buildings and near entrances, or isolated smoking rooms should be constructed with separate ventilation systems that exhaust directly to the outside.

### Biological contaminants

Potential biological contaminants in a building include the common problem of mold and mildew as well as bacteria, viruses, mites, pollen, animal dander, dust, and insects. Even protein in urine from rats and mice is an allergen.

*Molds* and *mildew* are microscopic organisms, types of fungi, which produce enzymes to digest organic matter. Their reproductive spores are present nearly everywhere. When exposed to these spores, people sensitive to molds and mildew may experience eye irritation, skin rash, running nose, nausea, headaches, and similar symptoms.

Mold spores require three conditions to grow: moisture, a nutrient to feed on, and a temperature range from 40°F to 100°F (4°C to 38°C). Many organic materials can serve as nutrients for organisms: wood, carpet, the paper coating of gypsum wallboard, paint, wallpaper, insulation, and ceiling tile, among others. A suitable temperature is always present in buildings, so the only ways to prevent and control mold are to prevent and control moisture where it should not be and to use materials that do not provide a nutrient. For example, metal framing can be used instead of wood framing.

## Causes of poor indoor air quality

There are four basic causes of poor indoor air quality. These are chemical contaminants from indoor sources, chemical contaminants from outdoor sources, biological contaminants, and poor ventilation. These factors may be present alone or combined with others to produce the various symptoms of poor indoor air quality.

One of the most common sources of poor indoor air quality is chemical contaminants from indoor sources, including VOCs, environmental tobacco smoke, respirable particles, carbon monoxide, and nitrogen dioxide. Lists of harmful chemicals can be obtained from the following sources.

- *Hazardous Chemicals Desk Reference,* Richard J. Lewis. New York: Van Nostrand Reinhold.
- The National Toxicology Program. (Lists chemicals known to be carcinogenic.)
- The International Agency for Research of Cancer (IARC). (Classifies chemicals that are known to be carcinogenic.)
- *Chemical Cross Index, Chemical List of Lists.* California Environmental Protection Agency. (Lists hazardous chemicals regulated by various state and federal agencies.)
- The California Office of Environmental Health Hazard Assessment. (Lists chronic reference exposure levels for hazardous chemicals recognized by this office, with links to more information about each chemical.)
- The California Health and Welfare Agency, Safe Drinking Water and Toxic Enforcement Act of 1986 (Proposition 65). (Lists chemicals known to cancer and reproductive toxicity.)
- The California Air Toxics Program, California Environmental Protection Agency, Air Resources Board (ARB).

Chemical contaminants from outdoor sources are introduced into a building when air intake vents, windows, or doors from parking garages are improperly located, allowing pollutants from the outside (carbon monoxide, for example) to be drawn into the building. Indoor pollutants from exhausts and plumbing vents can also be sucked back into the building through improperly located air intakes.

Biological contaminants such as mold, bacteria, and viruses may develop from moisture infiltration, standing water, stagnant water in mechanical equipment, and even from droppings from insects or birds that find their way into the building. These were discussed in the previous section.

Poor ventilation allows indoor pollutants to accumulate to unpleasant or even unhealthy levels and affects the general sense of well-being of building occupants. One of the most difficult aspects of providing proper ventilation is balancing the requirement for energy conservation. However, this problem can be solved by using heat exchangers and other mechanical engineering methods. For interior design projects, it is helpful to verify what types of mechanical equipment are installed in the building. Some of the minimum levels of ventilation are given in the following section on strategies for maintaining good IAQ.

## Symptoms of poor indoor air quality

There are many symptoms of poor indoor air quality, from temporary, minor irritations to serious, life-threatening illnesses. They are generally grouped into three classifications: sick building syndrome, building-related illnesses, and multiple chemical sensitivities. Problems with asbestos, lead, and radon are serious, long-term problems and are generally not included with these three classifications.

*Sick building syndrome* (SBS) is a condition in which building occupants experience a variety of health-related symptoms that cannot be directly linked to any particular cause. Symptoms generally disappear after the occupants leave the building. Noninclusive symptoms may include irritation of the eyes, nose, and throat, dryness of the mucous membranes and skin, erythema (redness of the skin), mental fatigue and headache, respiratory infections and cough, hoarseness of voice and wheezing, hypersensitivity reactions, and nausea and dizziness.

*Building-related illness* (BRI) is a condition in which the health-related symptom or symptoms of a building's occupants are identified and can be directly attributed to certain building contaminants. In the case of BRI, the symptoms do not immediately improve when the occupant leaves the building. Legionnaires' disease is an example of a BRI.

*Multiple chemical sensitivity* (MCS) is a condition brought on by exposure to VOCs or other chemicals. People with MCS may develop acute, long-term sensitivity and become symptomatic each time they are exposed to the chemicals. These sensitivities remain with some people for the rest of their lives. For many such people, even a slight exposure to the chemical can be enough to produce symptoms.

## Strategies for maintaining good indoor air quality

Many of the methods for maintaining good IAQ must be implemented by the architect or mechanical engineer with the approval of the building owner. However, there are several strategies that the interior designer can implement. These can be classified into four broad categories: eliminating or reducing the sources of pollution, controlling the ventilation of the building, establishing good maintenance procedures, and controlling occupant activity as it affects IAQ.

### Eliminating or reducing sources of pollution

- Early in the project, establish the owner's criteria for indoor air quality. This may be part of the programming process and should include establishing the available budget.
- Select and specify finish materials and furnishings with low emissions and low VOCs. The standards listed in the next section provide guidance in choosing materials. Because it is not always possible to eliminate all sources of pollutants, set priorities by identifying the materials that are the most volatile and those that are used in large quantities.
- Specify materials and finishes that are resistant to the growth of mold and mildew, especially in areas that may become wet or damp.
- Request emissions test data from manufacturers, such as material safety data sheets (MSDSs). OSHA regulations require all manufacturers to develop and supply MSDSs for those products that contain chemicals.

• Prior to occupancy, the HVAC system in a new building or occupied space should be operated at full capacity for two weeks to flush emissions due to outgassing chemicals and moisture. If it is possible to ventilate an individual space after the completion of construction, this should be suggested to the client.

### Controlling ventilation

• During the programming phase, determine the owners' and occupants' requirements for ventilation. Also determine the energy conservation code requirements.

• Verify with the mechanical engineer or building architect that minimum outdoor air ventilation is being provided. The American Society of Heating, Refrigerating and Air-Conditioning Engineers (ASHRAE) recommends minimum rates based on the specific activity of a building or individual space. These minimums, as given in ASHRAE Standard 62, range from 15 cfm/person to 60 cfm/person (8 L/s/person to 30 L/s/person). The absolute minimum now recommended is 15 cfm/person (8 L/s/person). 20 cfm/person (10 L/s/person) is recommended for office spaces. The high range of 60 cfm/person (30 L/s/person) is used for smoking lounges.

• Provide separate rooms and ventilation for equipment that emits high concentrations of pollutants. In an office, a high-volume copier might require a separate room. Health clubs, laboratories, and kitchens are other common locations for such equipment.

• Specify independent building commissioning and testing, adjusting, and balancing (TAB) of the HVAC system.

### Establishing good maintenance procedures

Once a building is completed it is important that it be properly maintained. Of course, the interior designer has little control over this aspect of indoor air quality, but through the proper selection of materials, development of maintenance manuals, and establishment of operating guidelines, the interior designer, architect, mechanical engineer, and other design professionals can provide the building owner with the basis for proper maintenance.

• Select and specify building materials and finishes that are easy to clean and maintain.

• Include in the specifications requirements for warranties and maintenance contracts.

• Suggest that the client and building owner conduct post-occupancy evaluations at regular intervals to review procedures for maintaining good IAQ.

• Require in the specifications that the contractor assemble an operation and maintenance manual from the various suppliers of HVAC and electrical equipment giving performance criteria, operation requirements, cleaning instructions, and maintenance procedures.

• Include in the maintenance manual materials and procedures for regular cleaning of specified products, including furnishings. Cleaning products should be low-emission products recommended by the manufacturer of each product or finish.

### Controlling occupant activity

As with maintenance procedures, the interior designer has little control over occupant activity once the building is completed. However, the designer can suggest to the client methods of controlling occupant activity as it affects IAQ. The interior designer can also add long-term occupancy IAQ suggestions to the operation and maintenance manual.

• Suggest a no-smoking policy for the space.

• Suggest that the building owner or manager monitor individual space use to determine whether major changes occur in occupant load, activities, or equipment. The building HVAC system may need to be adjusted accordingly.

• Install sensors for carbon dioxide ($CO_2$), carbon monoxide (CO), VOCs, and other products, which are connected to the building management system.

## Indoor air quality standards

The last few decades have seen the development of many laws, regulations, and standards enacted at the federal, state, and local levels that attempt to control and improve indoor air quality. The Occupational Safety and Health Administration (OSHA) has also proposed rules for IAQ. Some of the more important laws and regulations with which interior designers should be familiar are listed here.

For a listing of additional regulations and industry standards that relate to sustainability, refer to the section later in this chapter.

- The Clean Air Act (CAA) of 1970. This law regulates air emissions from area, stationary, and mobile sources. The CAA authorized the EPA to establish the National Ambient Air Quality Standards to protect public health and the environment. The CAA has been amended several times since 1970 to extend deadlines for compliance and add other provisions.
- The National Ambient Air Quality Standards. U.S. Environmental Protection Agency, 40 CFR 50. This standard implements part of the Clean Air Act.
- ASHRAE Standard 62-2001, *Ventilation for Acceptable Indoor Air Quality.* This is an industry standard and, as such, compliance with it is voluntary. However, most building codes incorporate all or a part of this standard by reference, thereby giving it the force of law. In addition to setting minimum outdoor air requirements for ventilation, the standard includes provisions for managing sources of contamination, controlling indoor humidity, and filtering building air, as well as requirements for construction, startup, operation, and maintenance of HVAC systems.
- ASHRAE Standard 62.2-2003, *Ventilation and Acceptable Indoor Air Quality in Low-Rise Residential Buildings.* This is also a voluntary industry standard. The standard applies to single-family houses and multifamily buildings of three stories or less, including manufactured and modular houses. It defines the roles of and minimum requirements for mechanical and natural ventilation systems as well as the building envelope.
- National VOC Emission Standards for Architectural Coatings (40 CFR Part 59). This rule implements part of the Clean Air Act and sets limits on the amount of volatile organic compounds that manufacturers and importers of architectural coatings can put into their products.
- South Coast Air Quality Management District (SCAQMD) Rule 1113, Architectural Coatings. This rule limits the VOC content of architectural coatings used in the South Coast Air Quality Management District in California. The limits it sets are more restrictive than the national VOC emission standard published by the EPA. Rule 1168 limits the VOC content of adhesives and sealants.
- The California Safe Drinking Water and Toxic Enforcement Act of 1986 (Proposition 65). This law prohibits businesses from discharging chemicals that cause cancer or reproductive toxicity into sources of drinking water and requires that warning be given to individuals exposed to such chemicals. The California Environmental Protection Agency's Office of Environmental Health Hazard Assessment (OEHHA) is the lead agency for the implementation of Proposition 65.
- The Greenguard Environmental Institute. This organization (described earlier in this chapter) tests products following ASTM Standards D5116 and D6670, the EPA's testing protocol for furniture, and the state of Washington's protocol for interior furnishings and construction materials. Greenguard has a list of the emission levels that products must meet before they are certified by the organization.
- *Threshold Limit Values and Biological Exposure Indices.* American Conference of Governmental Industrial Hygienists (ACGIH). This document gives exposure limits, called threshold limit values (TLV), for chemicals in the workplace.

• ASTM D5116, *Standard Guide for Small-Scale Environmental Chamber Determinations of Organic Emissions from Indoor Materials/Products.* This guide describes the equipment and techniques suitable for determining organic emissions from small samples of indoor materials. It cannot be used for testing complete assemblies or coatings. Another standard, ASTM D6803, is used for testing paint using small environmental chambers.

• ASTM D6670, *Standard Practice for Full-Scale Chamber Determination of Volatile Organic Emissions from Indoor Materials/ Products.* This practice details the method to be used to determine VOC emissions from building materials, furniture, consumer products, and equipment under environmental and product usage conditions that are typical of those found in office and residential buildings. It is referenced by other standards or laws as a standard way to determine the level of VOC emissions.

• ASTM E1333, *Standard Test Method for Determining Formaldehyde Concentrations in Air and Emission Rates from Wood Products Using a Large Chamber.* This test method measures the formaldehyde concentration in air and the emission rate from wood products in a large chamber under conditions designed to simulate product use.

## HAZARDOUS MATERIAL MITIGATION

Hazardous materials are chemical and other biological substances that pose a threat to the environment or to human health if they are released or misused. The interior designer should be aware of the potential existence of these materials, especially when working on a project in an older building. If any of these materials are suspected, the owner should be advised so that appropriate action can be taken. These contaminants need to be identified and removed in accordance with best practices and in compliance with federal, state, and local regulations. There are thousands of products and substances that can be defined as hazardous. Here are a few of the more common ones found in buildings.

### Asbestos

*Asbestos* is a naturally occurring fibrous mineral found in certain types of rock formations. After mining and processing, asbestos consists of very fine fibers. Asbestos is known to cause lung cancer, asbestosis (a scarring of the lungs), and mesothelioma (a cancer of the lining of the chest or abdominal cavity). Oral exposure may be associated with cancer of the esophagus, stomach, and intestines. In buildings, exposure generally comes from asbestos that is or has become friable (easily crumbled), or that has been disturbed either accidentally or by construction activities. Although generally not a problem in new construction, asbestos can be found in many types of existing building materials, including pipe and blown-in insulation, asphalt flooring, vinyl sheet and tile flooring, construction mastics, ceiling tiles, textured paints, roofing shingles, cement siding, calking, vinyl wall coverings, and many other products.

Asbestos is regulated under two federal laws and one federal agency restriction: the Clean Air Act (CAA) of 1970, the Toxic Substances Control Act (TSCA) of 1976, and the U.S. Consumer Product Safety Commission (CPSC). Under authority of the TSCA, in 1989 the EPA issued a ban on asbestos. However, much of the original rule was vacated by the U.S. Fifth Circuit Court of Appeals in 1991. Products still banned include flooring felt, corrugated and specialty paper, commercial paper, and rollboard. The ban also prevents the use of asbestos in products that have not historically contained asbestos. Under authority of the CAA, the National Emission Standards for Hazardous Air Pollutants (NESHAP) rules for asbestos banned the use of sprayed-on or wet-applied asbestos-containing materials (ACM) for fireproofing and insulation. These rules took effect in 1973. NESHAP also bans the use of ACMs for decorative purposes. This took effect in 1978. The CPSC bans the use of asbestos in certain consumer products such as textured paint and wall patching compounds.

Tests for asbestos and efforts at mitigation must be done by an accredited company following strict procedures. In many cases, asbestos that has not been disturbed can be left in place, because the EPA and the National Institute for Occupational Safety and Health (NIOSH) have determined that intact and undisturbed asbestos materials do not pose a health risk. The asbestos may be encapsulated to protect it from becoming friable or from accidental damage. During building demolition or renovation, however, the EPA requires asbestos removal. This must be done by a licensed contractor certified for this type of work.

## Vermiculite

*Vermiculite* is a hydrated laminar magnesium-aluminum-ironsilicate that resembles mica. It is separated from mineral ore that contains other materials, possibly including asbestos. When heated during processing, vermiculite expands into wormlike pieces. In construction, it is used for pour-in insulation, acoustic finishes, fire protection, and sound-deadening compounds. Vermiculite obtained from a mine in Montana is known to contain some amount of asbestos. This mine was closed in 1990. Vermiculite is still mined at other locations, but those have low levels of contamination. The current concern is with loose, pour-in insulation used in attics and concrete blocks.

The EPA recommends that attic insulation that may contain asbestos contaminated vermiculite not be disturbed, and that any cracks in the ceiling be sealed. If the insulation must be removed, only a trained and certified professional contractor should perform the work.

## Lead

*Lead* is a highly toxic metal that was once used in a variety of consumer and industrial products. Exposure to lead can cause serious health problems, especially to children, including damage to the brain and nervous system, slowed growth, behavior problems, seizures, and even death. In adults it can cause digestive and reproductive problems, nerve disorders, muscle and joint pain, and difficulties during pregnancy. Most exposure from lead comes from paint in homes built before 1978 and from soil and household dust that has picked up lead from deteriorating lead-based paint. The federal government banned lead-based paint from housing in 1978.

Federal law requires that anyone conducting lead-based paint removal be certified and that lead-based paint be removed from some types of residential occupancies and child-occupied facilities by a certified company using approved methods for removal and disposal. Removal of lead-based paint should not be done by sanding, propane torch, heat gun, or dry scraping. Sometimes, covering the wall with a new layer of gypsum wallboard or simply repainting is an acceptable alternative. Also, lead-coated copper—once used in flashing, sheet metal panels, gutters, and downspouts—is no longer used due to the potential for soil contamination.

## Radon

*Radon* is a colorless, odorless, tasteless, naturally occurring radioactive gas found in soils, rock, and water throughout the world. Radon causes lung cancer, with most of the risk coming from breathing air contaminated with radon and its decay products. Most radon exposure occurs in places where it accumulates, such as in homes, schools, and office buildings, so most remedial work is done in existing buildings. Testing for radon is easy and can be done by a trained contractor or by homeowners with kits available in hardware stores or through the mail. The EPA recommends that remedial action be taken if a radon level over 4 picocuries per liter (pCi/L) is found.

Remedial work should follow the radon mitigation standards of the EPA and ASTM E2121 and can include one or more of the following.

- sealing cracks in floors, walls, and foundations
- venting the soil outside the foundation wall
- depressurizing the voids within a block wall foundation (block wall depressurization)
- ventilating the crawl space with a fan (crawl space depressurization)
- using a vent pipe without a fan to draw air from under a slab to the outside (passive sub-slab depressurization)
- using a fan-powered vent to draw air from below the slab (active sub-slab depressurization)
- using a fan-powered vent to draw air from below a membrane laid on the crawl space floor (sub-membrane depressurization)

### Polychlorinated biphenyls (PCBs)

*Polychlorinated biphenyls* (PCBs) are mixtures of synthetic organic chemicals with physical properties ranging from oily liquids to waxy solids. PCBs were once used in many commercial and industrial applications, including building transformers, fluorescent light transformers, paints, coatings, and plastic and rubber products. PCBs are known to cause cancer and other adverse health effects afflicting the immune, reproductive, nervous, and endocrine systems. Because of concerns regarding the toxicity and persistence of PCBs in the environment, their manufacture and importation were banned in 1977 under the Toxic Substances Control Act (TSCA) of 1976. While there are some exceptions on the use of PCBs, the TSCA strictly regulates manufacturing, processing, distribution, and disposal.

If PCBs are discovered in building components or on-site, they must be handled by a certified contractor and disposed of by incineration, dechlorination, or placement in an approved chemical waste landfill.

## RECYCLING AND REUSE

Recycling and reuse of materials and products is an important part of the total life cycle of an interior space or building. There are many opportunities for the interior designer to recycle and reuse materials when designing and detailing. As many materials as possible should be recycled into other products or reused for their original purpose. In turn, new spaces and buildings should incorporate as many recycled and reused materials as possible to provide a market for those products. Ideally, all materials should be durable, biodegradable, or recyclable.

### Adaptive reuse

Adaptive reuse begins with reusing as much of the existing building stock as possible instead of constructing new buildings. Buildings can be updated to conform to their original uses or adapted to new uses. Turning an old warehouse into residences is a common example of adaptive reuse. A project can receive LEED credit for maintaining at least 75% of the existing building structure and shell, excluding window assemblies and nonstructural roofing material. Additional credit is also given for using at least 50% of the non-shell areas such as walls, doors, floor coverings, and ceiling systems.

At a smaller scale, individual products can be reused in new buildings. These include building elements such as plumbing fixtures, doors, timber, and bricks. For example, heavy timber can be reused by resawing and planing. In most cases, using these old materials adds to the architectural character of the new building. A project can receive LEED credit for using salvaged, refurbished, or reused materials, products, and furnishings for at least 5% of the total of all building materials. Additional credit is given for using 10%.

Reuse conserves natural resources, reduces the energy required to construct new buildings and products, lessens air and water pollution due to burning and dumping, and keeps materials from entering the waste stream.

### Recycled Materials

*Recyclability* is a previously used material's capability for use as a resource in the manufacture of a new product. Old steel that can be melted down to manufacture new steel is an example of recyclability. Recycling materials is often difficult because different substances must be separated so that they can be marketed separately. Most of this separating must be done by hand, and in some cases, such as with gypsum wallboard, the cost of separating all the component parts may be more than the cost of sending the material to a landfill.

Before selecting and specifying materials, the interior designer should ask product suppliers about the recycled content of their products. A project can receive LEED credit for using recycled materials if the sum of the post-consumer recycled content plus one-half of the post-industrial content constitutes at least 5% of the total value of the materials in the project. Additional credit is given for using 10%.

Recycling of consumer products can be encouraged by providing bins, recycling rooms, and other provisions as part of the building design. In some areas of the country local codes require that a portion of the trash area be reserved for recycling bins.

### Building disposal

If old products and materials cannot be reused or recycled, they must be burned or placed in a landfill for disposal. If a material is biodegradable it can break down quickly and return to the earth. Some materials, such as aluminum, most plastics, and steel, take a very long time to decompose naturally. A project can receive LEED credit for diverting at least 50% of construction, demolition, and land-clearing debris from landfill disposal to recycling or donation of usable materials to charitable organizations.

*Biobased products* may be used to minimize disposal problems while saving depletable raw materials. Biobased products are made using plant or animal materials as the main ingredient. Using these products also helps maintain good indoor air quality and provides a market for the rural economy. Biobased products include adhesives, composite panels, gypsum wallboard substitutes, ceiling tiles, and carpet backing. A project can receive LEED credit for using rapidly renewable building materials, made from plants that are typically harvested within a cycle of 10 years or less, for 5% of the total value of all building materials used.

## REGULATIONS AND INDUSTRY STANDARDS RELATED TO SUSTAINABILITY

(For a listing of standards and regulations that govern indoor air quality, refer to the previous section in this chapter.)

- ASHRAE Standard 90.1, *Energy Standard for Buildings Except Low-Rise Residential Buildings*. This is a voluntary industry standard that gives information on minimum energy efficiency standards, building envelope requirements, zone isolation, floor, ceiling, and roof insulation, and power allowance calculation. It is written in mandatory enforceable language suitable for code adoption.
- ASTM E1991, *Standard Guide for Environmental Life Cycle Assessment of Building Materials/Products*
- ASTM E2114, *Standard Terminology for Sustainability Relative to the Performance of Buildings*
- ASTM E2129, *Standard Practice for Data Collection for Sustainability Assessment of Building Products*
- Green Seal, GS-11, product standard for paints
- Green Seal, GS-13, product standard for windows

• The Toxic Substances Control Act (TSCA) of 1976. This law was enacted to give the Environmental Protection Agency the authority to track and regulate over 75,000 industrial chemicals produced or imported into the United States. It allows the EPA to ban the manufacture and import of those chemicals that pose an unreasonable risk.

## DEFINITIONS

*Coproduct*: a marketable by-product from a manufacturing process, which can include materials that are traditionally considered waste but that can be used as raw materials in a different process.

*Demand control ventilation*: a system designed to adjust the amount of ventilation air that is provided to a space in response to changes in occupancy. The system most often uses carbon dioxide sensors, but may also use occupancy sensors or air quality sensors.

*Embodied energy*: the total energy needed to extract, produce, fabricate, and deliver a material to a job site, including the energy used to collect, extract, and process the raw materials, to transport the materials from the original site to the processing plant or factory, to turn the raw materials into a finished product, and to transport the material to the job site

*Post-consumer*: referring to a material or product that has completed its life as a consumer item and has been diverted or recovered from waste destined for disposal.

*Post-industrial*: referring to materials generated in manufacturing processes, such as trimmings or scrap, that have been recovered or diverted from solid waste. Also called *pre-consumer materials*

*Pre-consumer materials*: see *Post-industrial*

*Recovered materials*: waste or by-products that have been recovered or diverted from solid-waste disposal. This term does not apply to materials that are generated from or reused within an original manufacturing process.

*Renewable product*: a product that can be grown, naturally replenished, or cleansed at a rate that equals or exceeds human depletion of the resource

*Sustainable*: able to meet the needs of the present generation without compromising the needs of future generations

# APPENDIX A-1: SUMMARY OF LATCHSET AND LOCKSET FUNCTIONS

| | types: 1000: mortise; 2000: preassembled; 4000: bored; 5000: interconnected | | | | | | | | | | | |
|---|---|---|---|---|---|---|---|---|---|---|---|---|
| | 1000 | 2000 | 4000 | 4000 | 4000 | 5000 | function | | | | | |
| | grades | | | | | | operating component | | method of locking | | method of unlocking | |
| description | 1,2,3 | 1 | 1 | 2 | 3 | 1,2,3 | out | in | outside | inside | outside | inside |
| passage | F01 | F36 | F75 | F75 | F75 | — | K | K | — | — | — | — |
| privacy, bedroom, or bath | F02 | — | — | — | — | — | K/R | — | — | turn | emergency release | turn |
| communicating | F03 | — | — | — | — | — | K | K | turn | turn | turn | turn |
| entry | F04 | — | — | — | — | — | K | K | stop or mechanical means | | key | knob |
| classroom | F05 | F42 | F84 | F84 | — | — | K | K | key | — | key | knob |
| classroom or hospital | F06 | — | — | — | — | — | K | K | key for knob | — | key | knob |
| holdback | — | F43 | F85 | — | — | — | K | K | key for knob (latchbolt may be locked in retracted position) | | key | knob |
| storeroom or closet | F07 | F44 | F86 | F86 | F86 | — | K/F | K | — | — | key | knob |
| front door | F08 | — | — | — | — | — | K | K | stop or mechanical means for outside; turn (DB) | | key (BB) | knob |
| apartment, exit, or public toilet | F09 | F45 | F88 | — | — | — | K | K | — | key | key | knob |
| apartment corridor | F10 | — | — | — | — | — | K | K | stop or mechanical means for outside; turn (DB) | | key (BB) | knob |

| | types: 1000: mortise; 2000: preassembled; 4000: bored; 5000: interconnected | | | | | | | | | | | |
|---|---|---|---|---|---|---|---|---|---|---|---|---|
| | 1000 | 2000 | 4000 | 4000 | 4000 | 5000 | function | | | | | |
| | grades | | | | | | operating component | | method of locking | | method of unlocking | |
| description | 1,2,3 | 1 | 1 | 2 | 3 | 1,2,3 | out | in | outside | inside | outside | inside |
| dormitory or exit | F11 | — | — | — | — | — | K | K | stop or mechanical means for outside; key (DB) | | key (latchbolt) | knob (BB) |
| dormitory or exit | F12 | — | — | — | — | — | K | K | stop or mechanical means for outside; key (DB) outside; turn (DB) inside | | key (DB) | knob (BB); turn (DB) |
| dormitory or exit | F13 | — | — | — | — | — | K | K | key (DB) | turn (DB) | key (DB) | knob (BB) |
| store door | F14 | F47 | — | — | — | — | K | K | key (DB) | key (DB) | key (DB) | key (DB) |
| hotel guest room | F15 | — | — | — | — | — | K/F | K | — | turn (DB) (restricts all keys except emergency) | key (latchbolt) | knob (latchbolt; turn (DB) or knob on both) |
| dead lock | F16 | — | — | — | — | — | C | C | key | key | key | key |
| dead lock | F17 | — | — | — | — | — | C | T | key | turn | key | turn |
| dead lock | F18 | — | — | — | — | — | C | — | key | — | key | — |
| privacy, bedroom, or bath | F19 | — | — | — | — | — | K | K | — | turn (DB) | emergency release | knob (BB) |
| apartment corridor | F20 | — | — | — | — | — | K | K | stop or mechanical means for outside; key (DB) outside; turn (DB) inside | | key (BB) | knob (BB) |
| room door | F21 | — | — | — | — | — | K | K | key (DB) | turn (DB) | key (DB) | turn (DB) |
| privacy, bedroom or bath | F22 | F37 | F76 | — | — | — | K | K | — | PB on all; turn for F22 | emergency release | knob |
| privacy, bedroom or bath | — | — | — | F76 | F76 | — | K | K | — | LD | emergency release | knob or LD in unlocked position |
| apartment or store door | F24 | — | — | — | — | — | TP | TP | — | key for outside; key (DB) | key (latchbolt) | TP |
| store door | F25 | — | — | — | — | — | TP | TP | key (DB) | key (DB) | key (DB) | key (DB) |
| patio or privacy | — | F38 | F77 | — | — | — | K | K | — | PB for all; LD for F77 | — | knob |
| patio or privacy | — | — | — | F77 | F77 | — | K | K | — | LD | — | knob or LD in unlocked position |
| communicating | — | F39 | F78 | F78 | — | — | K | K | TB in knob | TB in knob | TB in knob | TB in knob |
| entrance or storeroom | — | F40 | F81 | F81 | F81 | — | K | K | — | TB for all; LD for F81 | key | knob |
| entry | — | F41 | F82 | — | — | — | K | K | — | PB for all; LD for F82 | key | knob |

| | types: 1000: mortise; 2000: preassembled; 4000: bored; 5000: interconnected | | | | | | | | | | | |
|---|---|---|---|---|---|---|---|---|---|---|---|---|
| | 1000 | 2000 | 4000 | 4000 | 4000 | 5000 | function | | | | | |
| | grades | | | | | | operating component | | method of locking | | method of unlocking | |
| description | 1,2,3 | 1 | 1 | 2 | 3 | 1,2,3 | out | in | outside | inside | outside | inside |
| entry | — | — | — | F82 | F82 | — | K | K | — | LD | key | knob or LD in unlocked position |
| store door | — | F46 | F91 | — | — | — | K | K | key (both knobs) | key (both knobs) | key (both knobs) | key (both knobs) |
| hotel guest, clubhouse, dormitory, apartment | — | F48 | F93 | F93 | — | — | K/F | K | — | PB for all; LD for F93 (restricts all keys except emergency) | key | knob |
| communicating (knob and turn simultaneously locked) | — | — | F79 | F79 | — | — | K | T | TB in knob; LD | — | TB in knob; LD | — |
| communicating | — | — | F80 | F80 | — | — | K | K | key | key | key | key |
| exit (manually operated TB or LD unlocks outside knob) | — | — | F83 | F83 | F83 | — | K | K | — | TB; LD | — | knob |
| asylum, institutional | — | — | F87 | — | — | — | K/F | K/F | — | — | key | key |
| exit | — | — | F89 | F89 | F89 | — | K/F | K | — | — | — | knob |
| corridor (closing door releases PB or LD) | — | — | F90 | F90 | — | — | K | K | key | PB; LD | key | knob (releases PB or locking device) |
| service station | — | — | F92 | F92 | — | — | K | K | — | PB; LD | key (releases PB or LD except when locked) | knob (releases PB or LD except when locked) |
| exit | — | — | F89 | F89 | F89 | — | K/F | K | — | — | — | knob |
| entry | — | — | — | — | — | F95 | K | K | key | turn | key | knob |
| entry (key restores inside LD to unlocked position) | — | — | — | — | — | F96 | K | K | key (DB) | LD for outside knob; turn (DB) | key (latchbolt); key (DB) | knob (BB) |
| entry (manually operated LD unlocks outside knob) | — | — | — | — | — | F97 | K | K | key (DB) | LD for outside knob; turn (DB) | key (latchbolt); key (DB) | knob (BB) |
| storeroom | — | — | — | — | — | F98 | K/R | K | key (DB) | — | key (BB) | knob |
| dormitory (closing door releases LD) | — | — | — | — | — | F99 | K | K | key (DB) | LD for outside knob; turn (DB) | key (LD, DB) | knob (BB) |
| hotel/motel (indicator and shut out feature released by rotating knob) | — | — | — | — | — | F100 | K/R | K | key (DB) | turn (DB) (restricts all keys except emergency) | key (BB) | knob (BB); turn (DB) |

| | types: 1000: mortise; 2000: preassembled; 4000: bored; 5000: interconnected | | | | | | | | | | | |
|---|---|---|---|---|---|---|---|---|---|---|---|---|
| | 1000 | 2000 | 4000 | 4000 | 4000 | 5000 | function | | | | | |
| | grades | | | | | | operating component | | method of locking | | method of unlocking | |
| description | 1,2,3 | 1 | 1 | 2 | 3 | 1,2,3 | Out | In | outside | inside | outside | inside |
| hotel/motel | — | — | — | — | — | F101 | K/R | K | — | turn (DB) | key (latchbolt) | knob (BB); turn (DB) |
| handle set trim | — | — | — | — | — | F102 | TP | K | key (DB) | turn (DB) | key (DB) | knob (BB) |
| handle trim set | — | — | — | — | — | F103 | TP | K | key (thumb piece and DB) | LD (thumb piece); turn (DB) | key (BB) | knob (BB) |
| entry (key restores inside LD to locked position) | — | — | — | — | — | F104 | K | K | key (DB) | LD for outside knob; turn (DB) | key (BB) | knob; turn |
| entry (manually operated LD unlocks outside knob) | — | — | — | — | — | F105 | K | K | key (DB) | LD for outside knob; turn (DB) | key (BB) | knob; turn |
| dormitory (closing door releases LD) | — | — | — | — | — | F106 | K | K | key (DB) | LD for outside knob; turn (DB) | key (LD, BB) | knob (BB) |

K knob or lever handle
T turn
K/F knob, always fixed
K/R knob, always rigid or free spinning
TP thumb piece
C cylinder only
K/DB key, deadbolt
DB deadbolt
BB both bolts
LD locking device
PB push button
TB turn button

Note: See App. A-2 for a full description of all lock functions.

Source: Based on information from ANSI A156.2, A156.12, A156.13.

# APPENDIX A-2: HARDWARE LOCK FUNCTIONS

## SERIES 1000 MORTISE LOCK FUNCTIONS

F01 *Passage or closet latch.* Latch bolt operated by knob from either side at all times.

F02 *Privacy, bedroom, or bath lock.* Latch bolt operated by knob from either side. Dead bolt operated by turn from inside and by emergency release from outside.

F03 *Communicating lock.* Latch bolt operated by knob from either side. Two dead bolts or a split dead bolt operated independently by turns from both sides. This function should not be used on doors in rooms that have no other entrance.

F04 *Entry lock.* Latch bolt operated by knob from either side except when outside knob is made inoperative by a stop or mechanical means other than key. When outside knob is locked, latch bolt is retracted by key from outside or by rotating inside knob. Auxiliary dead latch.

F05 *Classroom lock.* Latch bolt operated by knob from either side except when outside knob is locked from outside by key. When outside knob is locked, latch bolt is retracted by key from outside or by rotating inside knob. Auxiliary dead latch.

F06 *Classroom or hospital lock.* Latch bolt operated by knob from either side except when outside knob is locked from outside by key. Latch bolt can be locked in a retracted position by key. When outside knob is locked, latch bolt is retracted by key from outside or by rotating inside knob, unless latch bolt has been locked in a retracted position. Auxiliary dead latch.

F07 *Storeroom or closet lock.* Latch bolt operated by key from outside or by rotating inside knob. Outside knob is always inoperative. Auxiliary dead latch.

F08 *Front door lock.* Latch bolt operated by knob from either side except when outside knob is made inoperative by a stop or mechanical means other than key. Dead bolt operated by turn inside. Key outside operates both bolts.

F09 *Apartment, exit, or public toilet lock.* Latch bolt operated by knob from either side, except when outside knob is locked by key from inside. When outside knob is locked, latch bolt is retracted by key from outside or by rotating inside knob. Auxiliary dead latch.

F10 *Apartment corridor door lock.* Latch bolt operated by knob from either side, except when outside knob is made inoperative by a stop or mechanical means other than key. Dead bolt operated by turn inside. Key outside operates both bolts. Dead bolt has 1 in (25.4 mm) throw.

F11 *Dormitory or exit lock.* Latch bolt operated by knob from either side except when outside knob is made inoperative by a stop or mechanical means other than key. Dead bolt projected by key from either side. Dead bolt retracted by key from outside. Both bolts retracted by inside knob.

F12 *Dormitory or exit lock.* Latch bolt operated by knob from either side, except when outside knob is made inoperative by a stop or mechanical means other than key. Dead bolt projected by key from outside and by turn from inside. Dead bolt retracted by key from outside and by turn from inside. Rotating inside knob retracts both bolts.

F13 *Dormitory or exit lock.* Latch bolt operated by knob from either side. Dead bolt projected by key from outside and turn from inside. Rotating inside knob retracts both bolts.

F14 *Store door lock.* Latch bolt operated by knob from either side. Dead bolt operated by key from either side.

F15 *Hotel guest lock.* Latch bolt operated by key from outside or by rotating inside knob. Outside knob is always inoperative. Dead bolt projected by turn from inside, and all keys except emergency and display key are shut out. Auxiliary dead latch. Indicator button. When so specified, rotating inside knob retracts both bolts.

F16 *Dead lock.* Dead bolt operated by key from either side.

F17 *Dead lock.* Dead bolt operated by key from outside only and by turn from inside.

F18 *Dead lock.* Dead bolt operated by key from outside only.

F19 *Privacy, bedroom, or bath lock.* Latch bolt operated by knob from either side. Dead bolt operated by turn from inside and emergency release from outside. Rotating inside knob retracts both bolts.

F20 *Apartment corridor door lock.* Latch bolt operated by knob from either side, except when outside knob is made inoperative by a stop or mechanical means other than key. Dead bolt operated by key outside or turn inside. Key outside operates both bolts. Dead bolt has 1 in (25.4 mm) throw. Rotating inside knob retracts both bolts. Latch bolt is deadlocked when outside knob is made inoperative or when the dead bolt is projected. When dead bolt is retracted, knob is unlocked by stop or mechanical means other than key.

F21 *Room door lock.* Latch bolt operated by knob from either side. Dead bolt operated by key from outside and turn from inside.

F22 *Privacy, bedroom, or bath lock.* Latch bolt operated by knob from either side except when outside knob is locked by inside turn or button. Operating inside knob, closing door, or operating outside emergency release unlocks outside knob.

F24 *Apartment or store door handle lock.* Latch bolt operated by thumb piece on both sides, except when outside thumb piece is locked by key from inside. When outside thumb piece is locked, latch bolt is retracted by key outside or by thumb piece inside. Auxiliary dead latch.

F25 *Store door handle lock.* Latch bolt operated by thumb piece from either side. Dead bolt operated by key from either side.

## SERIES 2000 PREASSEMBLED LOCK FUNCTIONS

F36 *Passage or closet latch.* Latch bolt operated by knob from either side at all times.

F37 *Privacy, bedroom, or bath lock.* Latch bolt operated by knob from either side. Outside knob locked by push button inside and unlocked by emergency release outside, rotating inside knob, or closing door.

F38 *Patio or privacy lock.* Latch bolt operated by knob from either side. Outside knob is locked by push button inside and unlocked by rotating inside knob or closing door. Auxiliary dead latch. This lock should not be used in rooms that have no other entrance.

F39 *Communicating lock.* Latch bolt operated by knob from either side. Turn button in either knob locks or unlocks opposite knob. Auxiliary dead latch. This lock should not be used in rooms that have no other entrance.

F40 *Entrance or store room lock.* Latch bolt operated by knob from either side except when outside knob is locked by turn button in inside knob. When outside knob is locked, latch bolt may be retracted by key from outside or by rotating inside knob. Turn button must be manually rotated to unlock outside knob. Auxiliary dead latch.

F41 *Entry lock.* Latch bolt operated by knob from either side except when outside knob is locked by push button in inside knob. When outside knob is locked, operating key from outside or rotating inside knob retracts latch bolt and releases push button. Closing door does not release push button. Auxiliary dead latch.

F42 *Classroom lock.* Latch bolt operated by knob from either side except when outside knob is locked from outside by key. When outside knob is locked, latch bolt may be retracted by key from outside or by rotating inside knob. Auxiliary dead latch.

F43 *Holdback lock.* Latch bolt operated by knob from either side except when outside knob is locked from outside by key. Latch bolt may be locked in a retracted position by key. When outside knob is locked, latch bolt may be retracted by key from outside or by rotating inside knob, unless latch bolt has been locked in a retracted position. Auxiliary dead latch.

F44 *Storeroom or closet lock.* Latch bolt operated by key from outside or by rotating inside knob. Outside knob is always fixed. Auxiliary dead latch.

F45 *Apartment, exit, or public toilet lock.* Latch bolt operated by knob from either side, except when outside knob is locked by key from inside. When outside knob is locked, latch bolt may be retracted by key from outside or by rotating inside knob. Auxiliary dead latch.

F46 *Store door lock.* Latch bolt operated by knob from either side except when both knobs are locked by key from either side. Auxiliary dead latch.

F47 *Store door lock.* Latch bolt operated by knob from either side. Dead bolt operated by key from either side.

F48 *Hotel guest room, clubhouse, dormitory, or apartment entrance lock.* Latch bolt operated by knob from inside at all times. Outside knob always fixed. Latch bolt operated by key from outside except when push button inside is depressed, thus shutting out all keys except the emergency key. Depressing push button operates visual indicator in face of cylinder, showing that the room is occupied. Turning inside knob or closing door releases indicator and shut out feature except when shut out is activated by a special procedure that shuts out all keys except emergency keys. Auxiliary dead latch.

## SERIES 4000 BORED LOCK FUNCTIONS

F75 Grades 1, 2, and 3. *Passage or closet latch.* Latch bolt operated by knob from either side at all times.

F76 Grade 1. *Privacy, bedroom, or bath lock.* Latch bolt operated by knob from either side. Outside knob is locked by push button or other locking device inside and unlocked by emergency release outside, rotating inside knob or closing door.

F76 Grades 2 and 3. *Privacy, bedroom, or bath lock.* Latch bolt operated by knob from either side except when outside knob is locked by locking device inside. Locking device shall automatically release when inside knob is turned or be in unlocked position before inside knob can be operated. Emergency release on outside permits outside knob to operate latch bolt.

F77 Grade 1. *Patio or privacy lock.* Dead locking latch bolt operated by knob from either side. Outside knob is locked by push button or other locking device inside and unlocked by rotating inside knob or closing door. This lock should not be used on doors in rooms that have no other entrance.

F77 Grades 2 and 3. *Patio and privacy lock.* Dead locking latch bolt operated by knob from either side except when outside knob is locked by locking device inside. Locking device shall automatically release when inside knob is turned or must be in the unlocked position before the knob can be operated.

F78 Grades 1 and 2. *Communicating lock.* Dead locking latch bolt operated by knob from either side. Turn button in either knob or locking device on either side locks or unlocks opposite knob. This lock should not be used on doors in rooms that have no other entrance.

F79 Grades 1 and 2. *Communicating lock.* Dead locking latch bolt operated from outside by knob and from inside by thumb turn. Turning button in knob or operating locking device locks both knob and thumb turn. Button or other locking device does not release unless manually restored to unlocked position.

F80 Grades 1 and 2. *Communicating lock.* Dead locking latch bolt operated by knob from either side. Turning key in either knob locks or unlocks its own knob independently. This lock should not be used on doors in rooms that have no other entrance.

F81 Grades 1, 2, and 3. *Entrance or store room lock.* Dead locking latch bolt operated by knob from either side except when outside knob is locked by turn button or other locking device inside. When outside knob is locked, latch bolt is operated by key in outside knob or by rotating inside knob. Turn button or other locking device must be manually operated to unlock outside knob.

F82 Grade 1. *Entry lock.* Dead locking latch bolt operated by knob from either side except when outside knob is locked by push button or other locking device on inside. When outside knob is locked, operating key in outside knob or rotating inside knob unlocks push button or other locking device and retracts latch bolt. Closing door does not release push button or other locking device.

F82 Grades 2 and 3. *Entry lock.* Dead locking latch bolt operated by knob from either side except when outside knob is locked by locking device on inside. When outside knob is locked, operating key in outside knob unlocks locking device. Locking device automatically releases when inside knob is turned or is in the unlocked position before the inside knob can be operated.

F83 Grades 1, 2, and 3. *Exit lock.* Dead locking latch bolt operated by knob from either side except when outside knob is locked by turn button or other locking device in inside. Turn button or other locking device manually operates to unlock outside knob. Rotating inside knob always operates latch bolt.

F84 Grades 1 and 2. *Classroom lock.* Dead locking latch bolt operated by knob from either side except when outside knob is locked from outside by key. When outside knob is locked, latch bolt is operated by key in outside knob or by rotating inside knob.

F85 Grade 1. *Holdback lock.* Dead locking latch bolt operated by knob from either side except when outside knob is locked from outside by key. Latch bolt may be locked in a retracted position by key. When outside knob is locked, latch bolt is operated by key in outside knob or by rotating inside knob unless latch bolt has been locked in a retracted position.

F86 Grades 1, 2, and 3. *Store room or closet lock.* Dead locking latch bolt operated by key in outside knob or by rotating inside knob. Outside knob is always fixed.

F87 Grade 1. *Utility, asylum, or institutional lock.* Dead locking latch bolt operated by key in knob from either side. Both knobs are always fixed.

F88 Grade 1. *Apartment, exit, or public toilet lock.* Dead locking latch bolt operated by knob from either side except when outside knob is locked by key room inside. When outside knob is locked, latch bolt may be retracted by key in outside knob or by rotating inside knob.

F89 Grades 1, 2, and 3. *Exit latch.* Dead locking latch bolt retracted by knob from inside at all times. Outside knob is always fixed.

F90 Grades 1 and 2. *Corridor lock.* Dead locking latch bolt operated by knob from either side except when outside knob is locked by key in outside knob or by push button or other locking device in inside. Key in outside knob locks or unlocks outside knob. Rotating inside knob releases push button or other locking device placed in a locked position. Closing door releases push button or other inside locking device. Inside knob always operates.

F91 Grade 1. *Store door lock.* Dead locking latch bolt operated by knob from either side except when both knobs are locked by key in knob from either side.

F92 Grades 1 and 2. *Service station lock.* Dead locking latch bolt operated by knob from either side except when outside knob is locked by push button or other locking device inside. Key outside, rotating inside knob, or closing door releases push button or other locking device unlocking outside knob except when slotted push button or other locking device is in a locked position. Inside knob always operates.

F93 Grades 1 and 2. *Hotel guest room, clubhouse, dormitory, or apartment entrance lock.* Dead locking latch bolt operated by knob from inside at all times. Outside knob always fixed or inoperable. Latch bolt operated by key from outside except when push button or other locking device inside is operated, thus shutting out all keys except emergency key. Operating push button or other locking device operates visual indicator outside, showing that the room is occupied. Turning inside knob or closing door releases indicator and shut out feature except when shut out is activated by a special procedure that shuts out all keys except emergency or display key.

## SERIES 5000 INTERCONNECTED FUNCTIONS

F95 *Entry lock.* Latch bolt operated by knob from either side. Rotating thumbturn from inside or key from outside will extend dead bolt to locked position. Both dead bolt and latch bolt are retracted to the unlocked position by rotating inside knob.

F96 *Entry lock.* Dead locking latch bolt is operated by knob on either side except when outside knob is made rigid or free spinning by locking device inside. When outside knob is locked, dead locking latch bolt is operated by key outside. Inside locking device must be manually operated to unlock outside knob. Rotating thumbturn from inside or key from outside extends the dead bolt to the locked position. Both dead bolt and dead locking latch bolt are retracted by rotating the inside knob. Closing the door does not release locking device inside.

F97 *Entry lock.* Dead locking latch bolt is operated by knob from either side except when outside knob is made rigid or free spinning by locking device inside. When outside knob is locked, dead locking latch bolt is operated by key outside. Inside locking device must be manually operated to unlock outside knob. Rotating thumbturn from the inside or key from the outside extends the dead bolt to the locked position. Both dead bolt and dead locking latch bolt are retracted by rotating the inside knob. Closing the door does not release locking device inside.

F98 *Storeroom lock.* Dead locking latch bolt is operated by key outside or rotating inside knob. Outside knob is always rigid or free spinning. Key outside projects or retracts dead bolt. Rotating inside knob or key outside retracts both dead bolt and dead locking latch bolt.

F99 *Dormitory lock.* Dead locking latch bolt is operated by knob from either side except when outside knob is made rigid or free spinning by locking device inside. When outside knob is locked, dead locking latch bolt is operated by key outside, restoring inside locking device to the unlocked position. Rotating thumbturn from inside or key from outside extends dead bolt to the locked position. Both dead bolt and dead locking latch bolt are retracted by rotating the inside knob. Closing door releases locking device inside.

F100 *Hotel/motel lock.* Dead locking latch bolt is operated by key outside or rotating inside knob. Outside knob is always rigid or free spinning. Rotating thumbturn from inside or key from outside extends dead bolt to the locked position. Both dead bolt and dead locking latch bolt are retracted by key outside or by rotating the inside knob. A visual occupancy indicator is operated from the inside and shuts out all keys except an emergency key. Rotating the inside knob releases the indicator and shut out feature unless fixed in a shut out position by a special tool.

F101 *Hotel/motel lock.* Dead locking latch bolt is operated by key outside or rotating inside knob. Outside knob is always rigid or free spinning. Rotating thumbturn from inside extends dead bolt to the locked position and indicates occupancy on the outside. Both dead bolt and dead locking latch bolt are retracted by rotating the inside knob. The occupancy indicator is released from the outside with a special key.

F102 *Handle set trim.* Latch bolt is retracted by thumbpiece on the outside and knob on the inside. Rotating thumbturn from inside or key from outside extends dead bolt to the locked position. Both dead bolt and latch bolt are retracted to the unlocked position by rotating inside knob.

F103 *Handle trim set.* Dead locking latch bolt is operated by thumbpiece outside or knob inside except when outside thumbpiece is locked or made inoperative by locking device inside or by key outside. When outside thumbpiece is locked or inoperative, dead locking latch bolt and dead bolt are retracted by key or key and thumbpiece operation outside by rotating inside knob. Rotating thumbpiece inside or key outside extends dead bolt to locked position. Thumbpiece outside remains locked or inoperative until unlocked by locking device inside or by key outside.

F104 *Entry lock.* Dead locking latch bolt is operated by knob from either side except when outside knob is made rigid or free spinning by locking device inside. When outside knob is locked, dead locking latch bolt is operated by key outside, restoring inside locking device to the unlocked position. Rotating thumbturn from inside or key from outside extends dead bolt to the locked position. Both dead bolt and dead locking latch bolt retract by rotating inside knob, key outside and thumbturn inside. Closing door does not release locking device inside.

F105 *Entry lock.* Dead locking latch bolt is operated by knob from either side except when outside knob is made rigid or free spinning by locking device inside. When outside knob is locked, dead locking latch bolt is operated by key outside. Inside locking device must be manually operated to unlock outside knob. Rotating thumbturn from inside or key from outside extends the dead bolt to the locked position. Both dead bolt and dead locking latch bolt are retracted by rotating inside knob, key outside, and thumbturn inside. Closing door does not release locking device inside.

F106 *Dormitory lock.* Dead locking latch bolt is operated by knob from either side except when outside knob is made rigid or free spinning by locking device inside. When outside knob is locked, dead locking latch bolt is operated by key outside, restoring inside locking device to unlocked position. Rotating thumbturn from inside or key from outside extends dead bolt to the locked position. Both dead bolt and dead locking latch bolt are retracted by rotating inside knob, key outside, and thumbturn inside. Closing door releases locking device inside.

# APPENDIX B: ABBREVIATIONS FOR INTERIOR DESIGN DRAWINGS

| | |
|---|---|
| Above finished floor | AFF |
| Above raised floor | ARF |
| Above suspended ceiling | ASC |
| Abrasive | ABRSV |
| Access door | AD |
| Access floor | AF |
| Access panel | AP |
| Acoustical | ACOUS |
| Acoustical insulation | ACOUS INSUL |
| Acoustical panel | ACOUS PNL |
| Acoustical plaster | ACOUS PLAS |
| Acoustical plaster ceiling | APC |
| Acoustical tile | ACOUS TILE |
| Acoustical wall treatment | ACWT |
| Adhesive | ADH |
| Adjacent | ADJ |
| Adjustable | ADJ |
| Aggregate | AGGR |
| Air conditioning | AC |
| Air conditioning unit | ACU |
| Air vent | AV |
| Alarm | ALM |
| Alarm annunciator panel | AAP |
| Alteration | ALTRN |
| Alternate | ALT |
| Alternating current | AC |
| Aluminum | AL |
| American National Standards Institute | ANSI |
| American wire gage | AWG |
| Ampere | AMP |
| Anchor | AHR |
| Anchor bolt | AB |
| Anodized | ANOD |
| Antenna | ANT |
| Apartment | APT |
| Approved | APPD |
| Approximately | APPROX |
| Architect | ARCH |
| Architect-Engineer | A-E |
| Architectural terra cotta | ATC |
| Area | A |
| Area drain | AD |
| Assembly | ASSY |
| Association | ASSN |
| Asymmetrical | ASYM |
| Attachment | ATCH |
| Audiovisual | AV |
| Automatic door closer | ADC |
| Automatic door seal | ADS |
| Automatic sprinkler | AS |
| Average | AVG |

| | |
|---|---|
| Back to back | B/B |
| Balcony | BALC |
| Base line | BL |
| Base plate | BP |
| Baseboard | BB |
| Baseboard radiation | BBRR |
| Basement | BSMT |
| Beam | BM |
| Bearing | BRG |
| Bedroom | BR |
| Below | BLW |
| Below ceiling | BLW CLG |
| Below finish floor | BLW FFLR |
| Bench mark | BM |
| Between | BETW |
| Bevel | BEV |
| Beveled plate glass | BPG |
| Bituminous | BITUM |
| Black iron | BI |
| Block | BLK |
| Blocking | BLKG |
| Board | BD |
| Bookshelves | BK SH |
| Both faces | BF |
| Both sides | BS |
| Both ways | BW |
| Bottom | BOT |
| Bottom face | BF |
| Bracing | BRCG |
| Bracket | BRKT |
| Brass | BRS |
| Brick | BRK |
| Bronze | BRZ |
| Brown and Sharpe gage | B&S |
| Building | BLDG |
| Bulletin board | BB |
| Burglar alarm | BA |
| Cabinet | CAB |
| Cabinet heater | CAB H |
| Cable television | CTV |
| Calking | CLKG |
| Canvas | CANV |
| Carpet | CARP |
| Casework | CSWK |
| Casing | CSG |
| Casing bead | CSB |
| Cast iron | CI |
| Cast stone | CS |
| Ceiling | CLG |
| Ceiling diffuser | CLG DIFF |
| Ceiling grille | CG |
| Ceiling height | CLG HT |
| Ceiling register | CLG REG |
| Center line | CL |
| Center to center | C TO C |
| Centimeter | CM |
| Ceramic | CER |
| Ceramic tile | CER TILE |
| Chalkboard | CH BD |
| Chamfer | CHAM |
| Change order | CO |
| Channel | CHAN |
| Chrome plated | CHR PL |
| Circle | CIR |
| Circuit | CKT |
| Circuit breaker | CKT BKR |
| Circular | CIRC |
| Classroom | CLRM |
| Cleanout | CO |
| Clear | CLR |
| Closed circuit television | CCTV |
| Closet | CLO |
| Cold water | CW |
| Cold-rolled | CR |
| Cold-rolled steel | CRS |
| Column | COL |
| Column line | CLL |
| Combination towel dispenser & receptable | CTD&R |
| Common | COM |
| Communication | COMM |
| Compartment | COMPT |
| Compressible | CPRS |
| Compressor | CPRSR |
| Concrete masonry unit | CMU |
| Concrete | CONC |
| Concrete floor | CONC FL |
| Conference | CONF |
| Connection | CONN |
| Construction | CONSTR |
| Construction joint | CJ |
| Continuous | CONT |
| Contract limit line | CLL |
| Contractor | CONTR |
| Control joint | CLJ |
| Convector | CONV |
| Cool white | CW |
| Cool white delux | CWX |
| Coordinate | COORD |
| Corner | CNR |
| Corner bead | COR BD |

| | |
|---|---|
| Corner guard | CG |
| Corridor | CORR |
| Countersunk | CSK |
| Cover | COV |
| Cover plate | COV PL |
| Cross arm | X ARM |
| Cubicle | CUB |
| Cylinder | CYL |
| Cylinder lock | CYL L |
| Damper | DMPR |
| Datum | DAT |
| Degree | DEG |
| Deluxe white | DW |
| Demolition | DEMO |
| Department | DEPT |
| Detail | DET |
| Detector | DET |
| Diagonal | DIAG |
| Diameter | DIAM |
| Diffuser | DIFF |
| Dimension | DIM |
| Dimmer control panel | DCP |
| Dining room | DR |
| Dishwasher | DW |
| Distribution panel | DISTR PNL |
| Ditto | DO |
| Division | DIV |
| Domestic water heater | DWH |
| Door closer | DCL |
| Door frame | DFR |
| Door louver | DLV |
| Door stop | DST |
| Double | DBL |
| Double acting | DBL ACT |
| Double-acting door | DAD |
| Double glazing | DBL GLZ |
| Down | DN |
| Downspout | DS |
| Drain waste & vent | DWV |
| Drawer | DWR |
| Drawing | DWG |
| Drinking fountain | DF |
| Dumbwaiter | DWTR |
| Duplex | DX |
| Duplicate | DUP |
| Dutch door | DD |
| Each face | EF |
| Each way | EW |
| Eased edges | EE |
| East | E |
| Eccentric | ECC |
| Electrical | ELEC |
| Electrical water cooler | EWC |
| Electrical water heater | EWH |
| Elevation | EL |
| Elevator | ELEV |
| Enamel | ENAM |
| Enclosure | ENCL |
| Entrance | ENTR |
| Equal | EQ |
| Equally spaced | EQL SP |
| Equipment | EQUIP |
| Escalator | ESCAL |
| Exhaust | EXH |
| Exhaust air | EXH A |
| Exhaust duct | EXH DT |
| Exhaust fan | EXH FN |
| Exhaust grille | EXH GR |
| Exhaust hood | EXH HD |
| Existing | EXST |
| Expansion bolt | EXP BT |
| Expansion joint | EXP JT |
| Extrusion | EXTR |
| Fabric wallcovering | FWC |
| Fabricate | FAB |
| Face of concrete | FOC |
| Face of finish | FOF |
| Face of masonry | FOM |
| Face of studs | FOS |
| Face to face | F/F |
| Far side | FS |
| Fiberglass | FGL |
| Finish | FIN |
| Finish floor | FIN FL |
| Fire damper | FDMPR |
| Fire extinguisher | FEXT |
| Fire extinguisher cabinet | FEC |
| Fire hose cabinet | FHC |
| Fireplace | FPL |
| Fireproofing | FPRF |
| Fixture | FXTR |
| Float glass | FLT GL |
| Floor | FL |
| Floor drain | FD |
| Floor finish | FLR FIN |
| Floor register | FLR REG |
| Flooring | FLG |
| Fluorescent | FLUOR |
| Folding | FLDG |
| Framed mirror | FR MIR |
| From floor above | FFA |

| | |
|---|---|
| From floor below | FFB |
| Front | FRT |
| Furnace | FUR |
| Furniture | FURN |
| Furring | FURR |
| Future | FUT |
| Gage | GA |
| Galvanized | GALV |
| Galvanized iron | GI |
| Galvanized steel | GALVS |
| Garage | GAR |
| Gas | G |
| General | GENL |
| General contractor | GC |
| Glass | GL |
| Glass block | GLB |
| Glaze, Glazing | GLZ |
| Glazed | GLZD |
| Glazed concrete masonry unit | GLZ CMU |
| Glued laminated | GLU LAM |
| Grab bar | GB |
| Grade | GR |
| Grille | GRL |
| Ground | GND |
| Ground fault interrupter | GFI |
| Grout | GT |
| Guardrail | GDR |
| Gypsum | GYP |
| Gypsum board | GYP BD |
| Gypsum plaster | GYP PLAS |
| Hand dryer | HD |
| Handrail | HNDRL |
| Hanger | HGR |
| Hardboard | HDBD |
| Hardware | HDW |
| Hardwood | HDWD |
| Head | HD |
| Heater | HTR |
| Heating | HTG |
| Height | HGT |
| Hertz | HZ |
| Hexagonal | HEX |
| High | H |
| High-intensity discharge | HID |
| High output | HO |
| Hold-open | HO |
| Hollow concrete masonry unit | HCMU |
| Hollow core | HC |
| Hollow metal | HM |
| Hollow metal door | HMD |
| Hollow metal frame | HMF |
| Horizontal | HORIZ |
| Hot water | HW |
| Incandescent | INCAND |
| Inside diameter | ID |
| Inside face | IF |
| Instantaneous water heater | IWH |
| Insulate | INS |
| Insulated panel | INSUL PNL |
| Insulation | INSUL |
| Intercommunication | INTERCOM |
| Interior | INTR |
| Janitor | JAN |
| Janitor's closet | JC |
| Joint | JT |
| Joist | JST |
| Junction box | JB |
| Kiln–dried | KD |
| Kilogram | KG |
| Kilovolt | KV |
| Kilovolt ampere | KVA |
| Kitchen | KIT |
| Knock down | KD |
| Knockout | KO |
| Laboratory | LAB |
| Ladder | LAD |
| Lamination | LAM |
| Landing | LDG |
| Large | LRG |
| Lateral | LATL |
| Lath and plaster | L&P |
| Laundry | LAU |
| Lavatory | LAV |
| Left | L |
| Left hand | LH |
| Left hand reverse | LHR |
| Length overall | LOA |
| Library | LIB |
| Light | LT |
| Light pole | LP |
| Lighting | LTG |
| Lightproof | LP |
| Lightweight | LT WT |
| Linear | LIN |
| Linear ceiling diffuser | LCD |
| Linear diffuser | LD |

| | |
|---|---|
| Linear foot | LF |
| Lintel | LNTL |
| Living room | LR |
| Load bearing | LD BRG |
| Locker | LKR |
| Locker room | LKR RM |
| Long leg horizontal | LLH |
| Long leg vertical | LLV |
| Louver | LVR |
| Low voltage | LV |
| Lumber | LBR |
| Manfacturing | MFG |
| Marble | MARB |
| Mark | MK |
| Masonry | MAS |
| Masonry opening | MO |
| Master bedroom | MBR |
| Material | MATL |
| Maximum | MAX |
| Mechanical | MECH |
| Medicine cabinet | MC |
| Medium density overlay | MDO |
| Metal | MET |
| Metal lath | ML |
| Meter | M |
| Mezzanine | MEZZ |
| Millwork | MLWK |
| Minimum | MIN |
| Minute | MIN |
| Mirror | MIR |
| Miscellaneous | MISC |
| Molding | MLDG |
| Mortar | MTR |
| Mounted | MTD |
| Mounting | MTG |
| Movable | MVBL |
| Mullion | MULL |
| Multiple | MULT |
| Nameplate | NPL |
| National Electric Code | NEC |
| National Fire Protection Association | NFPA |
| Natural | NAT |
| Near face | NF |
| Near side | NS |
| Negative | NEG |
| No paint | NP |
| Noise criterion | NC |
| Noise reduction | NR |
| Noise reduction coefficient | NRC |
| Nominal | NOM |
| North | N |
| Not applicable | NA |
| Not in contract | NIC |
| Not to scale | NTS |
| Number | NO |
| Obscure | OBS |
| Obscure glass | OGL |
| Obscure wire glass | OWGL |
| Office | OFF |
| On center | OC |
| Opening | OPNG |
| Opposite | OPP |
| Out to out | O/O |
| Outside diameter | OD |
| Outside dimension | OD |
| Outside face | OF |
| Outside radius | OR |
| Overall | OA |
| Overhead | OVHD |
| Owner furnished-contractor installed | OFCI |
| Owner furnished-owner installed | OFOI |
| Paint | PNT |
| Painted | PTD |
| Pair | PR |
| Panel | PNL |
| Panic bar | PB |
| Paper cup dispenser | PCD |
| Paper towel dispenser | PTD |
| Paper towel receptacle | PTR |
| Parallel | PAR |
| Particleboard | PBD |
| Partition | PTN |
| Passenger | PASS |
| Perforated | PERF |
| Perimeter | PERIM |
| Permanent | PERM |
| Perpendicular | PERP |
| Plaster | PLAS |
| Plastic laminate | PLAM |
| Plate | PL |
| Platform | PLAT |
| Plumbing | PLMB |
| Plywood | PLYWD |
| Polished | POL |
| Precast | PRCST |
| Prefabricated | PREFAB |
| Prefinished | PREFIN |
| Property line | PL |

| | |
|---|---|
| Public address | PA |
| Pull box | PB |
| Pull chain | PC |
| Purse shelf | PSH |
| Push button | PB |
| Quarry tile | QT |
| Quarter | QTR |
| Rabbet | RAB |
| Radiator | RAD |
| Radius | R |
| Receptacle | RCPT |
| Recessed | REC |
| Rectangular | RECT |
| Reference | REF |
| Refrigerator | REFR |
| Register | REG |
| Remote control | RC |
| Removable | REM |
| Required | REQD |
| Resilient | RESIL |
| Return | RET |
| Right hand | RH |
| Right hand reverse | RHR |
| Riser | R |
| Room | RM |
| Rough opening | RO |
| Round | RND |
| Sanitary | SAN |
| Schedule | SCHED |
| Screen | SCRN |
| Section | SECT |
| Service sink | SSK |
| Sheating | SHTHG |
| Sheet | SH |
| Sheet metal | SM |
| Shelving | SHV |
| Shower | SHR |
| Similar | SIM |
| Single | SGL |
| Sink | SK |
| Sliding | SL |
| Sliding door | SLD |
| Sliding glass door | SGD |
| Slip joint | SJ |
| Soap dispenser | SD |
| Solid core | SC |
| Sound transmission class | STC |
| South | S |
| Space | SP |
| Speaker | SPKR |
| Specification | SPEC |
| Sprinkler | SPKLR |
| Square | SQ |
| Square foot | SQ FT |
| Square inch | SQ IN |
| Square kilometer | SQ KM |
| Square meter | SQ M |
| Square yard | SQ YD |
| Stainless steel | SST |
| Steel | STL |
| Steel plate | STL PL |
| Storage | STOR |
| Supply air | SA |
| Supply-air grille | SAG |
| Supply diffuser | SD |
| Surface | SURF |
| Surfaced four sides | S4S |
| Surfaced two sides | S2S |
| Suspended | SUSP |
| Suspended ceiling | SUSP CLG |
| Switch | SW |
| Symmetrical | SYMM |
| System | SYS |
| Tackboard | TK BD |
| Tee | T |
| Telephone | TEL |
| Television | TV |
| Temperature | TEMP |
| Tempered glass | TMPD GL |
| Temporary | TEMP |
| Terra cotta | TC |
| Terrazzo | TER |
| Thermostat | T |
| Thickness | THK |
| Thousand | M |
| Threshold | THRES |
| To floor above | TFA |
| To floor below | TFB |
| Toilet paper holder | TPH |
| Tolerance | TOL |
| Tongue and groove | T&G |
| Top and bottom | T&B |
| Top of beam | TB |
| Top of concrete | TC |
| Top of finished floor | TFF |
| Top of joist | TJ |
| Top of pavement | TP |
| Top of slab | TSL |
| Top of steel | TST |
| Top of wall | TW |

| | |
|---|---|
| Total | TOT |
| Towel bar | TB |
| Towel dispenser | TD |
| Towel dispenser/ receptacle | TDR |
| Tread | T |
| Typical | TYP |
| Underwriters Laboratories, Inc. | UL |
| Unfinished | UNFIN |
| United States gage | USG |
| Unless otherwise noted | UON |
| Utility | UTIL |
| Variable air volume | VAV |
| Veneer | VNR |
| Vent pipe | VP |
| Vertical | VERT |
| Vertical grain | VG |
| Very high output | VHO |
| Vestibule | VEST |
| Video display terminal | VDT |
| Vinyl | VIN |
| Vinyl base | VB |
| Vinyl tile | VT |
| Vinyl wallcovering | VWC |
| Vitreous | VIT |
| Volt | V |
| Wainscot | WSCT |
| Wall to wall | W/W |
| Warm white | WW |
| Warm white deluxe | WWX |
| Waste | W |
| Waste receptacle | WR |
| Water closet | WC |
| Water heater | WH |
| Water resistant | WR |
| Waterproof | WP |
| Watt | W |
| Weather stripping | WS |
| Weight | WT |
| Welded | WLD |
| West | W |
| Width | WD |
| Wire glass | WGL |
| With | W/ |
| Without | W/O |
| Wood | WD |
| Working point | WP |

# READING LIST


## CHAPTER 1

Gypsum Association. *Fire Resistance Design Manual.* Washington, DC: Gyspum Association.

________. *Recommended Levels of Gypsum Board Finish.* Washington, DC: Gyspum Association.

United States Gypsum. *Gypsum Construction Handbook.* Chicago, IL: United States Gypsum Company.

## CHAPTER 2

American Society for Testing and Materials. ASTM C-635, *Standard Specification for the Manufacture, Performance, and Testing of Metal Suspension Systems for Acoustical Tile and Lay-In Panel Systems.* Philadelphia, PA: American Society for Testing and Materials.

________. ASTM C-636, *Installation of Metal Ceiling Suspension Systems for Acoustical Tile and Lay-In Panels.* Philadelphia, PA: American Society for Testing and Materials.

________. ASTM E-580, *Standard Practice for Application of Ceiling Suspension Systems for Acoustical Tile and Lay-In Panels in Areas Requiring Moderate Seismic Restraint.* Philadelphia, PA: American Society for Testing and Materials.

Ceiling and Interior Systems Construction Association. *Guidelines for Seismic Restraint for Direct-hung Suspended Ceiling Assemblies, Seismic Zones 3 and 4.* Skokie, IL: Ceilings and Interior Systems Construction Association.

________. *Recommendations for Direct-hung Acoustical Tile and Lay-in Panel Ceilings, Seismic Zones 0–2.* Skokie, IL: Ceilings and Interior Systems Construction Association.

## CHAPTER 3

Steel Door Institute. ANSI/SDI A250.8, *SDI 100 Recommended Specifications for Standard Steel Doors and Frames.* Cleveland, OH, Steel Door Institute.

________. SDI-108, *Recommended Selection and Usage Guide for Standard Steel Doors.* Cleveland, OH: Steel Door Institute.

________. SDI-111, *Recommended Standard Details for Steel Doors and Frames.* Cleveland, OH: Steel Door Institute.

________. SDI-118, *Basic Fire Door Requirements.* Cleveland, OH: Steel Door Institute.

Window and Door Manufacturers Association. I.S. 1-A, *Industry Standard for Architectural Wood Flush Doors.* Des Plaines, IL: Window and Door Manufacturers Association.

________. I.S. 6, *Industry Standard for Wood Stile and Rail Doors.* Des Plaines, IL: Window and Door Manufacturers Association.

________. ANSI/WDMA 1.5.6-A-01, *Industry Standard for Architectural Stile and Rail Doors.* Des Plaines, IL: Window and Door Manufacturers Association.

## CHAPTER 4

Door and Hardware Institute. *Basic Architectural Hardware.* Chantilly, VA: Door and Hardware Institute.

Steel Door Institute. SDI-109, *Hardware for Standard Steel Doors and Frames.* Cleveland, OH: Steel Door Institute.

## CHAPTER 5

Amstock, Joseph S. *Handbook of Glass in Construction.* New York: McGraw-Hill Professional Publishing.

Decicco, Paul R., ed. *The Behavior of Glass and Other Materials Exposed to Fire.* Amityville, NY: Baywood Publishing Co.

Glass Association of North America (GANA). *Glazing Manual.* Topeka, KA: Flat Glass Marketing Association.

## CHAPTER 6

Architectural Woodwork Institute. *Architectural Woodwork Quality Standards, Guide Specifications and Quality Certification Program.* Arlington, VA: The Architectural Woodwork Institute.

## CHAPTER 7

American Iron and Steel Institute. *Finishes for Stainless Steel.* Washington, DC: Committee of Stainless Steel Producers, American Iron and Steel Institute.

American Society for Metals. *Stainless Steel.* Metals Park, OH: American Society for Metals.

Copper Development Association. *Copper Brass Bronze Design Handbook.* Greenwich, CT: Copper Development Association.

Frisch, David, and Susan Frisch. *Metal: Design and Fabrication.* New York: Whitney Library of Design.

Zahner, L. William. *Architectural Metals.* New York: John Wiley & Sons.

## CHAPTER 8

National Terrazzo and Mosaic Association. *Terrazzo Information Guide.* Des Plaines, IL: The National Terrazzo and Mosaic Association.

Tile Council of America. *Handbook for Ceramic Tile Installation.* Princeton, NJ: Tile Council of America.

## CHAPTER 9

Hall, William R. *Contract Interior Finishes, A Handbook of Materials, Products, and Applications.* New York: Whitney Library of Design.

## CHAPTER 10

Amrhein, James E., and Michael W. Merrigan. *Marble and Stone Slab Veneer.* Los Angeles, CA: Masonry Institute of America.

Bradley, Frederick. *Natural Stone, A Guide to Selection: Studio Marmo.* New York: W.W. Norton & Company.

Jackman, Dianne R., and Mary K. Dixon. *Guide to Textiles for Interior Designers.* Winnipeg, Manitoba, Canada: Peguis Publishers.

Marble Institue of America. *Dimension Stone Design Manual.* Farmington, MI: Marble Institute of America.

________. *Interior Stone Wall Cladding Installation Guidelines.* Farmington, MI: Marble Institute of America.

Tile Council of America. *Handbook for Ceramic Tile Installation.* Princeton, NJ: Tile Council of America.

Yates, Marypaul. *Fabrics: A Handbook for Interior Designers and Architects.* New York: W.W. Norton & Company.

Yeager, Jan I., and Lura K. Teter-Justice. *Textiles for Residential and Commercial Interiors.* New York: Fairchild Books.

## CHAPTER 11

Ambrose, James E., and Jeffrey E. Ollswang. *Simplified Design for Building Sound Control.* New York: Wiley Interscience.

Cavanaugh, William J., and Joseph A. Wilkes, eds. *Architectural Acoustics: Principles and Practice.* New York: John Wiley & Sons.

Cowan, James P., ed. *Architectural Acoustics Design Guide.* New York: McGraw-Hill.

Cremer, Lothar. *Principles and Applications of Room Acoustics.* New York: Applied Science. (out of print, but worth looking for a used copy)

Egan, M. David. *Architectural Acoustics.* New York: McGraw-Hill. (out of print, but a classic with good information and worth looking for a used copy)

Mehta, Madan, James Johnson, and Jorge Rocafort. *Architectural Acoustics: Principles and Design.* Englewood Cliffs, NJ: Prentice Hall.

## CHAPTER 12

Templer, John. *The Staircase: Studies of Hazards, Falls, and Safer Design.* Cambridge, MA: MIT Press.

________. *The Staircase: History and Theories.* Cambridge, MA: MIT Press.

## CHAPTER 13

Hunt, Wayne, Eric Labrecque, and Gerry Rosentswieg. *Designing and Planning Environmental Graphics.* New York: Madison Square Press.

Miller, Collette. *Wayfinding: Effective Wayfinding and Signing Systems, Guidance for Healthcare Facilities.* London: NHS Estates.

## CHAPTER 14

Fennelly, Lawrence J., ed. *Effective Physical Security.* Boston, MA: Butterworth-Heinemann.

San Luis, Ed, Louis A. Tyska, and Lawrence J. Fennelly. *Office and Building Security.* Boston, MA: Butterworth-Heinemann.

## CHAPTER 15

International Organization for Standardization. ISO 11064, *Ergonomic Design of Control Centres.* Geneva, Switzerland: International Organization for Standardization.

Rhodes, John. *Videoconferencing for the Real World.* Boston, MA: Butterworth-Heinemann.

Simpson, Robert S. *Effective Audio Visual: A User's Handbook.* Woburn, MA: Focal Press.

U.S. Department of Defense. MIL-STD-1472F, *Design Criteria Standard, Human Engineering.* U.S. Department of Defense, August 23, 1999, www.combatindex.com/mil_docs/pdf/std/1400/MIL-STD-1472F.pdf (accessed 9/19/2006).

Wallace, E., and C. Diffley. *CCTV: Making It Work, CCTV Control Room Ergonomics.* PSDB Publication No. 14/98. Hertfordshire, UK: Police Scientific Development Branch.

## CHAPTER 16

Ambrose, James E. *Building Construction: Service Systems.* New York: Van Nostrand Reinhold.

Binggeli, Corky. *Building Systems for Interior Designers.* New York: John Wiley and Sons.

Gordon, Gary, and James L. Nuckolls. *Interior Lighting for Designers.* New York: John Wiley & Sons.

Kay, Gersil Newmark. *Fiber Optics in Architectural Lighting: Methods, Design, and Applications.* New York: McGraw-Hill.

Stein, Benjamin. *Building Technology: Mechanical and Electrical Systems.* New York: John Wiley & Sons.

Stein, Benjamin, and John S. Reynolds. *Mechanical and Electrical Equipment for Buildings.* New York: John Wiley & Sons.

## CHAPTER 17

Ambrose, James E. *Simplified Engineering for Architects and Builders.* New York: John Wiley & Sons.

Rupp, William, and Arnold Friedmann. *Construction Materials for Interior Design.* New York: Whitney Library of Design.

Salvadori, Mario George. *Why Buildings Stand Up: The Strength of Architecture.* New York: W.W. Norton.

## CHAPTER 18

American National Standards Institute. ICC/ANSI A117.1-2003, *Accessible and Usable Buildings and Facilities.* New York: American National Standards Institute.

Architectural and Transportation Barriers Compliance Board. *Americans with Disabilities Act (ADA) Accessibility Guidelines for Buildings and Facilities; Architectural Barriers Act (ABA) Accessibility Guidelines; Final Rule,* 36 CFR Parts 1190 and 1191.

Ballast, David Kent. *Handbook of Construction Tolerances.* New York: McGraw-Hill.

Department of Justice, Office of the Attorney General. *Nondiscrimination on the Basis of Disability by Public Accommodations and in Commercial Facilities,* 28 CFR Part 36.

Evan Terry Associates. *Pocket Guide to the ADA: Americans with Disabilities Act Accessibility Guidelines for Buildings and Facilities.* New York: John Wiley.

________. *Americans with Disabilities Act Facilities Compliance: A Practical Guide.* New York: John Wiley & Sons.

General Services Administration. *Uniform Federal Accessibility Standards.* Fed. Std. 795, U.S. Government Printing Office.

Goldsmith, Selwyn. *Universal Design: Manual of Practical Guidance for Architects.* Boston, MA: Butterworth-Heinemann.

Grist, Robert R., ed., Mary Joyce Hasell, Rocke Hill, and James I. West. *Accessible Design Review Guide: An ADAAG Guide for Designing and Specifying Spaces, Buildings, and Sites.* New York: McGraw-Hill.

Holmes-Siedle, James. *Barrier-Free Design: A Manual for Building Designers and Managers.* Boston, MA: Butterworth Architecture.

Stratton, Peter A., and Michael J. Crosbie. *A Basic Guide to Fair Housing Accessibility: Everything Architects and Builders Need to Know About the Fair Housing Act Accessibility Guidelines.* New York: John Wiley & Sons.

## CHAPTERS 19 AND 20

Building Officials and Code Administrators International, Inc. *National Building Code.* Country Club Hills, IL: Building Officials and Code Administrators International, Inc.

Ching, Francis, and Steven Winkel. *Building Codes Illustrated.* New York: John Wiley and Sons.

Harmon, Sharon Koomen. *The Codes Guidebook for Interiors.* New York: John Wiley & Sons.

International Code Council. *International Building Code.* Falls Church, VA: International Code Council.

________. *International Residential Code.* Falls Church, VA: International Code Council.

________. *2004 Supplement to the International Codes.* Falls Church, VA: International Code Council.

International Conference of Building Officials. *2000 IBC Handbook—Fire- and Life-Safety Provisions.* Whittier, CA: International Conference of Building Officials.

________. *Uniform Building Code.* Whittier, CA: International Conference of Building Officials.

Parish, Scott B. *Uniform Building Code Compliance Manual.* New York: McGraw-Hill.

Southern Building Code Congress International, Inc. *Standard Building Code.* Birmingham, AL: Southern Building Code Congress International, Inc.

Stephenson, John. *The Building Regulations Explained.* London: E & F N Spon.

## CHAPTER 21

American Institute of Architects. *Environmental Resource Guide.* Washington, DC: American Institute of Architects.

Associates III et al. *Sustainable Residential Interiors.* New York: John Wiley & Sons.

Bonda, Penny, and Katie Sosnowchik. *Sustainable Commercial Interiors.* New York: John Wiley & Sons.

Elizabeth, Lynne, and Cassandra Adams, eds. *Alternative Construction.* New York: John Wiley & Sons.

Kibert, Charles J. *Sustainable Construction.* New York: John Wiley & Sons.

Mendler, Sandra F., and William Odell. *The HOK Guidebook to Sustainable Design.* New York: John Wiley & Sons.

Spiegel, Ross, and Dru Meadows. *Green Building Materials: A Guide to Product Selection and Specification.* New York: John Wiley & Sons.

Tuluca, Adrian. *Energy Efficient Design and Construction for Commercial Buildings.* New York: McGraw-Hill.

U.S. Department of Energy and Public Technology, Inc. *Sustainable Building Technical Manual: Green Building Design, Construction, and Operations.* Washington, DC: Public Technology.

Yeang, Ken. *Ecodesign, A Manual for Ecological Design.* New York: John Wiley & Sons.

## GENERAL REFERENCE SOURCES

ARCOM, AIA. *The Graphic Standards Guide to Architectural Finishes.* New York: John Wiley & Sons.

Beylerian, George M., Jeffrey J. Osborne, and Elliot Kaufman. *Mondo Materialis: Materials and Ideas for the Future.* New York: H.N. Abrams.

Ching, Francis D. K. *Interior Design Illustrated.* New York: Van Nostrand Reinhold.

Ching, Francis D. K., and Cassandra Adams. *Building Construction Illustrated.* New York: John Wiley & Sons.

McGowan, Maryrose, and Kelsey Kruse. *Interior Graphic Standards.* New York: John Wiley & Sons.

________. *Specifying Interiors: A Guide to Construction and FF&E for Commercial Interiors Projects.* New York: John Wiley & Sons.

Mendler, Sandra, and William Odell. *The HOK Guidebook to Sustainable Design.* New York: John Wiley & Sons.

Reznikoff, S. C. *Specifications for Commercial Interiors.* New York: Whitney Library of Design.

Riggs, J. Rosemary. *Materials and Components of Interior Architecture.* Englewood Cliffs, NJ: Prentice Hall.

Rupp, William, and Arnold Friedmann. *Construction Materials for Interior Design.* New York: Whitney Library of Design.

Simmons, H. Leslie, and Harold B. Olin. *Construction: Principles, Materials, and Methods.* New York: John Wiley & Sons.

Spiegel, Ross, and Dru Meadows. *Green Building Materials: A Guide to Product Selection and Specification.* New York: John Wiley & Sons.

Staebler, Wendy W. *Architectural Detailing in Contract Interiors.* New York: The Whitney Library of Design.

# INDEX

F



G

H

## Q



## R

T

# MASTERFORMAT™ INDEX

| MasterFormat number | Book heading | Page |
|---|---|---|
| **Wood and plastics** | | |
| 062000 | Finish carpentry | 142–145 |
| 064116 | Laminates | 171–174 |
| 064000 | Finishes | 181, 182 |
| 064000 | Installation of architectural woodwork | 182, 183 |
| 064000 | Lumber | 145–151 |
| 064100 | Cabinetwork | 153–162 |
| 064200 | Paneling | 162–171 |
| 064216 | Veneer | 152, 153 |
| 064300 | Wood stairs | 289–291 |
| 064316 | Guard design | 296, 297 |
| 064600 | Standing and running trim | 174, 175 |
| 066116 | Solid surfacing materials | 180, 181 |
| **Doors and windows** | | |
| 081100 | Metal doors | 87–89 |
| 081113 | Steel doors and frames | 76–83 |
| 081116 | Aluminum doors and frames | 83, 84 |
| 081400 | Wood doors and frames | 68–75 |
| 083453 | Security doors | 318 |
| 083323 | Overhead coiling doors | 91–93 |
| 083500 | Folding and accordion doors | 89 |
| 084226 | Glass doors | 84–87 |
| 085656 | Security glazing | 318–320 |
| 087100 | Closing devices | 106–108 |
| 087100 | Door seals | 108–110 |
| 087153 | Door security | 110–114 |
| 087100 | Hinges and pivots | 95–102 |
| 087100 | Miscellaneous hardware | 114, 115 |
| 087100 | Operating devices | 102–106 |
| 087400 | Electronic hardware | 115–117 |
| 088100 | Common glass types | 121–126 |
| 088100 | Framed glazing | 129–132 |
| 088100 | Frameless glazing | 134–138 |
| 088100 | Guard design | 296, 297 |
| 088100 | Safety glazing | 137, 138 |
| 088100 | Special glazing | 126–129 |
| **Finishes** | | |
| 092113 | Lath and plaster partitions | 28–30 |
| 092113 | Plaster ceilings | 53, 54 |
| 092116 | Gypsum wallboard ceilings | 50–52 |
| 092116 | Gypsum wallboard partitions | 1–28 |
| 093000 | Tile | 215–223 |

| MasterFormat number | Book heading | Page |
|---|---|---|
| **Electrical** | | |
| 262000 | Power system requirements | 347–349 |
| 265100 | Light sources | 350–353 |
| 265300 | Exit signs | 309 |
| 273000 | Telephone and communication systems | 350 |
| 274000 | Teleconferencing | 336–339 |
| 281300 | Access control | 314–316 |
| 281600 | Intrusion detection | 313, 314 |
| 281600 | Notification systems | 316 |
| 265100 | Control devices | 353, 35 |